Art of Renaissance
FLORENCE

The publisher gratefully acknowledges the generous contributions to this book providedby Raymond Lifchez and the Samuel H. Kress Foundation.

The publisher also gratefully acknowledges the generous support of the Sonia H. Evers Renaissance Studies Endowment Fund of the University of California Press Foundation and the the Chairman's Circle of the University of California Press Foundation, whose members are:

Anonymous
Jeanne and Michael Adams
Stephen A. and Melva Arditti
Wendy Ashmore
Clarence and Jacqueline Avant
Elizabeth and David Birka-White
Mary Dingman
Sonia H. Evers
Carol and John Field
Walter S. Gibson
Mary-Jo DelVecchio Good and Byron Good
Adele M. Hayutin
Daniel Heartz
Edmund and Jeannie Kaufman
Lata Krishnan and Ajay Shah
John Lescroart and Lisa Sawyer
Judith and Kim Maxwell
Kenneth and Frances Reid
Loren and Frances Rothschild
Lisa See and Richard Kendall
Ralph and Shirley Shapiro
Michael Sullivan
Judy and Bill Timken

Art of Renaissance FLORENCE 1400–1600

LOREN PARTRIDGE

UNIVERSITY OF CALIFORNIA PRESS

University of California Press, one of the most distinguished university presses in the United States, enriches lives around the world by advancing scholarship in the humanities, social sciences, and natural sciences. Its activities are supported by the UC Press Foundation and by philanthropic contributions from individuals and institutions.
For more information, visit www.ucpress.edu.

University of California Press
Berkeley and Los Angeles, California

University of California Press, Ltd.
London, England

LIBRARY OF CONGRESS CATALOGING-IN-PUBLICATION DATA
Partridge, Loren W.
Art of Renaissance Florence, 1400–1600 / Loren Partridge.
p. cm.
Includes bibliographical references and index.
ISBN 978-0-520-25773-3 (cloth : alk. paper) — ISBN 978-0-520-25774-0 (pbk. : alk. paper)
1. Art, Renaissance—Italy—Florence. 2. Art, Italian—Italy—Florence.
3. Art and society—Italy—Florence—History—15th century.
4. Art and society—Italy—Florence—History—16th century. I. Title.
N6921.F7P37 2009
709.45'51109024—dc22
2009023613

Manufactured in Canada

20 19
10 9 8 7 6 5 4

The paper used in this publication meets the minimum requirements of ANSI/NISO Z 39.48-1992 (R 1997) (*Permanence of Paper*).

For the women who have made my life so fulfilling:
my wife, Leslie Martin; my daughters, Wendy and Amy;
and my sister, Shirley; and in memory
of my mother, Ruth Isaacson,
and my first wife, Rosemary.

CONTENTS

PREFACE AND ACKNOWLEDGMENTS

Art both mirrors and constructs its institutional and cultural contexts. Patronage and purpose, therefore, are of fundamental importance for interpreting works of art. Accordingly, following the introduction and a chapter on pre-Renaissance Florence, this book is divided chronologically into four sections that illuminate changes of style and content in response to the shifting political, religious, and intellectual currents across two centuries. These sections are defined by the governmental structure and principal patrons of each period—1400–1494 (Florence under the Albizzi and the Medici), 1494–1512 (Florence under Savonarola and Soderini), 1513–34 (Florence under the Medici popes), and 1531–1600 (Florence under the Medici dukes). Chapters within these sections focus on single genres of art: civic architecture, public piazzas, and their freestanding sculptural decoration; church architecture, including libraries within monasteries; ecclesiastical decoration, including altarpieces, burial chapels, and refectories; and palace architecture and decoration, including halls of state, chapels, freestanding sculpture, wedding chests, birth trays, *spalliera* painting, portraits, and devotional works. Regrettably, space constraints precluded consideration of confraternities, villas, statuettes, liturgical implements, ceramics, tapestries, drawings, prints, and book illustration.

The patrons of the works of art discussed in this book—bankers, merchants, clerics, popes, and dukes—were the social elite, acting privately or as agents of particular regimes or institutions. These patrons were closely connected to the major political, economic, intellectual, and religious issues of their cultural worlds, and the art they commissioned reveals much about their ideological claims to status and power as well as the period's aspirations and anxieties.

Religion was the underlying common denominator for nearly all genres of art, because most Renaissance Florentines—independent of class, occupation, education, or politics—were particularly concerned with leading moral lives to save their souls. Christian theology, liturgy, and devotion, therefore, are important themes of this book. An equally significant topic is the symbolic language or iconography of art, for a vast body of signs and symbols, drawn largely from theology, philosophy, mythology, and classical poetry, was routinely employed in the Renaissance. Since all symbols have multiple, even contradictory meanings, which can lead to under-, over-, or misinterpretation, a work's content and context have been used as the decisive factors in clarifying interpretation. Insights from recent gender studies have also been employed, particularly with regard to interpreting freestanding sculpture, bedroom decoration, devotional works, and portraits. Ancient and contemporary visual and literary sources, which often inspired and substantially conditioned a work's content, have been highlighted. Artists' social status, rivalries, and innovations have been particularly emphasized in the text, while techniques, media, or workshop practices of art production have been discussed primarily when these factors play a particularly important role in a work's interpretation. Finally, stylistic designations such as Gothic, early Renaissance, High Renaissance, or Mannerist have been employed as useful guideposts for understanding the general evolution of Renaissance art. But since they illuminate little about any individual work, such terms have been used with restraint.

To supplement the book's organization by periods and genres rather than by artist, an appendix of forty-eight artists' biographies has been included that summarizes each artist's major contributions and outlines chronologically his training, travels, and corpus of most important works, including works not discussed in the text. The back matter also includes a genealogy of the Medici family, timeline, glossary, bibliography, and annotated index.

Discussions of individual works are generally quite

in-depth, for successful art historical interpretation, in my view, requires deploying a multitude of perspectives proceeding from the work of art out to the cultural context and back again to the object while accounting both for the work's unique materiality and aesthetic properties, and for the ambiguities and conflicts of the circumstances of its making. My aim, in short, has been to achieve multileveled and nuanced interpretations that demonstrate how the culture *formally* registers in the work of art, and how the work of art *interactively* informs and often shapes the culture.

I am particularly indebted to the following friends and colleagues for commenting on the manuscript in whole or part: Paul Barolsky, Cristelle Baskins, James Clark, Sonia Evers, Evelyn Lincoln, Kendra Marcus, Leslie Martin, Wendy Partridge, Lisa Regan, Randolph Starn, Regina Stefaniak, and Barbara Wisch. Special thanks to Andrew Stewart and William S. Anderson for help with Latin translations and classical culture generally; to Sue Bolsom for acquiring the illustrations; to Charles Dibble for his keen copyediting; to Claudia Smelser for her artful book design; and to University of California Press editors Stephanie Fay, Sue Heinemann, and Eric Schmidt for their generous assistance. Meryl Bailey assisted with the genealogy, timeline, glossary, artists' biographies, and index. Bailey's stimulating graduate paper concerning the work illustrated in figure 189 also helped to shape my interpretation. Finally, my undergraduate and graduate students for the past forty years at Berkeley have been a constant source of challenge and inspiration.

For financial assistance, I am extremely grateful to Ralph Hexter, former dean of UC Berkeley's Division of Arts and Humanities for funding a portion of the sabbatical leave during which I drafted most of this book; to the current dean, Janet Broughton, for a grant to assist in acquiring the illustrations; and, lastly, to the Kress Foundation, Sonia Evers, and Ray Lifchez for grants to UC Press to assist in publication.

INTRODUCTION

RENAISSANCE

Renaissance, the French translation of the Italian *rinascita,* means "rebirth." The artist Giorgio Vasari (1511–74) coined the term *rinascita* in his celebrated *Lives of the Artists* (1550) to define at once a cultural movement and an artistic style characterized by the revival of classical Greek and Roman art and culture. This rebirth was preceded by an intervening Middle Age, a term introduced in 1437 by the historian Flavio Biondo (1392–1463), when a series of northern tribes, including the Goths, invaded Italy and imposed their art and culture, which from a Renaissance perspective was barbaric (i.e., Gothic).

Well before Vasari, the Florentine humanist and civil servant Matteo Palmieri (1406–75; see fig. 1) succinctly defined the character of the Renaissance in *On Civic Life* (c. 1432):

> The noble achievements of our far-off ancestors [the Greeks and Romans] are forgotten and have become impossible to modern men. Where was the painter's art until Giotto [Florentine painter, c. 1266/67–1337] tardily restored it? A caricature of the art of human delineation! Sculpture and architecture, for long years sunk to the merest travesty of art, are only today in process of rescue from obscurity; only today are they being brought to a new pitch of perfection by men of genius and erudition. Of letters and liberal studies it were best to say nothing. For these, the real guides to distinction in all the arts, the solid foundation of all civilization, have been lost to mankind for eight hundred years and more. It is but in our own day that men dare boast that they see the dawn of better things. We owe it, for example, to our Leonardo Bruni [Greek and Latin scholar and translator, and Florentine chancellor and historian, 1370–1444] that Latin, so long a byword for its uncouthness, has begun to shine forth in its ancient purity, its beauty, its majestic rhythm. Now, indeed, may every thoughtful spirit thank God that it has been permitted to him to be born in this new age, so full of hope and promise, which already rejoices in a greater array of nobly gifted souls than the world has seen in the thousand years that have preceded it.

The recovery of "letters and liberal studies"; the purging of Latin from its medieval corruptions to reveal its ancient "purity," "beauty," and "majestic rhythm"; and the "rescue from obscurity" of painting, sculpture, and architecture by renewed interest in ancient art and culture constitute the essence of the Renaissance. The Renaissance also includes a tumultuous movement to reform the abuses of the Catholic Church and to revive its original apostolic piety and zeal, termed the Protestant Reformation in northern Europe, and the Counter-Reformation or Catholic Reformation in Italy.

For Palmieri, Giotto had initiated the classical revival in art about 1300 just as the scholar and poet Petrarch (1304–74) had begun the recovery of classical languages and letters by the 1330s. But humanism, one of the most distinguishing features of the Renaissance, was largely a fifteenth- and sixteenth-century phenomenon. Humanists in turn fostered a distinctly Renaissance art quite different from fourteenth-century Gothic art by introducing political ideologies and subject matter appropriated from classical history, literature, and mythology, and by encouraging new approaches to portraiture and the representation of space, narrative, and the body. Humanism also promoted a new language of architecture and a new conception of artists' status.

HUMANISM

Renaissance humanism was an educational program that evolved from the recuperation of ancient culture and offered a distinctive conception of humanity and its relationship to the world. In contrast to scholasticism—the medieval program of education addressed primarily to clerics educated in monasteries, cathedral schools, and universities—humanism was taught largely to urban laymen in schools funded by courts or communes. Scholasticism was concerned with logical analysis, commentary, and compilations of texts regarded as authoritative in their fields, and focused primarily on philosophy (especially metaphysics) and theology. Scholastics aimed to refine human reason through Aristotelian logic and dialectic to understand Christian faith and divine grace in preparation for the hereafter. Humanists principally read ancient Greek and Latin history, literature, and moral philosophy—those reservoirs of human experience and emotion that spoke more to the heart than to the mind. They sought a broad and practical knowledge of the world so as to live effectively and ethically within complex contemporary society. So wide ranging was their curiosity that many humanists, such as Leon Battista Alberti (1404–72; see fig. 2), to name one of the most famously versatile, achieved such a degree of multifaceted accomplishment that they embodied the later notion of the well-rounded "Renaissance man." Alberti was a scholar of Greek and Latin, canon lawyer, papal secretary, priest, poet, satirist, dramatist, natural scientist, mathematician, surveyor, cartographer, cryptographer, architect, engineer, musician, and athlete. He also wrote influential treatises in Latin and Italian on painting, sculpture, architecture, education, domestic economy, love, friendship, moral philosophy, Roman antiquities, and horses.

Humanists, like scholastics, addressed complex debates on Christian dogma, such as the immortality of the soul, but they were more concerned with how to live moral Christian lives in an evolving and imperfect world. They believed in a perfect divinity but concentrated on paths to godlike human perfection through the exercise of will and reason. Although tainted by original sin, human beings, humanists believed, were fundamentally good, substantially able to control their destinies, perfect their characters, and acquire glory and fame in this world and the next by virtuous actions. Humanists were also pragmatists for whom truths were relative, not absolute. What was true was what worked. What worked in their worlds of scholarship, government, diplomacy, and religion were speaking and writing with Ciceronian rhetorical eloquence in Latin—the prime vehicle of Renaissance knowledge and communication—in order to delight, persuade, and move people to action.

The humanist recovery of classical culture, however, produced social and artistic anxieties and tensions. Medieval culture that survived into the Renaissance meshed awkwardly with classical attitudes and worldviews. Classical culture offered abundant models to imitate, yet whether to imitate slavishly or to innovate freely in order to adapt to changed cultural circumstances remained a topic of passionate debate. Or was it better not to imitate at all and to depend on experience and nature as guides? Was it nobler to live a contemplative life "in order to banquet with the gods while still on earth," as Pico della Mirandola (1463–94) wrote in his *Oration on the Dignity of Man* (1486), or to live an honorable and engaged life as a responsible citizen in service to society? Did virtue really bring its own reward, or did blind fate control the course of human events? Was it really possible to reconcile pagan culture and Christian dogma or believe, as did Petrarch, that "Cicero [106–43 BC] himself would have been a Christian if he had been able to see Christ and to comprehend his doctrine" (*On Ignorance,* 1367)?

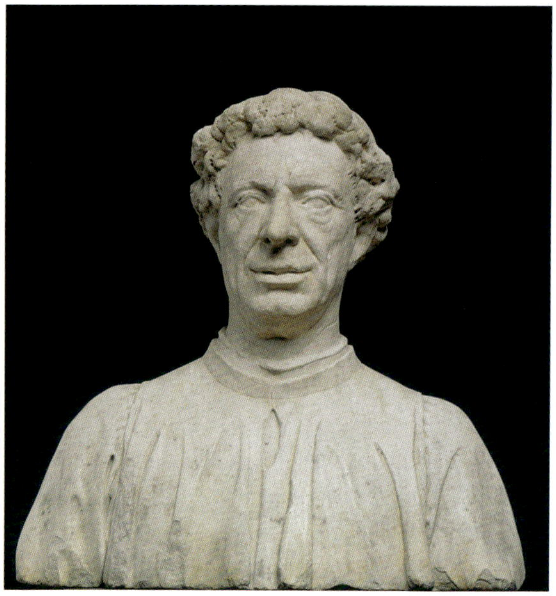

1. Antonio Rossellino (1427–79), *Matteo Palmieri,* 1468, marble, 21¼ in. (54 cm), Bargello, Florence.

Humanism initially flourished most vigorously in the republic of Florence and in the north Italian marquisates of Ferrara and Mantua, and soon spread to Rome, Venice, Naples, and most of the smaller political centers. In the volatile and highly competitive world of Italian politics, the political elite—whether advocating republican or authoritarian regimes—discovered that by commissioning art that referenced antiquity they could support claims to status, legitimacy, and sovereignty.

Matteo Palmieri, for example, commissioned a highly individualized portrait at age sixty-two with the effects of aging fully apparent to suggest a venerable sagacity (fig. 1).

The bust's lucid shape, wide-open eyes, and parted lips also evoked his lively intelligence. However, the unflinching realism—derived from early Roman commemorative and funerary busts—was a masquerade intended to associate Palmieri with the political engagement and civic responsibility of the leaders of ancient Rome and to underline the promotion in his treatise *On Civic Life,* quoted earlier, of a brand of ideal Florentine communal service modeled on the Roman republic.

INDEPENDENT PORTRAITS

From the fifteenth century onward, hundreds of independent portraits were produced in bronze, marble, and paint—a phenomenon paralleling the rise of Renaissance biographies, autobiographies, diaries, and dialogues. Many funerary and ruler portraits had been created in antiquity and to a much lesser extent in the Middle Ages, a tradition that continued with renewed vigor through the Renaissance. But as a direct result of the humanists' conception of human beings as intelligent, dignified, self-willed, and capable of moral responsibility and spiritual perfection, independent portraits of living individuals, who were neither rulers nor royals, appeared first in Renaissance Florence.

Alberti's youthful bronze self-portrait represents the earliest in the Renaissance of this type (fig. 2). Classical coins, medals, and gems inspired Alberti's oval format and profile presentation, linking his image to the ancient Romans whom he so admired. He wears a classical toga knotted at the neck and is identified by Roman block letters, L for Leon (lion), a name assumed only in adulthood, and BAP for Baptista, the Latin form of his baptismal name. His curly hair, thick neck, and alert eyes—classical portrait conventions indicating a leonine personality—signify his self-perceived strength, courage, and self-sufficiency.

In his dialogue *Little Rings* Alberti explained that the Egyptian-inspired winged eye under his chin signified the all-knowing, omnipresent divinity to whom humanity owed praise and devotion and whose absolute power spurred one to virtuous action. But it also symbolized godlike human intelligence with which one could choose to live an honorable and praiseworthy life. Alberti probably also intended the toga's knot to represent the philosopher's *nodus mundi* (knot of the universe), a classical symbol of the union between heaven and earth or, more precisely in this context, between God's omniscience and omnipotence, and his own will and intellect.

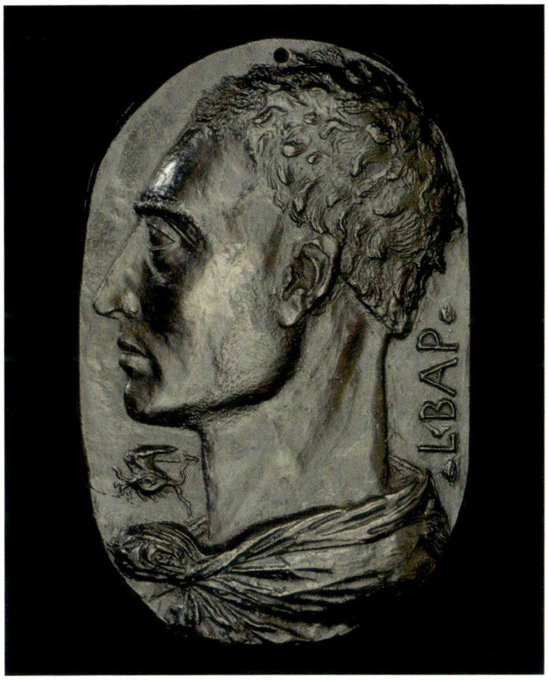

2. Leon Battista Alberti, *Self-Portrait,* 1430s, bronze, 7⅞ × 5⅜ in. (20.1 × 13.6 cm), National Gallery of Art, Washington, DC.

PERSPECTIVE

A method of representing three-dimensional space called one-point perspective first appeared in Florence sometime before 1425, although medieval surveying, map making, astronomy, urbanism, painting, geometry, and optical theory prepared for its invention by the Florentine artist and architect Filippo Brunelleschi (1377–1446). Brunelleschi's two painted demonstration panels have been lost and their dates disputed, but the techniques he employed were revised and publicized by Alberti in his 1435 treatise, *On Painting.*

Alberti understood vision as rays of light emanating from objects in nature focused cone-like at a single point within the eye. He conceived of a painting or relief as a square or rectangular section of this visual cone with the image's compositional lines focused at a single point, mirroring in reverse what the eye saw. Alberti's square or rectangular intersection of the visual cone revolutionized the perception and representation of space, challenging richly contoured Gothic windows and pictorial formats (see, e.g., figs. 18 and 54).

The bronze *Feast of Herod* by Donatello (1386–1466), the first extant fully developed example of one-point perspective, relates closely to Alberti's later description (fig. 3). Alberti instructed the artist to divide the bottom edge of his pictorial surface into an even number of modular units, a shorthand notation for a modular grid understood to cover the entire surface (fig. 4). Each modular unit (Donatello used five) represented for Alberti one *braccio,* a unit of measure about 23 inches (58.36 cm) in length. From each of the modular divisions Alberti instructed the artist to draw diagonal lines, called *orthogonals,* to a single point, the *focal point.* Ideally the focal point was located at the same height as the viewer's eye and usually at the center of the image. Next the artist was to draw a horizontal *horizon line* through the focal point and extend that line to a point at the edge or beyond the edge of the painting, called a *distance point.* A distance point further from the edge of the painting created a shallower space; a point closer to the edge created a deeper space. Finally, the artist drew lines from the distance point to the modular divisions on the bottom edge of the painting. Where these diagonals intersected the orthogonals, he drew horizontal lines called *transversals.*

Together the orthogonals and transversals created a boxlike space characterized by a receding tessellated (tiled) floor common to many Renaissance paintings and reliefs. Three floor squares determined the height of each approximately three-*braccia* figure measured from the square on which the figure was standing, a procedure that guaranteed the proper diminution of figures in space. The overall visual effect was a lucid geometrical space in which each element related to every other according to a mathematical ratio. In addition, the space was strongly illusionistic with forms diminishing systematically from foreground to background as in natural vision. The space also appeared to be related to that of the viewer, like the spatial continuum between inside and outside when looking through an open window.

It was precisely these characteristics, related to humanist ideals, that fostered the reception and development of perspective. The link to the eye of a single viewer supported the importance of each person, and the spatial

3. Donatello, *Feast of Herod* (Matthew 14:6–12; Mark 6:21–28), c. 1425, gilt bronze, 23⅝ in. (60 cm) square, Baptistery, Siena.

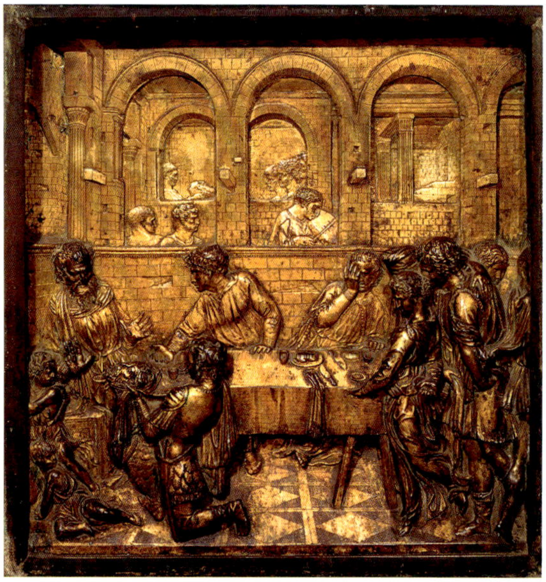

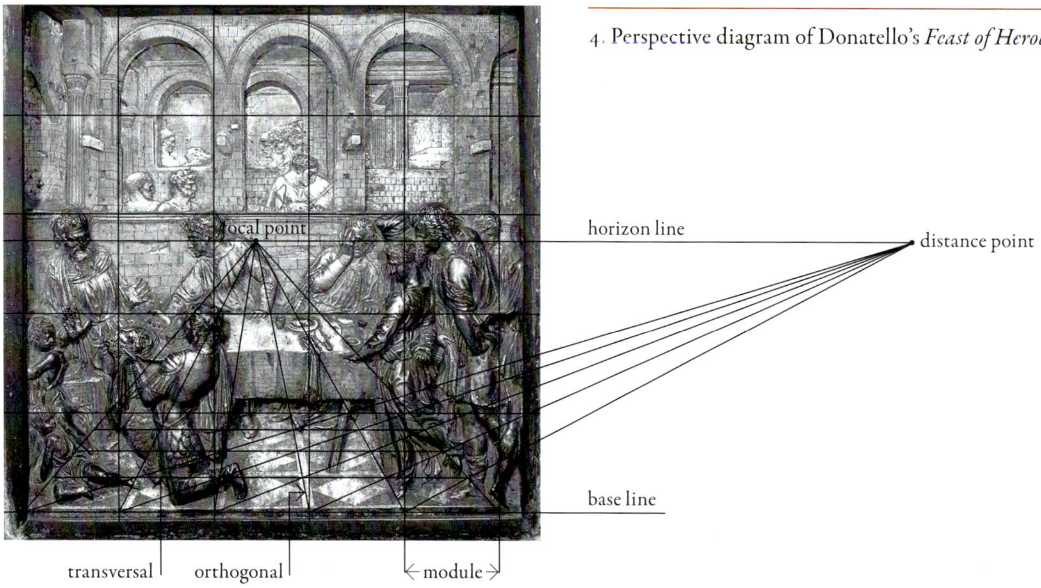

4. Perspective diagram of Donatello's *Feast of Herod.*

illusionism constructed a believable world where individuals could act autonomously. On the other hand, the geometrical perfection of space and the mathematical relationships between forms expressed the perfection of God and his creation as well as the potential for human perfectibility.

In the *Feast of Herod* Donatello exploited the illusion of continuity between viewer and image to intensify the drama's immediacy. He extended the space to the sides and rear to suggest amplitude appropriate to the sacred drama, while the geometrical space and proportional forms linked John the Baptist's life to the underlying perfection of God's plan.

NARRATIVE

In his treatise *On Painting* Alberti wrote that *istoria* (narrative) constituted art's highest goal. *Istoria* delighted the beholder by copious forms and diverse figures in varying postures and actions. Narrative also served to teach and persuade and thus required "the abundance to be graced with a certain moderation in variety, and marked with dignity and modesty." These narrative features were classical rhetorical prescriptions for eloquence in speech and writing, the highest aim of humanists. According to Alberti, an *istoria* should also be characterized by proper focus and subordination of parts, moving as in rhetorical speech from word, to phrase, to clause, to the full periodic sentence, which he translated for painted *istoria* as plane, member, body, and picture.

By the clarity yet complexity of its compositional and symbolic structure, Donatello's *Feast of Herod* (fig. 3) exemplified Alberti's *istoria.* The orthogonals draw the viewer's eye toward the musician in the middle ground playing a *lira da braccio* (early violin) for Salome's dance as two stewards to the left of the musician pause to listen. The musician's aural harmony, however, strikes a dissonant chord when the viewer suspects that the stewards have been carving meat for the feast, which anticipates the beheading of John, shown behind them. Furthermore, the grand classicizing architecture mixes arches, architraves, piers, columns, and colonnettes to create an oddly discordant environment, an appropriate visual expression for Herodias's rage when John the Baptist preached that Herod (r. as tetrarch 4 BC–AD 39) had breached Jewish law by marrying the ex-wife of his brother Philip (d. AD 39).

Herodias plotted her revenge by arranging a feast at which Salome, her daughter by Philip, performed an erotic dance for Herod. When Herod became aroused, she persuaded him to grant Salome one wish, prearranged to be a request for John's head. Salome dances rightward, her movement amplified by the gaze of two figures who look on from behind. Donatello enhanced her eroticism by deriving her figure from well-known examples of classical Maenads, orgiastic followers of Bacchus. The "cause" of Salome's dance is followed by the immediate "effect" of a soldier kneeling to present John's head on a salver, his action magnified by Herodias's movement, expression, and gesture. Herod's reaction of horror is underscored by the two terrified children at his side and the cringing banqueter to the right of Herodias. By staging the drama against the expectation of Western eyes trained to read from left to right, Donatello intensified Herodias and Salome's unnatural passion. Donatello further heightened the dramatic tension by contrasting the narrative's lateral flow with the onrush of orthogonals focused on an empty masonry wall. He arranged on the table in front of the wall a poignant still life of wine glass, plate of meat, knife, and napkin thematizing John's beheading.

THE HUMAN BODY

In the Middle Ages nudes were rarely represented except to illustrate punishments for bodily vices. When collections of ancient sculpture, carved gems, and coins were formed and studied in the Renaissance, however, contemporaries were impressed by the naturalism and beauty of classical nudes. Supported by certain strains of humanist thought that understood a human body's external grace as an expression of the soul's inner spiritual perfection made in the likeness of God, classicizing nudes—simultaneously realistic and idealized—became a major Renaissance art form for the first time since antiquity (see figs. 107, 132, 144, 164, 180, 181, 185, and 186).

Renaissance artists also learned from classical nudes the principle of *contrapposto,* a posture in which weight is carried on one leg while the other is relaxed, and the body is counterbalanced on either side of the rotated spinal axis to express movement or the potential for movement held in equilibrium against the force of gravity. *Contrapposto* is best exemplified by the *Doryphoros* of Polykleitos (fifth century BC; figs. 5 and 6). The well-toned, muscular athlete carries his weight on his right leg, forcing his right hip to thrust upward and his right shoulder and arm to lower. His left side counterbalances the right, with the leg relaxed, foot pulled backward, knee bent, hip lowered, and left shoulder and arm raised to support the (now missing) bronze spear. With his bodily axes in equilibrium and his head and torso

5. Polykleitos, *Doryphoros (Spear Bearer)*, marble, 6 ft. 6⅜ in. (199 cm), Museo Archeologico Nazionale, Naples, Roman copy after a Greek bronze original of c. 450–440 BC. Roman copies after the *Doryphoros* were not discovered until the nineteenth century, but the type was well known from freestanding life-size figures of Bacchus, Antinous, and Hercules, as well as smaller figures in relief sculpture.

6. Diagram showing the bodily axes underlying the *Doryphoros's contrapposto.*

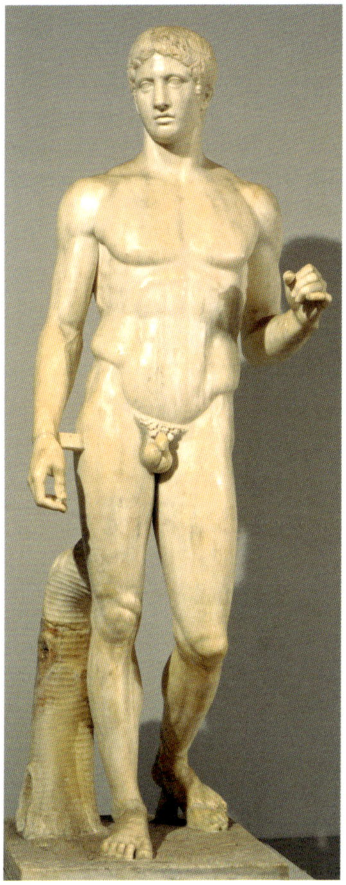

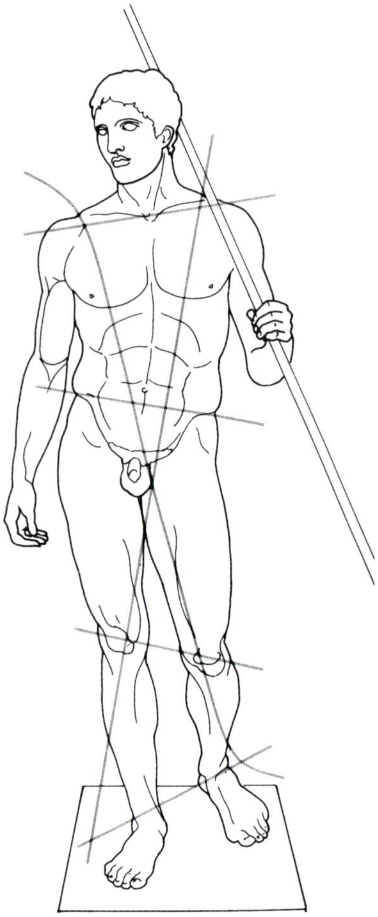

turned slightly to his right, he appears at rest, but poised to step forward.

The internal equilibrium and potential for movement achieved by the use of *contrapposto* graphically expressed the humanist belief in the ability of human beings to exercise their free will. Mastery of classical nudes also taught artists how to render more convincingly the movements and expressions of the draped body, greatly facilitating the composition of effective rhetorical narratives.

CLASSICIZING ARCHITECTURE

In about 1416, in the monastery of St. Gall, Switzerland, Poggio Bracciolini (1380–1459), Florentine humanist and papal secretary at the Council of Constance (1414–17), rediscovered a manuscript of *On Architecture* by Vitruvius (active 46–20 BC). The manuscript generated great excitement in Florence, for this was the sole treatise on the theory and practice of classical architecture to survive from antiquity. Vitruvius showed that classical architecture had its own complex vocabulary and grammar, vastly different from the prevailing fashion of Gothic architecture with pointed arches, attenuated columns, and complicated tracery. Just as the vocabulary and grammar of Latin had to be cleansed of medieval imperfections, so too, it was widely believed, did architecture need its medieval "deformities" purged.

Vitruvius, however, wrote an abominable Latin. As Alberti put it, "The Romans might think he wanted to appear Greek, while the Greeks would think that he babbled Latin." To better understand Vitruvius, humanists and architects began to measure and draw the Roman ruins that previously had served more as rock quarries than objects of serious study. Yet the ruins themselves were indeed fragmentary and difficult to understand—and they seldom conformed to the prescriptions of Vitruvius. This dilemma provoked a twofold response by humanists and artists.

On the one hand, to make the fragmentary whole, to clarify the obscure, to arrive at norms for the reform of

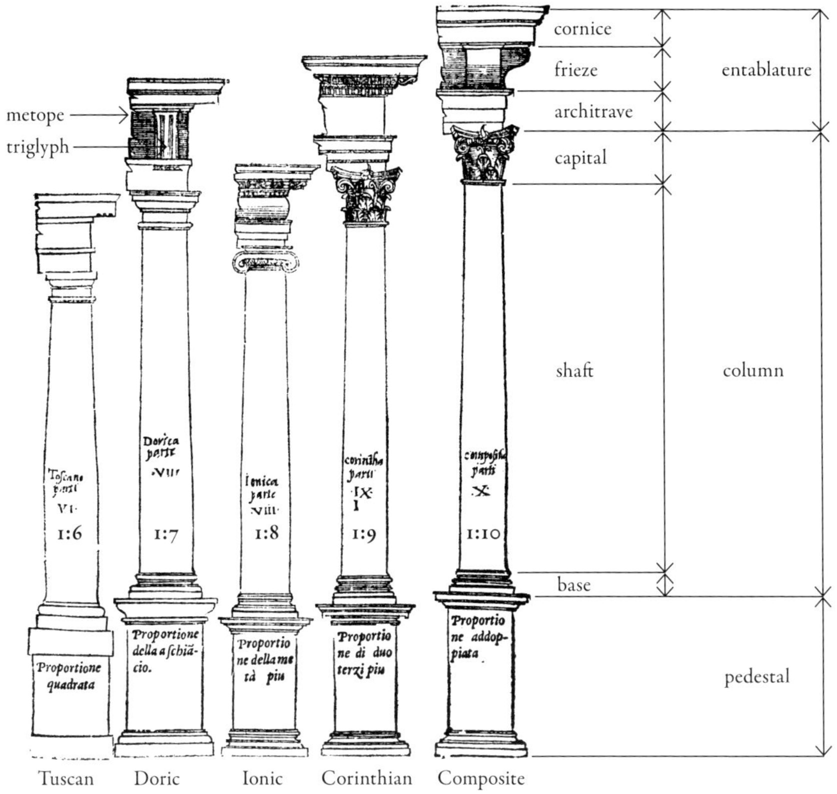

7. Sebastiano Serlio, *The Five Orders,* woodcut, from *Regole generali di architettura sopra le cinque maniere de gli edifici* (Venice, 1537), fol. 6r.

contemporary architecture, humanists and architects read the ancient literary and archaeological records with ever-greater attention and trust in their authority. By the mid-sixteenth century they had codified the classical language of architecture, especially the orders, far more rigidly and narrowly than had the ancients themselves. On the other hand, since knowledge of antiquity remained partial and classical building types—amphitheaters, basilicas, temples, public baths, triumphal arches, and the like—were mostly irrelevant to contemporary needs, scholars and architects depended on both tradition and innovation. In the early phases of the Italian Renaissance, with Gothic never having gained as strong a foothold in Italy as in the rest of Europe, there was less a revival of antiquity than a survival of eleventh- and twelfth-century Romanesque (see figs. 10 and 11), which in turn harkened back to Roman architecture. But by the mid-sixteenth century willful experimentation and breaking of rules resulted in a fanciful architecture (see, e.g., fig. 156) that would have appeared distorted and bizarre to Vitruvius. In the end, Renaissance humanists and artists invented the classical language of architecture as much as they relied on Vitruvius and classical ruins as models.

This classical language of architecture was grounded on the orders, the very name implying discipline and rule. Vitruvius distinguished the Doric, Ionic, Corinthian, and Tuscan, while Alberti in his influential mid-fifteenth-century architectural treatise, *On the Art of Building in Ten Books* (7.6), first described the Composite, a blend of the Ionic and Corinthian. The sixteenth-century architect Sebastiano Serlio (1475–c. 1554) was the first to present visually the five orders as a canonical set (fig. 7). All orders have an optional pedestal or supporting base and a vertical column composed of a base, a plain or fluted shaft, and a capital. Columns in turn carry a horizontal entablature consisting of an architrave, frieze, and cornice. A freestanding column-and-entablature structural system constitutes *trabeation. Arcuation* defines a series of piers and arches devised by the Romans to support heavy masonry vaults. Very often the two were combined by engaging a trabeated order with an arcuated structure. Flattened columns of the various orders engaged with piers or walls were called pilasters. The orders were also modular and proportional, the module equal to the lower diameter of the column. Proportions were based on simple mathematical ratios, such that the height of the sequence of orders might equal six, seven, eight, nine, or ten modules for ratios of 1:6, 1:7, 1:8, 1:9, and 1:10, as Serlio indicated by Roman numerals on his woodcut. The *intercolumniation,* or space between the columns, might be two, three, or even four modules, producing another set of ratios. According to Vitruvius, these proportional relationships imparted harmony to a building on the analogy to musical harmonies generated from simple mathematical ratios. As Pythagoras (sixth century BC) observed, two taut vibrating strings, one twice as long at the other (in a ratio of 1:2), sound a musical octave. A ratio of 3:4 produces a musical fourth, 2:3 a musical fifth. Plato (c. 428–348 BC) believed that the cosmos was constructed with harmonic ratios and thus produced a "music of the spheres." Vitruvius in turn thought that such architectural ratios "tuned" the building to "resonate" in harmony with the universe.

Vitruvius also related the ornamentation of classical architecture to the human body, introducing physical movement and gesture into architectural discourse. The 1:6 diameter-to-height ratio of a Doric column was, he claimed, derived from the same ratio between the length of a man's foot and his height resulting in a column that resembled "the proportion of a man's body, its strength and grace." The thinner and taller Corinthian order, by contrast, "imitates the slight figure of a maiden." Furthermore, just as the human body was composed of parts subordinate to the unity of the whole, so should a building's design adjust its "several members to the general pattern of the plan." Vitruvius illustrated this idea by noting that a man with outstretched arms and legs can be both circumscribed within and unified by the simple and perfect geometric forms of a circle and square, a concept visualized by many Renaissance artists, including Leonardo da Vinci (1452–1519; fig. 8). In both antiquity and the Renaissance, the stable square symbolized the terrestrial sphere, while the circle without beginning or end, every point equidistant from the center, signified the celestial sphere. The Vitruvian man, therefore, demonstrated the interaction between the micro- and the macrocosm, and humanity's dual material and spiritual nature.

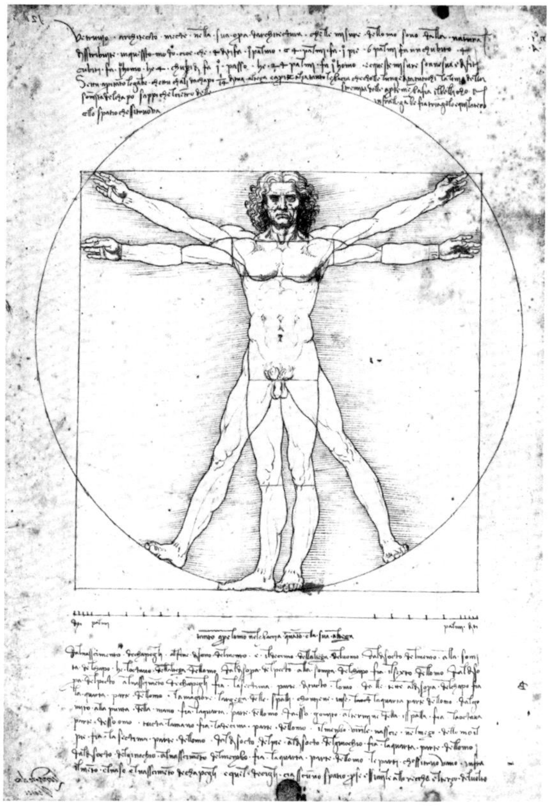

8. Leonardo da Vinci, *Vitruvian Man,* c. 1485–90, pen-and-ink drawing, 13½ × 9⅝ in. (34.3 × 24.5 cm), Accademia, Venice.

According to Vitruvius, the principle of decorum controlled the selection of orders used to articulate a building. The severe and robust Tuscan or Doric orders, for example, were most appropriate for temples honoring a male deity, while for a goddess, the elegant and ornamental Ionic or Corinthian were more apt. By resorting to decorum and proportion to order the composition of architectural forms, an architect achieved *eurythmia,* or overall syntactic harmony and integration.

The connection of architecture to language, ornament, and the body created an intertextual bridge to rhetoric with its syntactical rules, ornate speech, and physical gestures. Architecture was also perceived to have the same capacity as rhetoric to enthrall and inspire.

THE STATUS OF ARTISTS

Pliny the Elder (AD 23–79) wrote that Pamphilus (fourth century BC), the teacher of the famous classical Greek painter Apelles (active late fourth century BC) "was erudite in all branches of knowledge, especially arithmetic and geometry, without which, he held, an art could not be perfected. As a result of his prestige, freeborn boys in all Greece were given lessons in drawing and thus painting was received into the front rank of the liberal arts" (*Natural History* 35.75). Lucian (b. c. AD 120), by contrast, states that to be a sculptor "you will be nothing but a laborer getting meager returns, one of the swarming rabble. Even if you should become a Phidias [c. 500–432 BC] or Polykleitos [the two most famous sculptors of classical Greece], everyone would praise your craftsmanship, but none would wish to be like you; for whatever your achievement, you would be considered an artisan, a craftsman, one who lives by the work of his hands" (*The Dream* 9).

Lucian's prejudice against manual labor accorded with the medieval view that the visual arts belonged to the mechanical arts, an attitude that survived into the Renaissance. But we have already learned of Palmieri's belief that liberal studies were the "real guides to distinction in the arts." In forging a link between eloquence, *istoria,* and the language of architecture, Alberti and many other humanists subscribed to the famous simile of Horace (65–8 BC) *ut pictura poesis* ("as is painting so too is poetry" [*Ars poetica* 361]) by equating the goals of humanists and artists. Both art and rhetoric could teach human dignity and perfectibility. Both shared similar structural techniques for organizing visual and verbal fields. And both charmed and enlightened through eloquence and instructed viewers or auditors to lead ethical lives of good citizenship, virtuous action, and spiritual betterment. Furthermore, to understand perspective, classical subject matter, and the language of classical architecture, artists increasingly required knowledge of the liberal arts such as mathematics, ancient literature, history, and mythology. Artists, therefore, frequently saw themselves as rhetoricians and intellectuals.

All art, however, entailed manual labor. Nearly all Renaissance artists came from the lower artisan and shopkeeper classes and only rarely from the middle, professional, or patrician ranks. The educational opportunities accessible to those of position and wealth were closed to artists. Only Alberti, who was a humanist first and an architect second, had the privilege of a university education. Furthermore, the only way to learn and ultimately practice any art was to undergo a lengthy apprenticeship, which began around age ten after a basic grammar-school education and continued until about age twenty, when the artist joined one of the craft guilds as a journeyman or master. Despite these limitations, many artists were brilliant autodidacts. A few, such as Giorgio Vasari, learned basic Latin and wrote important treatises on art; others, such as Michelangelo Buonarroti (1475–1564) and Angelo Bronzino (1503–72), wrote first-rate vernacular poetry; still others through entrepreneurial skills and artistic virtuosity were invested with titles of nobility by the highest European sovereigns, such as Vasari and Giambologna (1529–1608), knighted by popes Pius V (1504–72, r. 1566–72) and Clement VIII (1536–1605, r. 1592–1605) respectively in 1571 and 1599.

The guild system of artistic training largely excluded women, who, however, did work as domestics, nurses, shopkeepers, and in the textile industry. Nevertheless, a few women did train as artists in the Renaissance, instructed by artist-fathers or, in the case of nuns, by artist-monks or artist-friars. Women were also art patrons, especially art for the home and convent.

In the later sixteenth century, in order to free themselves somewhat from the guilds' control of art training, marketing, and taxation, Florentine artists founded the first art academy in 1563, the Academy of Design, soon followed by several others elsewhere. The academy provided a forum where such essential liberal subjects as anatomy, mathematics, and perspective could be taught. Duke Cosimo I de' Medici (1519–74) sponsored the Academy of Design as a means to exercise greater centralized control over all the arts. He could, therefore, more efficiently stage the multimedia, largely ephemeral, extravaganzas to celebrate such events as births, deaths, marriages, and investitures that confirmed his legitimacy, authority, and dynastic continuity.

At Michelangelo's death in 1564, the academy seized the opportunity to promote its goals by staging an elaborate funeral for this greatest of Florentine artists, who had mastered supremely all the arts—sculpture, painting, architecture, and poetry. Such a grand state-sponsored ritual was unprecedented and indicative of the prominent social status that at least the most famous artists could achieve in the Renaissance. The educational program of the new academies, however, was of limited success, for apprenticeship in a master's workshop remained the essential method of art education in the Renaissance. But as academicians, artists could consider themselves scholarly practitioners of the liberal arts. As a compromise, they also served as courtiers, subservient to the demands of absolutist regimes.

PRE-RENAISSANCE FLORENCE

ROMAN AND EARLY MEDIEVAL FLORENCE

The Romans founded Florence at a strategic site on the banks of the Arno River as a *castrum* (military outpost) in the first century BC. In the sixteenth century Duke Cosimo I de' Medici commissioned his court artist, Giorgio Vasari, to paint this event in his principal audience hall (fig. 9). A priest in the background plows the outpost's fortified rectangular plan, while Roman legionaries construct the city, which includes an octagonal temple dedicated to Mars crowned with the god's equestrian image. To this day, the regular grid of streets and squares, standard in Roman planning, remains one of the principal features of Florence's urban core.

9. Giorgio Vasari, *Foundation of Florence by the Triumvirs Octavius, Mark Antony, and Lepidus,* 1563–65, oil on panel, ceiling, Sala Grande, Palazzo Vecchio. Aries, the zodiacal sign of March, represented in the sky, alludes to the belief that Florence was founded according to God's plan on March 25, the Feast of the Annunciation, giving the city a special sanctity and spiritual destiny as a new Jerusalem.

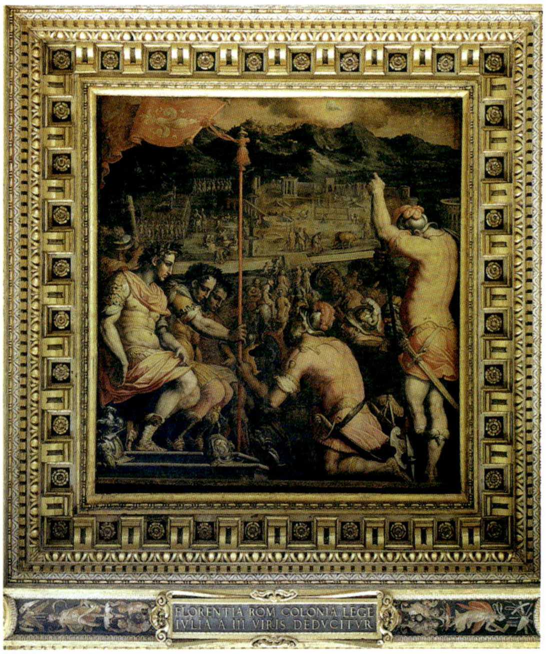

Beginning with the barbaric invasions in the fifth century, Florence (with a population of a mere two thousand or so) was dominated successively by the Ostrogoths, Byzantines, Lombards, Franks, and Germans. In the eleventh and twelfth centuries, a period of relative peace and prosperity under the margraves of Tuscany, Florence grew dramatically, and two new circuits of city walls were constructed, the first in 1078 and the second between 1173 and 1175, to accommodate populations grown to about twenty thousand and thirty thousand, respectively. Within this period two major Romanesque churches were built, the Baptistery of S. Giovanni Battista and S. Miniato al Monte (figs. 10 and 11, and see 12, nos. 3 and 4). In the Renaissance the Florentine Baptistery was considered a classical monument, for it was believed to be the ancient Roman temple dedicated to Mars—as depicted by Vasari (fig. 9)—that later had been modified for Christian use, as had the Pantheon in Rome. The Baptistery thus strongly influenced the revived classicism of early Renaissance architecture, as did the classicizing Romanesque style of S. Miniato.

The most characteristic feature of the twelfth century urban landscape, however, consisted of over one hundred and fifty towers that served as fortresses for clans of patrilineal noble families with feudal country estates. Many had ground-floor loggias open on one or more sides and supported on piers or columns where the clan gathered for banquets and celebrations of betrothals, weddings, political alliances, and religious holidays. Trained as sol-

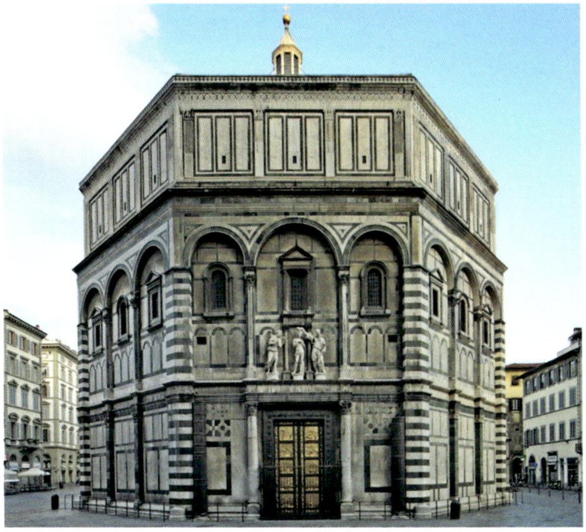

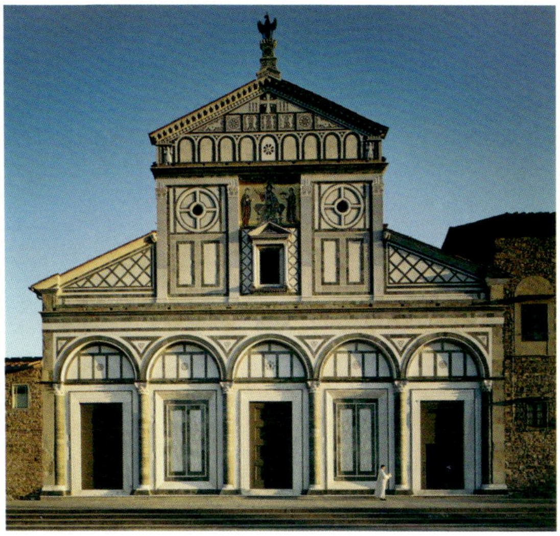

10. Baptistery, Florence, 1059–1150. Note the *Gates of Paradise* (fig. 49) by Lorenzo Ghiberti (c. 1381–1455) facing east. The marble *Baptism of Christ* above the door was executed in 1502 by Andrea Sansovino (c. 1467–1529).

11. S. Miniato al Monte, 1018–1207.

diers and aligned politically with the Ghibellines, supporters of German imperial authority in Italy, the men of these families squabbled primarily among themselves, periodically sallying forth from their towers to attack rival clans. These towers thus embodied the fragmented political order of magnates warring for family gain.

PEOPLE'S GOVERNMENT

By the mid-thirteenth century, Florence (now with a population of approximately seventy-five thousand) had developed a wealthy middle class of bankers, merchants, and professionals, a lower class of tradesmen and artisans, and a proletariat employed mostly in wool making, the city's economic mainstay. Also the power of the Ghibellines was increasingly countered by the rise of the Guelphs, supporters of papal authority. Within this evolving economic and political landscape, a coalition of major and minor guilds, formed to curb the magnates and the exploitative bankers and merchants, created in 1244 a republican government with statutes, representative councils, and executive officials. The executive and legislative branches of this government styled themselves "of the people." They were housed in a new Palazzo del Capitano del Popolo or Palazzo del Podestà, essentially a larger and more refined version of a magnate tower (see fig. 12, no. 5).

THE PRIORATE

After 1282, the economically more powerful major guilds succeeded in dominating the government and its new city council of priors selected by lot for short terms. The constitution of this new regime, the 1293 Ordinances of Justice, disenfranchised the magnates. As a visible sign of their disenfranchisement, the priors ordered their clan towers to be reduced to a height not to exceed 98 ½ feet (30 m). The priorate also deprived the nearly fifteen thousand proletarian wool workers of their political voice and civil rights, thereby provoking a rebellion in 1378. After a brief success, the so-called Ciompi Revolt was suppressed, and the Florentine republic remained under oligarchic control of the major guilds.

Florence reached the apex of its power and prosperity under the priorate in the thirteenth and fourteenth centuries. To celebrate its authority, provide for the common good, and promote the myth of Florence as a new Rome and a new Jerusalem, the priorate built some of the city's most imposing monuments and public spaces. Well-defined planning principles and strict building codes produced a high degree of urban order and harmony. Although celebrated as the "cradle of the Renaissance," Florence was urbanistically far more Gothic than Renaissance, as the early *View of Florence* demonstrates (fig. 12).

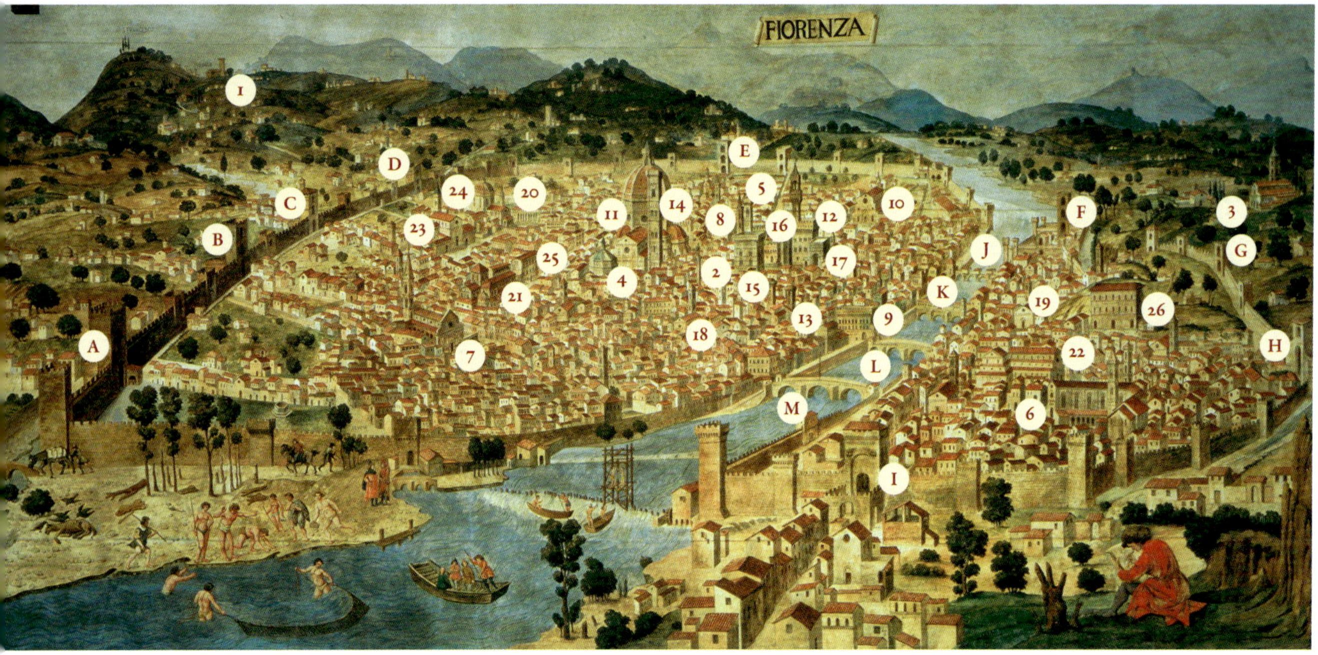

12. Anonymous, *View of Florence,* tempera on panel, Museo di Firenze Com'Era, Florence, based on a woodcut c. 1480 attributed to Francesco di Lorenzo Rosselli (1448–before 1513). In roughly chronological order: **1** Fiesole (Etruscan-Roman); **2** Column of the Mercato Vecchio, site of first-century BC Roman Forum; **3** S. Miniato al Monte (Benedictine until 1373, then Olivetan), founded by eighth century, rebuilt 1018–1207; **4** Baptistery, 1059–1150; **5** Palazzo del Podestà or Bargello, 1255–1345; **6** S. Maria del Carmine (Carmelite), begun 1268; **7** S. Maria Novella (Dominican), founded c. 1221, church c. 1246–78, façade c. 1457–78; **8** Campanile of Badia (Benedictine), founded 978, rebuilt 1285; **9** Palazzo Spini-Feroni, begun 1289; **10** S. Croce (Franciscan), founded 1228, begun 1295; **11** Cathedral, 1296–1467; **12** Priors' Palace, or Palazzo Vecchio, 1299–1315; **13** S. Trinita (Vallombrosan), founded in second half of eleventh century, rebuilt in fourteenth century, façade 1593–94; **14** Cathedral Campanile, 1334–60; **15** Or San Michele, 1336–1404; **16** Palazzo della Tribunale di Mercanzia, 1359; **17** Priors' Loggia, or Loggia dei Lanzi, 1374–82; **18** S. Pancrazio (Vallombrosan), documented by ninth century, begun 1370; **19** S. Felicità; **20** Foundling Hospital, 1419–45; **21** S. Lorenzo (Ambrosian), consecrated 393, rebuilt 1421–94; **22** S. Spirito (Augustinian), founded c. 1250, rebuilt c. 1434–96; **23** S. Marco (Silvestrine until 1436, then Dominican), begun 1299, rebuilt 1436–45; **24** SS. Annunziata (Servite), founded 1240, rebuilt 1444–1516; **25** Medici Palace, c. 1446–57; **26** Pitti Palace, 1458–66; **A** Porta al Prato; **B** Porta Faenza; **C** Porta S. Gallo; **D** Porta Pinta; **E** Porta S. Croce; **F** Porta S. Niccolò; **G** Porta S. Giorgio; **H** Porta Romana; **I** Porta S. Frediano; **J** Ponte alle Grazie; **K** Ponte Vecchio; **L** Ponte S. Trinita; **M** Ponte alla Carraia. For larger version, see insert following p. 148.

THE PRIORS' PALACE

The priorate built a huge baronial-style palace—more substantial than any previous Florentine palace—to house its armory, meeting rooms, administrative offices, chapel, and the priors' living quarters (figs. 12, no. 12; 13) and to loom over the city as a visible sign of the regime's legitimacy and power. Built on the site of the Uberti clan's residence, destroyed in 1258, and incorporating the Foraboschi family's tower in its campanile (bell tower), the Priors' Palace also signaled the suppression of the Ghibelline magnates. The rustication (masonry cut in massive blocks with beveled edges and left in a rough state) was derived from ancient Roman architecture to support the image of Florence as a new Rome. The crowning baldachin (canopy) on the bell tower also suggested the city's sovereignty and dominion. The north edge of the bell tower divides the square façade in half. The height of the bell tower equals the height of the façade. The heights of the battlements (defensive parapets) and the tower's crowning bell chamber each equal one-third the façade's total height. The façade's design, therefore, employed musical ratios of 1:1, 1:2, 1:3, and 2:3 to express the priorate's harmony and divine justice and to support

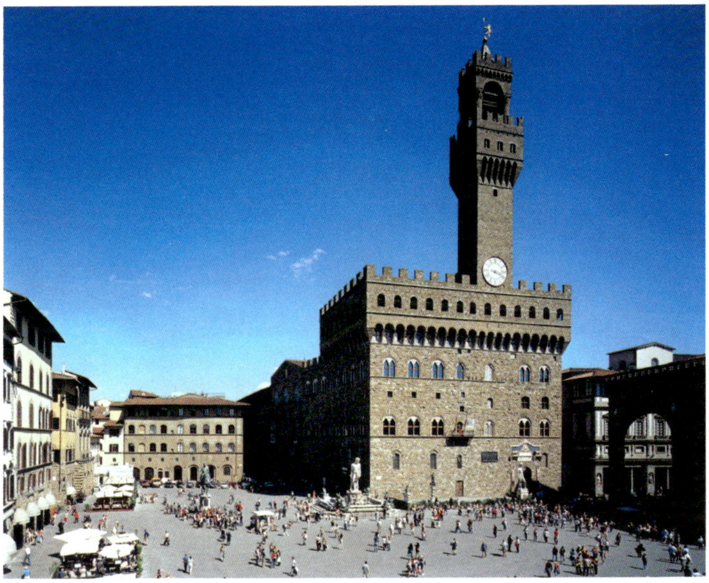

13. Arnolfo di Cambio (active 1245–c. 1302)?, Priors' Palace (Palazzo Vecchio after 1565), 1299–1315. The building block to the left of the Priors' Palace contains the Palazzo della Condotta (1337) and the Palazzo della Tribunale di Mercanzi (1359), housing, respectively, offices in charge of foreign mercenaries and the guilds' tribunal.

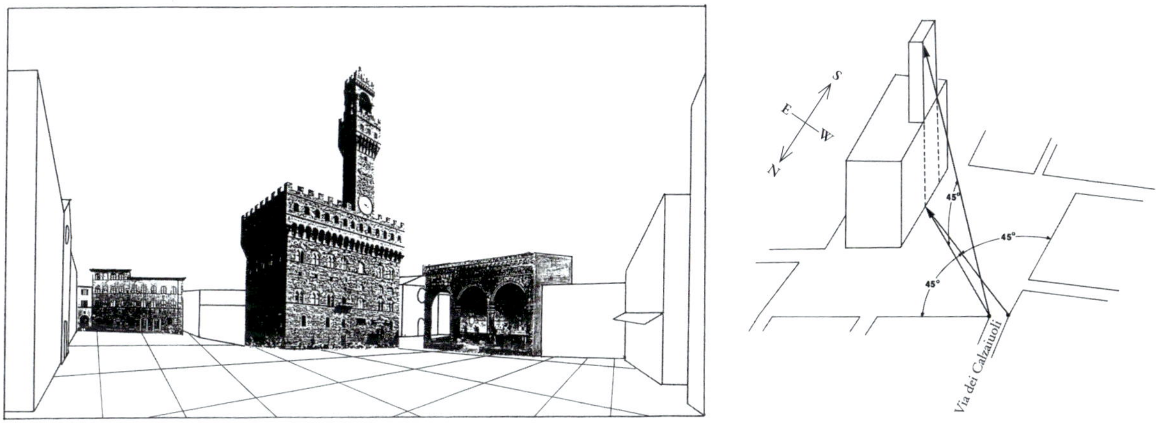

14. Diagram of the Piazza della Signoria.

the image of Florence as a new Jerusalem, an image underlined by the churchlike biforal (two opening) Gothic windows and the cloisterlike courtyard. Finally, the massive walls, high windows, and crowning battlements physically and visually served to counter resistance to the regime by the magnates on the right or the proletariat on the left.

PIAZZA DELLA SIGNORIA AND THE PRIORS' LOGGIA

From 1299 to 1387 the priorate cleared the L-shaped Piazza della Signoria to the north and west of the Priors' Palace and paved it in a grid pattern. The piazza (a public square or open space) accommodated civic spectacles of power that citizens were required to witness and verify. These included the bimonthly installation of priors, *parlamenti* (citizens' referendums and consultations), public executions, and maneuvers of the approximately four thousand–strong civic militia. From the principal entrance at the end of the Via dei Calzaiuoli, the piazza provided a 90-degree horizontal and a 45-degree vertical oblique view of the palace that concretized the ideals of spatial perception of contemporary optics, mathematics, and aesthetics (fig. 14). The priorate also added, at a near-right angle to the Priors' Palace, the Priors' Loggia (figs. 12, no. 17; 15), which sheltered communal rituals. Imitating but vastly outdoing baronial family loggias, the Priors' Loggia indicated the shift in power from the magnates to the priorate. Its cathedral-derived bay design also suggested the sanctity of the government and its divinely inspired justice.

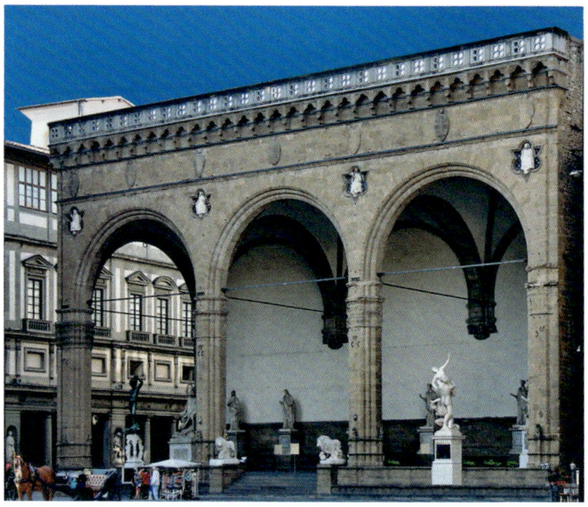

15. Benci di Cione (d. 1388) and Simone di Francesco Talenti (c. 1330/35–after 1383), Priors' Loggia (called Loggia dei Lanzi after the mid-sixteenth century), 1374–82. When the loggia became functionally obsolete under the autocratic Medici dukes, it was transformed into a sculpture gallery promoting ducal political ideology. Note the bronze *Perseus* (fig. 180) in the left arch, the marble *Rape of the Sabines* (figs. 185–86) in the right arch, and the Uffizi (figs. 174–78) to the left.

FINAL CIRCUIT OF WALLS AND FLORENTINE EXPANSION

The relative prosperity of the thirteenth and early fourteenth centuries promoted a rise in population to nearly a hundred thousand inhabitants, establishing Florence as one of the largest cities in Europe. This vast population was served by a number of religious orders that established their houses mostly outside the twelfth-century walls—first the Dominicans and the Franciscans in the 1220s, followed at various intervals throughout the century by the Servites, Augustinians, Carmelites, Silvestrines, and others (fig. 12, nos. 6, 7, 10, 13, 22, 23, and 24). From 1284 to 1333 the priorate constructed a final circuit of walls nearly five and a quarter miles long (about eight and a half km) to provide security for the expanding city and room for future growth. This momentous achievement was recorded by Vasari's painting on the ceiling of Duke Cosimo I's audience hall (fig. 16; cf. fig. 12). The new walls proved to be too expansive, when the 1348 pan-European Black Death killed a third or more of Florence's population.

The priorate also dramatically expanded the city's territorial empire from the mid-thirteenth century onward, conquering nearly all the important Tuscan centers, except Lucca and Siena, and founding a number of new towns. These conquests allowed the priorate to feed the growing populace, extract raw materials for industry, expand trade, secure an outlet to the sea, and provide fortresses to protect approaches to the city.

THE CATHEDRAL AND OR SAN MICHELE

No two buildings exemplified more fully the determination of the priorate to unify the commune, provide for its well-being, and glorify Florentine wealth and power than the new Duomo, or cathedral (seat of the bishop), and the civic granary and guild oratory, Or San Michele. In 1296, three years before beginning their governmental palace, the priors began to replace the Romanesque S. Reparata with a new cathedral large enough to accommodate nearly the entire population (fig. 17). Under the direction of the powerful wool manufacturers' guild, the Duomo became one of the largest churches in Christendom by its completion in 1467. It rose majestically above the city in the center of the final circuit of walls, a monument to Florentine unity and piety (fig. 12, no. 11). The dedication to S. Maria del Fiore (St. Mary of the Flowers) recalled both the Roman past of Florence, when it was called *Florentia* (city of flowers), and the spring Feast of the Annunciation (March 25), when it was supposedly founded. As a mighty symbol of the new Jerusalem and the new Rome, the cathedral unified Florence across space and time and evoked the communal hope for temporal prosperity and spiritual renewal.

In 1336 the priorate and the silk guild began a third great building project, Or San Michele, located between the cathedral and the Priors' Palace (figs. 12, no. 15; 18). The ground-floor groin-vaulted loggia, originally open on all sides, was designed as the communal grain exchange. The two floors above, echoing the style of the Priors' Palace (fig. 13), provided grain storage for periods of drought and famine. As the site of a miracle-working image of the Virgin and Child, the loggia also served as an oratory for the Florentine guilds, a role it played with more convenience and dignity when the arcade was closed in 1480 with Gothic windows. The interior of the oratory was embellished by images of the patron saints of various guilds and by the magnificent marble tabernacle (1355–59) by Andrea Orcagna (c. 1308–c. 1368) built by public donations as an expression of thanksgiving after the great plague of 1348. Other guilds had been assigned the fourteen exterior niches to fill with large sculpted images of their patron saints, although only three had been filled by 1404.

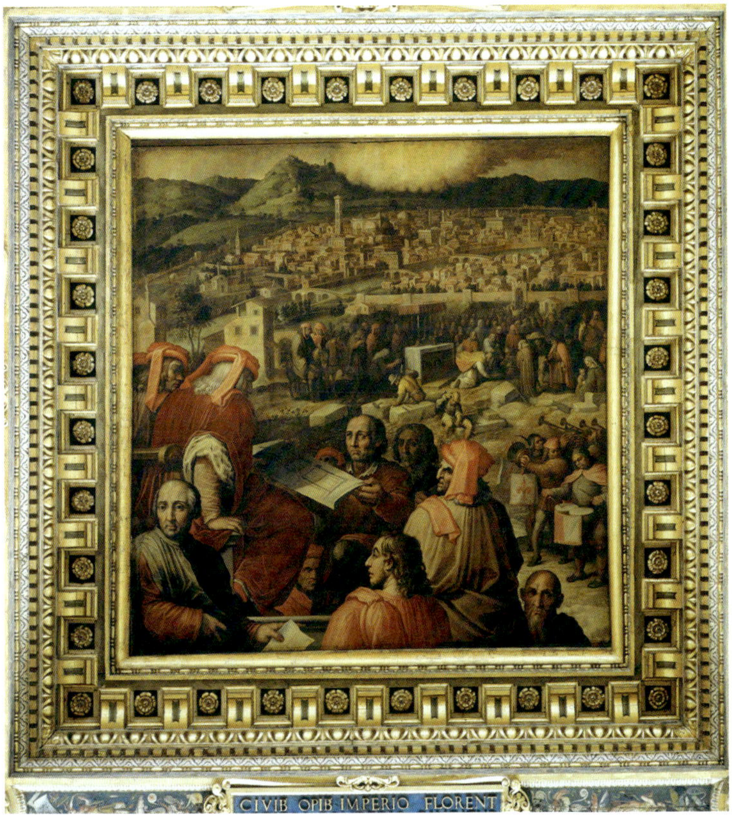

16. Giorgio Vasari, *Building the Third Circuit of Florentine Walls,* 1562–65, oil on panel, ceiling, Sala Grande, Palazzo Vecchio.

17. Aerial view of the cathedral and baptistery looking southeast. Arnolfo di Cambio designed the body of the cathedral (built 1296–1417) on a plan derived from that of the Church of the Holy Sepulcher in Jerusalem. Giotto designed the campanile (built 1334–60); Brunelleschi, the dome and lantern (built 1417–67). The cathedral was consecrated by Pope Eugenius IV (r. 1431–47) on March 25, 1436, and dedicated to S. Maria del Fiore, S. Reparata, and Christ.

18. Francesco Talenti (c. 1300/10–after 1369), Neri di Fioravante (active 1340–84), Benci di Cione, and Simone di Francesco Talenti, Or San Michele, north and west flanks, 1336–1404. On the north flank in the two niches to the right, note the *Four Crowned Saints* (fig. 23) and a copy of *St. George* (fig. 25).

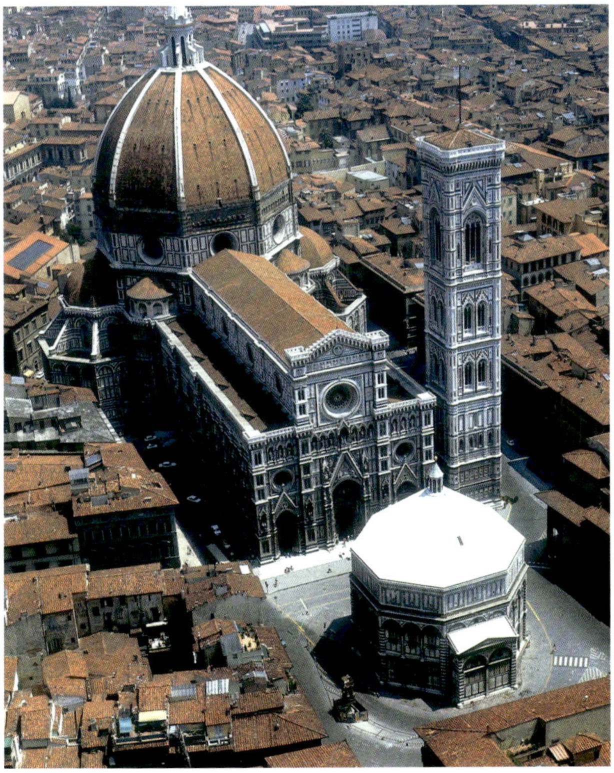

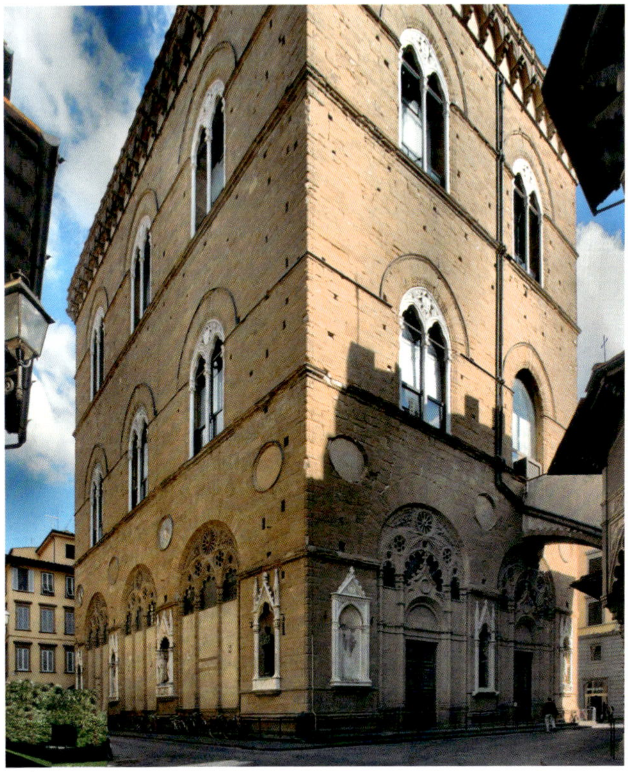

PART I

FLORENCE

under the Albizzi and the Medici

1400–1494

I

CIVIC ARCHITECTURE AND URBANISM

BRUNELLESCHI'S FOUNDLING HOSPITAL

The streets and squares of Florence changed but little in the fifteenth century. However, the earliest monument of *Renaissance* architecture, Brunelleschi's Ospedale degli Innocenti (figs. 19 and 20; see also fig. 12, no. 20), had important urbanistic implications for the sixteenth-century development of Piazza della SS. Annunziata.

When the Innocenti was solemnly inaugurated on April 11, 1445, by Fra Antonino Pierozzi (1389–1459, canonized 1523), the Dominican archbishop of Florence, it joined over forty other hospitals in Florence, but it was only the third to accept orphans. As a result of the Black Death of 1348 and subsequent cycles of plague, famine, and economic depression, the number of orphans and abandoned children kept increasing. The Foundling Hospital opened in 1445 with about 60 children, but by 1466 there were some 200 in-house children with an additional 450 or so living with wet-nurses; in 1506, about 450 in-house and 870 with wet-nurses; and by 1540, about 780 in-house and 1,500 with wet-nurses. By this point, the hospital's strained facilities and financial resources necessitated its reorganization and expansion under Duke Cosimo I.

The children were cared for by several visiting doctors and a permanent staff of mostly single women, some raised in the orphanage itself, who made a career of nursing and charitable service. They provided a minimal grammar-school education to prepare the boys for an apprenticeship in the trades and taught domestic skills to the girls, who usually outnumbered the boys by about three to one, for employment in hospitals, the textile industry, or private households.

The silk guild began construction of the Foundling Hospital in 1419, aided by a bequest of 1,000 florins from the estate of a merchant from Prato, Francesco Datini (c. 1335–1410)—less than one tenth of the eventual total building cost. The design commissioned from

19. Filippo Brunelleschi and successors, Foundling Hospital, Florence, 1419–45. In 1487 Andrea della Robbia (1435–1525/28) executed the blue and white glazed terracotta roundels with infants in swaddling clothes in the spandrels of the arches.

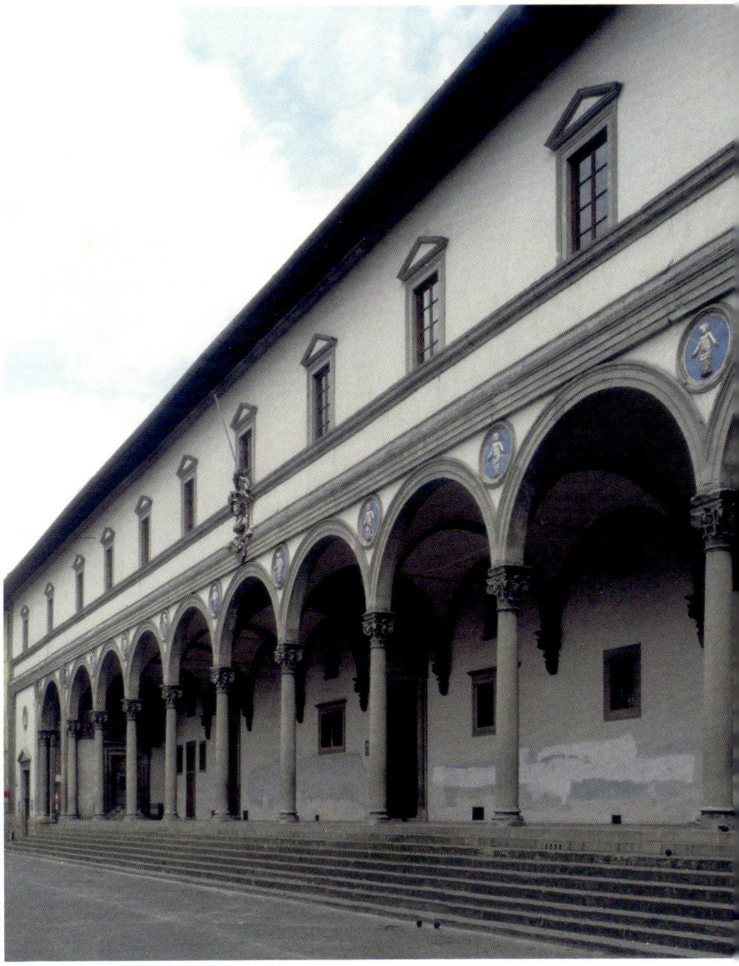

Brunelleschi, who as a goldsmith had been a member of the guild since 1404, featured elements common to most previous Florentine hospices for the sick, homeless, and orphaned, which in turn derived from monastic plans. The complex was built around a central square cloister surrounded by a groin-vaulted portico, five arched bays per side, supported on twenty Corinthian columns—a spatial island of therapeutic tranquility. To the north of the cloister, the tall timber-roofed Church of S. Maria degli Innocenti (18 × 54 *braccia,* a width to length ratio of 1:3) provided periodic solace for the children, staff, and public. To the west, two square (12 × 12 *braccia*) groin-vaulted rooms accommodated the administrative office and reception room of the *spedalingo* (director) and were flanked by three rectangular spaces containing a stairway, a groin-vaulted passageway to the cloister, and a barrel-vaulted chamber of uncertain use, perhaps a pharmacy. Dormitories reached by the stairway were located above

20. Plan, section, and elevation of the Foundling Hospital. The lower elevation reconstructs Brunelleschi's original design of the portico façade. 1 cloister, 2 S. Maria degli Innocenti, 3–4 office and reception room of the *spedalingo,* 5 pharmacy? 6 foundling ward, 7 women's entrance vestibule, 8 reception room, 9 nurses' common room, 10 women's refectory, 11 kitchen, 12 infirmary, 13 men's refectory, 14 kitchen.

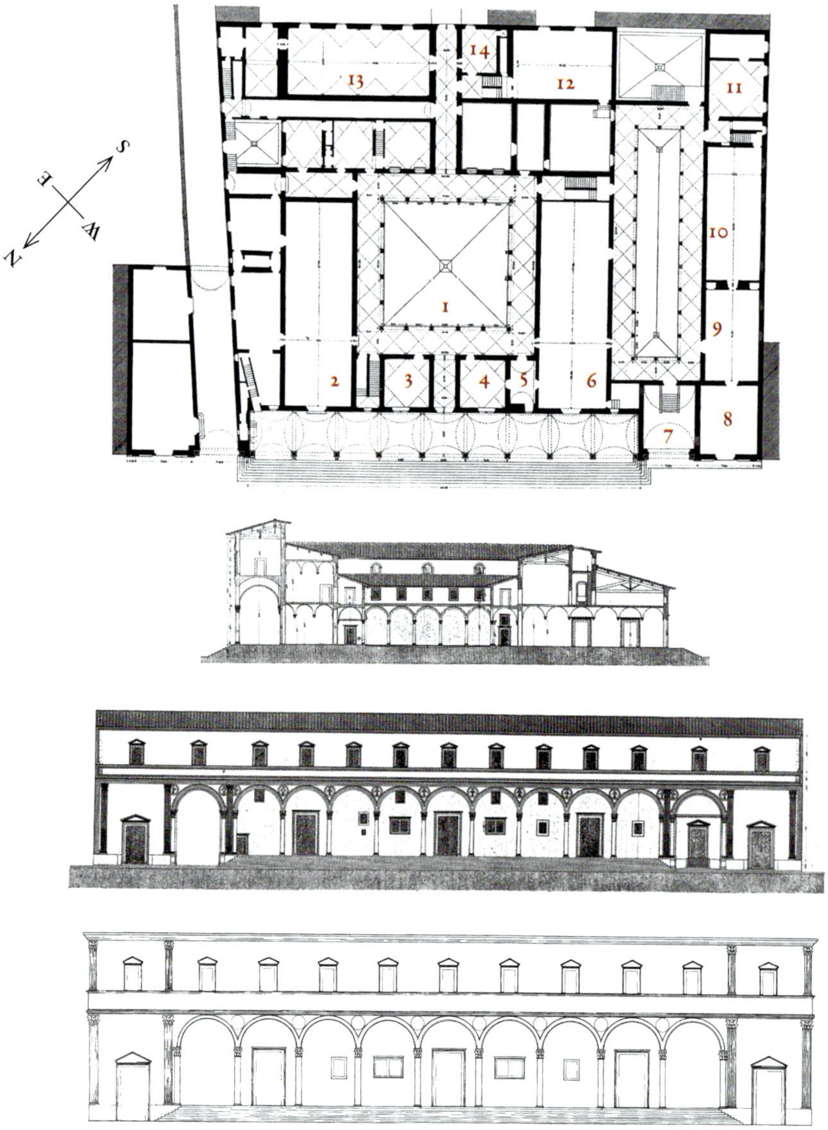

these spaces as well as over the façade's portico. To the south, the large foundling ward with an altar at the east end for daily services mirrored the church in plan and elevation, its high, well-ventilated, timber-trussed space designed to expel unhealthy air exhaled by the inmates. Further to the south, in an area reserved for women and girls, Brunelleschi's successor after 1427, Francesco della Luna (c. 1373–c. 1446), added a rectangular courtyard surrounded by a groin-vaulted portico supported by twenty-four Ionic columns, a reception room, a nurses' common room, a refectory (dining hall), and a kitchen. To the east at the rear of the complex were added, again after 1427, a refectory for men, a kitchen, and an infirmary. Storage and laundry facilities were located in basement rooms. An orchard and garden at the rear of the complex toward the east not only supplied produce for the orphanage but also provided a substantial income for its operating budget.

The entire complex was unified by an external façade incorporating a portico entered via a flight of eight steps. A portico was a common feature of many earlier hospitals, such as that of S. Matteo, built from 1388 to 1410 in the neighboring Piazza S. Marco (see fig. 142, no. 11). However, in a deliberate attempt to revive the spirit of classical antiquity, Brunelleschi appropriated most motifs of his façade from Tuscan Romanesque architecture (figs. 10 and 11), including a delicate arcade supported by unfluted monolithic Corinthian columns, a wide entablature, side bays flanked by fluted Corinthian pilasters, upper windows with triangular pediments, and an unexecuted crowning cornice.

As in classical practice, the façade's design was modular, the smaller module based on the lower diameter (5/6 *braccio,* or 48 cm) of the columns. Each column (including base, shaft, capital, and abacus) measured 517 cm, or 10.77 diameters, slightly higher than the ten-diameter height recommended by Vitruvius for the Corinthian order. The *axial* intercolumniation (the distance from column center to column center) of 10 *braccia* (5.837 m) left a *clear* intercolumniation (the space between the columns) of 9 1/6 *braccia* (5.35 m). Brunelleschi used this *clear* intercolumniation as a larger module. Thus, one large module measured the distances between the pavement of the portico to the springing of the arches (including the column's plinth, base, shaft, capital, abacus, and impost), between the springing of the arches to the top of the entablature's cornice (which also served as a windowsill), and between the entablature's cornice and the top of the unexecuted crowning cornice. Each arch of the portico defined a semicircle with a radius half of the large module (i.e., 2.68 m). Each of the loggia's nine bays up to the springing of the arches contained a spatial cube measuring one large module per side. Each bay was capped with a hemispherical sail or pendentive vault with a radius equal to one-half the diagonal of the bay's square plan. The entire façade, including the two flanking bays, was 120 *braccia* wide, with 90 *braccia* allocated for the portico and 15 *braccia* for the two end bays flanked by paired fluted pilasters, also 15 *braccia* high. Although the dimensions are not all quite exact, due to Brunelleschi's difficulty in coordinating classical and medieval modular and proportional planning techniques, his use of pendentive vaults and simple harmonic ratios of 1:1, 1:2, 1:3, and 3:4 based on modules derived from the column diameters and the clear intercolumniations imparted for the first time a convincing look of revived classicism.

PIAZZA DELLA SS. ANNUNZIATA

Brunelleschi located the façade of his Foundling Hospital on the east side of the Piazza SS. Annunziata, which already by 1300 had approximately its present size and shape and featured a weekly market. The façade was also parallel to the Via dei Servi, a street that ran from the cathedral, bisected the piazza, and focused on the center of the façade of the Church of SS. Annunziata (see fig. 142). SS. Annunziata was an important Servite pilgrimage church, begun in the mid-thirteenth century and completely rebuilt in the fifteenth and early sixteenth centuries by Michelozzo (1396–1472), Alberti, and their successors on a plan based on that of the Church of the Holy Sepulcher in Jerusalem (figs. 12, no. 24; 142). There is some inconclusive evidence that Brunelleschi made a wooden model for a redesign of the entire piazza in emulation of Vitruvius's description of a Roman forum (*Ten Books on Architecture* 5.1)—a bilaterally symmetrical rectangular space surrounded by porticos approached along a central axis focused on the façade of a major monument. In any case, it is certain that in 1478 Lorenzo de' Medici (il Magnifico; 1449–92) and his brother, Giuliano (1453–78), bought a parcel of land, 50 × 130 *braccia,* on the west side of the piazza directly opposite the Innocenti with the intention of building row houses to regularize the square and make it "more beautiful and honorable." The plan came to nothing, but it is clear that the Medici, major patrons of the Church of SS. Annunziata, planned to create a forumlike square, which by this date had also been promoted by Alberti in his mid-century architectural treatise, *On the Art of Building in Ten Books* (8.6).

2

FREESTANDING PUBLIC SCULPTURE

The extraordinary marble and bronze freestanding figures embellishing the public spaces of Florence constitute one of the great glories of Renaissance art. Bold and inventive, thanks to the intense pressure of public scrutiny and artistic rivalry, these monumental works represent some of the period's most significant aesthetic achievements; they also register the city's shifting political currents.

CATHEDRAL BUTTRESS FIGURES

Buttresses of medieval churches were commonly topped with freestanding sculptures, often prophets announcing the coming of the Savior. Upon the completion of the cathedral nave and tribunes in 1408, the Opera del Duomo (cathedral works), probably inspired by rivalry with the cathedrals in Milan and Siena, commissioned an *Isaiah* from Nanni di Banco (c. 1384–1421) and a *David* from Donatello. These were the first of an intended series of twelve life-size marble prophets for the buttresses of the three tribunes or apses (fig. 17).

Donatello's Marble *David*

The hip-shot stance and long arcs of drapery of Donatello's marble *David* (fig. 21)—here the adolescent giant killer, rather than king, psalmist, or prophet—create a lyricism characteristic of Gothic sculpture. However, the exposed weight-bearing left leg and the counterbalanced shoulders, arms, and hands suggest Donatello's incipient understanding of classical *contrapposto.* The outward glance, the wiry torso, and the arm akimbo express defiance and self-confidence, although the dreamy expression also connotes youthful vulnerability and innocence. The wreath of amaranth (Greek for "unfading," an early classical reference from Pliny's *Natural History* 21.47) and the severed head of Goliath signal David's nation-saving victory understood to prefigure Christ's self-sacrifice, which redeemed humanity from the consequences of original sin. In 1416 the sculpture was slightly re-cut and transferred to the Sala dei Gigli (see figs. 101 and 102) in the Priors' Palace, where its significance was inflected from an allegory of spiritual victory over evil and death to temporal triumph over Florence's enemies, Milan and Naples.

In 1409 either Nanni di Banco's or Donatello's statue was installed on one of the north tribune buttresses, where it was deemed too small and removed. Donatello replaced it the next year with a three-times-life-size white faux-marble terracotta *Joshua* (now lost). To carve such a colossal figure from marble must have been judged to be either technically impossible or impractical, which prompted Donatello and Brunelleschi to experiment in 1415–16 with a model for a *Hercules* (now lost) composed of gilt lead plates bolted over a stone core, a revived classical idea derived from Pliny's description of the Colossus of Rhodes (*Natural History* 34.41). The beginning of the cathedral's dome the next year (chapter 3), however, absorbed the energy and money of the wool manufacturers' guild for the next half century, temporarily ending the buttress-figure project.

OR SAN MICHELE, I

As noted earlier, in 1339 various guilds had each been assigned one of the fourteen exterior niches of the civic granary and guild oratory (see fig. 18) for statues of their patron saints, but by the turn of the century only three had been filled. By 1429, however, an impressive array of early Renaissance sculptures completed the project.

Donatello's *St. Mark*

From among the sculptors contributing to the Or San Michele project, Donatello made the first major breakthrough by employing a true *contrapposto* for his *St. Mark* for the south façade (fig. 22). Mark plants his right foot forward on the cushion, a product of the linen weavers and cloth drapers' guild that commissioned the work. Drapery falling like columnar fluting over his raised right hip registers the underlying upward surge of energy he expends to support his weight. The cloth draped over his right shoulder and across his chest further indicates that Mark has turned his lowered shoulder and arm into the niche. In dynamic counterpoint, he has relaxed his left leg, moved his foot sideward, and lowered his hip, setting off a lively cascade of folds around his jutting knee. In response to his left hand and shoulder, raised to support his gospel, his drapery loops around his forearm and draws taut over his outward-turned shoulder. The spiraling torsion of Mark's body—enhanced by the muscular power of his thick torso, massive limbs, and broad features—culminates in his tilted and turned head. His stately demeanor, frown, thick eyebrows, deep-set eyes, and cascading beard connote a vital intelligence encompassing the wisdom of the ages. A figure of such independent action and profound thought decisively marks the beginning of the Renaissance in freestanding sculpture.

Nanni di Banco's *Four Crowned Saints*

In his *Four Crowned Saints* Nanni di Banco demonstrated that he had mastered *contrapposto,* but he surpassed Donatello's example by applying it to a sculptural group (fig. 23). The relief on the niche's base portrays a mason, a carpenter, a stonecutter, and a sculptor plying the trades of the guild that commissioned the work. The patron saints of the stone- and wood-workers' guild—Castorius, Claudius, Symphorianus, and Nicostratus—were third-century Roman sculptors martyred by Emperor Diocletian (c. 240–313). They had refused to carve a statue of Aesculapius, the pagan god of health, in deference to their Christian god of healing, Christ.

21. Donatello, *David,* 1408–9, marble, 6 ft. 3¼ in. (191 cm), Museo dell'Opera del Duomo. The original bronze slingshot strap connecting David's right hand to the rock on Goliath's head has disappeared.

22. Donatello, *St. Mark,* 1411–13, gilt marble, 7 ft. 8⅞ in. (236 cm), Museo di Or San Michele.

23. Nanni di Banco, *Four Crowned Saints,* c. 1415–17, marble, 6 ft. (183 cm), north façade, Or San Michele.

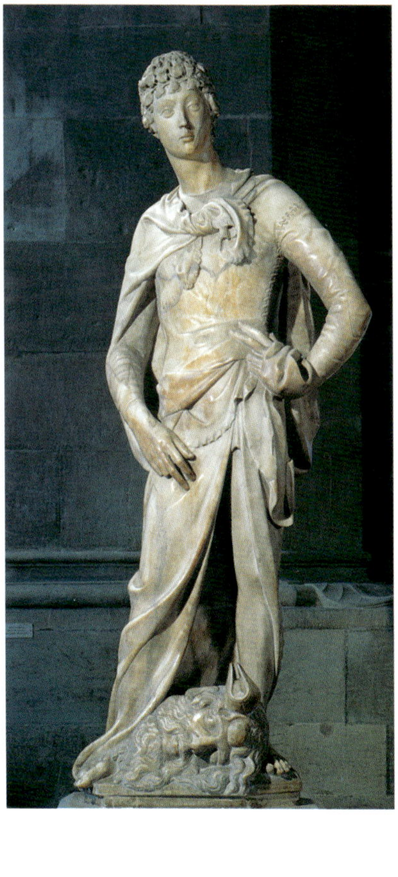

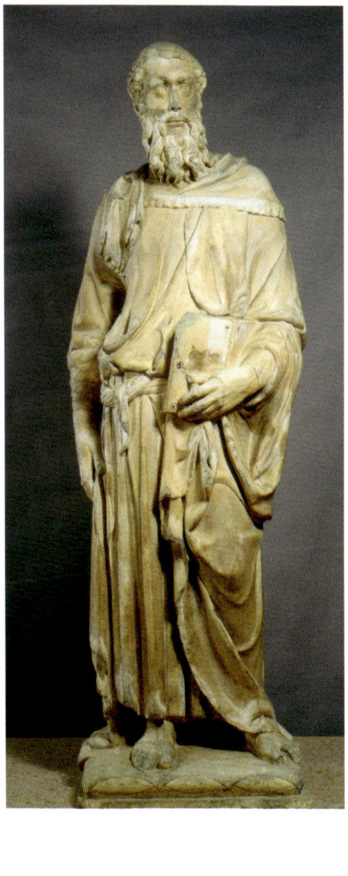

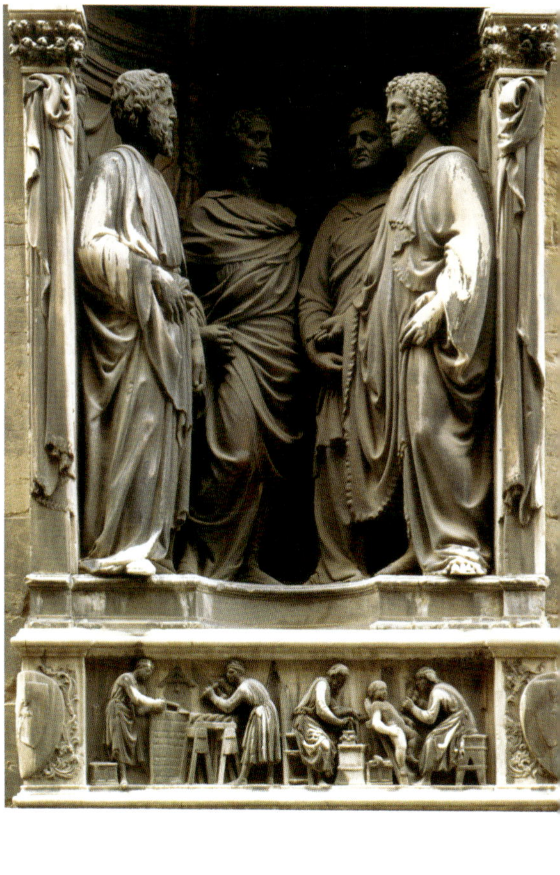

The rightmost martyr captures the viewer's attention by projecting his sandaled foot over the niche's edge. With an open mouth, knit brow, and right arm extended like an inspired classical orator, he appears to address the leftmost martyr, as if exclaiming, "No! I refuse to carve a pagan idol." The orator's solemn companion, carved from the same block of marble, receives the energy of the rhetorical gesture near his right hand and visually circulates it though his arm, shoulders, and drapery back to its source as he gazes diagonally across the niche at the orator's interlocutor.

This leftmost interlocutor engages the orator's eyes and mirrors the orator's *contrapposto,* including the relaxed outer leg with a turned foot extending beyond the niche's edge. The more youthful saint to the interlocutor's left also rivets his attention on the orator, as he shifts his weight to his left leg, firmly anchoring the group near its center. His drapery, pulled taut at his waist, draws attention to his clenched right fist, which adds a note of defiance to his bearing. His broad-featured classicizing head expresses inner spirituality but also a square-jawed determination to fight for the common cause voiced by the orator. In addition to the interconnected postures, gestures, and glances, Nanni unified the quartet by draping behind them a simulated cloth of honor, a distinction reserved for saints and sovereigns.

These remarkable toga-clad senatorial saints—dignified and distinct, yet joined in their solemn resolve to die for their shared beliefs—embodied the Renaissance ideal of civic virtue modeled on the ancient Roman republican *vir virtutis* (man of virtue) as espoused by such early humanists as Palmieri (fig. 1). The *vir virtutis*—needed precisely at this time, when the dukes of Milan and Naples were seriously challenging Florentine political liberty—exemplified the wise public-spirited citizen, versed in the arts of government and war and prepared to act with eloquence and courage to defend the commune's independent self-government.

Ghiberti's *St. John the Baptist*

Donatello's and Nanni di Banco's remarkable innovations are highlighted by comparison with the roughly contemporary *St. John the Baptist* by Lorenzo Ghiberti cast for the powerful cloth merchants' guild (fig. 24). In spite of contrasted feet and arms, the figure's frontal and level-shouldered body more nearly configures an S-shaped Gothic sway than a classical *contrapposto.* In addition, the lyrical surface patterns of the hair, beard, penitential hair shirt, tunic, and scroll obscure John's underlying anatomy and undercut the harsh reality of his austere wilderness life. Rather than classical models, Ghiberti drew inspiration from the ornate Gothic style of Burgundy (often called International Gothic), still much in vogue throughout Europe, to proclaim—along with the work's technical brilliance as the first large-scale cast-bronze statue in Florence—the guild's wealth and sophistication.

Donatello's *St. George*

Donatello's second work commissioned by the armorers and sword-makers' guild for the north side of Or San Michele, *St. George,* was as inventive as his first (fig. 25). The fourth-century knight, dressed in a hybrid of classical and Renaissance armor, stands flat-footed, his cross-inscribed escutcheon anchoring him firmly to the pedestal. His torso's silhouette continues the lines of his shield, transforming the warrior saint into an embodied aegis. Yet by means of a slight *contrapposto,* Donatello charged this abstract emblem of military preparedness with vital energy commensurate with the saint's toned body and outward gaze, as, with a gathering frown, he sizes up an adversary. This subtle dialectic between abstraction and dynamism powerfully evoked the humanists' prudent yet alert *vir virtutis* and offered a comforting mirage of civic military readiness in the face of the grim reality of Florence's ineffective militia, outmanned by the armies of Milan and Naples.

Donatello's *St. Louis of Toulouse*

The decoration of Or San Michele culminated in Donatello's magnificent *St. Louis of Toulouse* for the Guelph party's prominent central niche on the east façade facing the Via dei Calzaiuoli (fig. 26). Inspired by Brunelleschi's Old Sacristy at S. Lorenzo (see fig. 33), Donatello designed the first classicizing sculptural niche in Florence, which allowed him to create a dynamic interplay between architecture and figure. The spiral of the Ionic columns intensified the *contrapposto* of the slight body of St. Louis (1274–97), while the plain frieze of the Ionic entablature set off the unblemished features of the prince, who in 1296 at age 22, a year before his death and canonization, renounced the throne of Naples in favor of his brother Robert of Anjou (d. 1343) to become a Franciscan. His tilted crosier, countering the diagonal placement of his hands and the lean of his body, measured the height of the Ionic order and pointed to the apsidal shell, an ancient sign of fame and immortality, appropriately framing his bishop's miter. Donatello further heightened the figure's dynamism by the naturalistic cut, texture, and weight of his ample pluvial, or ceremonial robe.

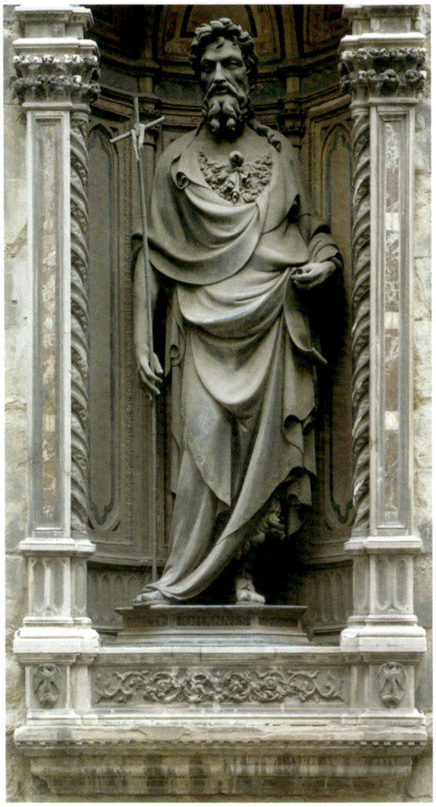
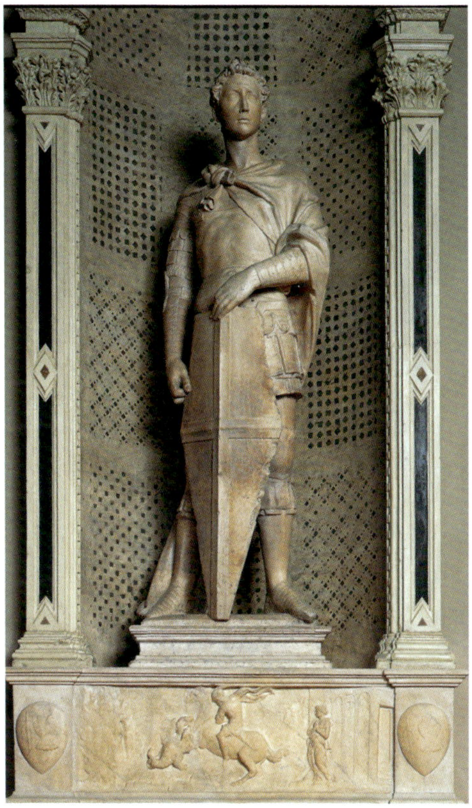
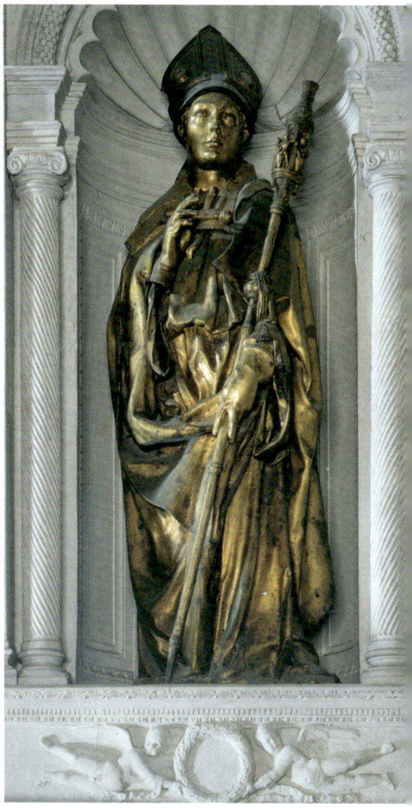

24. Lorenzo Ghiberti, *St. John the Baptist,* 1412–16, signed, gilt bronze, 8 ft. 4⅜ in. (255 cm), east façade, Or San Michele.

25. Donatello, *St. George,* c. 1416–17, marble, 6 ft. 10¼ in. (209 cm), Bargello. The scene on the niche's base, *St. George Killing the Dragon,* displays Donatello's influential invention of sketched low relief.

26. Donatello, *St. Louis of Toulouse,* c. 1422–25, fire-gilt bronze, miter partially enameled, 8 ft. 8¾ in. (266 cm), Museo dell'Opera di S. Croce. The statue was moved from Or San Michele to a niche on the façade of S. Croce in 1458–59. See fig. 29 for the original niche.

The awkwardly fitting miter and pluvial, however, not only suggest the saint's reluctance to hold the bishopric thrust upon him by Pope Boniface VIII (r. 1294–1303), but also connote an inner spirituality by their large internal volumes, which are largely unrelated to St. Louis' anatomy. The purity of his features, clarity of his silhouette, and oddity of his blessing hand—merely an empty glove fastened to the surface of his pluvial—further evoke his holiness. The saint's spirituality is underlined by the niche's architectural reliefs, representing two flying angels displaying a victory wreath at the base, winged victories sporting scrolls in the spandrels, winged cherubim carrying festoons in the entablature's frieze, and the Trinity (God the Father, the Son, and the Holy Spirit) soaring triumphantly within a winged wreath in the pediment. By the visual contrast between matter and spirit, Donatello captured St. Louis' struggle between the public responsibilities of his high office and the meditative life he sought in taking Franciscan vows.

CAMPANILE

An encyclopedic sculptural program for the cathedral campanile was all but completed by 1364. Spurred to action by the project at Or San Michele, the wool manufacturers' guild commissioned the remaining eight freestanding prophets for the upper-level niches on the north and east sides between 1415 and 1428, five from Donatello.

Donatello's *Abraham and Isaac*

Abraham's near-sacrifice of his innocent son Isaac prefigured Christ's sacrifice for humanity's salvation. Donatello's

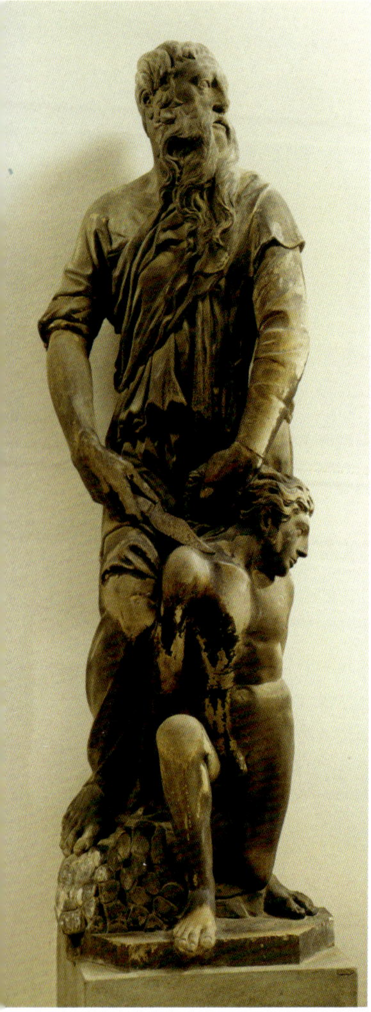

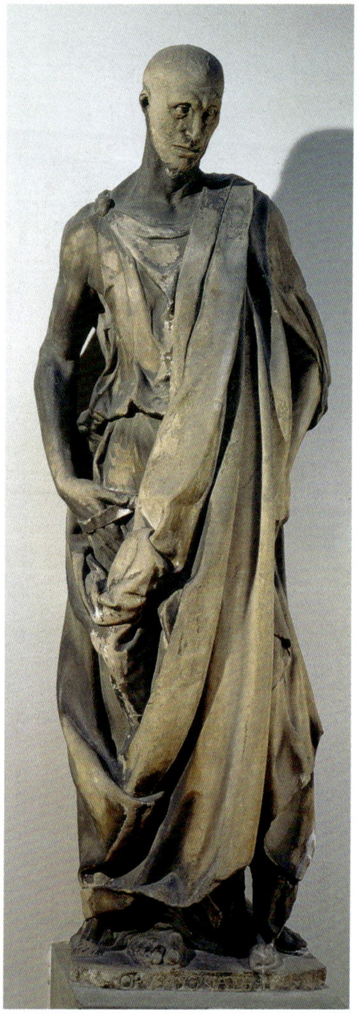

27. Donatello, *Abraham and Isaac* (Genesis 22:1–19), 1421, marble, 6 ft. 2 in. (188 cm), Museo dell'Opera del Duomo.

28. Donatello, *Zuccone (Elisha?)*, c. 1423–26, marble, 6 ft. 4¾ in. (195 cm), Museo dell'Opera del Duomo.

dynamic figural group emphasized the drama's pathos through contact—simultaneously violent and tender—between father and son (fig. 27). As if for protection, the kneeling Isaac leans against his father's legs, bowing his head in obedient resignation to expose his neck to his father's knife, as his arms, wrenched behind his back, register his distress. In preparation for the expected impact of his blade, Abraham pulls his son by his long hair toward him and steadies him against his bent leg, which rests atop the kindling readied for the sacrificial fire. But before Abraham can perform the horrifying deed by which God tests his faith, an angel stops him. This unseen messenger distracts him at the instant he begins to slit Isaac's throat, and Abraham's knife comes to rest harmlessly on Isaac's shoulder. Such drama within the narrow constraints of a single block of marble represents a truly innovative achievement.

Donatello's *Zuccone*

In his slightly later *Zuccone* ("baldy," or "squash head"), also for the campanile, Donatello created an even more intense series of counterbalancing contrasts (fig. 28). The figure's classic *contrapposto* implies anatomical energy and potential movement, heightened by his muscular neck and arms and by his inner garment, knotted at the shoulder, belted at the waist, and hugging his body. The strap that binds his right hand to his thigh, however, constricts his freedom of movement. His capacity to act is further compromised by the overly capacious outer robe, which swoops diagonally down from his left shoulder in gigantic loops, a garment so ill fitting that it appears to belong to another. Indeed, Donatello probably intended it to be the mantel that Elijah dropped on the shore when he ascended to heaven in a chariot of fire, which his disciple, Elisha (mocked for his baldness), then wore as a sign of his inheritance of Elijah's spiritual authority and the triumph of his spirit over matter (2 Kings 2:9–15). The robe registers a spiritual force that subsumes Elisha's physical energy, but the prophet also resembles an old man on the verge of mental breakdown, muttering to himself through his clenched teeth and gashlike mouth, his asymmetrical eyes staring wildly. Yet his possession by an inner demon also appropriately expressed the experience of spiritual ecstasy and prophetic vision. Hereafter Donatello often employed such frenzied expressions or aged bodies to express spiritual passion and wisdom.

OR SAN MICHELE, II

In 1463 the Università della Mercanzia, the court of commercial law, acquired the Guelph party's niche on Or San Michele. Piero de' Medici (1416–69), his son Lorenzo il Magnifico, and five Medici supporters sat on the committee that oversaw the niche's acquisition. Since the redecoration of the niche was designed in part to celebrate the rise of Medicean unitary rule in opposition to pluralistic Guelph oligarchic ideology, the committee must have intended that the new sculpture (fig. 29) commissioned from Verrocchio (1435–88) should outshine Donatello's *St. Louis of Toulouse* (fig. 26), which previously had occupied the niche.

Verrocchio's *Christ and Doubting Thomas*

Absent from Christ's first posthumous appearance to the Apostles, Thomas refused to believe in Christ's resurrection declaring, "Unless I put my hand into his side, I will not believe" (John 20:25).* Eight days later Christ reappeared, revealed his wound to Thomas, and said, "Put your finger here . . . do not be faithless, but believing" (John 20:27). Thomas, the archetypal skeptic, stands outside the niche in the full glare of daylight, resting his weight on the ledge as he turns from the street to examine Christ's wound with morbid fascination. The energy of his movement is expressed in his strong diagonal thrust toward Christ, yet in a kind of aborted *contrapposto,* he stops in mid-stride and pulls back as he recognizes the truth spelled out on his robe's hem, "My Lord, my God, savior of humanity" (based on John 20:38).

Christ mirrors nearly every detail of Thomas's stance, drapery, gesture, hair, and gaze. Appropriate for his resurrected state, however, Christ, a foot taller, stands on a pedestal withdrawn into the niche, a more mysterious and looming figure. His drapery is more graceful, and his bearing and demeanor more impassive. His movements are purposeful, not divided, as he leans back to brace himself against Thomas's penetrating assault while opening his drapery to expose his wound. The inscription on the hem of Christ's robe—"Because thou hast seen me, Thomas, thou hast believed. Blessed are they that have not seen and have believed" (John 20:29)—suggests that Christ's hand raised over Thomas's head, where it catches the light, expresses both mercy for Thomas's skepticism and rebuke for his lack of faith.

Christ's judgment tempered by clemency and Thomas's incredulity joined with a quest for truth made *Christ and Doubting Thomas* a common image of justice, well suited for the guilds' tribunal. Verrocchio's group also may have implied the justice of Medicean rule, for the Medici were closely associated with St. Thomas as major patrons of the Church of S. Tommaso on the Mercato Vecchio (fig. 12, no. 2). In any case, never before had the theme been rendered so dramatically with figures who, while appearing to move naturally, are caught at the very conflicted instant when Thomas both disbelieves and believes and Christ both blesses and reprimands. Nor had any artist before so successfully expressed the contrast between the materiality of Thomas and the spirituality of Christ, the former near, accessible, and filled with light, the latter elevated, removed, and shadowed.

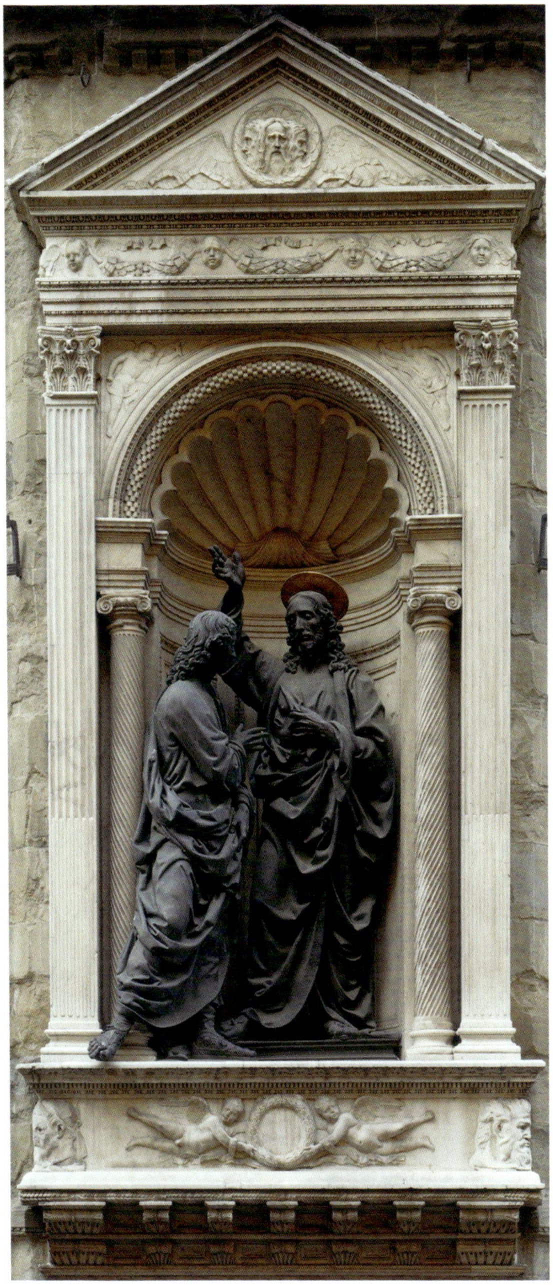

29. Verrocchio, *Christ and Doubting Thomas* (John 20:24–29), 1467–83, bronze, Christ 7 ft. 6½ in. (230 cm), Thomas 6 ft. 6¾ in. (200 cm), now moved to the Museo di Or San Michele.

* All biblical citations are from the Douay-Rheims English translation of the Latin Vulgate.

3

ECCLESIASTICAL ARCHITECTURE

THE CATHEDRAL DOME

In 1418 the Opera del Duomo held a competition for the design of the cathedral's dome that was won by Brunelleschi (fig. 30). Ever cautious, the Opera also appointed Brunelleschi's bitter rival, Lorenzo Ghiberti, to help oversee the construction. The engineering problems were daunting, for this was to be the highest and heaviest masonry vault ever attempted. An internal scaffold built from the ground would have required a prohibitively expensive forest of timbers. Brunelleschi, therefore, devised a ring of hung or flying scaffolding derived from smaller-scaled Gothic methods. Materials were raised up the center and positioned by a hoist and crane also of his invention. To reduce the dome's weight, Brunelleschi employed above the stone drum a double-shell structure, for which the Florentine Baptistery (fig. 10) and numerous domes in the Byzantine and Islamic areas of the Mediterranean offered suggestive but smaller and less complex precedents. He designed eight exterior marble-faced brick ribs and sixteen interior brick ribs to support the dome's internal and external masonry skin. Interconnected by horizontal brick arches in compression, these ribs arched upward to a stone compression ring 50 feet (15.24 m) across. The compression ring and arches, assisted by the dome's steep profile, counteracted the dome's tendency to fall inward toward the center. To counteract the opposite tendency to "kick out" near the bottom as the dome arched over the void, Brunelleschi installed above the drum several continuous stone and wooden chains under tension, linked together by iron clamps, bolts, and bands encircling the entire dome internally. For the dome's ribs and skin, Brunelleschi devised special lightweight modular bricks and fast-drying mortar. The bricks were laid horizontally in a herringbone pattern and vertically in spiraling courses so that the masonry twisted and compacted inwardly upon itself, stabilizing the dome as it rose.

By his sheer intellectual brilliance and technical inventiveness, far in advance of his contemporaries, Brunelleschi

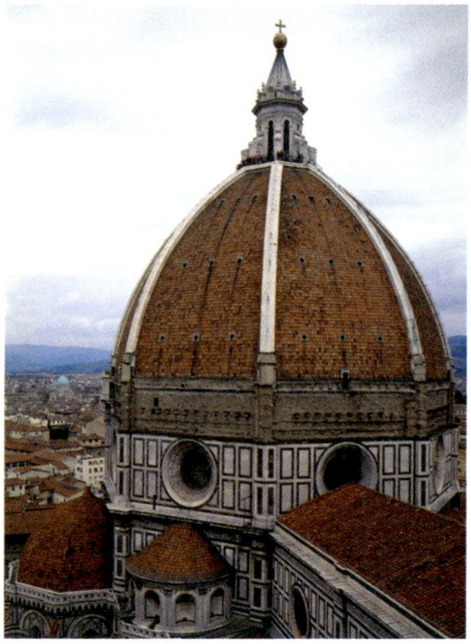

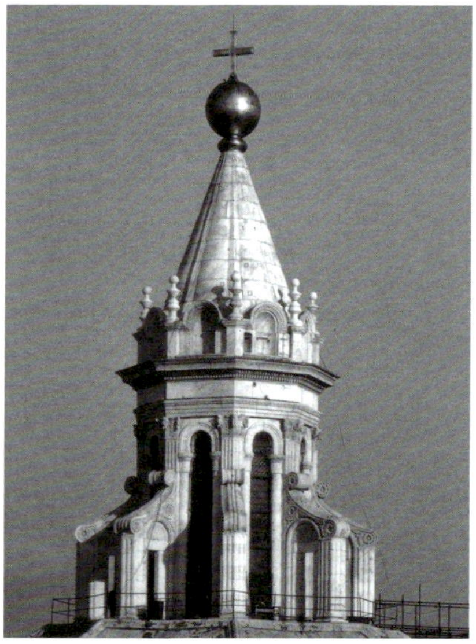

30. Filippo Brunelleschi, cathedral dome, Florence, designed 1417/18–20, executed 1420–36. The dome's width of 140 ft. (42.67 m) nearly equaled the diameter of 142 ft. (43.28 m) of the hemispherical dome of the Roman Pantheon (AD 118–28), while its height of 350 ft. 11¾ in. (106.98 m) was two and a half times greater.

31. Filippo Brunelleschi (completed by Michelozzo), lantern of the cathedral dome, Florence, designed 1436–38, executed 1444/45–67.

forced the meddlesome Ghiberti to the sidelines. When the dome (minus its lantern) was completed and the church consecrated on March 25, 1436, Brunelleschi had for the first time since antiquity established himself as an architect in the modern sense of the word—one who by technical expertise and creative imagination both creates a unique design and supervises its construction.

After the cathedral's consecration, Brunelleschi designed the marble lantern, its eight windows articulated with engaged columns, Byzantine-style capitals, and stilted arches between fluted Corinthian pilasters carrying an entablature with classical moldings (fig. 31). The lantern's eight flying buttresses, decorated with classicizing flutes, shell niches, volutes, and rosettes, created a visual focus for the ascent of the dome's ribs, while a steeply pointed spire resolved the dome's upward thrust and released its visual energy heavenward. Although Gothic in profile and structure, the classical details and regular geometry of the spire's niches, pinnacles, and crowning gilt-bronze globe marked the lantern as a Renaissance work.

Unique in architectural history to date, Brunelleschi's design of a soaring exterior dome was as noteworthy as its faceted interior. Conceived and built mostly during Florence's struggle to maintain its independence against Milan, the massive dome—visible from everywhere in the city and the surrounding Arno Valley, and, according to Alberti, "so ample as to cover the whole Tuscan people with its shadow"—rose triumphantly from the urban core (fig. 12, no. 11), a proud and daring symbol of Florentine resolve and unity in the face of grave external threats. In addition, the dome, as all domes, symbolized heaven, while its octagonal plan alluded to Christ's resurrection eight days after his entry into Jerusalem, appropriate symbolism for the cathedral's plan, inspired by that of the Church of the Holy Sepulcher in Jerusalem. A great beacon of faith, hope, and piety, Brunelleschi's dome marked Florence as a new Jerusalem.

S. LORENZO

S. Lorenzo was one of Florence's oldest churches and initially its cathedral. In the Renaissance it served as an important parish church for some of the city's leading families, including the Medici, whose palace was nearby (fig. 12, nos. 21 and 25). In a characteristic act of early Renaissance corporate patronage, the heads of these families formulated plans between 1415 and 1418 to share the cost of building a new church designed by Brunelleschi in exchange for burial rights in the side chapels (fig. 32).

32. Plan, S. Lorenzo: 1 Old Sacristy and 2 chapels of SS. Cosmas and Damian, designed 1419, executed 1421–28; 3 crossing, 4 transepts, 5 choir, and 6 transept side chapels, 1442–56; 7 nave, 8 aisles, and 9 aisle side chapels, 1460–94; 10 New Sacristy, 1519–34; 11 Laurentian Library and 12 vestibule, 1524–71.

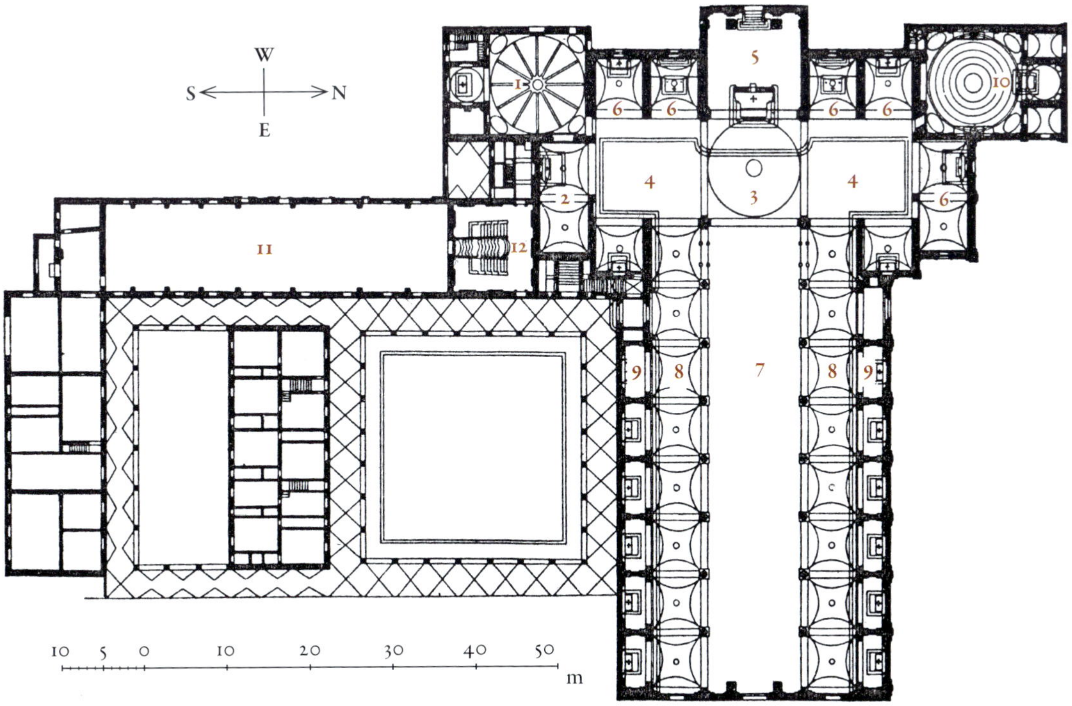

The Old Sacristy

The wealthy banker Giovanni di Bicci de' Medici (1360–1429) initiated the project by funding the construction of the Old Sacristy and the double chapel dedicated to the early Christian saints Cosmas and Damian between 1421 and his death in 1429 (figs. 33–35). In exchange he was allowed to display his family coat of arms in the vault's pendentives, dedicate the altar to his name-saint, John the Evangelist, and create a burial crypt for his family and their descendants.

In order to allude to Christ's redemptive sacrifice—an appropriate theme for a burial chapel—Brunelleschi created a centrally planned structure, 20 × 20 *braccia* square, emulating the well-known Chapel of the Holy Sepulcher in Jerusalem, including its most distinguishing feature, the exterior lantern capped by a spiral-ribbed dome carried on six colonnettes. He articulated the altar wall with a classical triumphal arch motif to imply victorious resurrection. And he used harmonic proportions to make the Old Sacristy a microcosm of God's universe, where the drama of salvation was enacted: the height of the Corinthian pilasters equaled that of the lunettes and of the chapter-room's vault, creating 1:3 or 2:3 ratios between the elevation's three zones; the width of the altar chapel's arch relates to the widths of the flanking arches in ratios of 3:2; the diameters of the hemispherical domes over the chapter room and the altar are equal to the diameters of their lunettes; the diameters of the *tondi* in the larger lunettes and pendentives are related to the diameter of the oculus of the melon dome in a ratio of 2:1.

The circular, semicircular, and hemispherical forms above the entablature evoke heaven, while the square spaces below represent earth. Brunelleschi appropriately articulated the transition between the symbolic heaven and earth with the entablature's continuous frieze of red seraphs and blue cherubs, symbols of divine love and wisdom.

Brunelleschi's double-shelled hemispherical dome carried on pendentives, modeled on Byzantine or Byzantinizing domes, was a new form in Florentine architecture. These domes were often decorated with the Pentecost (Acts 2:1–4), as at the Basilica of S. Marco in Venice. They illustrated the moment when the twelve Apostles received from the resurrected Christ the tongues of fire or gift of languages, and the charge to preach and convert. Similarly, Brunelleschi probably intended the central oculus to symbolize the resurrected Christ, while the twelve ribs and twelve peripheral windows represented the Apostles. Further evidence comes from the Old Sacristy's dedication to John the Evangelist and Donatello's representation of all twelve Apostles on the right bronze doors.

The Church

Between 1429 and 1442 all work at S. Lorenzo stopped owing to a series of disruptive events: a protracted war with Milan and Lucca; burdensome taxes; the exile in 1433 of Giovanni di Bicci's son Cosimo de' Medici (il Vecchio; 1389–1464), by the oligarchic regime of Rinaldo degli Albizzi (1370–1442); Cosimo's return from exile the following year and the subsequent exiling of Rinaldo; and an assault on the Florentine forces in 1439–40 by troops of Milan allied with the Florentine exiles led by Rinaldo. The defeat of the attackers at the Battle of Anghiari in May 1440 and the death of Rinaldo in 1442 finally ushered in a measure of peace. In 1442, therefore, Cosimo il Vecchio joined other wealthy parish families, mostly Medici supporters, to continue the church. In exchange for the rare privilege of burial rights in the crypt under the crossing and the right to display the Medici arms in the crossing, choir, and nave, Cosimo financed the construction of the west end except for the burial chapels on the transepts' periphery, which were paid for by other parish families. Michelozzo probably supervised the construction, completed by 1456, aided perhaps by Alberti and Antonio di Ciaccheri Manetti (c. 1402–60) for the design and construction of the crossing dome. In 1465, a year after his father's death, Piero de' Medici obtained exclusive rights over the nave, aisles, and side chapels, all of which were completed at Medici expense by 1494. So ended corporate patronage at S. Lorenzo, now transformed primarily into a pantheon for Medici self-glorification.

The choir, crossing, nave, and transepts revived the traditional early Christian basilical Latin-cross plan, symbolic of both the crucified Christ and the entire body of the Christian community, while the dome over the crossing symbolized heaven (figs. 32 and 36). The 20 × 20–*braccia* crossing constituted the module generating the entire design, conceived in terms of spatial units without regard to the masonry. Thus, each transept is 20 by 20 *braccia,* subtracting the width of the walls that divide the flanking eastern chapels; the aisle bays, 10 × 10 *braccia;* the aisle chapels, 9 ½ × 3 ½ *braccia;* the nave bays, 10 × 20 *braccia;* and the entire nave 80 × 20 *braccia,* subtracting the combined width of a file of columns. The module also determined three-dimensional relationships (fig. 37). The diameter of the dome is 20 *braccia;* the radii of the crossing's four triumphal arches, 10 *braccia;* and the radii of the aisle lunettes and the nave arches, 5 *braccia.* The

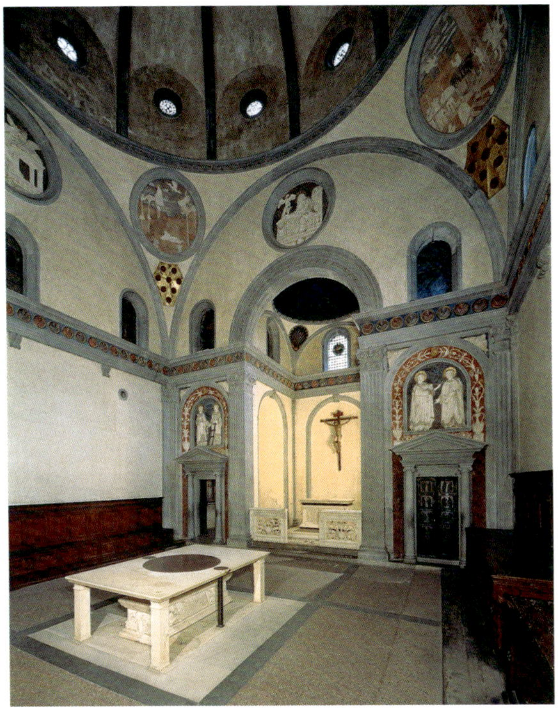

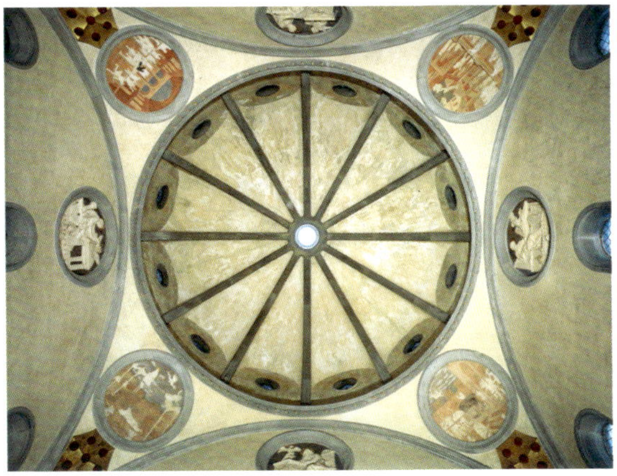

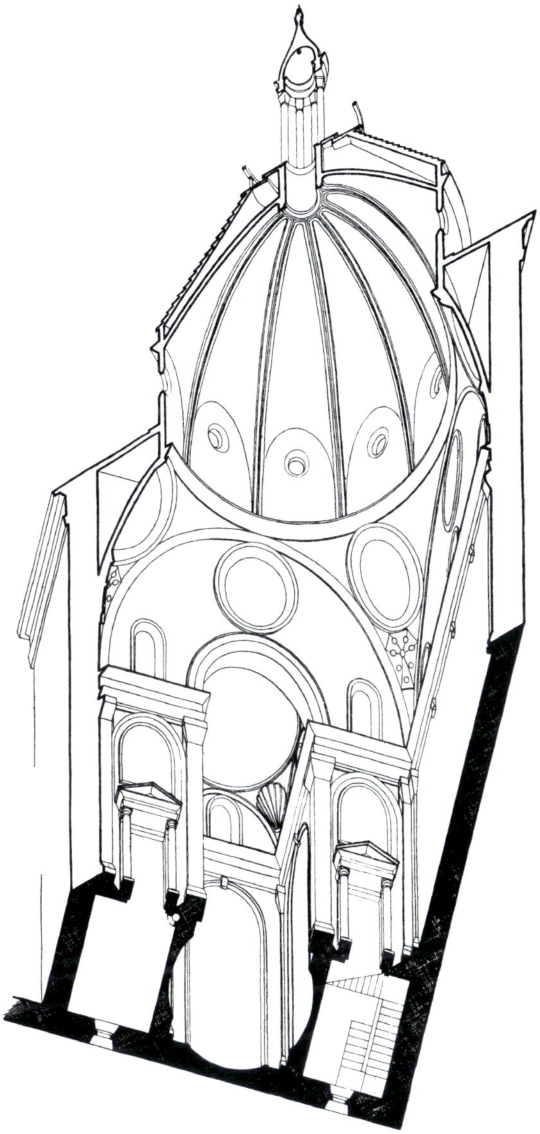

33. Brunelleschi, interior of the Old Sacristy, S. Lorenzo, designed c. 1418–19, executed 1421–28. The storage cabinets and benches along three walls provided for the room's triple function as chapel, sacristy, and chapter room for the Augustinian canons. See figs. 64–67 for details of the decoration.

34. Isometric diagram, Old Sacristy, S. Lorenzo.

35. Dome of the Old Sacristy, S. Lorenzo.

height from the floor to the top of the entablature surrounding the central cruciform space equals the diagonal of the crossing square. The simple mathematical ratios of these dimensions—1:1, 1:2, 1:3, and 1:4, graphically visualized by the pavement pattern—compose a harmonic plan that tuned the church to resonate with divine harmony following the prescriptions of Vitruvius. Although harmonic planning was also widely practiced in the late Middle Ages, S. Lorenzo's design is marked as Renaissance by its hemispherical crossing dome on pendentives with an oculus and stair-stepped exterior masonry loading derived from the Pantheon, the first Florentine revival of a classical dome. The combination of a circular dome over a square crossing also recalled the Vitruvian

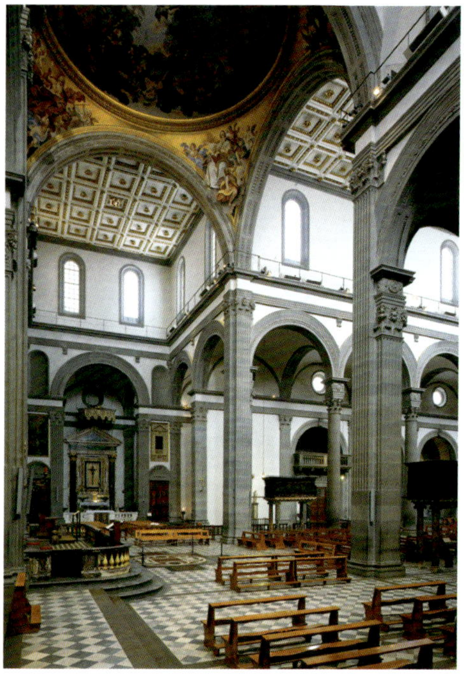

36. Crossing and dome, S. Lorenzo, 1442–56. The dome's oculus was originally open to the sky. See figs. 76–80 for details of the crossing decoration.

37. Nave, S. Lorenzo, 1442–94.

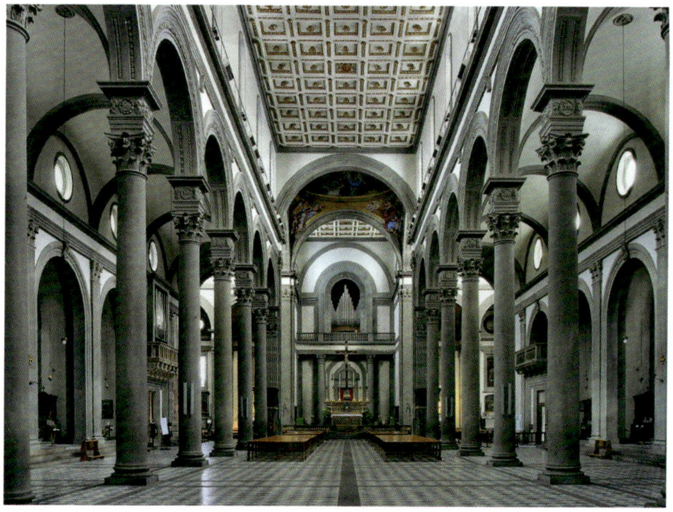

man (fig. 8), symbolically mediating between earth and heaven, humanity and God.

The main body of the church was designed to create a cross-axial progression from the low barrel-vaulted side-aisle chapels, to the higher hemispherical sail-vaulted aisle bays, to the highest nave bays with a coffered flat wooden ceiling, bays whose floor areas were respectively one-eighth, one-quarter, and one-half of the crossing's area. Furthermore, the design progressed from the dark windowless chapels, articulated with simple moldings and framed by fluted Corinthian pilasters, to the aisles dimly lit by oculi, to the nave defined by a Corinthian colonnade and flooded with light from the large clerestory windows. The nave was further enriched by the frieze of the colonnade's entablature, decorated with carved cherubim, seraphim, a lamb on an altar, and seven seals, symbols, respectively, of divine knowledge, divine love, Christ's sacrifice, and the Last Judgment. Classicizing details also decorated the faces and undersides of the arches. Finally, the continuous entablature carrying the clerestory above the arcade and the coffered ceiling unified the church's tall light-filled cruciform space. The rhythmic progression of the nave's arcade powerfully led the eye to the crossing and the high altar, where the design achieved its final resolution in the dome, symbolizing the aspiration for salvation.

S. MARCO

The Church and Monastery

In 1436 Pope Eugenius IV, who was then resident in Florence, ceded the old Silvestrine monastery of S. Marco to the Dominicans under the leadership of Fra Antonino Pierozzi, who became the archbishop of Florence in 1446 and was canonized in 1523 (fig. 12, no. 23). According to Vespasiano da Bisticci (1421–98) in his *Lives of Illustrious Men,* written in the 1480s, the pope also counseled Cosimo de' Medici (il Vecchio), whose bank handled papal finances, to pay for its complete renovation and expansion as a public act of contrition for his sins of usury (loaning money with interest). Over the next two decades, Vespasiano records, Cosimo spent over 40,000 florins on the project, supervised by his architect, Michelozzo (fig. 38).

The Library

In 1437 Niccolò Niccoli (1364–1437), an early Florentine humanist and bibliophile, bequeathed his extensive library—one of the finest collections of classical Greek and Latin manuscripts of its day—to the city of Florence with the stipulation that it be made available to all scholars. As one of sixteen trustees of Niccoli's estate, Cosimo agreed in 1441 to carry out the terms of the will by building a public library at his own expense as part of S. Marco's renovation. Throughout the rest of his life Cosimo also purchased additional books for the library to fill gaps in Niccoli's core collection.

Michelozzo's vaulted basilical-plan library, built over a groin-vaulted lower story, was conveniently located on the monastery's second floor near Cosimo's and the monks' cells (figs. 38 and 39). Hence, for the first time since the libraries of classical antiquity, books were contained within a fireproof and moisture-proof masonry envelope and accessible to the interested public. A central barrel-vaulted corridor supported on a delicate arcade of twenty-two Ionic *pietra serena* columns provided easy circulation to and from the twenty-four groin-vaulted square bays, twelve per side. Each bay originally contained three rows of high-backed desks, each row equipped with a bench seating up to four readers and a sloped lectern with shelves below accommodating the manuscripts, each chained to the desks (see fig. 157 for similar desks). Shuttered windows in each bay along the sides and the north end created a delightfully luminous space ideal for reading.

S. SPIRITO

Motivated by rivalry with the parishioners of S. Lorenzo, the principal families in the parish of S. Spirito commissioned Brunelleschi in about 1434 to design a replacement for their earlier parish church, although the civic unrest that stopped work at S. Lorenzo also delayed its construction (fig. 12, no. 22; figs. 40 and 41). Unlike the twenty-four unequally sized chapels at S. Lorenzo, most of them controlled by the Medici, the forty identical, individual family burial chapels at S. Spirito—the majority nearly equidistant from the high altar located directly under the dome—testify to the church's funding by a large group of egalitarian-minded patrons unsympathetic to the Medici's self-aggrandizement at S. Lorenzo.

Except for the side chapels, S. Spirito's plan, elevation, articulation, and dimensions are nearly identical to those of S. Lorenzo, yet its design far more elegantly blends a Latin cross and centralized plan. In both churches, the plan of the crossing constitutes the module. But at S. Lorenzo the module measures 20 × 20 *braccia* within the crossing piers, excluding the masonry. At S. Spirito it includes the masonry, measuring 22 × 22 *braccia* from the center of one pier to the center of the opposite pier. One such 22 × 22–*braccia* module also defined each transept and the choir, and four modules (88 × 22 *braccia* total) constituted the nave, all modules measured from center to center of its corner masonry supports. Each aisle bay measured 11 × 11 *braccia* from center to center of opposing

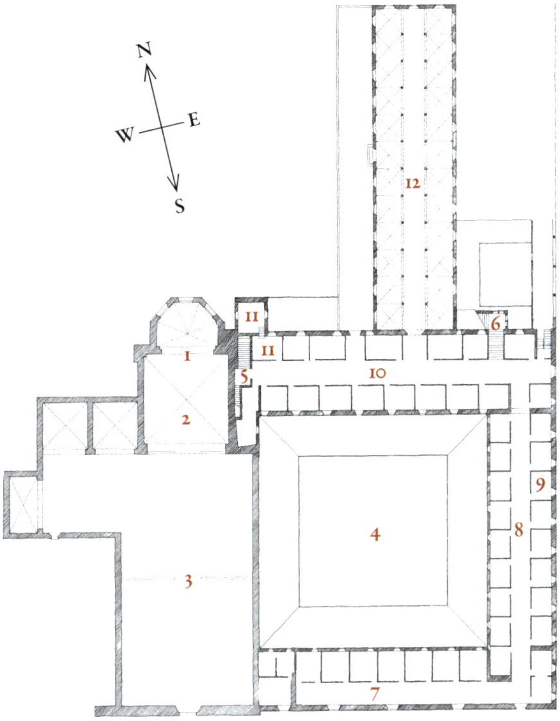

38. GROUND plan of the church and SECOND-FLOOR plan of the monastery and library, S. Marco, c. 1436–45: 1 apse and high altar with Fra Angelico's altarpiece (fig. 68), 2 enclosed monks' choir, 3 rood screen separating the upper church from the nave, 4 cloister, 5 staircase down to the monks' choir, 6 staircase down to the ground floor, 7 novices' south dormitory wing with guest rooms below, 8 clerics' east dormitory wing with kitchen and refectory below, 9 cell number 3 with Fra Angelico's *Annunciation* (fig. 69), 10 lay brothers' north dormitory wing with sacristy and chapter room below, 11 Cosimo il Vecchio's private cell, 12 library (fig. 39).

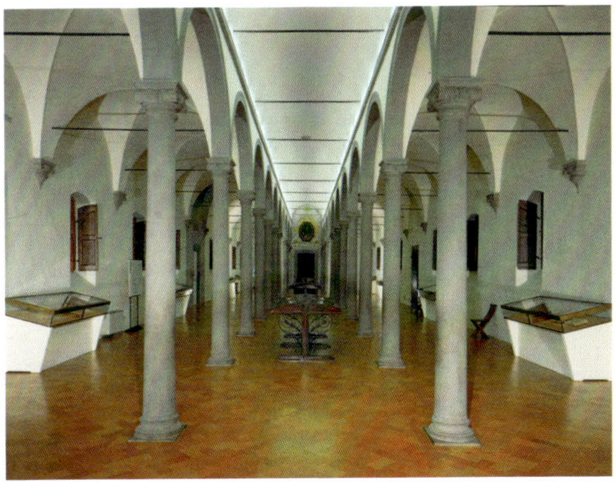

39. Michelozzo, library, S. Marco, c. 1442–43.

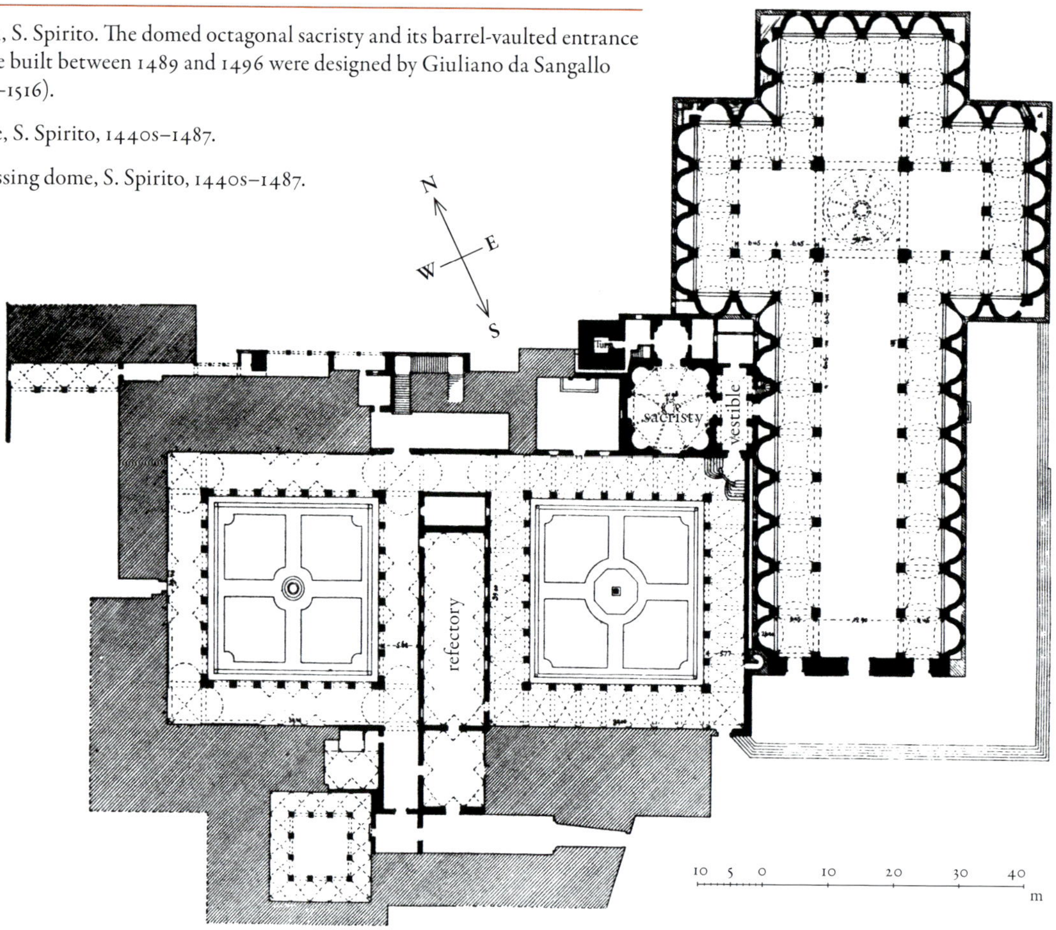

40. Plan, S. Spirito. The domed octagonal sacristy and its barrel-vaulted entrance vestibule built between 1489 and 1496 were designed by Giuliano da Sangallo (c. 1445–1516).

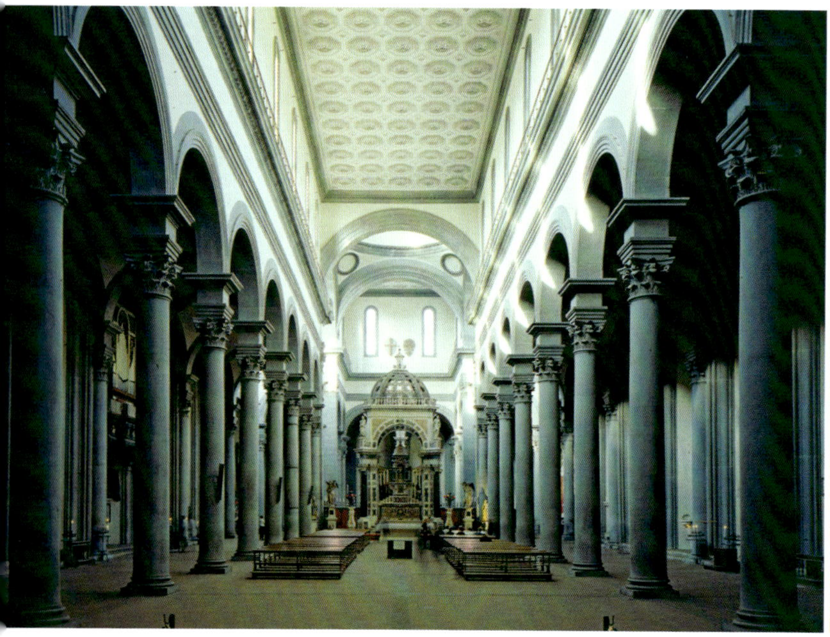

41. Nave, S. Spirito, 1440s–1487.

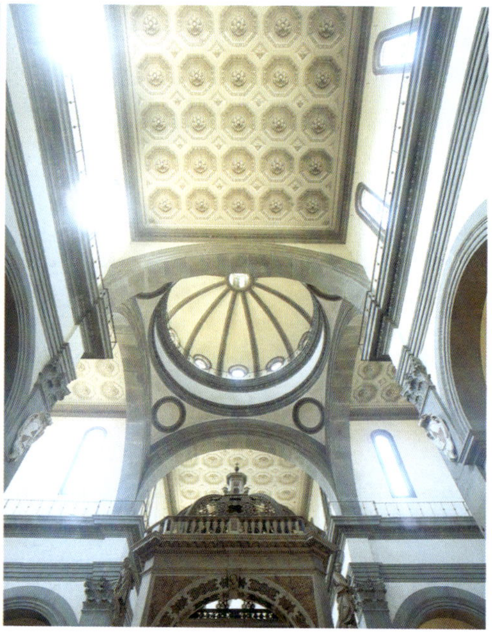

42. Crossing dome, S. Spirito, 1440s–1487.

supports, exactly one-quarter of the module's area. Very different from S. Lorenzo, these side bays formed a unifying ambulatory surrounding the entire cruciform central space.

In both churches the area between the crossing piers measures 20 × 20 *braccia,* and the diagonal of this square equals the height from the floor to the top of the entablature surrounding the cruciform space. In both churches the diameter of each Corinthian column measures 59 inches, or 150 centimeters. Yet at S. Spirito the columns are shorter (27 ft. 5 7/8 in. vs. 29 ft. 8 ¼ in., or 838 vs. 905 cm), necessitating taller entablature segments above the columns. Furthermore, in contrast to S. Lorenzo, the friezes of the entablature segments, as well as the undersides and faces of the arches, are free of carved decorative details, just as the crossing piers are unfluted. Compared with S. Lorenzo, the articulation of S. Spirito's cruciform space produced an effect of greater mass and unity.

The aisle bays and chapels were also more closely integrated into the overall design at S. Spirito. Engaged unfluted Corinthian columns flanking the chapels carried the aisles' hemispherical sail vaults in tandem with the colonnade's unfluted columns of the same height (in contrast to the fluted Corinthian pilasters, which are shorter than the opposite unfluted columns at S. Lorenzo). A circle with a 5 ½-*braccia* radius inscribed within each 11 × 11–*braccia* aisle bay determined the plan, including masonry walls, of each semicircular chapel. Furthermore, because of the importance of family burial sites at S. Spirito, the cylindrical, apsidal chapels not only reached nearly the same height as the colonnade's arches, but glowed with light from tall, narrow, arch-topped windows (in contrast to the lower, windowless, barrel-vaulted chapels at S. Lorenzo). Elegant curvilinear moldings provided the transition between the chapels and aisles at S. Spirito (in contrast to the flat, angular moldings at S. Lorenzo). In general, a dynamic lyricism expressive of spiritual harmony and grace distinguished S. Spirito from S. Lorenzo.

At both S. Lorenzo and S. Spirito, a dome surmounted the crossing. But the latter dome rests on a drum, and the height from the top of the crossing piers' entablature to the top of the drum equaled the diameter of the dome (fig. 42). The triumphal arches, pendentives, and drum at S. Spirito thus enclosed a cubic space, creating a more three-dimensional integration of the symbolic circle and square than at S. Lorenzo. Furthermore, in contrast to S. Lorenzo's Pantheon-like dome, S. Spirito's twelve-ribbed melon dome accommodated a lantern at its summit and twelve windows at its base, emblematic of the resurrected Christ surrounded by his twelve Apostles. Clearly, the patrons of S. Spirito were concerned more with spiritual than imperial symbolism.

THE FAÇADE OF S. MARIA NOVELLA

Remarkably few Florentine church façades were completed in the Renaissance, an important exception being S. Maria Novella (fig. 12, no. 7; fig. 43) commissioned by Giovanni Rucellai (1475–1525), whose palace was nearby (fig. 95). The inlaid marble inscription in the upper frieze records the patron's name and the date 1470. Rucellai's coat of arms is attached to each end of the attic, and thirty-nine repetitions of his personal device (a wind-filled sail, emblem of the patron's hope to sail safely to the harbor of salvation) are inlaid in the lower entablature's frieze and on the outside piers. Such self-promotion probably required Medici approval, and indeed the Medici's

43. Leon Battista Alberti, façade, S. Maria Novella, dated 1470, constructed c. 1457–78.

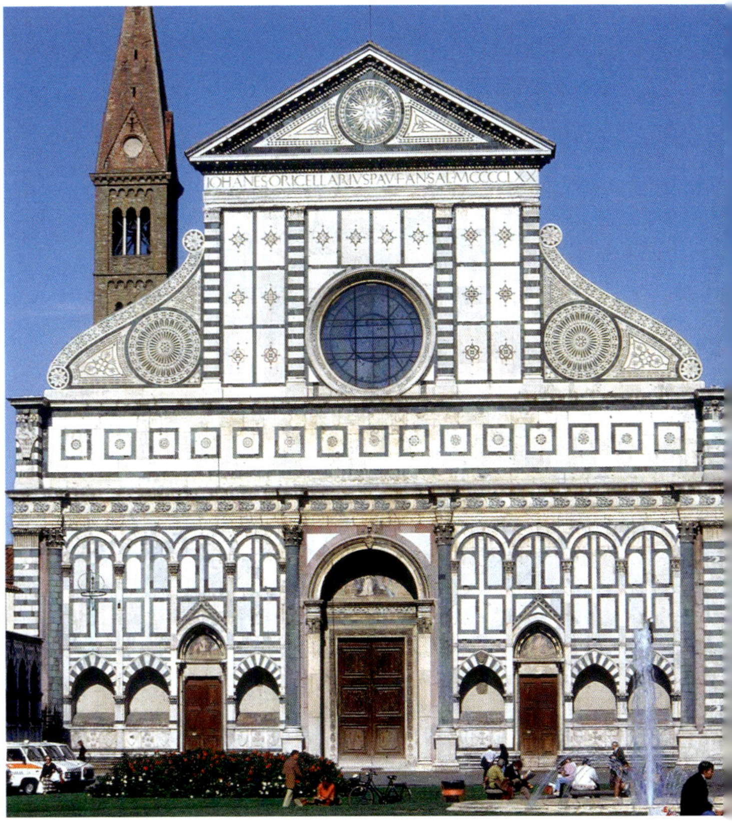

ostrich-feather and diamond-ring device repeated above the central door prominently advertised that Piero de' Medici was the godfather of Rucellai's eldest son, Bernardo (1448–1514), who was betrothed to Piero's daughter, Nannina (d. 1493) in 1461 and married her in 1466. Giovanni Rucellai had good reason to celebrate this alliance, because to survive and prosper in Florence as the son-in-law of and agent for the exiled Palla Strozzi (c. 1373–1462), one of the Medici's most distrusted enemies, required great patience, intelligence, and diplomacy as well as abundant good fortune—another meaning of the wind-filled sail.

By the mid-fourteenth century the Baldesi family, from whom Rucellai acquired his patronage rights in 1457, had completed only the lower portion of the marble façade, which consisted of an inlaid marble arcade of thirteen round arches (eight still visible) carried on fourteen tall Corinthian pilasters (ten still visible) framing ten tombs (six still visible) and three doors (two still visible). Leaving the previous decoration mostly intact, Alberti removed only the central door and its two flanking tombs to create the monumental entrance with a coffered barrel vault carried by Corinthian piers and framed by two colossal Corinthian columns. He also framed each side of the whole façade with a paired colossal Corinthian pier and column sharing a common pedestal, which was superimposed over the outermost tomb and arch. Alberti next designed a new entablature and attic carried by the colossal columns and piers. The attic in turn served as the base for the four pilasters supporting the entablature and triangular pediment that together defined the preexisting nave and oculus. The attic also masked the failure of the outer pilasters of the upper zone to continue vertically the articulating elements in the lower zone.

Although inspired by the twelfth-century Romanesque façades of the Baptistery (fig. 10) and S. Miniato (fig. 11), Alberti also borrowed motifs and harmonic proportions from classical antiquity. He derived the central doorway, for example, directly from the entrance to the Pantheon in Rome. In the upper zone he pioneered an ingenious solution to the difficult problem of adapting the form of a standard colonnaded and pedimented Roman temple front to a Christian church façade by using volutes curling around rosettes—introduced by Brunelleschi on the cathedral lantern (fig. 31)—to make an eloquent transition from the nave to the side aisles and to visually unite the upper and lower zones. In addition, Alberti circumscribed the entire façade within one large 60-*braccia* square, the upper temple-front within a 30-*braccia* square, and the lower zone within two side-by-side 30-*braccia* squares minus the attic's cornice (fig. 44a). He accommodated the areas with the rose window and the pediment each within two side-by-side 15-*braccia* squares (fig. 44b). He also subdivided the 15-*braccia* square into four even smaller squares (marked by dotted lines on the diagram), two of which define the area of two outer bays of the temple front (including in each case the outside pilaster), one the attic's height, eight the attic's length, and six the area of the central door (including the engaged columns). The sides of the squares containing the volutes relate to the height of the attic by a ratio of 5:3. By this progressive subdivision of squares, Alberti created a unified façade whose various elements relate to one another in simple mathematical ratios expressive of divine harmony. He also integrated squares and circles, symbols of matter and spirit, to express the fundamental duality of Christian theology, appropriately reserving the use of circles for the symbolic heavenly zone above the attic. Finally, within the pediment's circle he created an inlaid marble infant-faced sun disk, symbol of Christ's Incarnation and divine justice, to suggest the ultimate triumph of spirit over matter.

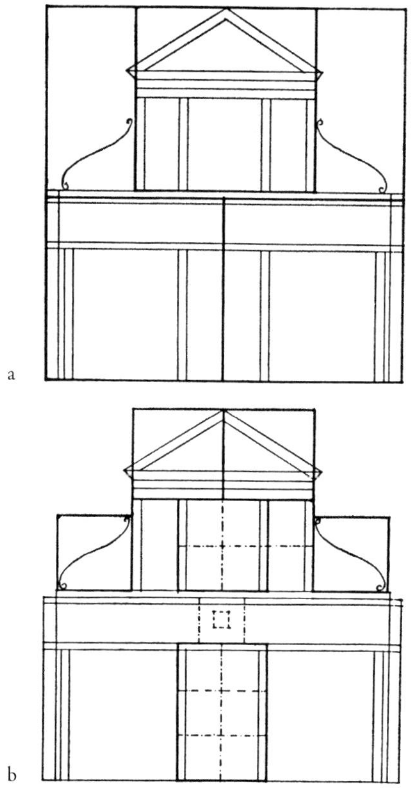

44. Façade diagrams of S. Maria Novella.

4

THE BAPTISTERY DOORS

The first set of bronze doors for the Baptistery's south entrance, featuring scenes from the life of John the Baptist, the city's patron saint, was commissioned from Andrea Pisano (c. 1295–c. 1348/49) in 1330 by the cloth merchants' guild. In 1401 the guild staged a competition for a matching set of doors for the east entrance facing the cathedral with scenes from the Old Testament. Each of the seven competitors was required to submit a bronze relief of the Sacrifice of Isaac (Genesis 22:1–19), although only Brunelleschi's and Ghiberti's entries were saved; the others presumably were melted down to recover the metal.

COMPETITION RELIEFS

Brunelleschi

In Brunelleschi's composition, the servants and donkey serve as a base for the stable triangular arrangement above of Abraham, Isaac, and the ram, which echoes the diagonal lines of the quatrefoil (fig. 45). Within this lucid geometric structure Brunelleschi created great aesthetic energy. Obedient to God's command, Abraham bears down on Isaac's twisted body with a look of grim determination as the ram, the boy's imminent substitute, scratches its ear. Employing the quatrefoil itself to emphasize forward flight, Brunelleschi represented the angel sweeping out of the left lobe to arrest at the last moment the death that foreshadowed Christ's sacrifice. Below the main action, one servant dips his cup into a stream, recalling baptism, while the wheat straw in the drinking donkey's packsaddle alludes to the Eucharistic bread. The second servant pulls a thorn from his foot, which Brunelleschi modeled on the most copied work of antiquity—the Hellenistic *Spinario* (*Thorn Puller*), displayed since the twelfth century in the Lateran Palace in Rome. The quotation was appropriate, for the sculpture had come to be understood as a metaphor for Christ the Good Shepherd plucking sin from the world by his sacrifice.

Ghiberti

Ghiberti approached the narrative quite differently (fig. 46). He divided the composition roughly in half vertically with the principal actors on the right. He designed the figures and landscape more gracefully than had Brunelleschi in response to the curves of the quatrefoil, and while his Abraham obeys God with equal determi-

45. Filippo Brunelleschi, *Sacrifice of Isaac* (Genesis 22:1–19), 1401–2, gilt bronze, c. 77 lbs. (c. 35 kg), 17¾ × 15 in. (45 × 38 cm), Bargello. Seven pieces (**1** ram, donkey, and lower rock; **2** left servant; **3** right servant; **4** Isaac and altar; **5** Abraham and upper rock; **6** tree; and **7** angel) were cast separately and soldered to the solid quatrefoil plate.

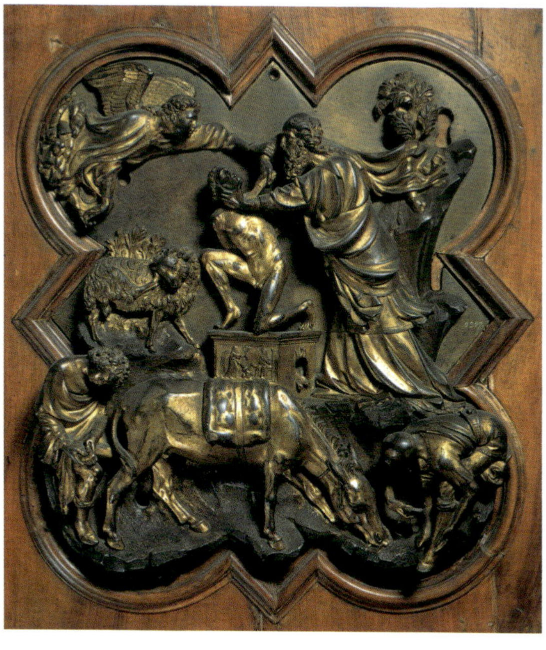

46. Lorenzo Ghiberti, *Sacrifice of Isaac* (Genesis 22:1–19), 1401–2, gilt bronze, c. 56 lbs. (25 kilograms), 17¾ × 15 in. (45 × 38 cm), Bargello. Except for the separately cast Isaac, all figures were hollow cast and integral with the background.

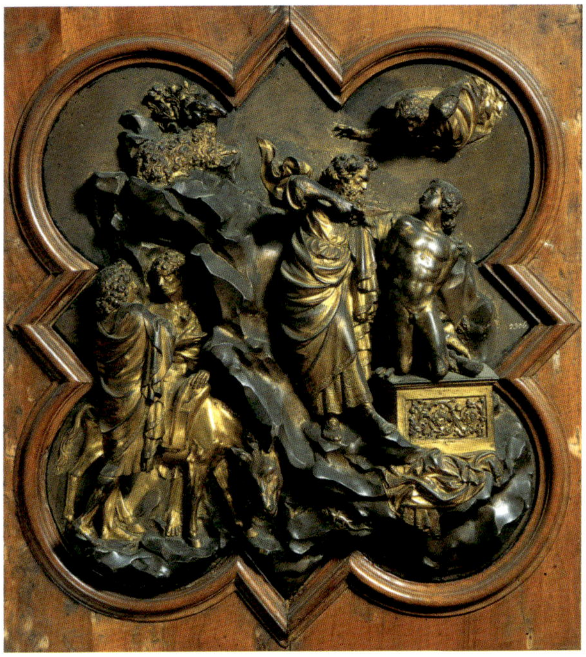

47. Lorenzo Ghiberti, *First Baptistery Doors,* 1403–24, signed, gilt bronze, 14 ft. 11⅞ in. × 8 ft. 2⅞ in. (457 × 251 cm) without frame, Baptistery. The doors were originally made for the east entrance, then moved in about 1452 to the north.

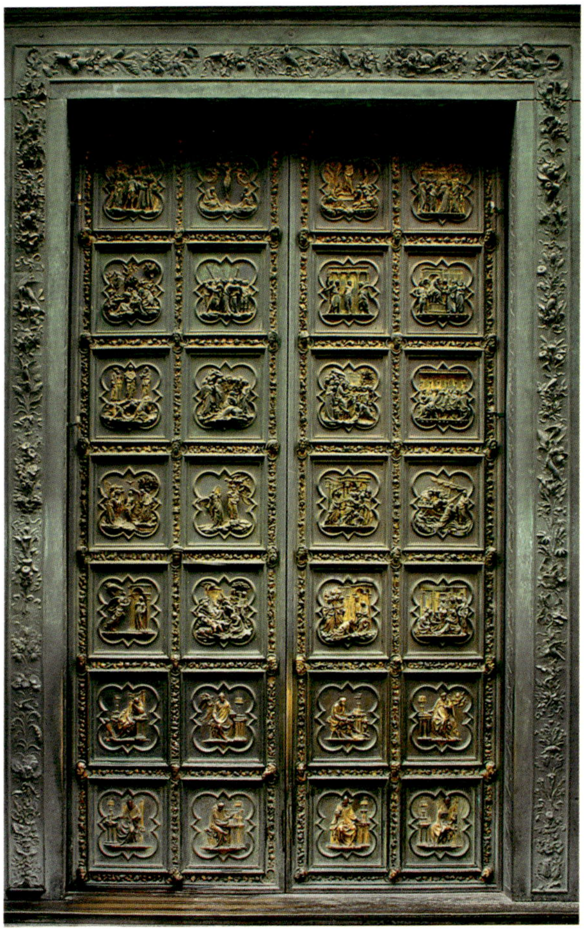

nation, he also lovingly embraces his son. Ghiberti's body of Isaac, inspired by images of classical athletes, is also far less contorted and thus more suggestive of the perfection and innocence of Christ, whom he prefigures.

Ghiberti's foreshortened angel appears to emerge from a more atmospheric background and to intervene less aggressively, as if to suggest that God's preordination of all history obviated the need for urgent action. The servants too—less active and physically isolated by the mountain—offer a commentary on the inevitability of the drama, much like the chorus in a Greek play. Ghiberti's narrative, in sum, appears more graceful and laconic, Brunelleschi's more dramatic and symbolic, although both achieved impressive results for sculptors in their early twenties.

In his *Commentaries* (c. 1450), Ghiberti boasted that he had won the competition outright. Antonio di Tuccio Manetti (1423–97) in his biography of Brunelleschi (c. 1480), however, reported a tie and an offer of a joint commission, which Brunelleschi refused. In any case, Ghiberti's use of about 30 percent less bronze probably weighed heavily in the guild's final decision to award the commission to Ghiberti.

GHIBERTI'S FIRST DOORS

After the competition, the guild changed the program from Old Testament scenes to twenty episodes from the life of Christ combined with representations in the bottom two rows of the four Evangelists and the four Church fathers (fig. 47).

Annunciation

The narrative series opened with the *Annunciation* (fig. 48). Exploiting the shape of the quatrefoil for dramatic effect, Ghiberti divided the composition in half, spiritual figures to the left, temporal to the right.

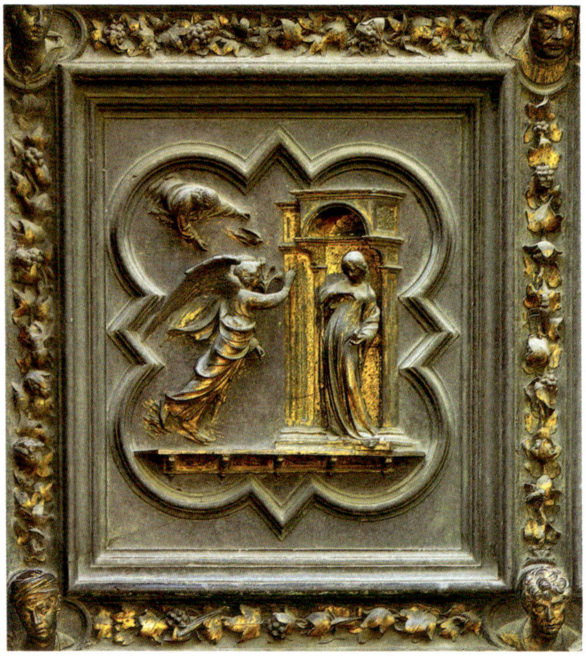

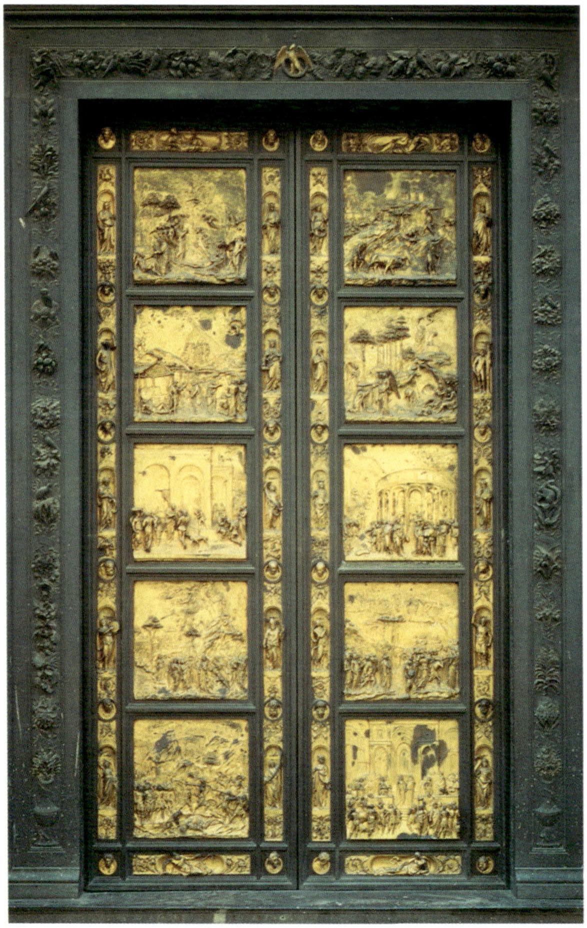

48. Ghiberti, *Annunciation* (Luke 1:26–38), c. 1404–7, gilt bronze, 15⅜ in. (39 cm) square. Detail of fig. 47.

49. Lorenzo Ghiberti, *Gates of Paradise,* 1424–52, signed, gilt bronze, 16 ft. 7¼ in. × 9 ft. 5 in. (506 × 287 cm) with frame, Baptistery. When completed in 1452, the doors were installed on the east facing the cathedral, and Ghiberti's earlier doors were reinstalled on the north. The restored original door is now displayed in the Museo dell'Opera del Duomo.

He aligned along one diagonal his foreshortened God and dove of the Holy Spirit emerging from clouds in the upper left lobe, and the wings and body of his airborne Archangel Gabriel along another diagonal.

Holding a book evocative of her piety and wisdom, the Virgin receives the archangel's announcement with trepidation and humility. Contrasting with the graceful and oblique movement of the left-hand figures, the Virgin stands planted within a classicizing aedicule, symbol of the Church she embodies. Her graceful S-shaped Gothic sway, however, associates her with Gabriel's sweeping drapery folds to express her spiritual grace. By the contrast yet interpenetration of curvilinear and rectilinear forms, Ghiberti visualized the essence of the narrative—the Word made flesh.

GHIBERTI'S GATES OF PARADISE

The great success of Ghiberti's first doors, installed in 1424, led to his commission without a competition for the final set of doors with Old Testament scenes for the north entrance (fig. 49). Ghiberti radically altered the design from the twenty-eight quatrefoils of the previous doors to ten large square panels, no doubt to allow greater narrative flexibility and spatial inventiveness in keeping with Brunelleschi's recent invention of one-point perspective and Donatello's experiments in low relief (figs. 3, 4, and 25). If Ghiberti himself was responsible for this new design, it constituted an early example of an artist striving to outdo both himself and his rivals in order to increase his fame and raise his social status.

Creation of Adam and Eve, Temptation and Fall, Expulsion from Paradise

The first panel includes four scenes, thirty-eight figures, and a variety of landscape features that diminish in scale and depth of relief from lower foreground to upper background, creating a deep atmospheric space (fig. 50). At the lower left Ghiberti represented

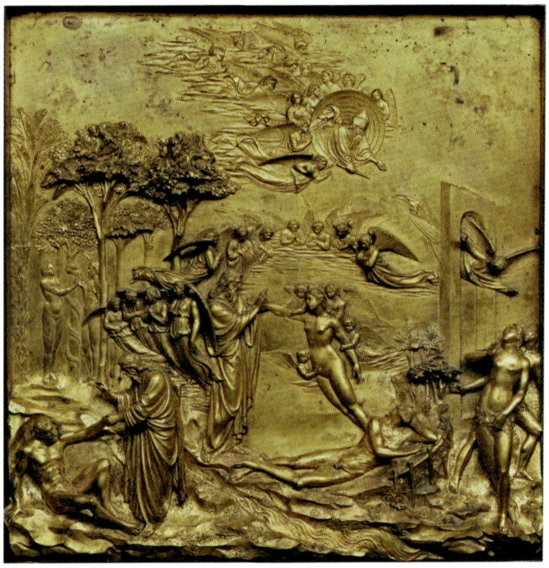

50. Ghiberti, *Creation of Adam* (Genesis 1:26–27), *Temptation and Fall* (Genesis 3:1–7), *Creation of Eve* (Genesis 2:21–25), and *Expulsion from Paradise* (Genesis 3:8–24), gilt bronze, 31½ in. (80 cm) square. Detail of fig. 49.

humanity's birth as God's creation of Adam. A semicircular choir of five angels witnesses the scene, expressing by their gazes and gestures God's love for humanity. Since the creation prefigured the Incarnation of Christ, Adam's heroic muscularity, shoulder-length hair, and short beard alluded to Christ, the second Adam, at the age of his sacrifice (33). Just above Christ, Ghiberti represented Adam and Eve's fall from grace to emphasize the necessity for a redeemer. The serpent's temptation of Eve, furthermore, was often understood as an antitype of Gabriel's annunciation to the Virgin, the second Eve and the vessel of the Incarnation. Traditionally viewed as sensuous and irresponsible, Eve appears to be the cause of original sin, for the female-headed serpent tempts only her, and only she reaches up to grasp the forbidden fruit, while Adam raises his hands in dismay. The framing palm and deciduous trees also evoke, respectively, Christ's frond-strewn entry into Jerusalem to begin his Passion and the regenerative promise of his sacrifice.

In the panel's center God's creative hand draws from Adam's side the figure of Eve—inspired by a classical Venus (see fig. 60)—carried aloft by a quartet of angels. The narrative merited pride of place, for it prefigured the foundation of the Church embodied by the Virgin. Ghiberti expressed the Church's perfection by the circularity of the episode's composition and by Eve's graceful body. The arc of adoring angels suggests the seven cosmic spheres and the Church's universality, as well as the virtues of the Virgin—the Seven Gifts of the Holy Spirit (Isaiah 11:1–2). Adam's sleep foreshadowed Christ's death, while the emergence of Eve from his side anticipated the piercing of Christ's side at the Crucifixion from which issued water and blood (John 19:34), symbols of baptism and the Eucharist. Finally, the River of Paradise flowing under Adam evinced the power of baptism to cleanse and regenerate the soul, an apt theme for baptistery decoration.

God appears for the third time near the panel's top wearing the triangular crown of the Trinity and carrying a baton of sovereignty. He is surrounded by the seven planetary spheres and a host of angels, symbols of his dominion. Responding to God's command, the Archangel Michael to the far right expels Adam and Eve from the gate of Paradise, his diagonal dive intensified by contrast with Eve's ascent in the center.

Jacob and Esau

Ghiberti rendered the two panels at the center of the door located just above a viewer's eye level in one-point perspective, their design close in time to Alberti's codification of perspective in his 1435 treatise, *On Painting*. The left panel represents the story of Jacob and Esau in seven episodes (fig. 51).

At the upper right God appears within clouds to the previously barren Rebecca. God tells her that "two nations are in thy womb [Esau and Jacob] and . . . one people shall overcome the other, and the elder [Esau] shall serve the younger [Jacob]." The episode was traditionally interpreted to mean that Christianity would supplant Judaism, with Jacob prefiguring Christ and Rebecca, the Virgin. In the left background Rebecca lies in her canopied bed after giving birth to her twins as the four young serving maids in the foreground—their drapery gracefully looping across their twisting bodies—excitedly discuss the births.

Later, when the twins are grown youths, Esau returns famished from hunting, and Jacob offers his older brother food on the condition that Esau yield to him his rights as firstborn. Esau consents, and Jacob (in the center middle ground seated at a table) hands a bowl of lentil soup to his hungry brother. Still later, the old and blind Isaac sends his firstborn and favorite, Esau (center foreground with his two dogs), on a deer hunt. A meal will be pre-

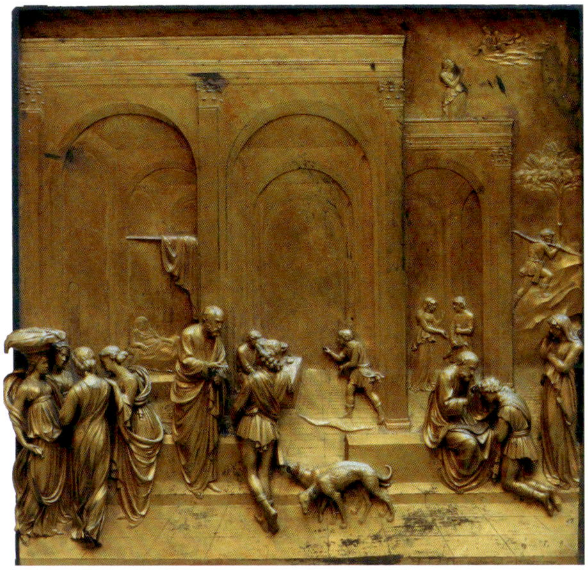

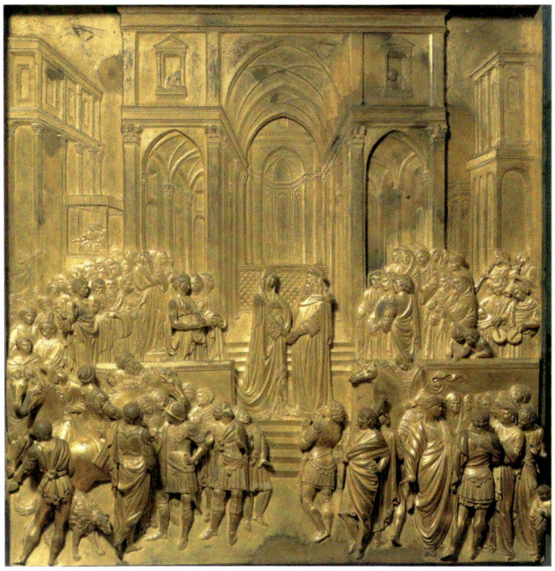

51. Ghiberti, *Rebecca Speaks to God* (Genesis 25:23), *Rebecca Gives Birth to the Twins Esau and Jacob* (Genesis 25:24–26), *Esau Sells His Birthright to Jacob* (Genesis 25:29–34), *Isaac Sends Esau on a Hunt* (Genesis 27:1–4), *Rebecca Instructs Jacob How to Deceive Isaac* (Genesis 27:6–17), and *Isaac Blesses Jacob* (Genesis 27:18–29), gilt bronze, 31½ in. (80 cm) square. Detail of fig. 49.

52. Ghiberti, *Meeting of Solomon and the Queen of Sheba* (3 Kings 10:1–9), gilt bronze, 31½ in. (80 cm) square. Detail of fig. 49.

pared from the venison, after which, in a formal ceremony of blessing, Isaac will confirm Esau's birthright to head the family. In the extreme right background, bow over his shoulder, Esau departs for the hunt.

Meanwhile, standing under a porch in the right middle ground, Rebecca instructs her favorite son, Jacob, to deceive Isaac by dressing in Esau's clothes and covering his hands and neck with a goat skin (which he holds) to simulate Esau's hirsuteness to his blind father's touch. She then prepares the ritual meal before Esau's return. The story concludes in the right foreground with Isaac blessing Jacob, whom he mistakes for Esau, as Rebecca looks on. God's plan has been fulfilled.

In composing the narrative, Ghiberti ingeniously exploited the real/ideal duality of perspective. In the foreground, a tessellated stage projects beyond the panel's frame to connect with the viewer's space. Here Ghiberti represented in high relief the serving maids, Isaac (twice), and Esau with his dogs. These accessible figures, seemingly free to act at will, are nevertheless unaware of God's purpose. Isaac is both literally and figuratively blind.

The diminished background figures, by contrast, operate furtively, their actions partially obscured by the foreground figures. Yet Rebecca and Jacob know the truth and act decisively to fulfill God's preordained plan, expressed by the space's geometrical and mathematical perfection. The breadth and harmony of the classicizing architecture also symbolize the grandeur of the Church to come.

Solomon and Sheba

The concluding panel, filled with nearly ninety figures, represents the queen of Sheba's reception by King Solomon in the Temple of Jerusalem (fig. 52). The story evoked such a wide range of symbolic meanings that Ghiberti gave the king and queen great visual prominence by their centrality and by the orthogonals that converge just above their heads. Bearing gifts to Solomon, the queen and her retinue prefigured the Magi's journey to the Nativity in Bethlehem, Christ's first revelation to the Gentiles. This epiphany was celebrated annually on January 6, often accompanied by a lavish pageant reenacting the procession of the Magi. Also celebrated on January 6 were the Marriage at Cana, where Christ performed his first miracle by turning water into wine, and the Baptism of Christ, the first (and only) revelation of the Trinity. On the same day, Florentine infants were baptized in the Baptistery into the Christian faith and the Florentine community. Finally, the handclasp pledging mutual faith between Solomon, a Christ type, and the queen of Sheba, a Virgin type, symbolized the union of Christ and his Church, and in this particular case perhaps also the union of the Eastern and Western Churches achieved briefly at the conclusion of the Council of Florence in 1439.

The Baptistery, as all baptisteries, was understood to be a gatehouse to Paradise, where the rite of baptism washed away original sin and opened the possibility of salvation. The east door, therefore, symbolized the east gate of Jerusalem through which Christ entered to begin his Passion on Palm Sunday, while the traditional octagonal plan evoked Christ's Resurrection eight days later on Easter Sunday. East doors were thus traditionally called the Gates of Paradise, as Michelangelo famously named them, according to Vasari. Ghiberti's brilliant gilding, then, was designed to reflect the rising sun, symbolically the dawn of renewed life. The doors also faced the cathedral, the principal image of Florence as a new Jerusalem. For this reason, Ghiberti employed Gothic architecture in the last panel to equate the cathedral's Gothic nave and aisles with the Temple of Jerusalem, an early use of style for an iconographical purpose.

5

ALTARPIECES AND CHAPELS

Altarpieces and chapels—major genres of Renaissance art—supplemented and visually enhanced the liturgy of the Mass, which reenacted Christ's birth, death, and resurrection (fig. 53). The climax of the Mass, accompanied by the ringing of bells, occurred when the priest consecrated the Eucharist (bread and wine). By a mystical process called Transubstantiation, he transformed the bread and wine into the Real Presence, Christ's actual body and blood. Immediately after the Consecration, the priest elevated the Eucharist toward heaven as a sign of Christ's resurrection and as a thanksgiving offering to God (Eucharist means "thanksgiving" in Greek). At this moment a divine presence mystically poured over the altar to join the earthly Mass with the celestial liturgy celebrated perpetually in heaven by angels and saints in praise of the triune divinity—God the Father, Christ, and the Holy Spirit (the Trinity).

Transubstantiation and Christ's birth, death, and resurrection were usually expressed in chapels by representations of the body of Christ, narratives from his life, or events from the lives of saints who followed Christ's example of virtue and self-sacrifice. Altarpieces also visualized the conjunction of heaven and earth during the Mass through some manifestation of divinity, such as angels, golden light, or one or more persons of the Trinity.

Altarpieces and chapels were commissioned and funded by a lay or ecclesiastical patron who could be an individual, family, or institution. A legal contract obligated the patron to decorate and maintain the altar or the entire chapel and to establish an endowment for its functioning. In return, the patron was granted such rights as burial near the altar, regular celebrations of requiem Masses for the soul's comfort, display of the family or corporate coat of arms, choice of the decoration's themes and artist(s), and sometimes even the selection of the altar's dedication—all subject to the approval of church authorities.

A name-saint, portrait, or inscription usually explicitly referenced the patron, a public display of piety and devotion believed to aid in his salvation. Also, the church authorities generally insisted upon some visual allusion to their interests and ideology. Finally, the decoration almost always indicated the altar's dedication, which, in the case of high altars, was normally the same as the church.

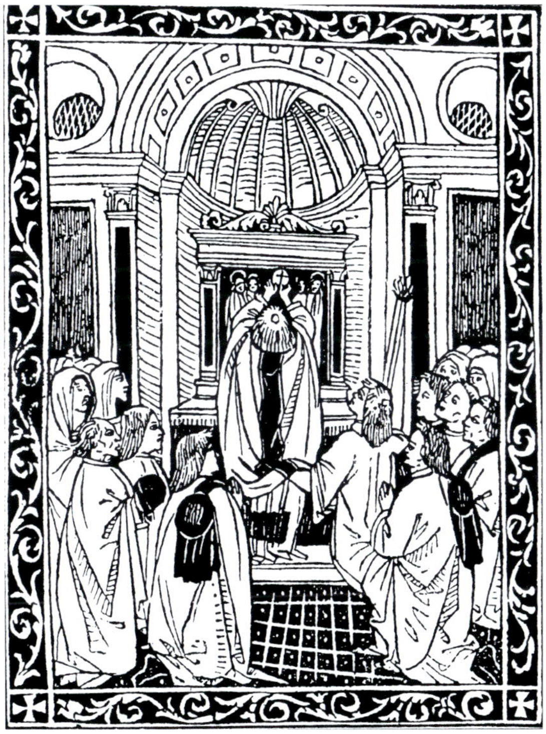

53. Anonymous, *Elevation of the Host,* woodcut, from Girolamo Savonarola (1452–98), *Tractato del sacramento e dei misterii della messa* (Florence, 1493).

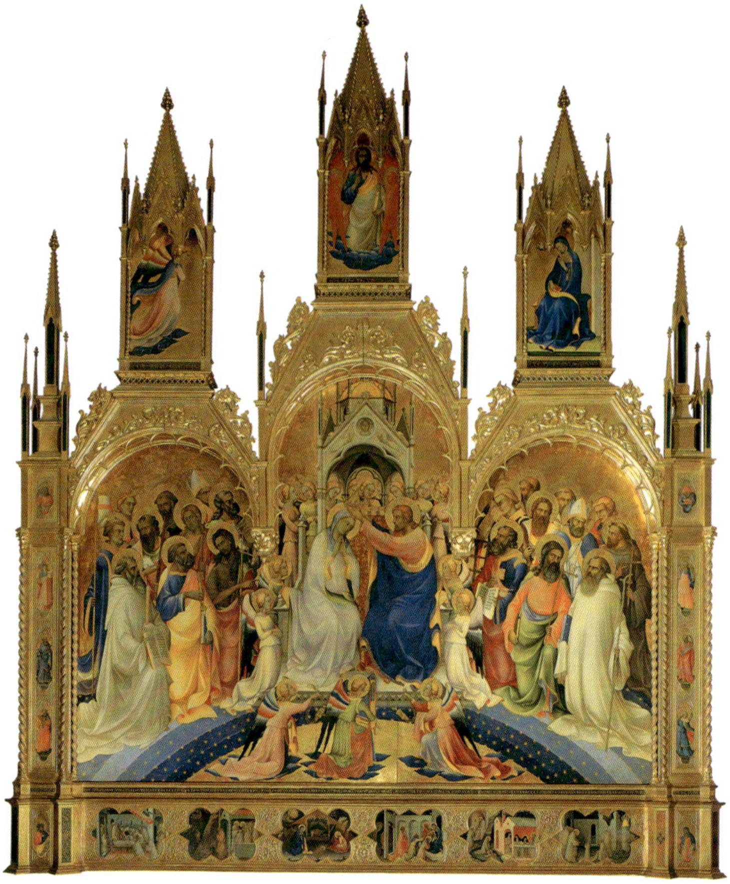

54. Lorenzo Monaco, *Coronation of the Virgin,* signed and dated 1414, tempera on panel, 16 ft. 9½ in. × 14 ft. 9 in. (512 × 450 cm), Uffizi.

S. MARIA DEGLI ANGELI: LORENZO MONACO'S *CORONATION OF THE VIRGIN*

The function of an altarpiece is well illustrated by the Gothic *Coronation of the Virgin* (fig. 54) by Lorenzo Monaco (c. 1370/75–c. 1425/30), originally on the high altar of the Camaldolese church of S. Maria degli Angeli. The *Annunciation* in the two outermost pinnacles at the top represents Christ's Incarnation, while the *Nativity* and the *Adoration of the Magi*—the two central scenes in the predella (the base of an altarpiece with narrative scenes related to the main panel[s] above)—depict his birth. The uppermost pinnacle representing the blessing cloud-born Christ adorned by red seraphim (symbols of divine love) as well as the two outermost predella panels—*Death of St. Benedict* (left) and *St. Benedict Resurrects a Young Monk* (right)—thematize Christ's death and resurrection. The mystery of Transubstantiation would have been visualized at the climax of the Mass, when the officiating priest elevated the Host in close proximity to the central image of the enthroned Christ. The celebration of the Mass on the high altar was also imitated by the three angels kneeling beneath the *Coronation,* two swinging censors and one playing a portative organ (the latter nearly effaced by a later tabernacle once installed here), thereby evoking the conjunction of the terrestrial and celestial liturgies. The *Coronation* also symbolized the union of the heavenly Church, embodied by Christ, and the earthly Church, embodied by the Virgin, a significance enhanced by the domed churchlike tabernacle behind them. The flooding of the altar with a divine presence during the Mass was suggested by star-studded arcs of the heavenly spheres, the haloed saints, and the late Gothic style of high-keyed colors, glittering surfaces, and graceful drapery patterns unrelated to underlying anatomies.

The altarpiece's patron was probably the banker Domenico della Frascha, who commissioned the work, as an inscription states, to commemorate "the soul of Zanobi di Ceccho della Frascha [1320s–1375] and his family." Domenico's father, Zanobi di Ceccho, was further referenced by his name-saint, Zenobius (d. 417), depicted in the second row of the heavenly court, second from the left. St. Zenobius was an early bishop of Florence and renowned for raising the dead, a talent most appropriate in this context of family memorialization.

The interests of the church authorities were expressed by the two outermost saints in the first row, dressed in white Camaldolese habits: on the right the founder of the Camaldolese Order, St. Romuald (c. 950–1027), and on the left St. Benedict (c. 480–c. 550), whose monastic rule the Camaldolese followed. The Virgin (also dressed in Camaldolese white) and her choir of angels indicated the high altar's dedication to St. Mary of the Angels, the same dedication as the church itself.

Finally, an altarpiece such as this, depicting a group of holy figures of different historical periods gathered together to form a heavenly court and engaged in "holy conversation," is known as a *sacra conversazione* type.

S. MARIA NOVELLA, I: MASACCIO'S *TRINITY*

The contrast between the *Coronation of the Virgin* by Lorenzo Monaco and the *Trinity* by Masaccio (1401–28) in S. Maria Novella (fig. 55; see also fig. 12, no. 7) vividly illustrates the vast stylistic difference between a late Gothic and an early Renaissance work.

The *Trinity* reconstructs in one-point perspective the Golgotha Chapel in the Church of the Holy Sepulcher in Jerusalem, which commemorated the "place of the skull" (Golgotha) where Christ was crucified. Although nearly contemporary with Donatello's *Feast of Herod* (fig. 3), the *Trinity* represents a far more accomplished spatial construction, suggesting that Brunelleschi himself might have assisted Masaccio. Extending the ribs or orthogonals of the coffered barrel vault upward to the bottom of the entablature establishes the inverted base line, divided into eight modular units (fig. 56). Extending the ribs downward locates the vanishing point on the horizon line at the top of the donor's ledge, the approximate eye level of a viewer standing in front of the fresco. From this ideal viewing position, the observer looks up into the coffered barrel vault, which is supported by eight Ionic columns. The four columns at the front and back carry red marble arches, while those at the sides support flat red marble cornices. Christ's tomb, one end of which is attached to the rear wall, extends forward to a position just behind the cross. The tomb's visible end is capped by a red marble corbelled cornice, on top of which stands God the Father supporting the cross.

A modular grid, derived from divisions of the inverted baseline, superimposed over the fresco as in the diagram (fig. 56), reveals that Masaccio composed the work according to three stacked *rectangles,* each eight modular units wide and six high; or, if the paired colonnettes and fluted

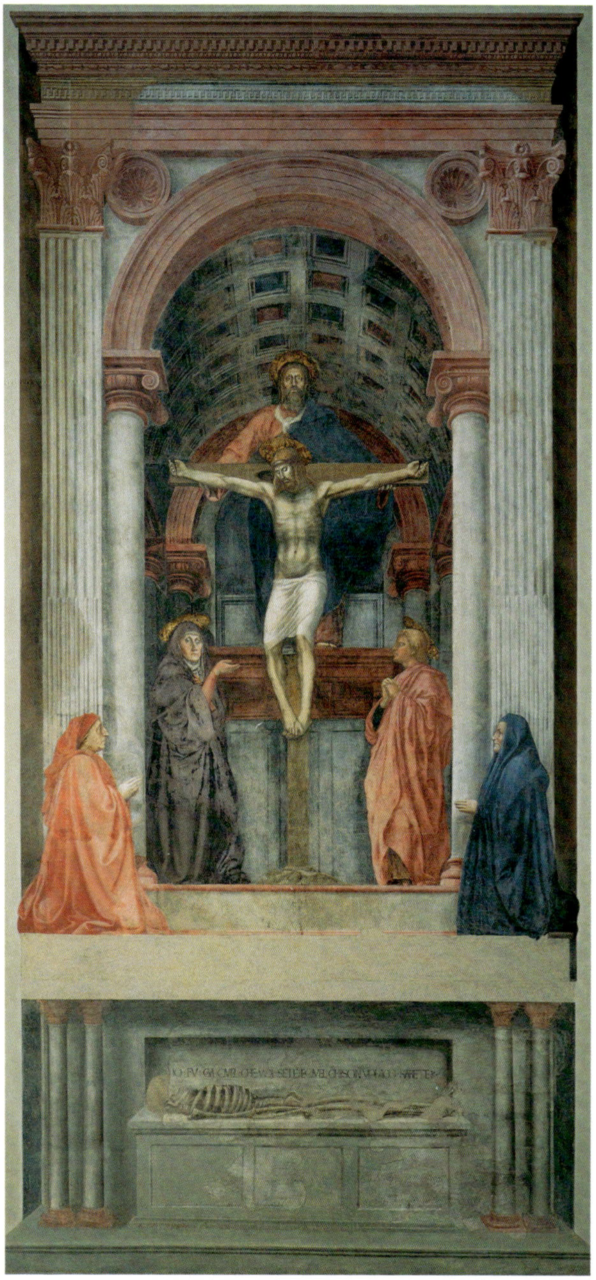

55. Masaccio, *Trinity,* c. 1425–27, detached fresco, 21 ft. 10⅝ in. × 10 ft. 4¾ in. (667 × 317 cm), S. Maria Novella. Damage to the fresco makes it impossible to determine with certainty, but Masaccio probably intended the colonnettes to support a fictive altar table. There may even have been a real altar table embedded in the wall with its outer edge supported by matching colonnettes, or perhaps a freestanding altar in front of the fresco. The identities of the life-size donors depicted kneeling on a ledge just outside the illusionistic chapel are uncertain.

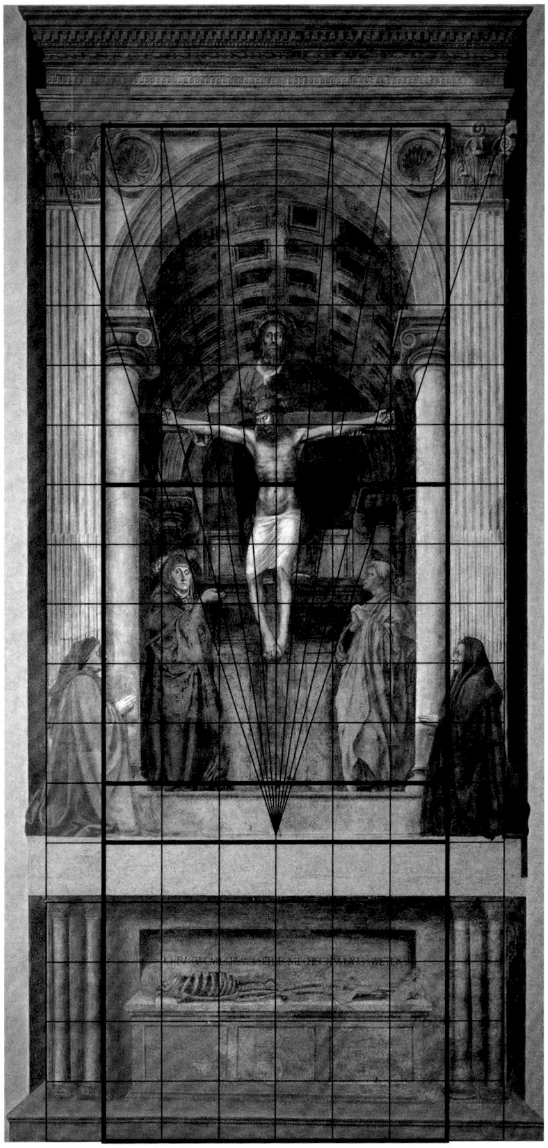

56. Perspective diagram of Masaccio's *Trinity.*

Corinthian pilasters on the sides are excluded, three stacked *squares,* each six by six modular units. The lower two rectangles or squares overlap by one modular unit.

The lower rectangle or square includes the sarcophagus, skeleton, altar table (?), donor's ledge, and base of the Golgotha Chapel. The skeleton, the most anatomically correct to date in Italian art, represents the first human, Adam (in Hebrew "everyman"), who was by tradition buried and redeemed at the foot of the cross. The bones address the viewer in an Italian verse inscribed just above: "I was once as you are; as I am you will also become." This zone thus represents the plenitude of history from humanity's beginning to the present, the visual equivalent of the third person of the Trinity, the Holy Spirit, which flows through all space and time.

The middle rectangle or square extends from slightly below the top of the donor's ledge to Christ's navel, traditionally understood as the center of the universe. It constitutes the zone of the second person of the Trinity, the Son, crucified at a specific moment in history. The chapel's ancient Roman architectural style underlines the historical moment of Christ's death within the Roman Empire. However, to indicate the continuing validity of Christ's redemptive sacrifice, Masaccio represented the actors in the Crucifixion—Christ, Mary, and John—as physically present and Christ's wounds as still bleeding. These massive, even heroic figures with foreshortened haloes stand within a shallow stage spatially continuous with the viewer's space, a continuity heightened by the Virgin's direct gaze at the observer as she gestures toward her lifeless son.

Similarly, the donors, probably deceased when Masaccio executed the work, simultaneously overlap Adam's zone, kneel within the viewer's space as if alive, and pray only inches away from the historic yet seemingly ongoing Crucifixion. Masaccio also linked the donors to Mary and John by costume, color, and gesture, and by the alignment of their heads along two contrary diagonals focused on Christ's navel. The artist, therefore, indicated the donors' desire, and that of all Christian viewers, for eternal salvation through Christ, merited by their manifest exercise of faith, hope, and charity.

The top rectangle or square extends from Christ's navel—or from the springing of the barrel vault at the rear of the chapel—to the inverted baseline at the bottom of the fresco's crowning entablature. Here the historic crucified Christ joins the first person of the Trinity, God the Father, and the white dove of the Holy Spirit (in descending flight between the heads of God and Christ) to form the image called the Throne of Grace or Throne of Mercy (based on Isaiah 16:5 and Hebrews 4:16), the symbolic judgment seat at the end of time. The vault (traditional sign of heaven), the hieratic nonforeshortened image of God (whose halo is tangent with the exact center of the coffered vault), and the framing triumphal arch mark this as the zone outside of space and time of the perfect and eternal Church Triumphant. If it is assumed that either a painted or actual altar table was intended above the colonnettes, then at the moment of the Eucharist's elevation near the feet of Christ, the entire fresco would have visualized the mediation of the Mass between here and hereafter, matter and spirit, death and renewed life.

Masaccio clearly poured much mental and physical energy into creating this work. He would certainly have understood the *Trinity* as a personal triumph, as a good work promoting the salvation of his own soul. Furthermore, by his command of classical architecture, mathematics, and rhetorical narrative, Masaccio could also claim to be a practitioner of the liberal arts.

S. MARIA DEL CARMINE: MASACCIO AND MASOLINO'S BRANCACCI CHAPEL

Before his death around 1366, Pietro Brancacci left a bequest to build a burial chapel dedicated to his name-saint, Peter, in S. Maria del Carmine (fig. 57; see also fig. 12, no. 6). In 1394, about five years after the chapel's completion, Pietro's twelve-year-old nephew, Felice Brancacci (1382–c. 1450), inherited the chapel's rights. About three decades later, Felice, now wealthy and politically active, commissioned Masaccio and Masolino (1383–c. 1447) to fresco the chapel with scenes from the life of St. Peter drawn from the thirteenth-century *Golden Legend* by Jacopo da Voragine (c. 1230–98), the Gospels, and the Acts of the Apostles. Not only was the life of St. Peter—Christ's successor, founder of the Roman Church, and martyr—appropriate for a burial chapel, but the Carmelite monks held Peter in the highest esteem. They claimed to have been founded by Elijah as an order of Jewish ascetics and then converted by Peter to become the first Christian monastic order. Owing allegiance directly to Peter and his successors, the Carmelites were ideologically committed to the Petrine Succession (the descent of Christ's authority through Peter to successive popes), papal supremacy (the pope's supreme spiritual authority over the entire Church hierarchy), and the mission of the Church to convert, baptize, heal, and preach.

Temptation and Fall and *Expulsion from Paradise*

Masolino's *Temptation and Fall* and Masaccio's *Expulsion from Paradise* on the upper level of the piers framing the chapel's entrance prefaced the decoration (figs. 58 and 59) and related directly to the Mass by illustrating the original sin that Christ died to redeem.

Using a late Gothic canon of anatomical form, Masolino conceived the sinners as refined courtly figures who register little emotion or energy. Almost completely lacking in *contrapposto,* they appear to be acted upon by the guile of the female-headed serpent rather than moved by their own free will.

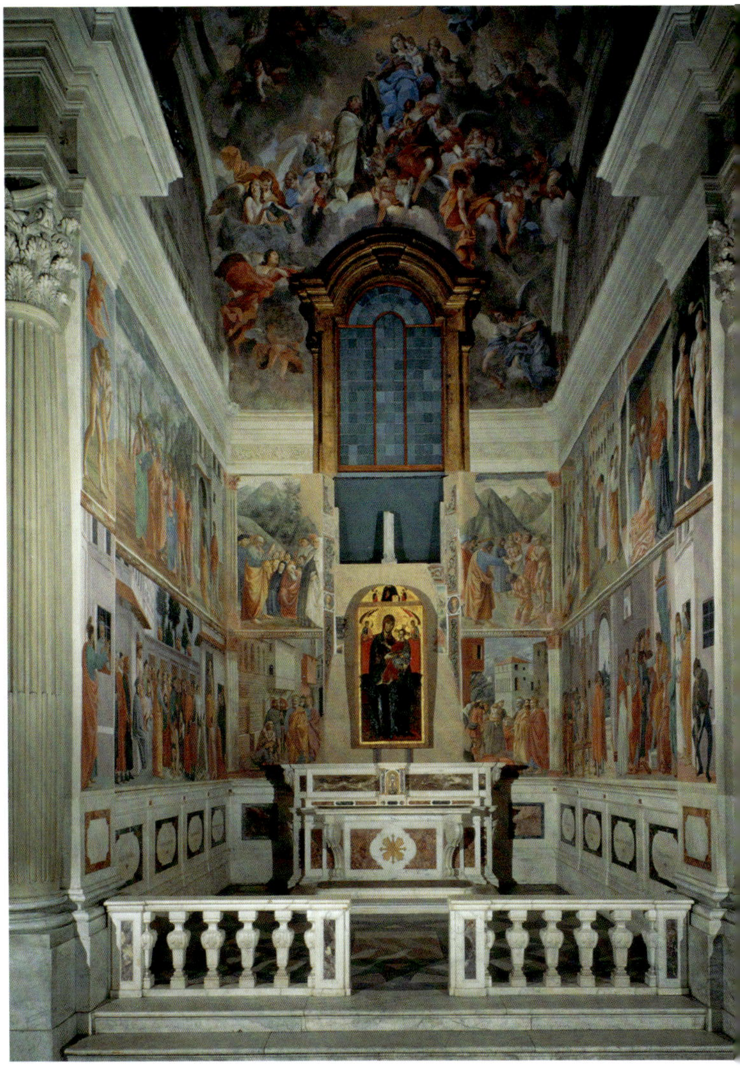

57. Masaccio and Masolino, Brancacci Chapel, S. Maria del Carmine, c. 1425–27. Between 1435 and 1460 the original altarpiece, probably depicting the crucifixion of St. Peter, was replaced by the present thirteenth-century *Madonna del Carmine*. The frescoes on the lower side walls were completed by Filippino Lippi (c. 1457–1504) between 1484 and 1485, and the vault was rebuilt and redecorated a few years after a fire in 1771.

In his *Expulsion* Masaccio all but completely rejected Gothic conventions as he developed a new early Renaissance style. His Adam and Eve are active and autonomous, bathed in strong focused light that casts shadows and sculpts their figures. Adam—toned and trim—strides forward while bowing his head and covering his face, as if convulsed in despair. Eve—softer and rounder—steps more awkwardly, covering her breasts

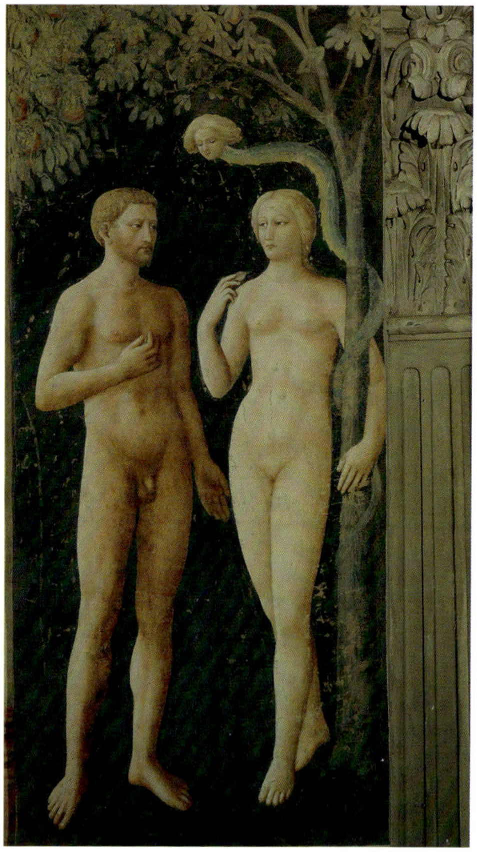

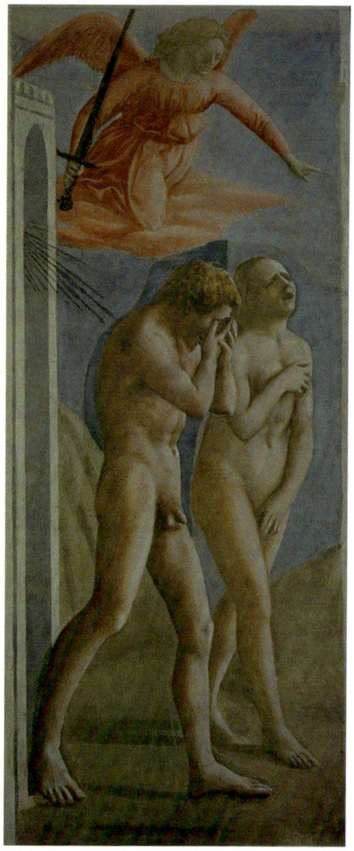

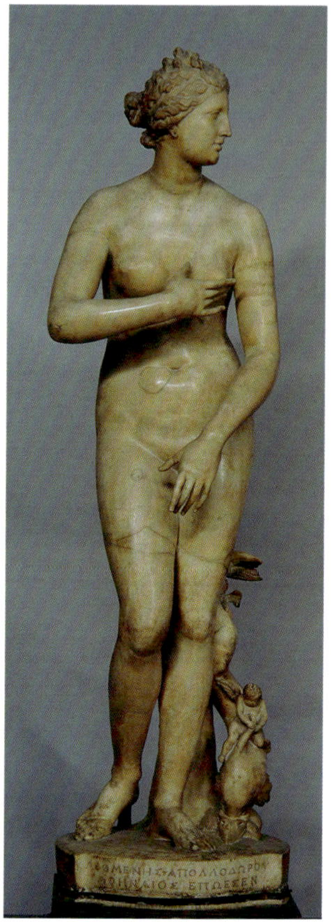

58. Masolino, *Temptation of Adam and Eve* (Genesis 3:1–7), fresco, Brancacci Chapel. Detail of fig. 57.

59. Masaccio, *Expulsion from Paradise* (Genesis 3:8–24), fresco, Brancacci Chapel. Detail of fig. 57.

60. *Venus pudica,* marble, 60¼ in. (153 cm), Uffizi, Roman copy of a Greek original of c. 350–340 BC.

and genitals in shame, a gesture inspired by the well-known classical sculptural type of the *Venus pudica* (*Modest Venus;* fig. 60). However, she throws back her head and, with knit brow, wails, her distress in sharp contrast to the calm self-assured *Venus pudica.* With his commanding sword and vigorous flight, the archangel demonstrates the supreme authority of divine justice and underlines the enormity of humanity's fall from grace as Adam and Eve enter a harsh and barren world.

Tribute Money

When Christ and his Apostles were journeying to Capharnaum, according to Matthew, Roman authorities demanded a head tax, the so-called tribute money (fig. 61). Christ commanded Peter to cast a hook into the sea and take a coin from the mouth of the first fish caught with which to pay the toll, represented on the far left. According to many biblical interpreters, Christ's payment for the Apostles foreshadowed his sacrifice for humanity's redemption, an interpretation most apt for a burial chapel and its liturgy. Since Christ made the payment through Peter, however, the event also demonstrated the preeminence of Peter, thus supporting the doctrines of the Petrine Succession and papal primacy, important for Carmelite and papal ideology.

In the years during which Masaccio was executing the *Tribute Money,* the Florentine government imposed hefty property taxes on Florentine citizens to help finance its struggle against Milan. It also assessed churches, noting that just as Christ had paid taxes to the Romans, so should the Church do its part for the war effort. Pope Martin V (r. 1417–31) refused, arguing that Christ was under no obligation to pay the tribute money. A compromise was finally reached that reduced the assessment by more than

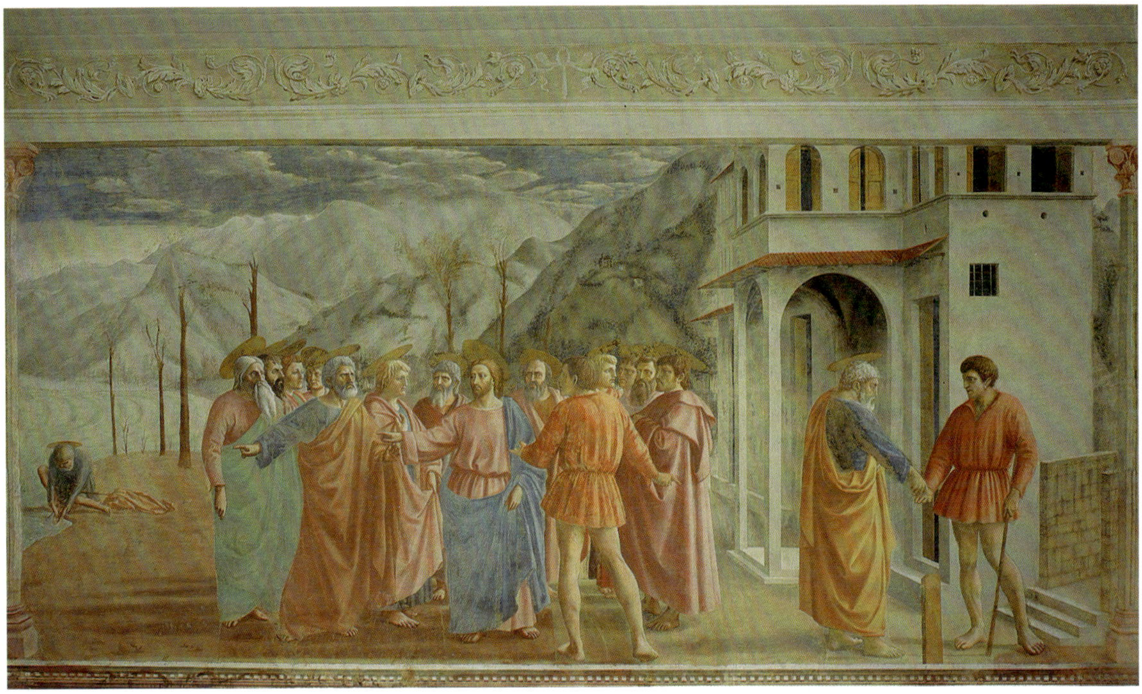

61. Masaccio, *Tribute Money* (Matthew 17:23–26), fresco, Brancacci Chapel. Detail of fig. 57.

90 percent, but the importance of this conflict between the Florentine government and the papacy no doubt accounts for the representation of the *Tribute Money* on such a monumental scale.

In the center of the composition the tax collector confronts Christ, demanding money while gesturing to the customs gate. Although he represents the awesome power of the Roman Empire, he cuts an unimpressive figure with his hunched shoulders and profiled face lost in shadow, especially in contrast to the exceptional bulk and gravity of Christ and the Apostles. Masaccio further emphasized Christ by locating the perspective's focal point at his head and by framing him with two trees, one dead against the dark mountain and one living against the light, to symbolize his death and resurrection. Inspired by Nanni di Banco's *Four Crowned Saints* (fig. 23), Masaccio also heightened Christ's spiritual majesty by arranging the Apostles in a semicircle. Finally, the directional impulse of the orthogonals, light, and Peter's outstretched arm impart great rhetorical power to Christ's command.

In previous representations of the tribute money, the miracle of the fish usually received the greatest emphasis. Yet Masaccio focused on Christ's conferral of authority on Peter, and dramatically contrasted Peter as the fisherman on the far left and as the fisher of men on the far right, exercising Christ's authority to damn and save. Monumentalized by the customshouse, Peter pays the tax symbolically to redeem humanity. His mighty gesture, countering the orthogonals, the light flow, and the movement of the first two narrative episodes, emphasizes the direction of Peter's action toward the altar, the locus of salvation. For its ingenious phrasing, structural clarity, and drama, Masaccio's *Tribute Money* represents a landmark of Western painting.

Peter Heals with His Shadow and *The Death of Ananias*

Masaccio coordinated the two scenes flanking the altar by perspective and light, for their light seems to originate from, and their vanishing points to be located within, the original altarpiece (figs. 62 and 63). Together the scenes also demonstrate the power of the keys conferred on Peter by Christ (Matthew 16:18–19) to save and damn.

On the right (fig. 63), Ananias lies in the foreground. He has been struck dead by Peter for holding back his personal resources, which he, like all the faithful of the early Church, had been expected to relinquish for redistribution by the deacons according to need. It is remarkable, however, that Peter's gesture—focused and

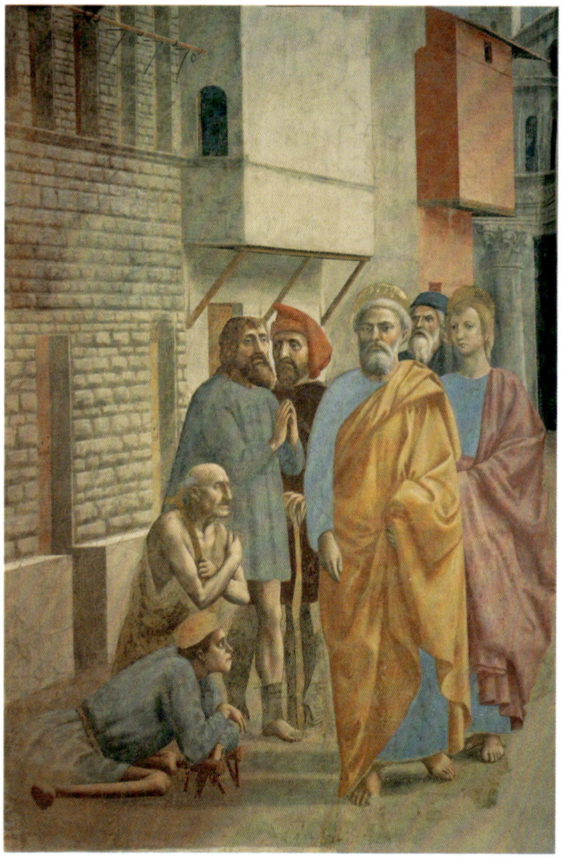

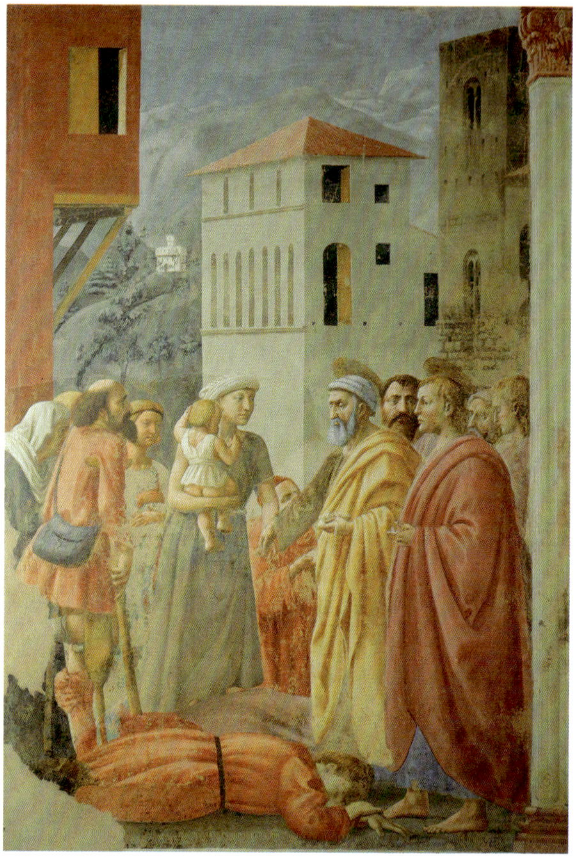

62. Masaccio, *Peter Heals with His Shadow* (Acts 5:12–16), fresco, Brancacci Chapel. Detail of fig. 57.

63. Masaccio, *Death of Ananias and Distribution of the Church's Common Goods* (Acts 4:34–35; 5:1–11), fresco, Brancacci Chapel. Detail of fig. 57.

monumentalized by the obliquely turned background palace—is not one of damnation, as in previous representations. Rather, Peter alone, without the deacons, performs the charitable act of distributing the Church's common goods to those in need. He thereby demonstrates his primacy and the papal claim to sole jurisdiction over all ecclesiastical property.

On the left (fig. 62), long orthogonals draw the viewer's eye to the background church as Peter, followed by John the Evangelist, walks solemnly forward, his shadow healing a trio of lame beggars. The awestruck beggar furthest back stands with his hands in prayerful adoration, as a companion steadies the crutch he no longer needs. The middle figure, also healed, begins to stand in humble reverence. Finally, Peter's shadow has fallen onto, but not yet healed, the beggar in the foreground, crumpled on his withered legs and crutches. Masaccio adeptly enhanced the stages of healing from kneeling, to rising, to standing by the projecting architectural elements, which also rise upward as the perspective draws the eye into space. The dramatic contrast between Peter and John's forward passage, the sequential rise of figures, and the receding architecture create one of the most captivating narratives of the early Renaissance.

S. LORENZO, I: OLD SACRISTY

Buggiano's Sarcophagus

Upon the deaths of Giovanni di Bicci de' Medici and his wife, Piccarda de' Bueri (1368–1433), their two sons, Cosimo il Vecchio and Lorenzo (1395–1440) de' Medici, commissioned Buggiano (1412–62), Donatello's adopted son, to carve a marble sarcophagus for their deceased parents (figs. 33 and 64). According to Renaissance funerary protocols and sumptuary laws (laws regulating extravagant expenditure and behavior), the chapel's founders were entitled to be buried in front of the altar, but as persons of non-ecclesiastical, non-noble, and non-professional rank, only in a floor tomb without an effigy. Thus, a freestanding floor sarcophagus located beneath a vesting table pushed the limits of decorum. In addition, the vesting table was inlaid with a red porphyry disk two *braccia* in diameter, symbolic of Christ's sacrifice, aligned with the vault's oculus, also two *braccia* in diameter, emblematic of Christ's resurrection, thereby creating a symbolic vertical axis focused on the sarcophagus, expressing Giovanni and Piccarda's hope for salvation through the Savior. Finally, the original altar was most likely placed further forward to allow the priest to officiate from behind to face into the chapter room, an early Christian practice in use when St. Ambrose (339–97) consecrated S. Lorenzo in 393. This revived arrangement would have linked the sarcophagus directly to the frequent memorial Masses and offices for the dead provided by Giovanni di Bicci's endowment of a canonry.

An inscription on the sarcophagus names only "chastity" as the virtue of Piccarda de' Bueri, while those of Giovanni di Bicci include "generosity toward all," "aid to the poor," and "support of friends." It also calls Giovanni the parent of his fatherland (*parente suo patria*) as though he deserved the ancient honorific title of *pater patriae* (father of his country) awarded by the Roman senate to such men as Furius Camillus (5th–4th century BC), Cicero, or all the emperors after Julius Caesar (100–44 BC) for extraordinary public service in defense of the *patria.* The sarcophagus's classicizing garlands, egg-and-dart moldings, and winged infants holding oak victory wreaths supported this verbal parallel between Giovanni di Bicci and the great heroes of antiquity. Furthermore, the porphyry disk over the "mausoleum," as the inscription terms the sarcophagus, staked bold claims to wealth and status, for rare and costly porphyry was reserved in classical Rome for imperial sites of court ceremony and burial, while in the Middle Ages it was employed almost exclusively for the burial monuments of high-ranking officials such as saints, popes, bishops, or sovereigns.

Donatello's Decoration

Immediately after returning from exile in 1434, Cosimo il Vecchio and his brother, Lorenzo, commissioned Donatello to execute *in situ* painted clay reliefs of the four Evangelists in the lunettes' *tondi*—the one above the altar reserved for the chapel's dedicatee, John the Evangelist (fig. 33). The artist also sculpted four episodes from John's life taken from the *Golden Legend* in the pendentives' *tondi.* The impressive *Apotheosis of John* is one of the earliest examples in Florentine art of a *dal sotto in su* (from below upward) perspective constructed to accommodate the oblique viewing angle of the viewer (fig. 65). By placing the focal point below the *tondo,* Donatello created a space that reveals the undersides of the porticoes and arcade and increasingly truncated figures the

64. Andrea il Lazzaro Cavalcanti (called Buggiano), *Sarcophagus of Giovanni di Bicci de' Medici and His Wife, Piccarda de' Bueri,* 1433, marble, Old Sacristy, S. Lorenzo. Buggiano also carved the altar rail, the marble altar (whose central panel was filled by Brunelleschi's *Sacrifice of Isaac* [fig. 45]), and probably the central vesting table shown in fig. 33.

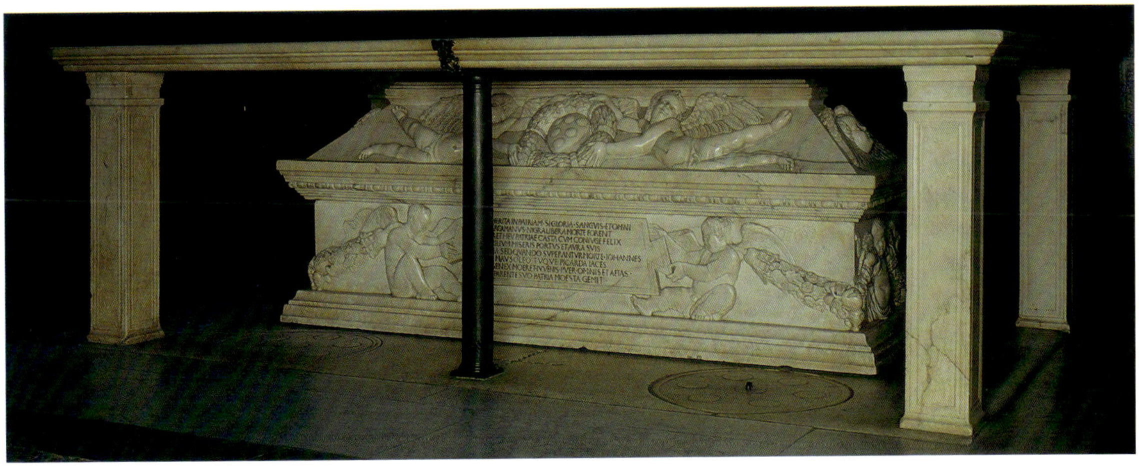

65. Donatello, *Apotheosis of St. John the Evangelist,* 1434–43, painted clay, diameter 7 ft. ⅝ in. (215 cm). Old Sacristy, S. Lorenzo. Detail of fig. 35.

66. Donatello, *Apostles' Doors,* 1434–43, bronze, 7 ft. 8½ in. × 3 ft. 6⅞ in. (235 × 109 cm), right doors. Old Sacristy, S. Lorenzo. See fig. 33. The figures that have attributes represent (top row, left to right) Florence's patron saint, John the Baptist (reed cross); Giovanni di Bicci's name-saint. John the Evangelist (book); and cofounders of the Roman Church, SS. Peter (keys) and Paul (sword and book); (second row) SS. Andrew (cross), James (pilgrim's staff), and Bartholomew (book and knife); (fourth row) Four Evangelists; and (bottom row) Four Latin Doctors.

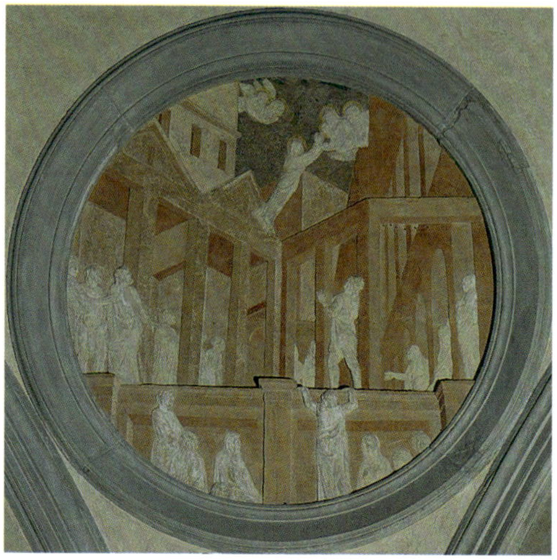

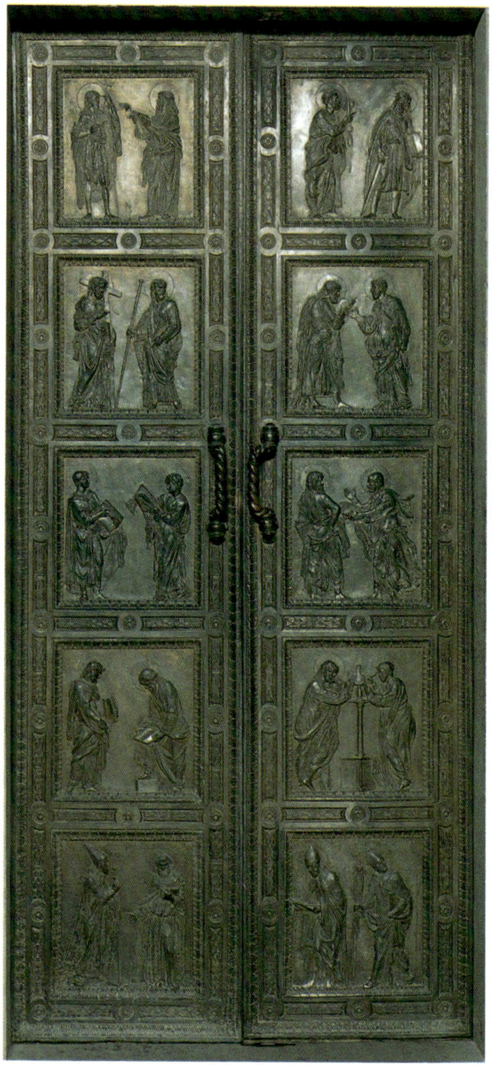

farther back they appear in space as the ground line slopes sharply downward. Donatello also arranged the buildings obliquely to the picture plane to create a lively pattern of plunging diagonals that contrasts dramatically with John's ascent heavenward toward Christ and SS. Peter and Paul. His ascension is underlined by the composition's abundant verticals and by the glances and gestures of the witnessing bystanders. Such a visually and emotionally charged narrative of salvation dramatically conveyed the promise of redemption, an appropriate theme for a burial chapel.

Over the right door (fig. 33) Donatello portrayed, in painted clay relief, SS. Cosmas and Damian, the early Christian martyred doctors (*medici*) and patron saints of the Medici family, with Cosimo il Vecchio's name-saint closest to the altar. Over the left door he added St. Stephen, the first Christian martyr, and (nearer the altar) St. Lawrence, the patron saint of the Church of S. Lorenzo and name-saint of Cosimo il Vecchio's brother, who died in 1440 as Donatello was executing the decoration. As the first deacon in charge of Church finances, St. Stephen (1st century) was also an important exemplar for the family that had made its fortune as the Church's banker. The role was first assumed by Giovanni di Bicci de' Medici in 1413, when he became the banker for John XXIII (r. 1410–15 as an antipope), and continued into the 1430s and 1440s, when Cosimo and Lorenzo performed the same service for Eugenius IV.

Donatello completed the Old Sacristy's decoration with two bronze doors for the openings between the columned and pedimented door frames, probably designed by Michelozzo (figs. 33 and 66). To enhance the revived classical and early Christian motifs and liturgy of the rest of the chapel, Donatello chose a typical late antique and early Christian low-relief style of paired figures against

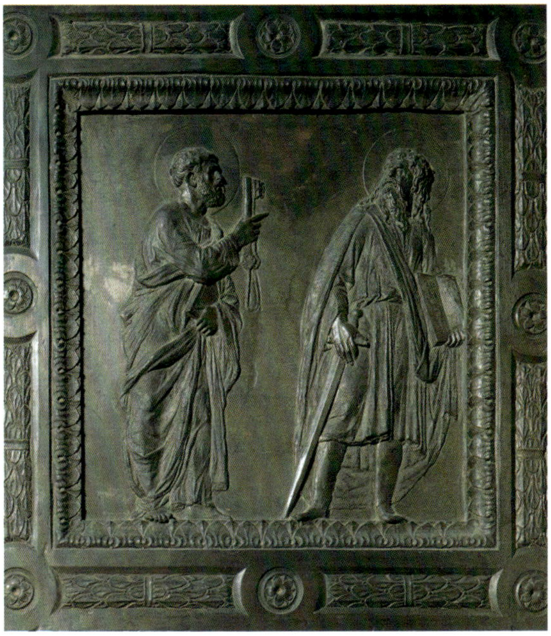

67. Donatello, *SS. Peter and Paul,* bronze. Detail of fig. 66.

spare backgrounds. Within the doors' twenty square compartments, he created a remarkably varied and dramatic series of paired figures, each dressed in richly patterned drapery stippled to pick up light, contrasting with the smoother, more atmospheric backgrounds.

In the upper right panel SS. Peter and Paul—embodiments of the Church for which the Medici served as bankers—engage in a heated debate (fig. 67). As in all panels for both doors, the figures' feet overlap the frame, imbuing them with a strong physical presence. Emphasized by the diagonal arrangement of his arms and drapery, Peter juts forward, thrusting his keys at Paul as if rhetorically punctuating some disputed point. Leaning back from Peter's forceful assault, Paul firmly holds his ground, and, as his cape majestically envelops his body, he gazes haughtily at his antagonist.

Bronze doors were of such prohibitive cost that previous Florentine examples had been commissioned only by major guilds supported by the communal government for the city's two most venerable religious monuments—three for the Baptistery and two for the cathedral's sacristies. By commissioning for their private burial chapel two bronze doors whose ten square fields emulated Ghiberti's *Gates of Paradise* (fig. 49), Cosimo il Vecchio and Lorenzo claimed wealth and power equal to that of the commune.

S. MARCO: HIGH ALTAR AND CELLS

Fra Angelico's *S. Marco Altarpiece*

Only a few years after Alberti's 1435 *On Painting,* Fra Angelico (c. 1400–1455) astutely employed a rigorous one-point perspective for the *sacra conversazione*–type high altarpiece for his own Dominican monastery church of S. Marco (fig. 68; see also fig. 12, no. 23, and fig. 38, no. 1). The painting's square format suggests the stability of the earthly Church, and is further underlined by the terrestrial globe held by the blessing Christ Child, traditional image of the *Salvator Mundi* (Savior of the World). Fra Angelico emphasizes the worldly Church by the open curtains and swags of white and red roses (symbols of the Virgin) that transform the lost frame into the proscenium of a perspective stage. Finally, the orthogonals of the Anatolian rug focus on the Virgin, embodiment of the Church, while Christ, St. Lawrence (d. 258), St. Cosmas, and an angel all look out at the priest and worshipers.

Yet even more emphatically, Fra Angelico created a vision of the heavenly Church. The court of saints, the opened curtains (age-old symbol of an epiphany), and John the Evangelist's book—labeled on its spine *Apocalypse* (the account of John's grand vision of the world's end)—all evoke eternity. The classicizing throne on a dais with its conch-shell apse and sumptuous embroidered gold and red cloth of honor, a sign of sovereignty, elevates Christ and the Virgin to the status of King and Queen of Heaven. Fra Angelico enhanced the spirituality of the attendant court by intensely coloring and partially gilding the costumes (even studding St. Lawrence's garb with painted jewels), scoring the gilt haloes with striations to reflect light, and draping an exquisite white, flowered fabric over the garden wall to serve as a cloth of honor, all Gothic conventions much influenced by the paintings of Gentile da Fabriano (c. 1385–1427). In addition, the figures' arrangement in a circle symbolizes their divine perfection, and the perspective construction—by definition geometrically abstract and mathematically proportional—suggests spiritual harmony. Finally, the eight angels flanking the Virgin and Child and the golden radiance illuminating the entire painting visually express the belief that at the Consecration and Elevation of the Eucharist the sacrament mediated between spirit and matter as the altar was mystically flooded with a divine presence.

To emphasize the mystery of the Incarnation, Fra Angelico added over the Holy Land in the exact center of Jesus' terrestrial globe the now mostly obliterated star of Bethlehem that guided the three Magi to the Nativity.

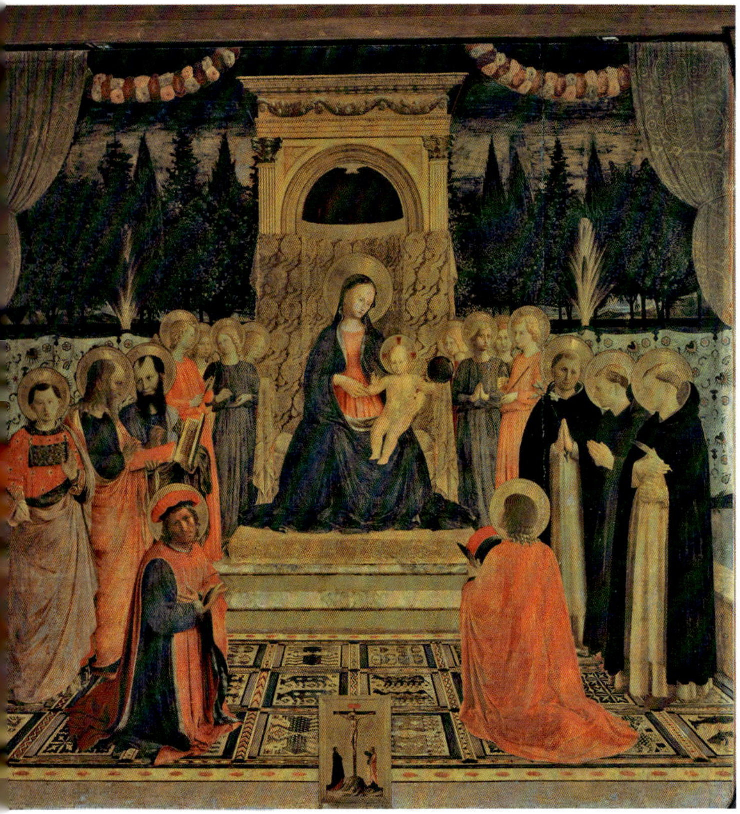

68. Fra Angelico, *S. Marco Altarpiece (Virgin and Child Surrounded by Eight Angels:* [left to right, standing] *SS. Lawrence, John the Evangelist, Mark, Dominic, Francis, Peter Martyr,* [kneeling] *SS. Cosmas and Damian;* and *Crucifixion),* c. 1438–41, tempera on panel, 7 ft. 2⅝ in. × 7 ft. 5⅜ in. (220 × 227 cm), Museo di San Marco.

The lily, the traditional attribute of St. Dominic (c. 1170–1221), also evoked the Annunciation, and the closed garden, the *hortus conclusus* from Song of Songs 4:12, suggested the Virgin's fertile yet unbreached womb.

Fra Angelico represented the Mass's commemoration of Christ's sacrifice through extensive symbols: the small simulated icon of the Crucifixion; Christ's cruciform halo; the instruments of the Passion held by the angels (pseudo-scepter, crown of thorns, flail, and nail denoting the Mocking [Matthew 27:27–30; Mark 15:16–19; John 19:2–3], Flagellation [Matthew 27:26; Mark 15:15; Luke 23:24–25; John 19:1], and Crucifixion); palm trees (recalling Christ's entry into Jerusalem, which began his Passion); and cypress trees (traditional emblems of death). The artist also visualized the Mass's reenactment of Christ's Resurrection by the lush garden, including orange trees that fruit only in the dead of winter.

The artist indicated the high altar's original dedication by locating St. Mark in the favored position closest to the Virgin's right hand. He also appealed to Dominican interests in a variety of ways, first by focusing on the Virgin, to whom the Dominicans were devoted. He also represented Dominic, the order's founder, in the second-most honored position (to the Virgin's left), and placed Peter Martyr (c. 1200–52), a major Dominican saint, on the painting's extreme right. In addition, Mark has opened his book to the sixth chapter of his Gospel. The clearly legible Latin text proclaims the Apostles' mission to set forth into the world two by two to teach humility though their poverty, preach the repentance of sins, cast out devils, and heal the sick. The Dominicans believed themselves to be new Apostles, whose authority came directly from Christ, with the same mission to preach, teach, and heal two by two through penance, humility, and poverty. Fra Angelico thematized this ideology by two Apostles, John the Evangelist and Mark, who converse and hold pens as if preaching and teaching; two Dominicans, Dominic, who humbly prays, and Peter Martyr, who with his split skull and palm of martyrdom imitates Christ's self-sacrifice; and two doctors, Cosmas and Damian, who embody healing by their medical profession.

The altarpiece's patron was Cosimo de' Medici (il Vecchio), who, as we have seen, spent a considerable fortune renovating and decorating the entire church and monastery. In exchange for his patronage, Cosimo il Vecchio was allowed to supplement the high altar's original dedication to Mark with a dedication to the Medici patron saints, Cosmas and Damian. In addition, he was given permission to include the name-saints of all the living and recently dead Medici males: John the Evangelist for Cosimo's father, Giovanni di Bicci, and his younger son, Giovanni (1421–63); Cosmas for Cosimo il Vecchio himself; Damian for Cosimo's twin brother, who died in infancy; Lawrence for Cosimo's recently deceased younger brother, Lorenzo; and Peter Martyr and Francis (1181–1226) for Cosimo's elder son, Piero, and Lorenzo's son, Pierfrancesco (1430–76).

Eugenius IV consecrated the restored church and its new altarpiece with great solemnity on January 6, 1443, the Feast of the Epiphany (Jesus' first revelation to the Gentiles). The consecration was the conclusion of an elaborate pageant staged every few years on Epiphany by the Confraternity of the Magi, headquartered in S. Marco and patronized by Cosimo. Dressed in sumptu-

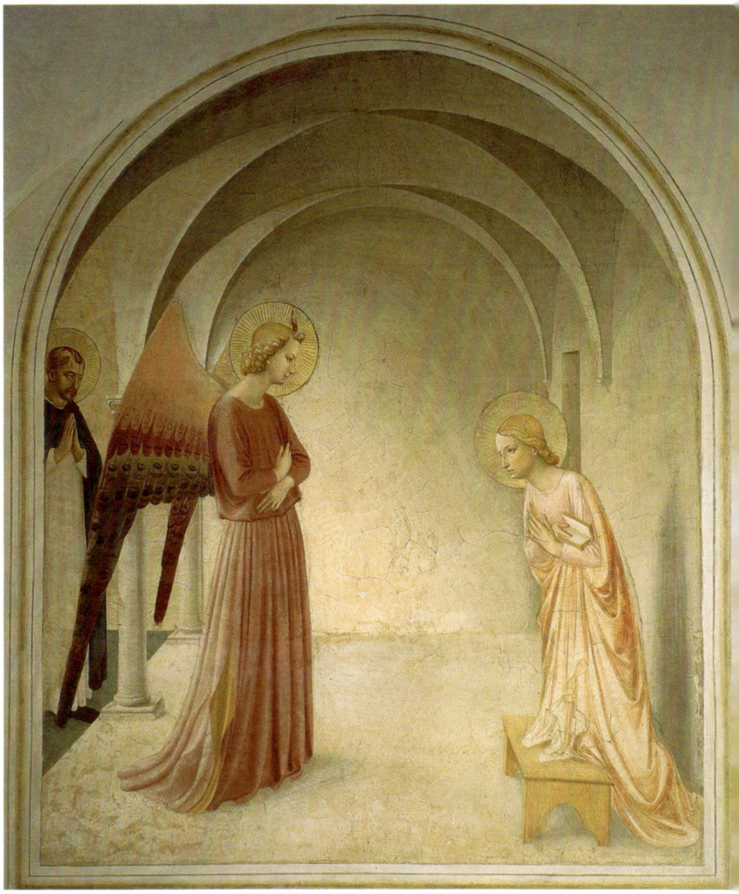

69. Fra Angelico, *Annunciation,* 1440s, fresco, cell 3, east dormitory (see fig. 38, no. 9), S. Marco.

ous costumes, hundreds of men from the wealthiest Florentine families reenacted the procession of the Magi by parading from the Priors' Palace, a symbolic Herod's Palace in Jerusalem, to S. Marco, a symbolic Bethlehem. At the procession's climax—viewing the newborn Christ Child on the high altar of S. Marco—Florentines would have witnessed Cosimo il Vecchio's public display of contrition and piety in the guise of his name-saint, Cosmas. The politically savvy would also have noticed that Cosimo had insinuated himself into the center of a major Florentine religious festival, not only to indicate his charity and hope for salvation, but also to exhibit his wealth and power to "heal" the commune and restore it to political health.

Fra Angelico was born Guido di Piero, but upon joining the Dominican order, he took the name Fra Giovanni to indicate that, like all Dominicans, he was a successor of the Apostles, specifically John the Evangelist, whom he represented second from the left. As a sign of Dominican humility, he did not include his signature. Yet he amply demonstrated his superb creative mind and visual intelligence—proving that he embodied the Dominican tradition for superior preaching and teaching—by his use of an advanced perspective system, the technical brilliance of his execution (much diminished by an inept nineteenth-century restoration), and the profound connections he made between the altarpiece, the liturgy, and the interests of both the Dominicans and the patron.

Fra Angelico's *Annunciation*

In the 1440s Fra Angelico and his workshop also decorated S. Marco's cloister, chapter room, refectory, and dormitory cells and corridors with more than fifty frescoes designed to enhance the friars' spiritual and liturgical life. The *Annunciation* in cell 3 constitutes a particularly masterful example (fig. 69; see also fig. 38, no. 9). At the extreme left, dressed in a Dominican habit, St. Peter Martyr observes the scene from outside the loggia. Standing with hands joined in prayer, he enacts the fifth of St. Dominic's nine methods of prayer (i.e., meditation), outlined in the thirteenth-century treatise on St. Dominic's mystical life, *De modo orandi* (*Modes of Prayer*), which all Dominicans were trained to use. As the visual stand-in for the cell's occupant, Peter Martyr not only would have stimulated meditation on the Annunciation, but also, with his split head of martyrdom, would have served as an exemplar of the Dominican life of ascetic self-sacrifice imitating Christ's. To strengthen the observing monk's personal identification with the scene, Fra Angelico painted the Annunciation's traditional loggia in the guise of Michelozzo's groin-vaulted Ionic cloister at S. Marco. While meditating and praying, the clerical viewer would have reflected on the joyous moment of the Incarnation, which initiated the process of redemption. He would also have recalled the liturgy of the Feast of the Annunciation (March 25), a major celebration from the *temporale*—the Dominican liturgical calendar of the major feasts commemorating key events of Christ's life and Passion—for which, as a parish priest, he would have had to deliver annual sermons. Uniquely from among the liturgies of the *temporale,* however, the Feast of the Annunciation also celebrated *the* principal event from the life of the Virgin, who was the Dominican Order's spiritual abbess and special protector. Thus, while contemplating the scene, the friar would have noted especially the Virgin's open book of scriptures, which both underlined Mary's piety and foretold Christ's fate. He would have observed that while Gabriel conveys his glad tidings to the Virgin by the subtlest of gestures (a raised right index finger), the artist had visually enhanced the momentous announcement by the thrust of the long left-hand orthogonal, the sweeping arcs of the angel's wings and the groin vaults, and the archangel's gaze. The Virgin indicates humble acceptance of her destiny by crossing her arms over her breasts and keeling on a prayer stool in submission.

The stability of the architecture, the naturalistic light flooding into the loggia from the left, and the shadows cast by Gabriel and Mary underline the event's historicity. However, the geometric perfection of the spare perspectival space, the flow of painted light contrary to the cell's natural light from the window on the right, the intensity of the golden radiance reflecting off the Virgin and the loggia's back wall, and the drapery patterns masking underlying anatomies all transmute the scene from an objective biblical illustration to an inner mystical experience. Fra Angelico's avoidance of such costly pigments as ultramarine also underlined the Dominican ideals of poverty and humility, while his almost exclusive use of shades of white, green, and red symbolized the Theological Virtues of Faith, Hope, and Charity. To an unusual degree, then, Fra Angelico's masterful work integrated the Dominicans' liturgical life of luminous preaching with their mystical life of structured prayer, while simultaneously expressing their monastic ideals of poverty, chastity, humility, and obedience.

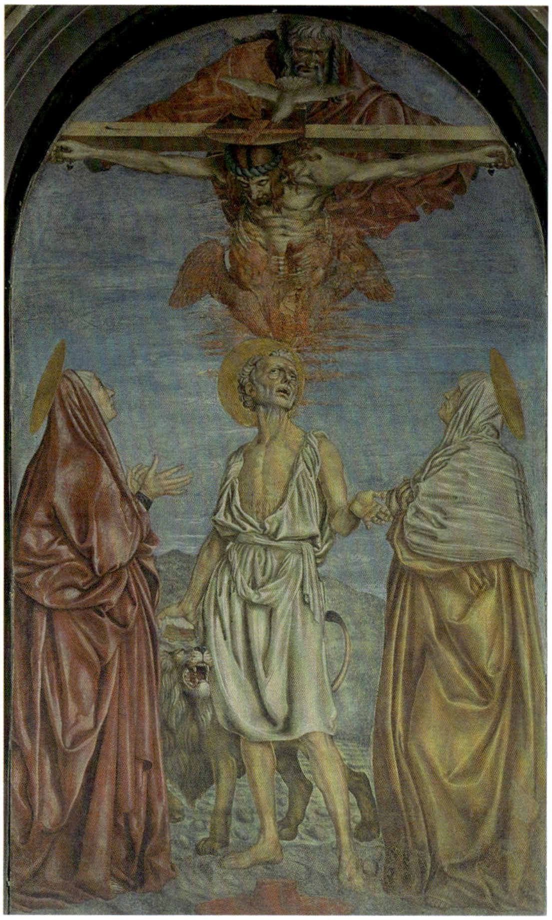

70. Andrea del Castagno, *Trinity with St. Jerome,* 1455, fresco transferred to canvas, 9 ft. 10⅛ in. × 5 ft. 10½ in. (300 × 179 cm), SS. Annunziata.

SS. ANNUNZIATA, I: CASTAGNO'S *TRINITY WITH ST. JEROME*

The large-scale 1455 altarpiece (fig. 70) for the Church of SS. Annunziata by Andrea del Castagno (c. 1421–57) indicates by its subject matter the dedication of its altar to the Trinity and the name-saint of its patron—businessman, moneylender, and trader Girolamo Corboli (see also figs. 12, no. 24, and 142, no. 3). Rejecting the deep illusionistic space of Fra Angelico's altarpiece at S. Marco (fig. 68), Castagno placed his life-size figures close to the picture plane within a stark desert. Early Christian ascetics and desert fathers such as St. Jerome (c. 341–420) retreated to the wilderness to live as virtuosi of self-denial—mortifying their flesh, fasting, and enduring extremes of temperature and isolation. Castagno expressed Jerome's deprivations by his emaciated and bleeding body, weatherworn face, rotten teeth, and unruly white hair. The acidic colors, angular drapery, and foreboding atmosphere also convey the hermit's perception of the physical world as a place of corruption, decay, and death. Ascetics strove to triumph over matter and to master the body's desires through ceaseless prayer, penitence, and contrition—a relentless process that Castagno indicated in the traditional way by depicting Jerome beating his chest with a rock. Through deprivation and self-mortification, hermits hoped to achieve a deeper understanding of divinity, particularly by means of beatific visions, such as that experienced here by Jerome and his disciples, the wealthy widow St. Paula (347–404) and her virgin daughter, St. Eustochium (370–c. 419). The radical foreshortening of the blood-red vision creates a powerful spatial disjunction that intensifies Jerome's tortured expression of ecstasy, an expression that closely parallels the manic rapture of Donatello's *Zuccone* (fig. 28).

The Trinity related closely to the Eucharistic liturgy. Just as the Mass conjoined heaven and earth through God's love of humanity, so at Christ's feet two seraphim, symbols of divine love, mediate between Jerome's material world and the spiritual world of his vision. The crucified Christ, as in Fra Angelico's altarpiece, visualized the body and blood of Christ contained in the consecrated and elevated bread and wine. Finally, as in Masaccio's fresco (fig. 55), the Trinity represented the Throne of Grace, marking the final judgment at the end of the world and thematizing the Mass's mediation between here and hereafter.

S. MINIATO AL MONTE: THE CARDINAL OF PORTUGAL'S CHAPEL

On August 27, 1459, the young Cardinal James of Portugal (1433–59), papal ambassador to Austria, died in Florence while en route from Rome to Vienna. His tutor and friend, Alfonso Alvaro of Silves, bishop of Evora and the executor of the cardinal's will, oversaw the building of a burial chapel in S. Miniato (figs. 71–75; see also figs. 11; 12, no. 3). Consecrated in 1466, the chapel was dedicated to SS. James (first century), Vincent (third–fourth century), and Eustace (second century). Cardinal James's descent from the royal house of Portugal and his relationships to the noble houses of Burgundy and Austria dictated the splendor of his burial chapel. His estate being insufficient, his family helped to cover the chapel's steep cost of 12,000 gold florins.

To underscore James's distinguished ancestry and renowned chastity, the chapel's architecture—most likely designed by Brunelleschi's pupil Antonio di Ciaccheri Manetti—revived the design of early Christian burial

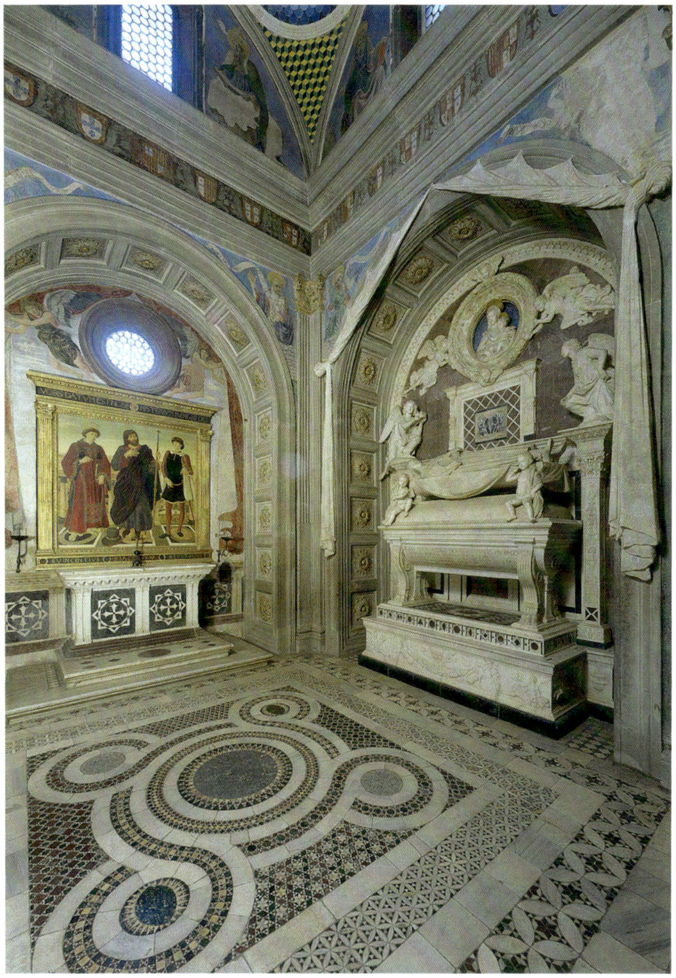

71. North altar wall and east tomb wall, 1460–68, Cardinal of Portugal's Chapel, San Miniato. Alessio Baldovinetti (1425–99) frescoed the prophets, patriarchs, and kings holding prophetic scrolls that populate the spandrels of the arches, as well as the coats of arms in the entablature's frieze indicating Cardinal James's royal lineage.

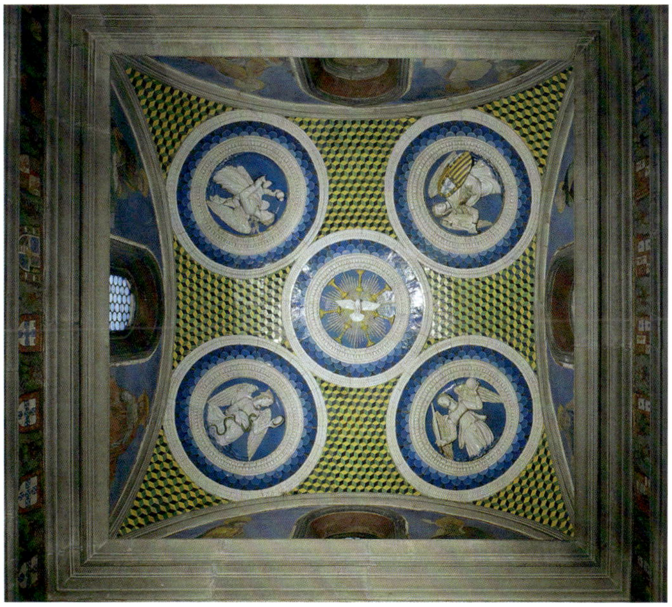

72. Vault, glazed terracotta with the *Holy Spirit and the Seven Golden Candlesticks of Revelation 1:12* surrounded by the *Cardinal Virtues* by Luca della Robbia (c. 1399/1400–1482). The vault's frescoed lunettes with the *Four Evangelists* and the *Four Latin Doctors* by Baldovinetti alluded to the cardinal of Portugal's erudition.

chapels for royalty and martyred saints, characterized by a vaulted square space with four barrel-vaulted extensions forming a Greek-cross plan. The mid-fifth-century mausoleum in Ravenna for Empress Galla Placidia (c. 390–450) and the mid-seventh-century burial chapel in Braga, Portugal, for St. Fructuoso (third century) represent two notable examples of such chapels. This design honored not only James but also the three dedicatees of the chapel and St. Minias (d. 250), the dedicatee of S. Miniato, all early Christian martyrs from the first through fourth centuries AD.

North Wall

Decorated between 1460 and 1468 by the Pollaiuolo brothers, Antonio (c. 1431–98) and Piero (1441–96), the north altar wall (fig. 71) includes two frescoed angels flanking an oculus who open ermine-lined curtains of red velvet to reveal a glimpse of heaven and an altarpiece representing the chapel's three dedicatees (fig. 73). The inscription on the altarpiece's frame—"To you it is given to know the mystery of the kingdom of God" (Mark 4:11)—also evokes divine revelation and the conjunction of heaven and earth in the Mass. These words, spoken by Christ to the Apostles, refer directly to the Apostle James Major, Cardinal James's name-saint, who peers out from the center of the altarpiece toward the cardinal's tomb on the east wall. The emphasis on St. James was particularly apt, for he was believed to have introduced Christianity to Spain and Portugal, just as St. Minias had done in Florence. St. Vincent, who looks out at the worshiper, was the patron saint of Lisbon, a Spanish deacon, and the protector of the royal house of Portugal. He alludes to Cardinal James's appointments as a cardinal deacon and the archbishop of Lisbon. St. Eustace, who gazes at the chapel's west wall, recalled the name of James's titular church in Rome, S. Eustachio.

The three saints, who stand on a lavish marble terrace before a balustrade with a ropelike bronze grille, are seen through a windowlike classicizing frame in a space continuous with that of the observer. The spatial illusion is heightened by the panoramic landscape background that mimics the view of the Arno Valley seen from S. Miniato. However, the saints' elevation above the horizon, gestures of humility, palms of martyrdom, lack of cast shadows, and sumptuous brocaded costumes transmute their physical presence to an otherworldly realm. The terrace pavement's inlaid squares and circles, signs of earth and heaven, also symbolize the saints' mediation between matter and spirit. Finally, Vincent's book and his pearl-

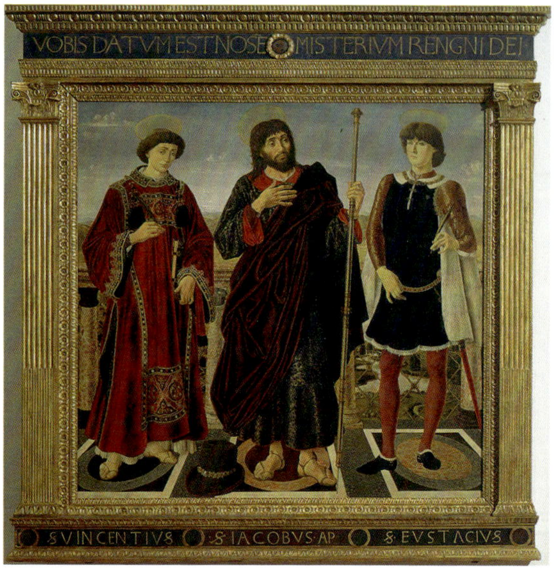

73. Antonio and Piero Pollaiuolo, *SS. Vincent, James Major, and Eustace,* 1466–68, oil and tempera on panel, 67¾ in. × 70½ in. (172 × 179 cm), Uffizi. Guiliano da Maiano (1432–90) executed the original frame. The altarpiece in the Cardinal of Portugal's Chapel today is a copy of this painting.

gem-encrusted priestly vestments, James's bejeweled pilgrim's hat and crystal staff, and Eustace's ermine-trimmed costume of a courtly knight all recall the high ecclesiastical rank, wisdom, humility, and regal lineage of the deceased cardinal.

East Wall

The face of the barrel-vaulted niche on the east wall with the tomb of the cardinal of Portugal by Antonio and Bernardo (c. 1407/10–64) Rossellino is draped with simulated open curtains—again the motif of divine epiphany—as if James were a saint (fig. 74). The niche itself, with its red porphyry back wall, once gilded to resemble a damask cloth of honor, suggests a triumphal gateway mediating between death and renewed life.

The cardinal's effigy, dressed in bishop's robes and miter, is laid out on a bier, reenacting perpetually James's state funeral in the Florentine cathedral. Six winged angels, who appear to have just arrived, highlight James's saintliness. Two hold the drapery covering the cardinal's bier, two display a crown and a now-missing palm—symbols of royal lineage and heavenly reward—and two (along with two cherubs) support the wreathed oculus. Within the oculus, the Virgin and Child appear as a vision, their divine perfection and spiritual fecundity suggested by the circular victory wreath surrounded by eight seraphs, embodiments of divine love. The Virgin tenderly cradles her son, while Jesus makes a sign of benediction. They embody the mediation of the Mass between here and hereafter and Cardinal James's hope for renewed life, as they turn toward the intercessory saints on the altar and look down at the effigy. Appearing against a blue background with gold stars within the eastern oculus (the direction of the rising sun), the mother and son also suggest, like the seven candlesticks in the vault (fig. 72), John's vision of the end of time (Apocalypse 12:1–5): "And a great sign appeared in heaven: A woman clothed with the sun . . . And she brought forth a man child who was to rule all nations . . . and her son was taken up to God, and to his throne."

West Wall

The elegant classicizing marble throne on the opposite west wall was probably designed for the abbot of S. Miniato when he celebrated the endowed requiem Masses commemorating the deaths of St. James, St. Minias, and the cardinal of Portugal (fig. 75). When not in use, it perhaps also alluded to James's throne as the bishop of Arras and archbishop of Lisbon, as well as his hope for a throne of glory in heaven. Yet, when empty, the throne also poignantly suggested absence and death.

Above the throne, Alessio Baldovinetti painted on a panel the *Annunciation*. The Virgin's long marble-veneer throne doubles as the closed wall of her *hortus conclusus* frescoed in the lunette above the panel. Behind the gilt rays of the Holy Spirit descending diagonally from the upper left, there appear fruit trees, emblems of regeneration, but primarily cypresses, symbols of death, illuminated by the setting sun in the western oculus.

The Cardinal of Portugal's Chapel was not only more sumptuous than the Old Sacristy in S. Lorenzo (figs. 33–35, 64–67) but also employed a wider range of artists (seven) and a greater variety of media, including carved and inlaid marble, fresco, painted panel, and glazed terracotta, as well as the now-lost gold and enamel crucifix, silver lamps, a bronze entrance grille, and carved benches inlaid with multicolored woods.

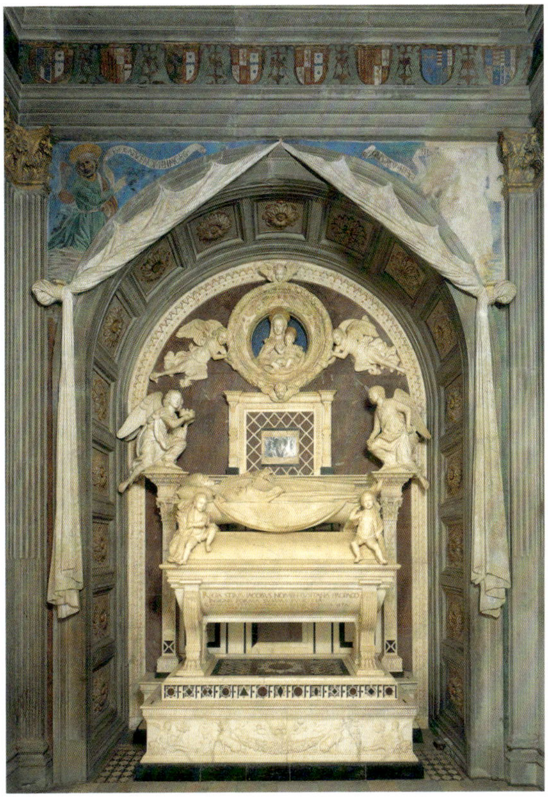

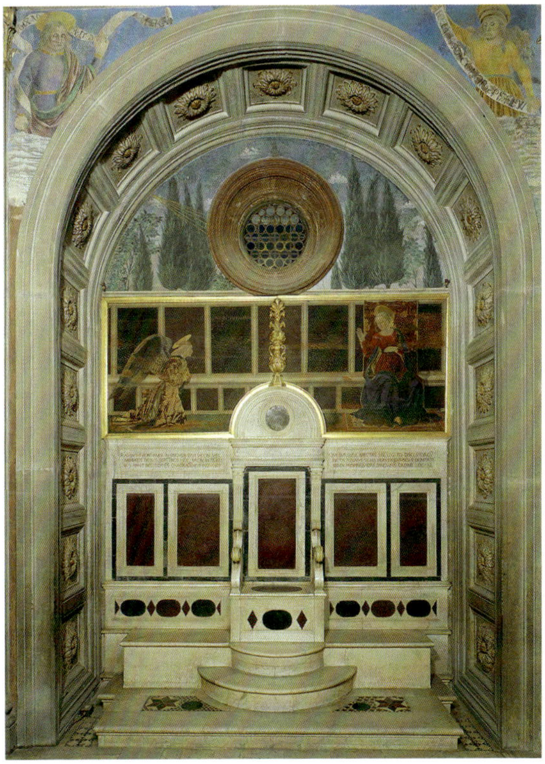

74. Antonio and Bernardo Rossellino, *Tomb of the Cardinal of Portugal,* 1461–66, marble, east wall.

75. West wall with Baldovinetti's *Annunciation* on panel.

S. LORENZO, II

Verrochio's Tomb of Cosimo il Vecchio

Cosimo de' Medici (il Vecchio) died on August 1, 1464. Although he had requested a simple burial, Cosimo's body was ceremoniously paraded through the streets of Florence by the Augustinian canons of S. Lorenzo before its provisional interment in the crypt of the church. The funeral services, attended by many foreign dignitaries, continued for the next thirty-two days.

Cosimo's firstborn son, Piero, was responsible for fulfilling the terms of Cosimo's will for a tomb monument, and in 1464 he commissioned Verrocchio to design a floor slab for the crossing of S. Lorenzo (figs. 36, 76, and 77). A floor slab without an effigy conformed to Renaissance protocols for a non-noble banker such as Cosimo. As the major patron of S. Lorenzo, however, he was entitled to be buried in front of the high altar and to display his coat of arms.

The black squares of the tomb slab symbolized earth and death, the white circle, heaven and renewed life. Similar to the Old Sacristy's design, the tomb's circle was aligned with the dome's oculus (fig. 36) to create a symbolic axis mediating between matter and spirit. Furthermore, the design within the marble circle—twelve interlocked circles and semicircles arranged on two crossing axes—derived from the oft-repeated seventh-century cosmic diagram of Isidore of Seville (c. 560–636); it illustrated the coordination of humanity with the cosmos through the four elements, seasons, temperaments, and humors. The design also recalled a well-known diagram in the sixth-century *On Arithmetic* by Boethius (480–c. 525) depicting the harmonic ratios underlying musical and cosmic harmony. The tomb, then, recalled the contemporary pun on the deceased's name to emphasize the hope that Cosimo would be received back into the cosmos.

76. Verrocchio, *Tomb of Cosimo de' Medici (il Vecchio)*, 1465–67, marble and bronze, 10 ft. 11⅞ in. (335 cm) square, crossing, S. Lorenzo.

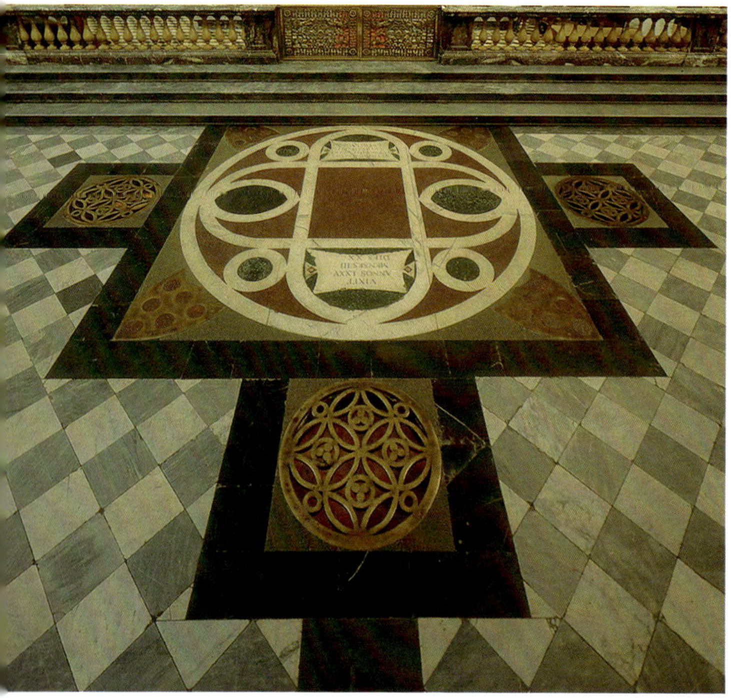

Word play and color also linked Cosimo to Christ. When interred on October 20, 1467, below his tomb slab in the crypt's central pier—the literal support of the crossing and S. Lorenzo's symbolic foundation stone—Cosimo's remains were associated with Christ, the "cornerstone" or "foundation stone" of the Church. In addition, calculating Cosimo's birth from his known death date and the length of his life recorded in the tomb's inscription ("75 years, 3 months, 20 days"), his birthday would have been on Palm Sunday, April 11, 1389. Cosimo almost certainly was not born on this date, which suggests that the inscription was carefully manipulated to associate him with the feast day commemorating the beginning of Christ's Passion. To merit renewed life, Cosimo offers Faith, Hope, and Charity, symbolized by the white, green, and red of the tomb slab's marble.

The honorific title "father of his country" (*pater patriae*), also inscribed on the tomb slab, was awarded posthumously to Cosimo by a vote of the Florentine government in March 1465. According to the speech announcing the honor by the humanist Donato Acciauoli (1429–78), "[Cosimo] bestowed the highest and most ample benefit on the Florentine Republic, both in peace and war, and always defended, sustained and aided his fatherland with all piety . . . and governed it with all care, zeal, and diligence, just as a *paterfamilias* governs his own household."

The humanists whom Cosimo patronized throughout his life paved the way for his posthumous title. Early in his career Niccolò Niccoli and Leonardo Bruni likened Cosimo to a wise Roman republican statesman, a selfless and prudent *vir virtutis,* who endured exile for the good of the commune, only to be recalled in 1434 to defend Florentine liberty against Milan. Cosimo was thus associated with Furius Camillus, who, as recounted by Livy (59 BC–AD 17), had been recalled to Rome from exile to defeat the Gauls in 386 BC, a deed for which he was honored with the title *pater patriae* by the Roman senate. In mid-career, Marsilio Ficino (1433–99) and Carlo Marsuppini (1399–1453) compared Cosimo to a just and moral philosopher/scholar in the tradition of rulers admired by Aristotle (384–322 BC). They drew parallels between Cosimo and Cicero, who had discovered and suppressed the Catiline Conspiracy, for which he was awarded the title *pater patriae* in 63 BC. Toward the end of his career, Cristoforo Landino (1424–1504) and others lauded Cosimo in the poetic tradition of the *Aeneid* by Virgil (70–19 BC). Like Emperor Augustus (63 BC–AD 14), proclaimed *pater patriae* by the Roman Senate in 2 BC, Cosimo was praised as a patron who used his wealth and power to commission great works of art and architecture for the public good.

The sheer sumptuousness of the materials used in the tomb, unprecedented in Florence, indeed suggested imperial wealth, status, and power. As it was the only tomb in the entire church visible outside the crypt, the entire sanctuary appeared to be Cosimo's private pantheon. Its placement directly under the hemispherical Pantheon-like dome made another connection between Cosimo and ancient Roman heroes. Florentines clearly understood the tomb's bold imperial and cosmic claims. When the Medici were expelled in 1494 and again in 1527, the inscription on Cosimo's tomb was twice effaced, only to be twice restored by Pope Leo X (r. 1513–21) and Pope Clement VII (r. 1523–34) after the Medici's restorations in 1512 and 1531.

Donatello's Bronze Pulpits

Cosimo il Vecchio also commissioned Donatello to flank his tomb with two bronze ambos or pulpits in the shape of ancient Roman sarcophagi supported on four Composite columns of rare oriental marbles (figs. 77–80; see also figs. 36 and 37). The early Christian tradition of paired pulpits, one for reading the Epistles, the other the Gospels, was long out of fashion by the Renaissance. But Cosimo drew attention to its revival by also facing the high altar toward the nave as in early Christian churches.

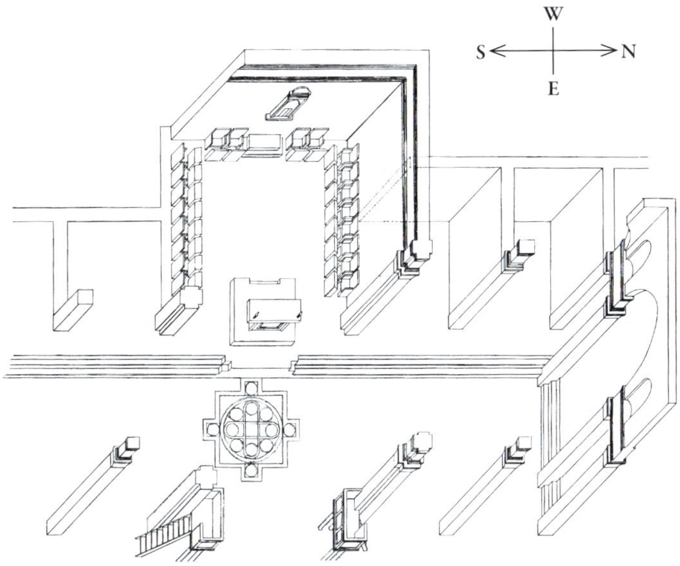

77. Conjectural reconstruction of the fifteenth-century west end of S. Lorenzo.

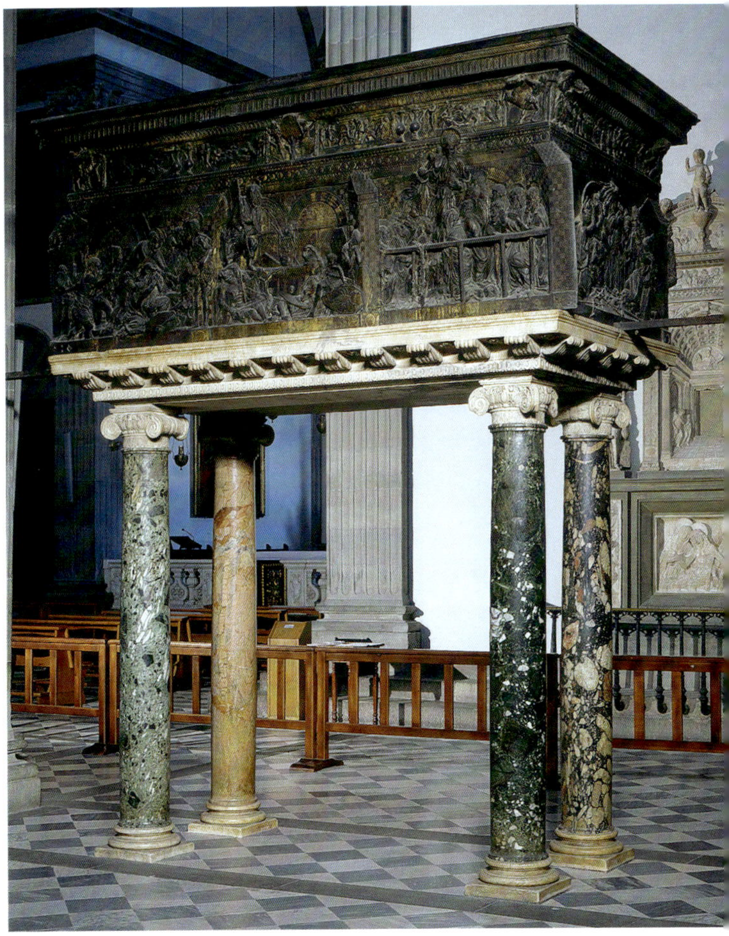

78. Donatello and successors, north pulpit, 1460–66, marble and bronze, 4 ft. 5⅞ in. × 9 ft. 2¼ in. (137 × 280 cm), S. Lorenzo. The tabernacle on the wall in the right background was executed in the 1460s by Desiderio da Settignano (1430–64) and his workshop and might originally have been located behind the high altar. See fig. 77.

By this arrangement of pulpits and high altar, Cosimo intended to evoke the first S. Lorenzo, founded by St. Ambrose in 393 as the first Florentine cathedral.

Scenes from Christ's Passion decorated the south pulpit. Notably missing was the *Last Supper,* in which Christ instituted the Eucharist. The regular Eucharistic celebrations on the high altar compensated for this absence. Post-Passion scenes and St. Lawrence's martyrdom adorned the north pulpit (fig. 78). Here, in the scene of *Christ in Limbo,* Christ carries the cruciform banner of the Church and lifts Adam as the crouching Eve presses her face against Christ's arm (fig. 79). Dressed in a camel-hair tunic, an emaciated John the Baptist greets Christ with an outstretched arm. Adam and Eve, the first humans, and John the Baptist, the last of the Hebrew prophets and Christ's precursor, combine with Christ to represent Christian history according to its traditional threefold division, before law (before Moses), under law (after Moses), and under grace (after Christ). Donatello expressed Christ's relentless grim-faced rescue of the righteous from hell by his powerful stride and the sweep of the background arches, the slipped keystones evoking Christ's epithet "keystone of the Church." Donatello enhanced Christ's charismatic authority by the ecstatic gestures of the saved souls, who gaze intensely at him. By contrast, two hideous and powerless devils are literally dwarfed by Christ's majesty.

The adjoining scene of the *Resurrection,* one of Donatello's last creative acts, suggests something of the artist's state of mind at the age of eighty (fig. 80). For the first time in a scene of the Resurrection, Donatello dared to represent Christ not as a centralized, transfigured, and triumphant figure, but rather as haggard, weighed down and encumbered by his shroud, lifting his foot to the edge of his sarcophagus. The sarcophagus's sharply pointed lid and the angular contorted postures of the sleeping soldiers, armed with shields, lances, and swords, suggest a hostile and sinful world of spiritual darkness. The whole scene expresses Christ's journey into hell. Yet even in dawn's gloom, flowering plants among the soldiers signify the hope of renewed life.

On March 11, 1459, Cosimo elevated S. Lorenzo to collegiate status by endowing a college for twelve clerics and a teacher for their religious education. On October 9, 1462, Cosimo also established an endowment for the clerics to celebrate at sunrise 365 days a year a votive Mass to the Virgin in his honor at the high altar facing his tomb. Cosimo was also specially commemorated as the church's founder with annual Masses at the high altar on the anniversary of his death and on the vigil of the feast of S. Lorenzo. In addition, just beyond the south transept in the Chapel of SS. Cosmas and Damian and in the Old Sacristy, endowed canons celebrated numerous liturgical rituals: daily Masses; offices of the dead every Monday for the benefit of all living and dead Medici; special anniversary Masses for every deceased Medici on the Wednesdays nearest the anniversary of their death; and feast-day Masses for SS. Cosmas and Damian and for St. John the Evangelist. In the Neroni Chapel just off the north transept, Masses were celebrated every Wednesday for S. Lorenzo. The location of his remains in the midst of these services demonstrated Cosimo's profound piety and de-

79–80. Donatello, *Christ in Limbo* and *Resurrection.* Details of fig. 78.

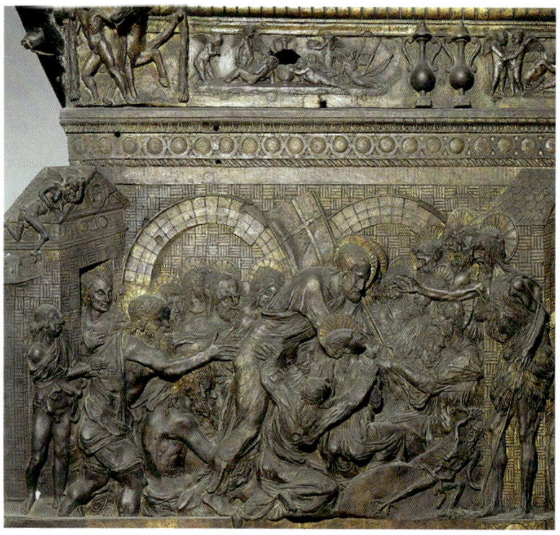

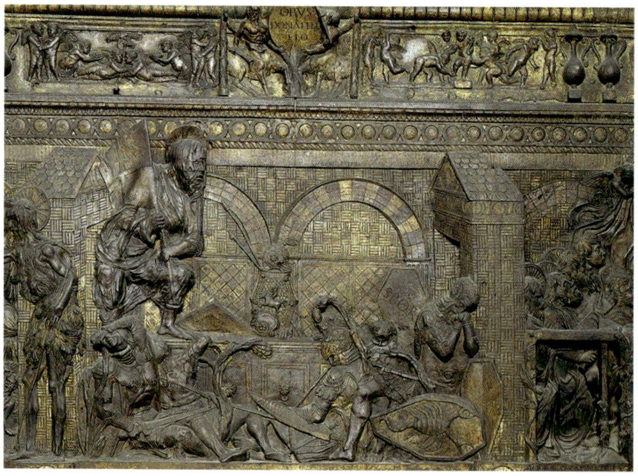

vout belief in the efficacy of the Eucharistic liturgy for his salvation. Yet he was also not above commemorating his worldly wealth, power, and status, nor associating himself with the heroes of Roman antiquity to further Medici political dominance of Florence.

Verrocchio's Tomb of Piero and Giovanni de' Medici, Old Sacristy

After Cosimo il Vecchio died in 1464, his son Piero became the behind-the-scenes ruler of Florence until his death five years later. It then fell to Piero's two sons, Lorenzo il Magnifico and Giuliano il Magnifico, to provide a tomb for Piero and his brother, Giovanni, who had died in 1463. Accordingly, they commissioned from Verrocchio in 1469 an arched double-faced monument (fig. 81). The arched opening with its distinctive bronze rope-like net allowed a spatial connection between the Old Sacristy and the Chapel of SS. Cosmas and Damian (fig. 32, nos. 1 and 2) that offered the deceased buried in the Old Sacristy the benefit of Masses celebrated in both chapels. The arch also constituted a symbolic liminal zone mediating between death and renewed life, a symbolism reinforced by its decoration of exquisitely carved garlands of alternating fronds and branches of palm, olive, and laurel growing from two classicizing vases. Palm fronds recalled the beginning of Christ's Passion on Palm Sunday, while the olive and laurel branches signaled the hope for peace and victory over sin and death through Christ's redemptive sacrifice. Bronze acanthus leaves, victory wreaths, and the shell-like cornucopias on the sarcophagus communicated the hope for renewed spiritual life merited by the Theological Virtues of Faith, Hope, and Charity symbolized by the white, green, and red marble. The lion's paws supporting the sarcophagus suggested the strength and magnanimity of Christ, often allegorized as the king of the beasts.

81. Verrocchio, *Tomb of Piero and Giovanni de' Medici,* 1469–72, marble, bronze, and *pietra serena,* 17 ft. 3⅞ in. × 8 ft. ½ in. (528 × 245 cm), east wall, Old Sacristy, S. Lorenzo.

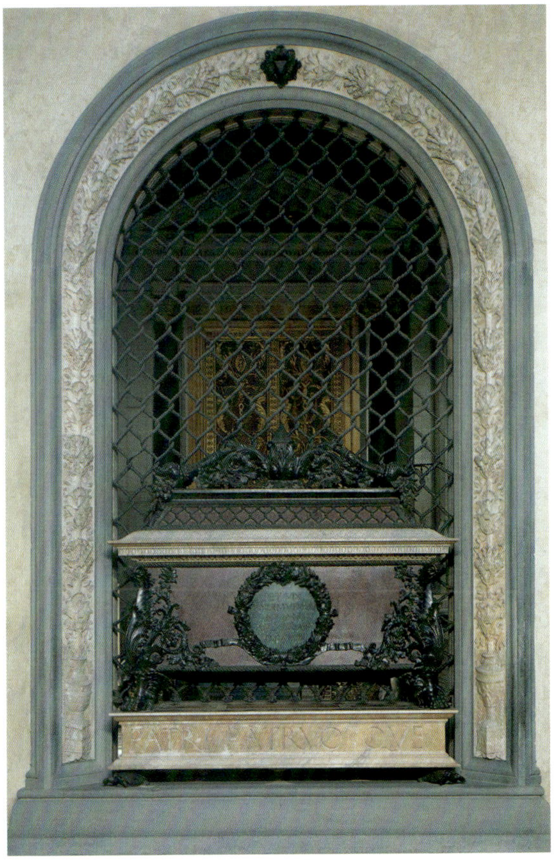

Carved in marble on the arch's frame are more than fifty representations of diamond rings entwined within the vegetation. Two large diamonds simulated in bronze atop the sarcophagus and the arched opening embrace a perfect imaginary circle or ring inscribable between them. As his personal emblem, the ring's diamond (*diamante*) was intended to suggest by a pun (*dio amante*) that Piero was a "lover of God," while the device's motto *semper* (always) evoked the constancy of his love for Christ. The brilliance and durability of diamonds and the circularity of rings also signified the everlasting purity and perfection of divine radiance.

The entire monument rests on four bronze tortoises, the personal device of Cosimo il Vecchio. The tortoise symbolized the cosmos in antiquity, for its shell suggested the vault of heaven, and, when fitted with strings, formed a lyre that produced cosmic harmony. Cosimo il Vecchio chose the tortoise not only to pun on "Cosimo" and "cosmos," but also to emulate the emperors Augustus and Constantine (272–337). Both emperors used the tortoise with a sail as their personal devices with the motto *festina lente* (make haste slowly) to signify prudence, a prime virtue of rule. The tortoises, then, recall the prudent founder of Medici fortunes as they appear to slowly transport the tomb heavenward.

The unprecedented splendor of materials and classical motifs supported the imperialism implicit in the tortoise motif. The acanthus masking the joins of the red porphyry slabs also created the impression of a monolithic sarcophagus similar to those associated with several well-known imperial tombs of antiquity. Finally, the tomb's format made claims, albeit exaggerated, to noble status, for all previous arched Florentine tombs had been reserved for knights or nobles.

SS. ANNUNZIATA, II: ANTONIO AND PIERO POLLAIUOLO'S *ST. SEBASTIAN*

The highest demonstration of Christian faith was martyrdom, an appropriate subject for altarpieces, which commemorated and reenacted Christ's sacrifice (fig. 82). St. Sebastian (third century AD) was an officer in the praetorian guard of Emperor Diocletian, as suggested by the classicizing battle relief in the passageway of the triumphal arch. The round scene in the arch's attic depicts the moment when Sebastian was tried before the emperor and condemned to death for refusing to recant his Christian faith. Sebastian was then shot with arrows, which failed to kill him, and later beaten to death and thrown into the Roman sewer. The similarity between arrow wounds and plague boils resulted in the belief that Sebastian was a particularly effective intercessor for those afflicted by the Black Death, a scourge recurring periodically in Florence throughout the Renaissance.

82. Antonio and Piero Pollaiuolo, *St. Sebastian,* 1474–75, tempera and oil on panel, 9 ft. 7 in. × 6 ft. 7⅜ in. (292 × 203 cm), The National Gallery, London.

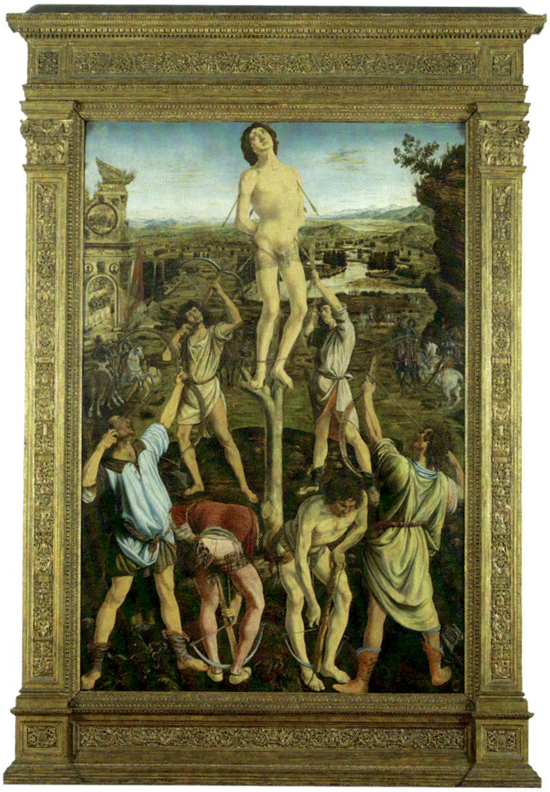

This impressive work was commissioned by Antonio Pucci (1418–84) for the Chapel of St. Sebastian in SS. Annunziata, built in the 1450s by the Pucci family (see fig. 142, no. 5), merchants and Medici supporters. It illustrates three major developments in Florentine painting to date: use of authentic classical motifs; accurately observed bodies in action; and a convincing landscape. By 1475 many Florentine artists had traveled to Rome, studied Roman antiquities, and recorded their observations in drawings that circulated among various workshops. This new antiquarianism is evident in the barrel-vaulted triumphal arch articulated with coffers and fluted Corinthian piers and decorated with reliefs, bull crania, swags, and winged victories. The ruined state of the arch thematized Christianity's triumph over paganism and Sebastian's victory over death.

Renaissance artists learned much about human anatomy from their study of classical sculpture, but they also drew from live models. Indeed, it appears that the Pollaiuolo brothers studied living archers with almost scientific interest and perhaps even crafted clay models. The two central crossbowmen in the foreground represent frontal and dorsal views of the same figure demonstrating how to cock a crossbow, while the remaining four symmetrically placed archers suggest variations on a single model illustrating the aim and discharge of longbows and crossbows. The Pollaiuolo brothers' expression of anatomical action considerably surpassed mere *contrapposto.*

Although the event was traditionally set in Rome, the artists have represented instead a view, remarkable for its breadth and depth, of the Tuscan Arno Valley. The panorama is heightened by one of the earliest uses of aerial perspective—the blurring and bluing of distant forms seen through an atmospheric haze. Familiarity with this vast landscape would have intensified for Florentine worshipers the immediacy of the drama.

Finally, to visualize the mediating function of the Mass between here and hereafter, the artists emphasized Sebastian's spiritual triumph in imitation of Christ's by placing him at the apex of a triangle, elevating him on a tree well above his tormenters, and silhouetting his torso against the sky, toward which he piously gazes.

S. TRINITA: GHIRLANDAIO'S SASSETTI CHAPEL

In 1480 Francesco Sassetti (1421–90) acquired patronage rights to his burial chapel in S. Trinita (fig. 12, no. 13) and had it frescoed by Domenico Ghirlandaio (1449–94) with six scenes from the life of his name-saint, St. Francis (figs. 83–86).

Confirmation of the Rule of St. Francis

In the lunette above the altar Ghirlandaio depicted the *Confirmation of the Rule of St. Francis* (fig. 84). Flanked by the College of Cardinals and enthroned on a baldachin-covered dais, the pope consigns to St. Francis and his eight kneeling followers the document authorizing the Franciscan order in the early thirteenth century. The wall behind the cardinals, decorated with a classical entablature and a sumptuous cloth of honor, recalls the newly decorated walls of the Sistine Chapel, which Ghirlandaio had helped to fresco in 1481–82. Although set historically in Rome, the scene's background represents the Florentine Priors' Palace (fig. 13), with its rostrum and heraldic lion, and the Priors' Loggia (fig. 15). Ghirlandaio's association of Florence with Rome evoked the age-old perception of Florence as a new Rome.

83. Sassetti Chapel, S. Trinita, 1483–85. In the vault, for the first time in a Renaissance chapel, the artist represented four classical sibyls who were believed to have prophesied the coming of Christ. Frescoed images of Sassetti and his wife, Nera de' Corsi (born c. 1444), kneeling in perpetual prayer within shallow illusionistic niches on either side of the altarpiece, publicly display their piety and charity. Their remains were placed in the black marble sarcophagi set within arched niches, signifying the transitory state between death and regenerated life.

84. Domenico Ghirlandaio, *Confirmation of the Rule of St. Francis,* fresco. Detail of fig. 83.

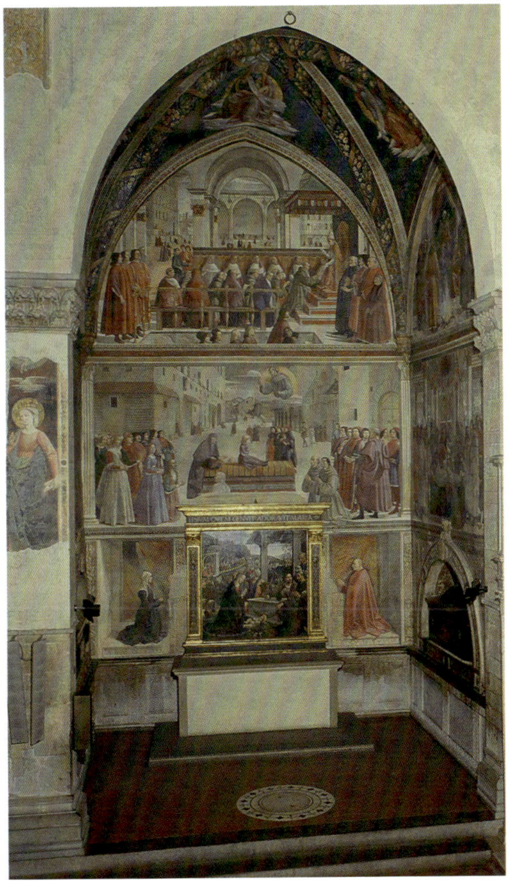

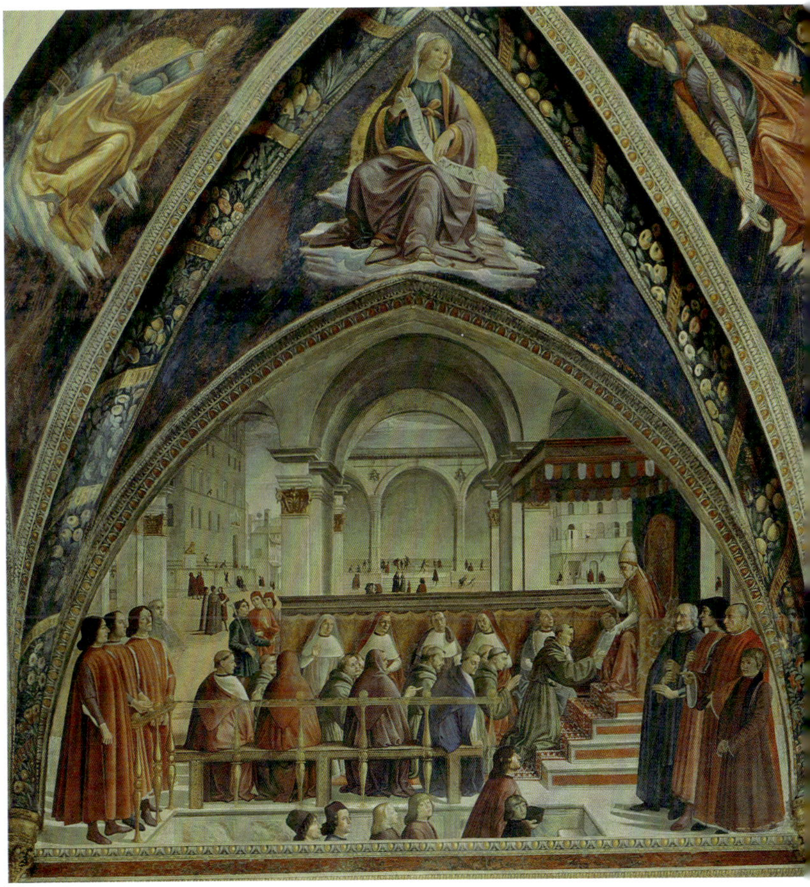

The conflation of Florence and Rome also recalled the recent conflict between the Florentines and Pope Sixtus IV (r. 1471–84). To further his scheme of incorporating Florence into the papal state, Sixtus IV had condoned the 1478 conspiracy by the Pazzi family to assassinate Lorenzo il Magnifico and his brother, Giuliano, while they attended Mass in the cathedral. Although Giuliano was killed, Lorenzo escaped by fleeing into the north sacristy. To avert this serious papal threat to Florence, Lorenzo soon negotiated a peace treaty with Sixtus IV's ally, King Ferrante I of Naples (1423–94) and then another with the papacy, thereby initiating two decades of relative peace. Humanist supporters of the Medici, especially Cristoforo Landino and Angelo Poliziano (1454–94), promoted this peace as marking the beginning of a new Laurentian (from "Lorenzo") golden age analogous to the universal peace established by Emperor Augustus in the first century AD. Ghirlandaio, therefore, depicted Lorenzo standing to the extreme right, making the classical gesture of pacification. He is flanked on his right by Antonio Pucci, who oversaw Medici affairs while he negotiated peace in Naples and Rome, and on his left by Francesco Sassetti, a lifelong Medici bank manager, and his son Federico (1472–90). The three adults ascending the stairs with Lorenzo's three sons (Giovanni, Piero, and Giuliano) embodied the flowering of Florentine learning and literature, a sign of the return of the golden age. From left to right they are the poet Luigi Pulci (1432–84), the humanist Matteo Franco (1448–94), and the poet, philologist, and professor of Greek and Latin in the Florentine university Angelo Poliziano. Sassetti participated in this golden age by serving as a governing officer of the university, promoting humanistic scholarship, and indulging his passion for ancient culture by collecting classical coins and manuscripts. Three more of Sassetti's five sons at the extreme left—Teodoro I (1460–79), Galeazzo (1462–1513), and Cosimo (1463–1527)—complete the roll.

St. Francis Resurrects a Boy Who Fell from a Palace Window in 1266

The concluding scene in the life of St. Francis above the altarpiece represents a posthumous appearance of the saint (fig. 85). Most accounts set the scene in Rome and identified the boy who fell as a six-year-old notary's son. Yet Ghirlandaio has again emphasized Florence as a new Rome by depicting the boy falling from the window of the Florentine Spini Palace opposite the medieval façade of S. Trinita (fig. 12, nos. 9 and 13). The prayers of two kneeling Franciscan friars at the foot of the boy's funeral

85. Domenico Ghirlandaio, *St. Francis Resurrects a Boy Who Fell from a Palace Window in 1266,* fresco. Detail of fig. 83. Portrait likenesses of Sassetti's five daughters and their husbands or fiancés, as well as (to the extreme right) Domenico Ghirlandaio and his brother Davide (1452–1525), witness the scene.

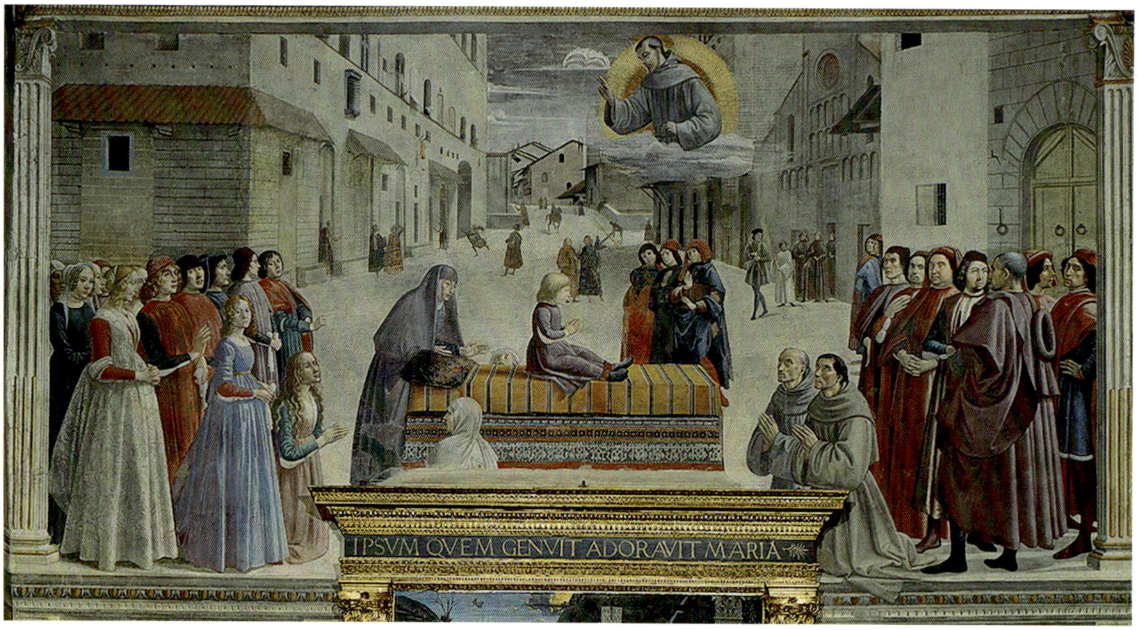

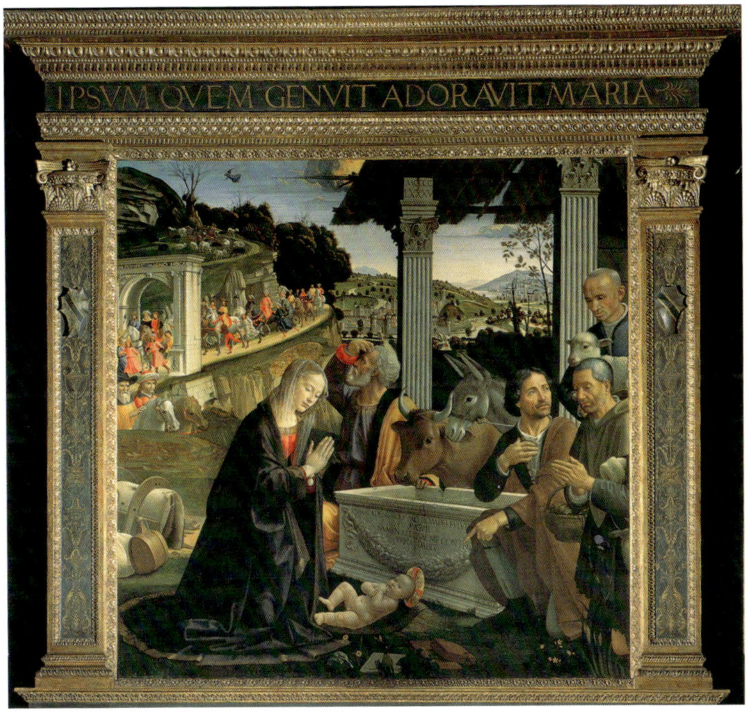

86. Domenico Ghirlandaio, *Nativity,* dated 1485, oil on panel, 65¾ × 66½ in. (167 × 169 cm), S. Trinita. The inscription on the frame translates, "He whom Mary begot [i.e., Jesus], Mary adores." The symbolism of the many details includes the Virgin as the vessel for Christ (the sun contained within a cloud, from Ecclesiasticus 24:6); the Incarnation (basket of eggs); Christ's sacrifice (lamb, goldfinch); the triumph of Christianity over paganism (ruined Corinthian architecture); death and renewed life (blasted tree and leafy tree between the piers, garland on the sarcophagus, flowering meadow); the Gentiles who accepted Christ as a savior (the ox and ass, from Isaiah 1:3); the old and the new dispensations (two books); Christ as the Church's cornerstone (square stone); the Sassetti family (rough stone or *sassetto*); and the Eucharist (Christ's pillow of wheat and the wine flask).

bier are answered by a vision of St. Francis, who resuscitates the boy with a gesture of benediction from within a golden aura.

The miracle commemorates a related event in Sassetti's life. In 1460, less than a year after his marriage, his wife gave birth to a son, Teodoro, who died in 1479 at the age of nineteen. Shortly afterwards, at the then late childbearing age of thirty-five, Nera de' Corsi "miraculously" gave birth to a "replacement" son, Teodoro II (1479–1546), Sassetti's tenth and last child, who would have been the same age as the first Teodoro when the frescoes were completed in 1485. The revived boy, probably a portrait of Teodoro II, would thus have suggested the power of the Mass to negotiate between death and renewed life and Sassetti's hope for salvation through Christ by the intercession of his patron saint.

Nativity

Ghirlandaio's altarpiece represents the *Nativity* and four related subjects: the Annunciation to the Shepherds, the Adoration of the Shepherds, the Adoration of the Virgin, and the Journey of the Magi (fig. 86). Ghirlandaio represented the mounted and crowned Magi riding three abreast through an arch inscribed "To Pompey the Great [106–47 BC], erected by the priest Hyrcanus," a reference to the conquest of Jerusalem by the Romans in the first century BC described by Flavius Josephus (c. 37–c. 100) in his *Jewish Wars* (1.13). In gratitude to Pompey for not despoiling the Temple of Jerusalem, Hyrcanus, the high priest of Israel, built a triumphal arch to honor the Roman general and triumvir.

The inscription on the sarcophagus refers to the same pre-Christian event: "Fallen by the sword before Jerusalem, the prophet Fulvius [first century BC] of Pompey's army proclaims, 'The tomb that contains me will bring forth a new God.'" With the sarcophagus now serving as Christ's manger, Fulvius's prophecy has been fulfilled, and Christianity has triumphed over paganism and Judaism. The esoteric historical references, perhaps furnished by the humanist Bartolomeo Fonzio (c. 1449–1513), and the classical motifs of sarcophagus, piers, and arch reflect the antiquarian interests of both Sassetti and Ghirlandaio, typical of this moment in the history of Florentine art.

S. MARIA NOVELLA, II: FILIPPINO LIPPI'S STROZZI CHAPEL

In 1486 Filippo Strozzi (1428–91) acquired patronage rights to a chapel dedicated to John the Evangelist in S. Maria Novella (fig. 43; see also fig. 12, no. 7) and was allowed to add Philip, his name-saint, to the chapel's dedication. The next year Strozzi commissioned Filippino Lippi to fresco the chapel with scenes from the lives of SS. John and Philip (see figs. 88 and 89) and shortly thereafter also commissioned the sculptor Benedetto da Maiano (1442–97) to carve a tomb (c. 1488–97) with a black marble sarcophagus set within a white marble arch with a Lamb of God keystone (fig. 87). Although his tomb was modeled in part on those in the Sassetti Chapel (fig. 83), Strozzi had it placed more boldly behind the altar so that the sarcophagus would be visible under the altar table, a revered space usually reserved for saints. Above the sarcophagus in white marble relief against a red porphyry background, Benedetto da Maiano carved an epiphany of the Virgin and Child encircled by a wreath of cherubs, stars, and roses and by four adoring angels and two cherubs. The sculptural ensemble, inspired by the cardinal of Portugal's tomb (fig. 74), serves as the chapel's altarpiece. Above the tomb within the lancet window, stained glass designed by Lippi portrays SS. Philip and John, the Virgin and Child, and the Sacrificial Lamb. Lippi frescoed the entire altar wall surrounding the lancet window with a simulated classical triumphal arch decorated with Strozzi arms and devices as well as skulls, bones, angels, muses (Euterpe and Melpomene, the muses of music and tragedy), and virtues (Charity and Faith)—all alluding to the triumph, promised by the Mass, of Strozzi's spirit over death.

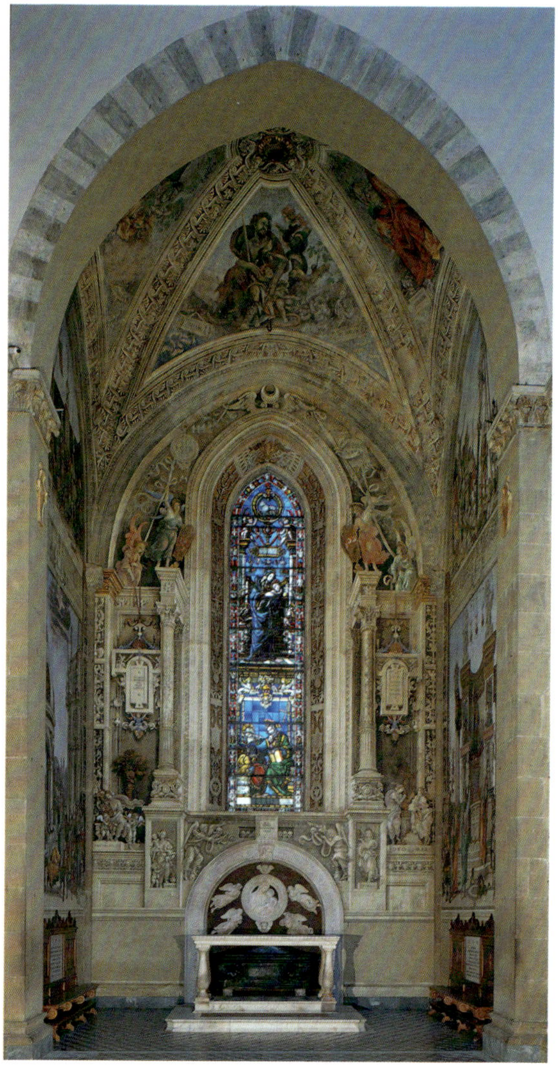

87. Strozzi Chapel, S. Maria Novella, 1487–1503.

St. John Raises Drusiana

The scene on the left wall depicts the supernatural powers of the chapel's first dedicatee, John the Evangelist (fig. 88). On his return from exile on the Aegean island of Patmos, John encountered on the outskirts of Ephesus in Asia Minor the funeral cortège of his friend Drusiana, whom he earlier had converted to Christianity. The pagan cremation ceremony is conducted by a priest carrying an urn for Drusiana's ashes and the priest's assistant holding a pitcher to pour libations on the funeral pyre and carrying a banner inscribed CONCLAMATVM (funeral lament). The standard is topped with symbols of time's flight and death—a winged circle, the underworld's guard dog, Cerberus, and a cypress branch. A crescent moon crowning the domed temple signals its dedication to Diana, whose cult was centered in Ephesus, while the altar's inscription ORGIA denotes the cult's secret orgiastic rites of initiation. The slab on top of the altar inscribed D[IIS] M[ANIBVS] (to the deified souls) records a classical formula used on pagan gravestones.

Clad in the green of hope and red of charity, John trumps this pagan, largely feminine world by resurrecting Drusiana with a single gesture, provoking the confused porters to drop Drusiana's bier. The youth and dynamism of the women and children in the funeral procession underline his miracle of renewing life. John also gestures heavenward to the source of his supernatural power, the sun enveloped within a cloud, a symbol from Ecclesiasticus 24:6 of Christ (the sun) incarnate within the pure vessel of the Virgin (the cloud). The Virgin, often symbolized by the moon basking in Christ's radiance, has supplanted the moon goddess Diana.

St. Philip Exorcises a Dragon

In the scene on the right wall, Lippi created a fanciful classical shrine to Mars, god of war. It is adorned with

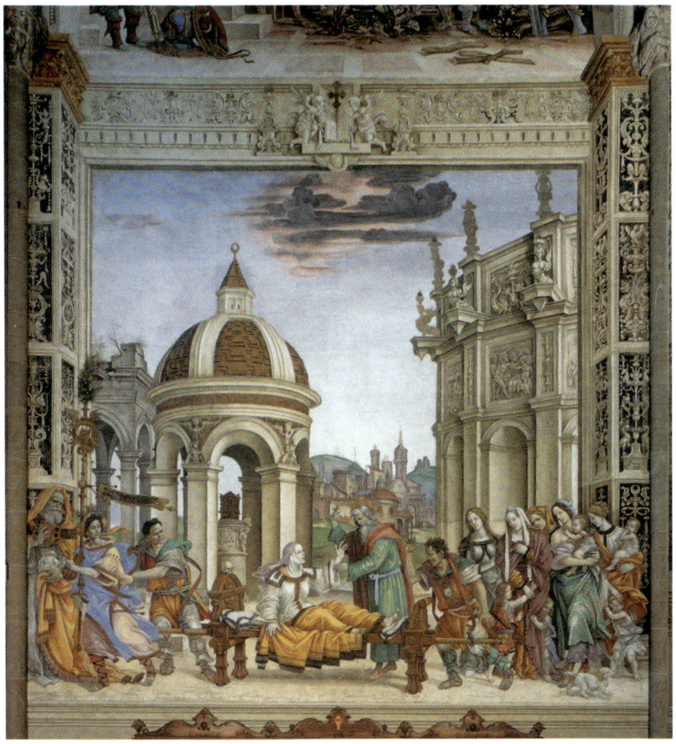

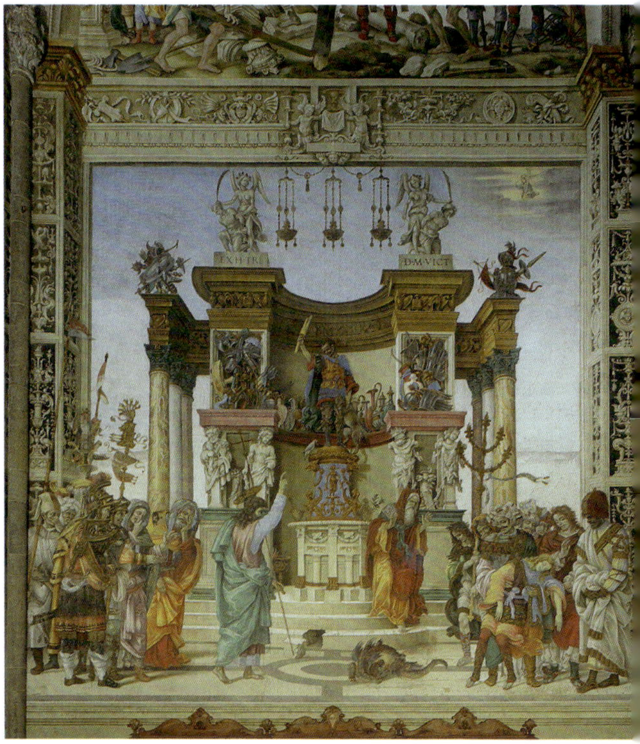

88. Filippino Lippi, *St. John Raises Drusiana* (*Golden Legend*), signed and dated 1502, fresco. Detail of fig. 87.

89. Filippino Lippi, *St. Philip Exorcises a Dragon* (*Golden Legend*), fresco. Detail of fig. 87.

trophies and topped with sculptures of two winged victories restraining conquered captives, inscribed "From this triumph, victory to the greatest god" (fig. 89). Mars, gripping a broken lance and a savage wolf, stands within a niche on an elaborately decorated pedestal dressed in classicizing armor with panther-skin kneepads. He is flanked by stone herms of Bacchus, Hercules, and two satyrs, figures often associated with frenzy, violence, irrationality, and bestiality. Three burning lamps, a flaming tripod, and two veiled priests dressed in golden robes indicate that a pagan sacrifice to Mars's victory is still in progress. It is attended entirely by males, many dressed in military garb and carrying standards.

A moment before, however, a dragon has escaped from under the steps of the shrine. With its pestilential breath, against which two worshipers hold their noses, the beast has killed a priest's son, who expires in the arms of an exotic Asian-featured bystander. St. Philip, armed only with a cross, commands the evil dragon to flee to the desert and revives the priest's son. With a rhetorical gesture he points to a vision in the sky of the resurrected Christ, by whose authority he exorcised the devil and resurrected the dead. He also indicates that the greatest god of the inscription is the compassionate Christ, not the warlike Mars. Together, Philip's and John's resuscitations offer hope for Strozzi's salvation.

In both frescoes Lippi employed an imaginative perspective to intensify the dramas' immediacy. He framed the openings with massive illusionistic piers and extended the floor between them, as if the scenes were being enacted on thrust stages projecting beyond the proscenium arches. Simultaneously, Lippi distanced the dramas archaeologically by his accurate re-creation of the motifs and ritualistic practices of Philip and John's pagan worlds. His antiquarian knowledge, acquired when he worked in Rome in the late 1480s and early 1490s, far exceeded that of previous Florentine artists. Yet Lippi rendered the classical motifs with a density and vibrancy found nowhere in antiquity. The resulting tension between visual intensity and archaeological distance underlined the clash between the old and new dispensations—between the demonic, destructive, and materialistic pagan world and the compassionate, healing, and spiritual Christian world.

6

REFECTORIES

S. APOLLONIA: CASTAGNO'S *LAST SUPPER*

Over two dozen monumental paintings of the Last Supper were painted on end walls of Florentine refectories from the fourteenth through the sixteenth century. Andrea del Castagno's *Last Supper* represents one of the most distinguished examples and the first to employ one-point perspective (fig. 90). According to the Gospels, Christ and the twelve Apostles celebrated the Passover feast in Jerusalem in "a large dining room" (Luke 22:12). During the feast Christ announced that one of the Apostles would betray him and indicated that his betrayer would be "He that dippeth his hand with me into the dish" (Matthew 26:23). He then immediately identified the traitor: "And when he had dipped the bread, he gave it to Judas Iscariot" (John 13:26).

Christ further stated to the Apostles, "Whither I go, thou canst not follow me now; but thou shalt follow hereafter" (John 13:36). As Judas left the banquet for the subsequent betrayal, Christ added, "Now is the Son of man glorified; and God is glorified in him" (John 13:31). By these words Christ alluded to his coming Resurrection, which promised salvation for all humanity. Finally, in the course of the paschal (Easter) feast, Christ instituted the sacrament of the Eucharist: "And taking bread, he gave thanks and broke it, and gave to them saying, 'This is my body which is given for you. Do this for a commemoration of me.' In like manner the chalice also, after he had supped, saying: 'This is the chalice, the New Testament in my blood which shall be shed for you' [or, as in, Matthew 26:28, 'which shall be shed for many unto remission of sins']" (Luke 22:19–20). Christ thus indicated that his death would atone for the original sin of Adam and Eve, and that the Mass commemorated his redemptive sacrifice.

Given the central importance of the Last Supper in Church doctrine and liturgy, the subject became one of the earliest subjects in Christian art and one particularly popular in Florence for the decoration of large monastic and mendicant refectories. In these *Last Suppers*, Christ and the Apostles, usually excluding the traitor Judas, faced into the refectory from behind a long table. They generally sat on straight wooden benches or, in an innovation introduced by Castagno, a U-shaped marble bench. The sacred figures, therefore, echoed the position of the monks, friars, or nuns who habitually ate seated on benches behind long tables arranged along the refectory's perimeter to indicate that the community of the Apostles and the sacrament of the Eucharist was shared by the monastic community.

For clear visibility, these scenes were elevated on the end wall and depicted with life-size or larger-than-life-size figures in a space apparently continuous with the refectory, as if Christ and the Apostles were feasting at an honored high table in an upper room. Castagno created a particularly sumptuous tile-roofed room set within a walled garden, the room's floor, ceiling, and walls encased in a lavish veneer of colored marbles. He also draped the marble bench with an exquisite blue cloth of honor embroidered with flowers, and covered the table with an intricate lace tablecloth.

All *Last Suppers* emphasized Christ's announcement of betrayal, typically by isolating Judas in front of the table near the center, and by contrasting him with Peter and John, who traditionally flanked Christ. Castagno has followed and even heightened these conventions by depicting Judas without a halo seated in front of Christ on a wooden stool holding the sop in his raised hand. Judas's features are sharp and sinister, and his hair and beard black. Trustful John, Christ's favorite Apostle, has fallen asleep in the precise center of the composition, the focus of the orthogonals and the gazes of Peter, Judas, and Christ, while Peter rhetorically raises his right hand in incredulity as if to query John, "Who is it of whom he speaketh?" (John 13:24).

Castagno visualized the obligatory theme of the insti-

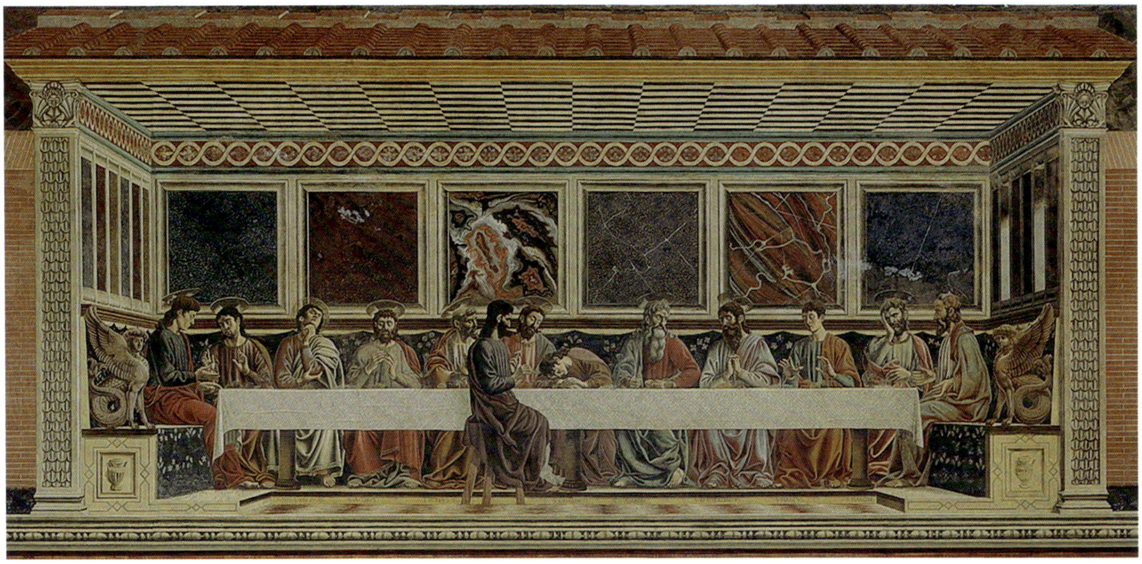

90. Andrea del Castagno, *Last Supper,* c. 1447–50, fresco, c. 15 ft. 5 in. × 31 ft. 6 in. (c. 470 × 960 cm), formerly Camaldolese Refectory, S. Apollonia.

tution of the Eucharist and its redemptive grace both by Christ's benediction and by the wine and bread scattered about the table. Peter's privileged position at Christ's right signaled his preeminence as the founder of the Church, charged with administering the sacrament. Castagno also bestowed enormous aesthetic energy on this drama of love, betrayal, disbelief, and sacramental ritual by the vibrant marble pattern over the heads of the central figures.

S. MARCO: GHIRLANDAIO'S *LAST SUPPER*

Three decades later, Domenico Ghirlandaio created a *Last Supper* for the smaller refectory of S. Marco behind the chapter room and under Michelozzo's library (figs. 38, 39, and 91). More rigorously than ever before, Ghirlandaio imitated the bays of the actual refectory, illusionistically extending the room by the depth of one bay and opening up the lunettes of the end wall to reveal a verdant garden behind. To fill this ample space, Ghirlandaio, developing Castagno's example, made the table as well as the bench U-shaped and placed two Apostles at each end. He alleviated the problem of the central corbel's lack of structural support by coordinating it with a background pier. Together corbel and pier focused attention on the central drama below, reinforcing the orthogonals' focus just above Christ's head. In contrast to Castagno's shadowless space, Ghirlandaio strengthened the illusionism by depicting the life-size figures casting distinct shadows in response to bright light from the left window. He also rendered such details as carafes, bowls, bread, fruit, flowers, trees, and birds with vivid realism.

Consistent with visual tradition, Judas, depicted without a halo, sits isolated from the rest of the Apostles on the opposite side of the table, holding the bread above the sleeping John. Although Judas is paired with a deceitful cat (enemy of the *Domini Canes,* or God's dogs, as the Dominicans liked to pun), his features appear benign, lacking the backdrop of the explosive marble pattern that expressed his treachery in Castagno's fresco. St. Peter, sitting in his usual favored position at Christ's right, frowns and grasps his knife, perhaps anticipating the moment when he will cut off Malchus's ear at Christ's arrest (John 18:10). But on the whole the Apostles' responses are far more restrained than those of Castagno's figures, undercutting the drama of betrayal, sacrifice, and renewal.

Rather, Ghirlandaio depended on symbols and an inscription to express the profound significance of the Last Supper. The vases of lilies and roses to the left and right alluded to the Incarnation and the Virgin. The palm tree in the garden recalled the beginning of Christ's Passion, when he entered Jerusalem on a road strewn with fronds. Cypress trees symbolized death; orange trees, rebirth and resurrection. Birds traditionally connoted liberated souls, but the dove in the left window specifically symbolized the Holy Spirit, and the peacock in the right window,

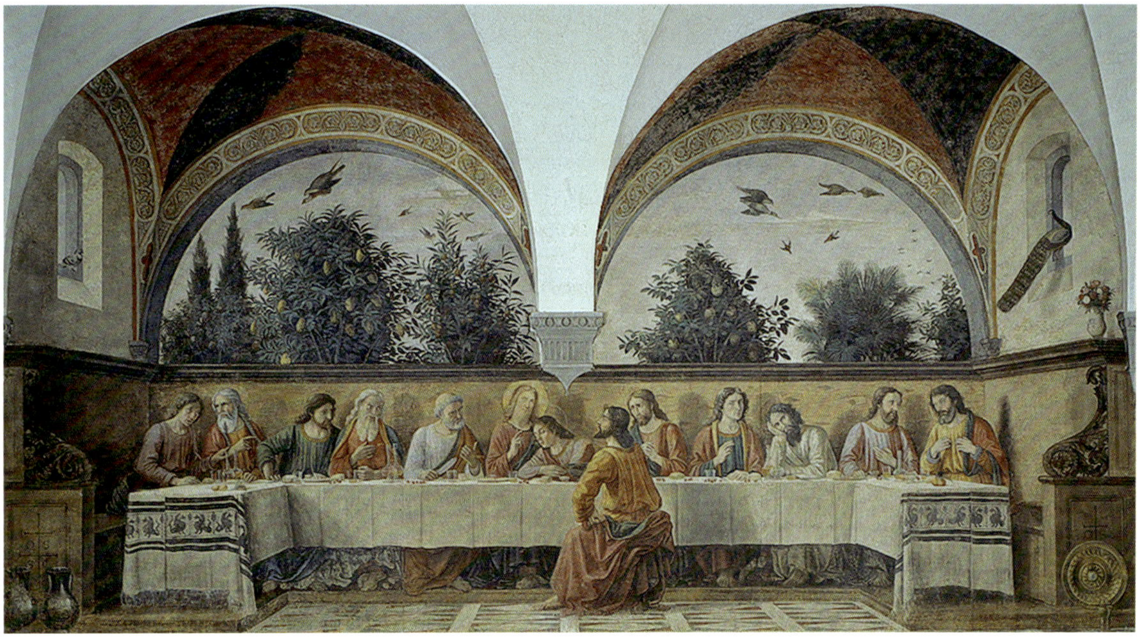

91. Domenico Ghirlandaio, *Last Supper,* c. 1480, fresco, 13 ft. 9⅜ in. × 25 ft. 7⅛ in. (420 × 780 cm), formerly Dominican refectory for guests, San Marco.

immortality, for a peacock's flesh was thought not to decay. Salvation promised by Christ's sacrifice was further signified by the star-studded vaults, the cherries on the table (known as the fruit of paradise), and Christ's words from Luke 22:29–30 inscribed in the bench's frieze ("And I dispose to you, as my Father hath disposed to me, a kingdom that you may eat and drink at my table, in my kingdom"). Finally, the water, bread, and wine on the table alluded to baptism and the Eucharist, the sacramental means to reach the kingdom of heaven.

7

PALACES

THE MEDICI PALACE

After the defeat of the Milanese allied with the Florentine exiles at Anghiari in 1440, and the death of Rinaldo degli Albizzi in 1442, Cosimo il Vecchio and his supporters held the levers of governmental power more securely than ever before. Cosimo, therefore, prepared to build a new palace commensurate with his political influence and wealth. He acquired from twenty-two different owners a site located on a bend in the Via Larga, where from the cathedral and Baptistery the new palace would offer an imposing sight (fig. 12, no. 25). His example sparked a palace-building boom in Florence facilitated by the new political and economic stability and by the recent exemption of palaces from taxation. Humanists, who promoted the family as the ideal model of political order, also supported palace building as an expression of civic harmony and pride. They justified the enormous expense and ostentatious display by reviving the classical theory of magnificence based on Aristotle's *Nicomachean Ethics* (1122a18–1123a30). The theory held that men of means had a moral duty to live in magnificent palaces for the benefit of themselves, their family, and society, a theory succinctly stated by Alberti in the prologue to his mid-fifteenth-century *On the Art of Building in Ten Books:* "When you erect a wall or portico of great elegance and adorn it with a door, columns, or roof, good citizens approve and express joy for their own sake, as well as for yours, because they realize that you have used your wealth to increase greatly not only your own honor and glory, but also that of your family, your descendents, and the whole city."

The identity of the architect of the new Medici Palace (figs. 92–94) is undocumented. Brunelleschi might have created the initial plan, since it relates closely to aspects of his earlier work, but Michelozzo, who supervised its construction, is generally credited with the design. In any case, the palace appears to have been conceived using a seven-*braccia* module with the dimensions of the original east façade (6 × 10 modules), south façade (6 × 9 modules), and south garden wall (2 × 4 modules) harmonically proportioned height to width in ratios of 3:5, 2:3, and 1:2. The courtyard was a three-module (21 *braccia*) square on column centers positioned four modules from the east and north, three modules from the south, and two modules from the west façades. Perhaps intended to evoke a cloisterlike sacred space, the courtyard's plan and portico echoed the crossing and colonnade of Brunelleschi's nearby S. Lorenzo, begun only a few years before (figs. 32, 36, and 37). Owing to the courtyard's off-center placement, the doors were placed asymmetrically in the main eastern façade. This arrangement resulted in a lack of alignment between the doors and the upper-story windows, a design feature characteristic of all previous Florentine palace façades.

Earlier private palaces often used exposed rusticated stone on the ground floor, but always plastered masonry above. The Medici Palace displays the first all-stone exterior on a Florentine private residence. The unprecedented scale of the massive stones that compose the ground-floor rustication, however, recalled ancient Roman rather than Florentine precedents. Equally new were the fine classical moldings surrounding the round-headed openings, the elegant voussoirs (wedge-shaped stones of an arch), and the display of the family coat of arms. Finally, the civic amenities of stone benches and wrought-iron hitching rings and torch holders suggested the palace's public character, designed to accommodate large numbers of visitors.

First appearing here on a private palace, the biforal windows resting on classicizing cornices echoed those of the Priors' Palace (fig. 13), which in turn had been derived from ecclesiastical architecture. But round classical arches have replaced the pointed Gothic versions of the prototype, and Medici arms and devices above the openings have supplanted communal symbols. In place of the

92. Filippo Brunelleschi and Michelozzo?, south and east façades, Medici Palace, c. 1446–57. Before its expansion in the seventeenth century by the Riccardi family, the east façade was originally only ten windows wide. Michelangelo closed the openings of the ground-floor corner loggia in 1517.

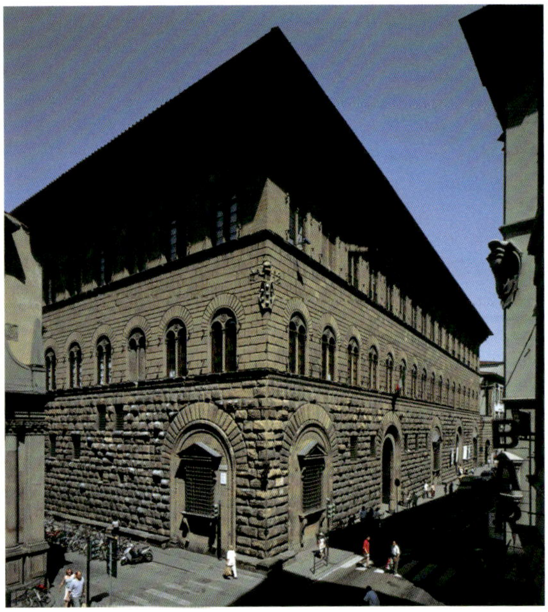

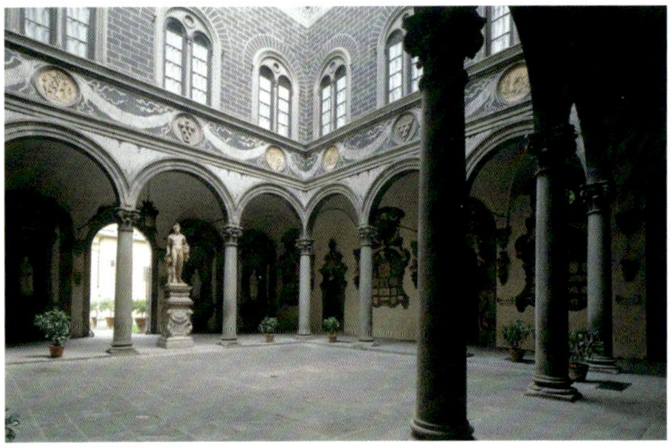

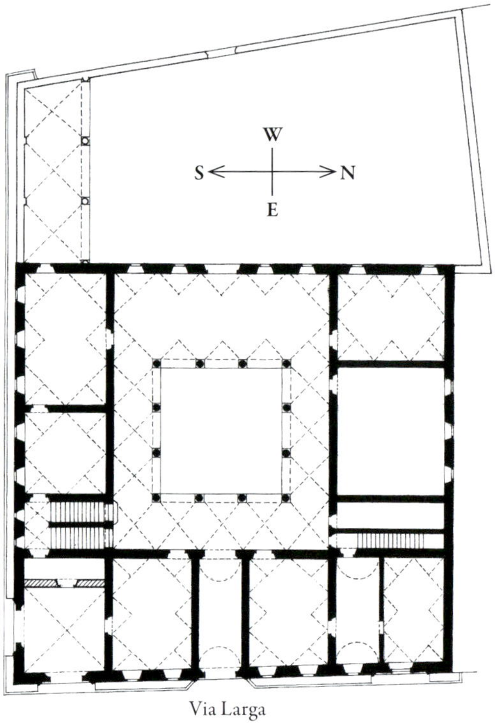

93. Ground-floor plan, Medici Palace. The sequential arrangement of entrance, barrel-vaulted vestibule, portico, courtyard, and garden, as well as the rich variety of ground-floor vaults—barrel, groin, and pendentive—constituted one of the earliest revivals of a Roman house described by Vitruvius. Donatello's bronze *David* and *Judith and Holofernes* (figs. 107 and 109) occupied the centers of the courtyard and garden, respectively, and by 1492 the *Battle of S. Romano* (figs. 99–100) by Paolo Uccello (1397–1475) decorated the northwest-corner bedroom. The Riccardi substantially altered the upper floors, including some modifications to the chapel (fig. 103).

94. Courtyard, Medici Palace. The marble *Orpheus* of c. 1517–19 (fig. 144) by Baccio Bandinelli (1488–1560) under the central arch of the Composite colonnade originally stood in the courtyard's center, replacing Donatello's *David* (fig. 107), which was confiscated by the Second Republic in 1494.

rustication surrounding the windows on the Priors' Palace, the designer here employed an elegant drafted *pietra forte* (a type of *pietra serena* prized for its lack of inclusions) on the *piano nobile,* and a smooth ashlar (dressed stone) on the top floor. The design also created a kind of optical recession reading upward from rough to refined surfaces and from taller to shorter stories that made the palace loom even larger. In place of the battlements on the Priors' Palace, the architect introduced a classical corbelled cornice embellished with dentils, egg-and-dart moldings, coffers, rosettes, and flutes. The cornice was scaled to serve as a crown for the entire building by projecting six feet beyond the façade and measuring one-third the height of the top floor.

The building's great height (approximately 80 ft. 4 5/8 in. or 24.5 m), all-stone façades, exterior corner loggia, central courtyard surrounded by porticoes, and three-bay garden loggia all had precedents in either noble or communal palaces. Yet the sophistication of the palace's design, its classicizing details, and its lavishly decorated interiors also discretely both refined and critiqued previous oligarchic palaces and the Priors' Palace. Was Cosimo signaling his allegiance to the communal government and its republican values, or to the nobles and their aristocratic ideals? Or both? Or was Cosimo subtly indicating that a shift in political power had occurred, from a consortium of the major guilds controlled by the leading families to a single man and his descendants, merited by his wealth, erudition, and piety? Did the new refined classicism of the Medici Palace simply honor the traditional vision of Florence as a new Rome, or did it also suggest that Cosimo, like a Roman statesman, was destined to lead this new Rome?

Answers to these questions are perhaps suggested by the following: From 1454 to the 1460s, beginning immediately after the establishment of a peaceful balance of power in Italy by the 1454 Peace of Lodi negotiated by Cosimo, the communal government commissioned Michelozzo to remodel the courtyard of the Priors' Palace. Cosimo's two sons, Piero and Giovanni, served during this same period either as a prior or as a member of the building committee of the Priors' Palace. Remarkably, Michelozzo designed the courtyard to recall that of the Medici Palace. So, while the Medici Palace originally drew its inspiration from aspects of the Priors' Palace, now the Priors' Palace under Medici leadership was brought into conformity with the Medici Palace. In addition, for the next half-century most builders of Florentine palaces expressed their allegiance to the Medici by closely following the Medici Palace paradigm, even as they often sought to outdo it.

THE RUCELLAI PALACE

Near the time he conceived the façade of S. Maria Novella for Giovanni Rucellai (fig. 43), Alberti also designed Rucellai's remarkable palace, created by remodeling eight earlier houses on the site and adding a uniform façade (fig. 95). As we saw in chapter 3, Rucellai had won Medici trust despite having served as the Florentine agent for his exiled father-in-law, Palla Strozzi, a major Medici opponent. His palace façade, therefore, diplomatically expressed his continued allegiance to the Medici by including the Medici device of the diamond ring with three feathers on the lower frieze. The façade was also designed with a number of features inspired by the Medici Palace: an all-stone façade divided into three stories carved to imitate a pattern of thick and thin stone courses; ground-floor benches; biforal windows resting on a cornice; and an overhanging corbelled cornice unifying the whole. But Rucellai also promoted his own classical erudition by employing a classical trabeated system of superimposed pilasters—Doric on the ground floor, Corinthian on the two floors above—carrying two full entablatures and the crowning cornice. In spite of the building's satisfying expression of load and support, apparently no other patron wanted to risk association with Rucellai, as his façade produced no immediate imitations. However, its classicism resonated with patrons in Rome, where it significantly influenced palace design.

When reflecting on his building activities in his memoirs, Rucellai added spiritual satisfaction as a component of the theory of magnificence: "Men do two important things in life: the first is to procreate, the second is to build. One must build more for necessity than just because one wants to, but in the course of building, one's desire to continue does not diminish but grows. I have given myself more honor and my soul more satisfaction by having spent money than by having earned it—above all with regard to the building I have done."

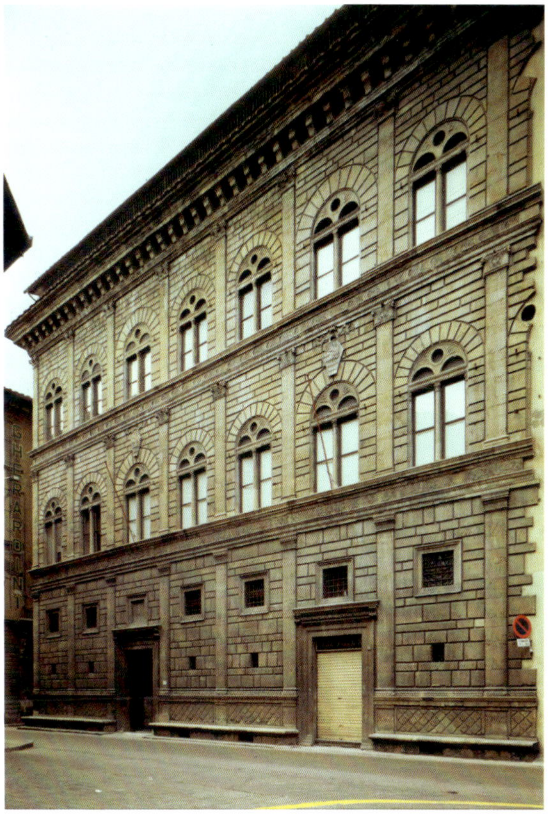

95. Leon Battista Alberti, Rucellai Palace, five bays to the left c. 1455–58, three bays to the right c. 1465–70. Rucellai's wind-filled sail device is carved on the upper frieze, and his coat of arms hangs above the two *piano nobile* windows over the two entrances.

THE PITTI PALACE, I

In about 1456–58, immediately after completion of the Medici Palace, Luca Pitti (1395–c. 1470) began construction of his huge palace on the opposite side of the Arno (fig. 96; see also fig. 12, no. 26). Pitti was a wealthy cloth merchant who had profited by his support of the Medici political faction and who frequently held various governmental offices. He boasted that his palace would so surpass Cosimo's achievement that the Medici Palace would fit in his courtyard. The palace was indeed large: about 177 feet 2 inches (approximately 54 m) wide and 118 feet 1 3/8 inches (approximately 36 m) high, a third again higher and wider than the Medici Palace. However, Pitti paid the Medici Palace the most sincere form of compliment: imitation. He subdivided the façade into three stories with three entrances on the ground floor. He rested the round-headed openings on the upper two floors directly on classicizing stringcourses that served as windowsills. The windows were defined by voussoirs within concentric semicircles and were intended to be in-filled with biforal windows. Pitti's designer employed the width of the openings as the module, each story three modules high, each opening two modules high, and each masonry pier between the windows one module wide. The entire façade was harmonically proportioned height to width in a ratio of 2:3. Finally, as in the Medici Palace, Pitti constructed his façade entirely from *pietra forte,* although he rusticated it throughout with far more massive stones from a nearby quarry, many weighing up to three and a half tons.

Yet the Pitti Palace also critiqued the Medici Palace by its greater unity. The doorways were arranged symmetrically and aligned with the upper windows; the crowning cornice was nearly identical to the two stringcourses; and elegant balustrades of Ionic colonnettes united each rank of windows, each story, and the entire ensemble. More directly than the Medici Palace, the façade expressed an impressive combination of harmony, proportion, symmetry, unity, and classical elegance, while the massive scale and the raw power of its masonry also imparted ancient Roman *gravitas* unique until now in Florence.

In 1465–66 Pitti made the mistake of opposing Cosimo's son Piero by leading a conspiracy to wrest control of the government from the Medici faction. His rebellion failed, he was voted out of office, and he went bankrupt. When he died about 1470, his palace remained incomplete.

THE STROZZI PALACE

Filippo Strozzi, patron of the Strozzi Chapel (figs. 87–89), also built the Strozzi Palace (figs. 97 and 98). His father, Palla Strozzi, had been a supporter of the Albizzi faction that had exiled the Medici in 1433. When the Medici prevailed in 1434, they exiled the Strozzi family along with many other Albizzi partisans. Young Filippo

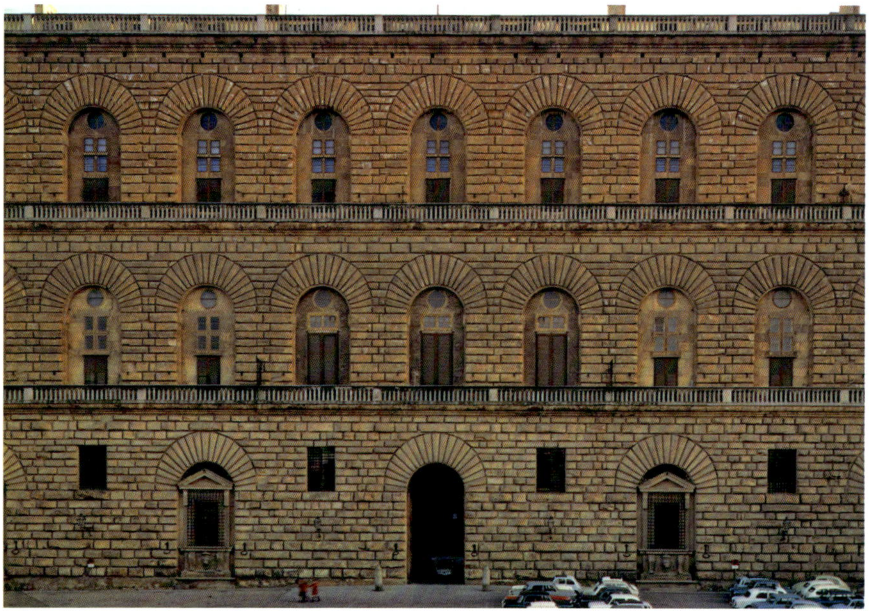

96. Luca Fancelli (c. 1430–c. 1495)?, Pitti Palace, 1458–66. The illustration shows the seven bays of the original façade, before its expansion by the Medici grand dukes in the seventeenth and eighteenth centuries.

was sent to Naples to apprentice with a relative in the banking business. By age thirty-five he owned his own bank and had become friend, advisor, and banker to King Ferrante I. In 1466, through his wealth and influence at court, he persuaded the Medici to lift his ban of exile, and that same year he returned to Florence, married, and opened a second bank. In 1480 he demonstrated his gratitude by helping Lorenzo il Magnifico on his diplomatic mission to King Ferrante, which forestalled Sixtus IV's threat to incorporate Florence into the papal state. Two years later Filippo opened a third bank in Rome, by which time he had become one of the wealthiest men in Florence.

Filippo Strozzi began acquiring land for his new palace in 1474 and started construction in 1489. So as not to provoke Medici resentment, Strozzi consulted Lorenzo il Magnifico on the design, which was said to have been relatively modest, with rental shops on the ground floor. Lorenzo, we are told, suggested a grander work to beautify the city in accord with the theory of magnificence, presumably the response Strozzi wanted. Having endured the disgrace and dislocation of exile, a bold expression of his family's permanence, cohesion, and honor—at a cost of 40,000 gold florins, one-third his total wealth—would no doubt have been a primary goal.

The final design paid careful homage to the Medici Palace (figs. 92–94), except for the overall rustication, which derived from the Pitti Palace (fig. 96). The borrowed features included a modular and proportional design; three stories diminishing in height from bottom to top; ground-floor benches and hitching rings; round-headed openings defined by elegant voussoirs within concentric semicircles; biforal windows resting on denticulated stringcourses; coats of arms and devices decorating the windows and corners; a massive corbelled cornice unifying the entire block, adorned with dentils, bead-and-reel and egg-and-dart moldings, coffers, and rosettes; and, finally, an internal courtyard surrounded by a Composite arcade (here three-by-five rather than three-by-three bays). However, the Strozzi Palace surpassed the Medici Palace by its greater scale, more elegant rustication, employment of masonry vaulting on the *piano nobile,* and, above all, the regularity of its plan, which was rigidly symmetrical on both its longitudinal and transverse axes, defined by a groin-vaulted and three barrel-vaulted entrances in the center of each façade.

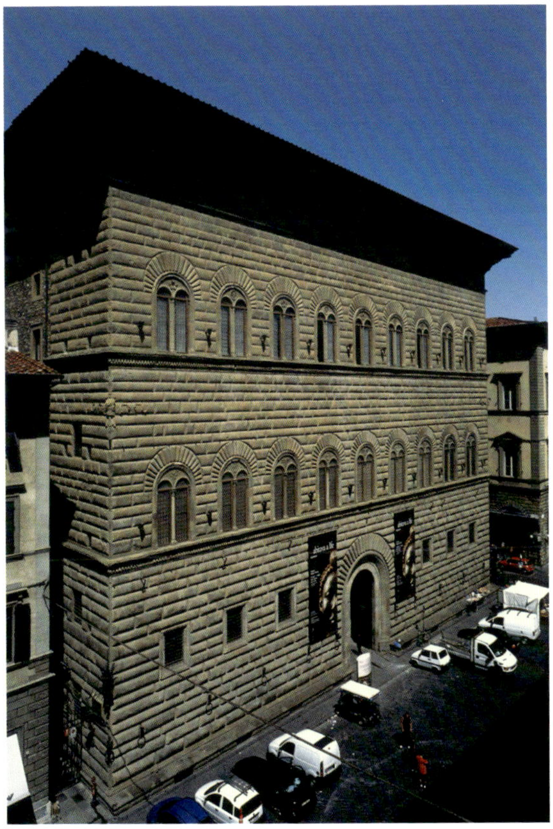

97. Giuliano da Sangallo, Giuliano da Maiano (1432–90), and Cronaca (1457–1508), Strozzi Palace, 1489–1536.

98. Ground plan, Strozzi Palace.

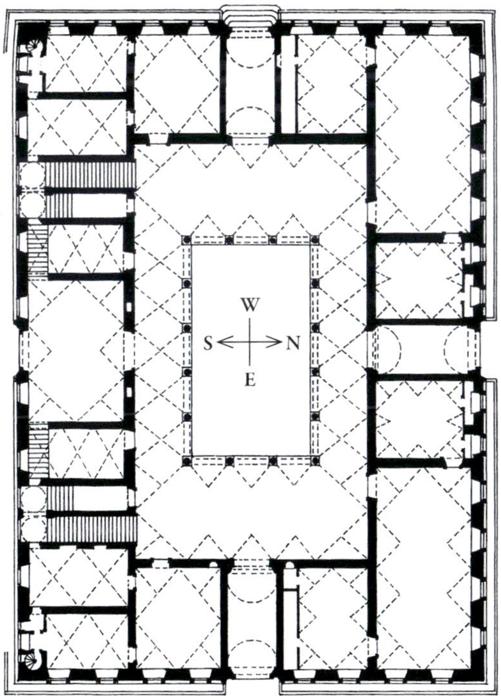

8

HALLS OF STATE

Palazzo Vecchio, I

Any reception or meeting room in a palace where political power was exercised constituted a hall of state. Its decoration, therefore, usually celebrated a regime's legitimacy, sovereignty, dominion, and victory over its enemies.

UCCELLO'S *BATTLE OF S. ROMANO*

The *Battle of S. Romano* by Paolo Uccello appears to be the earliest surviving Renaissance decoration for a Florentine hall of state (figs. 99 and 100). Uccello's paintings derived from a well-developed late medieval tradition of miniatures illustrating battles in Bibles, ancient histories, chronicles, and chivalric romances. But scenes on this scale had appeared previously only in Italian city halls commemorating civic victories, such as the well-preserved frescoes in the Sala del Mappamondo in the Sienese Palazzo Pubblico.

Unfortunately, the date, patron, and original location of Uccello's panels are unknown. Given their scale and communal precedents, however, one would expect them to have been commissioned by the Florentine government for the Priors' Palace to commemorate the victory at S. Romano on June 2, 1432, and to honor the mercenary commander Niccolò da Tolentino (c. 1350–1435). In September 1432, five months after the Battle of S. Romano, the government made Tolentino an honorary Florentine citizen. The next year in a civic ceremony on June 24—

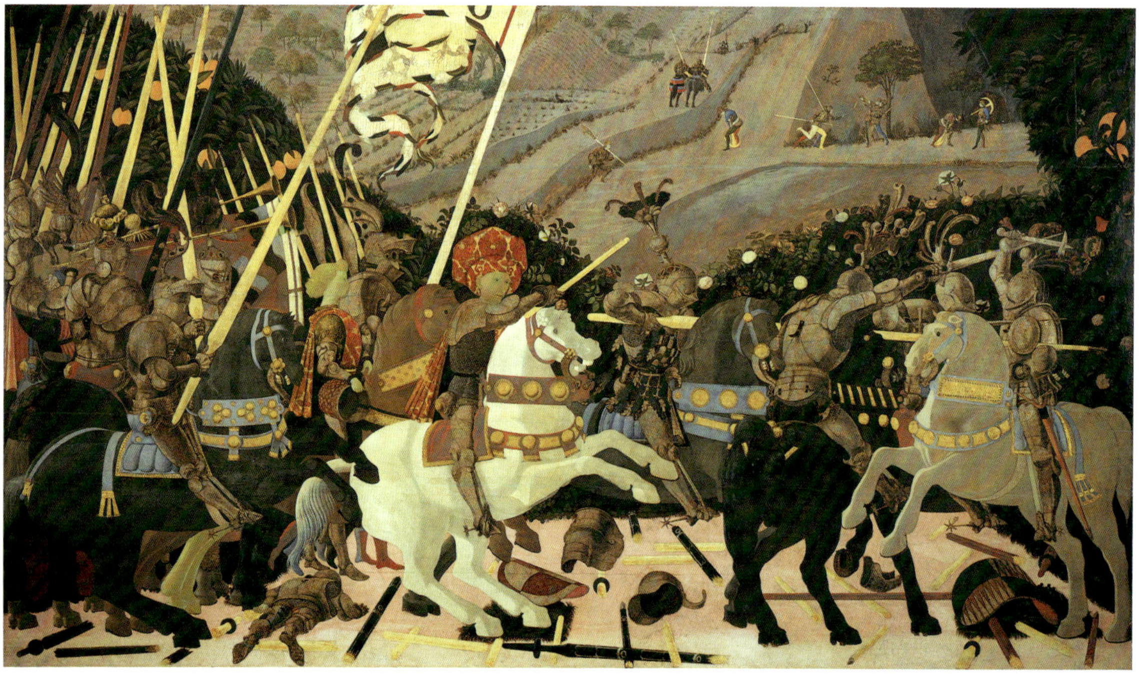

99. Paolo Uccello, *Battle of S. Romano,* c. 1435–36, tempera on panel, 5 ft. 11⅝ in. × 10 ft. 4¾ in. (182 × 317 cm), The National Gallery, London.

the feast of Florence's patron saint, John the Baptist—the Florentine chancellor Leonardo Bruni praised Tolentino for his heroic virtue and the great victory at S. Romano. He also presented him with a helmet, cape, baton, and caparisoned horse, probably similar to those shown in Uccello's London painting (fig. 99). After Tolentino died while campaigning in March 1435, the Florentine government displayed his body in the Baptistery, honored him with a civic ceremony in front of the Priors' Palace, and staged a state funeral and burial in the cathedral with a Mass officiated by Pope Eugenius IV. Therefore, if the government commissioned Uccello's paintings, as seems likely, it was probably just after his death in 1435.

Documentary evidence indicates that the paintings were purchased by three-time prior Lionardo di Bartolomeo Bartolini Salimbeni (1404–79) to decorate his villa, acquired between 1446 and 1451, at S. Maria a Quinto northwest of Florence. The documents offer no indication regarding the location of Uccello's panels or when they came into Salimbeni's possession. But, assuming that they had been painted for a council room in the Priors' Palace, Salimbeni probably bought them in 1459, when he held the office of standard-bearer of justice and when the Priors' Palace was undergoing extensive remodeling by Michelozzo, as mentioned in chapter 7. He would have wanted the paintings to commemorate his role as prior and quartermaster for short periods in the 1430s during the War of Milan (1423–40) and the related War of Lucca (1429–33), of which the Battle of S. Romano was one small episode.

In any case, it is documented that Lorenzo de' Medici (il Magnifico) acquired the paintings at some point between 1479 and 1486 from Lionardo's heirs, Damiano (b. 1453) and Andrea (1455–94) Bartolini Salimbeni. Lorenzo had their original lunette tops cut off, reframed them as rectangular paintings, and installed them as *spalliere* above the wainscoting in his ground-floor bedroom in the Medici Palace (fig. 93), where they are identified in a 1492 Medici inventory. For Lorenzo, the paintings would have celebrated the major role his grandfather, Cosimo il Vecchio, played in the wars of Milan and Lucca, including financial backing, service on the governmental commission directing the wars, and negotiation of the 1433 Peace of Ferrara, which ended the War of Lucca. It was also Cosimo who had persuaded his banking client, Eugenius IV, to release Tolentino from papal service in 1431 to assume command of the hitherto poorly performing Florentine forces. When serving Florence, Tolentino became Cosimo's close friend, and when the Albizzi faction sent Cosimo into exile in 1433, blaming him for the war's failure, Tolentino offered Cosimo his military support, an offer Cosimo refused.

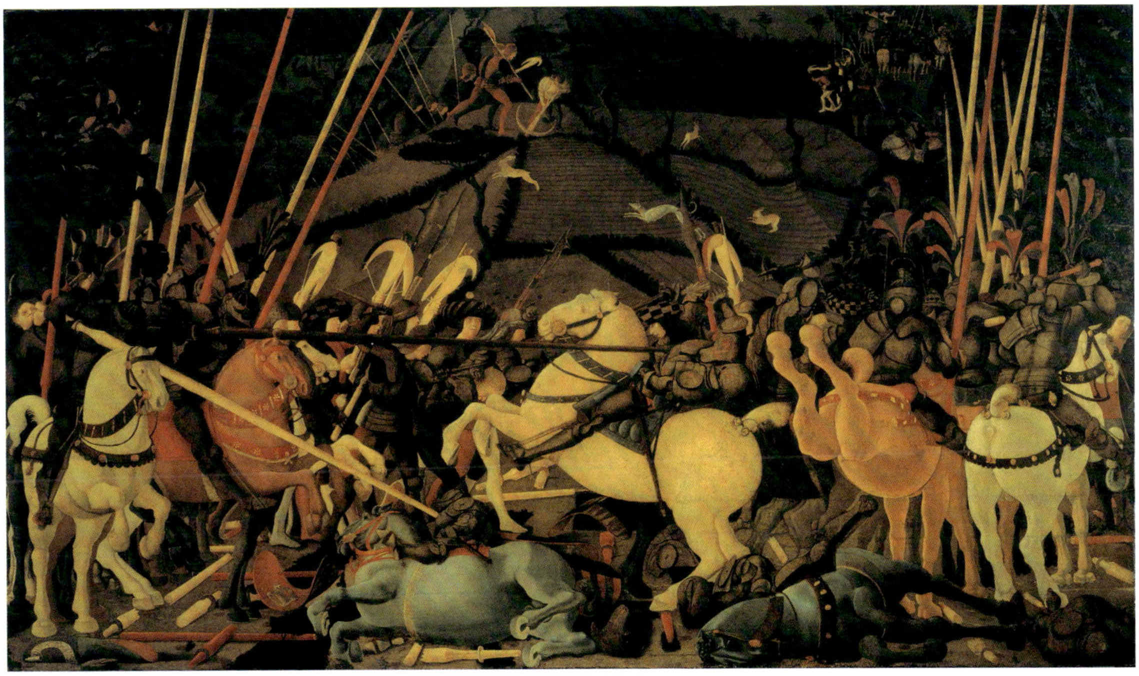

100. Paolo Uccello, *Battle of S. Romano,* c. 1435–36, signed, tempera on panel, 5 ft. 11⅝ in. × 10 ft. 7⅛ in. (182 × 323 cm), Uffizi. A third related panel is in the Louvre.

On his way up from Rome in 1432, Tolentino and his army of mercenaries defeated Bernardino della Carda and his Sienese troops, who had been attacking a Florentine fortress at Montopoli near S. Romano in the lower Arno Valley. The battle was celebrated the next day in Florence as a great victory, yet, oddly, the Florentine chronicles disagree on the number of captives, ranging from forty to ten thousand. Furthermore, Sienese chronicles record a *Sienese* victory with the capture of several important Florentine commanders and a minimal loss of life. Whatever the truth, the Florentine government chose to declare a victory in an otherwise disastrous war.

Rituals, uniforms, insignia, salutes, drills, and tactics had always been fundamental to giving shape to war's unpredictability and pandemonium. To make the formless chaos of battle intelligible, artists had likewise developed a series of endlessly repeated visual conventions. Those that Uccello adopted include a dense foreground frieze of rhythmically patterned armored knights, identified by brightly colored heraldic devices, engaged in a series of individual duels on rearing caparisoned horses; repetitive actions of hacking, chopping, or thrusting with lance, axe, sword, or dagger to kill and unhorse opponents; and a battlefield littered with fallen men, weapons, and horses. The large-scale battle scenes in the Sienese city hall also anticipated Uccello's representation of the civic infantry armed with pikes, halberds, crossbows, and trumpets supporting the mounted professional mercenaries, a tactic first developed in Italy in the fourteenth century in tandem with the rise of communes and their communal militias.

Drawing on a rich visual tradition in Gothic art, Uccello created panels strongly chivalric in character. But his panels differed from previous battle representations by including more detailed descriptions of armor, weapons, horses, trappings, and landscape. Uccello's armor, for example, can be precisely dated to the 1430s, and his landscape accurately portrays the fields and hedgerows that still define the area around S. Romano south of Florence. Previous city-hall battle representations, especially those in Siena, were characterized by the casual and episodic arrangement of a plethora of anonymous soldiers within an encyclopedic catalogue of notable topographic features of an entire region. Uccello, however, limited his representation to about a dozen foreground actors engaged in three decisive moments rationally controlled by a specific individual with a portrait likeness. The battle begins with Tolentino commanding the charge against the Sienese under a banner decorated with his personal device of Gordian knots (fig. 99), reaches its climax with the unhorsing of the Sienese commander (fig. 100, center), and ends with the retreat of the Sienese (fig. 100, right).

These differences reflect changes in the methods of recording battles. Late medieval Italian chronicles, such as the thirteenth-century *Florentine History* by Giovanni Villani (c. 1276–1348), listed abundant, often random facts and figures with many digressions. These chronicles offered little in the way of structure, point of view, personal voice, or overall plan. A battle was just one more fact in the undifferentiated flow of history and itself could occasion the listing of more facts, not unlike Uccello's tendency to catalogue almost endless details in the *Battle of S. Romano*. But by Uccello's day there had also appeared Latin histories such as Leonardo Bruni's *In Praise of Florence* (c. 1401) modeled on the rhetorical histories of classical Roman historians such as Livy, Julius Caesar, and Sallust (c. 86–35 BC). These histories, concerned largely with politics and war, understood battles as being controlled by human agency for predetermined political purposes and as having beginnings, middles, and ends in response to rational causes and effects—much like the episodes of Uccello's *Battle of S. Romano* under Tolentino's control. Uccello's paintings also manifest an awareness of one-point perspective codified in Alberti's 1435 treatise, *On Painting*. For the first time in a battle scene, Uccello created a perspectival foreground stage on which weapons and warriors fall neatly along orthogonals converging in the center of each panel, and many objects, especially the armor and the rumps and bellies of horses, are rendered geometrically. Finally, he followed Alberti's advice by depicting only a small number of principal actors and by composing his *istoria* with variety, abundance, and ornament, but also with moderation, dignity, and modesty.

Combining a chivalric style with a rhetorical style, Uccello's *Battle of S. Romano* is replete with inconsistencies, contrasts, abrupt transitions, and ambiguities. In a final ironic touch Uccello signed the Uffizi panel (fig. 100) on a shield claiming both authorship and armorial privilege, even though his father was merely a barber. Yet, as if recognizing the impossibility of capturing visually the full range of war's violence and confusion, he placed his signature on a fallen shield.

GHIRLANDAIO'S SALA DEI GIGLI

The Sala dei Gigli (figs. 101 and 102) on the second *piano nobile* of the Priors' Palace served as the meeting room for the *Signoria*—the government's highest executive and

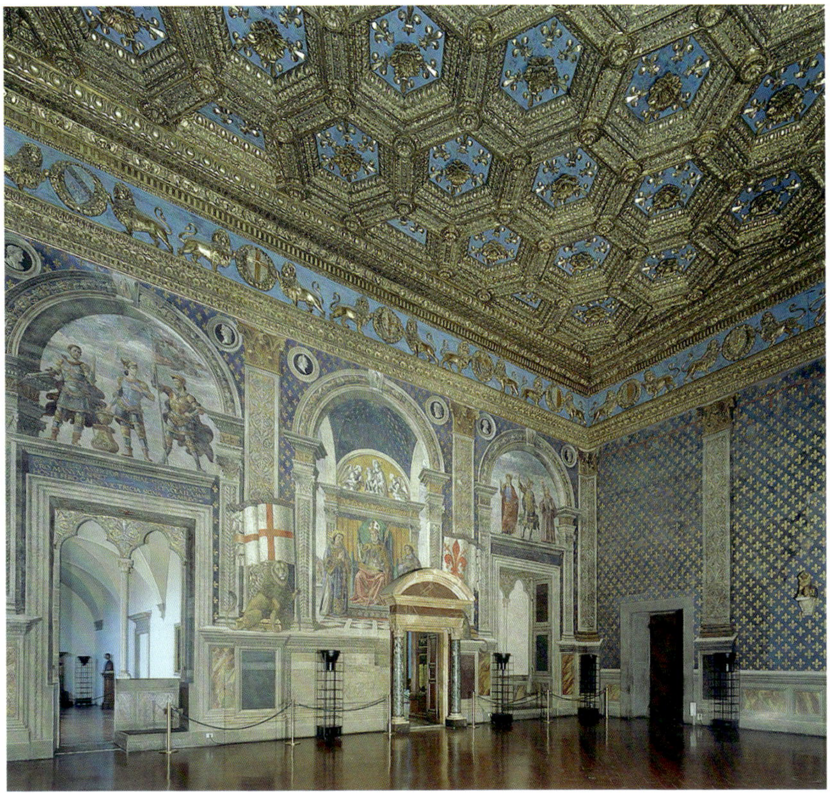

101. Ceiling, and east and south wall decoration, 1475–90, Sala dei Gigli, Palazzo Vecchio. Giorgio Vasari installed the columned door to Cosimo I's *guardaroba* in 1589.

judicial branch, comprising the eight priors and the standard-bearer of justice. Donatello's marble *David* (fig. 21) had been installed in this room in 1416 as a protector of Florence. The room was renovated during Lorenzo il Magnifico's regime (1469–92) under the direction of the palace works committee, staffed entirely by Medici supporters, with Lorenzo himself serving as one of the overseers in 1476, 1486, and 1488–92.

Domenico Ghirlandaio was commissioned to fresco the walls with regularly spaced illusionistic Corinthian pilasters to support visually the entablature carrying the ceiling and to suggest symbolically the government's stability. Emulating the classicizing ceilings in the Medici Palace, the brothers Giuliano and Benedetto da Maiano carved a painted and gilt wooden ceiling and a frieze of heraldic Florentine lions and coats of arms. The blue and gold and the six fleurs-de-lis (celestial lilies) surrounding the central rosettes in the hexagonal coffers symbolized heaven, thus signaling the aim of the *Signoria* to prepare its citizens for salvation by establishing peace and justice. These fleurs-de-lis together with those on the simulated blue cloth between the pilasters on the walls—designed by Ghirlandaio and executed by Bernardo Stefano Rosselli (active 1432–90) in 1489–90—also referred to the house of Anjou. After Charles of Anjou (d. 1285) defeated the Ghibellines at the Battle of Benevento in 1266, he was considered one of the protectors of Florentine liberty for facilitating the triumph of the Florentine Guelph party. But the fleurs-de-lis also had a specific Medicean connection. In 1465 King Louis XI (1423–83) gave Piero de' Medici and his descendants the privilege of adding three gold fleurs-de-lis on a blue ground to the upper *palla* of the Medici coat of arms.

On the east wall Ghirlandaio painted three arches between the pilasters with medallions of Roman emperors in their spandrels to create a classicizing triumphal arch behind the *Signoria*'s dais, signifying the triumph of Florence. In the spaces under the arches above the biforal windows Ghirlandaio painted six heroes from Livy's *History of Rome:* Junius Brutus (sixth century BC), Mucius Scaevola (second century BC), Furius Camillus, Decius Mus (both fourth century BC), Scipio Africanus (236–183 BC), and Cicero. Once protectors of the Roman Republic, they now symbolically defended Florence, the new Rome.

Between the heroes Ghirlandaio frescoed a simulated chapel to indicate that governmental authority and purpose derived from divine justice (fig. 102). The fictive marble relief in the chapel's lunette with two angels ador-

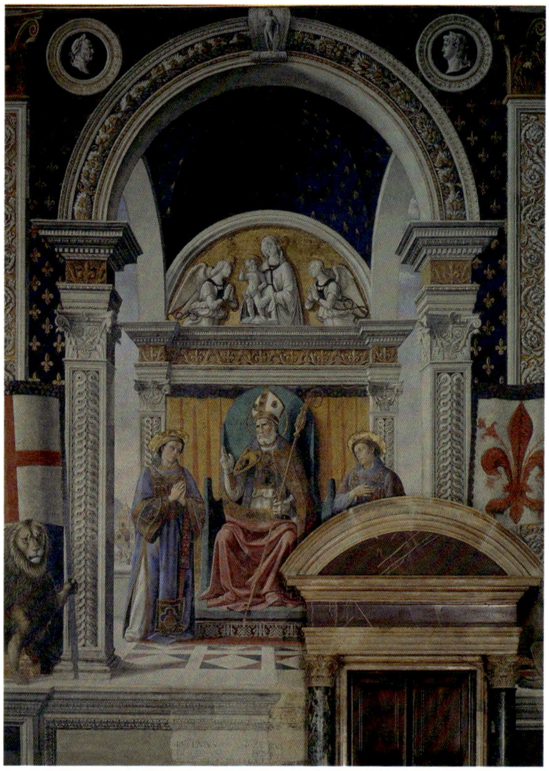

102. Domenico Ghirlandaio, *St. Zenobius Flanked by SS. Eugenius and Crescentius,* fresco. Detail of fig. 101.

ing the Virgin and the blessing Christ Child recalled the sacred founding of Florence in the first century BC on the Feast of the Annunciation. Flanked by his martyred deacons, SS. Eugenius and Crescentius (both fourth century AD), St. Zenobius, one of the earliest bishops of Florence, blesses and legitimates the *Signoria.* St. Zenobius was also an early protector of Florence, for he was said to have saved the city from defeat by the Goths in 405 by his prayers. Yet he also referred to the Medici, for his original bishop's seat was in S. Lorenzo, now a nearly completed Medici pantheon. Furthermore, during the 1478 Pazzi Conspiracy, Lorenzo il Magnifico believed that he had been saved from assassins by the saint's intervention, when he escaped into the cathedral's north sacristy, which housed St. Zenobius's relics. To reference Lorenzo's "miraculous" salvation and his brother's "martyrdom," Ghirlandaio must have been instructed to represent the cathedral at the left and to model his composition on Giuliano da Maiano's 1463–65 marquetry panels in the north sacristy representing the same three saints.

As mentioned in chapter 5, the Pazzi Conspiracy opened a two-year struggle between Florence and Sixtus IV allied with Naples. Lorenzo had avoided war by traveling at great personal risk to Naples to persuade King Ferrante I to join Milan in defending Florence. Sixtus IV bought time by signing a peace treaty with Florence, but he then turned on Naples in 1482 by offering Venice the papal fief of Ferrara in return for its aid against Naples, Florence, and Milan. In response, Florence and Milan prepared to defend Ferrara, and Spain joined in the defense of Naples. This forced the pope and the Venetians to back down and sign the Peace of Bagnolo on August 4, 1484. When Ghirlandaio executed the east wall in 1482–83, therefore, the peace that Lorenzo had negotiated in 1480, propagandized by Medici supporters as the return of the golden age, was in danger of devolving into a general Italian war. In this context, Ghirlandaio's six frescoed Roman republican heroes would have alluded to Lorenzo as a new Cicero, survivor of a conspiracy; a new Mucius Scaevola, unwavering in his defense of the republic and constant in the face of danger; a new Decius Mus, Furius Camillus, and Scipio Africanus, willing to throw his own body into enemy lines; and a new Junius Brutus, refounding the republic on impartial justice.

9

PALACE CHAPELS

The Medici Palace

In 1422 Martin V granted Cosimo il Vecchio and his wife the rare privilege of using a portable altar in their old palace, which probably served to authorize the construction of the sumptuous small chapel in Cosimo's new palace, designed by Michelozzo (figs. 103–106).

GOZZOLI'S *JOURNEY OF THE MAGI*

The fresco decoration by Benozzo Gozzoli (c. 1421–97), overseen by Cosimo il Vecchio's firstborn son, Piero, depicts on three walls the *Journey of the Magi*. The procession unfolds clockwise, beginning with Caspar, the young magus on the east wall dressed in white (fig. 104). Next come Balthazar, the mature black magus on the south wall in green, and Melchior, the old magus on the west in red. By their ethnicity, age, and color of dress, the Magi embodied the three continents (Asia, Africa, Europe), humanity's three ages (youth, maturity, old age), and the three Theological Virtues (Faith, Hope, and Charity). This tripartite scheme supported the chapel's dedication to the Trinity. Gozzoli portrayed each lavishly dressed, crowned, and bejeweled magus in profile and riding a richly caparisoned white mount derived from representations of a classical *adventus* (ceremonial entry into a city). Each magus is protected by six young foot-soldiers with five mounted pages leading the way. One page holds a sword, symbolic of Christ's sovereignty and justice, while others carry gifts for the Christ Child—gold, frankincense, and myrrh—emblems of Jesus' kingship, priesthood, and sacrifice.

On the east wall (fig. 104) a cavalcade following Caspar snakes its way down from a castellated hilltop town symbolizing Jerusalem, where Herod called the Magi before they made their way to Bethlehem (Matthew 2:1–9). The laurel behind Caspar and the Medici coats of arms on the caparison of his horse suggest that the magus alluded to Lorenzo il Magnifico (aged ten in 1459). Lorenzo was next in the line of primogeniture after Cosimo and Piero, and he was the youthful embodiment of the future political and dynastic aspirations of the Medici. The inclusion of portraits of three generations of Medici males within the procession behind Caspar signified not only the family's hope for the continuation of the dynasty, but also their quest for a Savior and regeneration at the end of life's pilgrimage.

Gozzoli painted the frescoes like colorful tapestries, the main figures parading close to the picture plane on a shallow rocky foreground stage. Many forms, especially

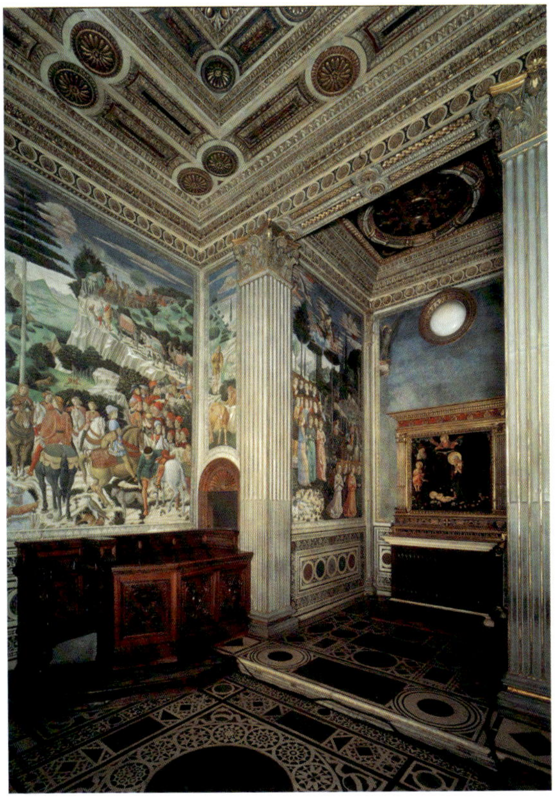

103. Medici Palace Chapel, c. 1449–59.

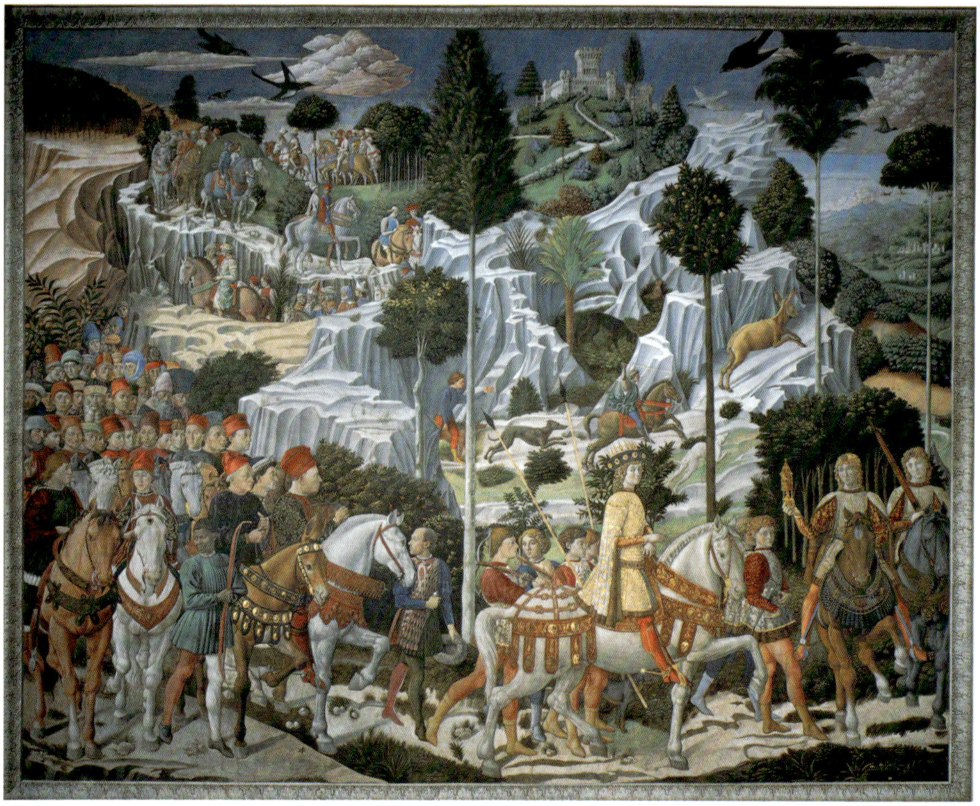

104. Benozzo Gozzoli, *Journey of the Magi,* 1459, fresco embellished with gold leaf, east wall, Medici Palace Chapel. Among the more than thirty portraits in the room, those here in the retinue following Caspar include (front row, right to left) Piero de' Medici on a white horse; behind Piero, Carlo de' Medici (1428–92), Cosimo's illegitimate son; Cosimo il Vecchio on a brown mule; Galeazzo Maria Sforza (1444–76), young son of Cosimo's ally, Duke Francesco Sforza (1401–66) of Milan, on a white horse; and Sigismondo Pandolfo Malatesta (1417–68), a Medici ally from Rimini, on a brown horse. The second row includes Cosimo's second son. Giovanni, and Piero's two sons. Lorenzo and Giuliano. In the center of the third row Gozzoli painted his self-portrait, signing his red hat.

105. Gozzoli, *Adoring Angels,* fresco, west chancel wall. Detail of fig. 103.

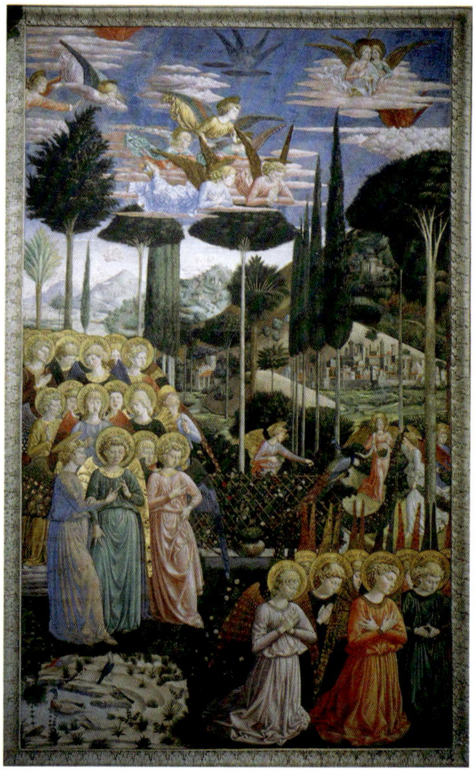

the horses, are foreshortened with great virtuosity. Drawing on his upbringing as a tailor's son and his early training as a goldsmith, Gozzoli represented the figures wearing exquisite outfits cut from facsimiles of the most opulent fabrics produced in Florence and such accessories as head brooches, jewel-studded belts, and golden spurs. The Magi's gem- and pearl-encrusted crowns and their gift vessels represent particularly imaginative and majestic examples of the goldsmith's art. The fanciful headgear of many within their retinues also exudes an oriental exoticism enhanced by the black African bowman in the Medici party, and by the camels, leopards, and monkey that precede Melchior on the west wall. The scene is populated with hill towns, farmhouses, and villas reminiscent of Medici holdings near Florence, where the family gardened and hunted. The verdant landscapes in the middle ground rise steeply behind the figures to a narrow deep-blue band of sky studded with birds and clouds. The countryside teems with activity, especially the noble sport of hunting with dogs and falcons.

Gozzoli rendered the outcroppings of barren, faceted rock according to the abstract conventions of earlier Gothic art. He depicted with uncanny precision the flora and fauna derived from Gothic pattern books, botanical treatises, and naturalistic painting, but transcended these sources by his highly original ensembles remarkable for their panoramic breadth, convincing evocation of the actual Florentine countryside, and exceptional variety. His decoration stands as a landmark in the history of Florentine landscape painting. It also powerfully evokes the two most common settings of Italian art and literature—foreboding woods and rocky wilderness—symbolic of humanity's spiritual journey in death's shadow through life's desert of trials and temptations.

The frescoed display of chivalric privilege, courtly rank, sartorial extravagance, and equine splendor might seem incongruous in a pragmatic merchant republic controlled, as Florence was, by strict sumptuary laws. Yet, as mentioned in chapter 5, on the Feast of the Epiphany (January 6), the Confraternity of the Magi staged every few years—with the participation and financial support of the Medici—an elaborate pageant reenacting the journey of the Magi. On horseback and on foot, dressed in the most exotic of finery, the spectacular parade featured many hundreds of citizens, including a multitude of youths in the guise of *Gloria*-singing angels. Gozzoli's frescoes reconstructed this procession in which the adults, including the Medici, played roles of potentates, knights, and nobility who humbly submit to the spiritual authority of the newborn Christ Child.

The decoration also displayed the ceremonial face that Florence assumed to honor visiting dignitaries in a manner worthy of comparison with rival Italian courts, such as the ceremonial entries of Pope Pius II (r. 1458–64) and Galeazzo Maria Sforza into Florence in April of 1459, just before Gozzoli executed the chapel. Gozzoli was undoubtedly also inspired by the presence two decades earlier of a host of eastern personages, including the Byzantine emperor John Palaeologus VIII (1392–1448) and delegations from other eastern Mediterranean countries. These visitors came to the 1439 Council of Florence, promoted and largely funded by Cosimo il Vecchio, to unite (if only briefly) the Eastern and Western Churches. Significantly, the doctrine of the Trinity—to which the chapel was dedicated—was one of the major issues dividing the two branches of Christianity.

On the walls of the chancel, Gozzoli painted nearly a hundred angels mediating between heaven and earth as they praise and adore Jesus, represented in the altarpiece toward which they turn (fig. 105). In the background within a *hortus conclusus*—symbolizing Paradise regained through the Virgin's fertile womb—four angels gather blossoms and branches to prepare celebratory festoons for Christ's birth, while a peacock, emblem of salvation, perches on a wicker fence. The pond and birds in the foreground evoke the cleansing water of baptism, which liberates souls from sin, just as the goldfinch, palms, and cypresses symbolize Christ's redemptive sacrifice, which made baptism efficacious. The rose-tinted clouds and the radiance illuminating the angels from the direction of the altar imply the dawn of a new era of grace. The city in the background, awash in this divine light, appropriately recalls Florence, which on the Feast of the Magi was symbolically transformed into a new Jerusalem.

FILIPPO LIPPI'S *NATIVITY*

The altarpiece by Fra Filippo Lippi (c. 1406–69) depicts along its central axis the Savior sought by the Magi as well as the Trinity of the chapel's dedication (fig. 106). The infant St. John, the patron saint of Florence, was the subject of a poetic life written by Lucrezia Tornabuoni (1425–82), Piero de' Medici's wife, which suggests that she played an active role in the patronage of the chapel. The inscription on John's banderole announces Christ's redemption of original sin (John 1:29, 36). The mountain stream alludes to John's baptism of Christ, celebrated on the same feast day as the journey of the Magi, and the only biblical episode in which the Trinity appears (Mat-

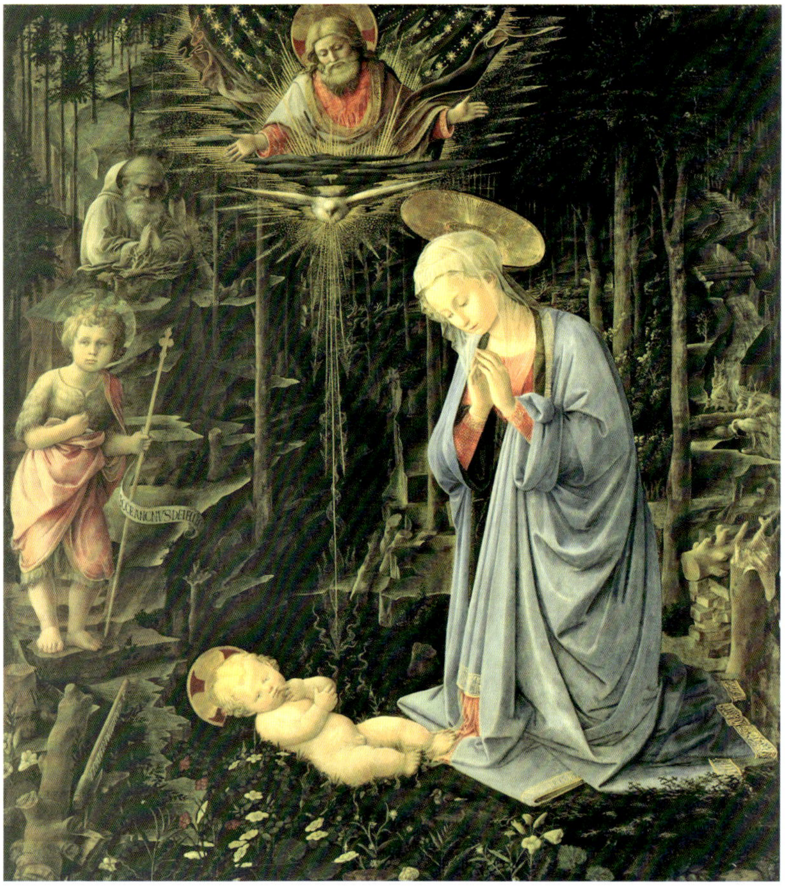

106. Fra Filippo Lippi, *Nativity (Trinity, Virgin Adoring Jesus, John the Baptist, and St. Bernard)*, c. 1459, signed, tempera on panel, 50 × 45⅝ in. (127 × 116 cm), Gemäldegalerie, Staatliche Museen zu Berlin. This original Medici Palace Chapel altarpiece was replaced in 1929 by a contemporary workshop variant. The painting includes the following symbolic references related to the birth, death, and resurrection of Christ celebrated in the Mass: lilies (Annunciation); flowers (renewed life); goldfinch, Jesus' cruciform halo, and John's cross (Christ's sacrifice); stork killing a snake (Christ's triumph over sin); and ax and tree stumps (death of the unfaithful and unrepentant, from Luke 3:9).

thew 3:16–17; Mark 1:9–11; Luke 3:21–22; John 1:29–34). The bearded Cistercian monk, his hands in adoring prayer echoing those of the Virgin, probably represents Bernard of Clairvaux (c. 1090–1153), the patron saint of the Florentine government and author of extremely popular works on the Nativity, the Virgin, and the Trinity.

Cosimo il Vecchio, all but immobilized by gout in the few years remaining before his death in 1464, often spent many hours a day in his chapel praying and receiving relatives, friends, clients, foreign dignities, and political allies. At the height of his influence, the aged patriarch must surely have cut an impressive figure. Seated in this consecrated space, which glittered in the flickering candlelight from the polished gold leaf and the intense blue made from crystals of lapis lazuli, and surrounded by symbolic references to the Mass, the Medici, and the Florentine government, he would have conveyed an awesome sense of piety, prosperity, and power—as if he were the sacred sovereign of Florence. No wonder, then, that after the expulsion of the Medici in 1494, officials of the second Florentine republic looted the chapel of its choir stalls, vestments, liturgical objects, relics, and altarpiece and carted them off to the Priors' Palace.

10

FREESTANDING PALACE SCULPTURE
The Medici Palace

When the Medici Palace (figs. 92–94) was nearing completion in the mid-1450s, it appears that Cosimo il Vecchio commissioned his friend Donatello to cast a pair of costly freestanding bronze sculptures, a *David* and a *Judith and Holofernes* for the center of his courtyard and garden, respectively (figs. 107 and 109), although Cosimo's patronage is undocumented.

107. Donatello, *David with the Head of Goliath,* c. 1455–60, bronze, 62¼ in. (158 cm), Bargello.

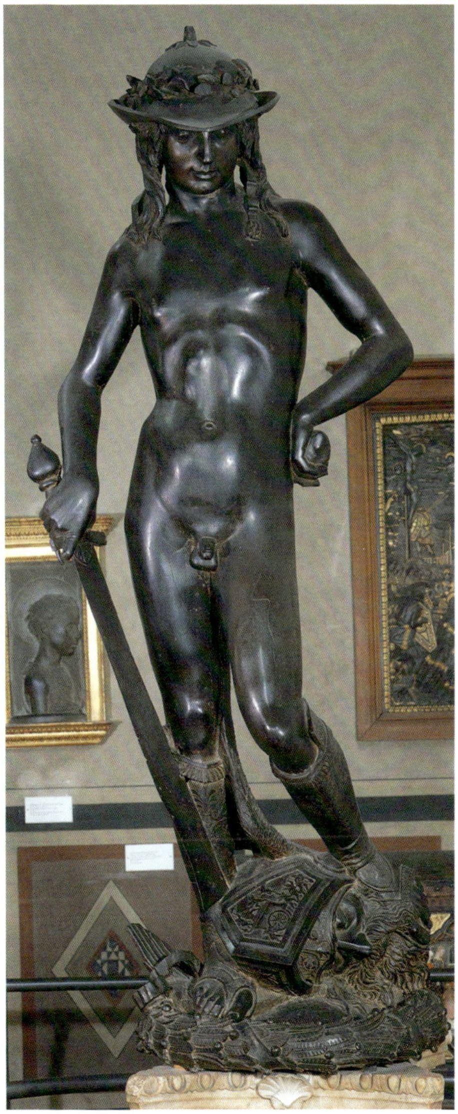

DONATELLO'S BRONZE *DAVID*

The *David*—Florence's first life-size, nude, freestanding bronze figure in classical *contrapposto* (cf. fig. 5)—would have been visible to passersby and accessible for closer inspection, when the entrance and courtyard of the palace were open to Medici clients and friends during the day. Once standing on a now-lost tall columnar base (by Desiderio da Settignano, according to Vasari), the *David* emulated a classical victory monument appropriate for a triumphant David.

A relief of *Hercules* on the cathedral was an important source for Donatello's knowledge of Polykleitan *contrapposto* (fig. 108). From the Priorate's founding in 1282, Hercules had been represented on the city's seal as a symbol of communal might and independence. In his *Labors of Hercules* (c. 1391), the humanist and Florentine chancellor Coluccio Salutati (1331–1406) wrote that Hercules embodied both fortitude and civic strength. In addition, Hercules was frequently interpreted as a Christ type, having achieved immortality through his self-sacrificial labors. The remarkable similarity between the marble relief and the bronze *David,* therefore, suggests that Donatello wished to combine David and Hercules to stress their identities as tyrant slayers, Christ types, and personifications of fortitude. Significantly, one traditional meaning of the name David in Hebrew was "strong of hand."

Donatello's bronze *David* also would have reminded politically active Florentines of his marble *David* in

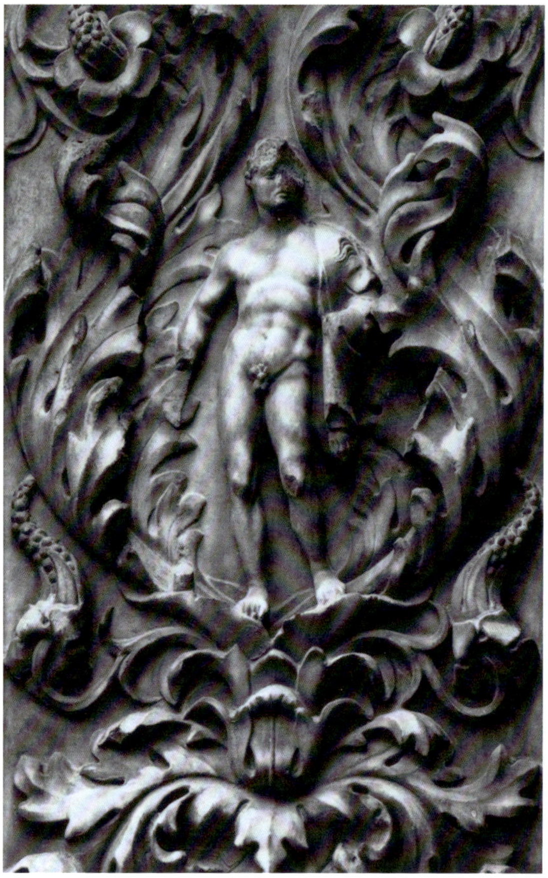

108. Nanni di Banco?, *Hercules,* c. 1400, marble relief, c. 15¾ in. (c. 40 cm), door jamb, Porta della Mandorla, north flank, Cathedral, Florence.

the Priors' Palace (fig. 21). The comparison was made all the more inevitable by the similarity of their Latin inscriptions:

> (marble *David*) To those who bravely fight for the fatherland, even against the most terrible foes, the gods will lend aid.
>
> (bronze *David*) The victor is whoever defends the fatherland. God crushes the wrath of an enormous foe. Behold! A boy overcame a great tyrant. Conquer, O citizens!

The latter inscription, composed about 1454 by Gentile de' Becchi (c. 1420/30–1497), the Medici's resident priest and humanist tutor of Cosimo's grandsons, Lorenzo and Giuliano, implied that the Medici, like David and Hercules, loyally defended Florentine liberty. Indeed, as mentioned in chapter 8, Cosimo had played major financial, diplomatic, and supervisory roles in the Florentine wars of Milan (1423–40) and Lucca (1429–33). In fact, the bronze *David* was probably commissioned in part to commemorate the concluding Peace of Lodi (1454), a treaty personally negotiated by Cosimo, which for the most part ended warfare between Florence, Milan, Venice, Rome, and Naples until the French invasion of Italy in 1494 upset the balance of power.

Born a lowly shepherd—and he wears a shepherd's hat of sorts over his down-turned head—David exemplified humility, especially in contrast to the pride of Saul, his predecessor. He was also the prototypical exile, called from the Judean desert by the prophet Samuel to become the second king of Israel. Thus, the bronze *David* would have reminded viewers that Cosimo, too, had humbly endured an Albizzi-imposed exile in 1433 before being recalled the next year to lead and defend Florence. The sculpture also would have implied a shift of governmental authority from the Priors' Palace to the Medici Palace and evoked, by its classicizing nudity and bronze medium, Cosimo's erudition and wealth. But whether situated in the Priors' Palace or the Medici Palace, David remained a prophet of Christ's coming, Christ's ancestor, and a Christ type whose victory over Goliath prefigured Christ's triumph over Satan. *David* thereby also served to construct an image of the Medici as pious servants of the Church.

To most modern observers, however, the bronze *David* appears less religious and heroic than homoerotic, with its introspective reverie and long, originally gilt hair intertwined with ribbons. David's stomach and buttocks swell and curve sensuously in profile, his limbs and torso appear soft and limp, his inner thigh is caressed by the feathered wing of Goliath's helmet, and the casually held hilt of his sword appears unusually phallic. One explanation for this narcissistic and erotic androgyny lies in an alternative Renaissance interpretation of the name David as "Beloved" and the biblical description of David as an adolescent youth "ruddy and beautiful, and of a comely face" (1 Kings 16:12; 17:42). The revival of classical Epicurean philosophy by humanists in the 1420s and '30s, a philosophy that emphasized the enjoyment of sensuous pleasures, would have supported an image of David as a desiring and desirable youth. In 1418 Poggio Bracciolini had rediscovered the Epicurean text *On the Nature of Things* by Lucretius (94–55 BC), a copy of which Cosimo owned by 1429. This text inspired *On Voluptuousness* (1427) by the humanist Lorenzo Valla (1407–57) and the equally Epicurean treatise of the same title (1458) by Marsilio Ficino. Antonio Beccadelli, called Panormita (1394–

1471), dedicated to Cosimo his *Hermaphrodite* (1425), an Epicurean text that sang the praises of the love of older men for younger boys. Indeed, homosexuality—encouraged by late marriages for most men due to dowry inflation and inheritance laws—was an important fact of Florentine Renaissance life. Yet, while the revival of Epicureanism and widespread homosexuality provided a social and cultural context for the homoerotic bronze *David,* Donatello and Cosimo surely did not intend the work to celebrate sodomy and pederasty, both illegal and immoral in the eyes of the law and the Church.

Rather, the bronze *David* reflected the world of Florentine confraternities, such as the Confraternity of the Magi sponsored and funded by the Medici, which provided moral, civic, and religious instruction for Florentine boys. During civic and religious celebrations these youths enacted religious dramas in public, including the stories of David and Goliath, and Judith and Holofernes—and, significantly, Piero de' Medici's wife, Lucrezia Tornabuoni, wrote a sacred play on the latter theme, which suggests that she might have been involved in the patronage of Donatello's works. Confraternal youth groups also led civic processions as utopian embodiments of renewed Florentine prosperity and innocence, just as an image of the young David traditionally embodied the city's ideal strength and righteousness. Donatello's bronze *David,* therefore, can be understood as having just performed with youthful promise and heroic strength a sacred drama to promote the political and spiritual regeneration of Florence. It also served as an example for the Medici and a projection of their self-perception.

The narrative relief on Goliath's helmet representing the Triumph of Eros inflected *David*'s eroticism toward an expression of the Platonic triumph of the soul over death through love (Eros). Platonic and Neo-Platonic thought had been well established in Florence by the 1450s and '60s. The complete works of Plato in Greek were available in Florence by 1424, and Leonardo Bruni had translated for Cosimo the *Phaedrus,* a key essay on Platonic love. The Greek Platonic scholar Georgius Gemistus Plethon (c. 1360–1452), who came to the Council of Florence of 1439 with Emperor John VIII Palaeologus, inspired further interest in Platonism, and another Greek scholar, Janos Argyropylos (1405–87), taught Greek and Greek philosophy in Florence from 1456 to 1471. According to Neo-Platonic thought, beauty inspired desire. Desire could lead to lust, sin, and ultimately death, or, controlled by reason, to victorious ascent toward pure transcendent love of God, to a state of internal grace reflected in the outward beauty of the body. From this perspective, *David*'s erotic beauty, grace, and introspection evoked the transformation of desire through reason to a chaste love of God. Donatello's bronze *David,* in short, embodied both the ideal Florentine state and the model Christian citizen. It projected an image of the Medici as humble, courageous, strong, wise, and striving through self-sacrifice for social justice and spiritual salvation.

DONATELLO'S BRONZE *JUDITH AND HOLOFERNES*

In contrast to the completed action of *David, Judith and Holofernes* represents a drama in progress (fig. 109). When Holofernes, Nebuchadnezzar's Assyrian general, was besieging the town of Bethulia, Judith, a wealthy and chaste widow, donned her most elegant clothes and jewels, and pretended to defect to the enemy camp with her maid, claiming to have a plan to help Holofernes conquer her city. Holofernes invited the lovely Judith to a banquet with the intention of seducing her. He soon passed out, having drunk "exceeding much wine, so much as he had never drunk in his life" (Judith 13:20). After commandeering Holofernes' sword, Judith prayed to God for strength, and decapitated him with two blows. She escaped with her maid, taking the bed canopy as a votive offering for God.

Proclaimed a savior of the Jewish people for slaying the Philistine general, Judith had been understood as David's counterpart by a long tradition, beginning with the *Psychomachia* by Prudentius (AD 348–after 405). Just as David's humility contrasted with Saul's pride, her modesty was opposed to Holofernes' arrogance. Like David, she symbolized fortitude and justice, emphasized by her raised, originally gilt sword. Just as David's victory over Goliath allegorized Christ's overcoming Satan, so Judith's triumph symbolized the Virgin's defeat of sin and evil. Judith also embodied chastity, in contrast to the lust and licentiousness of Holofernes, reinforcing her role as a Virgin type. Finally, the Latin inscription once inscribed on the group's pedestal indicated that the Medici understood Judith, like David, as a virtuous protector of Florence: "Kingdoms fall through luxury, cities rise through virtues. Behold the neck of pride severed by the hand of humility." Sometime after the death of Cosimo in 1464, his son Piero added another inscription, probably to commemorate his own victory over the 1466 Pitti-Neroni Conspiracy to wrest control of the government from the Medici: "The salvation of the state. Piero de' Medici son of Cosimo dedicated this statue of a woman both to

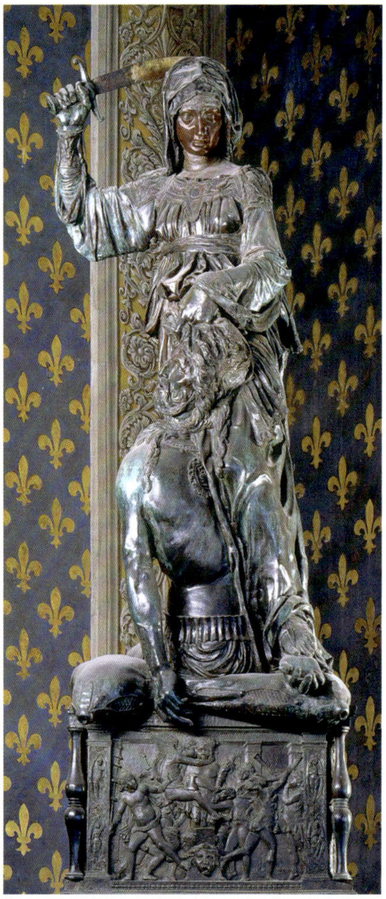

109. Donatello, *Judith and Holofernes,* c. 1455–60, signed, bronze, 7 ft. 8⅞ in. (236 cm), Sala dei Gigli, Palazzo Vecchio.

liberty and to fortitude, whereby the citizens with unvanquished and constant heart might return to the republic." Together the two inscriptions created an image of the Medici as humble, virtuous, strong, and loyal protectors of Florentine liberty.

Donatello represented Holofernes seated on an elaborate cushion dressed in silken shorts, symbols of luxury, his left hand pointing toward the bacchanalia on the base's relief, where infant bacchants enact his licentiousness. The medallion on his back represents a galloping horse, emblem of pride and unbridled lust. Judith's modest drapery, by contrast, evokes her chastity and humility, yet her costume is also elaborately decorated, as mentioned in the Book of Judith. Much as Donatello conceived *Abraham and Isaac* (fig. 27), the figures of Judith and Holofernes are intertwined in a manner that is oddly tender yet murderous. Grasping the tyrant's hair to hold him upright, Judith cradles his head and shoulders against her thigh. Seemingly transfixed, she raises her sword above her head to deliver what we understand—through the visible presence of a gash in Holofernes' neck—to be the second of her two decapitating blows. Two bands of drapery—suggestive of the bed canopy she offered as a votive—encircle Judith's body, one cinched tightly under her breasts, and the other encircling her thighs and legs, binding her to Holofernes. With head bowed, an introspective expression, and lips parted, Judith prays to God for strength, as she triumphs over Holofernes' lust. Neo-Platonically, through reason and faith, she has achieved a transcendent love of God.

However, the position of Holofernes' bearded head, the chest band emphasizing Judith's breasts, and the lower band binding the two figures together raised the issue of female sexuality—a disturbing concept in the Renaissance. A woman's domination of a man also related to several other equally troubling classical and biblical stories, such as Phyllis's enslavement of Aristotle or Delilah's defeat of Samson (Judges 14:5–9). These episodes were sometimes allowed expression at carnival time or in moralizing paintings as examples of unacceptable female behavior intended to reconfirm the patriarchal order.

The Medici Palace garden where the *Judith* stood is known to have contained an ancient herm of Priapus, and in a contemporary poem Judith is threatened with subjugation by "Priapus's weapon" (his erect member). If the poet understood the setting as a garden of erotic love, then Judith also could be interpreted as the proud and arrogant object of desire of chivalric romances or Petrarchan poetry who provoked intense suffering and anguish in her lover. These undercurrents of female sexual empowerment in a society where women almost by definition were expected to be chaste and silent surely accounts for the absence of any subsequent monumental representations of this subject.

Faced with constant threats to their political hegemony and the declining fortunes of their bank, the Medici chose to project their family image through two Old Testament servants of society and God particularly noted for their courage and humility. But by representing David as passive and androgynous and Judith as active and domineering, the Medici risked casting themselves either as sodomites and pederasts or as overbearing sexualized women. Nevertheless, *David* and *Judith* were such potent protectors and symbols of Florence, that, upon the Medici expulsion in 1494, the Second Republic confiscated both works, relocating the former to the courtyard and the latter to the rostrum of the Priors' Palace.

11

WEDDING CHESTS AND BIRTH TRAYS

The decoration of bridal bedrooms constitutes an important aspect of Florentine Renaissance art and serves as an accurate barometer of the anxieties and aspirations of Renaissance married life. Marriage among middle- and upper-class families was primarily an economic exchange. The bride (usually a teenager just past puberty) was regarded as a commodity to be bought or sold for social prestige and financial gain with little concern for her wishes. Whether between friendly or rival families, marriage negotiations were long and arduous. At issue were the size and payment of the bride's dowry in cash or land, and the counter-dowry of the groom (most often a man in his thirties or forties), which usually included the wedding dress, wedding feast, a portion of the bride's trousseau, the decoration of the nuptial chamber in the groom's family palace, and a cash payment at the marriage's consummation. The dowry negotiations continued until each family felt it had extracted maximum advantage from the other, fairly distributed the burdens and gains, and upheld its honor. A signed notarized document and a handshake sealed the negotiations. Later the couple was betrothed in the bride's palace by the exchange of vows and rings. The day the marriage was to be consummated, the groom and groomsmen triumphantly paraded the bride and her trousseau from her family's palace through the streets of Florence to the newly decorated bridal bedroom in the groom's palace. As Matteo Palmieri recounts, brides were "dressed up as much as possible, publicly displayed on horseback, and painted with lascivious cosmetics." With "trumpets calling the people," they were paraded "to jousting fields and circled around the piazzas to show that they are going to lose their virginity." This celebration concluded with a nuptial banquet for the two families hosted by the groom.

SCHEGGIA'S *RECONCILIATION BETWEEN THE ROMANS AND SABINES*

Palmieri fails to mention that the bride's trousseau was usually carried in a pair of painted *cassoni* (wedding chests) commissioned by the groom or male members of his family, such as the two now in a Copenhagen museum (fig. 110). The genre of painted *cassoni* flourished in Florence from about 1370 to 1520, with at least ten workshops producing some ten chests each year. Most have been disassembled to display their long narrative panels as independent paintings, of which more than three hundred still survive. Thematizing the conflicts, rivalries, and disparities in age, social status, and financial condition inherent in most marriages, as well as reinforcing the bride's submission to the dominant patriarchal order, a high percentage of these wedding chests deployed the age-old metaphorical association of love with military conquest by representing scenes of war and peace drawn from mythology, history, or contemporary life. The Copenhagen example depicts Hersilia standing in the center of a city gate pleading for peace between the leaders of two armies, one her father, the Sabine king Tatius, and the other her husband, Romulus, whom she was forced to marry when the Romans raped the Sabine women. She grasps the drawn swords of the two hostile kings, striking a pose personifying Justice, to prevent the Sabine women from being either widowed or orphaned by warfare between their fathers and husbands. So, too, Renaissance brides usually mediated between rival maternal and conjugal families to preserve social and political order.

A *cassone* also evoked sexual conquest, erotic intimacy, and fecundity, for *cassa* (box) was slang for female genitals. A number of wedding chests, therefore, like the Copenhagen pair, explicitly connoted sexual union by the representation of a reclining male and female nude on the underside of the lids.

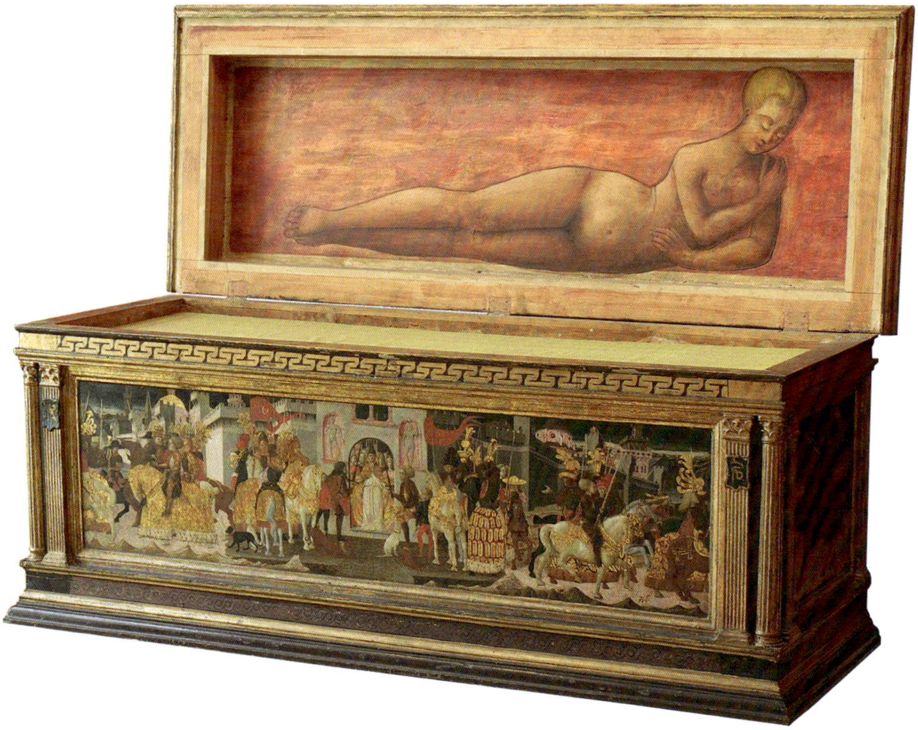

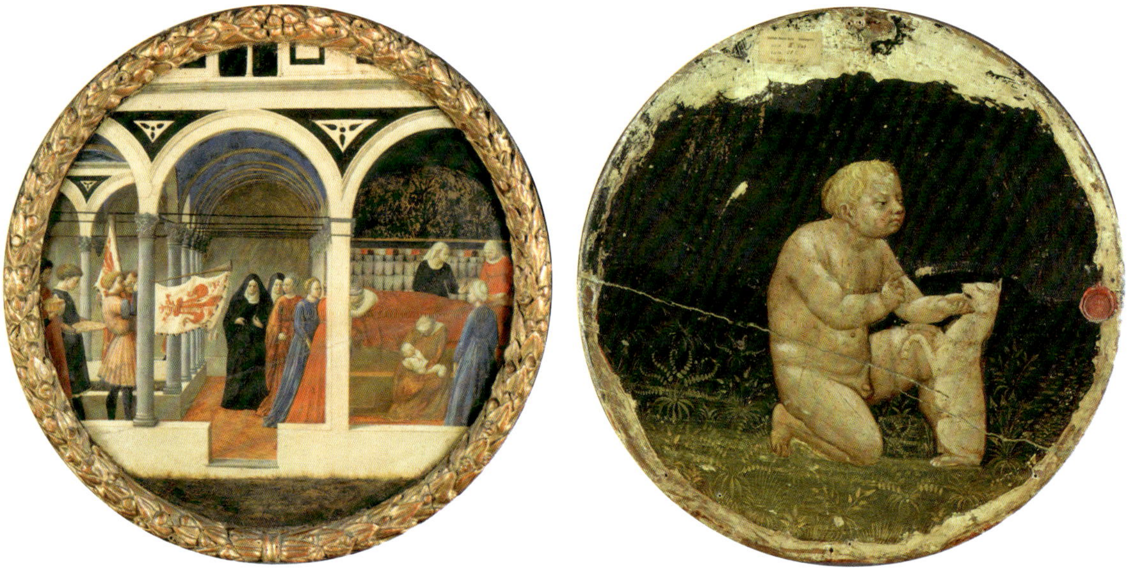

110. Giovanni di ser Giovanni (Scheggia, 1406–86), wedding chest (one of a pair) with *Reclining Nude Woman* and *Reconciliation between the Romans and Sabines* (Ovid, *Fasti* 3.199–228; Livy, *History of Rome* 1.13; Plutarch, *Lives* 2.19), c. 1460, tempera on wood, 21⅝ × 71¼ in. (55 × 181 cm), Statens Museum for Kunst, Copenhagen.

111. Masaccio, *Lying-in of a Florentine Lady* (recto) and *Infant Playing with a Dog* (verso), c. 1428, tempera on panel, diameter 22¼ in. (56.5 cm), 25⅝ in. (65 cm) with frame, Gemäldegalerie, Staatliche Museen zu Berlin.

MASACCIO'S *LYING-IN OF A FLORENTINE LADY*

A young bride's childbirth and her subsequent lying-in produced another important genre of bedroom art commissioned by fathers, friends, and relatives—the *desco da parto,* or birth tray (fig. 111). A recent catalogue records seventy-seven extant birth trays, but many hundreds more must have been produced in the Renaissance. *Deschi*—either round, twelve-sided, or sixteen-sided—commemorated births, served as platters on which to present gifts of food to new mothers, and then continued to function from generation to generation as household serving trays. On the recto of an early example in Berlin attributed to Masaccio, the left two-thirds of the tondo depicts a classicizing courtyard surrounded by a portico with pendentive vaults carried on Corinthian columns modeled on Brunelleschi's Foundling Hospital (fig. 19). From the portico a group of five women, including two nuns, prepares to enter the new mother's bedroom, its walls partially covered with fabric or leather. They are followed by four young men at the left, two bearing gifts, including a birth tray, and two carrying trumpets draped with the insignia of the Florentine republic—a red fleur-de-lis on a white field. The inclusion of the communal heralds, one of whom salutes the newborn with his instrument, as well as the elegant architecture, suggests that the drama is unfolding in the palace of a socially and politically prominent family.

Four servants attend the newborn child, wrapped in swaddling clothes, and the lying-in mother, apparently asleep in her large nuptial bed (called a *lettuccio*). By its similarity to images of the birth of Jesus, Mary, or John the Baptist, the scene has a quasi-religious character, which, combined with the presence of the heralds, may have been intended to evoke the humanist notion that a pious and fecund family was the basis and microcosm of the harmonious, just, and prosperous state.

The versos of the majority of birth trays were decorated with allegories (e.g., Justice), chess boards, family coats of arms or devices, or, most often, one or two nude infants, sometimes winged like angels. On the Berlin example a nude golden-haired male child plays with a dog in a flowering meadow. appropriately evincing fertility and carefree childhood innocence. Yet the infant, silhouetted against the deep blue vault of heaven, gazes into the distance with a serious, knowing, and perhaps even anxious expression as he strokes the pet's chin with his left hand and makes a gesture resembling a benediction with his right.. Thus, the scene might have been intended to evoke the Incarnation (the child) and the necessity of Faith (the dog) to merit the promise of Christ's sacrifice (the benediction) in order to achieve salvation (the sky and the round format).

12

SPALLIERA PAINTING

BOTTICELLI'S *PRIMAVERA*

Walls of bedrooms were often decorated with large narrative panels built into bed headboards or bench backs (*spalliere*), or, as in the case of the renowned *Primavera* by Botticelli (c. 1444/45–1510), hung above the wainscoting at about the height of one's "shoulders" (*spalla;* fig. 112).

When Cosimo il Vecchio moved into his new palace in the mid-1450s, he gave the neighboring old palace to the cadet branch of the family descending from Cosimo's brother, Lorenzo. When Lorenzo's son, Pierfrancesco de' Medici, died in 1476, the old Medici Palace passed to Pierfrancesco's son, the thirteen-year-old Lorenzo di Pierfrancesco de' Medici (1463–1503). Since Lorenzo di Pierfrancesco had not reached maturity, Lorenzo il Magnifico became his cousin's guardian and oversaw his tutoring by two celebrated humanists, Marsilio Ficino and Angelo Poliziano. When Lorenzo di Pierfrancesco turned 19, Lorenzo il Magnifico arranged his marriage on July 19, 1482, to Semiramide d'Appiano (d. 1523) and contributed a dowry of 2,000 florins. Either of the two Lorenzos could have commissioned the *Primavera,* which is first documented in a 1499 inventory hanging in a ground-floor room of the old Medici Palace.

The figural action in the right two-thirds of the composition was derived from Lucretius's *On the Nature of Things* (5.737–40): "On come Spring and Venus, and Venus's winged harbinger [Cupid] marching before, with Zephyr [the West Wind] and mother Flora a pace behind him strewing the whole path in front with brilliant colors and filling it with scents." This right-to-left procession of Zephyr, Flora, Venus, and Cupid enacting the coming of spring would have inspired hope for the bridal couple's fecund and happy union.

But who is the woman in front of Zephyr? In the *Fasti* (5.195–222) Ovid (43 BC–AD 17) explains her identity:

> I who am now called Flora was formerly Chloris [meaning "green"]: a Greek letter of my name is corrupted in the Latin speech. Chloris I was, a nymph of the happy fields.... 'Twas spring, and I was roaming; Zephyr caught sight of me; I retired; he pursued and I fled; but he was the stronger, and Boreas [the North Wind] had given his brother full right of rape.... However, he made amends for his violence by giving me the name of bride, and in my marriage-bed I have naught to complain of. I enjoy perpetual spring . . . the tree is clothed with leaves, the ground with pasture. In the fields that are my dower, I have a fruitful garden.... This garden my husband filled with noble flowers and said, "Goddess, be queen of flowers." Oft did I wish to count the colors in the beds, but could not; the number was past counting. . . . I was the first to scatter new seeds among the countless peoples; till then the earth had been of but one color.

The duo Chloris and Flora thus enact the metamorphosis from the initial greening of the earth in March to earth's full flowering in May as rape becomes a fruitful marriage. This drama related closely to the traditional conception of Renaissance marriages as conquest, capture, and triumph resolving, one would hope, into harmonious union.

Botticelli staged Zephyr's rape from right to left, contrary to a viewer's habitual reading direction, in order to intensify its violence. He heightened the aggression of Zephyr's sharply angled body by various devices: massive wings slicing through the trees; windblown hair; cold and harsh blue-green coloring; knit brow; puffed cheeks; inflated chest; grasping hands; and billowing drapery. Zephyr's onslaught also violently bends three laurels, traditional signs of victory and peace. The laurels were probably intended to recall Lorenzo il Magnifico's newly invented device of the *broncone* (laurel branch) with its motto, "Time Renewed" from Virgil's Fourth Eclogue, signaling the return of a golden age to Florence under his leadership. Seven barely visible green apples around Zephyr's wings also suggest the *palle* on the Medici coat of arms. The laurels' agitation and the apples' unripe color, however, imply that the golden age has not yet returned.

Botticelli represented Chloris fleeing Zephyr's grasping hands with such terror that she too appears airborne and desperate, her drapery agitated, hair disheveled, and backward glance fearful. Chloris's gauzy drapery fully reveals her sensuous body, further stimulating Zephyr's lust. Yet, as the rape reaches its climax, a subtle transformation occurs. Through an oral insemination of sorts, Zephyr blows golden rays of breath into Chloris's mouth. She immediately exhales a stream of flowers. Simultaneously, the gauzy drapery around her legs almost mystically reveals ghostly images of green flowers visible through the fabric's transparency. Her transformation from Chloris to Flora based on word play and Zephyr's *spiritus* penetrating her mouth also recalled the Incarnation, when the Virgin conceived through her ear by the divine Word.

With stunning virtuosity Botticelli transformed the panicked Chloris into Flora, a quintessential image of contentment and fulfillment. In contrast to the violence of Chloris's deflowering, Flora literally blossoms into the embodiment of both the ideal natural order (fertile spring) and the ideal social order (fecund marriage). Indeed, it is almost impossible to distinguish where nature ends and culture begins. Is Flora wearing a wreath around her neck, or is the neckline of her dress exquisitely wrought to resemble a wreath? Is her dress girdled with an actual climbing rose or rather an artfully woven belt? Are flowers embroidered or painted on her dress, or are they real flowers like those she scatters to color the earth?

Just as Ovid's *Fasti* posited marriage as the institutional agent of metamorphosis, so too at the moment of the Incarnation the Virgin Mary became the bride of God. Similarly, Semiramide at her marriage was metaphorically transformed into Flora, the personification of *Florentia* (Florence), the city of flowers, founded, according to legend, on March 25 on the Feast of the Incarnation. Although named after Semiramis, the ancient semi-legendary Assyrian queen famed for her beauty, cruelty, and lust, Semiramide by her marriage has been integrated into the civilized social and political order of Florence under the hegemony of Lorenzo il Magnifico. The seven, now golden, *palle* above Flora's head underline the return of the Medicean golden age. Given the probable date of

112. Sandro Botticelli, *Primavera,* c. 1482, tempera on panel, 6 ft. 7⅞ in. × 10 ft. 3⅝ in. (203 × 314 cm), Uffizi.

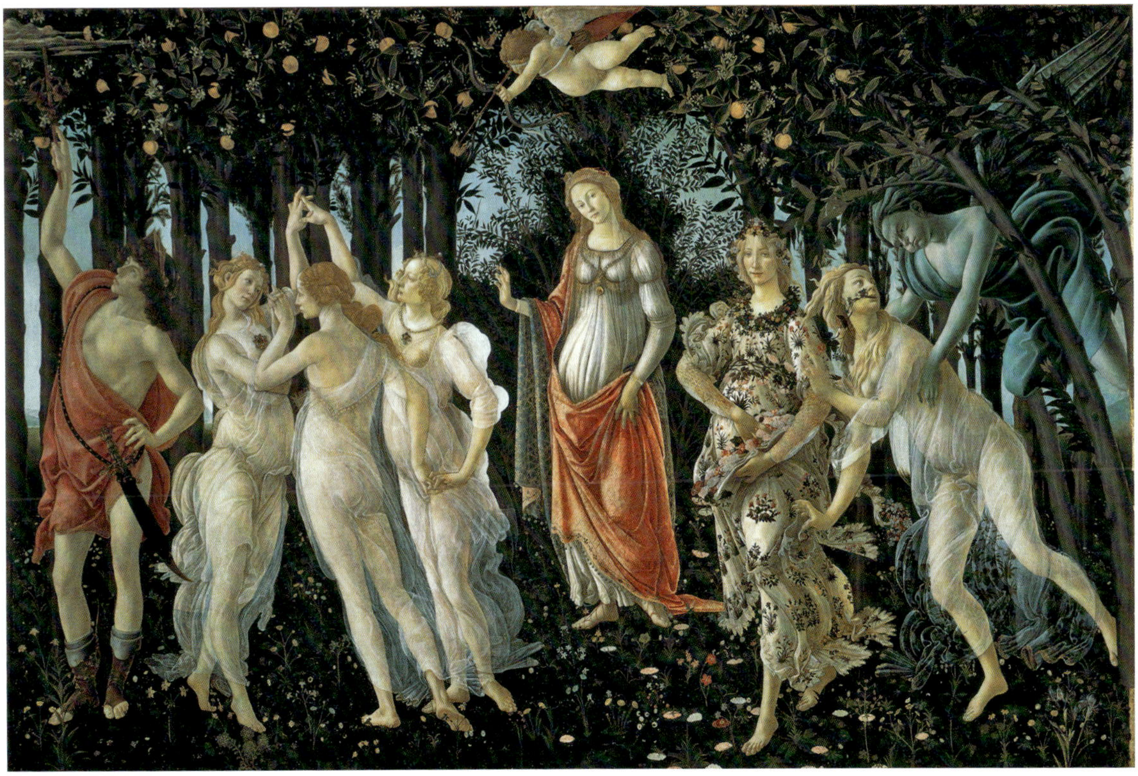

the painting, the advent of the golden age would refer specifically to the peace and prosperity that followed Lorenzo's 1479–80 negotiations with Sixtus IV and King Ferrante I, which defused their hostility toward Florence following the 1478 Pazzi Conspiracy.

The allusion to warfare and the depiction of rape recalled that the painting's central figure, Venus, the goddess of love, was born from conflict. According to the *Theogony* (188–200) by Hesiod (active c. 700 BC), when Cronus, the god of time and agriculture, castrated his father, Uranus, the sky god, Uranus's testicles fell into the sea and mixed with the water's foam to give birth to Venus, who floated ashore on a seashell. Generated from sky and sea, Venus embodied both heavenly and earthly love. As the goddess of April, Venus also exemplified spring and the creative principle of all nature enacted by Chloris and Flora as described by Lucretius (*On the Nature of Things* 1.1–27): "Through thee every generation of living things is conceived . . . for thee the wonder-working earth puts forth sweet flowers." However, silhouetted against evergreen and fragrant myrtle, a classical symbol of matrimony, and framed by a backdrop of stout trees whose branches, heavy with golden fruit, arch over her head to create a primitive shelter, Venus further personified the beginning of social order. She also implied the advent of political order, for in the Renaissance the family was a common metaphor for the ideal state. As Leonardo Bruni wrote, "The first community is that of man and wife from which, when multiplied, comes the republic."

By her gesture Venus welcomes Semiramide and Lorenzo di Pierfrancesco into her (now their) *locus amoenus* (fertile bower). Her costume's white and red fabric, the colors of chaste love, the golden flames of passion trimming her neckline and breasts, the swelling of her womb with love's new life, and the fullness of her breasts to nurture life, all heighten Venus's role as the goddess of terrestrial love. The reverse sky-blue side of her mantle, however, reminds the observer that Venus also personified a celestial planet and spiritual love, and in the Renaissance Venus often stood in for the Virgin Mary.

Cupid flying above Venus's head was derived from *On Agriculture* (10.192–214) by Columella (first century AD): "Now is the time when all the world is mating . . . , the spirit of the world in Venus's revel joins and is headlong urged by Cupid's goads . . . ; hence hills, hence even the whole wide world is celebrating spring; hence comes desire to man and beast and bird, and flames of love burn in the heart and in the marrow rage, till Venus, satiated, impregnates their fruitful members and a varied brood brings forth." Venus's son thus introduces desire into the painting, the force that stimulates carnal love for the procreation of humans, beasts, and birds. But desire's stimulus, as contemporary Neo-Platonists believed, could encompass the extremes of love—from bestial rape motivated by lust to transcendent spiritual love based on reason and faith. Having depicted a blindfolded Cupid shooting his flaming arrows randomly, Botticelli explicitly alluded to the dangers of lust. The leftward movement, however, cued by Venus's gesture and Cupid's arrow, directs the viewer's attention to the three Graces, embodiments of spiritual grace.

Horace in his *Odes* (1.4) described the Graces as the handmaids of Venus: "Keen winter is breaking up at the welcome change to spring and Zephyr. . . . Already Cytherean Venus leads her dancing bands . . . and the comely Graces . . . tread the earth with tripping feet." Seneca (4 BC–AD 65) in his *On Benefits* (1.3) further glossed the Graces as an allegory of the benefits of liberality or, in a Christian context, Charity, defined as *amor dei* (love of God) and *amor proximi* (love of neighbor):

> The Graces are three in number . . . , are sisters . . . , have their hands interlocked . . . , are smiling, youthful and virginal . . . , are clad in loosened and transparent garb . . . , and hand in hand dance in a ring. . . . Why?. . . . For the reason that a benefit passing in its course from hand to hand returns nevertheless to the giver; the beauty of the whole is destroyed if the course is anywhere broken, and it has most beauty if it is continuous and maintains an uninterrupted succession. In the dance, nevertheless, an older sister has special honor, as do those who earn benefits. They are young because the memory of benefits ought not to grow old. They are maidens because benefits are pure and undefiled and holy in the eyes of all; and it is fitting that there should be nothing to bind or restrict them, and so the maidens wear flowing robes, and these, too, are transparent because benefits desire to be seen. . . . Mercury stands with them.

Read from right to left, Botticelli's Graces dancing in a circle perfectly illustrate Seneca's allegory of giving a benefit, receiving it, and returning it to the giver.

But Florentine Neo-Platonists also understood the Graces as embodiments of the three stages of love: first, beauty stimulated love, then love provoked desire, and finally desire achieved fulfillment. In this formulation the figures read from left to right. The left Grace, the only one seen frontally displaying the full range of her charms, personifies beauty. The central Grace, her firm buttocks clearly delineated and one breast exposed, represents desire, and Cupid, the personification of desire, aims his flaming arrow toward her. The rightmost Grace—her body, gesture, and glance configuring a long ascending diagonal—embodies fulfillment. In this sense the trio stands in visual counterpoint to Zephyr (desire), Chloris (beauty), and Flora (fulfillment), but without carnal lust, for, as Seneca tells us, they are chaste virgins. Inspired by a well-known classical sculptural type of the three Graces, Botticelli expressed their chaste spirituality by graceful statuesque bodies dancing delicately in the grass and flowers to some unheard music, their transparent drapery and golden hair cascading in lovely eddies, their long fingers artfully interlacing, and their arms rhythmically patterned.

Although dancing in a circle, two of the graces turn leftward, drawing the viewer's eye to Mercury with his standard attributes of winged sandals, sword, helmet, and caduceus (serpent-entwined staff). As the god of commerce, Mercury evoked the commercial advantages afforded the Medici by a union with the Appiani family, who controlled the Elba iron mines. Therefore, the laurel branch crossing in front of his right foot marks Mercury as the fulfillment of the prosperous Laurentian golden age. As the god of May, Mercury was associated with the winds that blew dead branches from the trees and scattered inseminating seeds. Hence Botticelli depicted him wearing a Renaissance pruning knife and stirring the wind clouds with his caduceus as seeds float down around his boots to inseminate the soil. The painting's dependence on classical texts suggests that Mercury also represents the god of eloquence and reason. Finally, Mercury's red cloak adorned with yellow flames links him to Venus and the passion of love. But what kind of love?

Standing in a posture and gesturing upward in a way already anticipated by the rightmost Grace, Mercury could just as well be clearing away (as opposed to stirring up) the clouds in order to gain an unobstructed view of the heavens and enact his roles as a planetary deity and the messenger of the gods, mediating between heaven and earth. Furthermore, Mercury's caduceus—an ancient symbol of healing and emblem of the medical profession—and the painting's tapestry of identifiable plants and flowers with medicinal properties imply that Mercury represents a *medicus* (doctor or healer), a prefiguration of *Christus medicus* (the healing Christ), who through his love of humankind offered the possibility of salvation to those who, like the three Graces, reciprocally offer their chaste love to each other and to God. Botticelli underlined this point by modeling Mercury on Donatello's bronze *David* (fig. 107), ancestor of Christ and Christ type. Mercury, in short, has subordinated his passion to reason and cleared the clouds (and his intellect) to gaze lucidly at divine truth and justice. As the guide of souls to the underworld, however, Mercury would also have reminded the bride and groom that final transcendent love and ultimate knowledge of God come only through death.

In summary, the painting constructs a Neo-Platonic allegory of love compatible with Christian theology. Beauty (Venus), the source of love, provokes desire. Desire (Cupid) either leads humankind through lust to unbridled carnal passion and animalistic violence (Zephyr), or, through reason and faith (Mercury) to a chaste, pure, and spiritual love of God. Or as stated by Marsilio Ficino's Platonic *On Love* (1469):

> We are born or brought up inclined and disposed toward the contemplative, active, or voluptuous life. If we are disposed to the contemplative life [of reason], we are immediately elevated by the sight of bodily beauty to the contemplation of spiritual and divine beauty. If to the voluptuous life [of lust], we descend immediately from sight to the desire to touch. If to the moral and active life, we continue [chastely] in the mere pleasure of seeing. . . . The love of the contemplative man is called divine; that of the active man, human; that of the voluptuous man, bestial.

Ficino writes only about men, for desire and especially reason were understood primarily as the provenance of men, while women were simply the passive objects of desire. Not surprisingly, therefore, the three winged figures that frame Venus (Zephyr, Cupid, and Mercury), creating Botticelli's Neo-Platonic diagram, are males.

The *Primavera* is one of the masterpieces of Western art. Employing a refined mixture of styles and motifs, the painting is old and new, public and private, theatrical and poetic, chivalric and classic. This stylistic mode exactly paralleled the best contemporary Florentine literature, such as the poetry of Poliziano and Lorenzo il Magnifico, based on a Petrarchan and Dantesque vernacular style refined and purified in the light of classical Latin. Botticelli also quite literally created a visual and aural garden of art, drawing on painting, sculpture, architecture, music, dance, tapestry weaving, dressmaking, agriculture, horticulture, pharmacology, and medicine. He created an equally imaginative intellectual synthesis of poetry, politics, sociology, philosophy, and theology. Fulfilling Horace's famous simile *ut pictura poesis* (as is painting so too is poetry), Botticelli also produced here the first large-scale mythology and the first *poesia* (poetic invention) of the Renaissance.

113

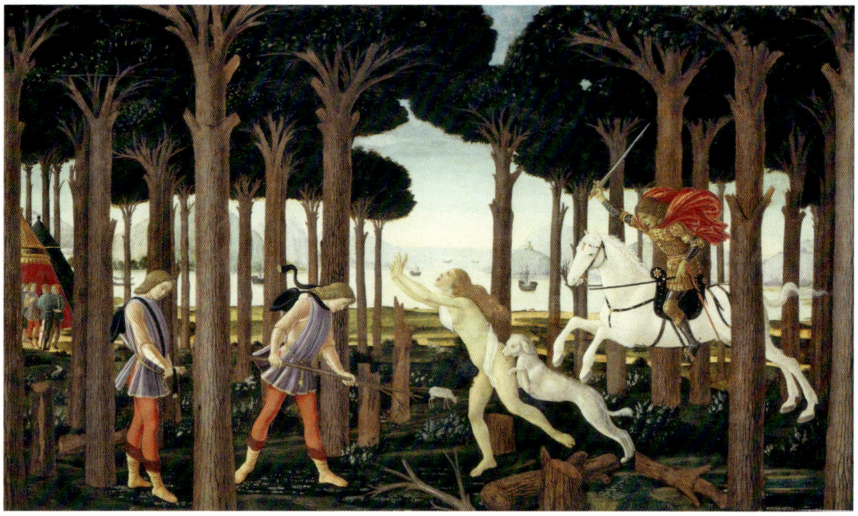

114

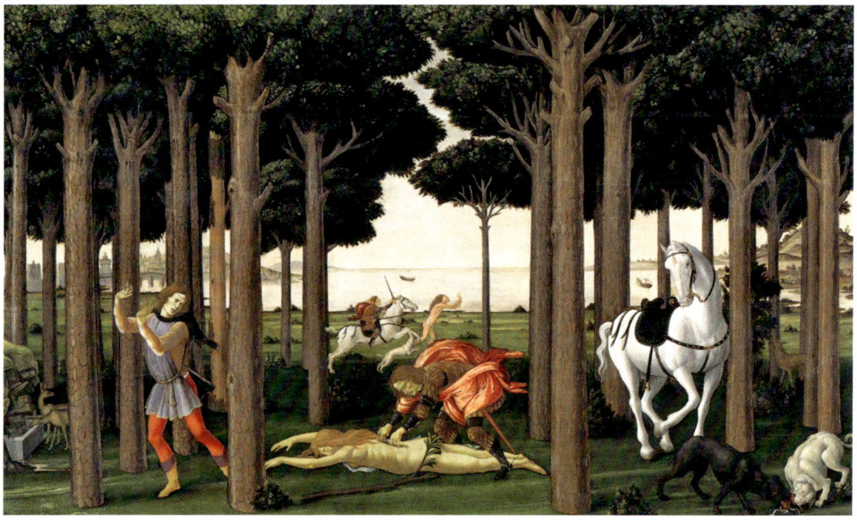

113–116. Sandro Botticelli, *Nastagio degli Onesti* (Boccaccio, *Decameron,* fifth day), 1482–83, four *spalliere* (or less likely *cassoni* frontals), tempera on panel, each 32⅝ × 55⅞ in. (83 × 142 cm), first three in the Museo Nacional del Prado, Madrid, fourth in a private collection.

BOTTICELLI'S *NASTAGIO DEGLI ONESTI*

While Botticelli's *Primavera* constructed an ideal social, political, and spiritual order, his four panels narrating the story of Nastagio degli Onesti, based on the *Decameron* by Boccaccio (1313–75), represented the cultural order seriously disrupted, but ultimately harmonized by marriage (figs. 113–16). The Florentine merchant Antonio Pucci, who earlier commissioned the Pollaiuolo brothers' *St. Sebastian* (fig. 82), ordered these panels for the 1483 marriage of his son Giannozzo to Lucrezia Bini. The Pucci family had been historically of modest social position but became more prominent and prosperous by loyal service to the Medici. Lorenzo il Magnifico acted as the intermediary between the two families in arranging the marriage, accounting for the Medici coat of arms in the center of figs. 115 and 116, flanked by the Pucci and the Pucci/Bini arms. Fig. 113 opens with Nastagio degli Onesti encamped in the woods in self-imposed exile from Ravenna, having been rejected by his more socially prominent ladylove. In seeking consolation, the lovesick Nastagio vacillated between wastefully consuming his inheritance in lavish entertainment of his friends (indicated by the tents and youths to the left) and morbidly contemplating suicide (signaled by the introspective Nastagio standing alone in the dark woods). Squandering love, money, and life grievously upset Renaissance norms of proper social behavior.

Nastagio's reverie is disrupted by the dramatic vision of the knight Guido degli Anastagi of Ravenna chasing down a woman who had long ago rejected him. Anastagi

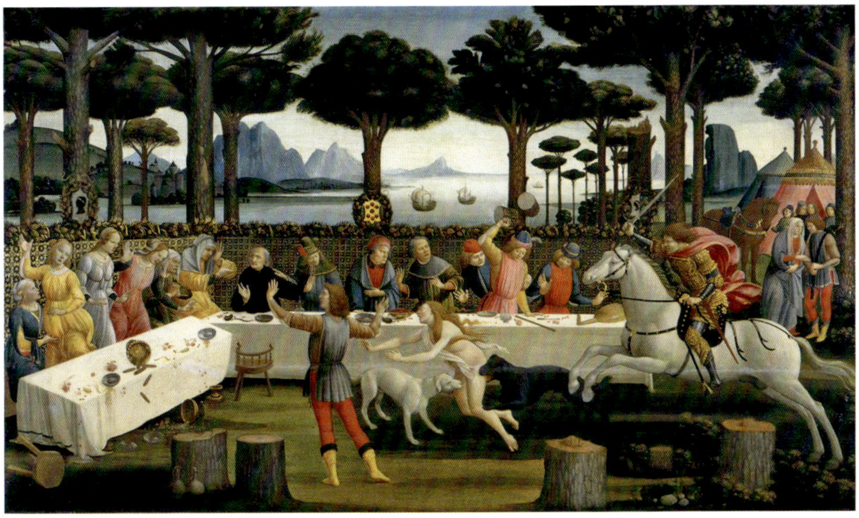

115

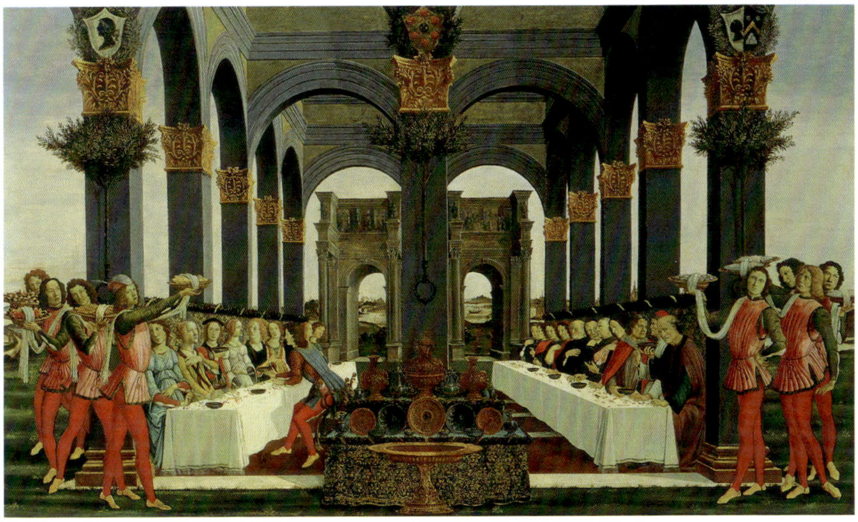

116

had killed himself in despair while his ladylove rejoiced. As punishment for committing suicide and rejecting love, both were condemned for eternity to repeat once a week a chase where Anastagi attacked and stabbed his ex-love in the back, ripped out her cold heart, and fed it to his dogs. Botticelli depicted this drama in the right half of fig. 113 and the center and extreme right of fig. 114.

The artist highlighted the woman by her blatant nudity and central placement framed by trees. The felled trees in fig. 113 allude to Anastagi's frustrated sexual desire and anticipate the woman's evisceration. In fig. 114 the zigzag pattern of light and the phallic limb with its leafy branch, which draws attention to the woman's buttocks, intensify the climax of Anastagi's violent revenge for her unrequited love.

Boccaccio drew a parallel between Nastagio and Anastagi's related love affairs by the similarity of their names and common birthplace, which Botticelli underlined by their similar physiques and physiognomies. Botticelli also gave them related but reversed roles to play. While Anastagi is depicted as the knight of chivalric romance, typically devoted to defending his chaste lady's honor, here he hunts and eviscerates his defenseless lady. Nastagio, scorned by his ladylove for not being sufficiently noble, completely lacks the trappings of knighthood, but like a true knight, he heroically tries to defend the woman with a dry branch in fig. 113. Furthermore, in fig. 114 Nastagio turns away in horror at Anastagi's butchery, his revulsion heightened by the skittish horse to the right. Yet, the aim of Nastagio's "weapon" in fig.

113 and the direction of his fascinated gaze suggest his own ignoble sexual desire.

Classical allusions compound the role reversals. Anastagi's antique garb evokes Mars, and Boccaccio's story was told on Tuesday, *martedi* (Mars's day). The woman's nudity suggests Venus, and Boccaccio writes that the vision reappeared every Friday, *venerdi* (Venus's day). But in the Mars and Venus myth, Venus conquers Mars. Similarly, a man gazing at a nude woman recalls Diana's transformation of the hunter Actaeon into a stag for spying on her bathing nude, which resulted in Actaeon's hunting dogs eating him alive. Yet in fig. 114 the dogs consume the woman, while in the background behind them a deer peacefully nibbles the leaves from a bush. A stabbed woman also evokes the early Roman victim of excessive male desire, Lucrezia, the namesake of the bride for whom these panels were painted. After Sextus, son of the Roman tyrant Tarquin, had blackmailed her into adultery, Lucrezia stabbed herself to prove her innocence. Her suicide led the Romans to revolt against Tarquin's tyranny and to found the Roman republic, forerunner of the Florentine republic. Yet rather than ideal chaste and loyal wives such as Lucrezia, the two women of Boccaccio's tale rejected marriage, thereby destabilizing the social order. Botticelli, in short, has created a disjointed world, a Dantesque hell of sorts, where women scorn love and men become effeminate by allowing themselves to be ruled by their passions.

Yet Botticelli included signs of purgatorial reform: the woods are ordered and well pruned—a version of Eden. In fig. 113 the woman is paired with a lamb, as if she were the innocent victim of Anastagi's savagery. And to the extreme left of fig. 114 two deer drinking at a fountain recall the soul's longing for union with God referred to in Psalm 41:1 ("As the hart panteth after the fountains of water; so my soul panteth after thee, O God").

Taking advantage of the weekly repetition of the gruesome vision to teach his ladylove a lesson, Nastagio invited her and her family to a Friday banquet in the woods shown in fig. 115. He has cut trees to make a stage and decorated the enclosure with garlands of pinecones, seed-bearing signs of regeneration. He has laid out on the tables a feast composed primarily of raw fruits and vegetables, marking Nastagio's cultural progress from savage hunting to civilized agriculture. As the guests feast, the ghastly vision is once again reenacted. But now Nastagio directs the event with rhetorical gestures, as if he were a sovereign presenting a theatrical interlude at a royal marriage feast. The dogs attack the woman with greater cruelty than before, and a felled tree amplifies the threat of Anastagi's drawn sword. However, a sign of marriage pacifies the violence of this fantasy of frustrated sexual desire: Anastagi's sword "impales" (the heraldic term for "joins") Bini's coat of arms with Pucci's.

Nastagio guides the spectacle toward the women's table placed at a right angle to the men's, indicating that the women are still at cross-purposes with their male counterparts. While her companions respond with terror, Nastagio's beautiful young lover (standing in the center dressed in virginal white) gazes attentively as she absorbs the vision's lesson. She raises her left hand to ward off the vision, while making a sign of peace with her down-turned right hand, as if now ready to accept Nastagio's love.

The man dressed in black opposite the empty chair, occupied by Nastagio before the theatrical interlude, represents the panels' patron, Antonio Pucci. His presence suggests that the message of Boccaccio's story was directly addressed to his new daughter-in-law, Lucrezia Bini. No matter that she came from a family of higher social standing, her proper behavior was to submit lovingly to his son Giannozzo.

In fig. 116, an episode not in Boccaccio, all the disruptions of the previous panels are resolved by marriage. Nastagio's father, again in the guise of Antonio Pucci, now sits at the center of the men's table opposite the newlyweds at the women's table. Here he ceremonially exercises his patriarchal authority to socialize his previously antisocial son. Nastagio has been purged of the roles of spendthrift, misogynist, and potential suicide and transformed into a noble husband, just as his bride has been transformed from a parsimonious virgin to a submissive and potentially fecund wife who will ensure the continuity of the Pucci patrilineal line.

Botticelli visualized the harmony and stability of the ideal matrimonial state and social order by his bilaterally symmetrical and perspectivally ordered wedding feast, set in a majestic family loggia. The tables construct the proper patriarchal order by their arrangement in parallel, the men's located on the heraldically superior right side, the women's on the subordinate left side. The foreground display of servants in livery and of silver and gold vessels on the sideboard serves to mark high social status. The servants' presentation of another elaborate course for the feast (sweetmeats?) also alerts the viewer that the bride and groom have now exchanged the cooked for the raw, or culture for nature. Laurel branches of Lorenzo il Magnifico's *broncone* device attached to the foreground Corinthian piers of the loggia and the triumphal arch in the background signal the victory of the Laurentian golden age, of which the Pucci/Bini marriage was a microcosm.

13

PORTRAITS

UCCELLO'S *YOUNG MAN*

About the same time that Alberti cast his self-portrait in bronze (fig. 2), independent painted portraits, emulating late Gothic northern European portraits of sovereigns, first appeared in Florence for palace decoration. About a dozen male portraits dating before the mid-fifteenth century survive. The panel attributed to Uccello in Chambéry (fig. 117) is one of the earliest. All these panels depict a youthful male in profile wearing a Florentine *mazzocchio* (a turban over a wire frame) usually behind a parapet, and all are nearly identical in format and style. The classicizing profile view and, in the case of the Chambéry example, the Roman block letters inscribed on the parapet suggest that these early portraits revived an ancient Roman tradition described by Pliny (*Natural History* 35.2.6–11). He writes that it was customary to display ancestor portraits in homes (he describes sculpted images, but many, now lost, independent painted portraits of individuals were made in antiquity): "In the halls of our ancestors, portraits were objects displayed to be looked at. Wax models of faces were set out each on a separate sideboard. Outside the houses on the walls and around the doorways there were other presentations of those mighty spirits, so that the houses eternally celebrated a triumph." Sallust in his *War with Jugurtha* (4.5–6) also notes that ancient ancestor portraits served as models for descendants to emulate: "Illustrious citizens of the state used to say that the sight of their ancestors' portrait masks fired their hearts with an ardent desire to merit honor . . . [and] that the memory of what others had accomplished kindles in the breasts of noble men a flame that is not quenched until their own prowess has won similar glory and renown."

The inscription on the parapet of the Chambéry likeness, "the end does all," implies that the life one lived would determine the soul's fate at the final reckoning. It indicates that this and the other early Florentine portraits were also created as examples of virtue for family and descendants to follow. The style suggests what virtues were being extolled. Projected against a dark background, the flattened and regularized features, lacking individual character traits, evoke intelligence by formal lucidity, prudence by visual balance, and moral perfection by geometrical abstraction. These portraits, in short, appear to communicate that through reason, discretion, and faith one might attain youthful immortality.

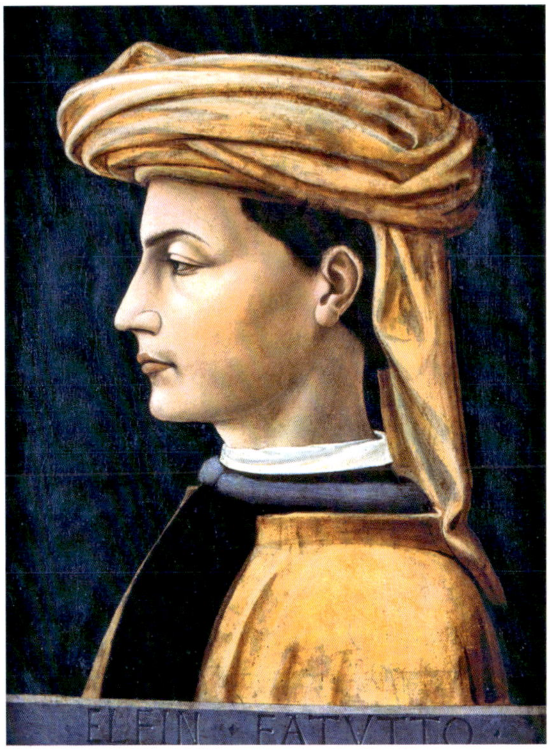

117. Paolo Uccello?, *Portrait of a Young Man,* c. 1435, tempera on panel, 18½ × 14⅛ in. (47 × 36 cm), Musée des Beaux-Arts, Chambéry.

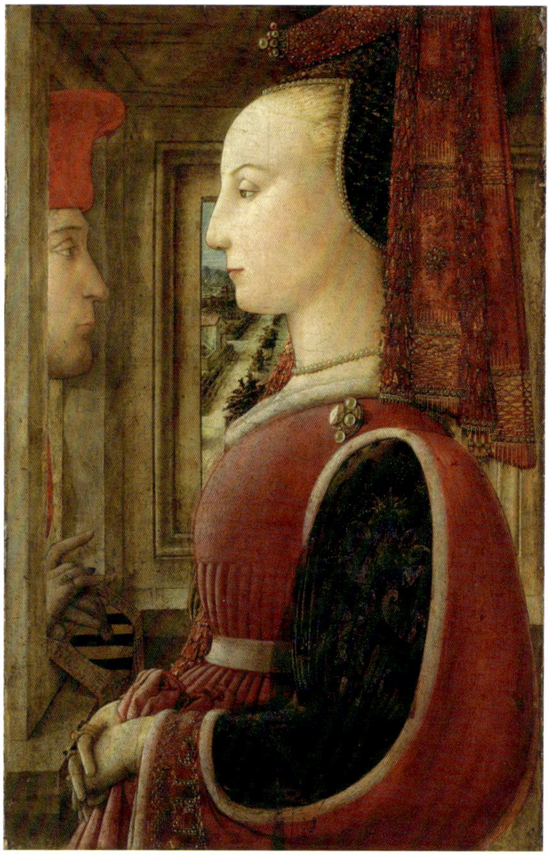

118. Fra Filippo Lippi, *Portrait of Lorenzo Scolari and Angiolo Sapiti,* c. 1438–45, tempera on panel, 25¼ × 16½ in. (64.1 × 41.9 cm), Metropolitan Museum of Art, New York. The shadow of the man's profile on the window casement may refer to the belief that painting originated by tracing on walls the shadows of loved ones to preserve their memory (Pliny, *Natural History* 35.15–16).

FILIPPO LIPPI'S *LORENZO SCOLARI AND ANGIOLA SAPITI*

Portraits of women communicated very different messages. In the earliest surviving example by Filippo Lippi (fig. 118), the Scolari coat of arms draped over the windowsill implies that the painting commemorated the 1436 marriage of Lorenzo di Ranieri Scolari (1407–78) to Angiola di Bernardo Sapiti. The bride is wearing five rings; a pleated fur-trimmed *giornea* (outdoor dress) with a cuff embroidered *Lealtà* (Loyalty) in gold and pearls; a brocaded *gamurra* (indoor dress) in velvet pile seen through the open sleeve of the *giornea;* a diamond and pearl shoulder brooch; a pearl necklace; a cap edged in pearls; and a pearl-encrusted headdress topped with a head brooch. The half-length format displays to full advantage her costly adornments. Together with the vineyard seen through the window, they very likely constituted a substantial part of the groom's counter-dowry. Apart from publicly displaying the bride's exchange value, the painting may also have been intended to record the groom's counter-dowry (legally always his property) to forestall future disputes with in-laws. In any case, the bride's many pearls also symbolized purity, perfection, and chastity. Her high plucked forehead, bleached hair, unblemished features, and swollen womb projected an image of pure, nubile, fertile youth, as well as fashionable beauty, enhancing her husband's wealth, lineage, and social standing.

Florentine sumptuary laws strictly limited to six years the time that a wife could wear the adornments of the counter-dowry. As formulated in 1472: "[Women] may wear necklaces, veils, and two brooches—one for the head and one for the shoulder. And these they may wear for three years from the day of their marriage. After the said three years, they may wear the necklace alone and only one brooch for another three years, and after that it is entirely forbidden to wear any of the above said things." Unless the bride is breaking the law, Lippi's painting probably dates to within three years of the 1436 marriage.

Women were subjected to such strict legal controls because men mistrusted the power of their beauty. Women were considered emotionally unstable and seductive like Eve, eager to lead men to perdition if not controlled by supposedly rational and trustworthy men. This misogyny was well expressed in a 1433 governmental decree certifying the election of the new administrators of the sumptuary laws. The laws were needed, the decree stated, to

> restrain the barbarous and irrepressible bestiality of women who, not mindful of the weakness of their nature, forgetting that they are subject to their husbands, and transforming their perverse sense into a reprobate and diabolical nature, force their husbands with their honeyed poison to submit *to them.* These women have forgotten that it is their duty to bear the children sired by their husbands and, like little sacks, to hold the natural seed which their husbands implant in them, so that children will be born. For women were made to replenish this free city and to observe chastity in marriage; they were not made to

spend money on silver, gold, clothing, and gems. For did not God Himself, the master of nature, say this?

Quite logically, then, Lippi boxed the bride within a room, doubly framed her by the picture frame and the window casement, and doubly subjected to her husband's gaze from within the painting and from outside, when the image hung in the Scolari Palace.

Men's rigid control of daughters and wives can also be gauged by what Lippi chose to censor out of the bride's representation: action, anatomical torsion, gesture, and emotion. Because it was widely feared that a woman's gaze could pierce a man's heart and provoke lustful passion, Lippi even placed the bride and groom's heads at different heights to avoid an exchange of glances. The costume also tends to desexualize the bride's body, and her covered ears, sealed lips, and vacant gaze suggest that she hears, speaks, and sees no evil. In summary, Lippi depicted the bride as a tightly closed (perhaps pregnant) container of seeds, a vessel of Scolari lineage. He also displayed her dowry of virtue expected of all wives: beauty, modesty, loyalty, obedience, and silence.

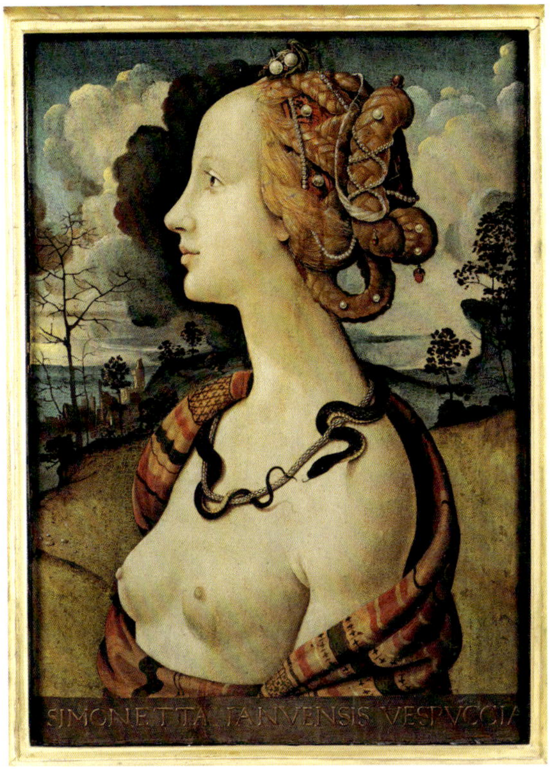

119. Piero di Cosimo, *Cleopatra,* c. 1480, tempera on panel, 22½ × 16½ in. (57 × 42 cm), Musée Condé, Chantilly.

PIERO DI COSIMO'S *CLEOPATRA*

A popular saying captured the largely misogynist conception of Renaissance women: "Women are [cynical] saints in church, [evil] demons in the house, [spying] owls at the window, [talkative] magpies at the door, and [lustful] goats in the garden." Four and a half decades after Lippi's double portrait, Piero di Cosimo (1462–1521) gave visual representation to this misogyny in his *Cleopatra* of c. 1480 (fig. 119). Cleopatra (69–30 BC), the queen of Egypt, was the supreme exemplar of an independent and ambitious woman, noted "for her greed, cruelty, and lust" (Boccaccio, *Famous Women* 88.1), who exploited her beauty for wealth and power. The artist depicted Cleopatra as an immoral, bare-breasted, and seductive temptress. She is ostentatiously adorned in exquisite silk, a sumptuous gold necklace coiled with an asp (suggestive of both her manner of dying and her evil spirit), luxurious pearls and gems interlaced within her serpentine hair, and a demonic animal-like head brooch. The barren ground, dead tree, and storm clouds connote the emotional turmoil and destructive passion that such a woman could provoke in men by vanity, artifice, deceit, and lust.

This may be the work painted for Francesco Giamberti da Sangallo (1404–80), whose portrait Piero di Cosimo painted, which Vasari described as "a very beautiful head of Cleopatra, with an asp wound around her neck." If so, the inscription identifying the subject as Simonetta [Cattaneo] Vespucci of Genoa (1453–75) was added to the parapet when the work was purchased by the Vespucci family in 1586.

However, it has recently been argued (not wholly convincingly) that the inscription is original and that the work is an idealized posthumous portrait of Simonetta commissioned by Lorenzo de' Medici (il Magnifico) to commemorate the platonic love of his brother, Giuliano. Under this interpretation, the negative symbols (barren ground, storm clouds, dead tree) suggest the tragic premature death of Simonetta, the asp almost biting its tail symbolizes immortality, the gold necklace (*catena,* or chain) and string of pearls (*vespaio,* or hair net) pun on her Cattaneo and Vespucci lineage, and her nudity evokes Neo-Platonic desire and transcendent love. This radically different interpretation points to the ambiguity of women's position in society and the difficulties of iconographical analysis.

MINO DA FIESOLE'S *PIERO DE' MEDICI*

The marble bust of Piero de' Medici, Cosimo il Vecchio's firstborn son, by Mino da Fiesole (1429–84) represents one of the earliest Florentine portraits to suggest a unique persona and psyche by characteristic features such as a knit brow, and anatomical movement by the turn of the head and eyes (fig. 120). Inspired by classical portraits, and medieval and early Renaissance portraitlike reliquaries of saints, such marble busts began to appear in great numbers in Florence at mid-century. It is documented that many, such as the bust of Matteo Palmieri (fig. 1), were placed over interior or exterior palace doorways, but many others (perhaps fig. 124) must have been displayed on "separate sideboards" or pedestals, just as Pliny's description of ancestor busts indicated.

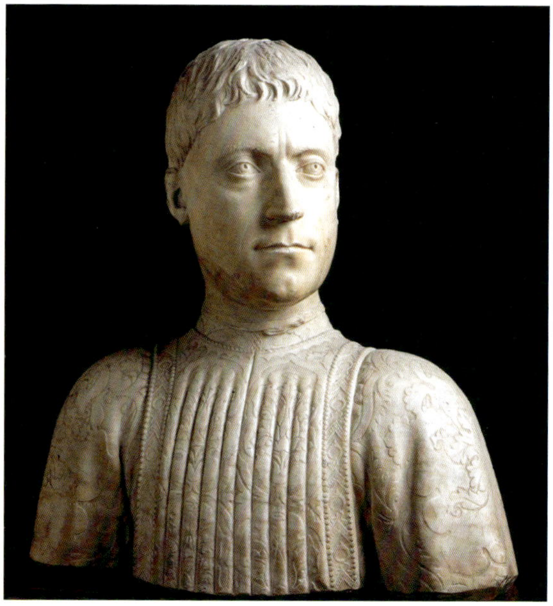

120. Mino da Fiesole, *Piero de' Medici,* signed and dated 1453, marble, 21⅝ in. (55 cm), Bargello.

BOTTICELLI'S *WOMAN AT A WINDOW*

Lippi's double portrait (fig. 118) and Mino's marble bust (fig. 120) inspired the palace setting and the individualized likeness of Botticelli's *Woman at a Window* wearing a white cap over a chignon, gemless necklace, white *camicia* (undergarment), red *gamurra,* and sheer *guarnello* (cotton duster; fig. 121). Illuminated by a biforal window and silhouetted against an open door and an angled shutter, the woman looks out at the viewer. One hand rests on the window frame, and the other holds a handkerchief over a swelling, perhaps pregnant, womb. While presented as a prosperous and fertile housewife, she is the first woman in Florentine portraiture to appear less as an emotionless commodity of exchange and more as an engaging, inquisitive, and intelligent individual.

BOTTICELLI'S *MAN HOLDING A MEDALLION OF COSIMO IL VECCHIO*

In his nearly contemporary *Portrait of a Man Holding a Medallion of Cosimo de' Medici (il Vecchio)* Botticelli created an even more vivid presence of a figure in three-quarter profile dressed in Florentine fashion of the era (fig. 122). Gazing directly at the viewer, the man displays, with highly individualized hands, a bronze profile portrait medallion inscribed "Great Cosimo de' Medici, first father of his country." The unknown man was probably a relative or supporter of the Medici, holding up for emulation the *vir virtutis,* Cosimo il Vecchio.

Seemingly natural outdoor light falls diagonally from the upper left, and the young man stands within an expansive landscape, his body enlivened by the undulating shores of a river or lake. While embedded within nature, he appears superior to it, dominating the distant trees and hills, which are viewed from a great height. Similarly, by placing his subject's head mostly above the high horizon and silhouetting it against the sky, the artist has located him within the objective world while creating the illusion of elevated and pious thoughts, presumably about the civic and family virtues exemplified by Cosimo il Vecchio.

LEONARDO'S *GINEVRA DE' BENCI*

Ginevra de' Benci (1457–c. 1520), daughter of Amerigo de' Benci (after 1431–before 1474), a wealthy Florentine banker and Medici supporter, was married on January 15, 1474. Her husband, Luigi Niccolini (c. 1441–1505), a member of a Florentine cloth-weaving family, was active in politics, and a recent widower almost twice Ginevra's age. Her portrait (fig. 123) was almost certainly commissioned by the poet and humanist Bernardo Bembo (1433–1519), the Venetian ambassador to Florence from 1475 to 1476, for his device with a laurel and palm is represented on the verso. But why would Bembo, living in Florence with his wife, commission a portrait of another man's wife twenty-four years his junior? The reason can only be his Platonic love affair with Ginevra, which was commemorated in about a dozen extant love poems of the 1470s by Cristoforo Landino, Alessandro Braccesi (1445–

1503), and Naldo Naldi (c. 1439–1520), all humanist literati of the Medici circle. Lorenzo il Magnifico and his brother Giuliano's Platonic love for the married women Lucrezia Donati (1449–1501) and Simonetta Cattaneo—the former celebrated in Lorenzo's poetry, the latter in Poliziano's 1478 *Poetry for the Joust [of 1475]*—had sparked the vogue for such chaste chivalric love affairs in precisely these years. They in turn emulated Dante Alighieri (1265–1321), who extolled his lover, Beatrice, in the *Divine Comedy,* and Petrarch, whose lyric love poems were addressed to his lover, Laura.

Fundamental to Petrarchan love poetry, derived in turn from such classical poets as Catullus (c. 84–c. 54 BC), Propertius (c. 50–c. 15 BC), and Tibullus (c. 55–c. 19 BC), was the existence of an actual beautiful woman who provoked the lover to write poetry—often exaggerated, idealized, and clichéd—in praise of her beauty and virtue. It was also important that the woman be married or otherwise unattainable. Her inaccessibility provoked intense longing and emotional turmoil in the poet, ranging from utter ecstasy for her slightest sign of notice to abject despair for the smallest slight. The poet's feelings for his lover, in short, expressed the torments of Neo-Platonic love. Her beauty and gaze could arouse his physical senses and plunge him into the emotional depths of lust. By contrast, her virtue and honor could awaken his reason and lift his soul to glimpse the divine, as in Dante's *Paradiso,* where Beatrice symbolized divine wisdom. The intense emotion provoked by the lover's beauty was understood as equivalent to poetic imagination and the lover as a symbol of his poetry, poetry based on true emotional experience, but creatively transformed into art. Leonardo understood these conventions perfectly and set out to prove that his image of Bembo's Platonic lover was the sign of *his* creative imagination, the very sign of painting itself, derived in his case from portrait rather than poetic traditions.

Leonardo, for example, embraced the hairstyle, out-

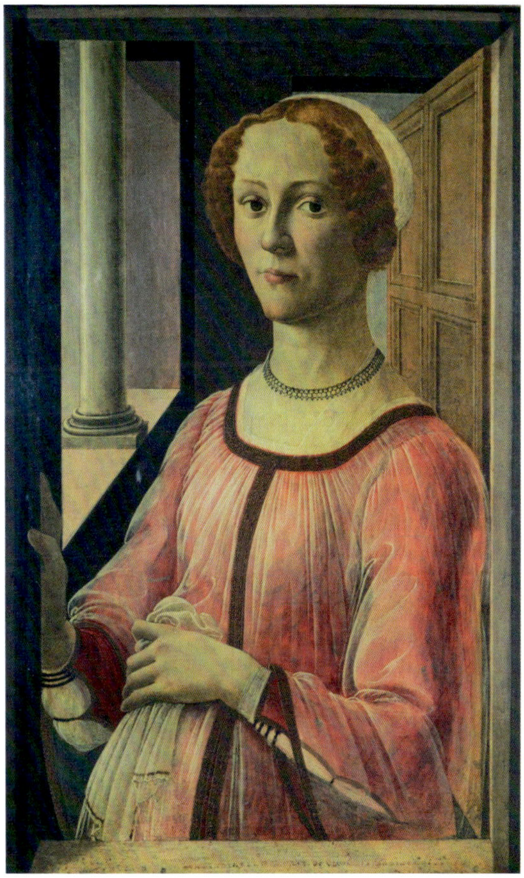

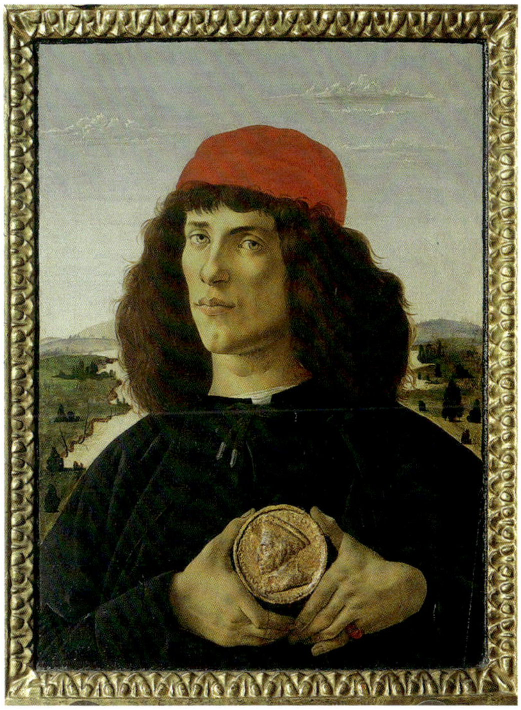

121. Sandro Botticelli, *Portrait of a Woman at a Window,* c. 1470–75, tempera on panel, 25⅞ × 16⅛ in. (65.7 × 41 cm), Victoria and Albert Museum. The seventeenth-century inscription on the windowsill identifying her as Smeralda Bandinelli is probably incorrect.

122. Sandro Botticelli, *Portrait of a Man Holding a Medallion of Cosimo de' Medici (il Vecchio),* c. 1475, tempera on panel, 22⅝ × 17⅜ in. (57.5 × 44 cm), Uffizi. The bronze medallion that Botticelli imitates in gesso was cast about 1465 to commemorate the Florentine government's posthumous conferral on Cosimo of the title *pater patriae* (see chapter 5).

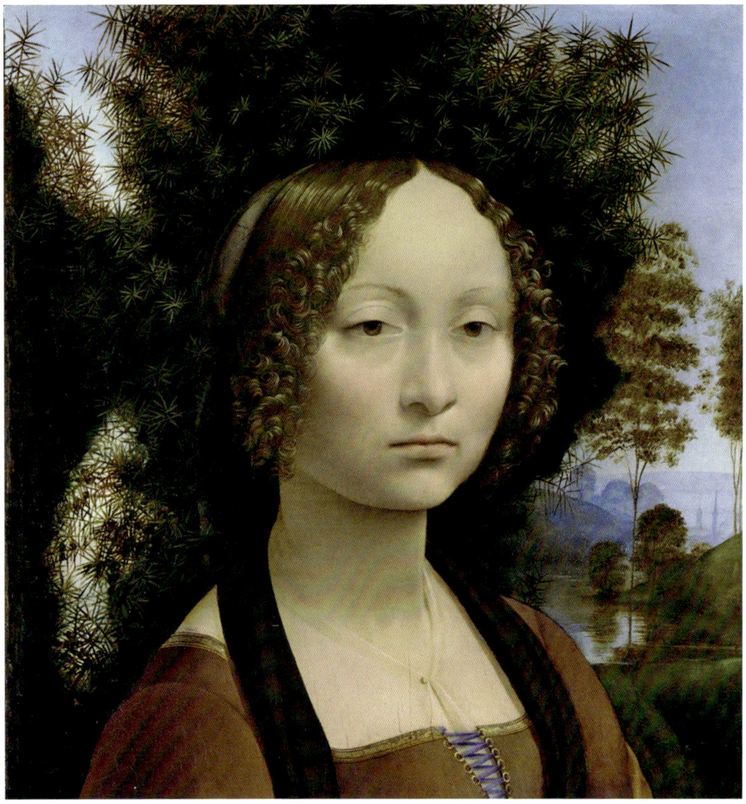

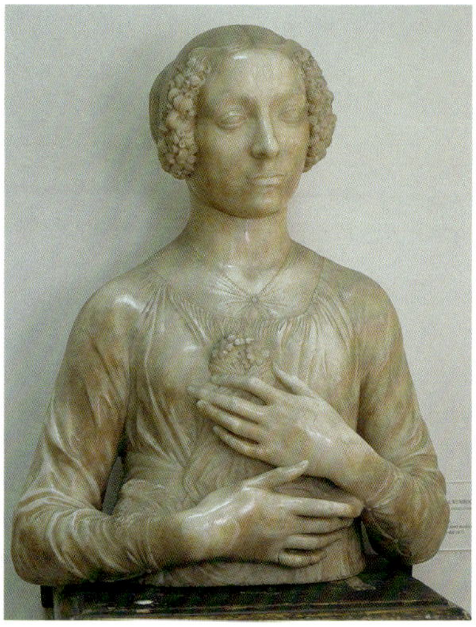

123. Leonardo da Vinci, *Portrait of Ginevra de' Benci,* c. 1475–76, oil on panel, 15 × 14⅝ in. (38.1 × 37 cm), National Gallery of Art, Washington, DC. Originally half-length, the painting was cut by about one-third at the bottom, reducing it to bust-length.

124. Verrocchio, *Woman with Flowers,* c. 1475, marble, 23⅝ × 18⅞ × 9⅞ in. (60 × 48 × 25 cm), Bargello.

ward glance, three-quarter profile, and half-length of Botticelli's *Woman at a Window* (fig. 121) and the landscape setting of the *Man Holding a Medallion of Cosimo il Vecchio* (fig. 122). He also cited the strikingly similar woman represented in a marble bust by his master, Verrocchio (fig. 124). A drawing of hands by Leonardo in Windsor Castle demonstrates that, before *Ginevra de' Benci* was cut down in size at some later date, Ginevra held flowers in her hands much like Verrocchio's sculpted image, perhaps as a sign of her fresh beauty or as a symbolic pledge of love. Equally important for Leonardo's revolution in perception were the portraits of such northern painters as Petrus Christus (c. 1410–75/76), whose work was known to have been in the Medici collection. These northern examples were also painted in oil, a technique that appears to have made its first appearance in Florentine portraiture with Leonardo's *Ginevra de' Benci.* Leonardo's portraits in oil allowed him to modulate psychological expression, surfaces, and light with much greater subtlety than in previous egg tempera portraits, as evident, for example, in Ginevra's extraordinarily sparkling and graceful curls. With such a highly developed ability to activate surfaces, Leonardo could then exaggerate the geometrical regularity of Ginevra's features and the aloofness of her bearing, transforming her into an even more perfect and inaccessible beauty.

In the late Middle Ages and early Renaissance, plants had long been accurately represented in botanical treatises for proper identification and correct use in pharmacology. Yet nothing within this tradition matches the accuracy of Leonardo's portrayal of juniper, let alone juniper viewed so convincingly through filtered light. While alluding to Ginevra's name, the juniper (*ginevra*) also delineates her personality. As a traditional symbol of chastity, the halolike juniper heightens her prickly aristocratic demeanor and transcendent virtue. The distant church within the deep landscape likewise underlines her unapproachable and unassailable moral rectitude. Yet the landscape's advanced demonstration of aerial perspective and reflected light—far more convincing than the landscape in the almost exactly contemporary Pollaiuolo brothers' *St. Sebastian* (fig. 82)—paradoxically sets Ginevra into a world that is realistic and accessible. By transforming a real woman into a transcendent work of art Leonardo stakes his claim to being an artist-poet fulfilling Horace's simile *ut pictura poesis.*

14

DEVOTIONAL WORKS

Devotional paintings and sculptural reliefs, designed as nonliturgical objects of domestic meditation, prayer, instruction, and aesthetic enjoyment, constituted one of the most popular genres of Renaissance art. Although documented in many different rooms of private and communal palaces, at least one would have hung in most bedchambers, usually the most lavishly decorated room in any palace, where spouses would have spent most of their time together.

By far the largest percentage of devotional images represented the Holy Family—sometimes with various other saints, often just the Virgin and Child—the supreme model of the virtuous and pious family. The Virgin exemplified the bride's expected humility, obedience, and chastity, and the infant Jesus fostered her desire to produce and raise beautiful children, especially males. Joseph demonstrated the groom's responsibility to love, protect, and support his family. And for the spouses' children, an image of the Holy Family inspired them to behave civilly, respect their parents, and prepare for their adult roles as parents. Although nonliturgical in function, devotional images, like altarpieces, also taught the essential tenets of Christian theology and offered hope for salvation. Finally, the four fifteenth-century *tondi* of the Holy Family that are documented in the Priors' Palace indicate that images of the Holy Family also served the priors as mirrors of the ideals of good government. The Holy Family, in short, presented a microcosm of the ideal social, religious, and political order.

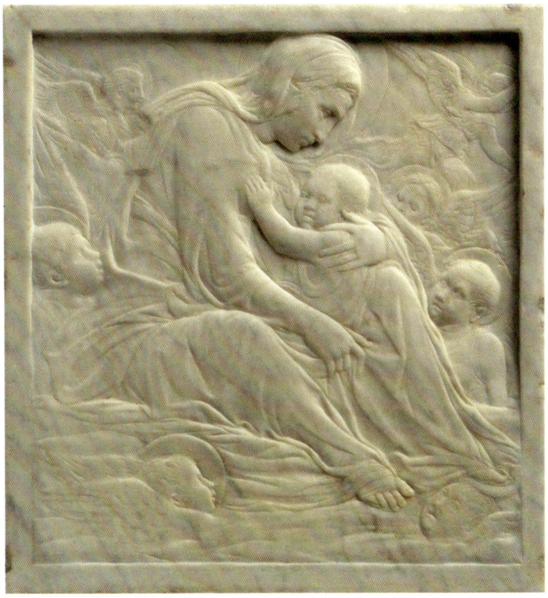

125. Donatello, *Virgin and Child with Seven Cherubs (Shaw Madonna),* c. 1430–32, marble, 13¼ × 12⅝ in. (33.5 × 32.2 cm), Museum of Fine Arts, Boston.

DONATELLO'S *SHAW MADONNA*

Donatello's early *Shaw Madonna* depicts the Christ Child leaning against his mother's raised thigh grasping her breasts, while the Virgin enfolds him in her embrace (fig. 125). The crossing diagonals of their limbs, torsos, and heads, and the sweeping folds of drapery further animate this image of tender, nurturing love. Yet Jesus appears distressed, his expression intensified by the anxious faces of the cherubs and the frantic action of the angel at the upper right. The Virgin with her bowed head and shaded eyes seems sadly introspective, akin to some seer of classical antiquity on whom she was probably modeled. The work's pervasive disquiet expresses the figures' foreknowledge that Christ must die to redeem original sin and nurture humanity.

Donatello derived his composition from a traditional type known as the Madonna of Humility depicting the Virgin seated on the ground. His Virgin, however, sits on clouds, transforming this small delicate work into a mon-

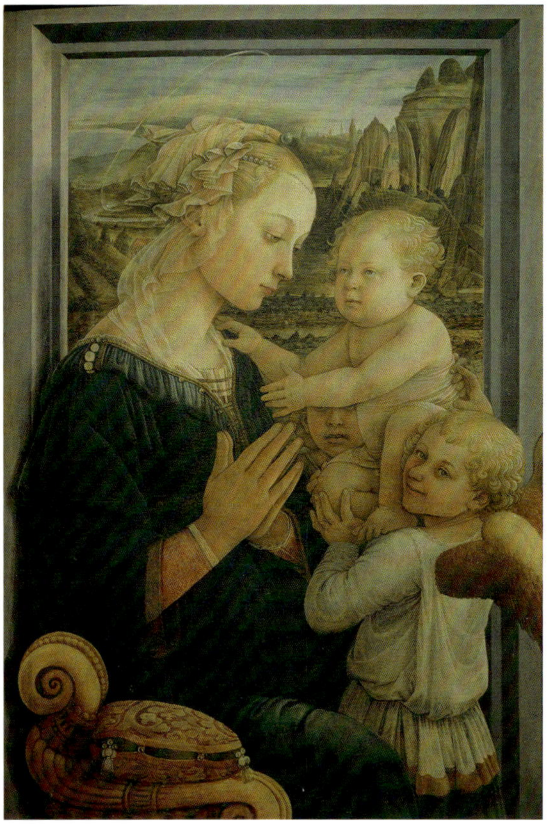

126. Fra Filippo Lippi, *Virgin and Child with Two Angels,* 1460s, tempera on panel, 36¼ × 25 in. (92 × 63.5 cm), Uffizi.

umental celestial vision that conveys the momentous consequences of Christ's destiny. The disparity in scale between the Virgin and the cherubs magnifies the Virgin's stature, befitting her role as the embodiment of the earthly Church, a role underlined by the square format and medium (marble). Yet by seating her triumphantly in heaven on a throne of clouds within a circular arrangement of haloed angelic heads and representing her in shallow, almost ethereal relief, Donatello also evoked her spiritual perfection and her role of mediator between earth and heaven.

FILIPPO LIPPI'S *VIRGIN AND CHILD WITH TWO ANGELS*

In his *Virgin and Child with Two Angels* the Carmelite monk Fra Filippo Lippi took a different approach, emphasizing the Virgin's earthy reality (fig. 126). The Virgin sits before an open palace window on a backless Renaissance chair with an embroidered cushion. The landscape accentuates the delicate lines of her unblemished features, long neck, and elaborate coiffure. Her bleached, braided hair has been twisted into a chignon intertwined with ribbons and pearls and covered with a gauzy veil, deftly tucked to form a series of tight folds before cascading down her neck. The white linen *camicia* that all Florentine women wore as an undergarment edges her neck and wrists. Over the *camicia* she wears a rose *gamurra* with long tight sleeves and a laced bodice. Over the *gamurra* she has donned a high-belted blue *giornea* whose neckline is trimmed in gold piping and pleated ruffles and fastened at the shoulders with pearl buttons. Any Florentine would have recognized this stunning woman as a Florentine bride wearing the expensive clothing and jewelry that constituted her dowry. Seemingly pregnant, dressed for outdoors, and meditative, she would also have been understood as a recently married woman prepared for church, one of the few places women were allowed to be seen in public.

The transparent halo, however, reveals her to be the enthroned Virgin. The wings on the impish urchin boldly insinuated between her legs identify him as an angel. He and a companion support the chubby haloed Christ Child reaching toward his mother while looking heavenward. The Virgin neither touches nor looks at her son, but glances downward with hands in prayer as signs of humility and piety, fundamental female virtues. Her seeming pregnancy further suggests that the Virgin is being presented with a vision of Christ before his birth, inwardly contemplating his humanity and divinity, just as the young bride for whom this painting was probably commissioned might have imagined her first child.

Various symbols accentuate the figures' divinity. The panoramic God's-eye view of the world transforms the window through which it is seen into a *fenestra caeli* (window of heaven), one of the Virgin's many epithets. The enclosed vineyard below the Virgin's chin evokes the *hortus conclusus,* sign of the Virgin's virginity and purity, and the light-filled cloud above her head recalls the Incarnation based on Ecclesiasticus 24:6. The rocky cliffs and the vineyard allude to Christ's sacrifice and the Eucharist; the river, baptism; and the distant city near a bay, the safe haven of the new Jerusalem to which the soul is guided by the Virgin, the *stella maris* (star of the sea). Far more than Donatello, Lippi emphasized the humanity of the Virgin, but then subtly transformed her through symbols into the Queen of Heaven.

BOTTICELLI'S *MADONNA OF THE MAGNIFICAT*

Botticelli painted his *Madonna of the Magnificat* as a *tondo,* a challenging but popular format symbolizing the cosmos and divine perfection (fig. 127). The *tondo* also represented the most perfect window onto the material world, for natural vision was conceived as a cone of light rays focused in the eye, and early Renaissance mirrors were generally round. By its very shape, then, the painting's format implied mediation between spirit and matter.

Like Lippi, Botticelli expressed the humanity of the life-size Virgin and Child by seating them before the stone sash of an open palace oculus giving onto a broad valley with a stream, symbolic of baptism. But Botticelli emphasized their divine natures by surrounding them with five radiant angels, two crowning the Virgin the Queen of Heaven, and two supporting an inkwell and book. The figures' exquisite fabrics, decorated with golden thread, are colored shades of red, white, ultramarine, and gold—suggestive of love, purity, heaven, and divinity. At the top, a glowing sun bathes the sacred figures in the aura of divine illumination.

Botticelli elegantly adapted the Virgin's posture to the circular format as she leans forward on her gold throne to embrace her son. As the embodiment of Wisdom, she dips her quill pen into the inkwell to inscribe the two texts from the Old and New Testaments announcing the end of the old dispensation and the beginning of the new. A standing angel leaning forward to embrace his two companions echoes her action to round out the composition. The infant Jesus holding a pomegranate with his mother likewise bends forward to indicate the Word he has just made flesh. He points specifically to the word characterizing his mother's greatest virtue, *humilitas* (humility). As in Lippi's devotional image, the Virgin's humble downward gaze and the Christ's poignant upward glance allude to their mediation between earth and heaven. Similarly, while the figures' close-knit actions of crowning, caressing, writing, and pointing unite them in earthly purpose, their actions have been transmuted into spiritual grace by the lyrical line and harmonious tones.

In classical antiquity the pomegranate was the attribute of Persephone, queen of the underworld, who was allowed to spend half of each year on earth, bringing in her wake spring and summer. The pomegranate, therefore, came to symbolize the Resurrection. Containing a multitude of seeds within a single strong husk, it also suggested the Church filled with the faithful, who, like seeds, were offered the possibility of regeneration. Finally, the sun and the crown associate the Virgin with John's account in Apocalypse 12:1–5: "And a great sign appeared in heaven: A woman clothed with the sun, and . . . on her head a crown of twelve stars . . . And she brought forth a man child, who was to rule all nations with an iron rod: and her son was taken up to God and to his throne." Botticelli thus evoked the fullness of Christian time: the Incarnation, the Resurrection, and the Second Coming at time's end.

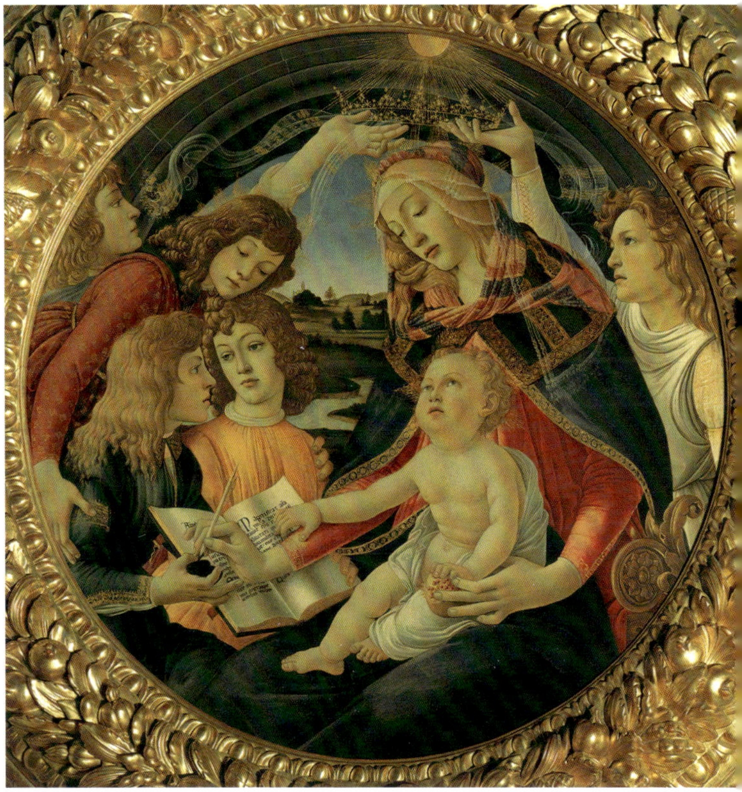

127. Sandro Botticelli, *Madonna of the Magnificat,* c. 1480–81, tempera on panel, diameter 46½ in. (118 cm), Uffizi. In the inscription on the book's left page (from Luke 1:68–79) Zachary prophesies John the Baptist's role as Christ's precursor; in the opposite inscription (from Luke 1:46–55, called the Magnificat) the Virgin glorifies the Lord.

MICHELANGELO'S *MADONNA OF THE STEPS*

In discussing Michelangelo's *Madonna of the Steps,* Giorgio Vasari astutely recorded that Michelangelo "wished to counterfeit the manner of Donatello" and that "he acquitted himself so well that it seems as if by Donatello's the earthly Church. The cubic throne also related to one of the Virgin's many epithets, *virgo super petram* (Virgin seated on a stone), indicating that Mary embodied the rock-solid Church founded on Christ, the cornerstone. In his 1493 Advent sermon, which Michelangelo may well have heard, Girolamo Savonarola, the fiery Dominican priest from S. Marco, also used stone as a metaphor for Christ and the Church: "The rock signifies the faithful Christians, square and stable in their faith. . . . The first rock is Christ the foundation of the Church. . . . The first period [of Christian history] is the primitive Church of living rock, Christians solid in their faith. These stones were made with the chisel and well squared and well fitted together with very strong cement. . . . The cornerstone was Jesus Christ, who joined two walls together, our Church and that of the Jews."

The Virgin tenderly embraces her Herculean son and lifts her drapery for him to nurse, an action emblematic of the nurture offered to the faithful by the Church. Her love is also thematized by the energetic children, two of whom at the top of the stairs caress each other, while the two below playfully tug at the Virgin's veil.

The Christ Child, however, has fallen asleep and turned his head from his mother's breast. Both his sleep and his dangling right arm suggest his redemptive sacrifice by recalling scenes of the Descent from the Cross, the Pietà, or the Man of Sorrows. As in Donatello's relief, the Virgin's sibylline scale and sober introspection allude to her foreknowledge of Christ's fate, and her veil, to which the children draw attention, commonly signified Christ's shroud.

Despite Michelangelo's insistence on solid corporeality, the stairway signaled divine transcendence by evoking the Virgin's common epithet "stairway to heaven" popularized by the *Book of the Stairway to Paradise* (Florence, 1477, 3rd ed. 1491). The treatise described Jacob's dream of a heavenly ladder with angels descending to earth and ascending to heaven (Genesis 28:10–22) as a prefiguration of the Virgin into whose womb the Holy Spirit descended to bring a Savior into the world so that the faithful could ascend to Paradise. Given this context the "children" become angels and the center of the composition configured as a circle, a sign of spiritual perfection.

Michelangelo, in short, captured through symbols and complex visual counterpoint the dualities of Christian theology concerning the Church's mediation between earth and heaven.

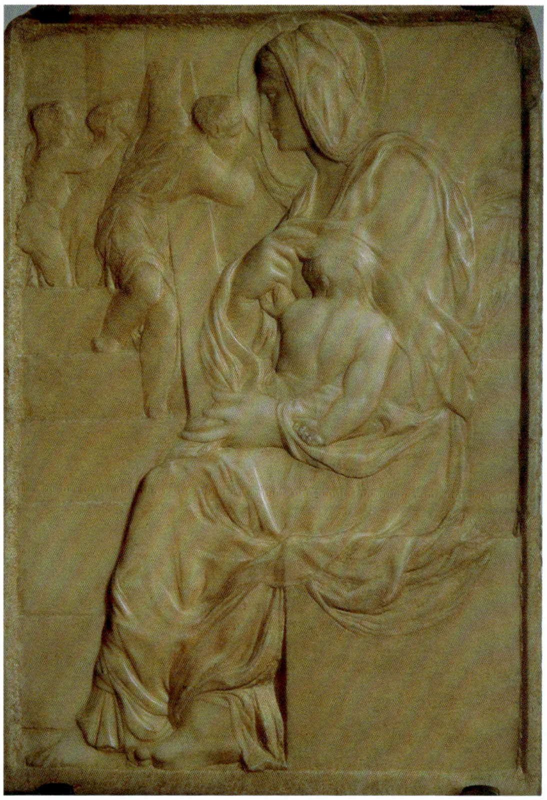

128. Michelangelo, *Madonna of the Steps,* c. 1491, marble, 21⅞ × 15¾ in. (55.5 × 40 cm), Casa Buonarroti. Carved when he was a precocious youth living within the Medici household, the relief may have been executed as a gift to decorate the Medici Palace.

hand, save that there may be seen in it more grace and more design" (fig. 128). Indeed, Michelangelo's choice of subject matter, flattened relief, sibylline Virgin, and meditative tone attest to his inspiration from Donatello (fig. 125).

But differences, rather than similarities, are more evident. Instead of a composition of short crossing diagonals concentrating attention at the center, Michelangelo composed his relief along two long crossing diagonals, defined by the Virgin's left leg and by the stair's balustrade, that divide his work into two unequal counterbalanced halves. While Donatello transformed the Virgin and Child into a celestial vision, Michelangelo emphasized the dense corporeality of the figures and hard stoniness of the throne, stairway, and wall to symbolize

PART II

FLORENCE

under the Second Republic

1494–1512

15

HALLS OF STATE

Palazzo Vecchio, II

SALA GRANDE, I

After the expulsion of the Medici on November 9, 1494 (the Feast of S. Salvador), Girolamo Savonarola, prior of the Dominican monastery of S. Marco, assumed leadership of a theocratic government that rewrote the Florentine constitution, modeling it on that of Venice. It featured a Great Council of some fifteen hundred citizens and an executive *Signoria* composed of eight priors and the standard-bearer of justice. To house a council of this size, the Sala Grande, modeled on the Venetian Sala del Maggior Consiglio, was built with exceptional speed just east of the Priors' Palace between 1495 and 1496 by Antonio da Sangallo the Elder (c. 1460–1534), Cronaca (1457–1508), and Baccio d'Agnolo (1462–1543; see figs. 129 and 179). A tribune and loggia framed by two windows in the center of the longest east wall of this enormous, slightly trapezoidal hall accommodated the *Signoria.* An altar framed by four windows was located directly opposite the tribune on the west wall.

Savonarola's increasingly puritanical and apocalyptic style of preaching and governing soon alienated the Florentine oligarchy, and his defiance of papal authority resulted in his excommunication. He was arrested by the government, tortured until he confessed to heresy, and burned at the stake in the center of the Piazza della Signoria on May 23, 1498.

Four years later, in 1502, Piero Soderini (1452–1522) filled the leadership vacuum left by the demise of the charismatic Savonarola when he was elected standard-bearer of justice for life. He appointed Niccolò Machiavelli (1469–1527), famed author of *The Prince* (1513), as his vice chancellor and secretary of state. To commemorate the Medici expulsion from Florence on the Feast of S. Salvador, the Soderini regime commissioned a marble statue of the Savior in 1502 from Andrea Sansovino for the top of the *Signoria*'s loggia, but it was left incomplete when the artist moved to Rome in 1505. In 1503 and 1504 the regime also commissioned two huge wall paintings to flank the tribune. They were to feature two notable Florentine military victories in order to inspire civic patriotism and promote Machiavelli's new civic militia for the ongoing and so far unsuccessful campaign to recapture Pisa after its revolt from Florence in 1494. Indeed, Pisa would be defeated only in 1509, after a fourteen-year struggle. In 1503 Leonardo da Vinci was contracted to depict the Battle of Anghiari of 1440 at the right of the tribune, and the next year Michelangelo was commissioned to fresco, on the left, the Battle of Cascina of 1364.

Leonardo's *Battle of Anghiari*

From chronicles of the battle near Arezzo and Leonardo's many surviving preparatory drawings, it appears that the artist designed a three-part composition. The main body of Florentine forces fought the enemy on the far right, while on the left the Florentine reserves prepared to charge across a bridge. In the center near the bridgehead, the opposing commanders engaged in the climactic moment of the battle. Abandoning the commission to work for the ducal court in Milan, Leonardo completed only the central section. The well-known drawing (c. 1603) by Peter Paul Rubens (1557–1640) in the Louvre is the most spirited of many replicas (fig. 130).

Leonardo structured the group using the standard convention of opposing diagonals created by two knights dueling on rearing horses, a formula with roots in classical antiquity used repeatedly throughout the Middle Ages and Renaissance, including Uccello's *Battle of S. Romano* (figs. 99 and 100), as we saw in chapter 8. But Leonardo enormously enlivened his composition by showing the two commanders screaming and their horses biting each other with teeth bared, nostrils flared, eyes bulging, bodies strained, manes agitated, and legs locked. On the right the Florentine commander, Micheletto Attendolo (c. 1390–1451), grips the Milanese standard with both hands as it begins to break. Immediately behind him, his second in command, Francesco Sforza, mounted on a rearing and whinnying horse, raises his sword and

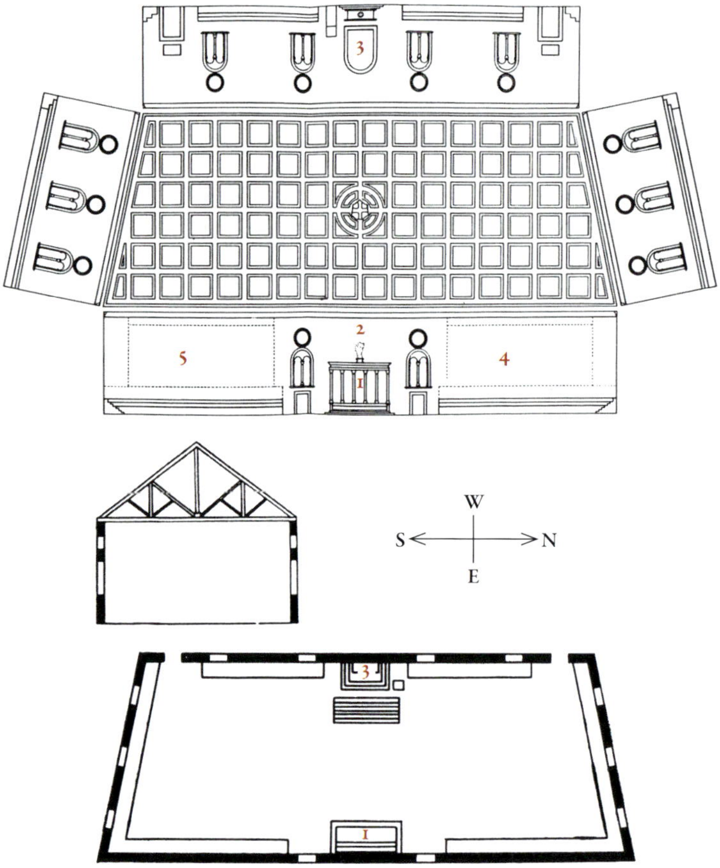

129. Antonio da Sangallo the Elder, Cronaca, and Baccio d'Agnolo, Sala Grande (reconstruction), 100 × 40 × 20 *braccia* (185 ft. 2 in. × 72 ft. 8 in. × 38 ft. 3⅞ in. or 56.44 × 22.15 × 11.68 m): 1 *Signoria's* tribune, 2 Andrea Sansovino's *Savior,* 3 altar with the *St. Anne Altarpiece* by Fra Bartolomeo (1471–1517) (fig. 136), 4 Leonardo's *Battle of Anghiari* (fig. 130), 5 Michelangelo's *Battle of Cascina* (fig. 131).

130. Peter Paul Rubens, partial copy after Leonardo, *Battle of Anghiari on June 29, 1440 (SS. Peter and Paul's Day),* c. 1604, black chalk, brown ink, gray and white heightening on paper, 17¾ × 25 in. (450 × 634 cm), Louvre. The drawing freely reproduces the battle's climax, the *Battle for the Standard,* of an unfinished, lost fresco (27 ft. 3 in. × 65 ft. 7⅜ in. [8 × 20 m]) of 1503–6 planned for the left side of the *Signoria*'s tribune on the east wall (fig. 129, no. 4).

131. Aristotile [Bastiano] da Sangallo (1481–1551), copy after Michelangelo, *Battle of Cascina on July 28, 1364 (Feast of St. Victor),* 1542, oil on panel, Earl of Leicester Collection, Holkham Hall, Norfolk. The grisaille painting reproduces the central section of a cartoon, *Sounding the Alarm,* for an unexecuted fresco (27 ft. 3 in. × 65 ft. 7⅜ in. [8 × 20 m]) of 1504–5 planned for the right side of the *Signoria*'s tribune on the east wall (fig. 129, no. 5).

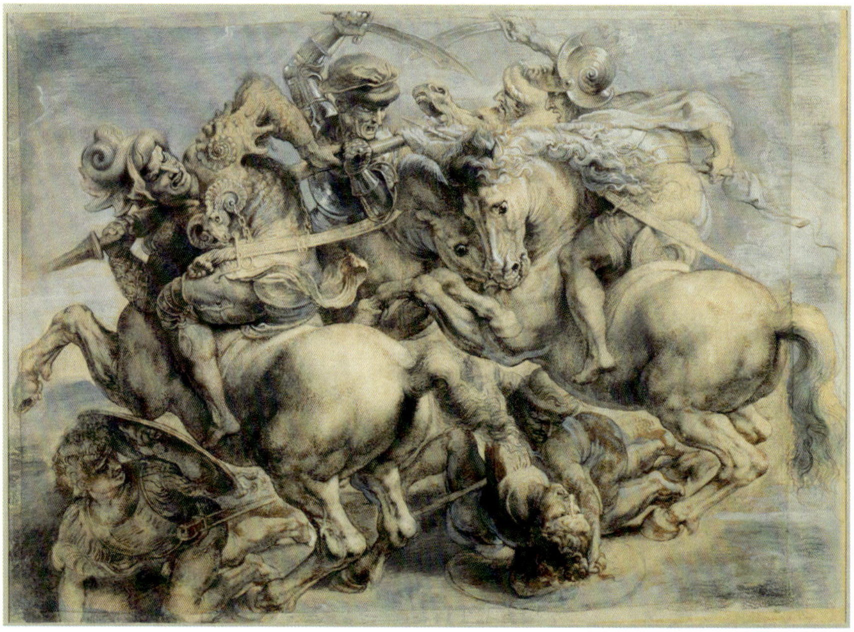

shouts as he parries the impending blow of the Milanese commander, Niccolò Piccinino (1386–1444).

To the far left, Piccinino's son, mounted on a rearing horse parallel to the Florentine commander's horse, awkwardly grips the standard with both hands in a wrenched posture. His body echoes, albeit awkwardly, that of the Florentine commander, but his horse turns its head inward, while Attendolo's horse turns its head outward, suggesting the potential for two similar, but opposite spiraling movements. Leonardo thematizes this potential movement by the double-helix design of the conch shells and ram's horns that decorate the shoulder, helmet, and breastplate of the son's armor.

Although the outcome of the battle has not yet been decided, Leonardo indicated that the Florentines will triumph. His visual cues include the strong right-to-left diagonal impulse of the two foreground horses toward the *Signoria*'s tribune and the contrast between the angular, contorted, and grimacing body of Piccinino's son and the fluid, controlled, and authoritative figure of the Florentine commander. The implicit victory was also underlined by a Florentine soldier about to dispatch a Milanese soldier on the ground under Attendolo's horse and by the defeated Milanese soldier cowering under his shield under the son's horse.

Michelangelo's *Battle of Cascina*

Michelangelo also seems to have planned a three-part composition with the Pisan army marching up the Arno Valley from the left, the Florentine forces caught unprepared for battle as they are bathing in the Arno River in the center, and the Florentines engaging the Pisans on the right near the tribune. He completed only the full-scale cartoon (drawing) for the central section, however, before abandoning the commission to work in Rome for Pope Julius II (r. 1503–10). The cartoon is lost but known from a grisaille painting by Aristotile da Sangallo in England (fig. 131). It shows a frieze of mostly nude Florentines who have been languidly relaxing on the riverbank but now are desperately dressing for the decisive battle toward the right. The scene provided an ideal opportunity for Michelangelo to demonstrate his superb command of classicizing nude male anatomy in the most widely varied postures imaginable. So rich was the demonstration that Benvenuto Cellini (1500–1571) called the cartoon "a school for the world." And, indeed, it was widely mined for ideas by nearly all following Renaissance artists and is generally considered one of the points of departure for Mannerism, a style that tended to emphasize aesthetic qualities over narrative content.

When the Medici returned to power in 1512, the Second Republic was abolished and the Sala Grande was used as a tax office and barracks. During the last Florentine republic (1527–30) the room was again used for its original purpose, but the Great Council was eliminated forever when the Medici returned definitively to power under Duke Alessandro (1511–37).

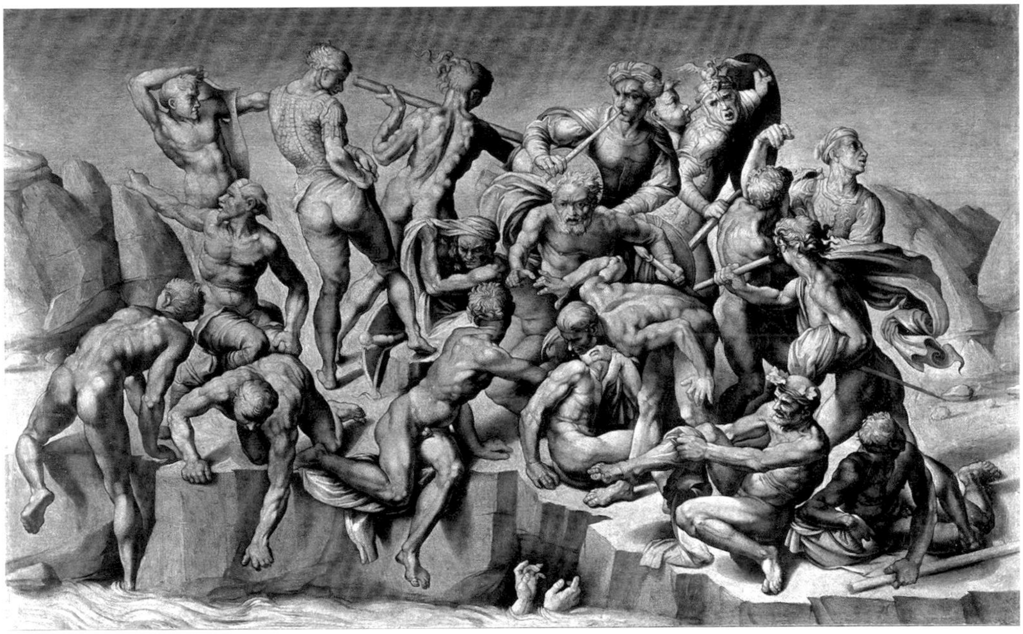

16

FREESTANDING PUBLIC SCULPTURE

MICHELANGELO'S *DAVID*

When the lantern of the cathedral's dome neared completion in 1463, the wool manufacturers' guild returned to the buttress-figure project (discussed in chapter 2) and commissioned a giant terracotta *Hercules* (now lost) from Agostino di Duccio (1418–before 1488) to complement Donatello's 1410 terracotta *Joshua* on the north tribune. The result was apparently satisfactory, for in 1466 Agostino was commissioned to execute another colossal figure, probably a David, but this time in marble from a block quarried in Carrare in 1464. For help with the technical difficulties, much greater in stone than clay, he appears to have turned to the aging Donatello; when Donatello died shortly afterwards, Agostino abandoned the marble block. A decade later, Antonio Rossellino attempted to complete the commission, but in 1477 he too gave up in defeat. In 1501 the guild commissioned Michelangelo to transform this supposedly ruined block into his *David* to serve as a buttress figure on the north tribune (figs. 132 and 133).

The cathedral's *Hercules* relief (fig. 108) served as one of Michelangelo's sources, just as it had for Donatello's bronze *David* (fig. 107). The similarity in stance, placement of arms, and turn of the head indicate that Michelangelo, like Donatello, intended to combine David and Hercules, a conflation justified by the nearly identical significance of the mythological and biblical heroes. Both killed tyrants, saved nations, protected liberty, embodied fortitude, and prefigured Christ.

But as the first freestanding marble nude on this scale since antiquity, Michelangelo's *David* presented difficult technical problems of design and execution, which the artist solved by studying in Rome several ancient freestanding life-size or over-life-size marble figures derived from Polykleitos's *Doryphoros* (fig. 5). However, he deviated from Polykleitan norms for his own expressive purposes. He created a lankier figure to combine the classical athlete with the lean adolescent David of the Florentine visual tradition. Although the state of the "ruined" marble block may have left few options, Michelangelo also gave *David* an unusually wide stance, much like the image of Hercules on the city's civic seal. He also diminished the expression of forward movement characteristic of classical *contrapposto* by projecting the non-weight-bearing left foot over the edge of the pedestal ahead of the weight-bearing foot. This less dynamic stance supported a narrative moment different from previous Florentine images of David, all of which had depicted Goliath's severed head at the hero's feet, the battle over. Here David—watchful and wary, his slingshot behind his back, not yet at the ready—sizes up the Philistine giant before the battle. To highlight the etymological meaning of David as "strong of hand," Michelangelo enlarged *David*'s hands and rendered their tendons and veins more prominently than in classical prototypes. He also exaggerated *David*'s head, perhaps to correct for optical foreshortening when seen high on a cathedral tribune buttress, but surely also to emphasize his intellect and reason as he calculates his plan of action for the momentous conflict ahead. In addition, Michelangelo turned from the Greek athlete to Roman imperial busts to revive the features of the classical leonine personality, expressed by bushy flamelike hair, fierce penetrating eyes, and knit brow (fig. 134). This expression further associated David with Hercules, the prototypical lion man, and suggested that David's reasoning would soon metamorphose into ferocious action. Finally, Michelangelo emphasized David's manliness beyond classical examples by rendering his pubic hair flamelike, similar to the hair on his head. Such emphasis on male virility could allude not only to David's strength, but to Christ's humanity and spiritual vitality as well.

But David's virility could equally have served as a metaphor for the artistic prowess of Michelangelo, just reaching the first peak of his artistic powers at age twenty-nine. In fact, three lines of poetry that Michelangelo wrote on a preparatory drawing for the statue now in the Louvre—"David with the sling / and I with the bow / Michelangelo"—demonstrates that the artist personally identified with David's strength and reason. Just as David defeated Goliath with his slingshot, so Michelangelo triumphed over the "ruined" marble with his bow. The bow *(arco)* of the drawing's inscription referred either to the bow that sculptors had used since antiquity to spin a drill to penetrate marble or to bowed calipers used to make proportional transfers from small models to large blocks of stone. In either case, the word also called to mind the common phrases *arco della schiena* (backbreaking work) and *arco dell' intelletto* (mental labor), evoking both the mental planning and the physical exertion that contributed to Michelangelo's victory.

Upon Michelangelo's completion of the *David* in January of 1504, a *parlamento* of twenty-eight citizens versed in art was called to advise on the work's placement. Suggestions included the north tribune buttress or the front steps of the cathedral, the central arch of the Priors' Loggia, and the rostrum or courtyard of the Priors' Palace. The rostrum was chosen, displacing Donatello's *Judith and Holofernes* (fig. 109), which was moved to the west arch of the Priors' Loggia. The new site might suggest that the artistic community desired a closer viewing position, where the overwhelming originality and authority of Michelangelo's achievement could be fully appreciated. But it is more likely that Piero Soderini, the standard-bearer of justice, engineered the *parlamento* and guided its outcome to exploit the *David* as a symbol of his regime's desperate need to promote itself as the strong and just defender of republican liberty against a trio of threats: the French, who had briefly conquered most of Italy in 1494; the Spanish, who had become the chief rivals of the French for control of Italy; and the Medici, who were maneuvering to return to Florence following their 1494 expulsion. Furthermore, after eight years of warfare, the Florentines had still failed to recapture Pisa.

The relocation of Michelangelo's *David* from the cathedral to the Priors' Palace altered the work's meaning in the same way that the significance of Donatello's marble *David* (fig. 21) was changed when it made the same transfer nearly a century before. From prophet, Christ-type, and savior most appropriate for its original ecclesiastical context, the emphasis shifted in its new secular setting to slayer of tyrants, embodiment of civic strength and justice, and defender of the Florentine republic.

132. Michelangelo, *David,* 1501–4, marble, 14 ft. 2⅞ in. (434 cm) without base, 16 ft. 11½ in. (517 cm) with base, Accademia. See also fig. 179, no. 1.

133. Michelangelo, *David.* Detail of fig. 132.

134. *Emperor Caracalla* (AD 188–217), third century AD, marble, c. 22½ in. (57 cm), Museo Archeologico Nazionale, Naples.

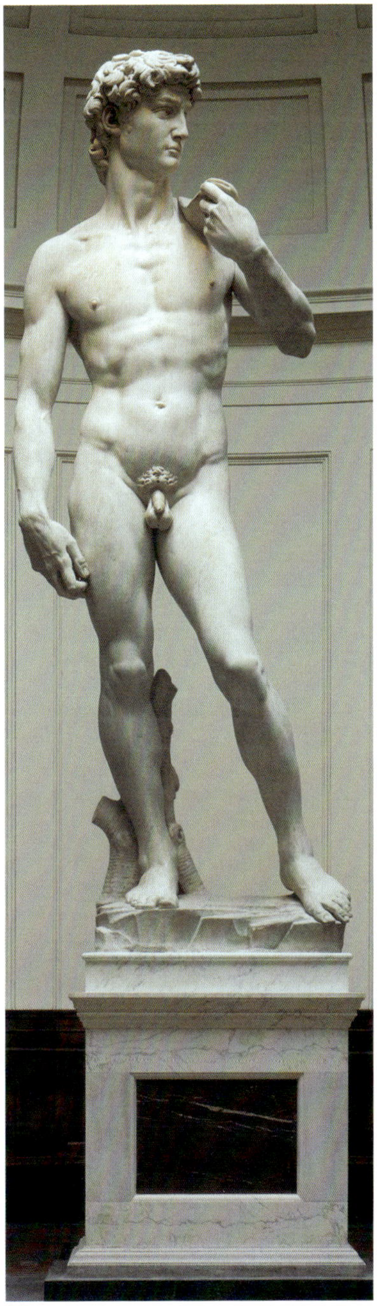

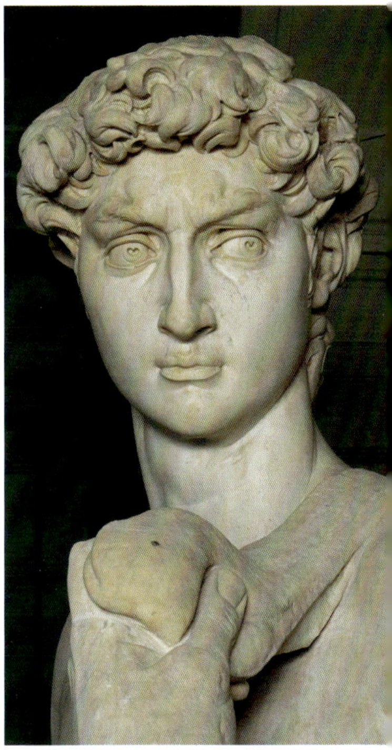

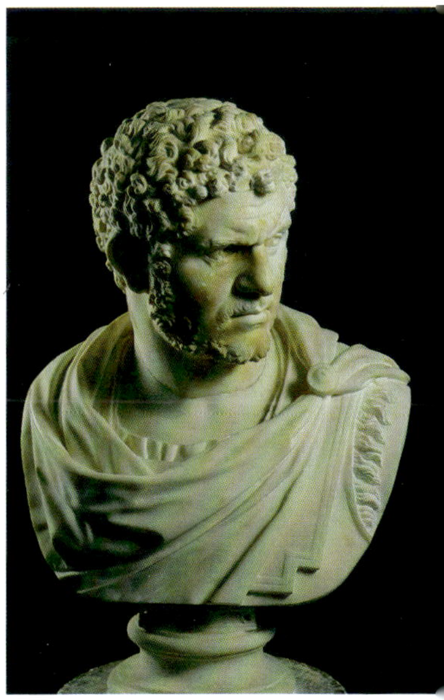

17

ALTARPIECES

SS. ANNUNZIATA: LEONARDO'S *ST. ANNE CARTOON*

When Leonardo da Vinci returned to Florence in 1500 after working about seventeen years for the duke of Milan, Ludovico Maria Sforza il Moro (1452–1508), he was, according to Vasari, commissioned by the Servites to paint the high altarpiece for their Church of SS. Annunziata (figs. 12, no. 24; 142, no. 6)—a monumental double-sided, eight-panel structure commissioned originally from Filippino Lippi in 1500 and eventually mostly completed by Perugino (c. 1450–1523) by 1507. Although he never executed any of the panels for the altarpiece, Leonardo did exhibit in the workshop provided by the Servites a full-scale cartoon, *Virgin and Child with St. Anne and the Infant John the Baptist Playing with a Lamb,* which, again according to Vasari, created a major artistic sensation. The original cartoon, known from copies, has been lost, but a similar cartoon dating from a few years later represents a close variation (fig. 135). If the lost cartoon was in fact made for the high altar—located at the junction between the nave and the circular choir chapel—it was probably a design for the central panel on the back side of the altarpiece facing the choir, as the Servites were especially devoted to the Virgin.

According to the ever-popular *Golden Legend,* Anne had remained childless after a long marriage to Joachim. One day an angel appeared separately to Joachim and Anne, informing each that Anne, well beyond childbearing age, would give birth. When Joachim and Anne met shortly later at the Golden Gate of Jerusalem and kissed at the joyful news, their daughter Mary was miraculously conceived. Many believed that the Virgin Mary was thus conceived divinely without original sin, a doctrine called the Immaculate Conception, which had long been promoted by the Franciscans, none more strongly than the Franciscan pope Sixtus IV.

Leonardo's cartoon represents Jesus seated on the lap of his mother, as if emerging from her womb, enacting the miraculous Incarnation. Mary seated on the lap of her mother alludes to the Immaculate Conception, which prefigured the Annunciation. By pointing heavenward, Anne underlines the mystery of the two conceptions. The Virgin seated on Anne also suggested that Christianity had supplanted Judaism, just as Leonardo's visual subordination of John the Baptist, the last of the Hebrew prophets, to Christ evoked the triumph of the new dispensation over the old. Finally, Jesus embodied the sacrament of the Eucharist, and John—the ascetic penitent and baptizer of Christ—the sacraments of penance and baptism. Together they constituted the three essential sacraments for salvation. Because Walter of Brienne (1304–56), duke of Athens, who had seized tyrannical control of Florence, had been expelled from the city in 1343 on the Feast of St. Anne (July 26), Anne was also considered one of the many protectors of Florentine republican liberty, a topic of renewed interest after the expulsion of the Medici in 1494.

Leonardo depicted the awkward subject of an adult seated on the lap of another naturally and spontaneously, even playfully. His light and shade subtly sculpted the life-size figures to convey their exceptional three-dimensionality. By slightly splaying and turning the legs of Mary and Anne and rotating their torsos toward the light, Leonardo managed to convey a sense of mass and torsion. Their limbs, bodies, and heads closely echo one another, and their expressions and joyous smiles convey their mutual trust and love. The Virgin tenderly cradles her chubby, curly-haired son as he rotates through nearly 180 degrees and, with a wistful expression, caresses and blesses John the Baptist as signs of love and redemption. Together Anne, Mary, and Jesus have been unified in a youthful, animated, and compact ovoid group expressive of spiritual renewal across three generations. The particularized yet monumental landscape highlights their immediacy and majesty. As is fitting, John kneels outside this family group. Yet he is still connected with

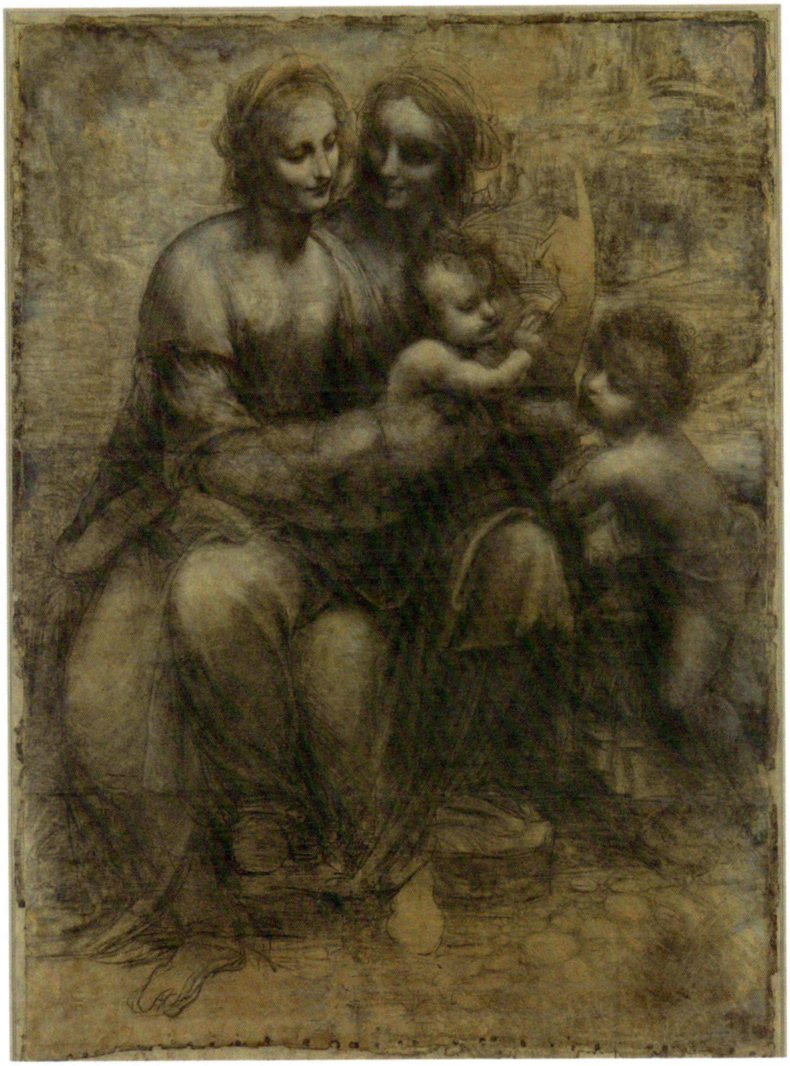

135. Leonardo da Vinci, *St. Anne Cartoon (Virgin and Child with St. Anne and the Infant John the Baptist),* c. 1505, charcoal on paper, 62⅝ × 39¾ in. (159 × 101 cm), The National Gallery, London.

Jesus by his echoing posture and expression as he humbly crosses his arms and raises his head in adoration and obeisance.

A High Renaissance style, which Leonardo first introduced to Florence with the commission for SS. Annunziata, can be defined in part as an accurate representation of humanity and nature in all their variety and movement. This much the Pollaiuolo brothers had already achieved (fig. 82), even though Leonardo's naturalism is more convincing and accurately observed. However, Leonardo has added—and this is the essence of his novel invention—a new depth of human emotion and breadth of landscape, a higher degree of anatomical grace and natural beauty, and a greater lyrical and rhythmical interweaving of animated figures within their natural environment. Leonardo expressed more than ever before the divine perfection and harmony that suffuse and transcend both humanity and nature.

PALAZZO VECCHIO, SALA GRANDE: FRA BARTOLOMEO'S *ST. ANNE ALTARPIECE*

Leonardo's example served as the starting point for Fra Bartolomeo in his development of an even more mature example of a High Renaissance style in his *St. Anne Altarpiece* (fig. 136).

The altarpiece for the altar opposite the *Signoria*'s tribune in the Sala Grande (fig. 129, no. 3) had been commissioned in 1498 from Filippino Lippi. By Lippi's death

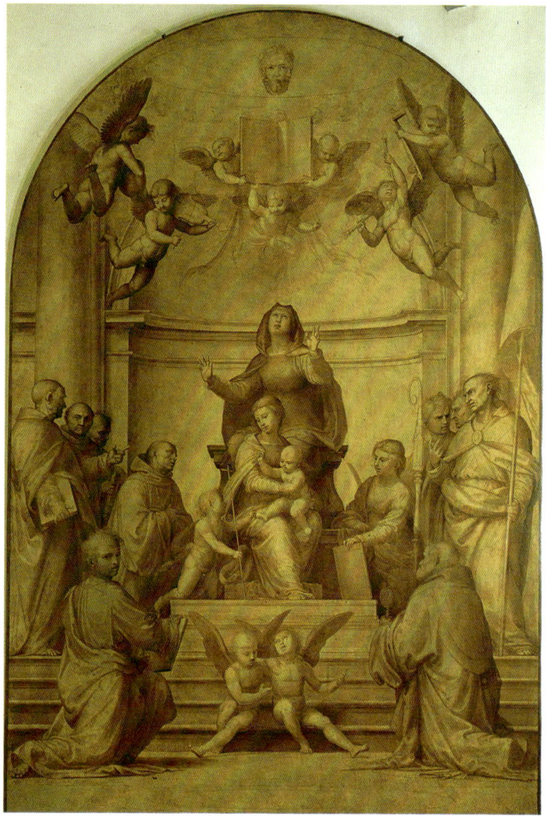

136. Fra Bartolomeo, *St. Anne Altarpiece* (unfinished), 1510–12, oil on canvas, Museo di S. Marco.

in 1504, only the frame had been completed, carved by Baccio d'Angolo following Lippi's design. On November 26, 1510, Fra Bartolomeo, a follower of Savonarola deeply committed to the Second Republic, was given the commission. By 1512, when the Medici returned to Florence and ended the Second Republic, Fra Bartolomeo had completed only the underpainting, yet the grandeur of his conception is clearly evident.

Vasari wrote in his *Lives* that the work "contains all the protecting saints of Florence and those on whose feast days the city has won its victories." Featured most prominently in the center are St. Anne, the Virgin, the Christ Child, and John the Baptist. The Virgin had been the protector of Florence since its founding, John the Baptist its principal patron saint, and St. Anne its liberator from the tyranny of Walter of Brienne, the duke of Athens. The other saints have too few attributes for positive identification, although the figure with the banner to the extreme right might be St. Victor, who guided the Florentines to victory at Cascina in 1364, the kneeling bishop just below is probably St. Zenobius, who assured victory over the Ostrogoths in 405, and one of the monks to the right is probably St. Bernard of Clairvaux, the patron saint of the Florentine government. SS. Peter and Paul, the patrons of the victory at Anghiari, would be expected but appear not to be included.

Fra Bartolomeo created a remarkably broad and deep spatial composition, and he imbued the central figures with enormous force by elevating them on a four-stepped platform, a two-stepped dais, and a grand throne. They are further monumentalized and constructed as embodying the earthly Church by the surrounding semicircle of saints and the background churchlike apse flanked by columns seemingly extending to infinity. The stable, yet dynamic triangular arrangement of the inner group draws the viewer's eye to a vision of the celestial Church in the upper zone with a semicircular arrangement of music-making angels, a book signifying the Word or Logos of divine truth, and the triune head of the Trinity surrounded by a ring of cherubim and seraphim, symbols of divine wisdom and love. The seven angels at the top of the composition and two at the bottom, as well as the symbolic circles of divine perfection inscribed in the foreground pavement and in the clouds surrounding the Trinity, were intended to serve as visual signs that heaven and earth were conjoined during the Mass.

Had the altarpiece been completed and placed on its intended altar, it would have suggested that the authority of the Florentine government derived from divine justice and that its mission was to prepare its citizens for salvation through law and order.

18

PORTRAITS

LEONARDO'S *MONA LISA*

About 1504 Leonardo began his portrait of Mona (*Madonna,* or My Lady) Lisa (Elizabeth) Gherardini and continued it for another decade or so, carrying it with him from Florence to Rome, Milan, and France (fig. 137). He never delivered it to the patron, presumably Mona Lisa's husband, the Florentine merchant Francesco del Giocondo.

Responding to the fundamental premise of classical and Renaissance theory that art had to be based on objective reality, Leonardo employed a number of devices to create a convincing physical and psychic presence. For the first time in Florentine female portraiture, he seated his subject parallel to the picture plane. Her left forearm and hand rest on and grasp the chair's arm while supporting her relaxed right hand and forearm, which recedes into space. He rotated her torso and head at an angle to the picture plane, and turned her eyes to gaze directly at the viewer. Although the portrait has much in common with Leonardo's earlier *Ginevra de' Benci* (fig. 123)—the landscape background, three-quarter profile, outward-gazing eyes, and hands crossed at the waist—it expresses a greater degree of anatomical torsion.

Leonardo also linked Mona Lisa's bodily torsion to the landscape. The road leading the eye into the left background reinforces the turn of her right shoulder away from the viewer. On the right, the river flowing down from a distant mountain lake and running under a bridge toward the foreground strengthens the rotation of Mona Lisa's left shoulder toward the beholder. The lack of continuity between the left and right landscapes signals Leonardo's manipulation of the landscape for aesthetic effect. Leonardo further heightened Mona Lisa's physical presence by placing her in a realistic environment, a loggia with a parapet supporting (originally) two framing columns. Like Lippi's and Botticelli's portraits of women (figs. 118 and 121), Mona Lisa is confined at home but within a far more ample architectural setting. Furthermore, the space is filled with natural light falling diagonally from the left. Leonardo transformed this light by his new *sfumato* (smoky) technique of adding shades of black to all the pigments. In this way he created a dark unity of color and a palpable atmosphere that blends Mona Lisa with the landscape background.

Leonardo also accentuated Mona Lisa's naturalism by the delicacy of her veil and the intricacy of her dress. Her sleeve falls into a complex system of folds that subtly reflect the light. Her bodice's neckline is decorated with a delicate design that draws attention to her cleavage. Her sensuality is emphasized by her loose hair, which falls in soft, graceful curls penetrated by light and air. Most remarkably, however, the subtle modulation of Mona Lisa's soft and fleshly features has captured the instant that an ambiguous expression passes across her face. She is either contracting her facial muscles to smile, or else, having already smiled, relaxing them. Furthermore, just as the juniper was a pun on Ginevra de' Benci's name, so the smile punned on Mona Lisa's married name, *Giocondo,* meaning jocund, cheerful, or genial. Leonardo, in short, has presented us with a vital and alert human being.

Yet this is only half the story, for Leonardo also created a transcendent supernatural woman. Her nearly symmetrical bell-shaped silhouette and regular ovoid head communicate a geometrical perfection underlying her vitality. Anchored to the chair and framed by the loggia, her body imparts permanence and solidity to her animation. Massive head, arms, and hands and a thick torso (emphasized by the roll of drapery arching over her shoulder) add power to her delicacy. Her loggia seemingly sits atop an exceptionally tall mountain. She is located within a vast, immensely old world, its enormous mountain ranges volcanically uplifted in the distant past and then gradually eroded over time by huge geological and meteorological forces. Her eyes at the level of the high horizon line combine with the mysterious *sfumato*

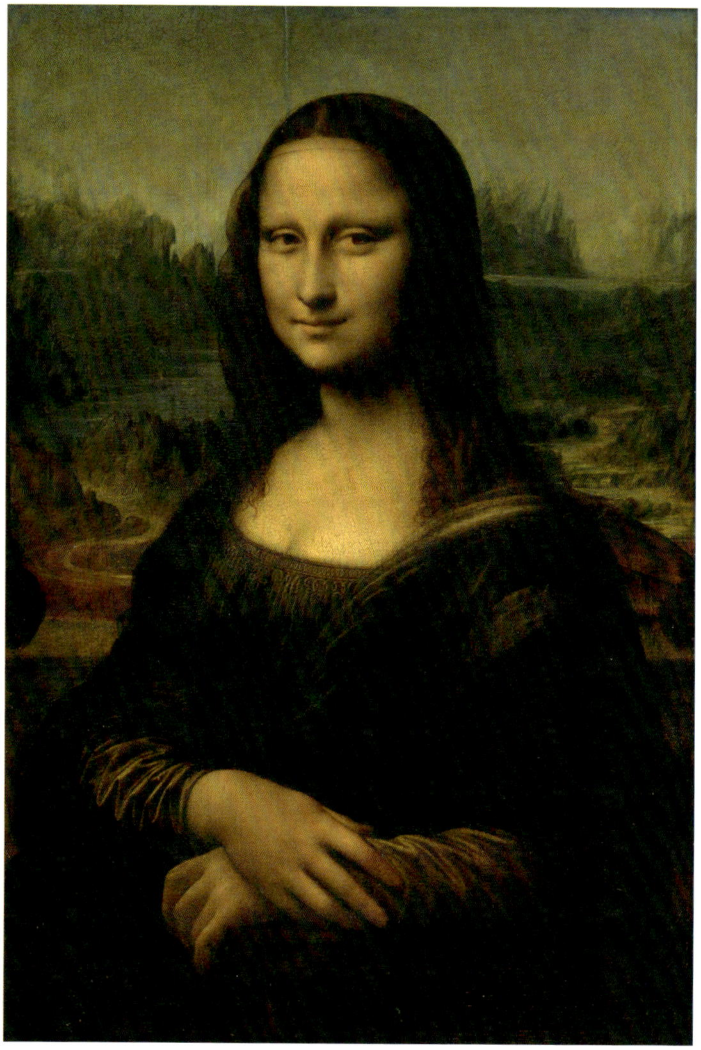

137. Leonardo da Vinci, *Portrait of Mona Lisa,* c. 1504–14, oil on panel, 38½ × 21 in. (97.8 × 53.3 cm), Louvre. A near-contemporary copy indicates that the painting has been cut on the sides, eliminating all but the bases of the original framing columns.

to convey sphinxlike wisdom. It is as if Mona Lisa were an earth goddess, the light around her head creating a cosmic halo to heighten her omnipotence. Leonardo, in short, has suggested that Mona Lisa possesses divine intelligence of universal scale. She confidently surveys the universe with *giocondità,* a word that means precisely spiritual serenity and psychological contentment derived from superior wisdom.

Mona Lisa, in summary, pulsates with life and psychological mobility. She both inhabits and embodies the world of flux, encompassing changes from bright light to intense dark, from minute muscular twitches to monumental metamorphoses of mountains over eons of geological time. She personifies, in short, the endless cyclical changes of nature, ranging from generation to decay, from decay to regeneration. Yet she also reflects the stability, perfection, and order underlying all God's creation. Ultimately, she mediates between the individual and the universal, death and renewal, contingency and permanence.

Far more than *Ginevra de' Benci*, *Mona Lisa* also signals Leonardo's own creative genius by mirroring his profound understanding of nature—from its most minute to its grandest cycles of birth, growth, death, and renewal—documented in his notebooks and drawings. The work also constructs Leonardo's classical conception—a conception that defines a High Renaissance style—that art should not only represent the natural world in all its complexity, multiplicity, and vitality, but also abstract and elevate nature to capture its transcendent mystery and majesty.

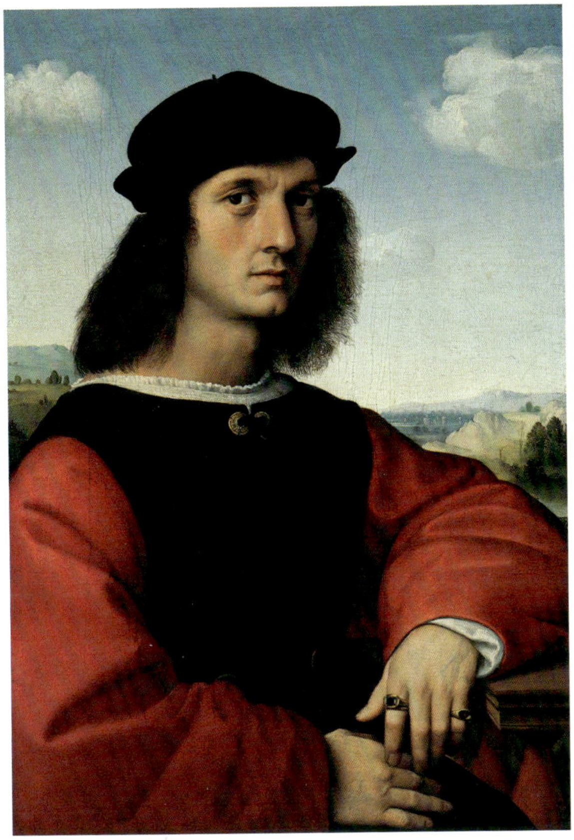

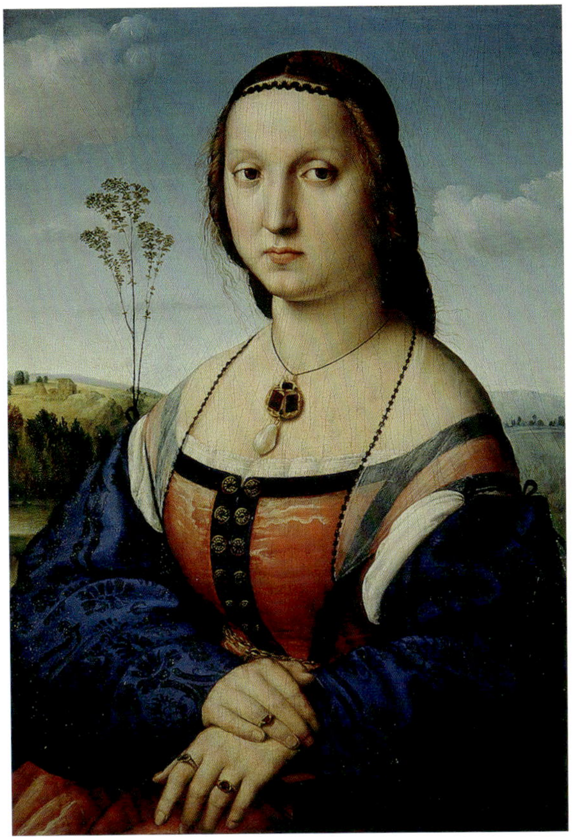

138. Raphael, *Portrait of Agnolo Doni,* c. 1506, oil on panel, 24¾ × 17¾ in. (63 × 45 cm), Pitti.

139. Raphael, *Portrait of Maddalena Strozzi Doni,* c. 1506, oil on panel, 24¾ × 17¾ in. (63 × 45 cm), Pitti. Maddalena probably wears Agnolo's counterdowry: three rings, gold belt, pendant with three large gems and a huge pearl, white chemise, red watered silk *gamurra* trimmed with black velvet and gold buttons, detachable blue damask sleeves, and transparent partlet (shoulder veil) edged with black stones.

RAPHAEL'S PORTRAITS OF AGNOLO AND MADDALENA DONI

About two years after the 1504 marriage of Agnolo Doni (1475–1539) at age twenty-nine to Maddalena Strozzi at age thirteen, Raphael (1483–1520) was commissioned to commemorate their union by a pair of portraits (figs. 138 and 139). In creating his two portraits, Raphael borrowed nearly every detail of Leonardo's *Mona Lisa* (fig. 137) including format, composition, posture, gaze, setting, light, and *sfumato.* So completely did he absorb Leonardo's example that Maddalena communicates an imperious grandeur beyond her young age. In emulating Leonardo, however, Raphael learned an important technique, one that constitutes a major characteristic of High Renaissance portraiture. Subjects in fifteenth-century portraits were usually depicted standing, the lower body rather abruptly truncated, but implying the continuation of the body below the frame (figs. 117–124). Yet Leonardo showed Raphael how to avoid this awkward discontinuity by portraying a seated subject with arms and hands locked to the pictorial field to create a contained aesthetic whole.

Far more than Leonardo, however, Raphael confronted the pivotal problem of portraiture: the creation of a vibrant individual likeness. He did so by loosening Leonardo's geometry and painting each figure with a livelier silhouette, extending beyond the frame and seated asymmetrically to one side of the vertical axis. He dressed his subjects in more contemporary-style clothing, gave them more individualized features, and set them in a more intimate landscape. One might imagine Agnolo and Maddalena walking down the streets of the Second Republic, but not Mona Lisa.

19

DEVOTIONAL WORKS

MICHELANGELO'S *DONI TONDO*

Around the time Agnolo Doni married Maddalena Strozzi in 1504 (see figs. 138 and 139) he commissioned Michelangelo to paint a *tondo* of the *Holy Family with John the Baptist* presumably to decorate their nuptial bedroom (fig. 140). In contrast to Botticelli, who disposed his figures to conform to the *tondo*'s circumference in his *Madonna of the Magnificat* (fig. 127), Michelangelo directed the anatomical energy of his Holy Family along the vertical axis, in tension with the format. The Virgin, a Madonna of Humility type seated with folded legs on the grass, has spiraled through 180 degrees to grasp her son. Dynamic and muscular, the Virgin represents a *mulier fortis* (valiant or strong woman, Proverbs 31:10, 19) embodying the vital and mighty Church. Her blue mantel, echoing the sky above, and her upward-turned eyes denote her spirituality. The rose hue of her tunic suggests her love of God and the marked book, signifying the Virgin's traditional identification with Wisdom (Ecclesiasticus 24:32), her foreknowledge of Christ's sacrifice. Daringly, Michelangelo also nestled the Virgin between the widespread legs of the squatting St. Joseph, rested her upper arm on his thigh, and placed her bare right foot next to his, as if to suggest carnal union.

In earlier art Joseph had played a more marginal role. But when humanists emphasized the family as a microcosm of the ideal state, Joseph increasingly came to be viewed as a perfect exemplar for Renaissance grooms, and his cult—fostered largely by the Franciscans—grew in popularity. The inclusion of his feast for the first time on the Roman liturgical calendar (on March 19) by an act of the Franciscan pope Sixtus IV, assured Joseph's new dignity as Jesus' legal father, guardian, and protector, and the Virgin's spiritual groom. A craftsman (carpenter), like the Master Craftsman, Joseph was also frequently regarded as God's earthly vicar. Thus Michelangelo depicted him just as God was traditionally represented—aged, bearded, bald, massive, draped in gold and purple (the colors of divinity and imperial majesty), and silhouetted against the sky. He thereby transmuted the implicit physical union between Mary and Joseph into a spiritual one.

Jesus' exceptionally dynamic bodily torsion, his Herculean form, his downcast eyes, and the Virgin's gesture, calling attention to his manhood, all underline his humanity. He steps up onto his mother's arm while pressing down on her head to suggest his willingness to step out into the world to accept his fate to redeem humanity. Yet, remarkably, Michelangelo chose not to represent Christ stepping out from the Virgin's lap, as he had done in his nearly contemporary marble *Bruges Madonna*. Rather, he suggested Christ's birth from the Virgin's womb by the green lining of Mary's mantel running from between her legs, up her back, and over her right bicep where Christ steps. He also depicted Jesus issuing from the thigh of Joseph/God to allude to the classical myth of the twice-born Bacchus, born once prematurely from the womb of his mother (Semele), and again at full term from the thigh of his father (Jupiter)—a common Renaissance allegory of the twice-born Christ, once from Mary's womb, and again from his tomb. Furthermore, by suggesting that Bacchus, the wine god, prefigured Christ, Michelangelo added mythic breadth and depth to his painting. Finally, by basing his infant Christ on one of several classical reliefs depicting infants stomping grapes, he further evoked the image of Christ/Bacchus as the mystic winepress, an allegory dating back to St. Augustine (354–430) connoting the Eucharist.

The infant John the Baptist standing behind a wall that divides the composition nearly in half implies that Michelangelo intended the background to be an image of the old dispensation. The man-made apselike wall, therefore, may be intended to recall the foundations of Judaism upon which the Church was built. It also resembles an early Christian baptismal font to remind the viewer that John, who stands within the structure, was Christ's baptizer. In addition, John's rustic cross and up-

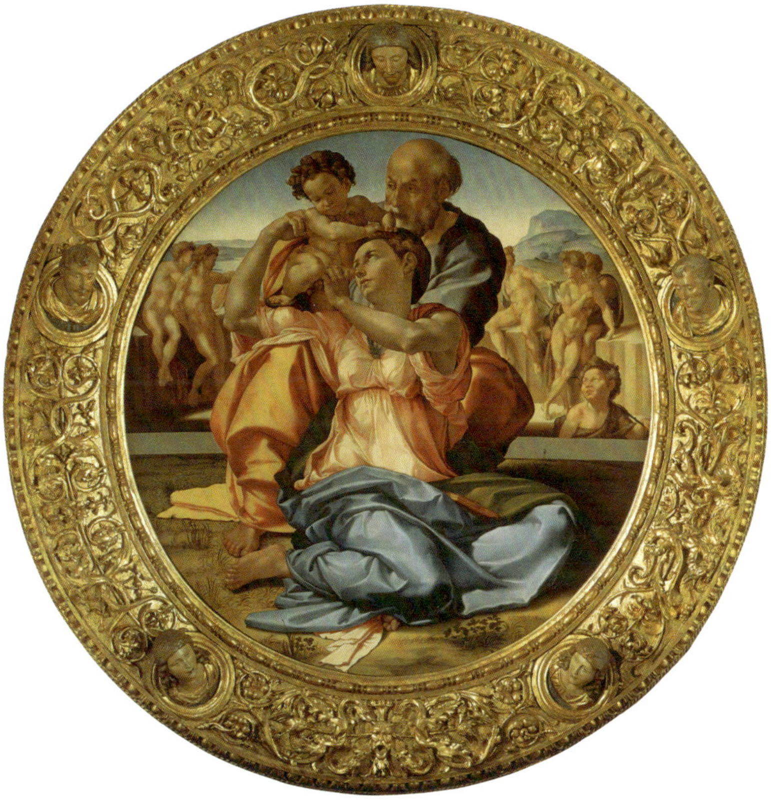

140. Michelangelo, *Holy Family with John the Baptist (Doni Tondo),* c. 1504–6, tempera on panel, diameter 47¼ in. (120 cm), Uffizi. Baccio di Montelupo (1469–1535) carved the original gilt frame with a bust of Christ on top and paired prophets and sibyls on the sides.

ward gaze at Christ recall his role as Christ's precursor while his camelhair shirt evokes the preacher of penitence. He embodies, in short, penance, baptism, and the Eucharist, the essential sacraments of salvation.

The significance of the five male nudes in the background has long been a puzzle. A recent suggestion casts them as Neo-Platonic divine energies, perhaps supported by Michelangelo's structure of the central vertical axis where Christ both descends into the world for his love of humanity and ascends into the loving arms of God the Father through the mediation of the Virgin. If so, the group to the right would suggest carnal love as one figure embraces another and pulls him between his legs. A third figure yanking on the drapery of the embracing couple (who quotes one of the sons in the famous ancient sculptural group of the *Laocoön* discovered in Rome on January 14, 1506) hints at the discord and ultimately the death of sensual love. The couple on the left, then, would signify celestial love as they gaze into the distance. In any case, the apselike foundation appears to embrace the viewer within a globelike universe encompassing the promise of a Savior from the beginning of time, to the Incarnation within time, to the sacramental pledge of salvation at the end of time.

At the moment just before both Raphael and Andrea del Sarto (1486–1530) fully embraced Leonardo's technique of melding soft rhythmical figures into a dark atmospheric *sfumato,* Michelangelo here engaged Leonardo in a *paragone* (comparison of the arts) by locating his Holy Family within a crystalline space with clear colors, incisive outlines, and hard surfaces, as if carved from a single block of stone. Leonardo had written that sculptors were dirty, sweaty, and boorish craftsmen, while painters were clean, elegant, and cultured intellectuals who created more inventive and convincing figures than sculptors. Michelangelo answered by his *Doni Tondo* that, with his sculptor's sensibilities, he could create paintings as fine as Leonardo's.

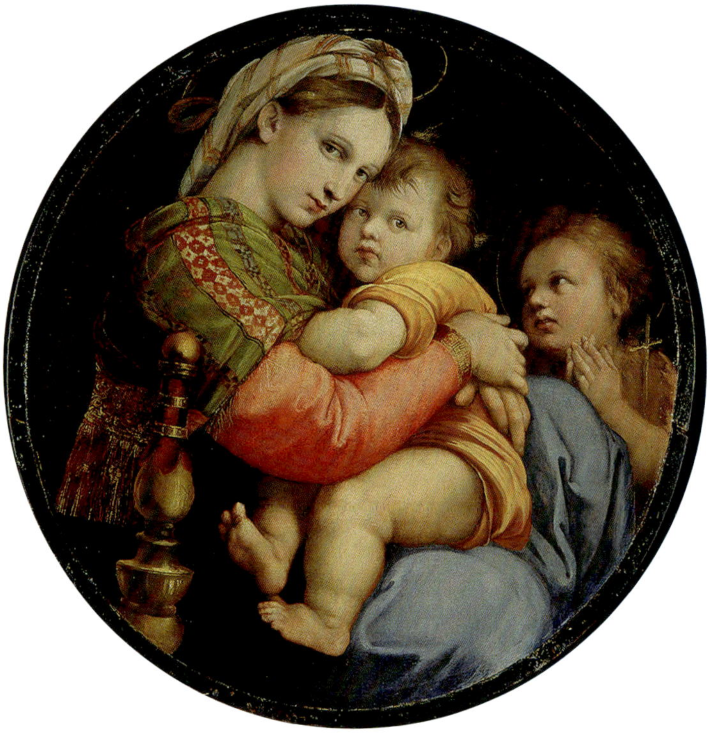

141. Raphael, *Madonna della Sedia,* c. 1514, oil and panel, diameter 28 in. (71 cm), Pitti.

RAPHAEL'S *MADONNA DELLA SEDIA*

Raphael painted his *Madonna della Sedia* (fig. 141) in Rome after he left Florence in 1508. But the work grows so fully out of, and so convincingly culminates the Florentine *tondo* tradition that it is proper to consider it here. As we have seen, the figures in Botticelli's *Madonna of the Magnificat* (fig. 127) conform to the *tondo*'s circularity, while in Michelangelo's *Doni Tondo* (fig. 140) they are in dynamic tension with it. In the *Madonna della Sedia,* the figures respond to both the *tondo*'s vertical and its horizontal axes, and their grouping echoes the circular format, filling it with a three-dimensional spheroid, at the center of which is Christ's elbow. The figures are also remarkably animated. The Virgin rotates in her chair (the *sedia* of the title), lifts her left leg to steady her son, coddles him within her encircling embrace, and turns her head. Jesus rotates his head and torso in the opposite direction, pausing to reach under his mother's shawl for her breast. In most previous devotional paintings, the Virgin and Child and any attendant figures appear preoccupied with each other within a self-contained whole. At most Christ, or occasionally another saint, glances outward. But here both the Virgin and Child simultaneously turn to meet the viewer's gaze, an action that intensifies the intimacy of their embrace.

So tender and affectionate is their mutual love that one almost forgets that the spherical harmony they lyrically construct recalls their status as deities. The luxuriant silk shawl and veil, the ornate throne, and the gilt halo adorning the transcendently beautiful Virgin evoke her role as the Queen of Heaven. Christ's gold tunic implies his kingship, and the glints of radiance at the top and sides of his head evoke his usual cruciform halo, just as John the Baptist's reed cross anticipates his Crucifixion. Jesus' slightly splayed toes and flexed feet and the Virgin's profound expression of pathos also remind us that he will soon step into the world to enact his preordained destiny. Finally, John—counterbalanced by the chair's lathe-turned upright—indicates by his hair shirt, gesture, and gaze the viewer's proper response to the divine figures: penitence, prayer, and loving faith. The indissoluble and self-contained unity between individual action and spiritual perfection, earthly warmth and divine love, and objective matter and ideal spirit expresses the essence of both Christian faith and High Renaissance art.

PART III

FLORENCE

under the Medici Popes

1513–1534

20

CIVIC ARCHITECTURE AND URBANISM

PIAZZA DELLA SS. ANNUNZIATA

After his elevation to the throne of St. Peter in 1513, one of Leo X's earliest acts was to signal renewed Medici domination of Florence by placing his papal coat of arms above the single-bay groin-vaulted entrance portico of the pilgrimage church of SS. Annunziata (figs. 12, no. 24; 142, no. 2), the mother church of the Servite Order founded in Florence in 1240 and dedicated to the service of the Virgin. He also commissioned the young Jacopo Pontormo (1494–1556) to flank his arms with frescoed personifications of Faith and Charity, as if to further indicate that he would treat the faithless Florentines charitably. Then on January 17, 1516, Cardinal Antonio Maria Ciocchi del Monte (1462–1533), legate for Leo X and protector of the Servites, consecrated the Church of SS. Annunziata, the rebuilding of which had been greatly facilitated by fifteenth-century Medici patronage. A week later, Leo X promulgated a papal bull officially confirming the cult of the Servite saint Filippo Benizi (1233–85),

142. Plan of the Piazza della SS. Annunziata: 1 Foundling Hospital, 1419–45 (figs. 19–20); 2 SS. Annunziata, begun 1240, rebuilt 1444–1516 (including the central bay of the entrance portico), entrance portico (except the central bay), 1599–1601; 3 Nave chapel with Castagno's *Trinity with St. Jerome* (fig. 70); 4 Michelozzo's 1448 marble tabernacle enclosing a miraculous fourteenth-century frescoed *Annunciation* on the inner façade; 5 Chapel of St. Sebastian, built in the 1450s by the Pucci family, originally containing Pollaiuolo's *Martrydom of St. Sebastian* (fig. 82); 6 high altar, probable intended location of Leonardo's unexecuted *St. Anne Altarpiece* (see fig. 135); 7 Servite Loggia, 1516–1614 (fig. 143); 8 *Equestrian Monument to Ferdinand I* by Giambologna (1529–1608), 1601–8 (fig. 143); 9–10 bronze fountains by Pietro Tacca (1557–1640), 1629; 11 Hospital of S. Matteo, 1388–1410.

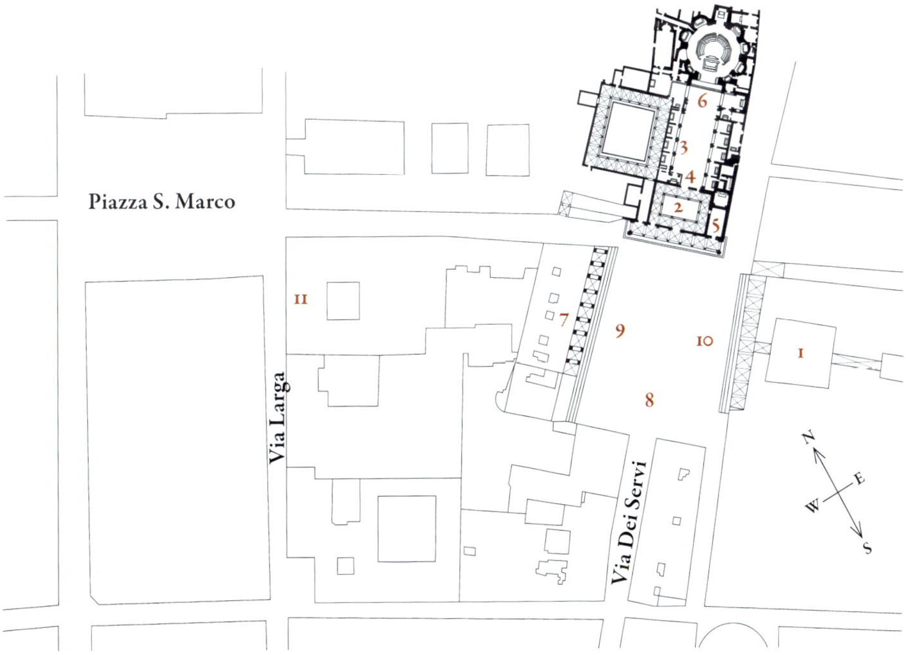

establishing his feast day on August 23. On Benizi's feast day of that same year (1516), the Servites began constructing on the west side of the Piazza SS. Annunziata eight income-producing row houses connected by a portico, the so-called Servite Loggia, under the supervision of Antonio da Sangallo the Elder and Baccio d'Agnolo (figs. 142, no. 7; 143). Although the construction was administered and largely financed by the Servites, Leo X, son of Lorenzo il Magnifico, certainly would have encouraged (and perhaps even mandated) the project as fulfilling his father's 1478 plan to build row houses, a plan that perhaps drew on an even earlier plan by Brunelleschi (see chapter 1). The transformation of the square into an ordered and harmonious Romanizing forum by the Servite Loggia would also have expressed the pontiff's own claims to universal spiritual and temporal sovereignty.

Whatever Leo X's degree of involvement in the project, the builders explicitly used Brunelleschi's Foundling Hospital as their model, employing the following identical features (cf. figs. 19, 20, 142, and 143): an overall length of 120 *braccia,* a Corinthian portico approached by a flight of eight steps, 10 × 10–*braccia* sail-vaulted bays of the same height, entablatures with a wide frieze above the arcade, *tondi* in the spandrels below the entablature, pedimented windows resting on the entablature, and a plan based on harmonic ratios. The differences result from different functions: the Servite portico originally had twelve open bays rather than nine (the western three were closed in the eighteenth century), and Servite emblems (an S interlaced with a lily), instead of infants in swaddling clothes, decorate the *tondi* of the spandrels. The Servite portico also lacks the framing lateral bays, but each of the eight apartments is 15 *braccia* wide (two apartments for every three bays), the same width as the end-bays of the Innocenti.

In strong contrast to the medieval urban plan of the Piazza della Signoria, where a tall primary solid dominated and shaped the secondary voids (figs. 13 and 14), the surrounding charitable, religious, and residential institutions of the Piazza SS. Annunziata were reduced to low frames bounding the dominant rectangular space. This effect was greatly reinforced by the construction, between 1599 and 1601, of an expanded seven-bay, pendentive-vaulted Corinthian portico across the front of SS. Annunziata commissioned by the Pucci family from Giovanni Battista Caccini (1556–1613).

Emulating the equestrian monuments of Roman emperors that focused and controlled the space of ancient forums, in 1608 Duke Ferdinand de' Medici (1549–1609) unveiled a monumental equestrian portrait in armor by Giambologna and his workshop that defined Piazza SS. Annunziata even more emphatically as a Medici "forum" (figs. 142, no. 8; 143). Giambologna located the monument to be viewed at about a 45-degree vertical and 90-degree horizontal viewing angle when entering the square from the Via dei Servi to emphasize visually that Ferdinand alone commanded this square and fulfilled Florence's Roman destiny for military strength and territorial dominion.

143. Antonio da Sangallo the Elder and Baccio d'Agnolo, Servite Loggia, Florence, designed 1516. The first three bays of the loggia closest to SS. Annunziata and the first row house behind were completed by 1525; all twelve bays of the loggia, by 1574; the second through fourth row houses, by 1578; and the fifth and sixth row houses, by 1614. The Compagnia of S. Filippo Benizi, founded on October 15, 1587, was assigned the last two row houses for its confraternity, which eventually resulted in the closure of the last three bays by the early eighteenth century.

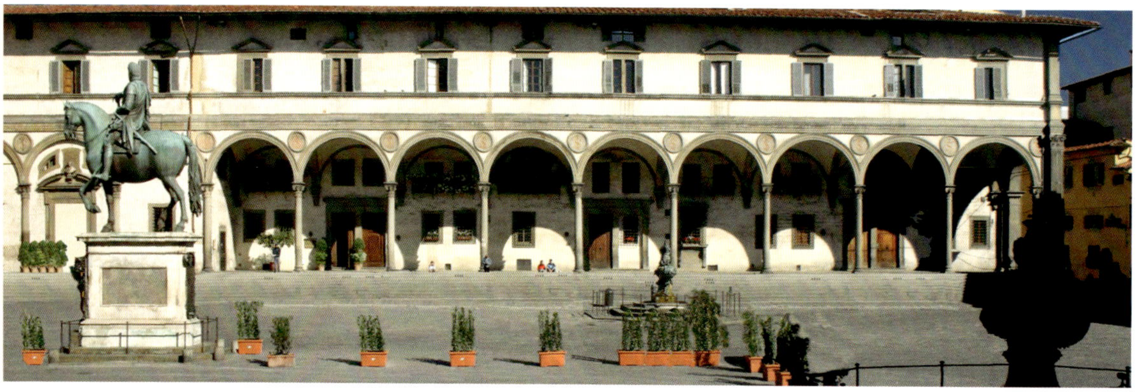

21

FREESTANDING PALACE SCULPTURE

The Medici Palace

BANDINELLI'S *ORPHEUS WITH CERBERUS*

About 1517–19 Pope Leo X and his cousin Cardinal Giulio de' Medici, the governor and bishop of Florence, commissioned Baccio Bandinelli to carve the first permanent freestanding sculpture of a pagan figure in Florence, a marble *Orpheus with Cerberus* (fig. 144) for the center of the Medici Palace courtyard (fig. 94), where Donatello's bronze *David* (fig. 107) had once stood.

According to classical myth, Orpheus sang to the accompaniment of a lyre so soothingly that he could charm wild animals and savages. When his wood-nymph wife, Eurydice, was mortally bitten by a snake and entered the underworld, Orpheus pursued her, charming with his music the three-headed dog, Cerberus, that guarded the entrance to Hades. Orpheus then enchanted Pluto, god of the underworld, who agreed to release Eurydice on the condition that he not look at her until returned to earth. Glancing back too soon, Orpheus lost Eurydice forever.

In the Renaissance, Orpheus—embodiment of eloquence, harmony, and reason—was often understood as the founder of the classical golden age of law and order. As a shepherd who descended into and returned from Hades, he also prefigured Christ, the Good Shepherd who descended into Limbo. As the charmer of wild animals, he recalled the peaceable kingdom of Isaiah (11:6–7), symbol of Paradise that Christ, through his sacrifice, opened to the faithful. Therefore, given that Leo X was himself a musician and Christ's vicar, the *Orpheus* alluded directly to the pontiff and his policy of bringing peace and harmony to Florence through his eloquence, wisdom, and justice.

Bandinelli modeled his *Orpheus* on the *Apollo Belvedere,* one of the best-known works in the papal collection of antiquities (fig. 145). The quotation was apt, for Apollo, the sun god, was also famed as a poet, a skilled musician on the lyre, and a type of Christ, the sun of justice. The reference also implied that governmental power now resided with the papacy in Rome and was administered from the Medici Palace through the papal legate, Cardinal Giulio de' Medici. But by substituting a bronze lyre (now lost) for *Apollo*'s restored bow and quiver (now removed), Bandinelli emphasized that papal power would be administered, not with violence, but with peace and harmony.

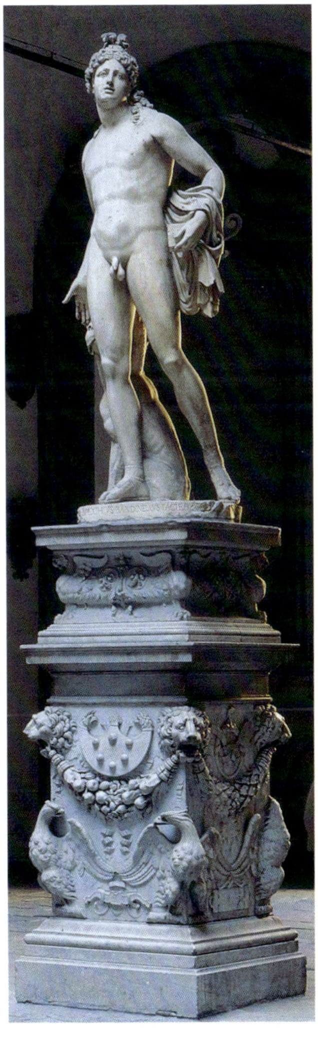

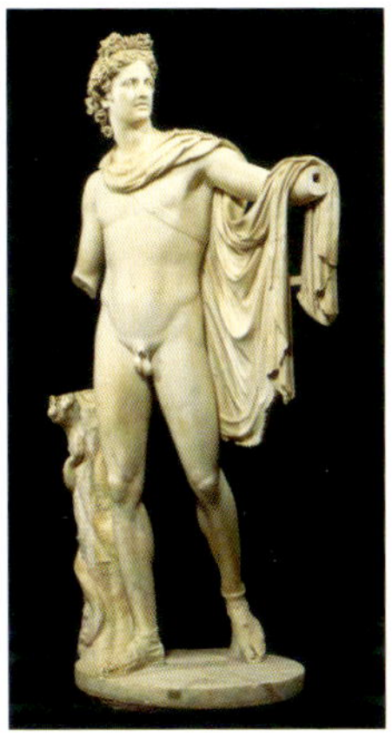

144. Baccio Bandinelli (and Benedetto da Rovezzano [1474–1552] for the base), *Orpheus with Cerberus* (Virgil, *Georgics* 4.444–527; Ovid, *Metamorphoses* 10.1–105 and 11.1–43; Horace, *Ars Poetica* 391–400), c. 1517–19, marble, over-life-size, Medici Palace.

145. *Apollo Belvedere,* marble, 7 ft. 4¼ in. (224 cm), Museo Pio-Clementino, Vatican, Roman copy of c. AD 130 after a Greek original of c. 330 BC.

22

CHAPELS AND LIBRARIES

S. Lorenzo

MICHELANGELO'S NEW SACRISTY

Just before Leo X commissioned the New Sacristy in 1519, the Medici had reached the height of their glory. As pope, Leo commanded great prestige and power, and he used his position to appoint his younger brother, Giuliano (1479–1516), captain of the Church in 1513, and captain general in 1515. A quiet literary man with no military experience, Giuliano principally served as Leo's advisor and liaison with Florence. Leo also arranged Giuliano's marriage in 1513 to Philiberte of Savoy (1498–1524), aunt of King Francis I (1494–1547) of France. Francis named Giuliano duke of Nemours in 1515, although Giuliano died the next year, before the title could be officially invested.

Leo also conferred great honor on Lorenzo (1492–1519), son of Leo's older brother Piero (1472–1503). Lorenzo was ambitious, pompous, and egocentric, hated by the Florentines as much as Giuliano was well regarded. Insanely jealous of Giuliano, Lorenzo demanded from Leo every title and privilege granted to his uncle. When Giuliano was granted his captaincy, Lorenzo insisted on an equivalent appointment as captain general of Florence, although he also lacked military experience. When Giuliano was designated duke of Nemours, Lorenzo, too, required a duchy, and in 1516 Leo awarded him the duchy of Urbino, a papal fief. However, Leo first had to fight a war to dislodge the reigning duke, Francesco Maria della Rovere (1490–1538), and Lorenzo died before he could be formally invested with the ducal title. When Giuliano married into a royal family, Lorenzo, too, had to have a royal bride, and in 1518 Leo arranged his marriage to Madeleine de la Tour d'Auvergne (1501–19). Before his death the next year, he fathered a single child, Catherine de' Medici (1519–89), who would later marry Henry of Valois (1519–59) and eventually became the queen of France.

By 1519 all the legitimate males of Cosimo il Vecchio's line had died, leaving only the two eight-year-old illegitimate sons of the duke-designates Lorenzo and Giuliano, Alessandro and Ippolito (1511–35), respectively. At the moment of this family crisis of succession, Leo commissioned Michelangelo to build the New Sacristy as the burial chapel for the two dukes-designate, a commission renewed in 1523 by Pope Clement VIII after Leo X's death in 1521. It was intended to commemorate the Medici's new, if never fully consummated, ducal status. Such celebration of Medici greatness would also help elevate the status of the two bastard sons. Indeed, in due course Ippolito was appointed a cardinal, and Alessandro became the first duke of Florence. The New Sacristy was also designed as the burial chapel for the two *magnifici,* also named Lorenzo and Giuliano: Lorenzo il Magnifico, Leo's father and de facto ruler of Florence from 1469 to 1492, and Giuliano the Magnifico, Lorenzo's brother, killed in the Pazzi Conspiracy in 1478.

Michelangelo followed Brunelleschi's plan for the Old Sacristy, designing a square, 20 × 20–*braccia* main room and a proportionally related square chapel (cf. figs. 32, no. 10; 33–35; 146–48). For the articulation of the lower walls, Michelangelo imitated Brunelleschi's use of a Corinthian triumphal arch motif in *pietra serena* but included the motif on all four walls and inserted piers to carry the central arch. Michelangelo also designed an entirely new intermediate zone above the main entablature and articulated it with pilasters carrying the cornice that supports the domes' lunettes and pendentives. Finally, like Brunelleschi, Michelangelo designed a hemispherical dome, but employed a far more classicizing coffered version derived from the Pantheon.

Michelangelo's modifications to Brunelleschi's design created a more symbolically significant architectural space (fig. 147). The lower zone, with its *pietra serena* pilasters and piers, expresses load and support, the quotidian realm of gravity and matter. Michelangelo cut this lower zone cleanly from the intermediate zone by encircling the entire space with the entablature's unbroken white frieze. The canonical classicizing palace-type windows in the intermediate zone also suggest the mundane, normal

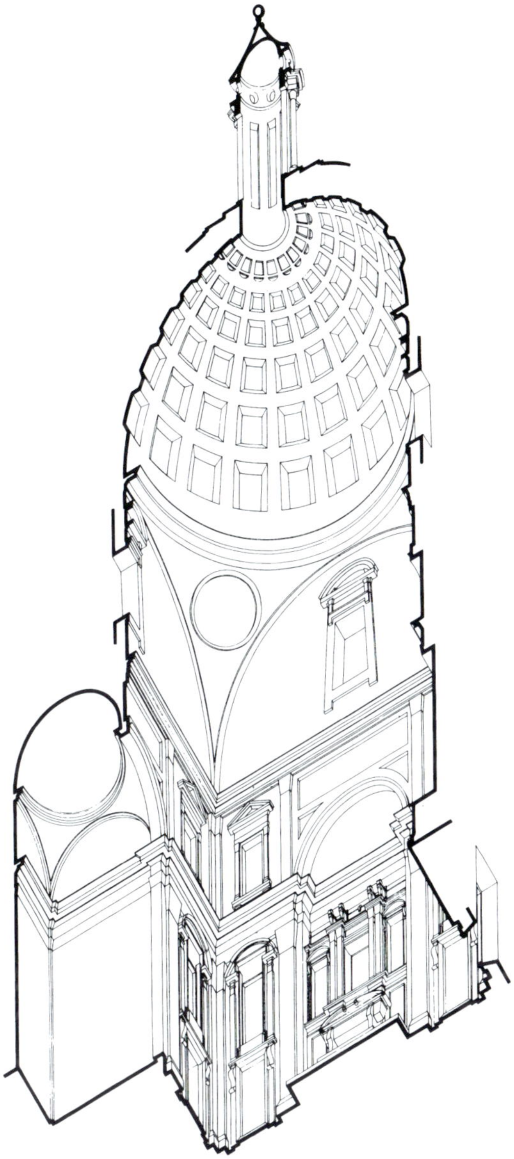

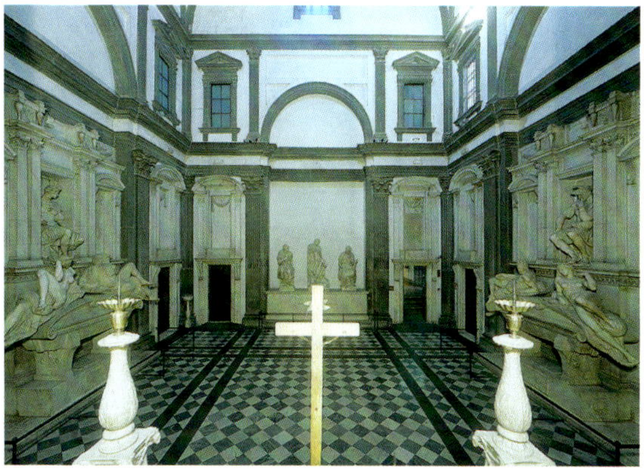

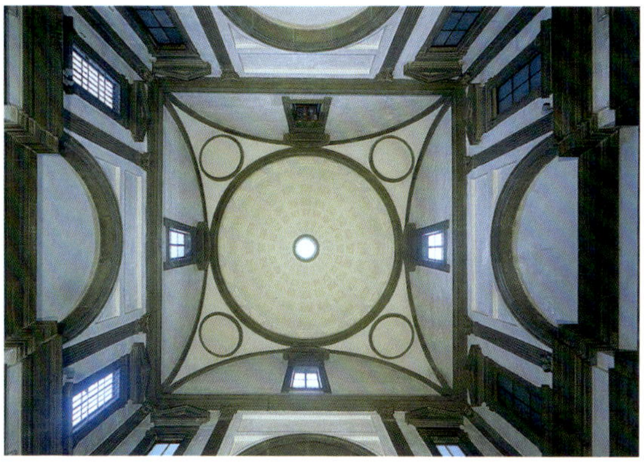

146. Isometric diagram, New Sacristy, S. Lorenzo.

147. Michelangelo, New Sacristy viewed from the altar toward the south wall, S. Lorenzo, 1519–34. After Leo X died in 1521, Clement VII renewed the commission in 1523; when Clement died in 1534, Paul III (r. 1534–49) called Michelangelo to Rome before the chapel was completed. Therefore, in the 1540s Giorgio Vasari and Niccolò Tribolo (1500–1550) assembled the chapel as seen today, a fragment of what Michelangelo intended.

148. Michelangelo, vault of the New Sacristy, S. Lorenzo.

world. Yet symbolically they evoked death, for six of the eight windows are blind and the setting western sun illuminates the other two. The palace windows reappeared in the lunettes, but filled with light from on high, they created an area where matter and spirit symbolically conjoin (fig. 148). Michelangelo imaginatively tapered the window frames to accelerate the eye's ascent toward the vault, symbol of heaven. The circles in the pendentives and the hemispherical vault expressed divinity's perfection, and the vault's narrowing coffers and ribs focus on the central lantern, the climactic architectural sign of the resurrected Christ. The Pantheon-derived dome provides the proper historical setting for the emblem of Christ, born into the Roman Empire under Emperor Augustus. However, it signaled as well the Medici family's ever-grander claims to imperial sovereignty and dominion.

At the lower level within the central arches to the east and west, Michelangelo located the marble tombs for the dukes-designate—wall tombs with effigies of the type reserved by protocol for the highest-ranking individuals (figs. 149 and 150). If Lorenzo and Giuliano had been actual dukes, the type would have been appropriate, but as only captains and dukes-designate they were overstepping the limits of decorum.

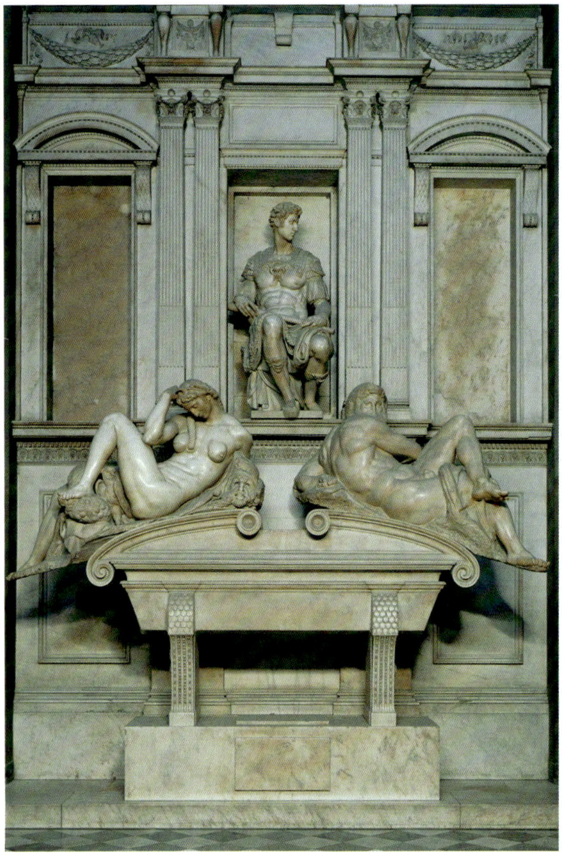

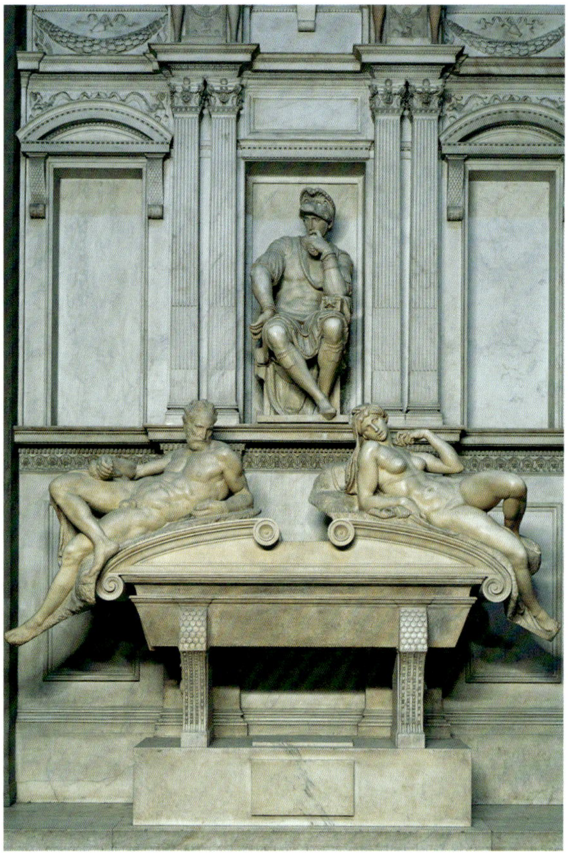

149. Michelangelo, *Tomb of the Baton Carrier (Lorenzo de' Medici)* with *Night* and *Day,* marble, *Baton Carrier* 68⅛ in. (173 cm) high, *Night* 6 ft. 4⅜ in. (194 cm) long, *Day* 9 ft. 4¼ in. (285 cm) long, east wall, New Sacristy. Although traditionally identified as Giuliano, the *Baton Carrier* almost certainly represents Lorenzo, as he holds the Florentine, not the papal, baton.

150. Michelangelo, *Tomb of the Thinker (Giuliano de' Medici)* with *Dusk* and *Dawn,* marble, *Thinker* 70⅛ in. (178 cm) high, *Dusk* 6 ft. 4¾ in. (195 cm) long, *Dawn* 6 ft. 9⅛ in. (206 cm) long, west wall. Traditionally identified as Lorenzo, the thoughtful *Thinker* far better suits the reputed character of Giuliano.

Michelangelo planned a pair of massive reclining river gods flanking each tomb, elevated from the floor by a low pedestal (fig. 151). His drawings and clay models show that he intended the river gods to be contorted figures expressive of vigorous, somewhat erratic movement. As embodiments of earth-eroding rivers, they would have reinforced the significance of the lower zone as an area of transformation and decay of matter. However, because rivers promote fertility, they equally would have expressed regeneration, especially as Paradise was traditionally believed to contain four rivers. On a political level the rivers might have signified Medici dominion.

From these embodiments of time's relentless flux and matter's endless metamorphosis, the viewer's eye moved upward to the allegories reclining on the lids of the sarcophagi. The allegories represented divisions within the cosmic cycle of time: Night and Day, Dusk and Dawn. Michelangelo represented *Night* (fig. 149) with a crescent moon and star on her lowered head, a dream mask under her arm, an owl under her leg, and poppies under her foot. Her sagging breasts and her flabby stomach indicate that her childbearing years have ended and that she has begun to approach old age and death. Her eyes, which are not fully closed, and her contorted posture suggest that her sleep is perturbed by poppy-induced hallucinations, and the erotically positioned owl adds sexual overtones to her nightmares. *Night,* then, embodies lust, which was believed to have been responsible for the downfall of Adam and Eve, resulting in the inevitability of death for all humanity. By contrast,

Michelangelo rendered *Day* as an alert muscular male with vast potential for life. Yet, literally muscle-bound, his potential is unrealizable. His face, if intentionally left unfinished, would also express lack of fulfillment.

As *Night* and *Day* symbolize the extremes of the temporal spectrum, so Michelangelo conceived them as visual opposites. One is turned frontally, the other dorsally; one female, the other male; one past childbearing, the other bursting with sexual energy. They are a mismatched pair indeed. Yet Michelangelo united them by their similar upward-curving bodies playing against the downward curl of the sarcophagus lid. They pull apart from each other, as if to allow the ascent of the soul from the tomb.

On the west wall Michelangelo conceived *Dusk* (fig. 150), like *Day* opposite, as a muscular male with one leg drawn up and crossed over his thigh. However, unlike *Day, Dusk* is more relaxed and older, his stomach muscles softer. *Dusk* thus suggests both the energy and power of the passing day and the dissolution and death of the approaching night. Michelangelo represented Dawn as a young female just awakening to face the day; she is still relaxed from sleep, but rousing herself and lifting her veil from her head and shoulders. In contrast to *Night* opposite, her large, firm breasts, toned abdomen, and raised left leg indicate potential sexual activity and childbearing. Yet Michelangelo has also suggested, by her weariness and pained expression, that her potential to produce offspring will not be realized.

Michelangelo designed *Dusk* and *Dawn* as a responsive, not contrasting pair like *Night* and *Day* opposite. Embodying the ambiguous times of day—not full day or full night—neither is fully awake nor fully asleep. Both lethargically turn toward the viewer, following the contour of the sarcophagus, as if in danger of slipping off the lid. Like *Night* and *Day,* they also constitute a mismatched pair: one is old and impotent, the other virginal and fecund.

Michelangelo created the dukes-designate as the very embodiments of everlasting worldly renown. He elevated their effigies far above the heads of viewers and withdrew them into niches in seated postures of triumph. He dressed them in costumes of Roman commanders and idealized their youthful features. He also portrayed them as a contrasting pair. The *Baton Carrier* (fig. 149) is active, muscular, and in a posture of spiraling *contrapposto.* Holding a baton of command in one hand and coins in the other, he exemplifies the spendthrift warrior ready to spring into action to expend his physical and material resources. The *Thinker* (fig. 150) exhibits a degree of *contrapposto,* yet he is far more relaxed. He sits with his legs crossed, one hand curled against his thigh, the other raised to his lips with his elbow resting on what appears to be a money box. In his left hand he holds a *mappa* (in imperial Rome, a cloth signifying consular or imperial rank) associating him with the imperial sovereignty. Yet rather than being prepared for action, he sits thoughtfully with shaded eyes, prudently saving himself and his goods. Together they emblematize arms and letters, the virtues of ideal rule.

In summary, Michelangelo conceived the east and west walls in opposition to each other: an older infertile woman is contrasted with a younger fertile one; a mature potent male with one older and impotent; and a warrior embodying the active life with another signaling the contemplative life. This dynamic series of contrasts evoked the earthly struggle to achieve salvation.

A sixteenth-century copy in Vienna after a drawing by Michelangelo, one of many such drawings, clarifies how Michelangelo intended to complete the ducal tombs to emphasize the progress upward from the flux of time, to the divisions of time, to worldly fame, to spiritual transcendence (fig. 151). He planned figures for the niches flanking the effigies, probably classical deities embodying the dukes' virtues. On the architrave above each effigy he envisioned ancient trophies, signs of victory, which were roughed out by assistants and are still extant. Each trophy was to have been flanked by paired angels holding sun disks, emblems of Christ and divine illumination, standing on symbolic thrones, symbols of divine presence. On either side of the trophy Michelangelo also designed pairs of mourning infant spirits, expressing both loss and the potential for renewed life.

Emulating Cosimo il Vecchio's early Christian placement of the high altar in S. Lorenzo (fig. 77), Michelangelo located his altar so that the priest faced into the main room (fig. 152). From here the priest gazed across to the south wall (fig. 147). A drawing in the British Museum in London indicates how Michelangelo intended to complete this south wall (fig. 153). At the upper level he planned his *Virgin and Child* to sit within a central tabernacle flanked by the spiritual intercessors for the Medici, *SS. Cosmas and Damian* (these two doctor saints were carved by assistants). At the intermediate level, below the *Virgin and Child,* he designed a figure of Fame holding two epitaphs. At the lowest level he placed two sarcophagi without effigies for the *magnifici.*

Michelangelo's exceptionally dynamic *Virgin and Child* represents the Virgin sitting in an unusual cross-legged spiraling *contrapposto* to elevate her son on her knee and bring her breast to his mouth (fig. 154). Christ in turn straddles his mother's thigh, turning around to grasp her breast and shoulder. Together they create a tightly interlocked pair, dramatizing nursing as they absorb the gazes of the priest and the effigies of the dukes-designate (fig. 147). In this work Michelangelo binds art and liturgy into a single dynamic image of the Church's spiritual nurturing. This liturgical and artistic drama was played out around the clock, for the Medici endowed two priests to celebrate three requiem Masses every day of the year, over one thousand Masses a year. Between Masses, the entire Psalter was recited continuously day and night, each Psalm followed by a prayer.

The New Sacristy was dedicated to the Resurrection. A drawing now in Windsor Castle, England, indicates that Michelangelo planned to fresco the lunette above the *Virgin and Child* with a scene of the *Resurrection*. On the drawing Christ leaps to the left from his tomb into the light. In the chapel left is east, from where the chapel receives its best morning light. In coordination with the new day's sun, then, the fresco would have dramatically reenacted the promise of salvation. The frescoed Resurrection in turn would have led the officiating priest's eyes to the vaults (fig. 148) flooded with light and defined by semicircular, circular, and hemispherical forms constituting an image of Paradise regained.

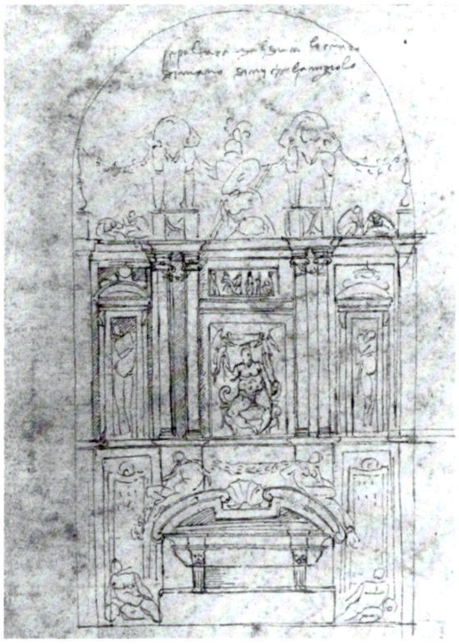

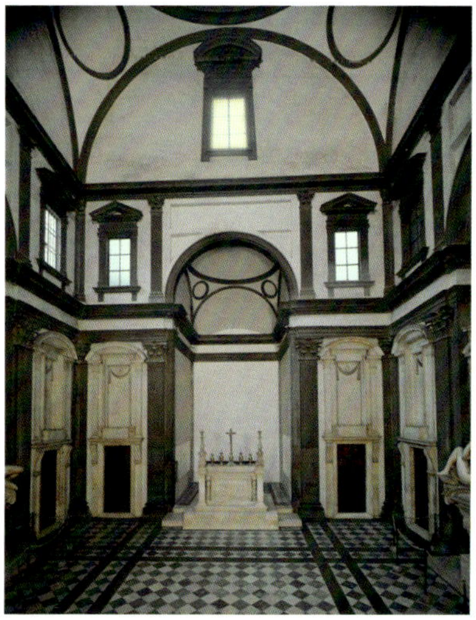

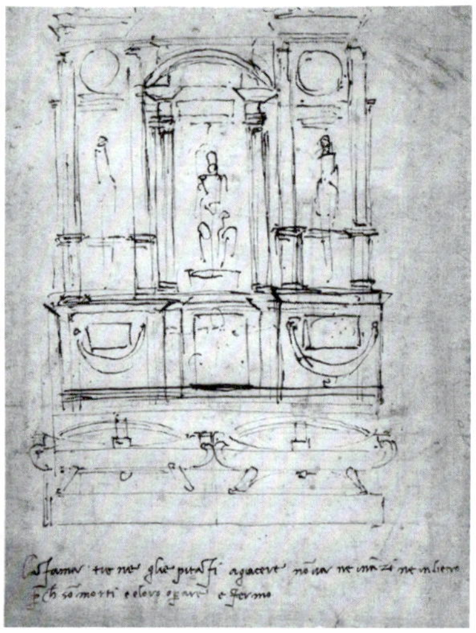

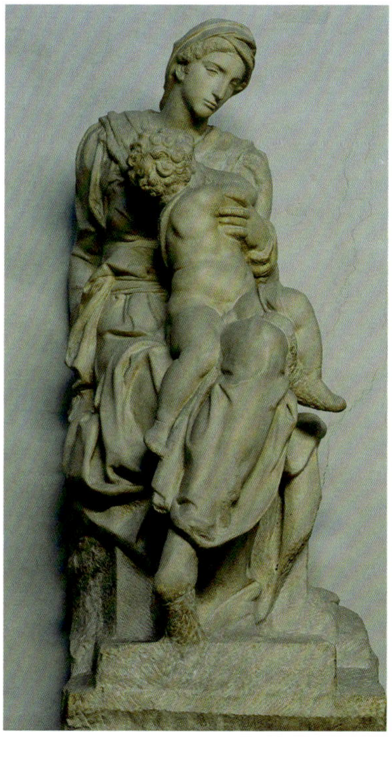

151. Giovanni Battista da Sangallo, called Il Gobbo (1496–1548), after Michelangelo, *Study for the Tomb of the Baton Carrier in the New Sacristy,* sixteenth century, pen and ink, 10⅞ × 8 in. (27.5 × 20.4 cm), Albertina, Vienna.

152. Michelangelo, altar chapel, north wall, New Sacristy.

153. Michelangelo, *Study for the South Wall of the New Sacristy,* 1519–34, pen and ink, 8¼ × 6⅜ in. (21 × 16.2 cm), British Museum, London. The inscription on the drawing reads, "*Fame* holds the epitaphs steady, for they [the *magnifici*] are dead and their work finished. It [fame] goes neither forward nor back."

154. Michelangelo, *Virgin and Child,* marble, height 7 ft. 5 in. (226 cm), south wall, New Sacristy.

MICHELANGELO'S LAURENTIAN LIBRARY

About the same time that Pope Clement VII renewed the commission for the New Sacristy, he also contracted with Michelangelo to design a public library for the monastery of S. Lorenzo (figs. 32, nos. 11 and 12; 155–57), emulating his great-grandfather Cosimo il Vecchio, who financed the building of the public library at S. Marco (figs. 38, no. 12; 39). Whereas the S. Marco library had been built as a repository for the private collection of Niccolò Niccoli, however, the Laurentian Library was constructed to house the much larger collection of Medici manuscripts and books. In addition, being attached to the Church of S. Lorenzo, which had become a pantheon for the burial of Medici dead, and located around the corner from the Medici Palace (figs. 12, nos. 21 and 25; 92–94), the Laurentian Library celebrated, more powerfully than the earlier library in S. Marco, the wisdom, wealth, and munificence of the Medici. Construction started in 1526, but only in 1571 was the library fully completed and opened to the public.

Since space was limited, Michelangelo built the library on top of the vaulted two-story west wing of the preexisting fifteenth-century cloister. This arrangement, like that of Michelozzo's S. Marco library, had the advantage of providing a fire- and moisture-proof foundation for the library and elevating it above the roof line of the cloister to provide superb light from a row of unobstructed windows on either side of the reading room. However, since the cloisters had not been designed for a third story, the site had the major disadvantage of not allowing a fireproof masonry vault to be built over the library, as at S. Marco. Rather, the walls had to be as thin and light as possible and could support only wooden trusses that carried the exterior sloping tiled roof and the interior flat wooden-beamed ceiling.

Michelangelo's design consisted of two spaces in counterpoint (fig. 155), the architectural equivalent of anatomical *contrapposto* so characteristic of his sculptural work. The *ricetto,* or vestibule, was essentially a stairwell leading from the second-floor monastic cells to the third-floor reading room (fig. 156). In keeping with its function, the space was tall and vertical and its articulation dynamic. By contrast, the reading room space was appropriately long and horizontal and its articulation serene (fig. 157).

To distribute the weight over the strongest part of vault below, Michelangelo designed the stairs of the *ricetto* to fill the center of the space and to avoid the walls. These *pietra serena* steps suggest molten lava flowing down in waves and curling inward where they meet the balustrade—a metaphorical river of knowledge cascad-

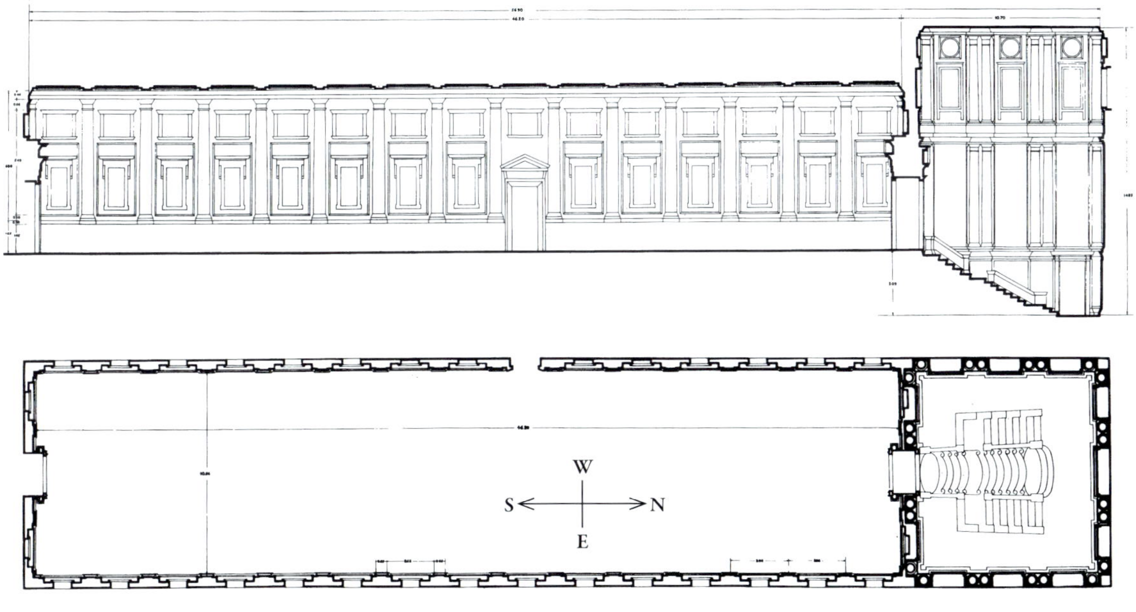

155. Michelangelo, plan and section, Laurentian Library and vestibule, S. Lorenzo, 1524–71.

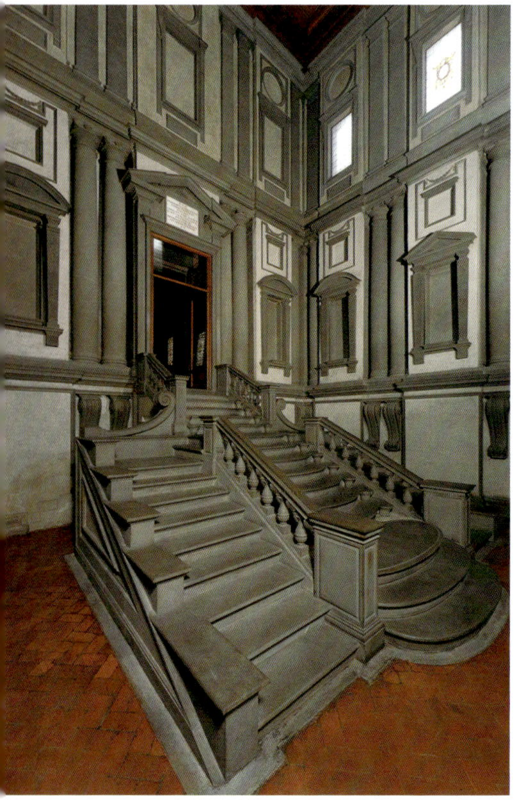

156. Michelangelo, vestibule, Laurentian Library, S. Lorenzo, 1524–27. The staircase, designed by Michelangelo in 1558–59, was executed by Bartolomeo Ammannati (1511–92).

157. Michelangelo, reading room, Laurentian Library, S. Lorenzo, 1524–27. The library opened to the public in 1571.

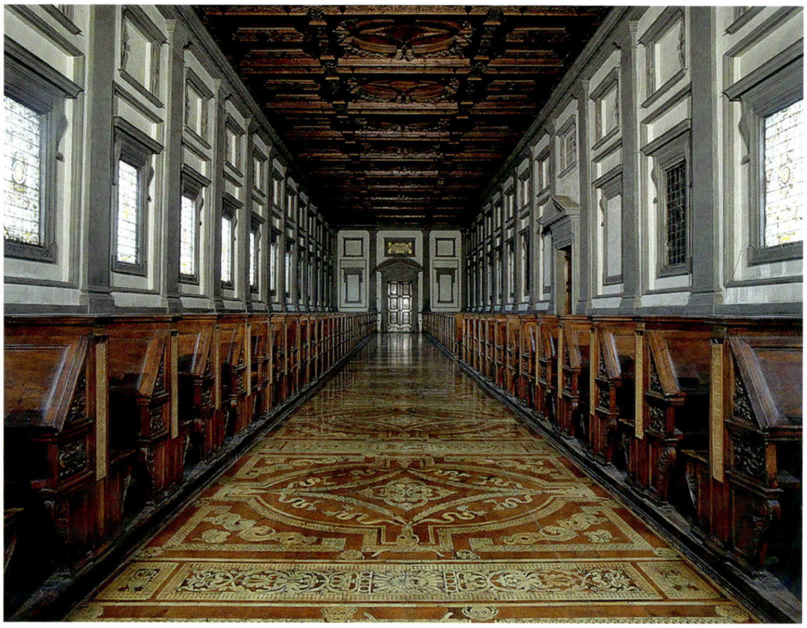

ing from the door of the reading room. For visitors ascending to the reading room against this current, the steps create a visual and psychological tension evoking the great effort required to acquire wisdom.

Similarly, Michelangelo designed the articulation of the walls with paradoxical inversions and deviations from classical norms. Paired columns with unconventional capitals are pressed into the wall and framed by pilasters rather than engaged or freestanding in front of the wall. They rest on consoles rather than pedestals. In each corner the columns are mated with a pier, counter to tradition. Between the columns Michelangelo installed windowlike frames of a type that might be found articulating windows on the *piano nobile* and mezzanine of a palace, yet they are on the interior rather than exterior, blind rather than open, and far too crowded by the columns. In addition, the pilasters of lower pedimented niches are oddly tapered with unusual fluting, while the frames above display strange U-shaped extensions from which hang garlands. The actual windows that light the *ricetto* are unusually high, as if the viewer were standing below ground level. While the columns and piers are actually important structural components of the thin walls, the wall articulation, combined with the stairway, engenders a space that appears discordant, irrational, and nonstructural, creating, metaphorically, a jarring and disjointed world outside the fount of knowledge and reason.

The reading room, by contrast, is harmonious, rational, and structural. Framed canonically, even while deeply inset into the mass of the walls, the windows flood the room with an even and warm light exactly where needed: above each of the sixty desks designed by Michelangelo. The pilasters project correctly from the walls, carry an orthodox entablature, and are coordinated with roof beams to create an integrated structural cage reflective of the basilical plan of Michelozzo's S. Marco library.

In the reading room, in sum, all decorative elements, including the nearly identical Michelangelo-designed patterns of the carved wooden ceiling and the inlaid marble pavement, appear restful, integrated, and structural. In the *ricetto* the articulation appears agitated, disintegrated, and capricious. This architectural *contrapposto* symbolically evokes the contrast, appropriate for a library, between ignorance and knowledge, irrationality and reason, discord and harmony.

23

ALTARPIECES AND DEVOTIONAL WORKS

S. FRANCESCO: SARTO'S *MADONNA OF THE HARPIES*

Every detail of the austere *Madonna of the Harpies* (fig. 158) by Andrea del Sarto, commissioned by the abbess of S. Francesco for her Florentine convent's high altar, evokes the reenactment of Christ's birth, death, and resurrection in the Mass, and the liturgy's mediation between earth and heaven. The chubby and curly-haired Christ Child places his right foot over his mother's womb, recalling the Incarnation, glances downward and squirms, eager to step down to accept his earthly destiny. He smiles joyously in anticipation of the spiritual bliss that awaits him after his Passion. The octagonal pedestal, shaped like a classical sacrificial altar, also connotes Christ's sacrifice and his Resurrection eight days after his entry into Jerusalem. John, present at the Crucifixion, and Francis, often called an *alter Christus* (another Christ) for his receipt of the stigmata (the five wounds of Christ), together allude to Christ's sacrifice. The lively *contrapposto* of the two saints and their gazes out at the viewer also evince Christ's promise of regeneration. As the embodied Church, the Virgin stands on a pedestal— a sculptural presence in a relaxed but active posture. The pedestal, however, elevates her as a deity, and its inscription—"The Queen is carried on high to the highest throne"—refers to her Assumption as the Queen of Heaven. As the Virgin emerges into the light from the mysterious Leonardesque *sfumato,* the supreme beauty of her veiled head, the introspection of her expression, the sublime harmony of the colors of her drapery, and the emblems of ancient Egyptian religious knowledge carved on her pedestal (sphinxes, not harpies, as traditionally called), all attest to her role as eternal Wisdom and to her acute awareness of her son's destiny foretold in her book. Even the glances of the two angels—one earthward, the other heavenward—thematize the Virgin and Child's dual human and divine natures. Similarly, the background architecture that structures the composition implies the visible Church, yet its expansion beyond the frame and its geometrically perfect convex dais and concave niche also call to mind the celestial Church. Finally, the puff of incense floating to the left of Christ's head refers both to the actual Masses celebrated regularly at the high altar and to the perpetual celestial liturgy of the heavenly court. Similarly, Sarto's signature in the imperfect tense, "Andrea del Sarto of Florence was making this," rather than the perfect "made this," alludes both to a past and an ongoing process of creation, a distinction made vivid to the Renaissance in Pliny's well-known *Natural History* (Preface, 26).

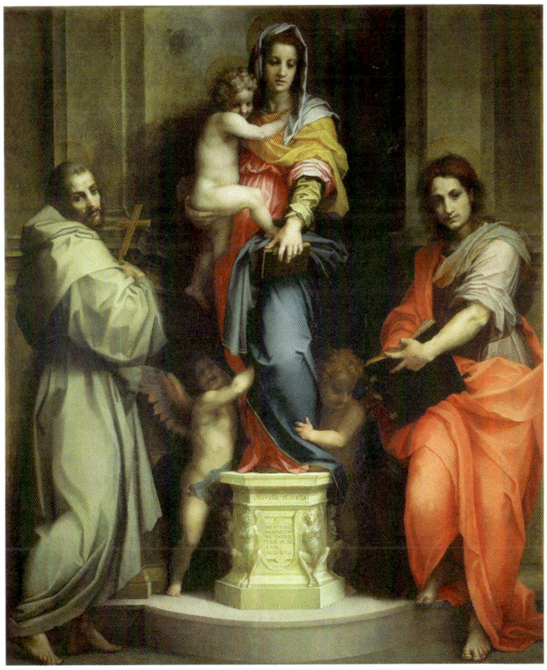

158. Andrea del Sarto, *Madonna of the Harpies (Virgin and Child with SS. Francis and John the Evangelist),* signed and dated 1517, oil on panel, 6 ft. 9½ in. × 5 ft. 10 in. (207 × 178 cm), Uffizi.

ROSSO'S *MOSES DEFENDING THE DAUGHTERS OF JETHRO*

In 1517, the year Sarto completed his *sacra conversazione* of the *Madonna of the Harpies,* Martin Luther (1483–1546) nailed his ninety-five theses on the doors of the church at Wittenberg. This particularly dramatic and defining act within the movement for Church reform had been gathering force for over two centuries, but it was only one of many challenges to the Church's traditional doctrines and liturgical practices in the period before the Council of Trent (1545–63). The political, economic, and military upheavals of the early sixteenth century in Florence and elsewhere in Italy compounded the religious crisis. Within this confusing atmosphere, many Catholics felt more dependent than ever on Christ's mercy and grace, and they sought more personal and immediate religious experiences than those offered by the elitist and worldly Church. Many Florentine artists responded by turning away from the balanced and cerebral High Renaissance styles of Leonardo, Raphael, and Sarto to more emotionally and spiritually charged modes, a style usually called first-generation Mannerism.

Moses Defending the Daughters of Jethro (fig. 159) by Rosso Fiorentino (1494–1540) represents an early example of such a Mannerist style. At the upper right the seven daughters of Jethro have gathered around the communal well outside of Midian to refresh their flock. They foreshadow the assembly of Christian faithful at the well of baptism. Prevented by a group of evil shepherds from using the well, they are defended by Moses, who drives away the shepherds. He thus prefigures the Good Shepherd's sacrificial triumph over sin and death reenacted in the Eucharist. Shortly thereafter, Moses married Zipporah, the daughter dressed in blue, anticipating Christ's union with the Virgin and the Church's foundation.

The painting is remarkably violent: Moses has knocked down three opponents and savagely pummels a fourth, as a fifth races to attack Zipporah. The figures' tousled hair, shouts, anatomical contortions, extreme foreshortening, and billowing drapery all heighten the intensity of the mêlée. Rosso's triangular composition of the foreground figures imposes a minimum of classical structure on the commotion, although the forms are more angular, aggressive, and harshly lit than in any High Renaissance art work. Furthermore, Rosso's display of nude or seminude bodies associates the violence with sexuality, as if to emphasize the widely believed notion that sex provoked humanity's downfall. This disturbing painting not only reflects something of the period's crises, but also Rosso's own disquiet spirit and the character of its patron, Giovanni Bandini (1498–1568), a brothel keeper known to have killed several men in duels (see chapter 31), who presumably commissioned the work for his family palace.

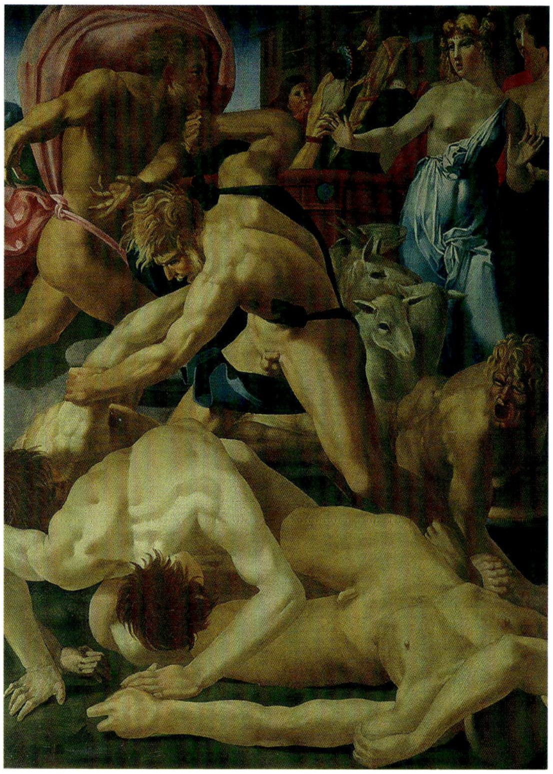

159. Rosso Fiorentino, *Moses Defending the Daughters of Jethro* (Exodus 2:16–22), 1523–24, oil on canvas, 63 × 46 in. (160 × 117 cm), Uffizi.

S. FELICITÀ: PONTORMO'S *DEPOSITION*

Between 1419 and 1423, in the Church of S. Felicità (fig. 12, no. 19), Brunelleschi had built the Barbardori Chapel, which was dedicated to the Annunciation. Ludovico di Gino Capponi (1482–1534) bought the chapel's patronage rights in 1525, added the Pietà to its dedication, and commissioned its decoration from Jacopo Pontormo, another Mannerist painter. Pontormo's altarpiece, traditionally called a *Deposition* (fig. 160), visualized the chapel's new dedication to the Pietà, a subject highlighted by the artist's quotation of Michelangelo's Roman *Pietà* for his figure of Christ. The subject matter, however, is not so straightforward.

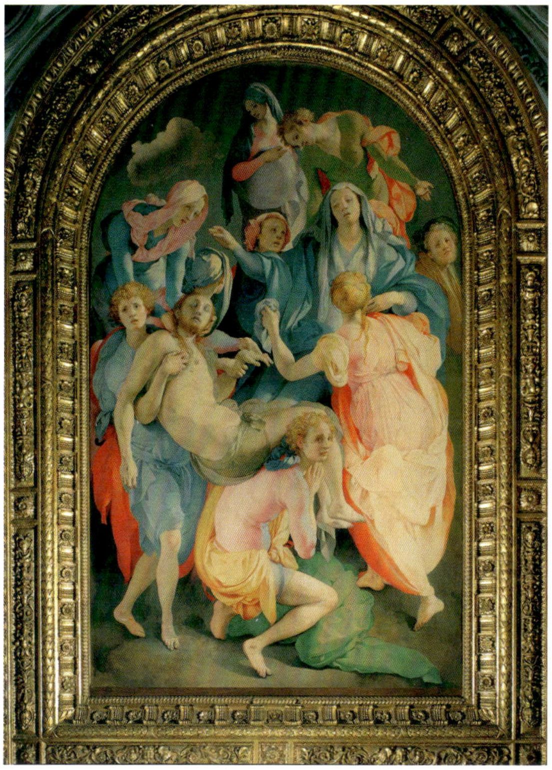

160. Pontormo, *Deposition,* 1525–28, oil on panel, 10 ft. 3¼ in. × 6 ft. 3⅝ in. (313 × 192 cm), Barbardori-Capponi Chapel, S. Felicità.

In response to the chapel's only window at the altar's right, the artist depicted the light falling diagonally from the upper right. Mary Magdalene rushes in frenetically from the lower right along a contrary diagonal to offer consolation to the grieving Virgin surrounded by four companions, including the androgynous John the Evangelist, who supports her from behind. Mary Magdalene's movement draws the eye to the upper left, where, in his preparatory drawing in Oxford, Pontormo had depicted a ladder, an attribute of a Deposition. In the altarpiece, however, he painted a cloud backlit from the left, contrary to the general light flow. The cloud invoked the Incarnation, the chapel's first dedication, based on Wisdom's speech in Ecclesiasticus 24:5–7, "I made that in the heaven there should rise light that never faileth, and as a cloud I covered all the earth." The sun ("light that never faileth") signified Christ; the cloud containing the sun, the Virgin as the vessel of the Incarnation; and the shadow covering the earth, the Church.

The painting's compositional division into two groups—one focused on Christ, the other on the Virgin—indicates that Pontormo has also illustrated Christ's separation from his mother and the transportation of his body to the tomb. The two foreground figures have just lifted Christ's heroic body from the Virgin's lap, the squatting figure acting as a pivot while the standing figure walks forward. Their coordinated actions have brought Christ's body into the foreground light, where it makes maximum visual impact when juxtaposed with the elevated Eucharist. As the drama of separation unfolds, the echoing rhetorical gestures of the Virgin, John, and Mary Magdalene, the pathos of the figures' expressions, the dissonant high-keyed color, and the intense light raise the painting's emotional pitch to a fervent Lamentation.

The crouching posture of the central foreground figure implies that the two transporters might be about to lower Christ's body onto the altar, Christ's symbolic tomb, in front of which the patron was buried. The crouching porter, however, effortlessly bears the weight of Christ's massive body on the tips of his toes, and his companion moves with a light-footed gait that also denies the cadaver's weight. These grief-filled porters, therefore, appear to be wingless angels carrying Christ's body as spirit, not matter. An upward-looking woman, who looms up from behind Christ, cradles and tips Christ's head upward suggesting that the angels might even carry the Son heavenward to join God the Father and the Holy Spirit that Pontormo had frescoed on the chapel's vault (destroyed in 1765–67). The animated green drapery at the knees of the crouching angel further suggests the promise of Christ's resurrection.

Deftly and poignantly, then, Pontormo alluded to the Incarnation, Deposition, Pietà, Lamentation, Leave Taking of Christ from the Virgin, Transportation of Christ to the Tomb, Entombment, and Resurrection—all as dramas in progress. Yet he suppressed the usual historical trappings and clustered the figures above a barren rocky shelf close to the picture plane with little comprehensible spatial connection to the ground or to each other. He also silhouetted the actors against an unnatural slate sky and painted their draperies in icy blues and acid pinks, reds, and yellows. Pontormo thus transmuted historical drama into a private, mystical, even hallucinatory vision with which he personally identified by including his self-portrait wearing an artist's beret to the extreme right in the guise of Nicodemus, traditionally believed to have been an artist.

24

PORTRAITS

SARTO'S *MAN WITH A BOOK*

Andrea del Sarto's seated *Portrait of a Man with a Book* (fig. 161) constitutes his response to, and development of, the High Renaissance portraiture of Leonardo and Raphael (figs. 137 and 138). Sarto created a more rigorously formal composition than those of his exemplars by reducing his color to a few deep and resonant tones; aligning the sitter's face and elbow along the painting's central vertical axis; projecting the figure against a shallow neutral background; and containing the sitter both two- and three-dimensionally within a diamond-shaped configuration.

Within this rather strict formal order, Sarto developed an exceptionally lively presence. The multiple compositional diagonals of book, arms, chair back, and beret express great dynamism. Having been absorbed in reading, with his back largely turned to the picture plane, the young man now suddenly turns to regard the viewer who has just walked into his space and consciousness. The bright light falling from the upper left, with its strong *chiaroscuro* (light and shadow modeling) powerfully sculpting the figure's faceted sleeve, further enlivens the composition and intensifies the sitter's physical immediacy. Sarto's characteristically harmonious colors are applied with broad and rapid brushstrokes throughout, including the background, which lightens toward the right to underline the oblique torsion of the sitter's body. The equilibrium Sarto achieved between dynamism and order, action and abstraction, constitutes the essence of a High Renaissance style.

SARTO'S *WOMAN WITH PETRARCH'S POEMS*

Sarto composed his *Woman with Petrarch's Poems* (fig. 162) in a manner very similar to the portrait just discussed. However, he made some adjustments, turning the arm of the chair at an angle to the picture plane, rotating the sitter's torso toward the viewer, aligning her face and book on parallel diagonals, and intensifying the blues and whites. He also created a more complex and nuanced expression. While the sitter appears self-possessed and intelligent like the *Man with a Book,* she is also coy and erotic. Furthermore, Sarto evokes the torments of the Petrarchan love, vacillating between misery and ecstasy, by depicting

161. Andrea del Sarto, *Portrait of a Man with a Book,* c. 1517, signed with a monogram, oil on linen, 28½ × 22½ in. (72.4 × 57.2 cm), The National Gallery, London.

his subject pointing to Petrarch's poem 152 on the left-hand page. In this poem the distraught poet begs for mercy because Laura ignores him, her heart cruel like that of a tiger or bear. Poem 153, which is legible at the top of the right-hand page, again attributes a cruel heart to Laura, but Petrarch's great love for her begins to transform his disquiet. Finally, poem 154, partially obscured by the woman's left hand, as if it were a promise waiting for fulfillment, finds Petrarch elevated by his transcendent love for Laura, whose eyes radiate sweetness, grace, chastity, and honor. Between the book and the face, a small bouquet underlines the ambiguity of Petrarch's poems and the woman's expression: the white flowers could constitute an emblem either of chaste and pure love or the transience of passion and beauty.

Like Leonardo in his *Mona Lisa,* Sarto envisioned his sitter's beauty as equivalent to the bravura and brilliance of his own artistic imagination. However, while Leonardo conceived the creative process as the expression of the full complexity of nature across the ages, Sarto focused more narrowly on capturing the nuances of human emotion.

ROSSO'S *YOUNG MAN*

The *Portrait of a Young Man* (fig. 163) in Berlin represents Rosso's response to the portraits of Leonardo, Raphael, and Sarto (figs. 137, 138, and 161). Rosso started with their same general format and composition, but depicted his subject with greater energy. He seems to stand rather than sit, his left arm is akimbo with the elbow turned toward the picture plane, and his right arm and shoulder are drawn back with his thumb tucked into his belt. The wide lapels of his coat form a wide dynamic V, drawing attention to the awkward way the young man juts his head forward.

The landscape backgrounds to the right and left are discontinuous, emphasizing the turn of the figure in space, an idea borrowed from Leonardo's *Mona Lisa* (fig. 137). To the left a river flows under a bridge toward the

162. Andrea del Sarto, *Woman with Petrarch's Poems,* c. 1526–28, oil on panel, 34¼ × 27⅛ in. (87 × 69 cm), Uffizi.

163. Rosso Fiorentino, *Portrait of a Young Man,* c. 1517, oil on panel, 31⅛ × 22½ in. (79 × 57 cm), Gemäldegalerie, Staatliche Museen zu Berlin. The attribution to Rosso is disputed.

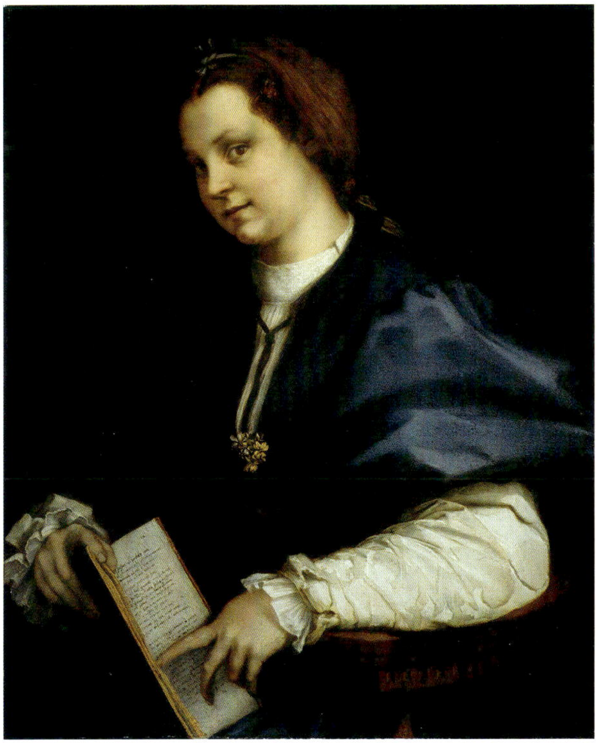

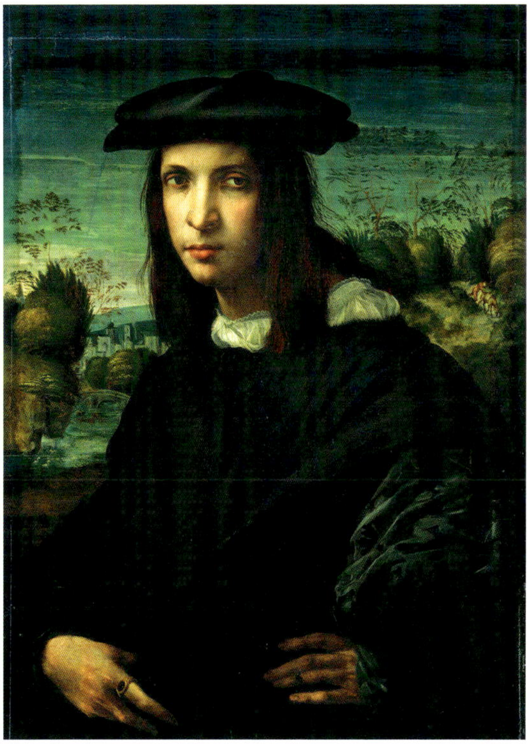

town in the background, heightening the turn of the man's right shoulder away from the picture plane, while to the right a figure beating a donkey walks down a country road, reinforcing the turn of the man's left shoulder toward the picture plane. The feathery vegetation, lively silhouette, and unruly hair further intensify the young man's torsion.

The darkened sky above the figure's head contrasts with the brightly lit horizon, and the rather acid palette and rapid Sarto-esque brushwork give the young man's intense and penetrating gaze a note of disturbed foreboding and nervous agitation. The final effect is one of febrile restlessness and eccentric intensity characteristic of first-generation Mannerism.

PART IV

FLORENCE

under the Medici Dukes

1531–1600

25

EARLIER FREESTANDING PUBLIC SCULPTURE

BANDINELLI'S *HERCULES AND CACUS*

After Leo X's death in 1521 and Cardinal Giulio de' Medici's ascension to the throne of St. Peter's in 1523 as Clement VII, the new pope commissioned Bandinelli in 1525 to sculpt a marble *Hercules and Cacus* (fig. 164) to stand next to Michelangelo's *David* (figs. 132 and 133) on the rostrum of the Priors' Palace (fig. 179, nos. 1 and 2). The work was intended to express Clement's political policy toward Florence and undercut the republican implications of Michelangelo's *David*. But before Bandinelli began work, the Medici were again expelled and replaced by the last Florentine republic (1527–30). When the Medici regained control of the city in 1531 with the aid of imperial troops and installed the illegitimate Alessandro de' Medici as the first duke of Florence on May 1, 1532, Clement VII and Alessandro renewed Bandinelli's commission as a victorious sign of the restoration of Medici rule in Florence.

To relate his sculpture to Michelangelo's *David,* Bandinelli represented Hercules vigilantly surveying the surrounding space with a fierce leonine expression. Yet with his thicker, more muscular body—exaggerated for greater legibility within the vast piazza—Hercules more closely resembled classical prototypes inspired by the *Doryphoros* (fig. 5) than any previous Florentine colossal sculpture. Remarkably, however, Bandinelli did not employ classical *contrapposto.* Rather, Hercules stands flat-footed and stable, recalling the stance of Donatello's *St. George* (fig. 25), the revered symbol of republican military preparedness. The comparison underscored Hercules' far greater strength and, by extension, the greater security offered by the Medici duke and pope.

Bandinelli also referenced Donatello's *Abraham and Isaac* (fig. 27). Abraham and Hercules both straddle a male figure, grip his hair with their left hands, hold their weapons in their lowered right hands, and turn their heads and torsos leftward to look outward. Just as Isaac was saved by divine intervention, so Hercules, contrary to the myth, is represented as sparing Cacus, to signify

164. Baccio Bandinelli, *Hercules and Cacus,* signed and dated 1534, marble, 16 ft. 3¼ in. (496 cm), Piazza della Signoria. Turbaned Atlantes on each face of the base signified capture and defeat. The merciful lion and loyal dog at the back of the base symbolized the clement and faithful Medici. A wild boar and a ferocious wolf on the front alluded to the violent enemies of the Medici.

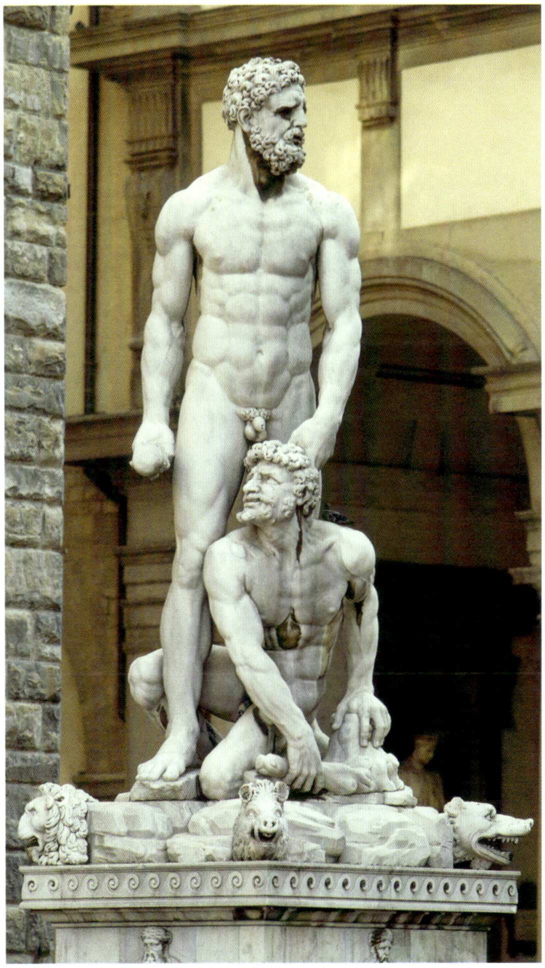

the divine clemency of Clement VII, who chose his papal name explicitly to refer to his policy of strong but clement rule of Florence. This policy was succinctly articulated by the great Florentine historian and Medici advisor Francesco Guicciardini (1483–1540): "There is nothing that men ought to desire more on this earth . . . than to see their enemy prostrate on the ground and at their mercy. This glory is greatly increased by. . . . showing mercy and letting it suffice to have conquered." Indeed, Cacus, prostrate at Hercules' feet with a pained expression of defeat, looks back toward the Priors' Palace, as if pleading for clemency. Clement's political strategy became all the more necessary when Alessandro—a cruel and vain libertine despised by most Florentines—proved from the beginning to be far from merciful.

Perhaps Bandinelli intended to complement Alessandro's domineering character by rendering his Hercules with a massive, muscled body and phallic club, but he may also have been responding to the looming crisis concerning the continuity of the Medici line. By May 1, 1534, when the sculpture group was dedicated, all Medici males had died except Clement VII, who would die in less than five months, the illegitimate Cardinal Ippolito, who died the next year, and the illegitimate Alessandro. If Alessandro's marriage in 1533 to the eleven-year-old illegitimate daughter of Charles V, Margaret of Austria (1522–86), were to produce no children (and it did not), then Cosimo il Vecchio's branch of the Medici family would become extinct with Alessandro's death (as it did when he was assassinated in 1537). With dynastic continuity in doubt, all the more reason for Bandinelli to emphasize manly prowess.

Like Michelangelo, Bandinelli would also have understood male virility as a metaphor for his own artistic powers. The bold signature—"Baccio Bandinelli of Florence made this in 1534"—carved in red porphyry on the base in Roman block letters, claimed Hercules' triumph over Cacus as a sign of Bandinelli's aesthetic victory over both Donatello and Michelangelo by creating the first freestanding Florentine sculpture to offer multiple views. While squaring the base and figures' lower limbs with the palace façade, Bandinelli dynamically rotated Hercules' and Cacus's torsos to provide a major oblique view from the rostrum's stairs. Bandinelli heightened the dynamism by contrasting the rock-hard mass and weight of Hercules with the energy of Cacus—a virtuoso *figura serpentinata* (serpentine figure) tightly contorted and coiled into a complex posture of maximum anatomical torsion. The net result was a work that read well from most perspectives.

According to Virgil's *Aeneid* (8.271) and Ovid's *Fasti* (1.581), Cacus plagued the region around present-day Rome by stealing cattle that he subsequently hid in a cave. Alerted by the cows' mooing, Hercules discovered the cave, killed Cacus, and founded Rome, one of several myths of Rome's foundation. Having restored peace and prosperity to the region, Hercules built a great altar (*ara maxima*) in the Forum Boarium at the site of his victory, where the citizens could worship him as the city's founder and liberator. Bandinelli's *Hercules and Cacus,* which both exudes *romanità* (Romanness) and stands on a base imitating an *ara maxima,* transformed the Piazza della Signoria into a new Forum Boarium and Florence into a new Rome. Having dedicated the group on May 1, 1534, the second anniversary of his investiture with the ducal title, Alessandro claimed to be a new Hercules, ending what the Medici viewed as the turmoil of republican rule.

In October 1532, six months after becoming duke, Alessandro ordered the Priors' Palace tower bell, called *la vacca* (the cow) to be melted down. For over two centuries the bell had called *parlamenti* and alerted Florentines to danger by its ring, called *la mugia* (the moo). Like Hercules, Alessandro had silenced the "mooing" forever, liberated Florence from republican instability, and claimed to have founded a serene and flourishing Medici regime, symbolized by the new coins he struck from the bell's bronze. There can be no doubt, then, that for Clement and Alessandro, the defeated Cacus—ever ready to spring into action, if not watched and restrained by strength and clemency—was understood to embody anti-Medici rebels.

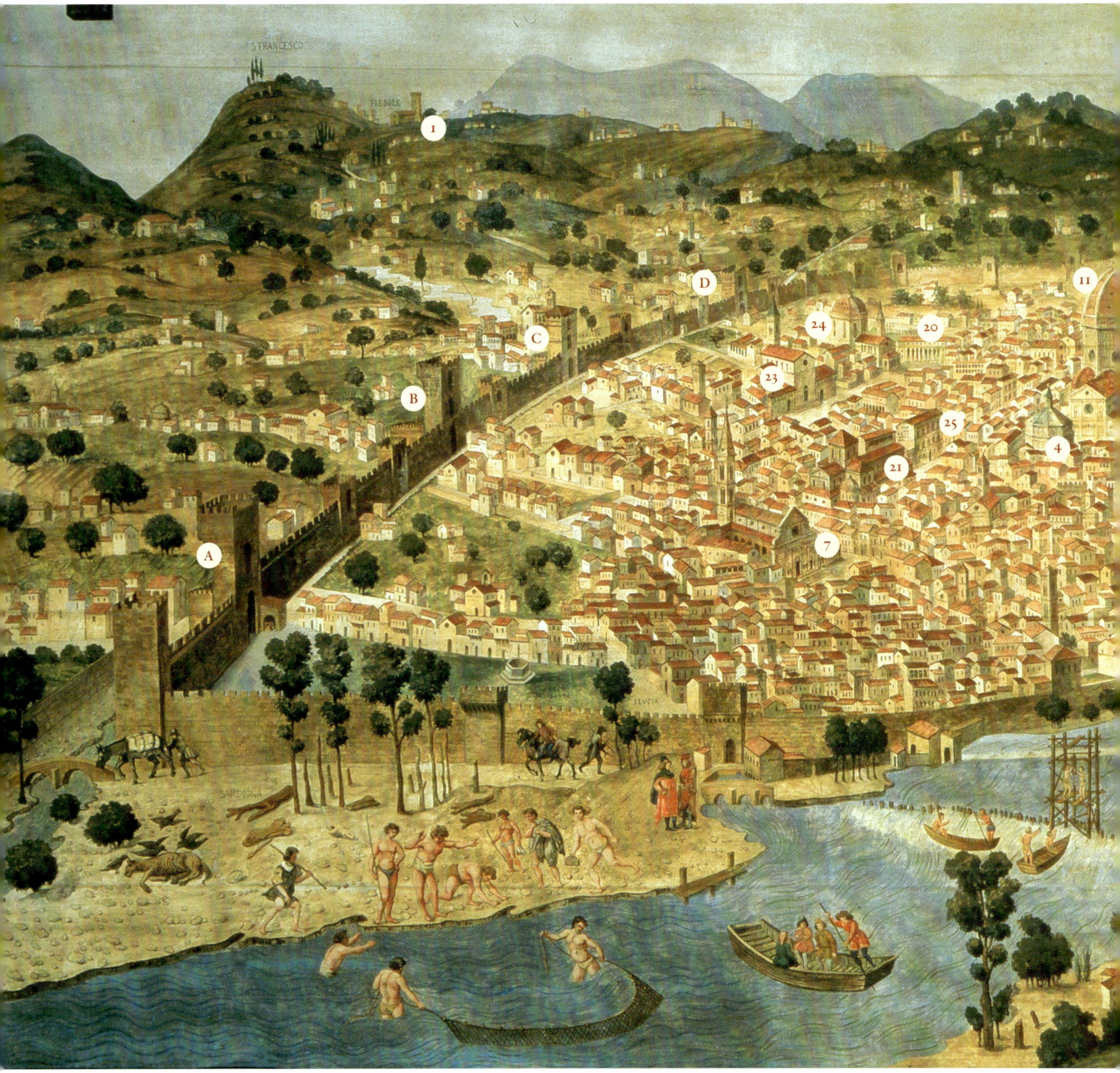

Anonymous, *View of Florence,* tempera on panel, Museo di Firenze Com'Era, Florence, based on a woodcut c. 1480 attributed to Francesco di Lorenzo Rosselli (1448–before 1513). In roughly chronological order: 1 Fiesole (Etruscan-Roman); 2 Column of the Mercato Vecchio, site of first-century BC Roman Forum; 3 S. Miniato al Monte (Benedictine until 1373, then Olivetan), founded by eighth century, rebuilt 1018–1207; 4 Baptistery, 1059–1150; 5 Palazzo del Podestà or Bargello, 1255–1345; 6 S. Maria del Carmine (Carmelite), begun 1268; 7 S. Maria Novella (Dominican), founded c. 1221, church c. 1246–78, façade c. 1457–78; 8 Campanile of Badia (Benedictine), founded 978, rebuilt 1285; 9 Palazzo Spini-Feroni, begun 1289; 10 S. Croce (Franciscan), founded 1228, begun 1295; 11 Cathedral, 1296–1467; 12 Priors' Palace, or Palazzo Vecchio, 1299–1315; 13 S. Trinita (Vallombrosan), founded in second half of eleventh century, rebuilt in fourteenth century, façade 1593–94;

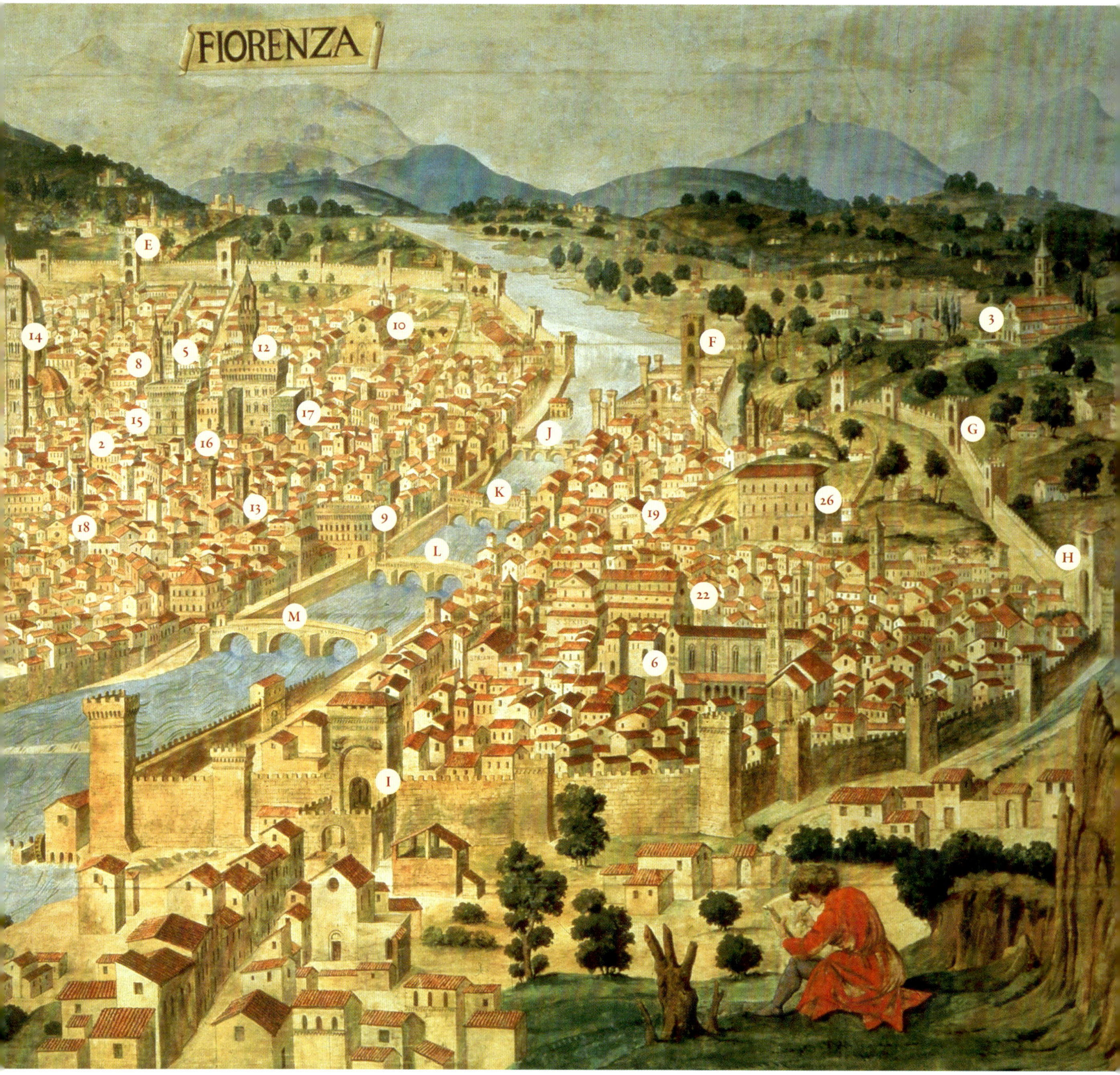

14 Cathedral Campanile, 1334–60; 15 Or San Michele, 1336–1404; 16 Palazzo della Tribunale di Mercanzia, 1359; 17 Priors' Loggia, or Loggia dei Lanzi, 1374–82; 18 S. Pancrazio (Vallombrosan), documented by ninth century, begun 1370; 19 S. Felicità; 20 Foundling Hospital, 1419–45; 21 S. Lorenzo (Ambrosian), consecrated 393, rebuilt 1421–94; 22 S. Spirito (Augustinian), founded c. 1250, rebuilt c. 1434–96; 23 S. Marco (Silvestrine until 1436, then Dominican), begun 1299, rebuilt 1436–45; 24 SS. Annunziata (Servite), founded 1240, rebuilt 1444–1516; 25 Medici Palace, c. 1446–57; 26 Pitti Palace, 1458–66; A Porta al Prato; B Porta Faenza; C Porta S. Gallo; D Porta Pinta; E Porta S. Croce; F Porta S. Niccolò; G Porta S. Giorgio; H Porta Romana; I Porta S. Frediano; J Ponte alle Grazie; K Ponte Vecchio; L Ponte S. Trinita; M Ponte alla Carraia.

26

PALACE CHAPELS

Palazzo Vecchio

After the assassination of Duke Alessandro in 1537, the eighteen-year-old Cosimo I de' Medici was first made the *capo* (head) of the Florentine government and shortly thereafter the second duke by a group of oligarchs who hope to manipulate the inexperienced youth to their advantage. Almost immediately after his appointment as *capo,* Cosimo faced his first major challenge, when the Florentine exiles attempted to drive the Medici from power yet once again. The exiles, however, were defeated by the Florentine forces at the Battle of Montemurlo on August 1, 1537. Since Emperor Augustus had defeated Cleopatra and Mark Antony (c. 83–31 BC) at Actium on the same day (August 1) in 31 BC, it was repeatedly emphasized within the ducal court that Cosimo had become a new Augustus who had renewed Florence's imperial destiny.

In 1539 at age twenty, Duke Cosimo I married the seventeen-year-old Eleonora da Toledo (1522–62) from a noble Spanish family and daughter of Don Pedro di Alvarez di Toledo, viceroy of Naples for Emperor Charles V (1500–1558). This marriage considerably raised Cosimo's status within the Florentine social order. The next year, in 1540, Cosimo and Eleonora moved from the Medici Palace (figs. 92–94) to the Priors' Palace (fig. 13), which, as the largest palace in Florence, was more commensurate with Eleonora's high social status. The huge palace also added dignity and majesty to Cosimo I's newly founded ducal regime and symbolically demonstrated that his regime had definitively supplanted the last republic. Finally, as the strongest and most defensible palace in Florence, the Priors' Palace provided greater security for Cosimo and Eleonora while Cosimo consolidated his still-tentative power. The move necessitated expanding, remodeling, and redecorating the palace, first under the direction of Giovanni Battista del Tasso (1500–1555) from 1540 to 1555, then under Giorgio Vasari from 1555 to 1574 (see fig. 179).

BRONZINO'S CHAPEL OF ELEONORA

The earliest part of the project included a new cubic chapel—approximately 13 × 13 × 13 feet (4 × 4 × 4 m) with a shallow pendentive vault—for the apartment of Eleonora created out of the so-called Green Room by the addition of two new walls. The chapel was decorated by Agnolo Bronzino from 1540 to 1546.

As the sixteenth-century papacy strengthened its authority in Italy and demanded conformity to traditional doctrines, Cosimo I simultaneously tightened his grip on Florentine religious, political, and cultural life and projected his power through sophisticated artistic displays of piety, strength, and erudition. In such an orthodox and authoritarian climate, personal and unconventional religious expression, such as Pontormo's *Deposition* (fig. 160), was deemed less acceptable. As a result, Florentine second-generation Mannerist religious art, exemplified by the Chapel of Eleonora, became ever more didactic, iconic, and refined. Duke Cosimo consciously intended not only to emulate Cosimo il Vecchio's display of piety, privilege, and wealth in the Medici Palace chapel (figs. 103–106), but also to associate his ancestor's accomplishments with the changed religious, political, and artistic circumstances.

Altarpiece

The chapel's altarpiece represents a Lamentation (fig. 165) derived largely from the *Deposition* of Bronzino's teacher, Pontormo (fig. 160). In the foreground John the Evangelist and Mary Magdalene, embodiments of love and penitence, support Christ's torso and feet. Under John's knee the crown of thorns, recalling the mocking of Christ, is balanced by Mary Magdalene's customary vessel of balm, with which she humbly washed Christ's feet (Luke 7:37–38). Behind John and Mary Magdalene two winged angels display a chalice and a corporal used in the Mass, suggesting the conjunction of the terrestrial and celestial liturgies. Standing in the background on the right, Joseph

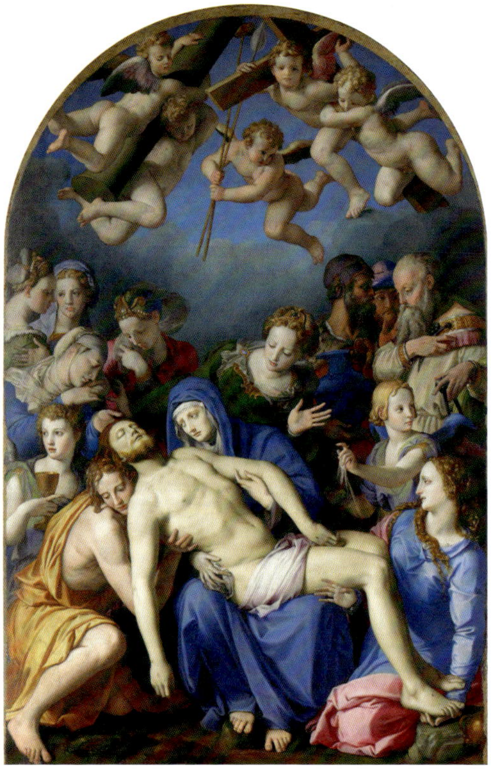

165. Bronzino, *Lamentation,* 1540–42, oil on panel, 8 ft. 9½ in. × 5 ft. 8⅛ in. (268 × 173 cm), Musée des Beaux-Arts, Besançon. Sent to France in 1545 as a diplomatic gift for Nicolas Perrenot de Granvelle (d. 1551), Charles V's vice chancellor, and replaced in the Chapel of Eleonora in 1553 by a copy (see fig. 166).

of Arimathaea, who gave his tomb to Christ, holds pincers and three nails in an allusion to Christ's Deposition. Nicodemus carries a lapis lazuli ewer filled with "a mixture of myrrh and aloe" (John 19:39) for Christ's burial. Angels in the lunette hold the instruments of the Passion. The column of the Flagellation parallels the torsos of John, Mary Magdalene, and the woman behind the Virgin, while the cross of the Crucifixion echoes the torsos of the Virgin and Christ. Carefully marked with all five wounds, Christ's body appears unambiguously material, emphasizing the Real Presence when serving as the visual backdrop for the elevated Eucharist. Compared with Pontormo's *Deposition* (fig. 160), which is characterized by aesthetic dynamism and narrative ambiguity, Bronzino's symmetrical X-shaped *Lamentation* is rich in traditional biblical and liturgical symbols that allude to Christ's Passion and its reenactment in the Mass.

The color blue is found in both Pontormo's and Bronzino's paintings, but Bronzino's pigment, composed of expensive crystals of powdered semiprecious lapis lazuli, is more luminous. In addition, the color progresses upward from the deep blue of the Virgin's robes and the dark storm clouds on the horizon, reported in the Gospels to have gathered at Christ's death, to the pale blue sky, a progression thematizing Christ's coming Resurrection. The luxurious fabrics, exquisite hairdos, and elegant jewelry of Bronzino's women recall the wealth and refinement of Cosimo's court. Whereas Pontormo's figures show real anguish, those of Bronzino express a more restrained sorrow in accord with courtly civility and dignity.

Bronzino, in short, created what Vasari called *la bella maniera* (the beautiful manner). This second-generation Mannerist style reflected and constructed the refined deportment and sophisticated erudition of Duke Cosimo's court. In this context, *bella maniera* was also visually clear, doctrinally orthodox, and biblically accurate. By its elegant gracefulness and splendid opulence, it expressed spiritual transcendence, much like Gothic tempera painting (fig. 54) communicated spirituality through sumptuous materials, high-keyed colors, and rhythmic line.

Altar Wall and *St. Michael*

The peripheral decoration of the east altar wall greatly enhanced the significance of the altarpiece (fig. 166). Elegantly composed by Bronzino within their cramped and awkward spaces, *David* and the *Erythrean Sibyl* appropriately observe and frame the *Lamentation,* for David prophesies the preceding Crucifixion, while the sibyl foresees the subsequent Resurrection. King David perhaps also prefigured and legitimated Cosimo I's rule, for about two decades later (1561) Cosimo's ambassador to Venice, Vincenzo Fedeli (d. before 1565), wrote, "Just as David, by God's wishes, was called to kingship from shepherding, so Cosimo was called to dukedom from birding and fishing."

John the Baptist, originally represented in a panel to the left of the altarpiece and now in the J. Paul Getty Museum in Los Angeles, preached the coming of a Messiah, as did David represented above him. John also embodied the sacraments of penance and baptism, which, together with the Eucharistic symbols in the *Lamentation,* constituted the sacraments of salvation. Originally to the right of the altarpiece, a panel depicting St. Cosmas (now lost), the doctor who healed the physically ill, was aptly paired with the Erythrean Sibyl, who foresaw the soul's cure through the Resurrection. John, the patron of Florence and name-saint of Cosimo I's father, was depicted in the guise of Giovanni delle Bande Nere de' Medici (1498–1526), just as Cosmas, name-saint of both Cosimo il Vecchio and Cosimo I, resembled the duke.

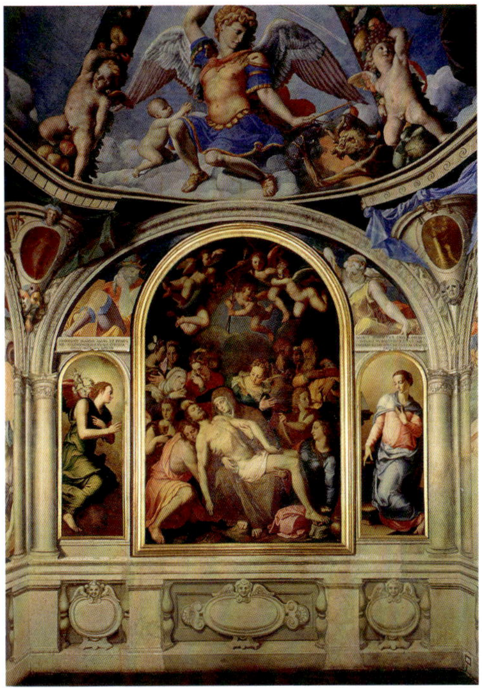

166. Bronzino, *Lamentation,* 1553, oil on panel, 8 ft. 9½ in. × 5 ft. 8⅛ in. (268 × 173 cm), a replacement for the original altarpiece (fig. 165); *King David,* 1540–46, fresco, inscribed "They have pierced my hands and my feet, they have numbered all my bones, David" (Psalm 21:17–18); *Erythrean Sibyl,* 1540–46, fresco, inscribed "He will die in death for three days; having undergone sleep and then having returned from the dead, he will come into the light, Erythea" (Sibylline Oracles 8.390–93, recorded in Lactantius [c. 240–320], *Divinae institutiones* 4.19); *Archangel Gabriel,* 1565, oil on panel; and *Annunciate Virgin,* 1565, oil on panel; east wall, Chapel of Eleonora, Palazzo Vecchio.

John the Baptist and *St. Cosmas* were replaced by the *Annunciation* in 1565 in preparation for the marriage of Cosimo's firstborn son and successor, Francesco I (1541–87), to Giovanna of Austria (1547–78), who, as the new duchess of Florence, was given Eleonora's apartment. The *Annunciation* not only closely related to the celebration of the Incarnation in the Mass, but also commemorated Florence's legendary founding on the Feast of the Annunciation (March 25) and the birth of Francesco, the city's new protector, on the same feast day in 1541.

In the vault above the altarpiece *St. Michael*—a dynamic and elegant pinwheel-like figure carefully adjusted to the difficult triangular space—defeats the hideous rebel angel Satan at the beginning of time with the sword and scales of divine justice (fig. 167). Bronzino also suggested St. Michael's role as the archangel of justice during the Last Judgment at the end of time by the emblem of resurrection on his shoulder—a chrysalis from which a butterfly will be born—and by the saved soul in the guise of an infant kneeling in prayer. On a political level, the victory of the prince of God's angelic army over Satan prefigured Cosimo's victory as the prince of the ducal army over the Florentine exiles at the Battle of Montemurlo. St. Michael's Roman armor, evoking portraits of Augustus, also evoked Cosimo's self-proclaimed role as a new emperor.

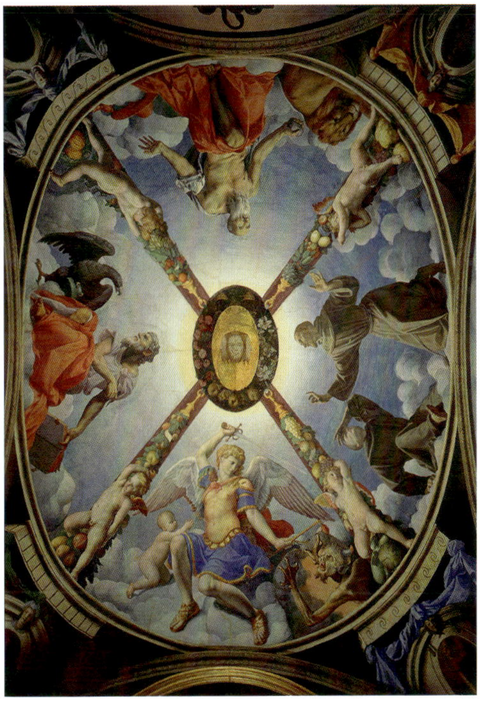

167. Bronzino, *St. Michael Defeating Satan* (east), *St. Francis Receiving the Stigmata on La Verna* (south), *Penitent St. Jerome* (west), *St. John the Evangelist on Patmos* (north), and *Trinity* (center), 1540–46 (*Trinity* is a 1565 replacement for the original *Medici/Toledo Coat of Arms*), fresco, vault, Chapel of Eleonora.

Crossing of the Red Sea and *St. Francis*

On the largest unbroken wall receiving direct light from the north window, the *Crossing of the Red Sea* was the most visible scene in the room (fig. 168). The seminude male to the left carries a bundle on his head with the dough for unleavened bread, a sign of the Host. A print engraved before the fresco was damaged shows that the woman to his left originally nursed two children, a standard personification of Charity as *amor proximi* (love of neighbor). The man with the dough also reaches down to help up a woman to his right (originally with a small child). She enacts Charity as *amor dei* (love of God) by gazing at the symbolic bread. The *Crossing of the Red Sea* was also commonly interpreted as humanity's redemption from original sin through the sacrament of baptism, a typology already mentioned by St. Paul (1 Corinthians 10:1–4). Politically the scene showing Moses freeing the Israelites from the oppression of the pharaoh suggested Cosimo's liberation of the Florentines from the threat of the exiles. Indeed, Baccio Baldini (d. c. 1585/90) in his 1578 biography of Cosimo called Cosimo's 1537 victory at Montemurlo a second crossing of the Red Sea. The white crescent on the red banner above the head of the man with the dough may well have referred to the crescents on the coat of arms of Filippo Strozzi (1489–1538), the leader of the exiles captured at Montemurlo and son of the patron of the Strozzi Chapel and Strozzi Palace (figs. 87–89, 97 and 98). It probably also suggested the larger sixteenth-century struggle of Christendom against the Ottoman Turks, a fight to which Cosimo contributed by founding, in 1561, the Pisan military Order of St. Stephen.

In the vault above the *Crossing of the Red Sea,* St. Francis receives the stigmata (fig. 167). This scene is most appropriate, for the Franciscans commonly called their founder a second Moses whose reception of the stigmata was prefigured by Moses's acceptance of the tablets of law. The Franciscans also believed their order to be on a perpetual pilgrimage, led by St. Francis through the desert of life in search of salvation. The exodus of the Israelites from Egypt and their trek through the wilderness in search of the Promised Land, therefore, foreshadowed the Franciscan journey. *St. Francis Receiving the Stigmata* also commemorated Cosimo and Eleonora's mid-1540 pilgrimage to the Monastery of La Verna in upper Tuscany, where St. Francis had received the stigmata. Earlier that year Eleonora had given birth to her first child, Maria (1540–57). Soon pregnant a second time, she made a pilgrimage with Cosimo to pray to St. Francis for a male heir, and, if their prayers were answered, vowed to name him Francis. On the extremely propitious date of March 25, 1541 (the Feast of the Annunciation and the anniversary of Florence's legendary founding), she gave birth to a boy and dutifully named him Francesco. He was baptized on August 1, the fourth anniversary of Cosimo I's victory at Montemurlo.

The *Crossing of the Red Sea* had probably been planned as early as 1540. However, it is likely that Bronzino added the scene in the right foreground only after the birth of Francesco. The scene shows Moses in the company of the priest Eleazar (dressed in blue to the left of Moses) appointing the startled and youthful blond Joshua as his successor. This act was commonly understood as presaging Christ's consignment of the keys to St. Peter (and Joshua grips a stone, symbol of the Church's foundation stone). Within the Florentine context, however, Joshua's appointment also would have suggested the dynastic descent of authority from Cosimo to his heir, Francesco. In this scenario Cosimo's absolutist regime would have been seen as divinely ordained, symbolized by the sword of divine justice at the lower right. Similarly, the pregnant woman behind Moses celebrated Eleonora's fecundity.

Despite the room's compact dimensions, Bronzino labored for an unusually long period—254 working days over more than five years—to achieve his high-keyed luminescent colors and refined compositions. Figures appear to inhabit an artificial crystalline atmosphere. While serpentine and foreshortened, they are so highly stylized that they exude striking, even erotic beauty and rhythmic grace. This highly polished and elegant style of *bella maniera* accurately mirrored ideal Florentine aristocratic courtly behavior, which masked emotions and motives behind eloquence and etiquette. In summary, Bronzino's chapel constructed the Florentine state as a pious, refined, and hierarchical work of art promising peace and ultimate transcendence.

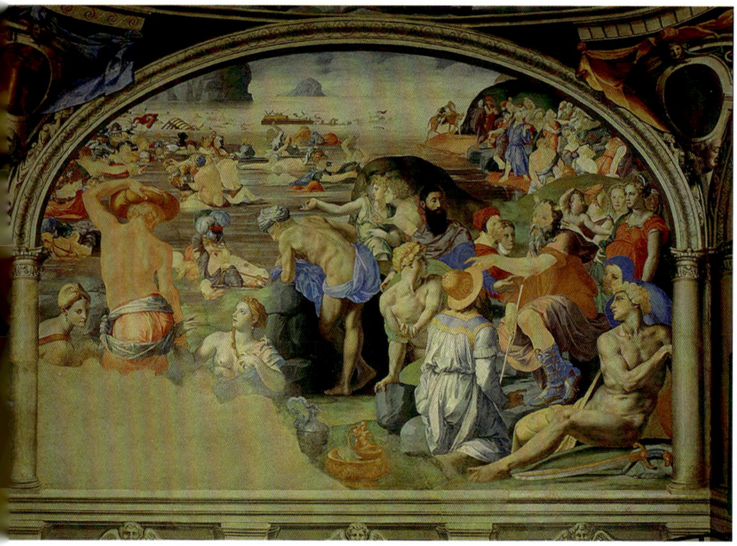

168. Bronzino, *Crossing of the Red Sea* (Exodus 12:33–39; 14:21–29; 15:1–21) and *Moses Appointing Joshua His Successor* (Numbers 27:18–23), 1540–46, fresco, south wall, Chapel of Eleonora.

27

PALACES
Pitti Palace, II, and Boboli Gardens

With the dowry of his wife, Eleonora da Toledo, Duke Cosimo I acquired in 1550 the unfinished Pitti Palace (fig. 96) and immediately commissioned Niccolò Tribolo to design the Boboli Gardens on the hillside behind (fig. 169). The interior of the old palace was completed in 1561; between 1561 and 1577 Bartolomeo Ammannati added two new wings and a courtyard embracing the natural theater of the Boboli Gardens (fig. 170); and in 1565 Giorgio Vasari constructed a long, elevated, covered corridor to connect the palace to the Uffizi and the old Priors' Palace (see figs. 169 bottom left and 179, no. 8). In 1565 Cosimo and Eleonora relocated to the Pitti Palace, leaving the old ducal residence, the Priors' Palace (henceforth called the Palazzo Vecchio), to Cosimo's firstborn son, Francesco, and his new bride, Giovanna of Austria.

In the Renaissance a garden was experienced as a tranquil and fertile refuge, a microcosm of the lost Garden of Eden and the promise of Paradise to come. As a ducal retreat, the Boboli Gardens also served as a metaphor for the abundant and serene Tuscan state. As Duke Cosimo gazed from the courtyard's central openings, aligned with the central axis of the garden theater, the architec-

169. Justus Utens (active 1588, d. before 1609), *View of the Pitti Palace,* 1599, tempera on canvas, 4 ft. 8¼ in. × 9 ft. 4¼ in. (143 × 285 cm), Museo Storico Topografico "Firenze Com'Era," Florence (from the Salone of the Villa di Artimino of Duke Ferdinand I). Vasari's 1565 corridor connecting the Pitti Palace to the Palazzo Vecchio runs along the bottom left (see also fig. 179, no. 8). Bernardo Buontalenti (c. 1531–1608) built the Belvedere Fortress, upper left, between 1590 and 1595.

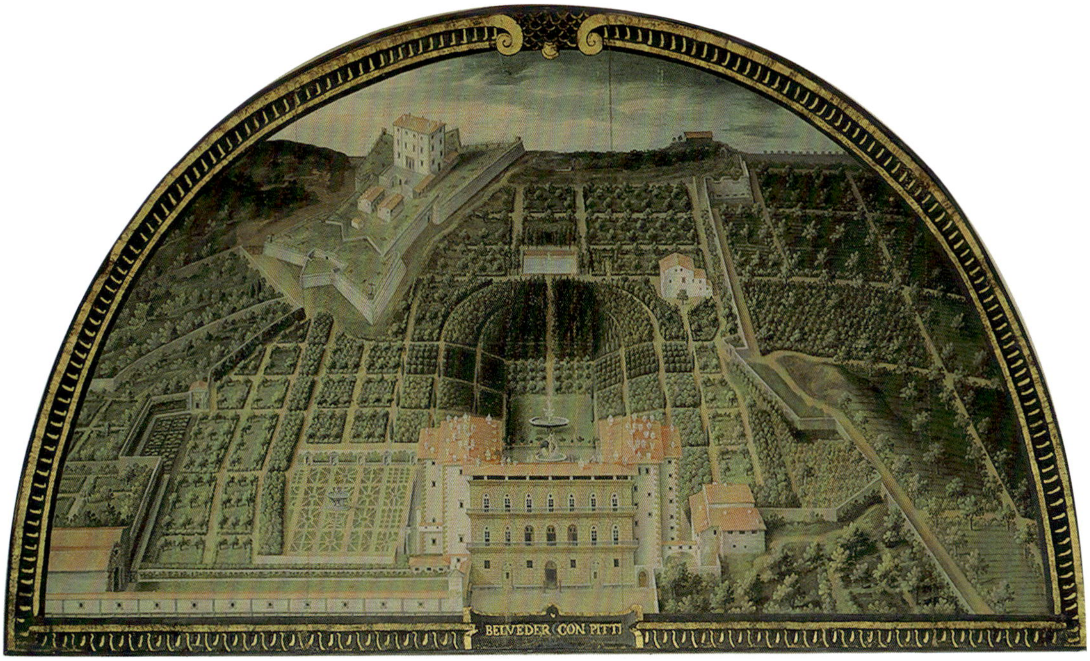

ture constructed a microcosmic image of his mastery of Tuscany. Cosimo I's imperial aspirations were further underlined by the Serlian motifs articulating the courtyard's central openings on all three floors—two trabeated engaged columns framing two smaller freestanding columns carrying an arch—derived from the appearance platforms of Roman emperors. The imperially scaled courtyard façades with massive porticoes, suggestive of Roman aqueducts, expressed his claims to dominion and sovereignty. So too did the courtyard's articulation—engaged Doric, Ionic, and Corinthian columns, a sequence given canonical status in the Renaissance by the example of the Roman Colosseum. Following the model of ancient Roman garden architecture, the orders were also rusticated to convey the informality of nature appropriate for the courtyard's embrace of the Boboli Gardens. Ammannati's design, in short, constructed an image of the ducal state as "naturally" peaceful, prosperous, and ordered under the supreme control of Duke Cosimo.

The progression from the Medici Palace (figs. 92–94) to the renovated Pitti Palace offers an accurate barometer of the Medici's rise from erudite citizen-bankers shrewdly controlling political power largely from behind the scenes with money and patronage, to aristocratic dukes ennobled by marriage, legitimized by imperial and papal grants of authority, and preserved in their absolutist state by an efficient bureaucracy and disciplined militia.

170. Bartolomeo Ammannati, courtyard, Pitti Palace, 1561–77. The Serlian motifs in the center of the two upper floors were originally open loggias.

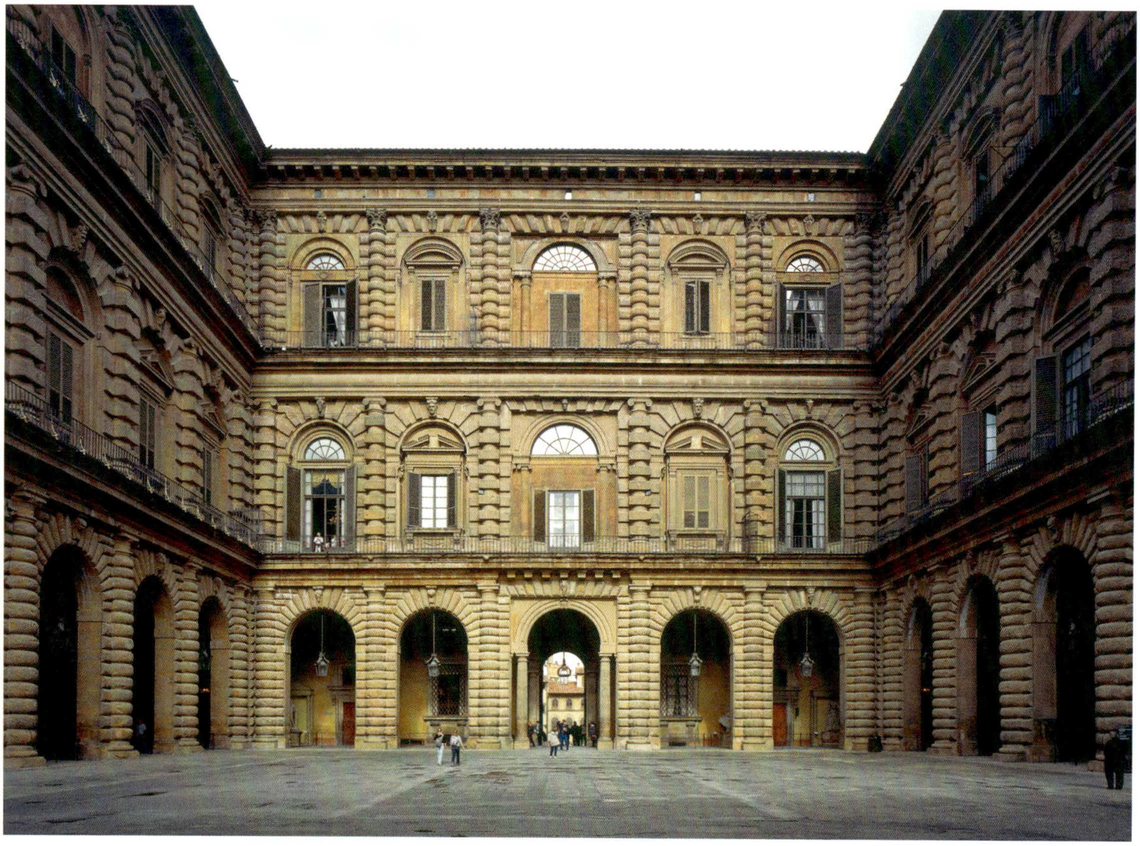

28

CHURCHES AND CHURCH DECORATION

VASARI'S RENOVATION OF S. CROCE AND S. MARIA NOVELLA

The most dramatic developments in sixteenth-century Florentine ecclesiastical architecture concerned not the construction of new churches, as in Rome and Venice, but rather the renovation from 1565 to 1577 of the two largest mendicant churches, S. Croce and S. Maria Novella (fig. 12, nos. 7 and 10). The Council of Trent, which had first convened in 1545 to reform the Church and answer Protestant challenges to papal authority, concluded its work in 1563. Its decrees, published the following year, defined and clarified key issues of doctrine, corrected most institutional abuses, and strengthened papal control over the Church. In response to the Protestant doctrines of justification or sanctification by faith alone and the priesthood of all believers—doctrines that had diminished or denied the importance of the Mass and the priestly hierarchy—the Council emphasized the daily celebration of the Mass by all priests and frequent attendance at the Eucharistic rite by the laity. Particularly stressed was Transubstantiation—the mystical transformation by the priest of the bread and wine into the actual body and blood of Christ during the Mass—and the necessity of a duly ordained priesthood empowered to perform this liturgy. Preaching also received new emphasis as a key tool of education and reform.

To accommodate architecturally these evolving Church rituals and the increasing numbers of priests and laity at sermons and Masses, a large unobstructed nave was required for preaching, a multitude of unencumbered side-aisle chapels for priests' daily celebration of the Eucharist, and a clear view of the high and side altars for lay participation in the Mass. Even when Mass was not being celebrated, the adoration of the Host on the high altar was strongly encouraged.

Eager to impress the papacy with his religious zeal in his ultimately successful campaign to be crowned grand duke in 1570, Cosimo I de' Medici updated the Gothic churches of S. Croce (fig. 171) and S. Maria Novella according to the new Catholic Reformation standards. To do so, he exercised a level of centralized control that would have been impossible in Florence before the establishment of his authoritarian regime. To open up the naves for preaching and for much enlarged congregations, and to give the laity a clear view of the high altar, he ordered his court artist, Giorgio Vasari, in 1565 to transfer the friars' chanting choir in each church from the nave in front of the high altar to the choir chapel behind. He also had Vasari destroy in both churches the huge rood screen, common to most medieval monastic and mendicant churches, which had shielded the cloistered monks

171. Interior, S. Croce, nineteenth-century engraving. The unencumbered nave focuses on Vasari's large monstrance on the high altar for the perpetual display and exultation of the Host, behind which is the new choir.

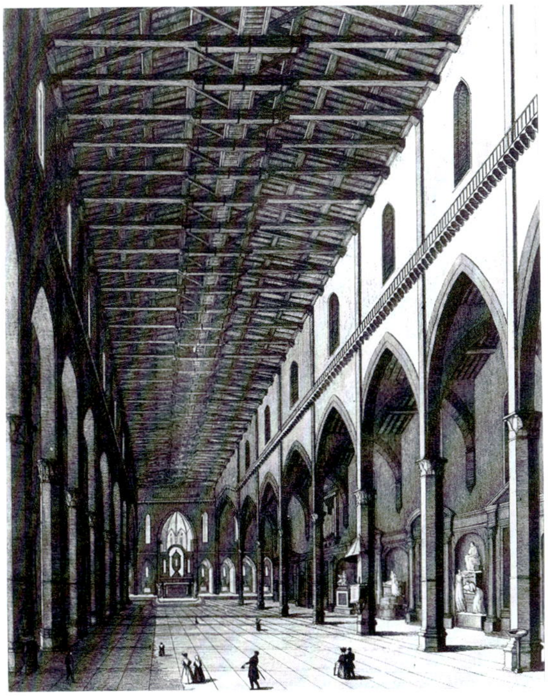

and friars from public view. Families with long-standing patronage rights to the side chapels had to finance the removal of most of the previous decoration and the construction of new altars and altarpieces framed in accordance with Vasari's uniform classical design. If families balked, patronage rights were transferred to others more willing to submit to ducal demands. This late sixteenth-century conception of a church as a spatial and decorative unity marked a radical new departure, one most fully realized in the next century, especially in Rome.

S. CROCE: VASARI'S *DOUBTING THOMAS*

In conjunction with the renovation of S. Croce and S. Maria Novella in the 1560s and 1570s, Duke Cosimo had obtained a papal bull to rededicate the altars in order to create a series of new altarpieces unified iconographically by a program devised by the humanist Vincenzo Borghini (1515–80). Twenty-five of the twenty-nine altarpieces by thirteen painters in the two churches were executed by the late 1570s, but the remaining four for S. Croce were not completed until the early seventeenth century. At S. Croce Passion and post-Passion scenes by Francesco Salviati (1510–63), Bronzino, and Vasari and his workshop began to the right of the high altar, continued down the right aisle, around the interior façade, and up the left aisle back to the high altar. This systematic and comprehensive focus on Christ's sacrifice and its liturgical reenactment represented a key component of much Catholic Reformation art.

Vasari's *Doubting Thomas* can serve as one example from the entire ensemble of altarpieces (fig. 172). Perhaps inspired by Verrocchio's version (fig. 29), Vasari represented St. Thomas stepping forward to thrust his finger at a radiant, resurrected Christ. Christ braces himself, exposing his wound, and raises his hand in an ambiguous gesture that could be interpreted as either a reprimand or an act of forgiveness for Thomas's impertinence. The ten Apostles flanking Christ and the two descending the central stairway intensify the narrative by their various individual responses, while Christ draws special attention with his left hand to the kneeling SS. Peter and Paul, founders of the Church. The drama is further heightened and focused by the massive barrel-vaulted Doric triumphal arch, symbolic of Christ's victory over sin and death. The central stairway, emblematic of the Virgin's epithet "Stairway to Paradise," mediates between heaven and earth.

Festoons, symbols of renewed life, drape across the top of the arch. In the spandrels, two infant angels, one holding a Eucharistic sheaf of wheat, conjoin heaven with earth. According to Borghini's program, the two winged allegorical figures hovering in front of the arch embody Paul's definition of faith in Hebrews 11:1. The left-hand figure holding a transparent veil represents faith as "the evidence of things that appear not," precisely what Thomas was unwilling to accept. Her companion, displaying an apple and flowers (symbols of humanity's fall from grace and regeneration), embodies faith as "the substance of things to be hoped for," which Thomas demanded. The paradox of faith as visible and invisible, substantial and insubstantial, related directly to the consecrated Eucharist regularly elevated before the painting, constituting both matter and spirit, both "the substance of things to be hoped for and the evidence of things that appear not." Compared with Bronzino's second-generation Mannerist *Lamentation* (fig. 165), Vasari's altarpiece is more symmetrical, spatial, focused, dramatic, and classical—a clear and accessible third-generation Mannerism often called classicizing *Maniera*.

172. Giorgio Vasari, *Doubting Thomas* (John 20:24–29), 1572, oil on panel, Guidacci Chapel (fourth, left aisle), S. Croce. Tommaso Guidacci (whose portrait appears to the extreme left close to his name-saint) and his brother Francesco commissioned the altarpiece.

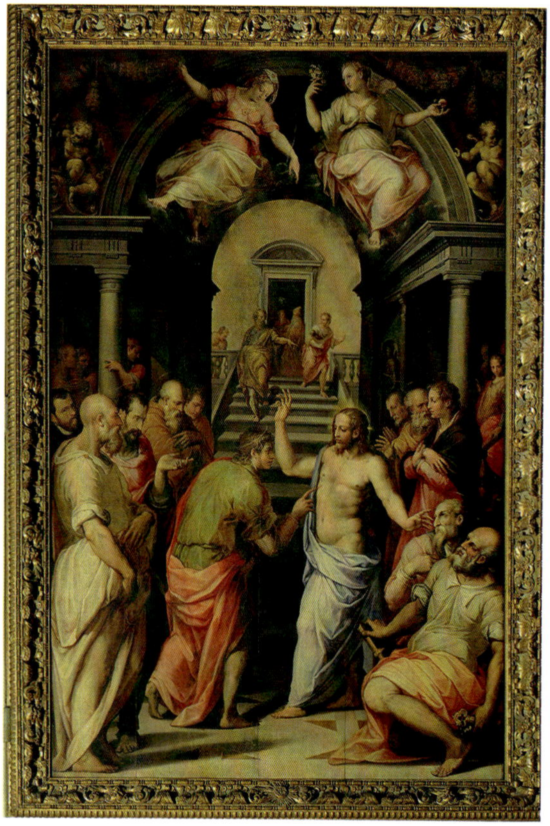

29

CIVIC ARCHITECTURE AND URBANISM

TASSO'S MERCATO NUOVO

Duke Cosimo I's first contribution to Florentine civic architecture and urbanism was the mid-century Loggia of the Mercato Nuovo (new market) built by his court architect for the gold and silk merchants who catered to the expensive tastes of the Medicean court (fig. 173). Built along the Via Calimala, the ancient Roman *cardo* (the central north-south street), the Mercato Nuovo recalled the medieval republican Mercato Vecchio (old market) two blocks north on the site of the old Roman forum (fig. 12, no. 2), while manifesting the superiority of the ducal regime by its greater geometrical regularity and structural solidity. Surrounded by just enough space to provide approximately a 45-degree vertical and a 90-degree horizontal viewing angle from either the northern or southern approaches along the Via Calimala, the Mercato Nuovo conformed to the medieval planning principles exemplified by the Piazza della Signora (fig. 14). As a permanent loggia with eight exterior sculpture niches, it was reminiscent of the loggia of Or San Michele a short distance away (fig. 18). The loggia's system of twelve bays with pendentive vaults, Corinthian columns, and wide entablatures echoed the early classicism of Brunelleschi's Foundling Hospital (fig. 19). This historical résumé of previous Florentine urbanism—coinciding with Vasari's first comprehensive account of Florentine art history in his 1550 edition of *Lives of the Artists*—was contained within the two principal façades at either end. Here huge square Doric corner piers embraced three massive barrel-vaulted arches carried on smaller Doric piers to express Roman imperial gravity, power, and authority. The loggia thus represented an architectural and urbanistic statement of Cosimo I's political ideology. This ideology held that Cosimo I had inherited the authority of the republic but, as a new Augustus embodying Florence's Roman destiny, had made the city more stable and ordered by replacing the chaotic and contentious rule of the republic with his efficient absolutism. Construction of the loggia directly over the spot where the medieval commune before every battle had displayed its battlewagon, a symbol of republican liberty and victory, drove home the message that Duke Cosimo had suppressed the republic and renewed peace and prosperity under the duchy.

VASARI'S UFFIZI

Cosimo I's most important urbanistic project, the Uffizi (offices), was designed by Vasari for both sides of a newly widened street, begun in 1546, that ran from the Priors' Palace to the Arno (figs. 174–79). Built to house the offices of Cosimo's reorganized and centralized ducal bureaucracy at the extravagant cost of 400,000 scudi, the three-story U-shaped Uffizi required the expropriation and destruction of about fifty buildings belonging to

173. Giovanni Battista del Tasso, Loggia, Mercato Nuovo, 1547–51.

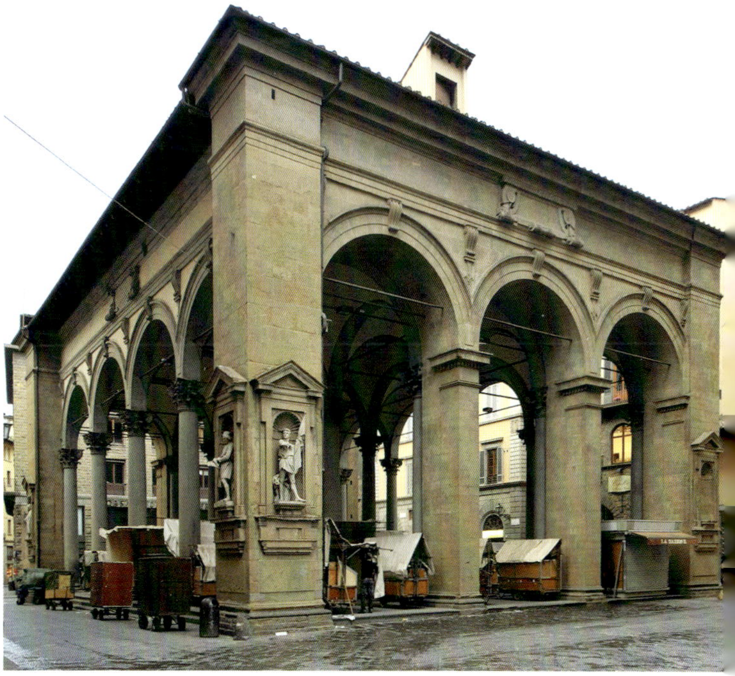

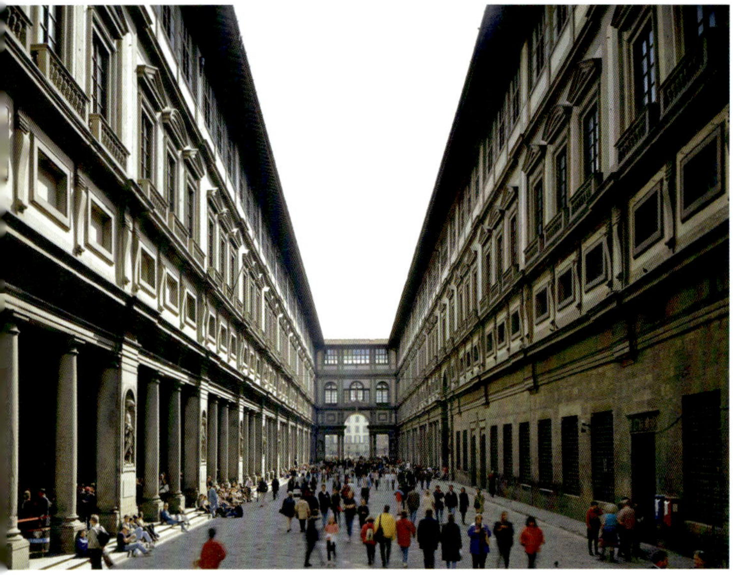

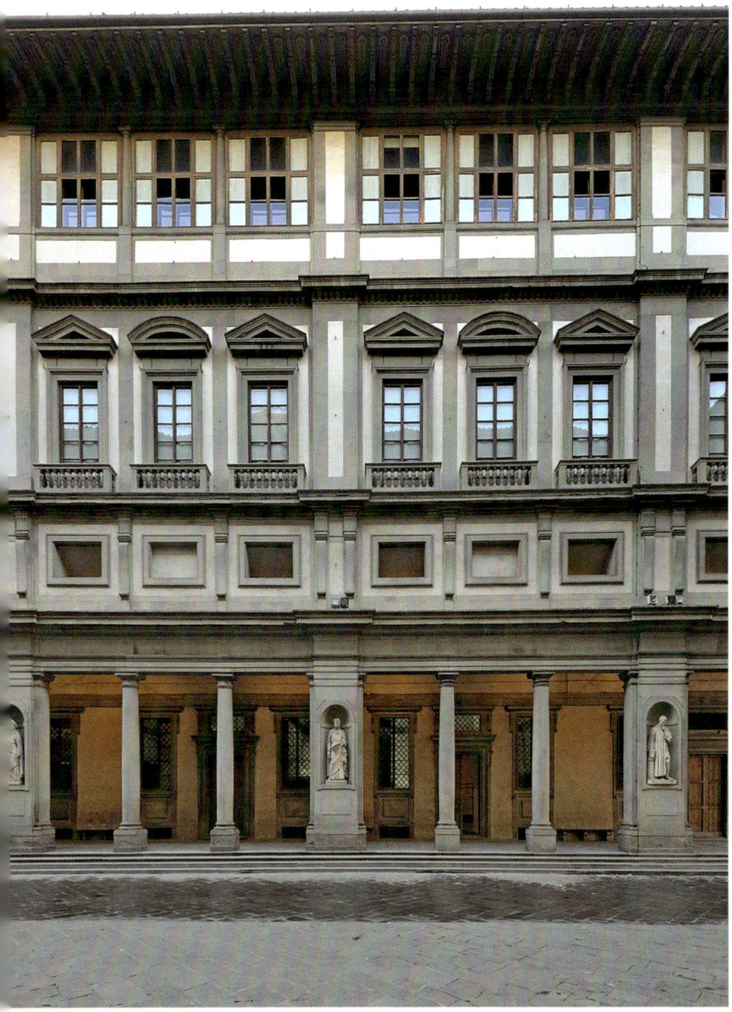

174. Giorgio Vasari and successors, Uffizi (looking south toward the Arno), 1560–80, c. 60 × 453 ft. (18 × 138 m). Today the Uffizi houses one of the world's richest collections of art.

175. Uffizi, east façade.

nearly three hundred owners. Each office on the ground floor behind a trabeated portico consisted of one or two large vaulted front rooms and smaller side and back rooms with a mezzanine for record storage. The upper two floors were reserved for ducal use.

Each ground-floor façade bay is framed by a pair of massive Tuscan Doric piers with sculpture niches on the front face and engaged pilasters on the sides (fig. 175). Between the piers two Tuscan Doric columns on plinths carry a full entablature. Above the entablature, paired and single stone bands in rhythmic alternation visually continue the lines of vertical support from the piers and columns below through the stories above. At the mezzanine level these bands with projecting consoles frame triplets of rectangular windows, the central one blind, the flanking ones light shafts for the barrel-vaulted portico behind. The *piano nobile* windows with balustrades are also organized in triplets, the central one crowned with a round pediment, those flanking with triangular pediments. The upper floor was originally an open loggia articulated with piers flanking two Doric columns resting on a parapet; it also served as part of the elevated corridor built by Vasari in 1565 connecting the Palazzo Vecchio and the Pitti Palace (figs. 169 bottom left, and 179, no. 8). Cosimo I planned the ground-floor pier niches—imitating those recorded in the Forum of Augustus in ancient Rome—to contain sculptures of famous Tuscans, a scheme carried out only in the nineteenth century.

Arcuated groin- or pendentive-vaulted porticos lining streets and piazzas were common in medieval and Renaissance Florence, but at the Uffizi Vasari was the first to emulate Roman trabeated barrel-vaulted examples (fig. 176). In his own life in the *Lives of the Artists* Vasari noted that he chose the Tuscan Doric at Duke Cosimo's request because it was "more secure and stable" and because "the form of the columns resembles Hercules," thereby showing "a certain solidity capable of sustaining the weight of the architraves, friezes, cornices, and the rest of the upper parts of the building." In other words, Vasari revived an imperial mode to underline Cosimo I's self-conception as a new Augustus and a new Hercules bringing peace, strength, and prosperity to Florence. The greater classi-

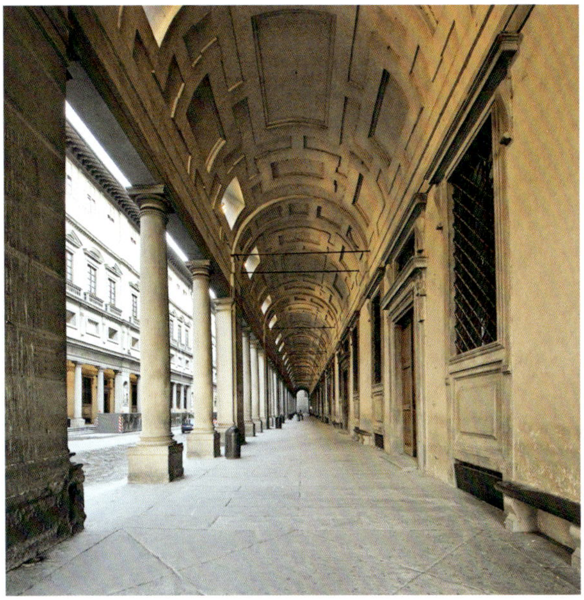

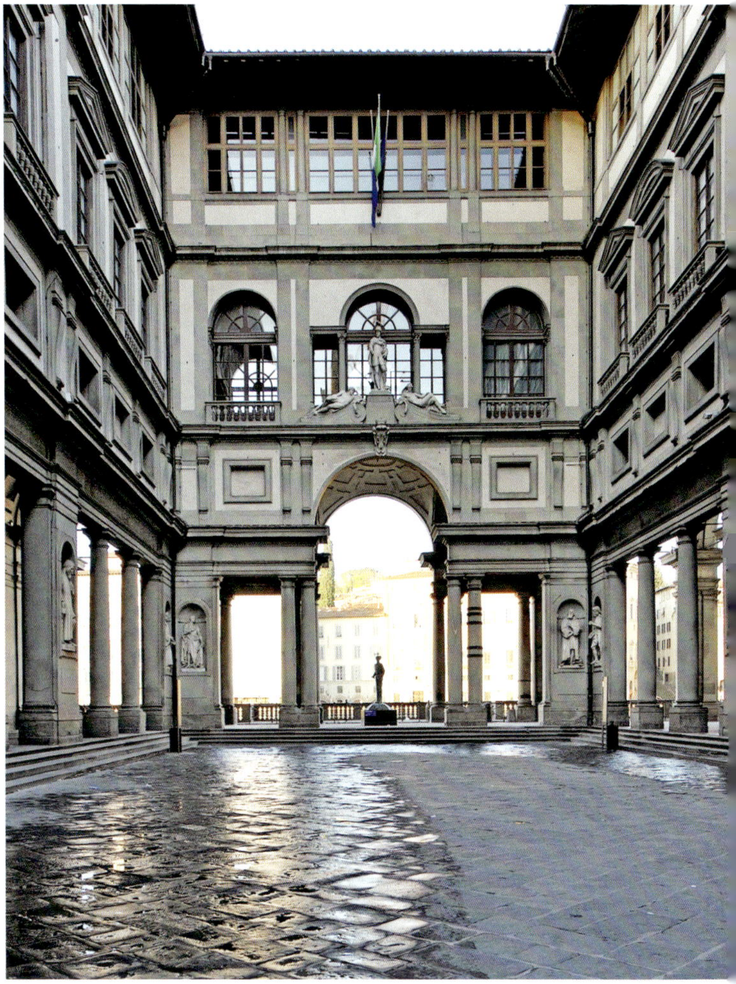

176. Uffizi, west portico.

177. Uffizi, watergate.

178. Uffizi, looking north toward the Palazzo Vecchio from the top floor of the watergate.

cism and uniformity of the Piazzale degli Uffizi compared with that of the republic's Piazza della Signoria (fig. 14) also symbolized the ducal regime's superior order and justice.

Vasari designed the portico at the south end of the Uffizi to recall a Roman triumphal arch opening onto the Arno River through three openings with coffered pendentive vaults (fig. 177). For the center of the watergate's *piano nobile,* he also employed the so-called Serlian motif (an arched central opening flanked by two narrower rectangular openings), which formed the ideal viewing position for the Piazzale degli Uffizi. Originating in antiquity as a framework for the appearance platforms of emperors, as mentioned in chapter 27, and first revived in the Renaissance by Bramante (c. 1443/44–1514) in 1507 for the window in the Sala Regia over the papal throne, the Serlian motif was associated with sovereignty, dominion, victory, and divine favor. Framed by the Serlian window, a sculpted image of Duke Cosimo commanded the major executive, administrative, judicial, and religious centers of ducal Florence (fig. 178). Both the Piazza della Signoria and Piazzale degli Uffizi were constructions of power and domination. Yet the ideal viewing position of the former at the beginning of the Via dei Calzaiuoli (fig. 14) was meant to be experi-

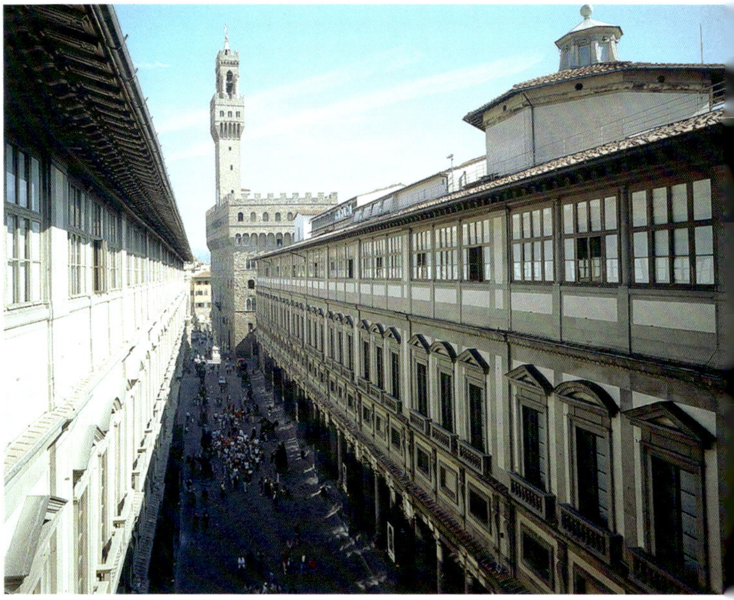

enced by all citizens of a highly participatory regime. The Piazzale degli Uffizi was experienced from its ideal viewing position exclusively by the effigy of the autocratic duke.

A row of sixteenth-century sculptures and the spatial "pull" of the Piazzale degli Uffizi screened and diminished the east side of the Piazza della Signoria (fig. 179, nos. 1, 2, 4, and 7). Florentine subjects of the duchy thus experienced an L-shaped piazza consisting of a larger trapezoidal space and a narrower rectangular space bounded by porticos that terminated in a watergate. A bell tower tied both spaces together vertically. This also describes the 1537 design by Jacopo Sansovino (1486–1570) for the Venetian Piazza and Piazzetta that Vasari knew from his visit to Venice in 1541–42. Vasari was also inspired by the trabeated porticos of Michelangelo's 1538 Capitoline Hill design. By these references Duke Cosimo not only emulated the civic centers of Venice and Rome, but claimed equality with pope and doge in sovereignty and dominion on both land and sea.

179. Plan of Piazza della Signoria and the Piazzale degli Uffizi: 1 Michelangelo's *David,* 1501–4 (figs. 132–33); 2 Bandinelli's *Hercules and Cacus,* 1534 (fig. 164); 3 Cellini's *Perseus Beheading Medusa,* 1545–54 (fig. 180); 4 Ammannati's *Neptune Fountain,* 1560–75 (figs. 181–82); 5 Danti's *Rigor* and *Equity,* 1564–66, and *Cosimo I as Hercules and Augustus,* 1572–73, replaced by Giambologna's *Cosimo I in Armor,* 1581 (figs. 183–84); 6 Giambologna's *Rape of the Sabines,* 1579–83 (figs. 185–86); 7 Giambologna's *Equestrian Monument of Cosimo I,* 1587–94 (fig. 187); 8 Vasari's Corridor, 1565.

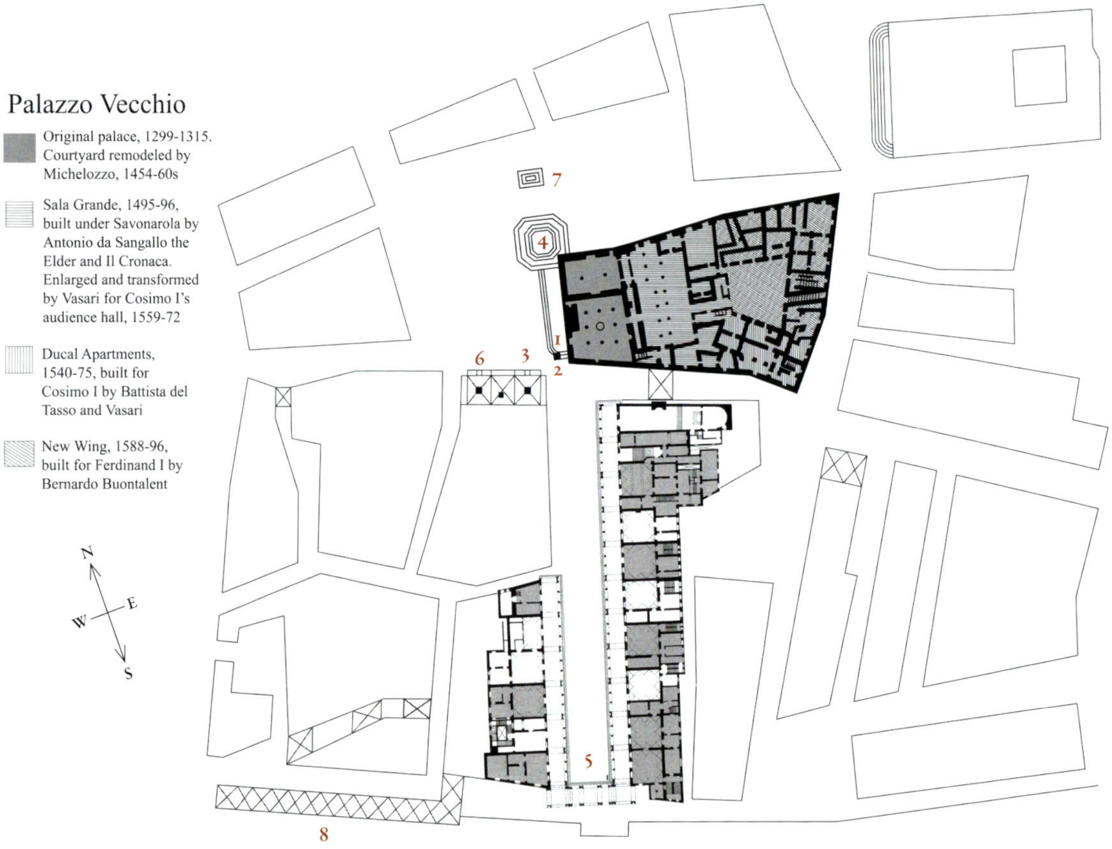

30

LATER FREESTANDING PUBLIC SCULPTURE

CELLINI'S *PERSEUS*

In 1545, five years after establishing the Priors' Palace as his ducal residence, Cosimo I commissioned Benvenuto Cellini to cast a bronze *Perseus Beheading Medusa* (fig. 180) for the left (eastern) arch of the Priors' Loggia (fig. 15; see also fig. 179, no. 3). Here it would balance Donatello's bronze *Judith and Holofernes* (fig. 109) in the right arch. In choosing the very subject his predecessor, Duke Alessandro, had struck on a medal as an emblem of his ducal authority, Cosimo I asserted his legitimate succession to the duchy. The sculpture also commemorated Duke Cosimo's victory over the Florentine rebels at the Battle of Montemurlo in 1537 by recalling the decapitation of vanquished rebels in the Piazza della Signoria. In addition, Perseus celebrated the duke's recent acquisition, in 1543, of the Florentine Fortezza da Basso and the fortresses in Pisa and Livorno (which had been occupied by imperial troops after the defeat of the last Florentine republic in 1530), and warned that Cosimo was prepared to defeat all who challenged his authority. The emphasis on Perseus's sexuality by the juxtaposition of his sword and genitals also celebrated the duke's procreative prowess. By 1545, after only six years of marriage, he had fathered two sons and three daughters, with two more sons and a daughter to follow before the sculpture was unveiled in 1554. Related through his mother, Maria Salviati (1499–1543), to Cosimo il Vecchio's now-extinct male line and

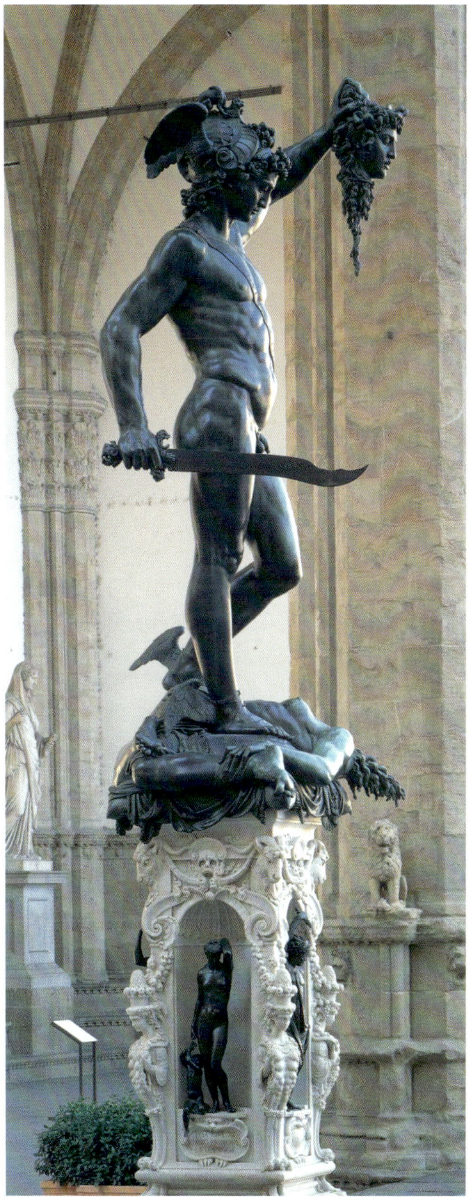

180. Benvenuto Cellini, *Perseus Beheading Medusa* (Ovid, *Metamorphoses* 4.765–86), signed and dated 1554, bronze, iron sword, and marble base; Perseus 10 ft. 6 in. (320 cm), base 6 ft. 6⅜ in. (199 cm), entire ensemble, including the relief, 19 ft. 8⅝ in. (601 cm), Loggia dei Lanzi, Piazza della Signoria. The four statuettes in the base's niches (originals also in the Bargello) represent Perseus's father, Jupiter; Perseus's mother. Danaë; Mercury, who gave Perseus his winged helmet and sandals; and Minerva, who donated her shield with which Perseus deflected in its polished surface the Gorgon's gaze, which turned men to stone.

through his father, Giovanni delle Bande Nere, to the cadet branch of the Medici, Duke Cosimo had assured the dynastic continuity of the Medici family. Finally, a virile male dominating an erotic and threatening female "corrected" the lack of decorum of Donatello's *Judith and Holofernes,* where "a woman killed a man," an impropriety voiced by the communal herald at the 1504 *parlamento* (see chapter 16).

As the centerpiece of his celebrated autobiography, Cellini dramatized the casting of Perseus as a nighmarish undertaking. . Exhausted and deathly ill with fever, Cellini was forced to his bed just as the late-night casting was to begin. But informed that his assistants were about to ruin the work by pouring improperly liquefied bronze, he leapt from his bed in a demonic rage. In the midst of a violent rainstorm with his workshop's roof on fire from the furnace's heat, he stoked the fire even higher and added an alloy. The furnace exploded with a blinding flash, and miraculously the molten metal filled his mold! By the artist's genius and God's grace, both Cellini and his *Perseus* arose at dawn revivified from near death and disaster.

According to his autobiography, Cellini boasted to Duke Cosimo that his *Perseus* would turn out three times better than Donatello's *Judith and Holofernes* and Michelangelo's *David* (figs. 109, 132, and 133). By creating the largest bronze since antiquity and casting Perseus in one piece (except for the accessories of sword, helmet, sandals, and Medusa's blood), Cellini trumped Donatello's smaller group composed of twelve separate parts. By choosing bronze as his medium—more prized than marble both in antiquity and the Renaissance—and by his heroic mastery of challenging casting techniques that "saved" the work on the verge of ruination, Cellini also outdid Michelangelo's rescue of *David* from a "ruined" marble block. Cellini further surpassed the earlier Piazza della Signoria sculptures by creating a lither, more energetic figure that appears to have been, an instant before, airborne, and now, with a dancer's buoyant step, touches down on Minerva's shield and Medusa's abdomen. In that same fraction of a moment, Perseus has sliced with his sword and elevated his severed trophy. The Gorgon's eyes and mouth are still open, and blood gushes from her head and neck. As the two gory geysers drain Medusa of life, Perseus is simultaneously empowered to turn his rivals to stone with Medusa's head. Victory is complete. There is no chance that Medusa will spring back into action as Cacus threatens to in Bandinelli's *Hercules and Cacus* (fig. 164).

Perseus celebrated his victory by offering sacrifices to his divine protectors, Jupiter, Minerva, and Mercury. Cellini alluded to this aspect of the myth by compactly arranging Medusa's body on a base emulating a classical altar, an altar/base far more elegant and classicistic than the *ara* that Bandinelli had designed for his *Hercules and Cacus.* He thus powerfully evoked Cosimo I's piety, divine favor, refinement, and erudition. In addition, at the precise moment Perseus beheaded Medusa, according to myth, the winged horse Pegasus, symbol of poetic inspiration and fame, sprang from her blood. By the simultaneous display of naked sword and jetting blood, Cellini expressed the duke's triumphant virtues of rule: arms and letters, or strength and justice.

The outpouring of blood further recalled the liquid bronze with which Cellini brought Perseus to life. In classical and Renaissance scientific and alchemical treatises, metal was thought to manifest its spirit only in a liquid state. The blood, then, signaled Cellini's extraordinary capturing of Perseus's living spirit through the fluidity and strength of the bronze, which allowed the dramatic extension of arms forward and back, up and down—an impossible feat in stone sculpture. According to contemporary poems of praise, Cellini's exceptionally animated yet gracefully counterpoised *Perseus* struck awe in his observers, emphasizing the dense stone of Michelangelo's *David* and Bandinelli's *Hercules,* both apparently petrified by their gazes at Medusa's head. A distinguished writer and a brave soldier who embodied the princely virtues of arms and letters, Cellini could legitimately claim the title "prince of Florentine sculptors" by the artistic genius evident in this career-culminating work.

AMMANNATI'S *NEPTUNE FOUNTAIN*

In 1560, six years after unveiling Cellini's *Perseus,* Cosimo I commissioned the *Neptune Fountain* from Bartolomeo Ammannati for the Piazza della Signoria (figs. 181 and 182; see also fig. 179, no. 4). The idea for the fountain had originated at least a decade earlier, when Bandinelli had roughed out a marble block for the figure of Neptune a year before his death in 1559. The colossal marble Neptune, unprecedented in size and mass, connoted Cosimo's emerging maritime power through his development of a Florentine navy based in ports at Pisa, Livorno, and Portoferraio. It also recalled his founding of the Pisan seafaring military Order of Saint Stephen. Neptune's bronze victory wreath of pine needles and pinecones suggested the forested hills feeding the Adriatic Sea that provided timbers for Cosimo's shipbuilding. In place of the usual trident, Neptune holds the reins of his chariot, drawn by four seahorses, and a baton of command. In his left hand he displays a cloth *mappa,* the classical Roman sign of consular or imperial rank used at the beginning of each year to start the games commemorating the renewal of peace and plenty. The fountain's narrative action of Neptune calming the turbulent sea—the so-called *Quos Ego* type derived from Virgil's *Aeneid* (1.125–43)—also served as a metaphor for Cosimo I's advancement of Tuscan peace and prosperity through naval power.

The bronze couples framing the fountain's basin enhanced the theme of sea-borne abundance. Doris (fig. 182), the mother of fifty sea nymphs, for example, turns her svelte nude body toward the viewer, raising a leg in a display of sexual availability and fertility. The octagonal basin, recalling the large baptismal font then in the Baptistery (fig. 10), and the water originally arching over Neptune from seventy surrounding jets to create a celestial-like dome, implied spiritual renewal and peace descending from the godlike Duke Cosimo. This suggestion was supported by the twelve zodiacal signs carved on the chariot wheels that mobilized the pun on "Cosimo" and "cosmos."

The fountain also staged the ideal social hierarchy of ducal ideology. At the center, the overpowering, virile Neptune personified absolute ducal authority. The bronze couples in the intermediate zone embodied Cosimo I's sophisticated court by their poise and refined features. On the periphery, frenzied and convulsive satyrs and fauns—primitive terrestrial deities mediating between the basin's emblematic sea and the land beyond—symbolized the unruly populace reined in by the commanding authority of Neptune/Cosimo.

Although constrained by the roughed-out marble block inherited from Bandinelli, Ammannati entered the rolls of artistic one-upmanship by the disdainful expression his Neptune casts at *David* (figs. 132 and 133) and *Hercules and Cacus* (fig. 164). While closely related in posture to Bandinelli's *Hercules,* Ammannati's *Neptune* stands in a more fluid *contrapposto* and straddles three dynamic Tritons originally blowing jets of water from their conch shells. Ammannati also drew inspiration from noted Venetian works. His spirited horses derived from the four ancient bronze horses on the façade of the Basilica of S. Marco, and his *Neptune* recalled the *Neptune* (1554–56) by Jacopo Sansovino, one of Ammannati's teachers, in the courtyard of the ducal palace. These references suggested that Duke Cosimo controlled a prosperous maritime dominion equal to that of Venice. The great size of Ammannati's *Neptune* (four heads taller than Sansovino's) even implied the presumptive superiority of Florence over its rival.

181. Bartolomeo Ammannati and Workshop, *Neptune Fountain,* 1560–75, marble and bronze, Neptune 18 ft. 4½ in. (560 cm), Piazza della Signoria. According to a near-contemporary source, the semi-reclining figures flanked by fauns and satyrs at the four corners of the basin represent Doris (SW), the daughter of Oceanus; Doris's husband, Nereus (NW); Pelius (NE), father of Achilles; and Pelius's wife, Thetis (SE).

182. *Doris, Faun,* and *Satyr.* Detail of fig. 181.

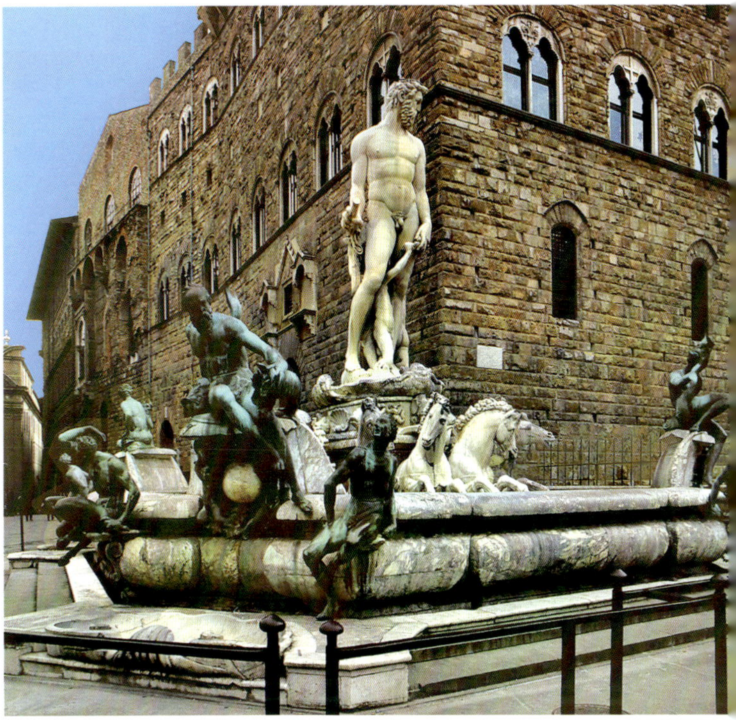

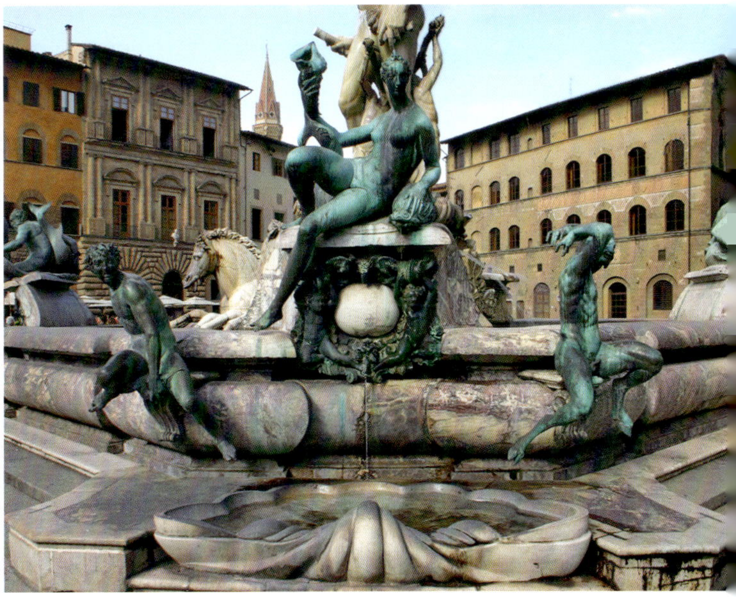

DANTI'S *RIGOR, EQUITY,* AND *COSIMO I AS AUGUSTUS*

While the Uffizi was still under construction, Cosimo I commissioned Vincenzio Danti (1530–76) to carve for the center of the south watergate a marble *Rigor* and *Equity,* personifications of his virtues of rule (fig. 183). By their cornucopias and male/female pairing, the statues also alluded to the prosperity and abundance that his virtues promoted.

Seven years later, as part of the same commission, Danti installed above the reclining virtues in the center of the triumphally arched window a standing *Cosimo I as Augustus* (fig. 184). Here in the guise of Emperor Augustus, one of the triumvirs who founded Florence (see fig. 9), Cosimo stood militantly and triumphantly in the classic *contrapposto* of the *Doryphoros* type (see fig. 5), dressed in Roman leather armor and holding a shield, symbol of strength (rigor), and fasces, sign of justice (equity). The epaulettes with dolphin heads connoted Augustus and Cosimo's shared device of the dolphin and anchor with the motto *festina lente* (make haste slowly), an allusion to the virtue of prudence. They also shared the same birth signs, as indicated by the reliefs of the Corona Borealis and Capricorn carved on the shield (not visible in the illustration). Just as Vasari had written that the Uffizi's Doric columns evoked Hercules by their strength and stability, so too the statue alluded to Florence's mythological protector by its lion-headed helmet. In short, Danti's image of Duke Cosimo—the strong, just, and prudent new Hercules and the new Augustus—surveyed a new forum as the agent of Florence's renewed peace and plenty, and embodied the city's divinely ordained imperial destiny.

GIAMBOLOGNA'S *COSIMO I IN ARMOR*

Perhaps wishing to more aggressively assert Medici power after Cosimo I's death had left the regime weakened, Francesco I, Cosimo's heir and third duke of Florence, commissioned Giambologna in 1581 to replace Danti's classicizing image with *Cosimo I in Armor* (fig. 183). For

183. Vincenzio Danti, *Rigor* (left) and *Equity* (right), 1564–66, marble, each 6 ft. 6¾ in. (200 cm) long, and Giambologna, *Cosimo I in Armor,* 1581–85, marble, 9 ft. 2¼ in. (280 cm).

184. Danti, *Cosimo I as Augustus,* 1572–73, marble, 9 ft. 2¼ in. (280 cm), Bargello.

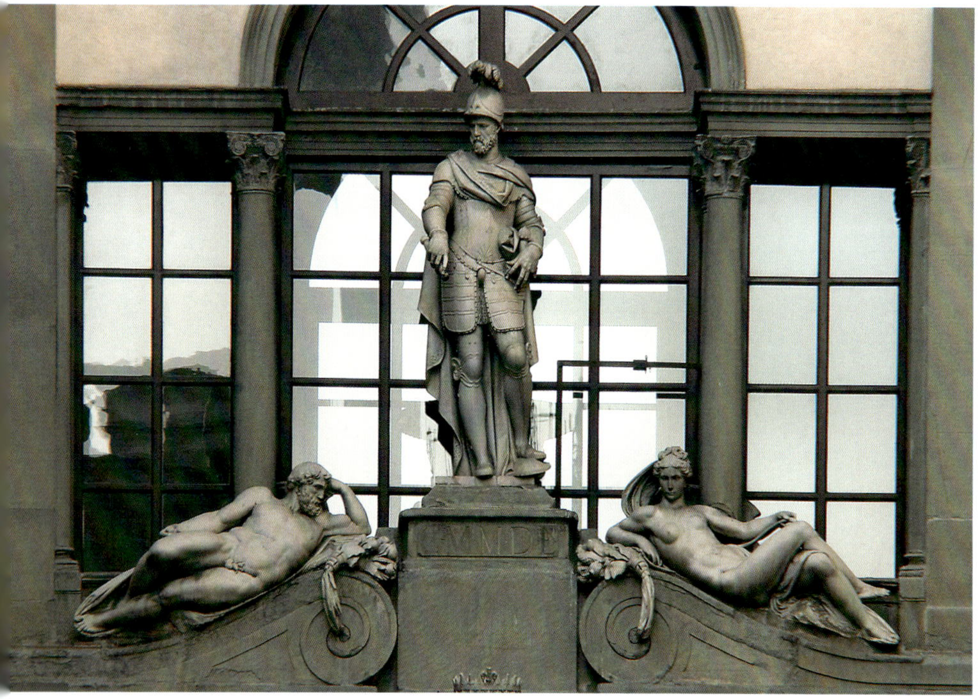

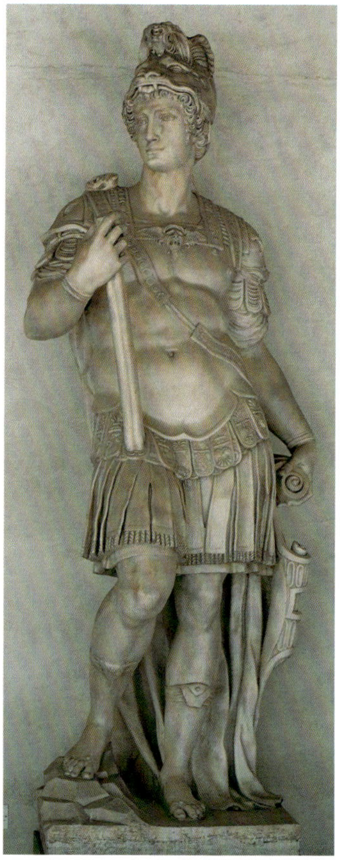

the first time in the realm of public sculpture, allegorical allusion was rejected in favor of a straightforward realistic portrait of Cosimo I in full contemporary armor with a commander's cape, baton, and sword. The prominent codpiece also signified the manly prowess by which Duke Cosimo had founded the Medici ducal dynasty, again an issue of increasing anxiety now that all but three of Cosimo's eight children had died and Francesco had sired no offspring.

GIAMBOLOGNA'S *RAPE OF THE SABINES*

In the competitive aesthetic arena of the Piazza della Signoria, Giambologna challenged all previous works with his *Rape of the Sabines* (figs. 185 and 186). A topos from antiquity held that the most skillful stone sculpture was carved without error from a single block. Michelangelo had succeeded with his single figure of *David* (figs. 132 and 133), but for his *Hercules and Cacus* (fig. 164) Bandinelli had employed twenty pieces of marble. Giambologna was the first to succeed in carving from a single block of marble a complicated group of three adult figures in extreme states of anatomical torsion with all viewpoints equally effective. Furthermore, he sharply differentiated the figures by age, gender, posture, and expression. Reading upwards as the group faces the square (fig. 185), the thoroughly vanquished old man at the bottom crouches awkwardly, looking up in pain. Straddling him, the young captor seen from the rear looks excitedly to his left and leans in the opposite direction. His young victim, seen in three-quarter profile, twists her body diagonally in his arms, exposing her breasts as she looks up in terror. Although the bodies of the old man and the young woman arch along similar diagonals, the man cowers on splayed legs, steadying himself with a stone that he grips behind his back and shielding himself with his left arm, which he has reflexively jerked in front of his head. The woman, by contrast, crosses her feet at her ankles and desperately flails her arms. Unlike Michelangelo's *David,* which communicates only the *potential* for movement through *contrapposto,* the powerful captor here strides forward. The group's exceptionally open silhouette, with light penetrating at several points between the forms and the woman's limbs suspended precariously in space, obscures the original shape of the block and defies the fragility of marble under tension. The subtle modulations of the surfaces, suggesting pliant flesh over vibrant muscles, equally belie the marble's unyielding stony mass.

Within these many contrasts and contradictions, Giambologna created overall harmony and unity by presenting the drama of the figures' actions and glances as a consistent counterclockwise spiral ascending in a crescendo from compression to extension. As they turn in space, Giambologna's figures also link to one another rhythmically with consummate artistic grace.

In a letter of June 13, 1579, Giambologna wrote that the design had been conceived without a commission or a subject, a project simply "chosen to give scope to the knowledge and study of art," that is, to demonstrate his highly sophisticated aesthetic values and technical virtuosity. And once again the artist equated aesthetic triumph with sexual prowess by ironically carving his bold and assertive signature and date between the splayed legs of the impotent old man.

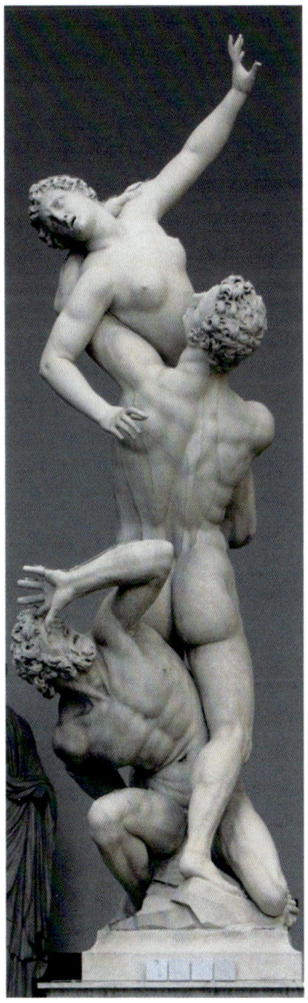

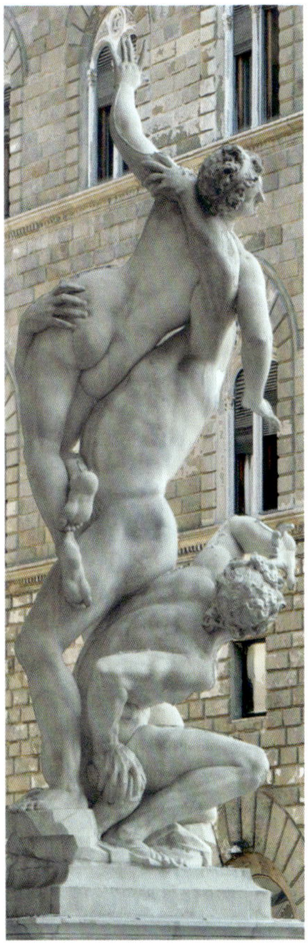

185. Giambologna, *Rape of the Sabines* (Livy 1.9, Plutarch (before AD 50–after AD 120) 2.14), signed and dated 1582, marble, 13 ft. 5⅜ in. (410 cm), Loggia dei Lanzi, Piazza della Signoria.

186. Giambologna, *Rape of the Sabines,* back view of fig. 185.

The work was purchased in 1582 by Duke Francesco I and installed in the western arch of the Loggia dei Lanzi (figs. 15; 179, no. 6), displacing Donatello's *Judith and Holofernes* (fig. 109), which was moved to the side arch of the Loggia dei Lanzi facing east. Various subjects were proposed, including Paris's Rape of Helen, Pluto's Rape of Persephone, and Phineus's Rape of Andromeda. Although the latter would have formed a fitting sequel to Cellini's *Perseus,* the subject that was chosen marked the moment when the earliest Romans transformed themselves from conquering warriors to fathers and founders of Rome. By association, therefore, the work celebrated Duke Francesco as the virile founder of a new Rome. In this reading, Giambologna's young Sabine woman symbolized Florence, but—unlike Cellini's *Medusa* (fig. 180)—her seductive power advanced prosperity rather than devastation. Although Giambologna's art for art's sake statement quoted above has promoted the understanding of *Rape of the Sabines* as a quintessential demonstration of Mannerism, that is, an excessive concern for aesthetic form at the expense of naturalistic narrative, the work's conceptual refinement and technical brilliance also reflected an essential aspect of its context—the rarified preciousness of Duke Francesco's court.

GIAMBOLOGNA'S *EQUESTRIAN MONUMENT TO COSIMO I*

When Francesco died in 1587, he left no children and was succeeded by his younger brother, Ferdinand, age forty-six. Never expecting his fourth-born son to become duke, Cosimo had arranged an ecclesiastical career for Ferdinand, securing his appointment as a cardinal in 1563 at age fourteen. Now unexpectedly becoming the fourth duke of Florence, Cardinal Ferdinand—celibate and unmarried—faced the problem of establishing his legitimacy and ensuring dynastic succession. He immediately commissioned from Giambologna Florence's first freestanding equestrian monument in permanent materials in order to symbolically legitimate his own rule and glorify the founder of the Medici dynasty, Cosimo I (fig. 187; see also fig. 179, no. 7). By the time the work was formally unveiled on June 5, 1595, Ferdinand had renounced the cardinalate and married Christine of Lorraine (1565–1637). She produced nine children, including his first-born son and successor, Cosimo II (1590–1621).

Giambologna represented for the first time and on a colossal scale a Medici duke mounted on horseback as commander-in-chief of land forces. The work, therefore, complemented the *Neptune Fountain* (figs. 181 and 182) celebrating Cosimo's maritime power. It also joined *Cosimo I in Armor* on the Uffizi watergate (fig. 183) to bracket the lineup of sixteenth-century sculptures with two militaristic images of Ferdinand's father (see fig. 179, nos. 5 and 7). Inspired by the ancient bronze equestrian monument of Marcus Aurelius (121–180) on the Capitoline Hill in Rome, Giambologna depicted the horse performing a parade gait. This standard motif of a Roman imperial *adventus* (triumphal entry) signified domination and pacification—an appropriate theme for a work with a bronze relief on its base commemorating Cosimo I's conquest of Siena in 1555, which nearly doubled the size of Florence's Tuscan empire. Cosimo's association with Marcus Aurelius—noted in the Renaissance for his piety, divine favor, justice, and military victories—was underlined by those same virtues attributed to Cosimo I

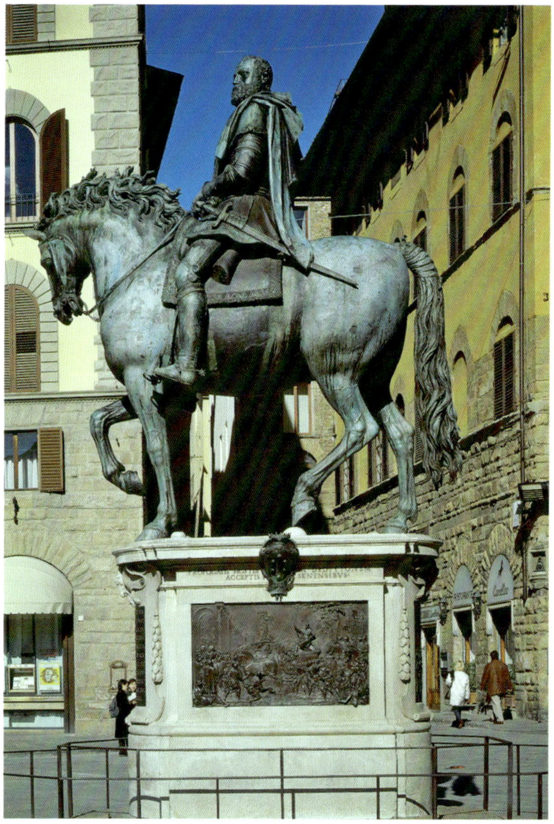

187. Giambologna and Workshop, *Equestrian Monument to Cosimo I,* signed and dated 1594, bronze and marble, 22 ft. 11⅝ in. (700 cm) including base, 14 ft. 9⅛ in. (450 cm) horse and rider alone, Piazza della Signoria. The bronze relief on the pedestal's south face depicts Cosimo I's triumphal entry into Siena in 1555.

in the monument's bronze dedicatory inscription on the front of the pedestal. Seated erect and effortlessly holding the reins and the baton of command—the very image of virility and strength—Cosimo completely dominates the spirited stallion with its rippling muscles, straining neck, agitated mane, and flowing tail. Sheathed sword, body armor draped with a commander's cape, and the chain of the Order of the Golden Fleece hanging from his neck completed Cosimo's image of authority and dominion. The monument thus boldly transformed the Piazza della Signoria into a new imperial forum under the control of the duke's watchful eyes, just as Giambologna's earlier *Cosimo I in Armor* dominated the forumlike Piazzale degli Uffizi by its gaze (figs. 178 and 183).

So compelling was this image of sovereign power that it almost immediately spawned a series of equestrian monuments of royalty all over Europe that continued until horsemen became obsolete in warfare some three centuries later. One of the earliest such monuments was Ferdinand's own equestrian image by Giambologna and assistants for the Florentine Piazza SS. Annunziata (figs. 142, no. 8; 143), unveiled in 1608 during the wedding celebrations for his firstborn son, Cosimo II, to Maria Maddalena of Austria (1587–1629).

31

PORTRAITS

BRONZINO'S *UGOLINO MARTELLI*

Ugolino Martelli (1519–92) had studied with the Florentine exile and humanist Benedetto Varchi (1503–65) in the Paduan literary Academy of the Impassioned. In 1542 Martelli became a member of the Florentine Academy—established by Cosimo I on March 25, 1541, to bring humanist scholarship under state control. Martelli was joined the next year by his mentor, when Duke Cosimo lifted Varchi's ban of exile. In his *Portrait of Ugolino Martelli* (fig. 188) Bronzino presented the young scholar in a dynamic three-quarter-length *figura serpentinata* spiraling through nearly 180 degrees, derived in part from Michelangelo's New Sacristy *Baton Carrier* (fig. 149). Bronzino located the sitter in a palace with the Martelli family's Donatellesque marble *David,* now in the National Gallery of Art, Washington, attributed to either Antonio Rossellino or Desiderio da Settignano. Bronzino also imaginatively employed Michelangelesque architectural forms to create a lively and contrapuntal foil to the sitter. The architecture abruptly recedes into space at the left and plunges forward at the right in opposition to the turn of the figure's shoulders. It also makes a turn at the center of the composition to create a small off-center flat plane that focuses attention on Martelli. Bronzino counterbalanced the orthogonal thrust of the architecture by the diagonal fall of diffused light from the upper left. This creative manipulation of form acts as a visual counterpoint to the humanist scholar's agile intellectual prowess implied by his three books.

The books from left to right are inscribed with the name of Virgil, the beginning of Book 9 from Homer's *Iliad* with its legible Greek text visible to the viewer, and the name Pietro Bembo (1470–1547). They indicate Martelli's command of Latin, Greek, and Italian, and suggest that Bembo's poetry—written in the Tuscan vernacular, which he championed despite his Venetian birth—equaled that of Homer and Virgil, the two greatest poets of antiquity. This message was completely in accord with Cosimo's mission for the Accademia Fiorentina: to promote Tuscan literature and standardize the Tuscan language.

Martelli points to the Homeric text (*Iliad* 9:307–429) that recounts Achilles' refusal to fight during the siege of Troy because Agamemnon had stolen his beautiful concubine. These lines perhaps subtly allude to a feud that took place in 1530, just before the fall of the last Florentine republic. Ugolino's cousin, Ludovico Martelli, and Giovanni Bandini, brothel keeper and patron of Rosso's *Moses Defending the Daughters of Jethro* (fig. 159), had been competing for the favors of one Marietta de' Ricci. The feud was exacerbated by differing political loyalties, for Bandini supported the pro-Medici imperialists be sieging the city, while Martelli championed the Florentine republic. After Bandini insulted Martelli, the protagonists fought a duel on March 12, 1530, in which Martelli was killed. Ugolino might, therefore, have wished to allude subversively to his own anti-Medici political sympathies, especially since his symbolic alter ego, the Martelli *David,* symbolized Florentine republican liberty.

In any case, Bronzino rejected in this portrait the High Renaissance ideal/real synthesis, emphasizing instead a sophisticated and charged aestheticism at the expense of individual psychological expression. This new Mannerist style constructed the mannered elegance and stylish grace of Cosimo I's court but also reflected his regime's oppressive authoritarianism, which discouraged individual emotional expression.

BRONZINO'S *COSIMO I AS ORPHEUS*

Just as Pope Leo X alluded to himself as a new Orpheus when he commissioned Baccio Bandinelli's *Orpheus* (fig. 144), so too it appears that Cosimo I requested a painting from Bronzino depicting himself as a nearly life-size nude Orpheus (fig. 189). It has been suggested that the painting was an intimate gift for Eleonora of Toledo just before or just after their marriage in 1539.

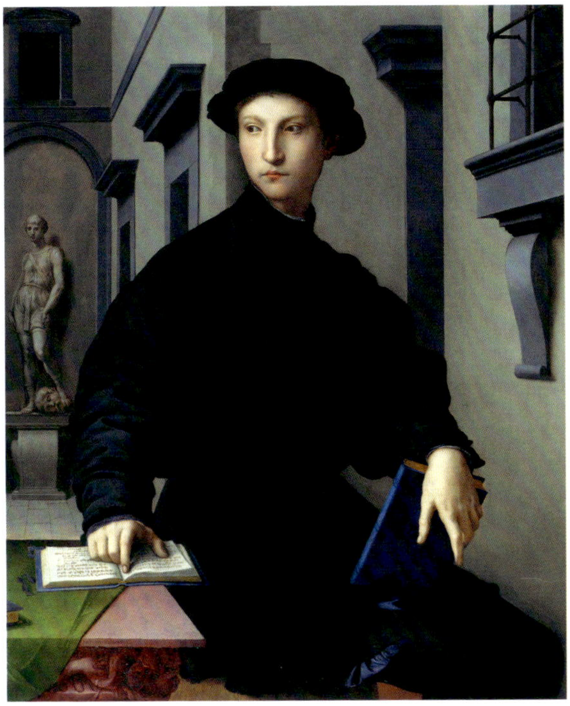

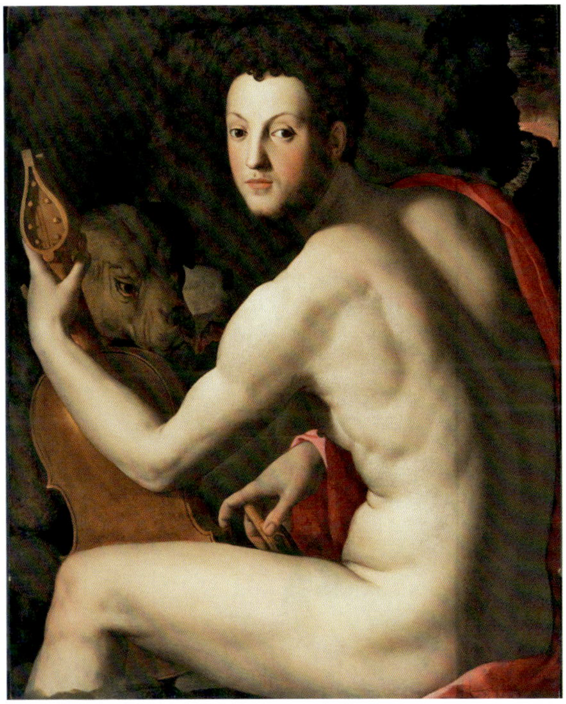

188. Agnolo Bronzino, *Portrait of Ugolino Martelli,* c. 1540, signed, oil on panel, 40⅛ in. × 33½ in. (102 × 85 cm), Gemäldegalerie, Staatliche Museen zu Berlin.

189. Agnolo Bronzino, *Portrait of Cosimo I as Orpheus,* late 1530s–early 1540s, oil on panel, 37 × 30⅝ in. (93.9 × 77.7 cm), Philadelphia Museum of Art.

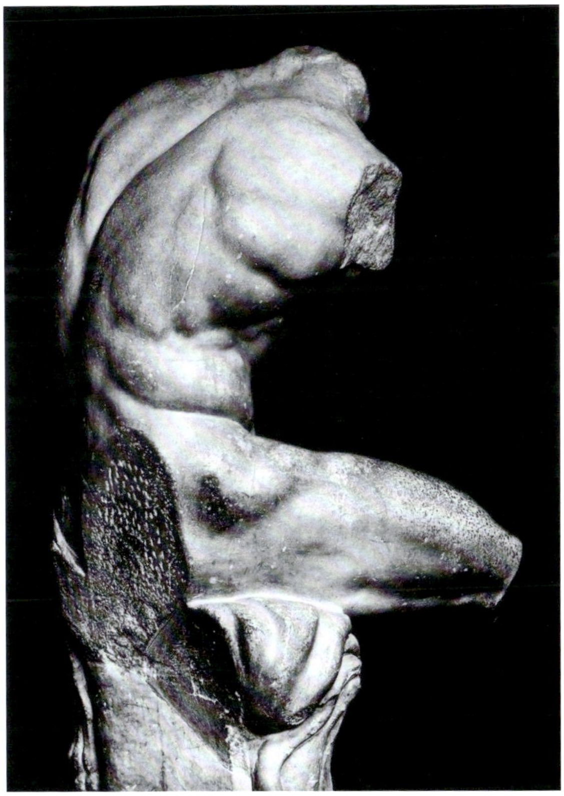

190. Apollonios, *Torso Belvedere,* mid-first century BC, marble, 62⅝ in. (159 cm), Museo Pio-Clementino, Vatican.

Seated before the fires of Hades at the upper right, Orpheus holds a bow and *lira da braccio,* having just subdued by his music Cerberus, the vicious three-headed dog guarding the entrance to the underworld, into which Orpheus descended to rescue his lover, Eurydice (Ovid, *Metamorphoses* 10–11; Virgil, *Georgics* 4.444–527). Just as the Vatican *Apollo Belvedere* (fig. 145) inspired Bandinelli's *Orpheus,* so Bronzino's *Orpheus* quoted the Vatican *Torso Belvedere* (fig. 190) believed to represent Hercules, the mythical protector of Florence and alter ego of Duke Alessandro (fig. 164). A Herculean Orpheus was appropriate, because Hercules had also descended to the underworld to subdue Cerberus (Diodorus Siculus [first century BC] 4.24.4–25) and had learned to play the lyre, with which he killed his teacher, Linus, the brother of Orpheus (Diodorus Siculus 3.66.67). Cosimo thus appears to have presented himself to his noble wife as a devoted husband and the legitimate descendant from the Medici line of the Orpheus-like Pope Leo X and the Hercules-like Duke Alessandro. In addition, Cosimo might have wished to embody the eloquence and reason of Orpheus, by which he restored to Florence a golden age of law and order, as well as the courage and strength of Hercules, by which he protected Florence from rebels and dissidents. In this interpretation, he personified the virtues of the ideal prince: arms and letters.

Uniquely in Renaissance portraiture, however, Bronzino's *Orpheus* expressed a blatant eroticism. Orpheus/Cosimo has positioned his bow to suggest an erect member, and placed between his legs a *lira da braccio* whose shape resembles a nude female body. The shape of the instrument's peg box and the arrangement of pegs within even appear vulgarly to associate the Medici coat of arms with female genitalia. The strained over-the-shoulder outward gaze and the somewhat hunched and paunchy torso, which seems to parody its Herculean classical source, recall that in the end Orpheus was less than heroic. By his impatient backward glance as he ascended from Hades, he lost Eurydice forever, and then by rejecting women for the love of young boys, as Hercules also did on occasion, he was torn to pieces by frenzied Maenads. Indeed, Orpheus/Cosimo's small head—baby-faced, rosy-cheeked, and red-lipped—awkwardly joined to a somewhat flaccid nude body suggests androgyny, while the owlish expression created by the arched eyebrows evokes a common burlesque code word for sodomy, "owl." Bronzino might even have intended the slender bow to disparage the size of Orpheus/Cosimo's sexual equipment, and certainly one of the heads of Cerberus stares fixedly at his groin with a quizzical, perhaps disdainful raised eyebrow. Finally, by casting Orpheus as Hercules, Bronzino might be comically questioning whether the *lira da braccio* was Orpheus's instrument of harmony or Hercules' brutal murder weapon. Would the overt sexuality and satire of such a painting have been appropriate for the pious and aristocratic Eleonora or tolerated by a still-insecure Cosimo?

No mention of the painting as a Medici possession has ever come to light. It may be documented in a 1650 Florentine inventory of goods stolen from the poet Simone Berti, whose father, Giovanni Berti, was a literati with connections to the Florentine Academy. Bronzino, a self-taught intellectual, also wrote sonnets and burlesque verse and was a founding member in 1540 of the Accademia degli Umidi, which Cosimo I refounded as the Accademia Fiorentina in 1541 and to which Bronzino was admitted as a member in 1542. It has been suggested, in fact, that the painting commemorated Cosimo's patronage of the Florentine Academy, and certainly the academicians would have been an ideal audience to delight in the painting's sophisticated ambiguities and paradoxes, bawdy humor, and veiled classical references. Was the portrait, then, painted for one of these (perhaps anti-Medici) literati, who wished to mock the political and sexual prowess of Cosimo before he had fully consolidated his autocratic authority? Or in the spirit of the Florentine Academy's love of burlesque verse, would Cosimo himself, not otherwise noted for humor or irony, have delighted in the painting's combination of praise and parody? Whatever the case, Bronzino soon become Cosimo's official and only portraitist in painting, just as Apelles was the only artist whom Alexander the Great (356–323 BC) allowed to paint his portrait.

BRONZINO'S *COSIMO I IN ARMOR*

In May 1543 Emperor Charles V returned the Fortezza da Basso in Florence and the fortresses in Pisa and Livorno to Duke Cosimo for a huge payment of 150,000 florins. Now fully in control of Florence and Tuscany, Cosimo was the master of his own destiny as never before. He celebrated the occasion by commissioning Bronzino to paint a much-copied portrait as a military commander dressed in armor (fig. 191). To enhance visually Cosimo's stature, Bronzino based the painting on the lost portrait of Charles V in armor of c. 1533–34 by Titian (c. 1488/90–1576), an image widely circulated in a woodcut by Giovanni Britto (c. 1500–after 1550).

Bronzino rotated Cosimo's shoulders and turned his head and eyes toward the light to create a dynamic bodily tension. He further animated Cosimo by the light glinting off the polished armor, the bluish cloth of honor draped behind him, and the V-shaped position of his right arm. The pointed besagues (armpit protectors) evoke a pair of sharp eyes looking right, complementing his real eyes to communicate a sense of wariness for the slightest signs of danger or challenge. Yet Bronzino tempered this hard, spiky, and alert image of military strength by removing Cosimo's helmet and depicting him not in battle dress, but in elaborately engraved parade armor made in Austria to suggest a victorious man of peace.

BRONZINO'S *ELEONORA OF TOLEDO WITH HER SON GIOVANNI*

Bronzino's *Portrait of Eleonora of Toledo with Her Son Giovanni* (fig. 192) transformed the paradigm of Leo-

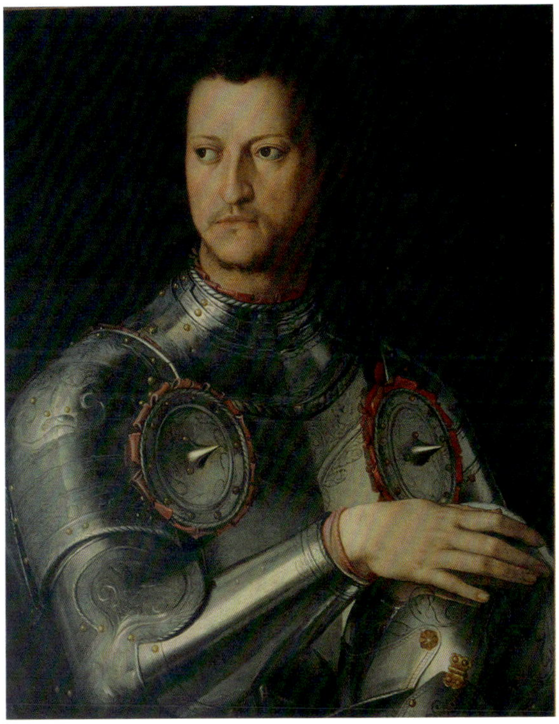

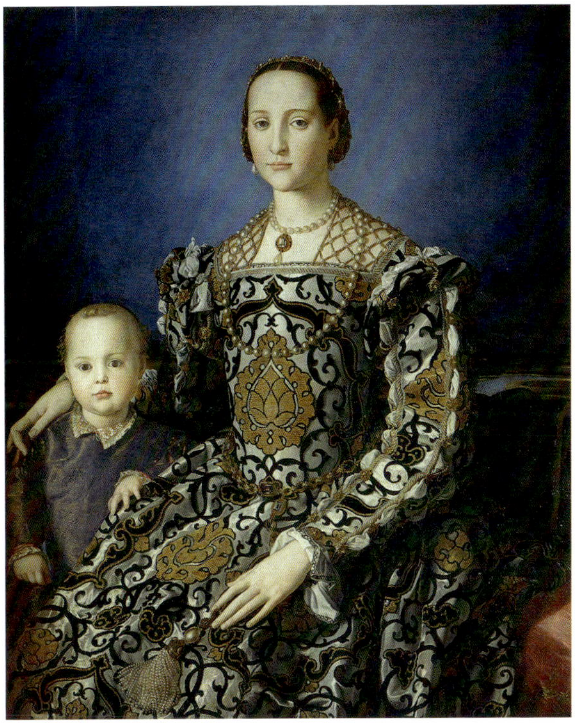

191. Agnolo Bronzino, *Portrait of Cosimo I in Armor,* c. 1543, oil on panel, 29⅛ × 22⅞ in. (74 × 58 cm), Uffizi.

192. Agnolo Bronzino, *Portrait of Eleonora of Toledo with Her Son Giovanni,* c. 1545, oil on panel, 45¼ × 37¾ in. (115 × 96 cm), Uffizi.

nardo's *Mona Lisa* (fig. 137) into a state portrait employing an over three-quarter-length sitter and a large, nearly square format. In contrast to Mona Lisa's relatively simple costume and absence of jewelry, appropriate for a symbolic nature goddess, Eleonora's voluminous dress with puffed and slashed sleeves and her immensely valuable jewelry evoke the great wealth and the prosperity of Cosimo's regime. With microscopic precision, Bronzino rendered Eleonora's adornments: two pearl necklaces, one with a diamond and pearl pendant; pearl earrings; a pearl-studded partlet (shoulder veil) and snood (hair net); and a gem-studded gold belt with a pearl tassel. Like Mona Lisa, Eleonora sits in a loggia, but here the parapet has became a broad throne upholstered with a red cushion and a draped back appropriate for a duchess. While the landscape and posture of Mona Lisa expressed the immense complexity and contingency of the universe, the landscape in Bronzino's portrait depicts the Arno Valley as a symbol of Cosimo I's dominion and sovereignty. Eleonora's aristocratic bearing, steady emotionless gaze, and elegant tapered fingers reflect the exquisite manners, refined taste, and cultural sophistication of the Medici court. As in the *Mona Lisa,* the sky creates a radiant aura of sanctity around the sitter's head. In Leonardo's work the light underlined Mona Lisa's expression of universal knowledge and divine wisdom. In Bronzino's portrait the nocturnal lunar light and the multitude of pearls, symbolic of purity and chastity, associate Eleonora with Diana, goddess of chastity and childbirth, basking in the light of her Apollonian sun, Cosimo I. While Mona Lisa's portrait communicated the generative potential of all nature, Eleonora's more narrowly celebrates the continuity of the ducal patrilineal dynastic line by representing her—one of the first instances in Florentine female portraiture—with one of her offspring, here her second-born son, Giovanni (1543–62), who was destined for an ecclesiastical career had he not died at age nineteen. Despite his subject's manifest fecundity, Bronzino has suppressed even a hint of sexuality or eroticism. Rather, he has depicted her skin as ivory-white marble, her bearing as erect and effortlessly graceful, her outward-directed gaze as glacial and distant, and her features as flawless—all set within a crystalline blue empyrean. The artist, an accomplished poet, as we have seen, has portrayed Eleonora as Petrarch's Laura, a paragon of chaste, timeless, and radiant beauty whose supreme perfection and virtue induce the viewer to contemplate divinity.

VASARI'S *APOTHEOSIS OF COSIMO I*

Just as Charles V had abdicated his throne in 1556 in favor of his son Philip II (1527–98) two years before his death, so Cosimo ceded most of his power in 1564 to his firstborn son, Francesco, who became the third duke of Florence. In preparation for Francesco's betrothal in 1564 and his wedding the next year to the illegitimate daughter of Charles V, Giovanna of Austria, Vasari and his workshop rushed to complete the ceiling of Cosimo I's new audience hall in the Palazzo Vecchio (see chapter 32). The center of the ceiling provided an opportunity for Vasari to paint a valedictory portrait of Cosimo I, summarizing the accomplishments of his ducal career (fig. 193). Seating his subject triumphally in heaven, silhouetted against a radiant sun and accompanied by a multitude of angels, Vasari presented the duke as an immortal god—a new Apollo and a virtual cosmos unto himself within a circular format symbolic of his divine perfection. Cosimo dominates the three shields of Florence and the twenty-one shields of the guilds tied to the balustrade of the oculus. They symbolize the governmental, commercial, financial, industrial, military, juridical, and artistic institutions of Florence. Flanking him, two angels display the cross of the Pisan naval Order of St. Stephen founded by Cosimo in 1561, the chain of the prestigious Burgundian military Order of the Golden Fleece, and the ducal crown of Florence and Siena—insignias of sovereignty, dominion, power, authority, and legitimacy. Behind him, bare-breasted Flora, personification of Florence's fertility and prosperity, crowns Cosimo with an oak wreath like that awarded by the Roman senate to Emperor Augustus in 27 BC for meritorious service to the empire.

As a new Augustus being honored for his service to Florence, Cosimo appropriately dons a Roman military costume and sits on an imperial folding field throne. Equally appropriately, Vasari derived Cosimo's posture from the Roman emperor represented on the Arch of Constantine in Rome distributing largesse to the Roman populace after military victory. By extension, Cosimo now delivers prosperity and dominion to the Florentines. His posture also cited Michelangelo's New Sacristy *Baton Carrier* (fig. 149) to legitimate Cosimo by linking him with the line of Cosimo il Vecchio.

The gulf in style and content between these last two portraits and the Chambéry portrait of a young man (fig. 117) and Lippi's image of Angiola Sapiti (fig. 118) represents the great distance between a republican man of virtue and an absolutist duke, between a middle-class citizen bride and a foreign-born noble duchess. Since the role of women had changed far less than had the political system in Florence throughout two centuries, the portrait of Angiola Sapiti shares far more with that of Eleonora of Toledo than the Chambéry *vir virtutis* does with the portrait of Duke Cosimo.

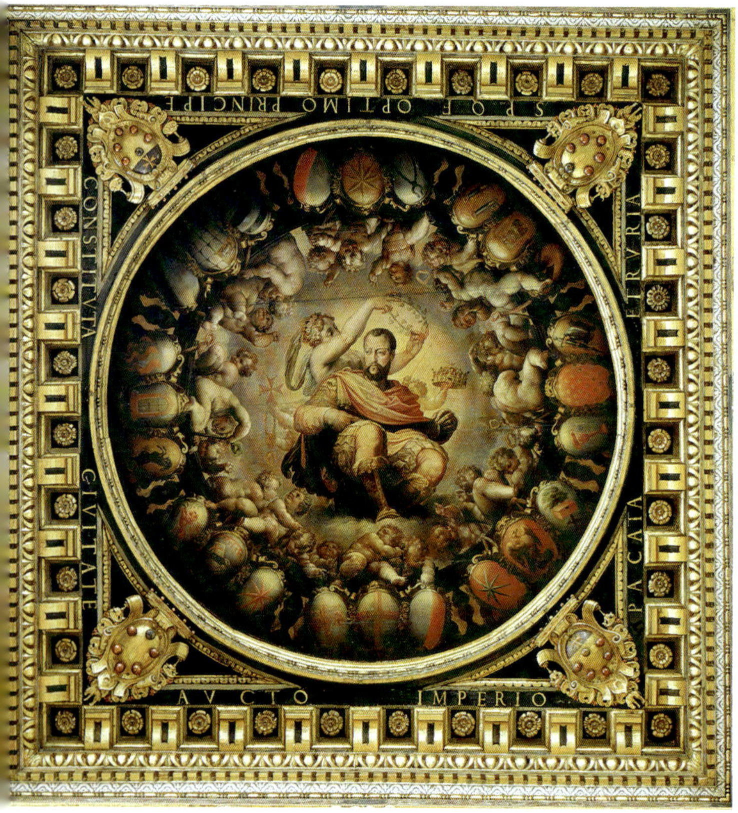

193. Giorgio Vasari, *Apotheosis of Cosimo I,* 1563–65, ceiling, Sala Grande (fig. 197), Palazzo Vecchio. The inscription translates, "The supreme prince of the senate and people of Florence founded the state, enlarged the empire, and pacified Etruria [Tuscany]."

32

HALLS OF STATE

Palazzo Vecchio, III

SALVIATI'S SALA DI UDIENZA

In 1543, three years after establishing the Priors' Palace as his new ducal residence, Cosimo I commissioned Francesco Salviati (1510–63) to fresco the walls of his new audience hall, the Sala di Udienza (figs. 194–196). The decoration commemorated his victory over the exiles at Montemurlo in 1537 and the return of the fortresses at Florence, Pisa, and Livorno to ducal control in 1543. The Sala di Udienza originally had served as the audience hall for the republican *Signoria*. Its classicizing carved and gilt wooden ceiling and marble entrance on the east wall with intarsia doors and a marble personification of Justice had all been executed at the same time and by the same artists who had remodeled the adjoining Sala dei Gigli (figs. 101 and 102). By continuing and outdoing in decorative refinement a project begun under the regime of his maternal great-grandfather, Lorenzo il Magnifico, Cosimo I registered his legitimacy as the heir to the Laurentian golden age.

To discourage petitioners from approaching Cosimo I too abruptly or directly, his throne was elevated on a dais at the north end and approached through the door from the Sala dei Gigli. This created the bent-axial ceremonial

194. North and east walls, Sala di Udienza, Palazzo Vecchio.

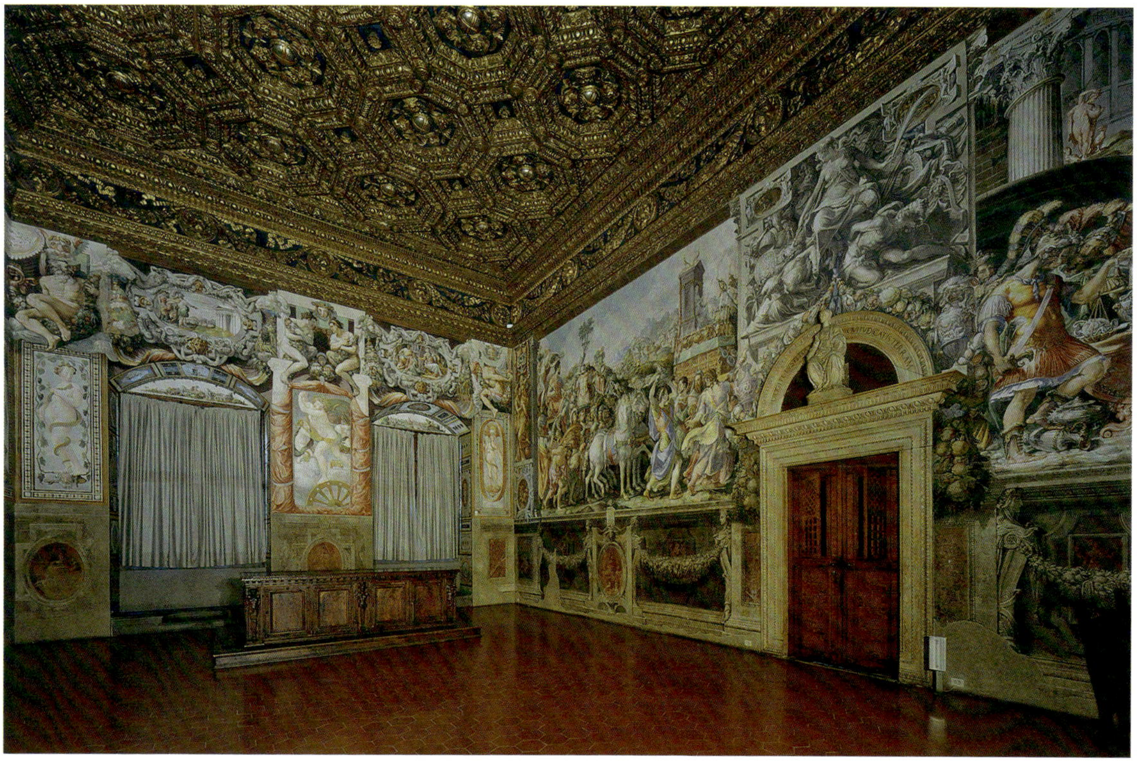

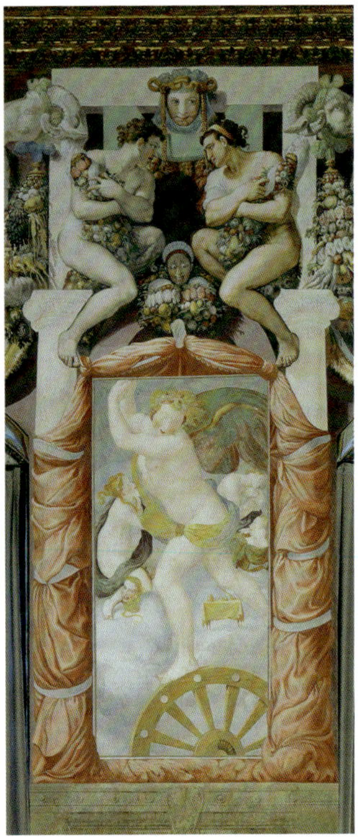

195. Francesco Salviati, *Fortuna,* 1543–45, fresco. Detail of fig. 194.

196. Francesco Salviati, *Triumph of Furius Camillus over the Etruscans at Veii in 396 BC,* 1543–45, fresco. Detail of fig. 194.

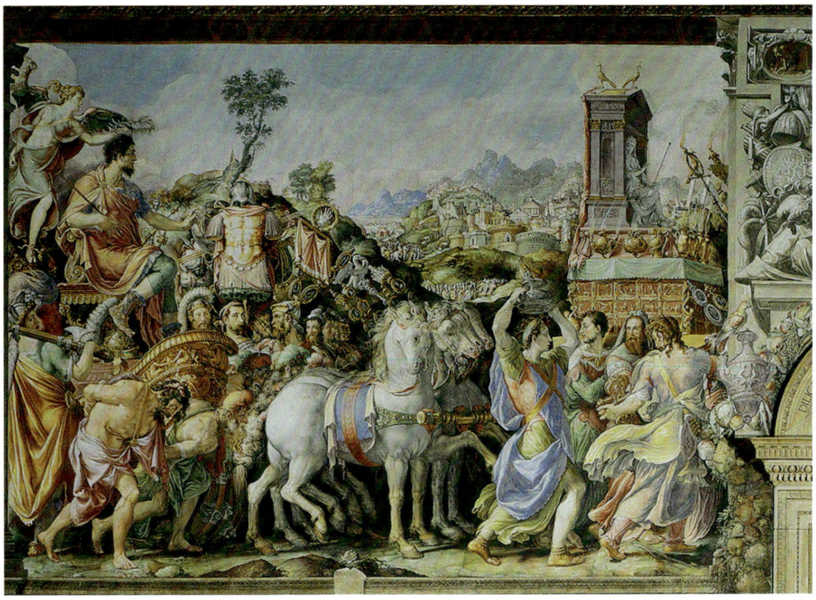

route common to most halls of state. Salviati emphasized the first leg of this processional way by frescoing above the door a classicizing personification of Peace, dominating Benedetto da Maiano's earlier marble *Justice* below (fig. 194). *Peace* torching a heaped pile of arms, armor, and bound captives signified the end of war and factionalism under Cosimo I and his initiation of a new *pax fiorentina* (Florentine peace) analogous to the *pax romana* (Roman peace) of Augustus.

The windows behind the throne would have tended to blind and intimidate a petitioner, a device used in many halls of state. A scene behind the throne defining the sovereign's source of authority was also a standard feature of halls of state. Here Salviati frescoed a winged Fortuna standing on a wheel to indicate fate's instability (fig. 195). The personified vices surrounding Fortuna (Envy, Lust, Sloth, and Malice) and the table displaying the rewards of good fortune (a bishop's miter, crown, and scepter) suggested that Cosimo I had rejected vice and mastered fortune to achieve its rewards of authority, sovereignty, and divine favor. The two columns framing *Fortuna,* emblems of strength, justice, and territorial dominion, further indicated the fruits of Cosimo's good fortune. In addition, the canopy or baldachin attached to the columns signaled divine favor and sovereignty, while the two Michelangelesque nude youths holding large festoons of fruits and vegetables symbolized abundance and prosperity.

Narrative scenes unfolding down the east wall and across the south wall illustrated deeds of Furius Camillus taken from Livy's *History of Rome* (5.19–end). Furius Camillus was one of the republican heroes in the Sala dei Gigli important for Lorenzo il Magnifico (fig. 101). Even earlier, Cosimo il Vecchio's recall from exile in 1434 had been paralleled to Furius Camillus's return to Rome in 390 BC to save the city from the attacking Gauls. The selection of the subject matter, therefore, evoked the notion that Cosimo I continued and fulfilled earlier Medicean rule in Florence. The first scene is the *Triumph of Furius Camillus over the Etruscans at Veii in 396 BC* (fig. 196). Seen between illusionistic piers faced with fluted Corinthian pilasters, as if the events were unfolding in real time on a shallow stage, Camillus sits enthroned on a *quadriga* (four-horse chariot) with the Etruscan city of Veii in the background. While crowned with laurel by a winged victory, Camillus parades toward Rome with captives, trophies, and his troops—impressive "like a Jupiter," as recorded by Livy. Salviati portrayed Camillus in the guise of Cosimo I to suggest that Camillus's conquest of Etruria (Tuscany) prefigured Cosimo I's victory at Montemurlo in 1537 and that he fulfilled Florence's great destiny for empire stemming from its foundation by Rome in the first century BC (fig. 9). The prominent severed laurel tree sprouting a new branch on the hilltop near Cosimo I/Camillus further alluded to the *broncone* device of Lorenzo il Magnifico to indicate that Cosimo I had continued Lorenzo's bloodline and established a new period of peace and prosperity.

According to Livy, Camillus was not only a brilliant commander but also a pious leader, donating 10 percent of his booty to the temple of Apollo in Rome just as Duke Cosimo tithed a portion of his income to the Church. Camillus also rededicated to Apollo the Etruscan image of Juno, shown here holding a scepter while carried in a shrine. In Medici circles Eleonora da Toledo was often allegorized as a new Juno, supreme goddess of marriage and childbirth. The scene implied, then, that the duke and duchess embodied the spiritual authority of classical Rome, founding a new Medici dynasty and ushering in a new golden age.

Salviati plundered the winged victory, *quadriga*, captives, trophies, standards, costumes, and the friezelike composition from classical imperial reliefs. His parade of ancient trophies aptly supported the triumphal subject matter. But never before had Florentine art sought to awe its viewers by exhibiting such a vast antiquarian display of classical knowledge. The use of specifically Roman imperial motifs for a Roman republican narrative also indicated ideologically that Cosimo I had absorbed Florence's republican past but now had constructed a new authoritarian government based on the model of imperial Rome. Salviati's Mannerist style was thus a tour de force of creativity, graceful refinement, and vibrant rhythm far richer than any of his classical models. This finely wrought courtly style was itself part of a message that signaled erudition, prosperity, power, and triumph.

BANDINELLI AND VASARI'S SALA GRANDE, II

About two years after moving into the Priors' Palace in 1540, Cosimo I began to convert the Sala Grande (fig. 129) into his principal audience hall. While the *Signoria* had sat within the Great Council on a tribune in the center of the east wall, Cosimo I changed the hall's orientation by commissioning Bandinelli to build a vast dais at the north end enclosed by a now-dismantled balustrade (fig. 197). Bandinelli's triumphal arch motif articulating the end wall of the dais (1542–60) was modeled on Jacopo Sansovino's Venetian Loggetta of 1538–45 to suggest that Cosimo I's sovereignty equaled that of Venice. The paired freestanding columns flanking the ends of the dais expressed strength, justice, and dominion—similar to the columns framing *Fortuna* in the Sala di Udienza (fig. 195).

In 1559 Cosimo I commissioned Vasari to oversee the decoration of the ceiling and walls of the Sala Grande with paintings commemorating his annexation of Siena in 1555, which nearby doubled the size of the Florentine state. Between 1559 and 1563, Vasari had the height of the ceiling raised by 13 *braccia* (approximately 25 ft. or 7.6 m) in order to insert windows high on the end and side walls to properly light the paintings, and then had the old ceiling reinstalled, after it had been modified to achieve its present Venetian-style compartmentation, carving, and gilding (1559–63). Vasari and his workshop also built a monumental double-ramped stairway (1561–72) leading to the center of the west wall to provide the traditional bent-axial processional route to the throne, painted the ceiling panels (1563–65), and frescoed the walls (1566–71). By reusing the republican Great Council hall, Cosimo I suggested continuity between the republic and the duchy. But the greater scale and richer decoration of the renovated Sala Grande also revealed the duchy's superiority.

When enthroned on his dais, the duke would have been backlit by the windows of the triumphal arch and blessed by a statue of Pope Leo X (fig. 198), as if the pontiff were legitimating his rule with divine and genealogical authority.

Arranged chronologically along the central longitudinal axis of the ceiling in corresponding pairs on either side of the central *tondo,* a brief history of Florence in six scenes prefigured the even greater accomplishments of Cosimo I. The *Foundation of Florence* (fig. 9), for example, foreshadowed Cosimo's refounding of ducal Florence in an imperial mode, justifying his claim to be a new Augustus. The corresponding scene at the opposite end of the ceiling, *Building the Third Circuit of Florentine Walls* (fig. 16), anticipated Cosimo's construction of fortifications all over Tuscany. The two *tondi* at the far ends of the ceiling's central axis represented the four quarters and the sixteen neighborhoods of Florence, and the sixteen square panels on either side of the *tondi* represented the twenty-three cities and sixteen regions of Tuscany that constituted Cosimo I's territorial dominion (fig. 197). The signs and symbols in these panels also comprehensively catalogued the vast agricultural, mineral, industrial, military, cultural, religious, and judicial

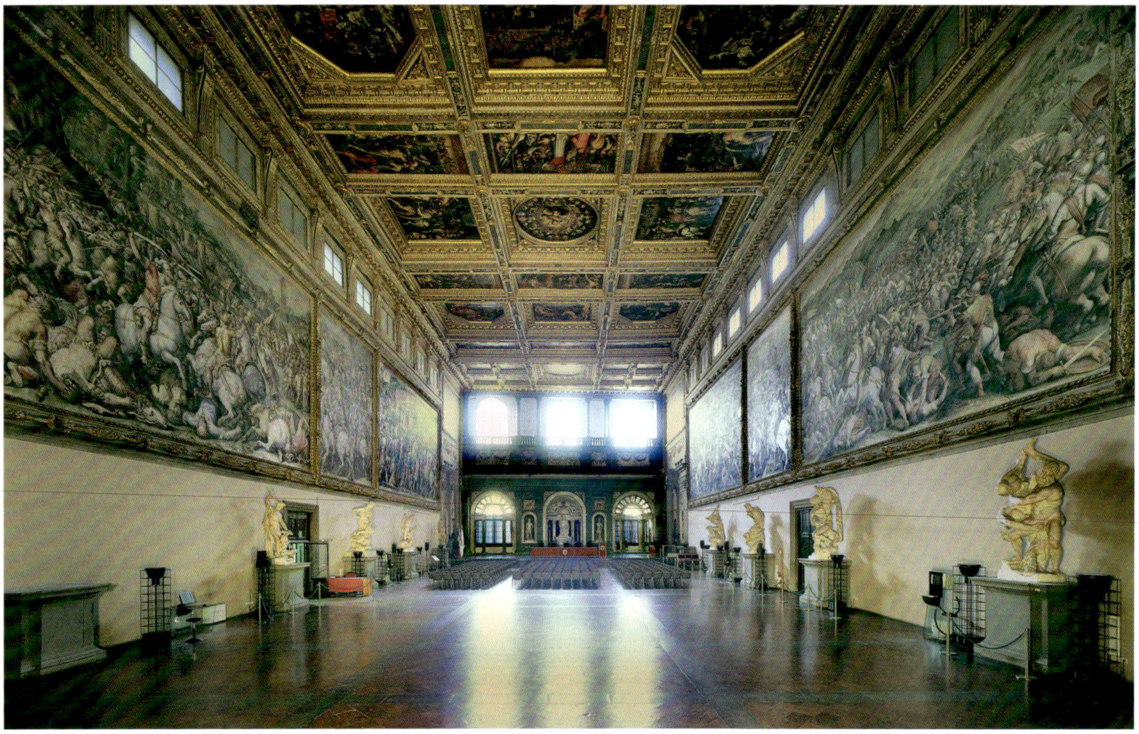

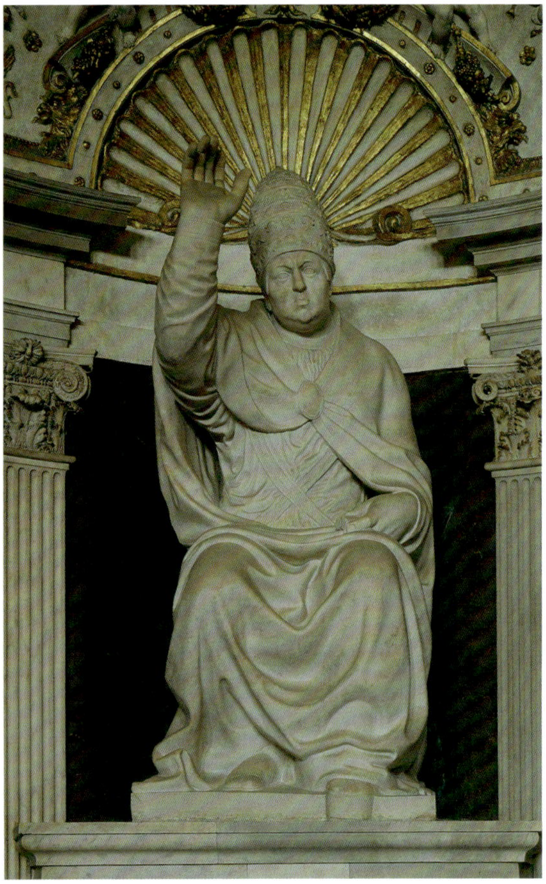

197. View north toward the dais, Sala Grande, 185 ft. 2 in. × 72 ft. 8 in. × 63 ft. 1⅞ in. (56.44 × 22.15 × 19.25 m), Palazzo Vecchio.

198. Baccio Bandinelli, *Pope Leo X,* 1542–65, marble. Detail of fig. 197.

resources and institutions of Tuscany. In addition, they depicted over two hundred images of classical spirits (pagan deities, winged putti, and zodiacal signs). From the moment of its foundation, in short, Florence was shown to have been destined to be both a great spiritual and temporal center.

The remaining twenty scenes—seven on each side of the ceiling's central axis and three on each of the two side-walls—represented events from the fourteen-year Pisan War (1494–1509) on the west and the fourteen-month Sienese War (1554–55) on the east. Vasari contrasted visually the ten scenes on the west with the corresponding scenes on the east to distinguish the protracted, divisive, and inefficient Pisan War under the republic from the brief, unifying, and efficient Sienese War under Cosimo I. In one scene, *Florence Declares War against Pisa,* for example, Vasari shows the Florentine *Signoria* and its councilors in the Sala dei Dugento in the Priors' Palace fervently debating their course of action motivated by an allegory of Nemesis (the classical goddess of vengeance and retributive justice) holding a flaming sword with which to punish the Pisans for the hubris

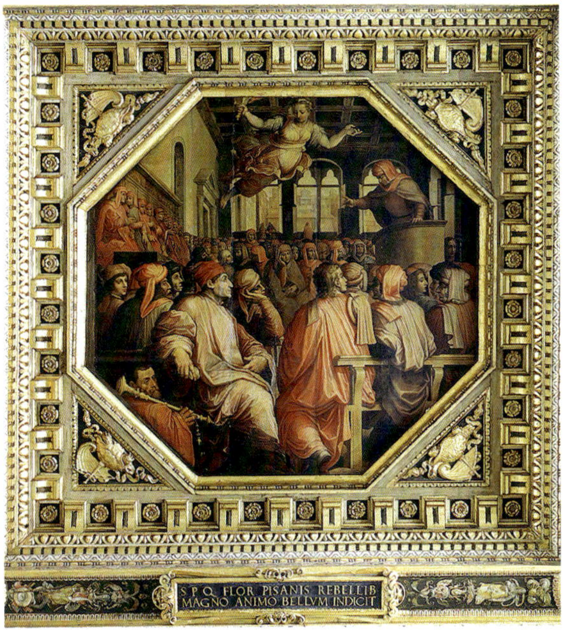

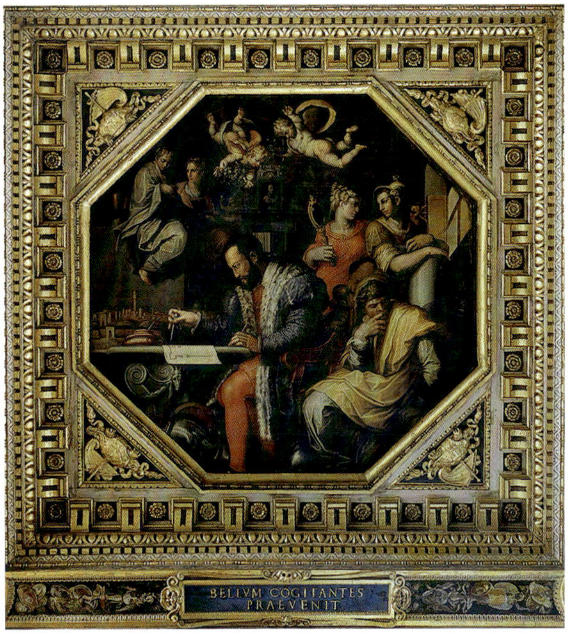

199. Giorgio Vasari and Workshop, *Florence Declares War against Pisa,* 1563–65, oil on panel. Detail of fig. 197.

200. Giorgio Vasari and Workshop, *Cosimo I Plans the War of Siena,* 1563–65, oil on panel. Detail of fig. 197.

of their rebellion (fig. 199). In his *Ragionamenti* describing the Palazzo Vecchio's program, Vasari identifies the gesticulating orator in the rostrum as Antonio Giacomini, whom Francesco Guicciardini in his celebrated 1561 *History of Italy* had explicitly criticized as being so passionate and so lacking in caution that "audacity overcame prudence," leading to chaos on the battlefield and prolongation of the war effort.

By contrast, in the corresponding scene, *Cosimo I Plans the War of Siena,* on the opposite side of the ceiling, Cosimo makes his plans entirely alone (fig. 200). Wearing ermine-lined ducal robes and the chain of the Order of the Golden Fleece with his armor resting at his feet, he efficiently designs his strategy, like a skillful architect, with a compass, square, quill pen, plan, and model of Siena. Rather than acting precipitously with passionate vengeance, the surrounding personifications suggest that Cosimo rationally planned his tactics with Patience (urn), Vigilance (lamp), Prudence (mirror), Fortitude (column), and Silence (finger to lips). The imperial-style bust of Cosimo over the door implies that his efforts will fulfill Florence's Roman destiny for empire. Above the duke's head two angels signal the war's outcome by a laurel crown of victory, an olive branch of peace, and a palm of immortality.

Vasari created equally dramatic contrasts between corresponding battle scenes of the Pisan and Sienese wars. In the *Florentine Defeat of the Pisans at Torre di S. Vincenzo in 1505,* for example, Vasari depicted in the foreground a tight cluster of individual duels between knights on rearing horses amidst a clutter of fallen horses, warriors, and weapons (fig. 201). He even included a battle for a standard that recalled Leonardo's lost *Battle of Anghiari* (see fig. 130). But who is winning? The chaotic background skirmishes do little to clarify the issue, and were it not for the inconspicuous Florentine banner at the extreme left, the Florentines could not even be distinguished from the Pisans, especially since all wear identical classical military garb. Vasari, in short, showed the republican forces as disorganized, ineffective, and poorly commanded—winning only by virtue of Florence's classical destiny.

In the *Battle at Scannagallo in the Val di Chiana in 1554* directly opposite, by contrast, nearly all of Cosimo I's troops are dressed in contemporary armor, as if impelled less by destiny than by Cosimo I's will and design (fig. 202). Under the efficient leadership of Giangiacomo de' Medici (b. 1497) who carried out Cosimo I's tactics, the Florentines sweep across the countryside in highly disciplined and carefully organized formations. This unstoppable force meets mild resistance in the center middle ground, but otherwise completely routs the enemy.

The scenes of the Pisan and Sienese wars culminate with two triumphal entries into Florence in 1509 and

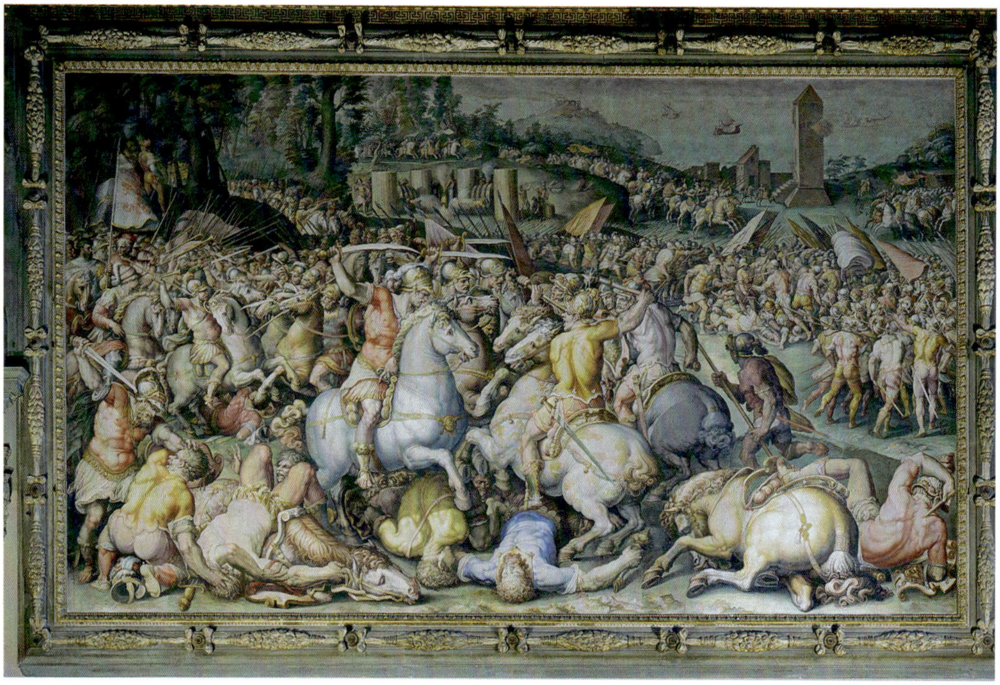

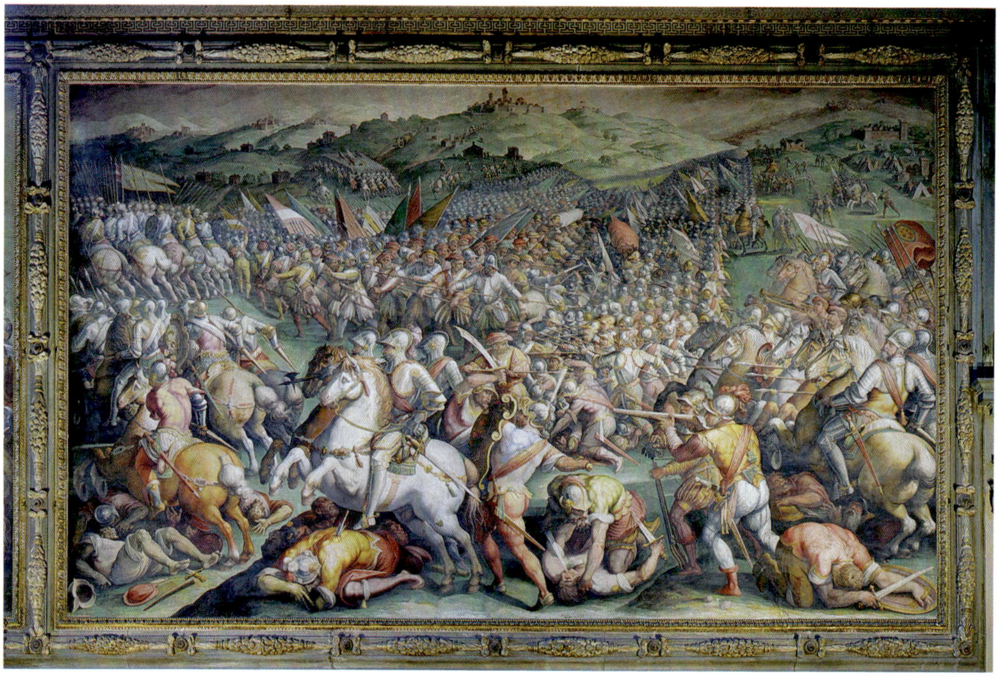

201. Giorgio Vasari and Workshop, *Florentine Defeat of the Pisans at Torre di San Vincenzo in 1505,* 1566–71, fresco. Detail of fig. 197.

202. Giorgio Vasari and Workshop, *Battle at Scannagallo in the Val di Chiana in 1554,* 1566–71, fresco. Detail of fig. 197.

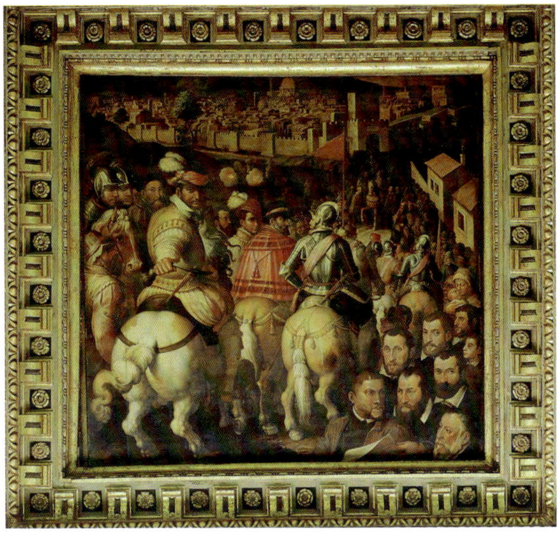

203. Giorgio Vasari and Workshop, *Triumphal Entry into Florence after the Conquest of Siena,* 1563–65, oil on panel. Detail of fig. 197.

1555, respectively, flanking the central *tondo* (figs. 193, 197, and 203). In other words, the entire decoration was organized around the central *tondo,* which was oriented toward the dais. Thus, when the victorious duke was enthroned, he only had to lift his eyes heavenward to view his triumphant image in heaven. The decoration thus implied that Cosimo alone had inherited all Florentine institutions and territories and now sat like an imperial god directing the temporal history and spiritual destiny of this new Rome and new Jerusalem.

The *Triumphal Entry into Florence after the Conquest of Siena* (fig. 203) contains at the lower right an unprecedented group portrait as a signature: in the center Giorgio Vasari, impresario and commander-in-chief of the decoration, holds what is presumably the Sala Grande's program; he is flanked in front by the humanist Vincenzo Borghini and the historian Giambattista Adriani (1513–79), who together wrote the program; behind Vasari stand his artist-lieutenants, Giovanni Stradano (1523–1605), Jacopo Zucchi (c. 1540–89/90), and Battista Naldini (c. 1537–c. 1591). All are dressed like scholars and gentlemen. By locating the portrait-signature in this particular scene, Vasari claimed an artistic triumph as great as Cosimo I's military victory, while acknowledging that the duke commanded both the military and artistic campaigns. This portrait-signature also indicated that a huge decorative project such as the Sala Grande, produced under tight deadlines, had become by necessity a disciplined, intellectually complex, logistical exercise, with a chain of command descending from the duke down through the planners and designer-in-chief to a multitude of specialists, including architects, masons, carpenters, sculptors, stone carvers, stucco workers, figure painters, landscape painters, grotesque painters, gold beaters, gilders, glass makers, color grinders, and a host of assistants. Between 1543 and 1565 nearly seventy individual artists and craftsmen are mentioned in the payment records. The responsibility for such a vast enterprise provided Vasari with power, wealth, and prestige, transforming him into a prince of artists, but like all courtiers, subject to the will of the duke.

The decoration fluctuates to an unprecedented degree between a focus on Duke Cosimo—his person, deeds, and virtues—and his dispersion across Florentine history and territory. The centrality of the duke on the dais and in the central ceiling *tondo* emphasized his authority, legitimacy, and leadership, while his diffusion across time and space underlined the vast extent of his sovereignty, dominion, and power as well as the abundance of his material and cultural resources. The dispersed and focused decorative structure also formed a precise aesthetic analogue to the characteristics of the martial subject.

But the structural oscillation between center and periphery, contraction and expansion, command and execution also suggested underlying tensions and anxieties. The apotheosis of the duke masked his anxiety about his death and place in history. The emphasis on male virility and female fertility called forth concerns about impotence and dynastic discontinuity. Victorious battles and triumphs glossed over the real risks and sacrifices of war. Claims to have continued and fulfilled Florence's republican past ignored the program's self-serving manipulation of republican history and the political ruptures and social dislocations provoked by the establishment of an absolutist duchy. The many signs of abundance and prosperity concealed deep fears of famine, plague, and economic stagnation. The many emblems of rank and status constructing social and military hierarchies suppressed anxieties about factionalism, sedition, and rebellion, just as the scenes of command and control overlooked the typical inertia and entrenched conservatism of bureaucracies and armies.

But in a hall of state—a theater for the display of the state's ideology, a site for staging the state as a work of art—all the contingencies of real life could be overcome and frozen in time. Here, whole worlds could be claimed and controlled despite the inevitable subtext of doubts, threats, and instabilities.

GENEALOGY OF THE MEDICI FAMILY

Cosimo il Vecchio, *pater patriae*
(1389–1464)
Ruled Florence, 1434–1464
Buried in Old Sacristy, before high altar, under crossing dome
m. Contessina dei Bardi (d. 1473)

Carlo
(1428–92)

Piero il Gottoso
(1416–69)
Ruled Florence, 1464–69
Buried in Old Sacristy, Verrocchio's Tomb
m. Lucrezia Tornabuoni (1425–82)

Giovanni
(1421–63)
Buried in Old Sacristy, Verrocchio's Tomb
m. Ginevra degli Albizzi (d. after 1476)

Cosimino
(1454–59)

Giuliano il Magnifico
(1453–78)
Killed in Pazzi Conspiracy
Buried in New Sacristy,
Madonna Wall

Bianca (Pazzi)
(d. 1488)

Nannina (Rucellai)
(d. 1493)

Lorenzo il Magnifico
(1449–92)
Ruled Florence, 1469–92
Buried in New Sacristy, Madonna Wall
m. Clarice Orsini (1450–88)

Giulio
(1478–1534)
Illegitimate
Ruled Florence, 1512–27
Archbishop of Florence, 1513
Pope Clement VII, 1523–34
Buried in Rome,
S.M. sopra Minerva

Piero
(1472–1503)
Ruled Florence, 1492–94
m. Alfonsina Orsini
(1472–1520)

Giovanni
(1475–1521)
Pope Leo X, 1513–21
Patron of New Sacristy
Buried in Rome,
S.M. sopra Minerva

Giuliano
(1479–1516)
Captain of Church, 1513
Captain general of Church, 1515
Named duke of Nemours, 1515
Buried in New Sacristy
m. Philiberte of Savoy (1498–1524)

Cosimino
Contessina (Ridolfi)
(d. 1515)

Maddalena (Cibo)
(1473–1519)

Lorenzo the Younger
(1492–1519)
Captain general of Florence, 1515
Named duke of Urbino, 1516
Buried in New Sacristy
m. Madeleine de la Tour Auvergne (1501–19)

Clarice (Strozzi)
(1493–1528)

Ippolito
(1511–35)
Illegitimate
Cardinal 1530

Alessandro
(1511–37)
Illegitimate
Duke of Florence 1531–37
m. Margaret of Austria
(1522–86)

Catherine
(1519–89)
m. Henry II of France

Lucrezia (Este)
(1545–61)

Isabella (Orsini)
(1542–76)

Pietro
(1554–1604)
m. Eleonora da Toledo
(1553–76)

Maria
(1540–57)

Ferdinando I
(1549–1609)
Cardinal, 1563
Grand duke of Florence, 1587–1609
m. Christine of Lorraine (1565–1637)

Averardo di Bicci
m. Jacopa de Spini

Giovanni di Bicci
(1360–1429)
Buried in Old Sacristy,
sarcophagus under vesting table
m. Piccarda Bueri (1368–1433)

Lorenzo
(1395–1440)
Buried in Old Sacristy Crypt
m. Ginevra Cavalcanti (d. after 1464)

Pierfrancesco the Elder
(1430–76)
m. Laudonia Acciajuoli

Giovanni il Popolano
(1467–98)
m. Caterina Sforza (1462–1509)

Lorenzo il Popolano
(1463–1503)
Semiramide d'Appiano
(d. 1523)

Pierfrancesco the Younger
(1487–1525)
m. Maria Soderini

Laudomia (Salviati, Strozzi)
(1518–after 1558)

Lorenzino
(1514–48)

Giuliano
(1520–88)

Maddalena (Strozzi)

Lucrezia (Salviati)
(1470–1550)

Maria Salviati = **Giovanni delle Bande Nere**
(1499–1543) (1498–1526)

Cosimo I
(1519–74)
Duke of Florence, 1537–70
Grand duke, 1570–74
m. Eleonora da Toledo (1519–62)
m. Camilla Martelli (1545–90)

Giovanni
(1543–62)

Garzia
(1547–62)

Francesco I
(1541–87)
Grand duke of Florence, 1574–87
m. Giovanna of Austria (1547–78)
m. Bianca Cappello (1548–87)

Virginia (Este)
(1568–1615)

Bia
(c. 1536–42)

Giovanni
(1567–1621)

TIMELINE

Politics, Religion, and Culture

1400–1402 Troops of Gian Galeazzo Visconti, duke of Milan, invade Florentine territory. Florence liberated when Visconti dies of plague in 1402.

c. 1401 Bruni's *In Praise of Florence.*

1406 Florence conquers Pisa.

1414–18 The Council of Constance resolves the Great Schism and reunifies the Church. Schism ends with the election of Pope Martin V in 1417.

1416 Florentine humanist Poggio Bracciolini discovers Vitruvius's *On Architecture* at St. Gall in Switzerland.

1418 Discovery of Lucretius's *On the Nature of Things* sparks an interest in Epicurean philosophy.

1423–40 War of Milan.

1425 Panormita's Epicurean *Hermaphrodite* dedicated to Cosimo il Vecchio.

Architecture and Sculpture

1401 Competition for Baptistery bronze doors won by Ghiberti.

1403–24 Ghiberti's first bronze doors.

1404–29 Or San Michele niche sculpture completed by the guilds, including Donatello's *SS. Mark* (first true *contrapposto*), *George,* and *Louis of Toulouse,* Nanni di Banco's *Four Crowned Saints,* and Ghiberti's *John the Baptist.*

1408–9 Donatello's marble *David.*

1415–28 Campanile niche sculpture completed by wool manufacturers' guild, including Donatello's *Abraham and Isaac* and *Zuccone.*

1415–28 Brunelleschi's Old Sacristy at S. Lorenzo commissioned by Giovanni di Bicci de' Medici.

1416 Donatello's marble *David* transferred to the Priors' Palace.

1417 Main body of the cathedral completed.

1418–36 Brunelleschi's cathedral dome.

1419–45 Brunelleschi's Foundling Hospital.

1419–23 Brunelleschi's Barbardori Chapel in S. Felicità.

1424–52 Ghiberti's *Gates of Paradise.*

c. 1425 Donatello's bronze *Feast of Herod,* first extant demonstration of one-point perspective.

Painting

1414 Lorenzo Monaco's Gothic *Coronation* for the high altar of the Camaldolese S. Maria degli Angeli.

Before 1425 Brunelleschi invents one-point perspective, transforming Renaissance painting and relief sculpture.

1425–27 Masaccio and Masolino's Brancacci Chapel frescoes in S. Maria del Carmine with scenes from the life of St. Peter.

Reigns of Popes

Note: Antipopes in italics and family names in parentheses.

1389–1404 Boniface IX (Tomacelli)

[AVIGNON] ***1394–1423*** *Benedict XIII (De Luna)*

1404–6 Innocent VII (Migliorati)

1406–15 Gregory XII (Correr)

[PISA] ***1409–10*** *Alexander V (Filargo)*

[PISA] ***1410–15*** *John XXIII (Coscia)*

1417–31 Martin V (Colonna)

[AVIGNON] ***1423–29*** *Clement VIII (Muñoz)*

Politics, Religion, and Culture

1427 Lorenzo Valla's Epicurean *On Voluptuousness.*

1429–33 War of Lucca.

1432 Battle of S. Romano commanded by Niccolò da Tolentino, who was made an honorary Florentine citizen five months after the battle.

1433 Peace of Ferrara between Florence, Venice, and Milan negotiated by Cosimo il Vecchio, ending the War of Lucca.

1433 Albizzi faction exiles Cosimo il Vecchio.

1434 Cosimo il Vecchio recalled from exile by Medici faction.

1435 Niccolò da Tolentino dies in battle and is given state funeral by the Florentine government.

1436 Eugenius IV consecrates the cathedral on March 25.

1436 Eugenius IV cedes the old Silvestrine monastery to the Dominicans under the leadership of Fra Antonino Pierozzi (canonized as St. Antoninus).

1438–45 Council of Ferrara, Florence, and Rome briefly reunifies Eastern and Western Churches. Emperor John VIII Palaeologus and Greek scholar Giorgius Gemistos Plethon visit Florence.

1440 Florence, allied with Venice, defeats the Milanese, allied with Florentine exiles, at the Battle of Anghiari commanded by Rinaldo degli Albizzi.

1442 Rinaldo degli Albizzi dies.

1445 Fra Antonino Pierozzi (later canonized as St. Antoninus), the archbishop of Florence, inaugurates the Foundling Hospital.

Architecture and Sculpture

1430s Alberti's bronze *Self-Portrait* relief.

c. 1430–32 Donatello's marble *Shaw Madonna.*

1433 Buggiano's Medici sarcophagus for the Old Sacristy of S. Lorenzo.

1434–43 Donatello's decoration for the Old Sacristy, including vault *tondi* and bronze doors.

c. 1434–87 Brunelleschi's S. Spirito.

1436–38 Brunelleschi's cathedral lantern designed; completed by Michelozzo in 1467.

1436–45 Michelozzo's church, monastery, and library of S. Marco financed by Cosimo il Vecchio.

1442–92 S. Lorenzo rebuilt on a design by Brunelleschi.

c. 1443–57 Medici Palace, commissioned by Cosimo il Vecchio, sets the norms for Florentine palace design for the next half-century or more.

Painting

c. 1427 Masaccio's *Trinity* fresco in S. Maria Novella, rigorous early demonstration of one-point perspective.

c. 1428 Masaccio's birth tray, *Lying-in of a Florentine Lady.*

1435 Alberti's *On Painting* refines and disseminates Brunelleschi's one-point perspective.

c. 1435 Paolo Uccello's *Portrait of a Young Man.*

c. 1436 Paolo Uccello's *Battle of S. Romano,* perhaps painted for the Priors' Palace, first applies one-point perspective to a battle scene.

c. 1438–41 Fra Angelico's *S. Marco Altarpiece* commissioned by Cosimo il Vecchio combines Gothic and Renaissance elements.

c. 1438–45 Filippo Lippi's *Portrait of Lorenzo Scolari and Angiola Sapiti.*

1442–45 Fra Angelico's frescoes for the cloister, chapter house, refectory, corridors, and cells in S. Marco.

c. 1447–50 Castagno's *Last Supper* fresco for the Camaldolese refectory in S. Apollonia, first rigorous one-point perspective applied to a Last Supper scene.

Reigns of Popes

[AVIGNON] ***1425–30*** *Benedict XIV (Garnier)*

1431–47 Eugenius IV (Condulmer)

[AVIGNON] ***1440–49*** *Felix V (Amadeus of Savoy)*

1447–55 Nicholas V (Parentucelli)

Politics, Religion, and Culture

1452 Alberti's *On the Art of Building in Ten Books* presented to Pope Nicholas V.

1452 Ghirberti's *Gates of Paradise* completed.

1456–71 Janos Argyropylos teaches Greek and Greek philosophy in Florence.

1458 Ficino's Epicurean treatise *On Voluptuousness*.

1459 Cosimo il Vecchio elevates S. Lorenzo to a collegiate church for twelve clerics.

1459 Ceremonial entrance of Pope Pius II and Duke Galeazzo Maria Sforza into Florence.

1464 Cosimo il Vecchio dies. His son Piero takes behind-the-scenes control of Florence.

1465 Cosimo il Vecchio, like the heroes of classical Rome, honored by the Florentine government with the posthumous title "father of his county" (*pater patriae*).

1466 The Pitti-Neroni Conspiracy against the Medici fails.

1469 Piero de' Medici dies, and his son Lorenzo il Magnifico assumes control of Florence.

1469 Ficino's Platonic *On Love*

1474 Marriage between Ginevra de' Benci and Luigi Niccolini.

Architecture and Sculpture

1453 Mino da Fiesole's marble bust of Piero de' Medici, one of the first such busts in Florentine art.

1455–60 Donatello's bronze *David* and *Judith and Holofernes* for the courtyard and garden of the new Medici Palace.

c. 1455–70 Alberti's Rucellai Palace for Giovanni Rucellai. First use of classical orders on a Florentine palace façade.

c. 1457–78 Alberti's façade for S. Maria Novella commissioned by Giovanni Rucellai.

1458–66 Pitti Palace commissioned by Luca Pitti. Construction abandoned when Pitti involved in an anti-Medicean conspiracy.

1460–66 Donatello's bronze pulpits for S. Lorenzo imitating early Christian ambos.

1460–68 Alfonso Alvaro of Silves oversees the building and decoration of the Cardinal of Portugal's Chapel in S. Miniato, including Antonio and Bernardo Rossellino's *Tomb of the Cardinal of Portugal*.

1465–67 Verrocchio's *Tomb of Cosimo il Vecchio* in the crossing of S. Lorenzo.

1467 Brunelleschi's cathedral lantern completed.

1467–83 Verrocchio's bronze *Doubting Thomas* on Or San Michele for the merchants' tribunal replaces Donatello's *Louis of Toulouse* for the Guelph party.

1468 Antonio Rossellino's marble bust of Matteo Palmieri.

1469–72 Verrocchio's *Tomb of Piero and Giovanni de' Medici* for the Old Sacristy of S. Lorenzo.

c. 1475 Verrocchio's marble bust, *Woman with Flowers*.

Painting

1455 Castagno's *Trinity with St. Jerome Altarpiece* for SS. Annunziata commissioned by Girolamo Corboli.

1457–59 Gozzoli's *Journey of the Magi* frescoes for the chapel in the Medici Palace, which make an important contribution to Florentine landscape painting.

c. 1459 Filippo Lippi's *Nativity Altarpiece* for the Medici Chapel.

c. 1460 Scheggia's Copenhagen wedding chest, *Reconciliation between the Romans and Sabines*.

1460s Filippo Lippi's Uffizi devotional *Virgin and Child with Two Angels*.

1461–68 Baldovinetti's *Annunciation* for the Cardinal of Portugal's Chapel.

1466–68 Antonio and Piero Pollaiuolo's *SS. Vincent, James Major, and Eustace Altarpiece* for the Cardinal of Portugal's Chapel.

c. 1470–75 Botticelli's *Portrait of a Woman at a Window*.

1474–75 Antonio and Piero Pollaiuolo's *St. Sebastian Altarpiece* for SS. Annunziata commissioned by Antonio Pucci. Important for its classical motifs, figural action, and landscape.

c. 1475 Botticelli's *Portrait of a Man Holding a Medallion of Cosimo il Vecchio*.

1475–76 Leonardo's *Portrait of Ginevra de' Benci* commissioned by the Venetian ambassador to Florence, Bernardo Bembo.

Reigns of Popes

1455–58 Callistus III (Borgia)

1458–64 Pius II (Piccolomini)

1464–71 Paul II (Barbo)

1471–84 Sixtus IV (della Rovere)

Politics, Religion, and Culture

1477 *Book of the Stairway to Paradise*, 1st ed.

1478 Poliziano's *Poetry for the Joust [of 1475]*.

1478 Giuliano de' Medici killed at Mass in the Pazzi Conspiracy supported by Pope Sixtus IV. His brother, Lorenzo il Magnifico, is wounded but survives by escaping to the cathedral's north sacristy.

1480 Lorenzo il Magnifico travels to Naples to make peace with King Ferrante I and then to Rome to make peace with Pope Sixtus IV.

1482 Marriage between Lorenzo di Pierfrancesco de' Medici and Semiramide d'Appiano arranged by Lorenzo il Magnifico.

1483 Marriage between Gianozzo Pucci and Lucrezia Bini mediated by Lorenzo il Magnifico.

1484 Peace of Bagnolo ending the conflict between Florence (allied with Ferrara, Milan, Naples, and Spain) and the papacy (allied with Venice).

1486 Pico della Miradola's *Oration on the Dignity of Man*.

1489–98 Dominican friar Savonarola preaches in S. Marco and the cathedral against the immoral behavior of Florentine citizens. Defying papal authority, he is excommunicated and forbidden to preach in 1497 and executed for heresy in 1498.

1492 Giovanni de' Medici, son of Lorenzo il Magnifico, created a cardinal.

1492 Lorenzo de' Medici dies. His son Piero briefly assumes leadership of Florence.

1493 Savonarola's *Tractato del sacramento dei misterii della messa (Treatise on the Eucharistic Sacrament)*.

1494 Charles VIII invades Italy, the Medici escape into exile, and the Second Republic is established with a new constitution modeled on that of Venice.

1494–1509 Pisan War.

Architecture and Sculpture

1475–81 Giuliano and Benedetto da Maiano's carved wooden ceilings and marble and intarsia doors for the Sala dei Gigli and the Udienza in the Priors' Palace.

c. 1488–97 Benedetto da Maiano's *Tomb of Filippo Strozzi* in the Strozzi Chapel of S. Maria Novella.

1489–1536 Giuliano da Sangallo, Giuliano da Maiano, and Cronaca's Strozzi Palace, one of the largest and most refined buildings of its period.

c. 1491 Michelangelo's marble *Madonna of the Steps*.

1495–96 Antonio da Sangallo the Elder, Cronaca, and Baccio d'Agnolo's Sala Grande added to the Priors' Palace for the new Great Council modeled on the Sala del Maggiore Consiglio in the Doge's Palace in Venice.

Painting

c. 1480 Ghirlandaio's *Last Supper* for the guests' refectory in S. Marco.

c. 1480 Piero di Cosimo's *Cleopatra*.

c. 1480–81 Botticelli's *Madonna of the Magnificat*.

c. 1482 Botticelli's *Primavera* for the old Medici Palace.

1482–83 Botticelli's *Nastagio degli Onesti* commemorating the Pucci/Bini marriage.

1482–89 Ghirlandaio's fresco decoration for the Sala dei Gigli in the Priors' Palace.

1483–85 Ghirlandaio's frescoes of the life of St. Francis for the Sassetti Chapel in S. Trinita commissioned by Francesco Sassetti.

1485 Ghirlandaio's *Nativity Altarpiece* for the Sassetti Chapel.

1486–1503 Filippino Lippi frescoes of the lives of SS. John and Philip for the Strozzi Chapel in S. Maria Novella commissioned by Filippo Strozzi.

Reigns of Popes

1484–92 Innocent VIII (Cybo)

1492–1503 Alexander VI (Borgia)

Politics, Religion, and Culture

1502 Piero Soderini elected standard-bearer of justice for life of the Second Florentine Republic.

1504 *Parlamento* of twenty-eight artists and citizens called to decide the location of Michelangelo's *David.*

1505 Battle of Torre di S. Vincenzo, part of the Pisan War.

1512 Medici return to power in Florence.

1513 Machiavelli's *The Prince.*

1513 Giovanni de' Medici, son of Lorenzo il Magnifico, elected Pope Leo X.

1513 Marriage between Giuliano de' Medici and Philiberte of Savoy.

1513–15 Giuliano de' Medici appointed first captain and then captain general of the Church by Leo X.

1515 Giuliano de' Medici designated duke of Nemours by King Francis I of France.

1515 Lorenzo the Younger de' Medici appointed captain general of Florence by Leo X.

1516 Lorenzo the Younger de' Medici designated duke of Urbino by Leo X.

1516 Giuliano de' Medici dies.

1517 Martin Luther nails his ninety-five theses on the door of the church at Wittenberg. He is excommunicated in 1521.

1518 Marriage between Lorenzo de' Medici the Younger and Madeleine de la Tour Auvergne.

1519 Lorenzo de' Medici the Younger dies.

1519 Cardinal Giulio de' Medici, illegitimate son of Giuliano de' Medici, becomes archbishop of Florence.

1521 Pope Leo X dies.

1523 Cardinal Giulio de' Medici elected Pope Clement VII.

Architecture and Sculpture

1501–4 Michelangelo's marble *David* placed on the rostrum of the Priors' Palace.

1516–1614 Antonio da Sangallo the Elder and Baccio d'Agnolo's Servite Loggia on the Piazza SS. Annunziata completes the square as a Roman-style forum.

c. 1517–19 Bandinelli's marble *Orpheus with Cerberus* commissioned by Pope Leo X and Cardinal Giulio de' Medici for the center of the courtyard of the Medici Palace, where Donatello's bronze *David* once stood.

1519–34 Michelangelo's New Sacristy in S. Lorenzo commissioned by Pope Leo X, a commission renewed by Pope Clement VII. Michelangelo abandons the project when he is called to Rome by Pope Paul III. Marble sculpture includes *Night, Day, Dawn, Dusk, Baton Carrier, Thinker,* and *Virgin and Child.*

1524–71 Michelangelo's Laurentian Library commissioned by Pope Clement VII.

Painting

c. 1500 Leonardo's lost *St. Anne Cartoon* for SS. Annunziata initiates the High Renaissance style in Florentine art.

1503–6 Leonardo's unfinished *Battle of Anghiari* for the Sala Grande in the Priors' Palace.

1504–5 Michelangelo's unfinished *Battle of Cascina* for the Sala Grande in the Priors' Palace.

c. 1504–6 Michelangelo's *Doni Tondo.*

c. 1504–19 Leonardo's *Mona Lisa.*

c. 1506 Raphael's *Portrait of Agnolo Doni* and *Portrait of Maddalena Strozzi Doni.*

1510–12 Fra Bartolomeo's unfinished *St. Anne Altarpiece* for the Sala Grande in the Priors' Palace.

c. 1514 Raphael's *Madonna della Sedia.*

1517 Sarto's *Madonna of the Harpies* commissioned by the abbess of S. Francesco for the high altar.

c. 1517 Sarto's *Portrait of a Man with a Book.*

c. 1517 Rosso's *Portrait of a Young Man.*

1523–24 Rosso's *Moses Defending the Daughters of Jethro,* a first-generation Mannerist painting, commissioned by brothel keeper Giovanni Bandini.

Reigns of Popes

1503 Pius III (Todeschini Piccolomini)

1503–13 Julius II (della Rovere)

1513–21 Leo X (de' Medici)

1522–23 Adrian VI (Florensz)

1523–34 Clement VII (de' Medici)

Politics, Religion, and Culture

1527 The Medici once again expelled from Florence, and the Third (and last) Florentine Republic established.

1527 Rome is brutally sacked by imperial troops, and Pope Clement VII flees to the Castel Sant'Angelo.

1529–30 Florence besieged by imperial troops and ultimately capitulates, bringing an end to the Third Republic.

1530 Ludovico Martelli killed in a duel with Giovanni Bandini.

1530 Charles V crowned emperor by Pope Clement VII in Bologna.

1532 Alessandro de' Medici becomes the first duke of Florence.

1533 Marriage between Duke Alessandro and Margaret of Austria.

1537 Duke Alessandro assassinated, leaving no heirs.

1537 Cosimo I becomes the second duke of Florence.

1537 Battle of Montemurlo and the defeat of the Florentine exiles.

1539 Marriage between Duke Cosimo I and Eleonora da Toledo, daughter of the viceroy of Naples.

1541 Francesco I, Duke Cosimo I's heir is born.

1541 The Florentine Academy established by Duke Cosimo I to promote Tuscan literature and language.

1543 Duke Cosimo I gains control of the Fortezza da Basso in Florence and the fortresses of Pisa and Livorno by paying a tribute of 150,000 florins to Emperor Charles V.

1545–63 The Council of Trent meets in three sessions—1545–47, 1551–52, and 1562–63—to reform the Church in response to the Protestant Reformation.

Architecture and Sculpture

1534 Bandinelli's *Hercules and Cacus,* commissioned by Pope Clement VII and Duke Alessandro de' Medici, installed on the rostrum of the Priors' Palace next to Michelangelo's *David.*

1540 Duke Cosimo I establishes the Priors' Palace as his new ducal residence.

1540–55 Tasso remodels and expands the Palazzo Vecchio.

1542–60 Bandinelli builds the dais in the Sala Grande in the Palazzo Vecchio commissioned by Duke Cosimo I.

1545–54 Cellini's bronze *Perseus,* commissioned by Duke Cosimo I, for the Loggia dei Lanzi in the Piazza della Signoria.

1547–51 Tasso's Mercato Nuovo commissioned by Duke Cosimo I for the gold and silk merchants.

Painting

1525–28 Pontormo's *Deposition* commissioned by Ludovico Capponi for his burial chapel in S. Felicità.

c. 1526–28 Sarto's *Woman with Petrarch's Poems.*

c. 1539 Bronzino's *Portrait of Duke Cosimo I as Orpheus.*

c. 1540 Bronzino's *Portrait of Ugolino Martelli.*

1540–46 Bronzino's second-generation Mannerist Chapel of Eleonora in the Palazzo Vecchio.

1543–45 Salviati's frescoes with scenes of the life of Furius Camillus in the Sala di Udienza in the Palazzo Vecchio commissioned by Duke Cosimo I.

c. 1543 Bronzino's *Portrait of Duke Cosimo I in Armor.*

c. 1545 Bronzino's *Portrait of Eleonora of Toledo with Her Son Giovanni.*

Reigns of Popes

1534–49 Paul III (Farnese)

1550–1575

Politics, Religion, and Culture

1550 First edition of Vasari's *Lives of the Artists.*

1554–55 Sienese War. By the conquest of Siena, Cosimo I nearly doubles Florence's Tuscan empire.

1554 Battle of Scannagallo, part of the Sienese War.

1559 Treaty of Cateau-Cambrésis, establishing peace between the Valois and Habsburgs, brings greater stability to the Italian peninsula.

1561 Duke Cosimo I founds the maritime crusading Order of St. Stephen headquartered in Pisa.

1561 Guicciardini's *History of Italy.*

1563 Council of Trent closed.

1563 Ferdinand I de' Medici created cardinal at age fourteen.

1563 Academy of Design founded.

1564 The canons and decrees of the Council of Trent published, addressing Church abuses, standardizing and clarifying Church doctrines, reforming the religious orders, and renewing the Church's missionary objectives.

1564 Michelangelo dies in Rome. An elaborate funeral is staged in S. Lorenzo in Florence by the Academy of Design.

1565 Marriage between Duke Francesco I and Giovanna d' Austria, for which elaborate spectacles are staged.

1568 Second enlarged and revised edition of Vasari's *Lives of the Artist.*

1569–70 Cosimo I named grand duke of Tuscany and crowned in Rome in 1570 by Pope Pius V.

1574 Cosimo I dies and is succeeded by his son Francesco I as grand duke of Tuscany.

Architecture and Sculpture

1550 With the dowry of his wife, Eleonora da Toledo, Duke Cosimo I acquires the unfinished Pitti Palace and its surrounding grounds for a ducal residence.

1550 Tribolo designs the Boboli Gardens behind the Pitti Palace.

1555–74 Vasari completes the remodeling and expansion of the Palazzo Vecchio.

1559–63 Vasari oversees raising the roof of the Sala Grande in the Palazzo Vecchio, installing clerestory windows, and reinstalling the much-modified coffered wooden ceiling.

1560–75 Ammannati's *Neptune Fountain* in the Piazza della Signoria.

1560–80 Vasari's Uffizi and the Piazzale degli Uffizi for the administrative offices of the Florentine duchy.

1561–72 Vasari's new double-ramped stairway for the Sala Grande in the Palazzo Vecchio.

1561–77 Ammannati's two new wings for the Pitti Palace embracing the Boboli Gardens.

1564–66 Danti's marble *Rigor* and *Equity* for the Uffizi watergate.

1565 Vasari's corridor linking the Palazzo Vecchio and the Palazzo Pitti.

1565–77 Vasari oversees the renovation and redecoration of S. Croce and S. Maria Novella.

1572–73 Danti's marble *Cosimo I as Augustus* for the Uffizi watergate.

Painting

1563–65 Vasari and workshop's panels for the ceiling of the Sala Grande in the Palazzo Vecchio completed in time for the marriage of Francesco I and Giovanna d'Austria.

1566–71 Vasari and workshop's frescoes on the walls of the Sala Grande with scenes of the Pisan and Sienese wars.

1567–75 Vasari and his workshop complete twenty of the twenty-nine altarpieces for S. Maria Novella and S. Croce. Two mid-sixteenth-century altarpieces by Salviati and Bronzino in S. Croce are incorporated into the new iconographical program.

1572 Vasari's third-generation Mannerist *Doubting Thomas* for S. Croce commissioned by Tommaso and Francesco Guidacci.

Reigns of Popes

1550–55 Julius III (Ciocchi del Monte)

1555 Marcellus II (Cervini)

1555–59 Paul IV (Carafa)

1559–65 Pius IV (de' Medici)

1566–72 St. Pius V (Ghislieri)

1572–85 Gregory XIII (Buoncompagni)

Politics, Religion, and Culture	Architecture and Sculpture	Painting	Reigns of Popes
1587 Duke Francesco I dies and is succeeded by his brother Ferdinand as grand duke of Tuscany after he renounces the cardinalate. **1589** Marriage between Duke Ferdinand and Christine of Lorraine.	**1579–82** Giambologna's marble *Rape of the Sabines.* Purchased in 1582 by Duke Francesco I and installed in the Loggia dei Lanzi in the Piazza della Signoria. **1581–85** Giambologna's marble *Cosimo I in Armor* for the Uffizi watergate. **1594** Giambologna's *Equestrian Monument of Cosimo I* for the Piazza della Signoria, commissioned by Duke Ferdinand.	**1575–1613** Vasari's followers complete the remaining seven altarpieces for S. Maria Novella and S. Croce.	**1585–90** Sixtus V (Peretti) **1590** Urban VII (Castagna) **1590–91** Gregory XIV (Sfondrati) **1591** Innocent IX (Facchinetti) **1592–1605** Clement VIII (Aldobrandini)

GLOSSARY

a secco Lit. dry; a technique of painting on plaster that has already dried; cf. fresco.

abacus The flat slab on top of a capital.

adventus A triumphal entry.

aedicule An opening or niche framed by two columns or piers, often supporting an entablature and pediment.

aerial perspective The blurring of distant forms as if seen through an atmospheric haze.

aisle The lower part of a church flanking the nave and often the transepts and choir.

alter christus Another Christ.

ambo A raised pulpit for reading the Epistles and Gospels.

ambulatory In church architecture, a vaulted passageway or aisle around the apse with the high altar.

amor dei Love of God, an aspect of Charity.

amor proximi Love of neighbor, an aspect of Charity.

amphitheater An elliptical or circular structure with rising tiers of seats.

Annunciation According to Christian doctrine, the angel Gabriel's announcement to the Virgin of Christ's conception.

antipope A person elected or claiming to be pope in opposition to the pope already lawfully chosen.

apse A vaulted semicircular or polygonal termination of a chancel or chapel.

arcade An arched passageway or walkway.

arch A curved structural member spanning an opening or serving as a support.

architrave The lowest division of an entablature, resting on the capital of a column.

arcuation A structural support system based on the principle of the arch; cf. trabeation.

articulated Defined by architectural features.

ashlar Dressed stone.

attic The low story above the principal entablature, as on a triumphal arch.

baldachin or **baldacchino** An honorific canopy, usually over a sovereign or an altar.

balustrade A row of short supports topped by a rail.

banderole A scroll bearing an inscription or device.

baptistery Part of a church or a separate building used for baptism.

barrel vault A continuous vault, semicircular in section, unbroken in its length by cross-vaults.

basamento The lower portion of a wall, sometimes decorated.

basilica In ancient Roman architecture, an oblong aisled building terminating in an apse used for public assembly and as a law court. In Renaissance architecture, a church with nave, side aisles, crossing, transepts, and apse; also a Catholic church with special ceremonial privileges.

bastion A projecting part of a fortification.

battlement A defensive parapet with open spaces surmounting a wall.

bay In architecture, the main division or compartment of the exterior or interior of a building marked by fenestration, vaulting, the use of an order, etc.

bead-and-reel An ornamental molding formed by beads alternating with disks, placed edge-on in a row.

bella maniera The beautiful manner or style; second-generation Mannerism.

belvedere An open loggia on top of a tower for commanding a view.

biforal window A window with two openings.

blind arcade A row of shallow arches running along a wall.

braccio (pl. ***braccia***) Lit. an arm's length; a unit of measure approximately equal to 23 inches (58.37 cm).

breviary A liturgical book containing psalms, hymns, lessons, and prayers.

broncone Laurel branch; the device of Lorenzo de' Medici (il Magnifico).

buttress A projecting structure for supporting a wall or building.

caduceus A staff with two entwined snakes and two wings at the top, an attribute of Mercury.

camicia An undergarment, usually of white linen.

campanile A bell tower.

canon A clergyman staffing a cathedral or collegiate church.

canonry An endowment that financially supports a canon.

capital The uppermost part of a column or pilaster.

cardinal The highest-ranking Roman Catholic ecclesiastical official after the pope, who is appointed by the pope to serve as an advisor within the College of Cardinals.

Cardinal Virtues Justice, Fortitude, Prudence, and Temperance; known as the virtues of rule from Plato's *Republic.*

cardo In a Roman town, the central north-south street.

cartoon A drawing used to transfer a design to a panel, canvas, wall, or tapestry.

caryatid A sculpted female figure supporting an entablature.

cassone A large wedding chest, often containing part of the dowry.

cathedral A church that is the seat of a bishop.

chancel The part of a church containing the high altar and seats for the clergy, often used interchangeably with choir.

chase In bronze casting, to smooth, polish, or ornament the surface of the metal.

cherub (pl. **cherubim** or **cherubs**) A winged infant angel, usually colored blue, symbolic of divine wisdom.

chiaroscuro The use of light and shadow to model form in paintings, prints, and drawings.

choir The part of a church where divine service is sung, usually containing the high altar; cf. chancel.

Christus medicus The healing Christ.

Church Militant The earthly Church.

Church Triumphant The heavenly Church.

clerestory The upper walls of a church's nave, pierced by windows above the roofs of the aisles.

coffer A decorative recessed panel in a ceiling or vault.

colonnade A series of columns set at regular intervals, supporting a wall or roof.

colonnette A small column.

column A round supporting pillar consisting of a base, shaft, and capital.

confraternity A lay society dedicated to religious and charitable activities.

consecration In liturgy, the moment in the Mass when the priest transforms the bread and wine into the body and blood of Christ. See Transubstantiation.

console An architectural member with a compound curved outline projecting from a wall to form a bracket or support.

contrapposto Lit. to set in opposition. A posture in which weight is carried on one leg and the other is relaxed, and the body is counterbalanced on either side of the rotated spinal axis.

Conventuals Franciscan friars who accumulated common property and followed a mitigated Rule of St. Francis. See Observants.

corbel An architectural member that projects from a wall to support a weight.

cornice The upper part of an entablature, or a projecting horizontal member that crowns a structure.

corporal A linen cloth on which the bread and wine are consecrated during the Mass.

crenellation In architecture, a defensive parapet with alternating indentations (embrasures) and raised portions (merlons).

crossing In a church, the space at the intersection of the nave, chancel, and transepts, often domed.

crown of a vault The highest point from the floor.

Crucifixion Christ's sacrifice on the cross (Matthew 27:33–56; Mark 15:22–41; Luke 23:33–49; John 19:18–27).

cruciform Cross-shaped.

cuirass An ancient Roman breastplate.

cupola A dome.

dais A raised platform denoting the high status of a seated individual or individuals.

***dal sotto in su* perspective** Perspective constructed to be seen from below looking obliquely upward.

dentil or **denticulation** An ornamental motif consisting of small blocks resembling teeth.

desco da parto A decorated wooden tray given to a woman who has just given birth.

device A personal emblem, often with a motto.

disegno Drawing and design; defining form by outline.

distance point In perspective, a point level with the horizon line whose position determines the illusion's depth.

distemper Pigment bound in animal size; cf. tempera.

dome A vault of even curvature erected on a circular or polygonal base or drum.

drum A circular or polygonal wall supporting a dome.

ducat A unit of currency.

Ecclesia The Church.

effigy An image or representation of a person.

egg-and-dart An ornamental molding based on alternating ovals and pointed arrows.

ekphrases A rhetorical literary form consisting of an ornate verbal description of a visual, often imaginary, work of art.

elevation In architecture, the vertical plane of an interior or exterior wall; (cap.) in liturgy, the moment in the Mass when the priest raises the Eucharist heavenward in thanksgiving.

enfilade Doors aligned to produce a view through a series of rooms.

engaged column A column attached to a wall.

entablature The upper horizontal beam of an order, consisting of architrave, frieze, and cornice.

entasis The slight convexity of a column.

epiphany A divine appearance or revelation; (cap.) the Feast of the Magi (Jan. 6) commemorating Christ's first appearance to the Gentiles.

Eucharist The Mass; the bread and wine transubstantiated into the body and blood of Christ.

Evangelists SS. Matthew, Mark, Luke, and John.

exedra A semicircular recess.

façade The exterior wall of a building.

fasces Bundled rods often with an ax, an ancient Roman emblem of peace and judicial authority.

fenestra caeli The window of heaven; epithet of the Virgin.

festina lente Make haste slowly, a motto for some devices.

figura serpentinata A serpentine figure.

florin A unit of currency that originated in medieval Florence.

flying buttress An arch or half-arch transmitting thrust to an outer support.

focal point In perspective, the point to which the orthogonals converge.

foreshortening The proportional contraction of a form to create the illusion of projection or recession in space.

fresco A technique of painting on freshly spread moist lime plaster; cf. *a secco*.

friar A member of a mendicant order.

frieze The plain or ornamented band on an entablature, between the architrave and cornice.

gamurra Indoor dress.

gesso A plasterlike paste used to create a smooth ground on panel and canvas, and to create relief on paintings and frescoes.

Ghibelline Supporter of German imperial authority in Italy.

giornea An outdoor dress.

Golden Legend An immensely popular collection of stories and legends compiled in about 1260 from a wide variety of sources, recounting the lives of the saints, Christ, and the Virgin arranged according to the liturgical calendar by Jacopo da Voragine (c. 1230–98), Dominican friar and archbishop of Genoa from 1292. The *Golden Legend* was the source for much Renaissance narrative art.

Golgotha Lit. place of the skull; Calvary outside of Jerusalem where Christ was crucified.

Gothic sway In figural sculpture or painting, an S-shaped posture.

grisaille Lit. grayish; painting in tones of a single color, especially gray, to produce three-dimensional effects.

groin vault A vault produced by the intersection at right angles of two barrel vaults.

guarnello A cotton duster.

Guelph Supporter of papal authority in Italy.

harmonic ratios Ratios of whole numbers that produce musical harmonies; e.g., 1:2 = a musical octave, 3:4 = a fourth, and 2:3 = a fifth.

herm A pillar terminating in a bust.

horizon line In perspective, the horizontal line intersecting the focal point.

hortus conclusus Lit. enclosed garden; in art, often a symbol of the Virgin Mary's virginity and fertility (from Song of Songs 4:12; Ezekiel 44:2–3); cf. *porta clausa*.

Host The consecrated bread or wafer that, along with the wine, is the focus of the Eucharistic rite.

iconography The study of the signs and symbols in art.

imitatio Christi Imitation of Christ's self-sacrifice.

Immaculate Conception According to Catholic doctrine, the Virgin Mary's conception free from original sin in the womb of her mother, St. Anne.

in situ In its original position.

Incarnation According to Christian dogma, the union of the divine Word and human flesh in Jesus Christ.

intarsia Inlaid wood; marquetry.

intercolumniation The distance, measured in column diameters, between adjacent columns.

intrado The interior curve of an arch.

istoria Lit. history; a narrative or historical scene in art.

jamb The vertical face of an archway, doorway, or window.

keystone The central, wedge-shaped stone at the crown of an arch or a rib vault, often symbolic of Christ.

lantern A small windowed turret crowning a roof or dome.

lapis lazuli A blue semiprecious stone sometimes ground to make a blue pigment.

Last Judgment According to Christian theology, humanity's judgment by God at the end of the world.

Latin Doctors SS. Ambrose, Augustine, Gregory the Great, and Jerome.

leonine personality Having a lionlike character, depicted in classical and Renaissance images by a knit brow, piercing gaze, and curly flamelike hair.

lintel A horizontal beam bridging the top of a door or window.

lira da braccio An early violin.

loggia A room or structure open on one or more sides, usually supported on piers or columns

lunette A semicircular opening or surface.

Maenad Drunken follower of Bacchus, Roman god of wine.

Magnifico (pl. ***magnifici***) Magnificent, a title of respect.

mandorla An almond-shaped halo.

mappa In imperial Rome, a cloth held in the hand signifying consular or imperial rank.

marzocco Heraldic lion of Florence.

Mass Liturgical celebration of the Eucharist.

mazzocchio Turban over a wire frame.

medico (pl. ***medici***) Doctor.

medicus A doctor or healer.

melon dome A ribbed dome, circular in plan.

mendicant order A religious order, such as the Franciscans or Dominicans, combining monastic life and outside religious activity; originally a begging order.

metope The square block between two triglyphs in the frieze of the Doric order, often decorated in relief.

mezzanine In architecture, a low story between two higher ones or under the roof.

module A unit of measurement regulating a building's proportions.

monk A male member of a religious order who lives in a monastery; cf. friar.

mosaic A picture or decoration formed of small colored pieces of material.

Nativity The birth of Jesus Christ.

nave The main central body of a longitudinally planned church.

navicella A boat or ship symbolic of the Church.

Nereid A sea nymph.

niche A recess, often concave and arched, in a wall or pier, usually containing a statue or other decoration.

nodus mundi Lit. knot of the universe; ancient philosophers' sign of the union of heaven and earth.

nun A female member of a religious order who lives in a convent.

Observants Reformed Franciscan friars who observed exactly the primitive Rule of St. Francis; cf. Conventuals.

oculus A circular opening in a wall or dome.

one-point perspective A method of representing three-dimensional space on a flat surface.

Opera del Duomo Cathedral works.

***orant* posture** An early Christian posture of prayer with raised arms and hands.

order A column, pier, or pilaster supporting an entablature, the whole ensemble decorated and proportioned according to one of the accepted classical modes, including the Tuscan, Doric, Ionic, Corinthian, and Composite orders; a monastic or mendicant society or fraternity.

orthogonal In linear perspective, diagonal lines converging at the focal point.

palle (sing. ***palla***) Balls; device on the coat of arms of the Medici family.

papal supremacy The pope's supreme spiritual authority over the entire Church hierarchy.

paragone Comparison of the arts, often between painting and sculpture.

parapet A low wall placed to protect a place where there is a sudden drop.

parlamento (pl. ***parlamenti***) In Florence, a citizens' referendum or consultation.

partlet A shoulder veil.

Passion According to Christian doctrine, the suffering of Christ between the Last Supper and his death.

pater patriae Father of his country.

patera Libation dish.

pedestal A base supporting a column, statue, or other superstructure.

pediment A triangular architectural member that forms the gable of a low-pitched roof, or a similar structure above a window or door.

pendentive A concave triangular architectural member supporting the base of a circular dome over a square space.

Petrine Succession The unbroken descent of Christ's spiritual authority through Peter to each successive pope.

piano nobile The main floor, usually over the ground floor.

piazza A public square or open space surrounded by buildings.

pier A pillar, usually rectangular in cross section, as distinguished from a column.

pietra forte A type of *pietra serena* prized for its lack of inclusions.

pietra serena A fine-grained gray Tuscan sandstone.

pilaster A shallow pier or flattened column projecting only slightly from a wall.

plinth The projecting base of a wall or column pedestal.

Podestà In an Italian commune, a foreign executive official with broad administrative powers.

poesia (pl. ***poesie***) Lit. poetry; imaginative invention or a poetic mythological painting.

polychromy Decoration with multiple colors, usually sculpture or glazed ceramics.

polyptych A multiple-paneled altarpiece.

pope The head of the Roman Catholic Church and bishop of Rome, elected from and by the College of Cardinals.

porphyry Rare stone composed of feldspar crystals embedded in a compact dark red or purple groundmass.

porta clausa Closed door; often a reference to the Virgin's virginity from Ezekiel 44:1–2.

portico A roofed or vaulted walkway at the entrance of a building or around a courtyard or square, often colonnaded.

predella The base of an altarpiece with narrative scenes related to the main panel(s) above.

prior A high official elected for a two-month term. Eight priors and the standard-bearer of justice constituted the *Signoria,* the executive branch of the Florentine government.

proscenium The stage on which the action takes place in a theater.

putto (pl. ***putti***) An infant boy.

quadriga A four-horse chariot.

quadrivium Four of the seven Liberal Arts: music, arithmetic, geometry, and astronomy; cf. *trivium.*

quatrefoil An ornamental form with four lobes superimposed over a diamond shape.

quoin Solid block of stone articulating and protecting a building's corner.

Real Presence According to Christian doctrine, the Eucharistic bread and wine transformed into the actual sacrificial body and blood of Christ.

refectory A dining hall.

relief A mode of sculpture in which forms are raised from a flat surface.

reliquary A container for relics.

rib vault A framework of diagonal arched ribs carrying the cells covering the spaces between.

rinascita Rebirth.

rinceaux An ornamental scroll of foliage.

rood screen A screen set across a church's nave, closing off the chancel or choir.

rosette A rose-shaped architectural ornament.

rostrum A raised platform for public speaking.

roundel A round panel, window or niche; cf. oculus, *tondo.*

rustication Masonry cut in massive blocks with beveled edges, often left in a rough state.

sacra conversazione An altarpiece depicting holy figures of various historical periods gathered together in a heavenly court and engaged in "sacred conversation," as opposed to one that represents a single biblical drama, such as a Crucifixion.

sacristy A room in a church, usually adjacent to the choir, used for storing sacred vessels and vestments, sometimes also used as a chapel and or chapter room.

sail vault A dome over a square space such that the diagonal of the square is the diameter of the dome.

salone A large hall.

Salvator mundi Savior of the world.

scudo A unit of currency.

sepulcher (or **sepulchre**) A burial place.

seraph (pl. **seraphim** or **seraphs**) The highest order of winged angels, colored red, symbolic of divine love.

Serlian motif An archway or window with three openings, the central one arched and wider than the flanking side openings, which are lower in height and rectangular in shape; used in Roman antiquity as the frame for imperial appearances. Named after Sebastiano Serlio, who first illustrated the motif in his 1537 *Regole generale;* also called a Palladian motif, after Andrea Palladio, who used the motif frequently in his designs.

sfumato Lit. smoky; a technique in painting in which black is added to hues, tones are subtly graduated, and contours blurred to create a soft, hazy appearance; developed by Leonardo da Vinci and widely imitated by successive artists.

sgraffito A monochrome fresco technique in which a design is etched into fresh plaster.

sibyl A female seer of classical antiquity, equivalent to Old Testament prophets, who were believed to have prophesied the coming of Christ.

signori (sing. ***signore***) Lords.

Signoria In Florence, the executive branch of government consisting of the eight priors and the standard-bearer of justice.

sill The lower horizontal part of a window frame.

sol invictus Invincible sun.

sol iustitiae Sun of justice.

spalliera A painting installed in the back panel of a bed frame or bench, or hung above wainscoting at the height of one's shoulder (*spalla*).

spandrel The space between the exterior curve of an arch or vault and an enclosing right angle.

spedalingo Director of a hospital (*spedale*).

spire A tall, pointed structure rising from a tower or roof.

standard-bearer of justice Chief executive official of the Florentine government.

Stella maris Star of the sea, an epithet of the Virgin.

stigmata The five wounds of Christ.

stipple To ornament artworks by means of engraved or painted dots or short strokes.

stringcourse A continuous horizontal molding set in a wall.

studiolo (pl. ***studioli***)A study.

sumptuary laws Laws enacted in most Italian cites to regulate extravagant expenditure and behavior.

swag A festoon or garland.

tableau vivant Lit. a living picture.

tempera A technique of painting using pigment mixed with egg yolk.

temple-front motif Triangular pediment carried on a row of columns, piers, or pilasters.

tessellated Tiled.

Theological Virtues Faith, Hope, and Charity.

titular church A Roman church assigned to each cardinal for his financial maintenance and spiritual charge.

tondo (pl. ***tondi***) A round painting or relief.

trabeation Construction using a post and beam principle; cf. arcuation.

tracery Open interlocked ornamental stonework in Gothic windows.

transept The shorter transverse arms of a cross-shaped church.

Transubstantiation The mystical transformation of the bread and wine into the body and blood of Christ performed by a priest at the consecration of the Mass.

transversals In one-point perspective, the lines parallel to the horizon line.

tribune A church's apse or a dais.

triglyph A stone block with two vertical grooves at the center and half-grooves at the edges, placed between the metopes in a Doric frieze.

Trinity According to Christian doctrine, the unity of the Father, Son, and Holy Spirit as three persons in one Godhead.

triptych A three-paneled altarpiece.

Triton A sea-god, half man and half fish.

triumphal arch A freestanding commemorative monumental gateway.

trivium Three of the seven Liberal Arts: grammar, rhetoric and dialectic; cf. *quadrivium.* In urbanism, three streets branching from a single point; a trident.

umbrella vault A circular dome divided into curved webs.

usury Loaning money with interest, considered a sin by the Renaissance Church.

ut pictura poesis Lit. as is painting so too is poetry (from Horace, *Ars poetica* 361).

vir virtutis Man of virtue.

virgo super petram Epithet of the Virgin "seated on a stone" symbolizing her embodiment of the earthly Church.

volute A spiral scroll on an Ionic, Corinthian or Composite column's capital; a spiral scroll often used on the façades of Renaissance churches to mark the transition from the nave to the aisles.

voussoir The wedge-shaped stone of an arch.

wainscoting Paneled wooden lining on a wall.

ARTISTS' BIOGRAPHIES

N.B.: Figure numbers refer *either* to works of art *or* to their locations, depending on whether the work or only the site is discussed in the text. For the location of works, the following abbreviations are used: BARGELLO (Museo Nazionale del Bargello, Florence), LONDON (National Gallery), LOUVRE (Musée du Louvre, Paris), PITTI (Galleria Palatina, Palazzo Pitti, Florence), UFFIZI (Galleria degli Uffizi, Florence), VATICAN (Pinacoteca), and WASHINGTON (National Gallery of Art, Washington, DC).

ALBERTI, LEON BATTISTA (1404–72). Educated as a humanist and canon lawyer in Padua and Bologna, Alberti worked mostly in Rome as a papal secretary (1432–64) but also accompanied the papal court to Florence, Bologna, and Ferrara (1434–43), and later to Mantua (1459). His influential treatises *On Painting* (1435), *On Sculpture* (1440s), and *On the Art of Building in Ten Books* (1452)—the latter based on Vitruvius, but far more systematic and coherent—profoundly influenced Renaissance art. His codification of Brunelleschi's linear perspective and his concept of *istoria,* derived from classical rhetoric, provided the theory for a new approach to narrative realism, drama, and decorum in painting and sculpture. His clarification of the vocabulary, syntax, and spatial composition of classical architecture helped to shape subsequent Renaissance urbanism and building. He designed the first Renaissance bronze portrait plaquette (1430s; fig. 2) and many influential buildings—in Rimini, the Tempio Malatestiano (1450) for Sigismondo Malatesta; in Florence, the Rucellai Palace (c. 1455–70; fig. 95), the façade of S. Maria Novella (c. 1457–78; fig. 43), and the Rucellai Chapel (S. Pancrazio, c. 1464–67) for Giovanni Rucellai; and in Mantua, S. Sebastiano (1460) and S. Andrea (1470) for Ludovico Gonzaga (1412–78). As friend and frequent guest of Federico da Montefeltro (1422–82), Alberti probably consulted on the design of the Ducal Palace in Urbino (c. 1450–80s).

AMMANNATI, BARTOLOMEO (1511–92). Trained by Baccio Bandinelli in Florence and Jacopo Sansovino in Venice and strongly influenced by Michelangelo, he worked for patrons in Pisa, Naples, Urbino, Venice, Padua, Vicenza, Rome, Florence, Lucca, Volterra, and Arezzo. He contributed to the sculpture on Jacopo Sansovino's Venetian Library (1540s) but is best known for the tomb of Marco Mantova Benavides (Eremitani, Padua, c. 1546), the Del Monte tombs (S. Pietro in Montorio, Rome, c. 1553), the design (with Jacopo Vignola [1507–73] and Giorgio Vasari) of the Villa Giulia (Rome, early 1550s), the Juno Fountain (south end, Sala Grande, Palazzo Vecchio, 1555–63; fig. 197), the Neptune Fountain (1560–65; figs. 181 and 182), the Palazzo Pitti courtyard (1561–67; fig. 170), and the Ponte S. Trinita (1567–70; fig. 12, L). In 1550 he married the poet Laura Battiferri (1523–89), whose portrait was painted by Bronzino. Deeply influenced late in life by the Jesuits and Counter-Reformation piety, he denounced—in letters to the Florentine Academy of Design (1582) and to Ferdinand I de' Medici (c. 1590)—the public display of nude sculptures as immoral.

ANDREA DEL CASTAGNO (c. 1421–57). His figures, influenced by Florentine sculpture, are strongly contoured and three-dimensional, while exhibiting a fine sense of color. He frescoed the now-lost images of condemned traitors hanging upside down on the Florentine Bargello (fig. 12, no. 5) shortly after the Battle of Anghiari (1440). In 1442 he frescoed the vault of the S. Tarasio Chapel in Venice, and in 1444 he designed a round stained-glass window for the drum of the Florentine cathedral (fig. 17). His principal Florentine works, all in fresco, include the *Last Supper* (1447–50; fig. 90), *Famous Men and Women* (Villa Carducci, Legnaia, 1449–51, now Uffizi), *Trinity with St. Jerome* (1455; fig. 70), and *Equestrian Monument to Niccolò da Tolentino* (cathedral, 1455–56).

ANDREA DEL SARTO (1486–1530). Trained by Piero di Cosimo and influenced by Raphael, Michelangelo, Leonardo, Fra Bartolomeo, and Andrea Sansovino (c. 1467–1529), he became the most prolific and important of the Florentine High Renaissance painters. His paintings—notable for their atmospheric and vibrant color, dramatic and monumental compositions, and warm and intimate figures—include the life of St. Filippo Benizi (forecourt, SS. Annunziata, 1509–10; figs. 12, no. 24; 142, no. 2), the life of John the Baptist (cloister, Scalzo, 1509–26), *Madonna del Sacco* (cloister, SS. Annunziata, 1515), *Madonna of the Harpies* (1517; fig. 158), *Man with a Book* (c. 1517; fig. 161), *Tribute to Caesar* (Salon, Villa Medici, Poggio a Caiano, 1519–21),

Woman with Petrarch's Poems (c. 1526–28; fig. 162), and the *Last Supper* (S. Salvi, 1526–27). In 1518 he went to France to serve as court painter for Francis I, king of France, but lonely for his wife, Lucrezia del Fede, whom he portrayed in many works, he returned the following year. His pupils included Pontormo, Rosso, Vasari, and Salviati. In the late Renaissance his works, including his brilliant drawings, inspired many artists to reform Mannerism through a revival of his High Renaissance style.

ANGELICO, FRA (Guido di Piero, c. 1400–1455). Trained as an illuminator, he entered the Dominican order in Fiesole (fig. 12, no. 1) about 1417–25. Although influenced by Masaccio's use of perspective, monumental figures, and dramatic narratives, his first major work, the Linaiuoli Tabernacle (1433–36, with a marble frame by Ghiberti), reveals his brilliant high-keyed palette of saturated color derived from earlier, especially Sienese, late Gothic painting, which he used to express a deeply felt spirituality characteristic of all his work. About 1437–38 he worked in Umbria (Cortona and Perugia), and between 1438 and 1445 he and his workshop decorated the newly renovated Dominican monastery of S. Marco (figs. 12, no. 23; 38) financed by Cosimo de' Medici il Vecchio, including the church's high altarpiece (fig. 68) and over fifty frescoes in the chapter room, dormitory cells (fig. 69), and corridors (where the *Annunciation* at the head of the dormitory stairs remains perhaps his most famous work). Between about 1446 and 1450, he decorated several rooms in the Vatican Palace, although only the chapel of Pope Nicholas V (r. 1447–55) survives, as well as part of the vault of the S. Brizio chapel in Orvieto (summer 1447). Between 1449 and 1452, he served as prior of S. Domenico in Fiesole, during which period he executed for the Medici the Bosco ai Frati altarpiece and the shutters for the silver votive cabinet in Michelozzo's new marble tabernacle enshrining the miraculous image of the Virgin in SS. Annunziata (figs. 12, no. 24; 142, no. 4). In the 1450s he returned to Rome, where he died and was buried in the Dominican church of S. Maria sopra Minerva.

BACCIO D'AGNOLO (Bartolomeo d'Agnolo di Donato Baglioni, 1462–1543). Trained as a woodworker, Baccio became a leading Florentine craftsman of wood-carved furnishings such as intarsia paneling, coffered ceilings, and picture frames. From 1496 to 1502 Baccio was the principal woodcarver for the furnishings of the Sala Grande (fig. 129), which included a coffered ceiling; a tribune for the *Signoria* with a columned and trabeated loggia and intarsia paneling; an elevated and paneled gallery around the walls with two rows of benches reached by steps and enclosed by banisters for the city's magistrates; a chapel opposite the tribune with an altar, two candelabra, a gilt frame for the altarpiece, stalls, a pulpit for preaching and oratory, and a balustraded enclosure; special inlaid benches surrounded by banisters in front of the chapel for the city's judges and the Ten of the Balìa (war council); and, finally, rows of benches within the hall for approximately fifteen hundred council members. From 1499 until his death, with only a few interruptions, Baccio was the head (*capomaestro*) of the palace works responsible for extensive furnishings throughout the Priors' Palace (fig. 13). He was also an important architect, designing many ecclesiastical and secular buildings, including collaboration with Antonio da Sangallo the Elder on the Servite Loggia (1516–20; fig. 143). Although most of his work followed Florentine traditions (e.g., the Palazzo Taddei-Ginori, c. 1513), his most ambitious building, the Palazzo Bartolini-Salimbeni (1520–23), introduced to Florence principles of planning and articulation characteristic of Roman Renaissance palaces, which he learned from his trip to Rome in about 1510–11. Finally, Baccio oversaw the completion of the Strozzi Palace (figs. 97 and 98) and designed the piazza in front.

BANDINELLI, BACCIO (1488–1560). Trained by his father, a Medicean goldsmith, he remained a lifelong Medici partisan, the success of his career thus fluctuating with the Medici fortunes. Medici favoritism and his irascible, megalomaniacal personality incurred the animosity of many Florentine sculptors, especially the volatile Benvenuto Cellini. Medicean works include *Orpheus with Cerberus* (c. 1517–19; fig. 144), *Hercules and Cacus* (1525–34; fig. 164), tombs of Leo X and Clement VII in S. Maria sopra Minerva in Rome (1536–42), the Sala Grande dais and niche sculptures (1542–60; figs. 197 and 198), sculpture for the Florentine cathedral's octagonal choir (1547–55), and the figure of Neptune for the *Neptune Fountain* (1559; fig. 181), the latter only roughed-out at his death. His social-climbing ambitions were crowned with success when Clement VII and Charles V created him, respectively, a Knight of St. Peter and a Knight of the Order of Santiago.

BARTOLOMEO, FRA (Baccio della Porta, 1472–1517). A major painter and draftsman of the Florentine High Renaissance, Fra Bartolomeo was the first to understand and develop Leonardo's *sfumato* technique and his dynamic and harmonious compositions in a distinguished series of altarpieces and devotional works. He was trained in the 1480s and early 1490s in the workshop of Cosimo Rosselli (1439–1507) primarily by Piero di Cosimo, who introduced him to the oil painting techniques of Netherlandish masters and to German printmakers, such as Albrecht Dürer (1471–1528) and Martin Schongauer (1435/50–91). In the Rosselli workshop he met his close friend Mariotto Albertinelli (1474–1515), with whom he established a joint workshop intermittently from about 1495 until 1515 where he painted both collaborative and independent works. Profoundly moved by the preaching of Savonarola (whose posthumous portrait he painted, Museo di S. Marco, Florence) and one of his defenders when S. Marco was stormed and the friar captured in 1498, he joined the Dominican Order of S. Domenico in Prato in 1500 taking the name Fra Bartolomeo and renounced painting (although he continued to draw and provide studies for Albertinelli). He transferred the next year to the S. Marco congregation in Florence, where, encouraged by the biblical scholar Sante Pagnini (d. 1541), then prior of S.

Marco, he resumed painting in 1504. His visits to Venice in 1508 and Rome in 1513–14 enriched his palette, repertory of figural forms, and compositional techniques. His major altarpieces include the *Vision of St. Bernard* (Uffizi, 1504–7; commissioned by Bernardo del Bianco for the Florentine Badia), *God the Father with SS. Mary Magdalene and Catherine of Siena* (Villa Guinigi, Lucca, dated 1509; commissioned by the Dominican monastery of S. Piero Martire in Murano, but installed in S. Romano, Luca), two versions of the *Mystic Marriage of St. Catherine of Siena* for S. Marco (Louvre, dated 1511, and Accademia di Belle Arti e Liceo Artistico, Florence, dated 1512), the unfinished *St. Anne Altarpiece* (1510–12; fig. 136), *Madonna of Mercy* (Villa Guinigi, Lucca, dated 1515; commissioned by Fra Sebastiano Montecatini-Lombardi for S. Romano, Lucca), and *Christ as Salvator Mundi and Four Evangelist* (Pitti, dated 1516; commissioned for the Salvatore Billi Chapel in SS. Annunziata). All these altarpieces are remarkable for their dramatic intensity, grandeur of conception, harmony of composition, and deep religiosity. A master of pen and ink and a pioneer of black/red chalk and landscape drawing, Fra Bartolomeo produced over one thousand drawings throughout his career, a high percentage of which are still extant. These drawings were inherited by Fra Paolino (c. 1490–1547), a Dominican pupil and assistant of Fra Bartolomeo, who in turn bequeathed them to his pupil Suor Plautilla Nelli (1523–88), a nun in the Florentine convent of S. Caterina di Siena and a successful painter said to have trained several other nuns in painting.

BOTTICELLI, SANDRO (c. 1444/45–1510). Trained by Filippo Lippi, he reached maturity during the rule of Lorenzo de' Medici (il Magnifico), and, apart from three scenes frescoed on the walls of the Sistine Chapel in Rome (1481–82), his greatest paintings of the 1470s–1480s were mostly commissioned by Lorenzo de' Medici and his circle, many of whom he commemorated in vivid portraits. Outstanding domestic paintings include *Primavera* (c. 1482; fig. 112), *Nastagio degli Onesti* (1482–83; figs 113–116), *Birth of Venus* (Uffizi, c. 1484), and *Mars and Venus* (London, c. 1485). They expressed the renewed Laurentian golden age of peace and prosperity, and mirrored, through a mix of courtly and classical styles and subjects, the literature of the Laurentian period that had refined the vernacular of Dante and Petrarch through the lens of classical Latin poetry. Botticelli's Gothic naturalism, ornamentalism, and lyricism combined with classical grace, movement, and harmony also brilliantly expressed the fusion of matter and spirit in his many religious paintings (fig. 127). The Medici's expulsion from Florence in 1494 and Savonarola's subsequent reign of religious fanaticism resulted in his intensely spiritual, otherworldly, and apocalyptic late works, such as the *Mystic Nativity* (London, 1501). Although he often added oil to his egg yolk medium, he never abandoned tempera painting, and while his innovative work was fundamental for the High Renaissance, the works of Leonardo, Michelangelo, and Raphael eclipsed his late paintings.

BRONZINO, ANGOLO (1503–72). Trained by Pontormo and a champion of Michelangelo's *disegno,* he developed a sophisticated and graceful Mannerist style of great technical virtuosity and opulence. As a talented poet, founding member of the Accademia degli Umidi in 1540, and member of the Florentine Academy in 1542, he was connected with the Florentine intellectual and aristocratic elite, for whom he painted various portraits (fig. 188) and devotional works. In 1539 he became Cosimo I de' Medici's court painter and meticulously executed the exquisite, jewel-like Chapel of Eleonora (1540–46; figs. 165–168), numerous portraits of the ducal family (figs. 189, 191, and 192), and many tapestry designs (1545–57) woven in the ducal tapestry works. Among his several elegant allegorical works, the marmoreal *Venus, Cupid, Folly, and Time* (London, c. 1544–45) reigns supreme. Vasari gradually usurped his position as the dominant Florentine painter beginning about 1555. His last ducal commission was the large Michelangelesque fresco for S. Lorenzo, the *Martyrdom of St. Lawrence* (1565).

BRUNELLESCHI, FILIPPO (1377–1446). Trained as a goldsmith, he competed for the commission for the Florentine Baptistery doors (1401–2; fig. 45), and before 1425 invented one-point perspective. An ingenious and self-taught architect, he designed the cathedral dome (1417/18–36; fig. 30) with its lantern (1436–67; fig. 31), one of the greatest engineering achievements of the fifteenth century. He initiated the architectural Renaissance with his Foundling Hospital design (1419–45; figs. 19 and 20) by using classical vocabulary and a modular and proportional scheme based on ancient Roman and Tuscan Romanesque models. His Old Sacristy (1419–28; figs. 32–35), plan for S. Lorenzo (designed 1420s, executed by others 1442–94; figs. 32, 36, and 37), and Scolari Oratory (S. Maria degli Angeli, begun 1434) all anticipated his masterpiece, S. Spirito (1436–82; figs. 40–42). As son of a notary, he ranked higher than most Florentine artists and held several important governmental positions, including that of prior in 1425.

CELLINI, BENVENUTO (1500–1571). Ever restless, Cellini trained as a goldsmith in workshops in Florence, Siena, Bologna, Pisa, Rome, and Mantua. He served popes Clement VII and Paul III in Rome (1529–40), mainly as a minter and medalist in the papal mint, while interspersing trips to Naples, Venice, Padua, Paris, and Ferrara. Works of this early period are mostly lost, often melted down for their gems, gold, and silver. While employed as a sculptor and goldsmith by Francis I in Paris and Fontainebleau (1540–45), he created his famous saltcellar (Kunsthistorisches Museum, Vienna, 1540–43), a Mannerist tour de force, and the elegant bronze relief *Nymph of Fontainebleau* (Louvre, c. 1543). The remainder of his life he worked in Florence, principally for the Medici court, creating a bronze portrait of Cosimo I (Bargello, 1545–48), the masterful bronze *Perseus* (1545–54; fig. 180), and a marble *Crucifix* (Escorial, 1557–61) planned for his own tomb. His eventful life and colorful personality—he was arrogant, vain, quarrelsome, promiscuously bisexual, a murderer, and a thief (of precious metals and gems entrusted to his care by patrons)—is richly detailed in his autobiography, written with great literary flare in competition with Vasari's *Lives of the Artists* while under house arrest for sodomy (1557–61). He also wrote treatises on goldsmithing and sculpture (1565; published 1568).

CRONACA (Simone di Tomasso del Pollaiuolo, 1457–1508). Trained as a stonecutter and mason, Cronaca early in his career studied and measured ancient Roman ruins with such diligence that upon his return to Florence he "described the marvels of Rome and of other places with such accuracy, that from that time onwards he was called Cronaca, . . . truly a chronicle of information, . . . for it was evident from his works how good an imitator he was of antiquities . . . the rules of Vitruvius and . . . Brunelleschi" (Vasari). Between 1490 and 1504 he was first the chief stonecutter and then from 1497 the chief architect of the Strozzi Palace (figs. 97 and 98), designed initially by Giuliano da Sangallo; Cronaca was responsible for the design of the exterior crowning cornice (derived from the Forum of Nerva, Rome) and the upper levels of the interior courtyard. Between 1495 and 1497 he was chief architect jointly with Antonio da Sangallo the Elder of the Sala Grande that was added to the east side of the Priors' Palace (figs. 13, 129, and 179). These same two architects also designed in 1504 the plinth for Michelangelo's *David* (fig. 132). From 1495 until his death in 1508 he was the chief architect of the Florentine cathedral (fig. 17), now largely completed except for minor interior work, and between about 1490 and 1504 he designed and constructed the austere Church of S. Salvatore al Monte just below S. Miniato al Monte (fig. 11) for the Observant Franciscans under the patronage of the cloth merchants' guild. As a close follower of Savonarola, Cronaca developed a severe and straightforward classicism that appears to reflect the sobriety of the Savonarolan period.

DANTI, VINCENZIO (1530–76). Trained in Perugia as a goldsmith by his father, Giulio Danti (1500–1575), he studied anatomy in Rome with Michelangelo and Daniele da Volterra (1509–66) before moving to Florence in 1557, where he learned marble carving, probably from Bandinelli. In 1560 he competed for the commission of the Neptune Fountain (figs. 181 and 182) and in 1561 completed for Sforza Almeni, Cosimo I's chamberlain from Perugia, *Honor Triumphant over Falsehood* (Bargello), one of the most distinguished marble sculptures of the Florentine Renaissance. He also executed for the Uffizi "Serlian" arch *Rigor* and *Equity* (1564–66; fig. 183) and *Cosimo I as Emperor Augustus* (1572–73; fig. 184), and for the Baptistery a bronze *Beheading of John the Baptist* (1571). He was a founding member of the Academy of Design in 1563 and joined the Florentine Academy in 1565. The latter membership was merited by the first chapter of an unrealized fifteen-chapter treatise on *disegno* and perfect proportion based on human anatomy. He had learned anatomy from over eight dissections.

DONATELLO (Donato di Niccolò di Betto Bardi, 1386–1466). Trained in the workshops of Ghiberti and the cathedral works (1404–7), he evolved into the most imaginative, versatile, and prolific sculptor of fifteenth-century Florence. The works of this sharp-witted and rough-mannered artist are characterized by drama, pathos, and ecstasy. Well versed in the ancient sculptural remains of Pisa and Rome and the works of Brunelleschi and Masaccio, he introduced classical *contrapposto* to freestanding sculpture, as well as one-point perspective and *rilievo schiacciato* (flattened or sketched relief) to relief sculpture. His works include the marble *David* (1408–9; fig. 21); *St. John the Evangelist* for the cathedral façade (1408–15); *St. Mark* (1411–13; fig. 22); *St. George* (c. 1416–17; fig. 25); *Abraham and Isaac* (1421; fig. 27); *Tomb of Pope John XXIII* (Baptistery, 1421–28); *St. Louis of Toulouse* (c. 1422–25; fig. 26); *Zuccone* (c. 1423–26; fig. 28); bronze *Feast of Herod* (c. 1425; fig. 3); *Shaw Madonna* (c. 1430–32; fig. 125); *Cantoria* or cathedral organ loft (Opera del Duomo, Florence, 1433–39); Cavalcanti *Annunciation* (S. Croce, 1430s); marble *Feast of Herod* (Lille, Palais des Beaux-Arts, c. 1435); clay reliefs and bronze doors for the Old Sacristy (1434–43; figs. 33, 65–67); high altar for S. Antonio (Padua, c. 1447–50); *Equestrian Monument of Gattamelata* for Padua (1447–53); *Mary Magdalene* for the Florentine Baptistery (1453–55); bronze *David* (c. 1455–60; fig. 107); *Judith and Holofernes* (c. 1455–60; fig. 109); and the S. Lorenzo pulpits (1460–66; figs. 78–80). His friend Cosimo de' Medici (il Vecchio) honored the artist's genius by providing for his burial near his own tomb in S. Lorenzo's crypt.

FANCELLI, LUCA (c. 1430–c. 1495). Vasari's attributions to Fancelli of the Pitti Palace (fig. 96) and other Florentine buildings remain undocumented. For Ludovico and Federico Gonzaga (1441–84) of Mantua, he constructed (between c. 1450 and c. 1485) influential palaces, villas, fortifications, and churches, including Alberti's designs for S. Sebastiano and S. Andrea. Before his death, he also worked in Milan and Florence.

GENTILE DA FABRIANO (c. 1385–1427). An important late Gothic painter from Fabriano (Marches) noted for naturalistic and ornate detail, rhythmic line, and novel light effects. He executed frescoes in Venice (Sala del Maggior Consiglio, Doge's Palace, 1409–14, destroyed in the fire of 1577), where he trained Jacopo Bellini (c. 1400–1470/71). He served as the court painter for Pandolfo Malatesta (1370–1427) in Brescia (1414–19) before moving to Florence (1420–25) where he painted for Palla Strozzi his famous Uffizi *Adoration of the Magi* (originally for the sacristy, S. Trinita, 1423; fig. 12, no. 13), a work that influenced Masolino, Fra Angelico, and Domenico Veneziano (active 1438–61). He also worked in Siena and Orvieto (1425–26), ending up in Rome (1527), where he died while executing the now-destroyed frescoes of the life of John the Baptist in the Lateran.

GHIBERTI, LORENZO (c. 1381–1455). After training as a goldsmith by his stepfather, he entered and won the cloth merchants' competition for the Baptistery's second bronze doors (1401–2; fig. 46). He completed the doors in 1426, including the jambs and lintel (figs. 47 and 48), during which time he also executed for Or San Michele the bronze *St. John the Baptist* (1412–16; fig. 24) for the cloth merchants' guild, the bronze *St. Matthew* (1419–22) for the money-changers' guild, two bronze reliefs (1416–27) for the Sienese baptistery, and a model for the Florentine cathedral dome competition (1418–20). Between 1424 and 1452 he executed the *Gates of Paradise* (figs. 49–52), the wool manufacturers' guild's bronze *St. Stephen* (1425–29) for Or San Michele, and bronze shrines for the relics of SS. Protus, Hyacinth, and Nemesius (Bargello, 1428) and St. Zenobius (cathedral, 1432–42). During his career he also designed twelve stained-glass windows for the cathedral and late in life (c. 1447–55) wrote his incomplete *Commentaries,* an important forerunner of Vasari's *Lives of the Artists.* The treatise includes a discussion of classical art, drawn mostly from Pliny and Vitruvius, an outline of art's history from the fall of antiquity to the Renaissance, including an autobiography and a discussion of the science of sculpture that drew on optics, anatomy, and proportion. Ghiberti's large workshop employed many important artists (e.g., Donatello, Masolino, Uccello, Michelozzo, and Gozzoli), and his work influenced countless others.

GHIRLANDAIO, DOMENICO (1449–94). A master of perspectivally ordered painted compositions, brightly colored sculptural forms, realistic details (including portrait likenesses), and clear narratives, he ran a large Florentine workshop with his brother Davide (1452–1525) specializing in large-scale fresco decoration. These include *St. Jerome in His Study* and the *Last Supper* in Ognissanti (c. 1480), the *Last Supper* in S. Marco (c. 1480; fig. 91), *Roman Heroes and St. Zenobius* in the Palazzo Vecchio (east wall, Sala dei Gigli, 1482–83; figs. 101 and 102), scenes from the life of St. Francis in the Sassetti Chapel (S. Trinita, 1483–85; figs. 83–85), and scenes from the lives of the Virgin and John the Baptist in S. Maria Novella (Tornabuoni Chapel, 1485–90; fig. 12, no. 7). In Rome he frescoed two scenes on the walls of the Sistine Chapel (1481–82). He was also a talented panel painter, especially altarpieces (fig. 86) and independent portraits. Among the latter, *Lucrezia Tournbuoni* (Thyssen-Bornemisza Collection, Madrid, c. 1488) and an *Old Man with Rhinophymia and a Boy* (Louvre, c. 1490) are memorable. In the late 1480s the young Michelangelo apprenticed in his workshop.

GIAMBOLOGNA (1529–1608). A Fleming trained as a sculptor in Flanders, he traveled to Rome in 1550–52 to study ancient and Renaissance sculpture. He then settled permanently in Florence, opened a large workshop, and served as the court sculptor for grand dukes Francesco and Ferdinand de' Medici. Much influenced by Michelangelo and Cellini, his works are characterized by lithe movement, graceful elegance, and technical virtuosity. His principal sculptures for the Medici include *Florence Triumphant over Pisa* (Sala Grande, Palazzo Vecchio, 1563–75; fig. 197), *Samson Slaying a Philistine* (Victoria and Albert Museum, London, 1564–75), the *Apennines Fountain* in Pratolino (1570–80), the *Ocean Fountain* in the Boboli Gardens (1574–75; fig. 169), *Rape of the Sabines* (1579–82; figs. 185 and 186), *Equestrian Monument to Cosimo I de' Medici* (1587–94; fig. 187), and *Hercules Slaying a Centaur* in the Loggia dei Lanzi (1595–1600; fig. 15). He also executed the *Neptune Fountain* in Bologna (1563–66). The dissemination throughout Europe of his avidly collected bronze statuettes, including his famous "flying" *Mercury* (c. 1565), made him the most influential sculptor of the second half of the sixteenth century. He was knighted by Pope Clement VIII in 1599.

GOZZOLI, BENOZZO (c. 1421–97). Trained probably by Fra Angelico, he assisted the master in frescoing the cells of S. Marco in Florence (c. 1440–45; figs. 12, no. 23; 38), the Chapel of Nicholas V in the Vatican Palace in Rome (c. 1448–50), and the vault of the S. Brizio Chapel in Orvieto (1448). Before going to Rome, he helped Ghiberti chase the *Gates of Paradise* (1445–47; figs. 49–52). A specialist in fresco painting, his major cycles include the *Life of St. Francis* in Montefalcro (S. Francesco, 1452), *Journey of the Magi* in Florence (Medici Palace, 1459; figs. 103–5), *Life of St. Augustine* in San Gimignano (S. Agostino, 1563–65), and twenty-four large, severely damaged Old Testament scenes in Pisa (Camposanto, 1468–85). He died while working in Pistoia.

LEONARDO DA VINCI (1452–1519). Trained by Verrocchio, he became the greatest polymath of the Renaissance (painter, draftsman, sculptor, theater and pageant designer, architect, art theorist, engineer, scientist, and musician) and inventor of a High Renaissance style that profoundly shaped the course of Western art through his influence on Bramante, Michelangelo, Raphael, Andrea del Sarto, Giorgione (1477–1510), Correggio (c. 1489–1534), Albrecht Dürer, and many others. His productive life divides into six periods: 1464/69–81/83 in Florence completing his apprenticeship, enrolling in the painters' guild, and establishing an independent practice; 1481/83–99 in Milan as court artist for Ludovico Sforza; 1500–1506/8 in Florence again (by way of Mantua and Venice) including a year (1502–3) in the service of Cesare Borgia (1475–1507) in Urbino and elsewhere; 1506/8–13 in Milan again serving the French court; 1513–16 in Rome working at the papal court; and 1516–19 in France as court artist for Francis I. Major paintings in the first Florentine period include parts of Verrocchio's *Baptism* (Uffizi, c. 1472), the Uffizi *Annunciation* (c. 1473), *Ginevra de' Benci* (c. 1475–76, fig. 123), the *Benois Madonna* (Hermitage, St. Petersburg, c. 1479–81), and the unfinished *Adoration of the Magi* (Uffizi, 1481–82). In his first Milanese period he painted several portraits, including that of the duke's mistress, Cecilia Gallerani (Czartoryski Collection, Kraków, c. 1489–91), and the *Belle Ferronière* (Louvre, 1490s), as well as the *Virgin of the Rocks* (Louvre version, 1483–c. 1490) and the *Last Supper* (S. Maria delle Grazie, Milan, 1495–97). He also completed a full-scale clay model of a horse (c. 1490–94) for an unexecuted bronze equestrian monument commemorating the duke's father, Francesco Sforza. In the second Florentine period he perfected his *sfumato* technique in the *Virgin and Child with St. Anne* cartoon (1500–1501, lost), the unfinished *Battle of Anghiari* (Sala Grande, Palazzo Vecchio, 1503–5; lost, but see fig. 130), and the *Mona Lisa* (c. 1504–14; fig. 137). In his second Milanese period he appears to have completed the London cartoon of the *Virgin and Child with St. Anne* (c. 1505; fig. 135), the London version of the *Virgin of the Rocks* (late 1490s–1506/8), the Louvre *St. John the Baptist* (c. 1508–9), and the Louvre *Virgin and Child with St Anne* (c. 1513–14). Combining classical and medieval knowledge with his own observations, experiments, and dissections, he produced from his first Milanese period to the end of his life about thirty-five hundred pages of unsystematic notebook entries and drawings of unprecedented precision, nuance, and technical brilliance that demonstrate an insatiable curiosity about the physical and natural world and a remarkable ability to visualize the structures, forces, and movements of its component parts. He had a superior command of, and often made original contributions to, a vast array of subjects, including perspective, optics, color theory, engineering (aeronautical, hydraulic, nautical, military, structural, civil, and mechanical), mathematics, geometry, proportion, geology, meteorology, botany, zoology, anatomy, physiology, physiognomy, caricature, church and palace design, and town planning. Painting was the means by which he attempted to synthesize his vast erudition. Epitomizing the artist as both superb technician and universal genius, he did much to raise the social status of Renaissance artists.

LIPPI, FILIPPINO (c. 1457–1504). Trained by his father, Filippo Lippi, and Botticelli, and much influenced by Verrocchio, he introduced new energy into later fifteenth-century Florentine painting by his vibrant line, dramatic figures, and fanciful antiquarianism. His principal works include the completion of the lower register of the side walls of the Brancacci Chapel (1484–85; fig. 57); an altarpiece for the Pugliese Chapel in the Badia (*Vision of St. Bernard,* c. 1485–87), an altarpiece for the communal government in the Priors' Palace (*Virgin and Child with Saints,* Uffizi, 1486), the fresco decoration of the Carafa Chapel in S. Maria sopra Minerva in Rome (1488–93), the fresco decoration of the Strozzi Chapel in Florence (1487–1503; figs. 87–89), and the high altar for the Monastery of S. Donato a Scoperto outside Florence (*Adoration of the Magi,* Uffizi, 1496), which substituted for Leonardo's 1481–82 unfinished painting of the same subject.

LIPPI, FRA FILIPPO (c. 1406–69). When orphaned, he took vows as a Carmelite monk (1421) at S. Maria del Carmine (fig. 12, no. 6). His artistic training is unknown, but his residency in Florence, Siena (1429), and Padua (1434–35) exposed him to many influences. His early *Tarquinia Madonna* (Museo Nazionale, Palazzo Barberini, Rome, 1437) shows his acquaintance with Flemish art. His *Barbadori Altarpiece* (Louvre, c. 1437–39) for S. Spirito (fig. 12, no. 22; figs. 40–42) and *Coronation of the Virgin* for S. Ambrogio (Uffizi, c. 1439–47) established him as one of the leading Florentine painters. He enjoyed the patronage of the Medici, who commissioned the *Annunciation* (c. 1438) for S. Lorenzo (Chapel of SS. Cosmas and Damian, fig. 32, no. 2), the *Virgin and Child with Saints* (Uffizi, c. 1445) for the Novitiates' Chapel in S. Croce (fig. 12, no. 10), and the *Nativity* for the Medici Palace chapel (c. 1549; fig. 106). He painted some of the earliest Florentine independent portraits (c. 1438–45; fig. 118) and important devotional images, including the Pitti tondo of the *Virgin and Child* (1452–53) and the Uffizi *Virgin and Child with Two Angels* (1460s; fig. 126). His late works include fresco cycles in the cathedral of Prato (*Life of St. Stephen* and *Life of John the Baptist,* 1452–64) and the cathedral of Spoleto (*Life of the Virgin,* 1466–69). Ill suited to monastic life, he was thrice tried for fraud (1450–55), and in 1456 in Prato he fathered a son with a nun, Lucrezia Buti, whom he abducted from the Augustinian convent where he was the chaplain. He trained his son Filippino, Botticelli, and several other painters.

LORENZO MONACO (c. 1370/75–c. 1425/30). Lorenzo the Monk, a member of the Camaldolese Order, appears to have been trained as an illuminator in the renowned Florentine scriptorium of S. Maria degli Angeli. His work represents the culmination of the late Gothic style in Florence, occupying about the same position in painting as Ghiberti's contemporary work in sculpture. Although he continued to profess a religious life, he operated an active workshop outside the monastery that produced exquisitely crafted panel paintings in brilliantly colored tempera, including altarpieces, cut-out crosses, devotional works, and one fresco cycle (the badly damaged *Life of the Virgin,* Bartolini Salimbeni Chapel, S. Trinita, 1420s). The inscription on his masterpiece, the 1414 *Coronation of the Virgin* (fig. 54) for the high altar of the church of his own monastery, insists that the work was a collaborative enterprise of his entire workshop: "This work is by Lorenzo di Giovanni, a monk of this order, and his associates."

MAIANO, BENEDETTO DA (1442–97). While trained in the family workshop, Benedetto was strongly influenced by Desiderio da Settignano and by Antonio Rossellino (perhaps assisting him in the Chapel of the Cardinal of Portugal, figs. 71 and 74, c. 1466). As did his older brother Giuliano, Benedetto produced work for various Italian cities (e.g., Arezzo, Faenza, Loreto, Naples, San Gimignano, and Siena), but his principal Florentine sculptures are the marble portrait busts of the bankers Pietro Mellini (Bargello, dated 1474) and Filippo Strozzi (Louvre, 1475); marble door frames for the Sala dei Gigli (figs. 101 and 102) and the Sala di Udienza (fig. 194) in the Priors' Palace with the figures of the young *John the Baptist* and *Justice* (1476–81); the pulpit for S. Croce with five marble reliefs representing scenes from the life of St. Francis (commissioned by Pietro Mellini, 1481–85), his greatest work; and the altar and tomb monument for the Strozzi Chapel in S. Maria Novella (fig. 87; c. 1488–97).

MAIANO, GIULIANO DA (1432–90). Firstborn son of woodworker and mason Leonardo (Nardo) d'Antonio (d. before 1469), originally from Maiano near Fiesole, in about 1455 he became the head of the family woodcarving, intarsia, and sculpture workshop in Florence with his two younger brothers, Giovanni (c. 1438–78) and Benedetto. About 1461 Giuliano began to devote most of his attention to architecture, while in 1473 Benedetto became largely a marble sculptor, leaving most of the woodcarving and intarsia to Giovanni. Among the picture frames, benches, stalls, cabinets, candelabra, tabernacles, crucifixes, pulpits, inlaid wainscoting, coffered ceilings, doors, beds, chairs, and chests produced by the workshop throughout the last half of the fifteenth century, the two most important extant Florentine projects are the illusionistic intarsia panels for the north sacristy of the cathedral (*Sacrestia delle Messe,* 1463–65) and the ceilings and doors for the Sala dei Gigli and the Udienza in the Priors' Palace (figs. 101, 102, and 194; 1476–81). Aside from several projects in Florence, including service as the chief architect for the cathedral (1477–88), Giuliano produced architectural designs for patrons all over Italy (e.g., Arezzo, Loreto, Orvieto, Recanati, San Gimignano, and Siena). The cathedral for Faenza (1474–86), however, represents his most important ecclesiastical work. From 1485 to 1490, now the leading architect of his generation, he served Alfonso II of Aragon (1448–95), duke of Calabria, as his court architect in Naples, where his most influential building was the villa at Poggio Reale (1487–90, now destroyed).

MASACCIO (1401–28). He founded Renaissance painting by combining the monumentality of Giotto, the figural and drapery style of Donatello, the architectural vocabulary and linear perspective of Brunelleschi, and motifs from classical antiquity with his own brilliantly controlled lighting, compositional structure, and narrative drama. A frequent collaborator with Masolino, his Florentine works include the S. Giovenale triptych (1422), the St. Ambrogio altarpiece with Masolino (Uffizi, *Virgin and Child with St. Anne,* c. 1423–24), the now-dispersed Pisa altarpiece (central panel London, 1426), the Brancacci Chapel frescoes with Masolino (c. 1425–27; figs. 57, 59, 61–63), the *Trinity* fresco perhaps with Brunelleschi (c. 1427; figs. 55 and 56), and a birth tray (fig. 111, c. 1428). In Rome, where he died prematurely, he painted one wing (London, *SS. Jerome and John the Baptist*) of the S. Maria Maggiore high altarpiece, which was completed by Masolino (c. 1428–32).

MASOLINO DA PANICALE (1383–c. 1447). According to Vasari, he trained as a goldsmith and painter with Ghiberti and Gherardo Starnina (c. 1360–c. 1413), but Gentile da Fabriano and Masaccio were even more formative influences. In Florence he painted with Masaccio the S. Ambrogio altarpiece (Uffizi, *Virgin and Child with St. Anne,* c. 1423–24) and the Brancacci Chapel (c. 1425; figs. 57 and 58) before going to Hungary (1425–c. 1427/28) to work for the mercenary Pippo Spano. In Rome he completed the now-dispersed S. Maria Maggiore altarpiece begun by Masaccio (main panels, Capodimonte, Naples, c. 1428–32) as well as a frescoed chapel in S. Clemente (c. 1428–32) commissioned by Cardinal Branda Castiglione (1350–1443). He also frescoed the baptistery and choir vault of the Collegiata (c. 1432–35) in the cardinal's Lombard birthplace of Castiglione Olona.

MICHELANGELO (Michelangelo Buonarroti, 1475–1564). With his profound knowledge of anatomy, he became the most brilliant artist of the human form in the Renaissance. Throughout a seventy-year career, he practiced superbly sculpture, painting, drawing, and architecture and wrote a distinguished body of poetry. Apprenticed as a painter to Ghirlandaio in about 1488 and probably trained a little later as a sculptor by Bertoldo di Giovanni (c. 1430/40–1491), the precocious youth soon entered the Medici household, where he probably carved the marble reliefs of the *Madonna of the Steps* (c. 1491; fig. 128) and the *Battle of the Centaurs* (Casa Buonarroti, Florence, c. 1491). After the expulsion of the Medici from Florence, he went to Rome (1496) where he carved a marble *Bacchus* (Bargello, 1495–97) and a marble *Pietà* (St. Peter's, 1497–1500) only to return to Florence in 1500 to carve his colossal marble *David* (1501–4; figs. 132 and 133), complete a cartoon of the *Battle of Cascina* (1504–5, lost; but see fig. 131) for a never-executed fresco in the Sala Grande of the Priors' Palace, paint the *Doni Tondo* (c. 1504–6; fig. 140), and execute the marble *Bruges Madonna* (Onze Lieve Vrouw, Bruges, c. 1504–6). In 1505 he was called back by Pope Julius II to Rome, where he began the early stages of the *Julius Tomb* (1505–16), frescoed the Sistine Chapel ceiling (1508–12), and carved the marble *Risen Christ* (S. Maria sopra Minerva, 1514–21). Under the Medici popes, Leo X and Clement VII, he returned to Florence, where he executed the New Sacristy in S. Lorenzo with its sculptural decoration (1519–27, 1530–34, left incomplete and assembled by others; figs. 147–154), designed the Laurentian Library (c. 1524–27, 1530–34, completed by others under his supervision, 1549–71; figs. 155–157), and carved a marble *Victory* (Sala Grande, Palazzo Vecchio, Florence, c. 1533; fig. 197). With the election of Pope Paul III in 1534, he was recalled to Rome, where he remained for the rest of his life. For Paul III he frescoed the *Last Judgment* in the Sistine Chapel (1534–41); designed the Capitoline Hill (1538–64, completed by others by 1605); continued the Farnese Palace (1547–64, completed by others in 1589); and painted the *Crucifixion of Peter* and *Conversion of Paul* in the Pauline Chapel in the Vatican Palace (1542–50). In the same period he also completed the final version of the *Julius Tomb* in S. Pietro in Vincoli (1542–45). At the death of Antonio da Sangallo the Younger (1484–1546) in 1546, Paul III appointed Michelangelo chief architect of St. Peter's, where he oversaw the construction of his own radically different design until his death. Toward the end of his life he also carved the unfinished marble *Pietà* for his own tomb (Opera del Duomo, Florence, c. 1547–55) and designed for Pope Pius IV (r. 1560–65) the Porta Pia (1561–65). At his death he left unfinished the marble Rondanini *Pietà* (Castello Sforzesco, Milan).

MICHELOZZO (1396–1472). Trained as coin engraver for the Florentine mint (he became its director in 1435), he also worked as a sculptor assisting Ghiberti on his Baptistery doors (1403–52; figs. 47–52) and the bronze casting of *St. Matthew* for Or San Michele (1419–22). He established a partnership with Donatello (1420s) and collaborated on the *Tomb of Pope John XXIII* (Baptistery, 1421–28), *Tomb of Cardinal Rinaldo Brancaccio* (S. Angelo a Nilo, Naples, 1426–28), *Tomb of Bartolomeo Aragazzi* (Montepulciano, now dismantled, 1427–38), and the exterior pulpit of Prato's cathedral (1428–38). He was also a distinguished architect patronized principally by the Medici. Medici commissions include the Monastery of S. Francesco in Bosco ai Frati (1420s); the villas at Trebbio, Cafaggiolo, Careggi, and Fiesole (1420s–1450s); the construction, with modifications, of Brunelleschi's S. Lorenzo (begun 1442; figs. 32, 36, and 37); the monastery, library, and church of S. Marco (1437–44; figs. 38 and 39); the Medici Palace (c. 1446–57; figs. 92–94); the Novitiate or Medici Chapel at S. Croce (1440s; fig. 12, no. 10); the cloister, forecourt, chapel of S. Sebastian, nave tabernacle, and circular tribune of SS. Annunziata (1444–55; fig. 142, nos. 2, 4, and 5); and the tabernacle of the crucifix in S. Miniato (1448; fig. 12, no. 3). For Montepulciano he designed the Palazzo Comunale (1440). After Brunelleschi's death, he was appointed master of the cathedral works (1446–60), essentially the official architect of Florence, and supervised the construction of Brunelleschi's cathedral lantern (1444/45–67; fig. 31), the remodeling of the courtyard of the Priors' Palace (1454–1460s), and various communal fortifications.

MINO DA FIESOLE (1429–84). The first Renaissance sculptor to carve marble portrait busts, Mino excelled in the new medium represented by such works as *Piero de' Medici* (Bargello, dated 1483; fig. 120), *Niccolò Strozzi* (Skulpturengalerie, Berlin, 1454), *Astorgio Manfredi II* (Washington, 1455), and *Diotislavi Neroni* (Louvre, 1464). Mino also specialized in tombs, including the *Tomb of Bishop Leonardo Salutati* (cathedral, Fiesole, c. 1466), the *Tomb of Bernardo Giugni* (Badia, Florence, dated 1466), and the *Tomb of Count Hugo of Tuscany* (Badia, Florence, 1469–81). Mino also worked extensively in Rome (in 1454, 1461–64, and 1474–80) and once in Naples (1455).

NANNI DI BANCO (c. 1384–1421). He was trained as a sculptor by his father, a Florentine stone carver, and strongly influenced by Donatello. His principal works include a marble *Isaiah* (cathedral, Florence, 1408), a companion to Donatello's marble *David* (fig. 21), and four sculptures for niches on Or San Michele: *St. Luke* (1408–13), *St. Eligius* (c. 1411–14), *St. Philip* (c. 1412–15), and *Four Crowned Saints* (c. 1415–17; fig. 23). He also carved the marble relief with the *Assumption of the Virgin* above the cathedral's Porta della Mandorla (1414–1421).

PIERO DI COSIMO (1462–1521). Trained as a painter in the workshop of Cosimo Rosselli, whose name he adopted, and influenced by Filippino Lippi, Leonardo da Vinci, and Netherlandish painting (especially Hugo van der Goes, c. 1440–82), Piero di Cosimo painted in tempera and oil a wide variety of works of great imagination and fantasy, including altarpieces, devotional paintings (especially *tondi*), portraits, wedding chests, and *spalliere,* very few of which are dated or easily datable. He also made important contributions to landscape painting and designed ingenious floats and other decorations for public festivals (e.g., the *Triumph of Death* for the carnival pageant of 1506, described by Vasari, and the triumphal entry of Pope Leo X in 1515). Major altarpieces include the *Virgin and Child with Saints* (Saint Louis Art Museum, c. 1481–85), the *Visitation* (Washington, 1489–90), the *Virgin and Child with Saints* (Spedale degli Innocenti, Florence, c. 1493), the *Incarnation* (Uffizi, c. 1504), and the *Immaculate Conception* (S. Francesco, Fiesole, c. 1515–16). Examples of his domestic painting—his most imaginative, exotic, and eccentric work, often based on classical mythology, especially Ovid—include *The Hunt* and *Return from the Hunt* (Metropolitan Museum of Art, New York, c. 1485–1500), *Finding of Vulcan on Lemnos* (Wadsworth Atheneum, Hartford, c. 1490s), *Return of New Life to Lemnos* (National Gallery of Canada, Ottawa, c. 1490s), *Death of Procris* (London, c. 1495–1500), *Venus, Cupid, and Mars* (Gemäldegalerie, Berlin, c. 1495–1505), *Forest Fire* (Ashmolean Museum, Oxford, c. 1495–1505), *Discovery of Honey* (Art Museum, Worcester, MA, c. 1500), *Misfortunes of Silenus* (Fogg Art Museum, Cambridge, MA, c. 1500), *Battle of the Lapiths and Centaurs* (London, c. 1500–1510), and *Liberation of Andromeda* (Uffizi, c. 1510–13). Principal portraits include the pendants *Giuliano da Sangallo* and *Francesco Giamberti* (Rijksmuseum, Amsterdam, c. 1485–90) and *Cleopatra* (fig. 119; c. 1485). Piero di Cosimo's pupils included Fra Bartolomeo, Mariotto Albertinelli, Andrea del Sarto, and Pontormo, but he also influenced many other more conservative artists.

POLLAIUOLO, ANTONIO (c. 1431–98) and PIERO (1441–96). The more talented elder brother, Antonio, was a goldsmith, embroidery designer, sculptor, engraver, and painter, while Piero was more exclusively a painter, but they collaborated on most projects produced in their joint Florentine workshop. Their preoccupation with human anatomy and figures in action, derived from life studies and clay models, the use of atmospheric perspective in landscapes, fostered by the use of oil, and the employment of classical models and motifs greatly influenced the next generation, including Leonardo, Michelangelo, and Raphael. Their major works include *Hercules and the Hydra* and *Hercules and Antaeus* (Uffizi, 1460s), small replicas on panel of three large (now lost) canvases for the salon of the Medici Palace (figs. 92–94); decoration for the altar wall of the Cardinal of Portugal's Chapel (1460–68; figs. 71 and 73); six *Virtues* for the Tribunale di Mercanzia (Uffizi, 1469–70, mainly by Piero); *Dancing Figures* (fresco, Villa Gallina, late 1460s–early 1470s); *Annunciation* (Berlin, c. 1470; mainly by Piero); *Battle of the Ten Nudes* (c. 1470), the largest engraving of the early Renaissance; *Martyrdom of St. Sebastian* (1474–75; fig. 82); *Hercules and Antaeus* (bronze statuette, Bargello, c. 1475–80); and *Coronation of the Virgin* (S. Agostino, S. Gimignano, signed and dated 1483 by Piero). In 1484 the brothers moved their workshop to Rome, where they executed for St. Peter's the two most impressive papal tombs of the fifteenth century, the *Tomb of Sixtus IV* (dated 1493) and the 1492–98 *Tomb of Innocent VIII* (r. 1484–92).

PONTORMO, JACOPO (1494–1556). Trained by Piero di Cosimo and Andrea del Sarto and influenced by Fra Bartolomeo, his first major work, the *Visitation* (fresco, forecourt, SS. Annunziata, 1514–16; fig. 142, no. 2), has the breadth, depth, and narrative drama typical of the High Renaissance. However, by the time of the *Visdomini Altarpiece* (S. Michele Visdomini, Florence, 1518) and *Joseph in Egypt* for Pierfrancesco Borgherini's bedroom (London, c. 1518) he had evolved a Mannerist style characterized by visual disjunctions and psychological intensity. In *Vertumnus and Pomona* (fresco, Villa Medici, Poggio a Caiano, 1520–21) he created a tension between the relaxed sun-drenched atmosphere of a naturalistic pastoral idyll on the one hand, and, on the other, abstractly patterned form and color, taut contours, flattened space, and forceful emotions. In his frescoed Passion cycle (Certosa del Galluzzo, 1523–26) he drew directly from Albrecht Dürer's *Small Passion* woodcuts to create a visual world of broken lines, faceted draperies, elongated and distorted figures, compressed spaces, and discordant colors that captured the spiritual anguish provoked by the plague, from which he had sought refuge in the Certosa outside of Florence. Intense spirituality also typifies his mature works—e.g., the *Deposition* (1525–28; fig. 160) and the *Visitation* (S. Michele, Carmignano, late 1520s)—although now much more strongly influenced by Michelangelo. His neurotic, melancholic, and eccentric personality revealed by his diary (1554–56), appears to have heightened his sensitivity to the nuanced character of his portrait subjects—e.g., *Cosimo il Vecchio de' Medici* (Uffizi, 1519), *Alessandro de' Medici* (Philadelphia, 1534), and the *Halberdier/Cosimo I de' Medici* (J. Paul Getty Museum, Los Angeles, 1537–38). His nearly four hundred surviving drawings are among the most expressive of the Renaissance. He exerted a strong influence on his major pupil, Bronzino.

RAPHAEL (Raffaello Sanzio, 1483–1520). Trained as a painter by his father, Giovanni Santi (c. 1435/40–1494), and by Perugino, the precocious youth worked until 1504 largely in the Marches and Umbria. Two altarpieces—*Marriage of the Virgin* (Pinacoteca di Brera, Milan, 1504) and *Ansidei Madonna* (London, 1505)—and two pairs of small courtly paintings of about 1504—*St. George* and *St Michael* (Louvre), and the *Dream of Scipio* and *Three Graces* (Musée Condé, Chantilly)—are among the most important works of this period. In and out of Florence from 1504 to 1508, where he was greatly influenced by Leonardo and Michelangelo, he created a remarkable series of large-format devotional works—*Madonna of the Meadow* (Kunsthistorisches Museum, Vienna, 1505), *Madonna del Cardellino* (Uffizi, c. 1506), *Belle Jardinière* (Louvre, 1507), and the *Bridgewater Madonna* (Edinburgh, National Gallery of Scotland, c. 1508)—two portraits of Agnolo Doni and Maddalena Doni (c. 1506; figs. 138 and 139), and a major altarpiece for Perugia, the *Entombment* (Galleria Borghese, Rome, 1507). In Rome for the remainder of his short life, Raphael developed a large and well-organized workshop to meet the ever-increasing demands of popes Julius II and Leo X for the frescoes in the Vatican Palace *stanze*—Stanza della Segnatura (1508–11), Stanza d'Eliodoro (1511–14), Stanza dell'Incendio (1514–17), and Sala di Costantino (1519–24)—the cartoons for the Sistine Chapel tapestries (Victoria and Albert Museum, London, 1515–16), and the decoration of the Vatican Loggia (1518–19). But he also found time to paint the *Galatea* (1511) and the Loggia of Cupid and Psyche (1518–19) in the Palazzo Chigi/Farnesina, four major altarpieces—the *Madonna di Foligno* (Vatican, c. 1511–12), *Sistine Madonna* (Gemäldegalerie Alte Meister, Dresden, c. 1513), *St. Cecilia* (Pinacoteca Nazionale, Bologna, c. 1514–16), and *Transfiguration* (Vatican, 1517–20); several devotional works—the *Alba Madonna* (Washington, c. 1511) and *Madonna della Sedia* (c. 1514; fig. 141); and a remarkable series of portraits, including *Julius II* (London, 1511–12), *Donna Velata* (Pitti, c. 1514), *Baldassare Castiglione (1478–1529)* (Louvre, c. 1514–15), and *Leo X with Cardinals Giulio de' Medici and Luigi de' Rossi* (Uffizi, c. 1517–18). As an architect, he directed the construction of the new St. Peter's after Bramante's death in 1514, designed the Chigi Chapel (S. Maria del Popolo, c. 1513–16), S. Eligio degli Orefici (c. 1515–20), the Palazzo Branconio d'Aquila (c. 1515–20), and the Villa Madama (1518–20). He was such a celebrated artist and gracious courtier that he was offered the hand of the niece of Cardinal Bernardo Bibbiena (1470–1520), for whom he painted the bathroom or *stufetta* (1516) and *loggetta* (1519) in his Vatican apartment. When he died, he was honored by burial in the Pantheon. Through his paintings and frescoes, engravings after his designs by Marcantonio Raimondi (c. 1470–c. 1527), and the works of his assistants—principally Giulio Romano (c. 1499–1546), Giovanni da Udine (1487–1564), Gianfrancesco Penni (c. 1496–c. 1528), and Perino del Vaga (1501–47)—he exerted an enormous influence on Renaissance art.

ROSSELLINO, ANTONIO (1427–79). Antonio was trained by this older brother, Bernardo, a sculptor and architect, best known in Florence for his *Tomb of Leonardo Bruni* (S. Croce, 1444–50) and his supervision of the construction of Alberti's Rucellai Palace (fig. 95). Antonio shared Bernardo's workshop until 1469, when he established his own productive shop that supplied numerous tombs, reliefs, and statues for various cities outside of Florence (Pistoia, Prato, Empoli, Venice, Ferrara, and Naples). His earliest dated work is the marble bust of the physician *Giovanni Chellini* (Victoria and Albert Museum, London, 1456), which was followed in 1468 by the bust of *Matteo Palmieri* (fig. 1). Although the two contracts of 1461 for the tomb of the cardinal of Portugal (figs. 74 and 75) mention both Bernardo and Antonio, the figural sculptures appear to be the first fully mature work of Antonio. Motifs from the tomb of the cardinal of Portugal were often repeated with variations in subsequent workshop production, but Antonio's tomb monument for Francesco Nori (S. Croce, 1478) is wholly unique. Antonio also attempted, but failed, to carve the marble block that became Michelangelo's *David* (figs. 132 and 133).

ROSSO FIORENTINO (1494–1540). Although trained in Andrea del Sarto's workshop, his first major work, the *Assumption* (forecourt, SS. Annunziata, 1513–14; fig. 142, no. 2), already displays the dissonant colors, staccato rhythms, distorted forms, and spiritual disquiet more fully developed in the *Virgin and Child and Four Saints* (Uffizi, 1518), an altarpiece for the Ospedale di S. Maria Nuova that so shocked its patron that he rejected it outright, believing that the figures resembled devils more than saints. His *Deposition* for Volterra (Pinacoteca Comunale, 1521) and *Moses Defending the Daughters of Jethro* (1523–24; fig. 159) used even more jarring and hallucinatory aesthetic effects to express personal identification with the subjects and a troubled spirituality, although the *Marriage of the Virgin* (S. Lorenzo, Florence, 1523) is more restrained. Between 1524 and 1527 Rosso worked in Rome, where he was deeply influenced by the works of Michelangelo and Raphael and their followers, even though his arrogance and caustic tongue alienated him from the artistic community. Major Roman works include the *Creation Eve* and the *Fall of Adam* (fresco, Cesi Chapel, S. Maria della Pace, 1524), the haunting and eccentric *Dead Christ* (Museum of Fine Arts, Boston, 1525–26), and sophisticated engravings after his drawings depicting gods in niches and the erotic loves of the gods. After the 1527 Sack of Rome he traveled widely in central and northern Italy, creating for the Compagnia dei Battuti in Borgo Sansepolcro a *Pietà* (S. Lorenzo, 1527) and a *Christ in Glory* (1529–30) for the cathedral of Città di Castello. For the last decade of his life he served as a court artist for Francis I in France, where his elegant Mannerist frescoes and stuccowork in the Galerie François I in Fontainebleau helped to change the course of French art.

SALVIATI, FRANCESCO (Francesco de' Rossi) (1510–63). Trained by Bandinelli, Andrea del Sarto, and others, the precocious and temperamental youth was taken in 1531 to Rome in the service of Cardinal Giovanni Salviati (1490–1533), whose name he adopted. His study of antiquity, Michelangelo, Raphael, Perino del Vaga, and Baldassare Peruzzi (1481–1536) is evident in his 1538 *Visitation* (fresco, Oratory, S. Giovanni Decollato), yet these influences are incorporated into an early manifestation of his own elegant second-generation Mannerist style. From 1539 to 1541, he worked in Bologna, Venice, and Mantua, where he absorbed the works of Parmigianino (1503–40), Giulio Romano, and the Venetian school, before returning to Rome to execute the Margrave Chapel in S. Maria dell'Anima (begun 1541, completed c. 1549–50). From 1543 to 1548 he worked in Florence for Cosimo I de' Medici, painting his brilliant frescoes in the Sala dell'Udienza (1543–45; figs. 194–196) and a number of tapestry designs for the ducal tapestry works. To the same period belong the allegory of *Charity* (Uffizi, c. 1545) and the *Deposition* for S. Croce (c. 1547), which translated Rosso's Volterra *Deposition* (Pinacoteca Comunale, 1521) and Daniele da Volterra's Roman *Deposition* (Trinità dei Monti, Rome, 1541–45) into the *bella maniera* of High Mannerism. Aside from some now-lost work at the French court (1555–56), he spent the rest of his life in Rome, where his major works include the decoration of the Palio Chapel in the Palazzo della Cancelleria (1548–50) and the Sala dei Fasti Farnesiani (1552–55) in the Palazzo Farnese, both for the Farnese family; the *Birth of the Baptist* (1551) for the Oratory of S. Giovanni Decollato; scenes from the life of David (1552–54) in the salon of the Palazzo Ricci-Sacchetti for Cardinal Giovanni Ricci (c. 1497–1574); and the *Meeting of Alexander III and Frederick Barbarossa* (1562–63) in the Vatican Sala Regia for Pope Pius IV. The latter, as well as two walls of the Sala dei Fasti Farnesiani were unfinished at his death and completed respectively by Giuseppe Salviati (c. 1520–c. 1575) and by Taddeo (1529–66) and Federico (c. 1541–1609) Zuccari. Together his fresco cycles constitute the most inventive, complex, elegant, and poetic body of Mannerist decorative work of the Renaissance.

SANGALLO, ANTONIO DA, THE ELDER (c. 1460–1534). Antonio was trained as a woodworker, sculptor, architect, and engineer by his father, Francesco Giamberti da Sangallo (1404–80), and by his older brother, Giuliano da Sangallo, with whom he shared a workshop from about 1480 to 1516, collaborating on many projects. Between 1499 and 1501 he designed and executed the Sala Grande (fig. 129), for which Cronaca did most of the interior furnishings, and in 1504 he again joined Cronaca in designing the plinth for Michelangelo's *David* (fig. 132). Between 1516 and 1520 he joined Baccio d'Agnolo in designing and constructing the Servite Loggia (figs. 142, no. 7; 143). His architectural masterpiece is the central-planned Greek-cross pilgrimage church of the Madonna di S. Biagio, Montepulciano (begun 1518 and completed after his death).

SANGALLO, GIULIANO DA (c. 1445–1516). Trained as a woodworker by his father, Francesco da Sangallo, the young Giuliano was responsible for carving the inlaid stalls in the chapel of the Medici Palace (figs. 103–106; c. 1465). Shortly thereafter he spend a number of years in Rome, where he evolved, like many woodcarvers, into an architect and military engineer by studying and drawing ancient ruins, which he extensively documented in two sketchbooks (Biblioteca Comunale, Siena, and Codex Barberini, Vatican Library). Two early architectural commissions after his return to Florence in the 1470s are the Palazzo Scala (1470s) for the Florentine chancellor Bartolomeo Scala (1430–97) and a wooden model for SS. Annunziata (1480–83; figs. 12, no. 24; 142, no. 2) designed to connect the nave to the new round tribune added by Michelozzo and Alberti. His masterworks, however, commissioned by Lorenzo de' Medici (il Magnifico), are the centralized umbrella-domed Greek-cross church of S. Maria delle Carceri in Prato (1485–99) designed to enshrine a miraculous image; the octagonal domed sacristy with a barrel-vaulted vestibule for S. Spirito (fig. 40); and the Medici villa at Poggio a Caiano (1485–94; completed 1515–19 by others). The latter incorporates a symmetrical H-shaped plan within a square and the first classicizing temple-fronted, barrel-vaulted entrance portico in Renaissance architecture with a wide pediment carried on two Ionic piers, four Ionic columns, and an Ionic entablature. The temple-front entrance anticipated the villa designs of Andrea Palladio (1508–80). In 1484 Giuliano designed the still-extant wooden model for the Strozzi Palace (fig. 97), a design modified somewhat by the construction supervisor, Cronca. In 1490 Giuliano also designed the elegant Palazzo Gondi for Giuliano Gondi (1421–1501). From the 1490s until his death in 1516 Giuliano mostly designed fortifications, palaces, and churches outside of Florence (Loreto, Sansepolcro, and Rome). In 1506 in Rome in the company of Michelangelo he was the first to identify a newly excavated multifigure marble group as the *Laocoön* described by Pliny.

SCHEGGIA (Giovanni di ser Giovanni Guidi, 1406–86). Scheggia ("Splinter") may have received his nickname owing to his small stature compared to his older brother Masaccio ("Big Tom"). He appears to have been trained as a painter in part by the late Gothic painter Bicci di Lorenzo (1373–1452), in whose workshop he is documented in 1420–21, and in part by Masaccio, with whom he collaborated and shared a workshop in the 1420s. He was also a friend of Brunelleschi, according to the architect's biographer, Antonio Manetti. Although he painted at least one signed fresco cycle (in his hometown of S. Giovanni Valdarno), he specialized in small devotional works and furniture painting, including wedding chests (fig. 110), *spalliere,* and birth trays, including the round salver commissioned for the birth of Lorenzo de' Medici (il Magnifico) depicting the Triumph of Fame on one side and a Medici device on the other (Metropolitan Museum of Art, New York, 1449).

SERLIO, SEBASTIANO (1475–c. 1554). Trained as a perspective painter in Bologna, he was in Rome about 1514–20 and 1523–25 studying Renaissance architecture and measuring Roman ruins with Peruzzi, as well as making many drawings of the designs of Bramante and Peruzzi, as well as ancient Roman architecture. From around 1527 until 1541 he lived in Venice, working as a minor architectural consultant and designer as well as continuing his study of Roman ruins in the Veneto. He also began publishing in Venice a seven-book architectural treatise with a supplement: in Book 4 (*Regole generale,* 1537) he first codified the five classical orders (fig. 7) and included plans and elevations of Bramante's Tempietto (S. Pietro in Montorio, Rome, c. 1502–10), in Book 3 (*Della antichità,* 1540) he provided a comprehensive survey of ancient Roman architecture. In 1541 he moved to France, where he remained the rest of his life working as a painter and architect in the French court and completing his treatise. Book 1 (on geometry) and Book 2 (on perspective) were published in Paris in 1545. Book 2 contained his reconstructions of the classical tragic, comic, and satiric stage sets, which influenced many artists. Book 5 (on ancient temples and Renaissance churches) was printed in Paris in 1547, while Book 6 (on French- and Italian-style domestic architecture) was published only in 1966. The supplement on Mannerist doorways came out in Lyon in 1551 and Book 7 (on architectural accidents) appeared in Frankfurt in 1575. The entire treatise (minus Book 6) was published in Venice in 1619 as *Tutte l'opere d'architettura e prospetiva* and was soon translated into several languages. While not as learned as Alberti's *On the Art of Building in Ten Books* (1452) or Andrea Palladio's *Four Books of Architecture* (1570), nor as focused and precise as Jacopo Vignola's *Rule of the Five Orders of Architecture* (1562), Serlio's treatise, with its lucid illustrations and succinct text, was immensely popular, and, more than any other, responsible for spreading classical and Renaissance architectural ideas throughout Europe and the New World.

TASSO, GIOVANNI BATTISTA DEL (1500–1555). Tasso was trained as woodcarver by his family of woodworkers. Much of his early production has been lost, but his masterwork still survives: the ceiling and desks designed by Michelangelo for the Laurentian Library (figs. 155 and 157). Late in his career he won the confidence of Duke Cosimo I and became his court architect, designing the Mercato Nuovo (1547–51; fig. 173), overseeing various fortifications, and expanding and remodeling between 1549 and 1555 the Priors' Palace (figs. 13 and 179) to serve as the new seat of the Medici duchy, which included the design and construction of the Chapel of Eleonora decorated by Bronzino (figs. 165–168). He was also one of the artists invited to participate in Benedetto Varchi's famous *paragone* (comparison of the arts) debate concerning the superiority of painting or sculpture.

UCCELLO, PAOLO (c. 1397–1475). Trained in the late Gothic style of Ghiberti's workshop, he soon absorbed new Florentine developments in perspective and narrative codified in Alberti's 1435 *On Painting.* Uccello's interest in geometry and mathematics is evident in his works by the precise application of linear perspective and the geometrical rendering of natural forms. Other than brief periods working as a mosaicist in Venice (1425–27), and as a painter in Padua (1445–46) and Urbino (1465–68/69), his career was spent in Florence. His works are particularly difficult to date, but to the 1430s appear to belong frescoed scenes of the Creation (c. 1430) in the Chiostro Verde of S. Maria Novella (fig. 12, no. 7), the *Portrait of a Young Man* (c. 1435, fig. 117), the *Battle of S. Romano* (c. 1435–36, figs. 99 and 100), and the frescoed illusionistic equestrian monument of Sir John Hawkwood (1436) in the Florentine cathedral (fig. 12, no. 11; fig. 17). Later works include frescoed scenes, again in the Chiostro Verde, of the life of Noah (1440s–50s), including the dramatic *Flood* (c. 1445–55), and the *Hunt in the Forest* (Ashmolean Museum, Oxford, c. 1470).

VASARI, GIORGIO (1511–74). As a precocious youth in Arezzo he studied Latin and painting before attracting the attention of Cardinal Silvio Passerini (1470–1529), who took him to Florence, where from 1524 to 1527 he was tutored in classics with Passerini's wards, Alessandro and Ippolito de' Medici. He also furthered his artistic training with Andrea del Sarto and Bandinelli until the expulsion of the Medici in 1527. Before becoming the court artist and artistic entrepreneur for Duke Cosimo I de' Medici in 1554, he worked throughout Italy (Arezzo, Florence, Camaldoli, Modena, Bologna, Naples, Venice, Rimini, Rome, and Cortona). Works from this period include portraits of Lorenzo il Magnifico and Alessandro de' Medici (both Uffizi, 1534); an *Immaculate Conception* (SS. Apostoli, Florence, 1541); a stage set for Pietro Aretino's *La Talanta* and ceiling paintings for the Palazzo Corner Spinelli (both Venice, 1542); the fresco decoration of his palace in Arezzo (1542–48); and the fresco decoration of the Sala dei Cento Giorni (1546) commissioned by Cardinal Alessandro Farnese (1520–89) for the Palazzo della Cancelleria in Rome. After the death of Tasso in 1555, he was commissioned to continue the remodeling of the Palazzo Vecchio (figs. 13 and 179), Cosimo I's new ducal residence, and to begin the interior fresco decoration. He conceived the decorative program—one of the most extensive and coherent of the Renaissance—in collaboration with Cosimo Bartoli (1503–72), Vincenzo Borghini, and Giambattista Adriani. Vasari's *Ragionamenti* (begun 1558, published 1588) contains a detailed explanation of the complex program. The most important room was the monumental Sala Grande, with scenes of Florentine history culminating in the apotheosis of Cosimo I (1562–71; figs. 9, 16, 129, 193, 197–203) painted in conjunction with Francesco de' Medici's 1565 wedding, the decorations for which Vasari also supervised. Vasari's major architectural projects include the Uffizi in Florence (1560–80, figs. 174–178); the Palazzo dei Cavalieri (1562–69) and the Church of S. Stefano (1563–68) in Pisa for the Order of St. Stephen founded by Cosimo in 1561; the dome of the Madonna dell'Umiltà in Pistoia (1563–68); the remodeling of S. Maria Novella and S. Croce (begun 1565; fig. 171), and the Loggia in the Piazza Grande, Arezzo (1572). Near the end of his life Vasari decorated the salon of his Florentine palace (c. 1569); oversaw the decoration of Francesco de' Medici's *studiolo* in the Palazzo Vecchio (1570), which included his *Perseus and Andromeda;* directed the installation of new altarpieces in S. Maria Novella and S. Croce, including his own *Doubting Thomas* (1572, fig. 172); began the fresco decoration of the Florentine cathedral dome with a *Last Judgment* (1572); and completed the frescoes in the Sala Regia in the Vatican Palace (1572–73). While in Rome, Pope Pius IV knighted him (1571). To produce such a vast quantity of art, often at a frenetic pace, Vasari established a large workshop with many specialized assistants. Along with Borghini, he founded the Florentine Academy of Design in 1563. His *Lives of the Artists* (1550; revised and enlarged, 1568) was the first critical history of style, establishing him as the father of art history. His characterization of the flowering of Florentine art as a *rinascita* or rebirth of antiquity (source of the term "Renaissance"), his division of Italian art into three eras—infancy (Giotto and followers), adolescence (Masaccio and followers), and maturity (Leonardo, Michelangelo, Raphael, and followers)—and his concept of *disegno* as the unifying principle of all the arts were all extremely influential.

VERROCCHIO, ANDREA DEL (1435–88). Trained as a goldsmith in Florence, Verrocchio brought the techniques and delicacy of jewel-making to his work as a painter and sculptor, yet he also added great dynamism to his figures. As the leading sculptor of Florence during his lifetime, he worked for illustrious private patrons as well as for the communal government on such important public projects as the bronze *Christ and Doubting Thomas* (1467–83, fig. 29) on Or San Michele (fig. 18) and the small silver relief *Beheading of St. John the Baptist* (1477–80) for the altar in the Baptistery (fig. 10). His many commissions from the Medici include the *Tomb of Cosimo il Vecchio* (1465–67, fig. 76) in the crossing at San Lorenzo (figs. 36 and 37), the *Tomb of Piero and Giovanni* (1469–72, fig. 81) in the Old Sacristy (figs. 33–35), the bronze *Putto with a Dolphin* (late 1460s or early 1470s), and the bronze *David* (Bargello, c. 1475). Other works include the marble *Woman with Flowers* (c. 1475, fig. 124) and the *Baptism of Christ* for S. Salvi (Uffizi, c. 1475–85), an altarpiece to which Leonardo contributed several passages. For the Venetian Senate, Verrocchio executed an *Equestrian Monument to Bartolomeo Colleoni* (Campo SS. Giovanni e Paolo, c. 1479–92) noted for its forceful realism, the *contrapposto* of horse and rider, and the technical achievement of balancing the horse on three legs. He ran highly successful and productive workshops in both Florence and Venice, and counted Perugino and Leonardo da Vinci among his pupils.

SELECTED BIBLIOGRAPHY

N.B.: Authors who use double names (usually family and married) have been alphabetized according to the second name unless hyphenated. Family names with particles (d', da, de, de', del, de la, della, di, van, von) have been alphabetized without respect to the particle.

Ackerman, James S., "Architectural Practice in the Italian Renaissance," *Journal of the Society of Architectural Historians* 13 (1954), 3–11.

———, *The Architecture of Michelangelo,* 2nd ed. (Chicago: University of Chicago Press, 1986).

Adelson, Candace J., "The Tapestry Patronage of Cosimo I de' Medici, 1545–1553," 4 vols. (PhD diss., New York University, 1990).

Ahl, Diane Cole, *Benozzo Gozzoli* (New Haven: Yale University Press, 1996).

———, *Fra Angelico* (London: Phaidon, 2008).

———, ed., *The Cambridge Companion to Masaccio* (Cambridge: Cambridge University Press, 2002).

Ajmar-Wollheim, Marta, and Flora Dennis, eds., *At Home in Renaissance Italy,* exh. cat., Victoria and Albert Museum, London (London: V & A Publications, 2006).

Alberti, Leon Battista, *On Painting and On Sculpture,* English and Latin texts of *De Pictura* [1435] and *De statua* [1460s], ed. and trans. Cecil Grayson (London: Phaidon, 1972).

———, *On the Art of Building in Ten Books* [*De re aedificatoria* (1452)], trans. Joseph Rykwert, Neil Leach, and Robert Tavernor (Cambridge, MA: MIT Press, 1988).

Allegri, Ettore, and Alessandro Cecchi, *Palazzo Vecchio e i Medici: Guida storica* (Florence: Studio per Edizioni Scelte, 1980).

Ambrosini, Alberto, *Immaginazione visiva e conoscenza: Teoria della visione e pratica figurativa nei trattati di Leon Battista Alberti, Lorenzo Ghiberti, Leonardo da Vinci* (Pisa: Plus Pisa University Press, 2008).

Ames-Lewis, Francis, "Early Medicean Devices," *Journal of the Warburg and Courtauld Institutes* 48 (1979), 122–43.

———, *Drawing in Early Renaissance Italy* (New Haven: Yale University Press, 1981).

———, *The Intellectual Life of the Early Renaissance Artist* (New Haven: Yale University Press, 2000).

———, ed., *Cosimo "il Vecchio" de' Medici, 1389–1464* (Oxford: Clarendon Press, 1992).

———, ed., *The Early Medici and Their Artists* (London: Birkbeck College, 1995).

——— and Joanne Wright, eds., *Drawing in the Italian Renaissance Workshop,* exh. cat., University Art Gallery, Nottingham (London: Victoria and Albert Museum, 1983).

——— and Anka Bednarek, eds., *Decorum in Renaissance Narrative Art: Papers Delivered at the Annual Conference of the Association of Art Historians* (London: Birkbeck College, 1992).

——— and Mary Rogers, eds., *Concepts of Beauty in Renaissance Art* (Brookfield, VT: Ashgate, 1998).

——— and Paul Joannides, eds., *Reaction to the Master: Michelangelo's Effect on Art and Artists in the Sixteenth Century* (Burlington, VT: Ashgate, 2003).

d'Ancona, Mirella Levi, *Miniatura e miniatori a Firenze dal XIV al XVI secolo: Documenti per la storia della miniatura* (Florence: Olschki, 1962).

Andreatta, Emanuella, and Francesco Quinterio, "La Loggia dei Servi in Piazza SS. Annunziata a Firenze," *Rivista d'Arte* 40 (1988), 169–331.

Andres, Glenn M., John M. Hunisak, and A. Richard Turner, *The Art of Florence,* 2 vols. (New York: Abbeville Press, 1988).

Andrews, Lew, *Story and Space in Renaissance Art: The Rebirth of Continuous Narrative* (Cambridge: Cambridge University Press, 1996).

Anstey, Tim, "Theology and Geometry in the Façade of S. Maria Novella," *Albertiana* 6 (2003), 27–49.

Appelstadt, Eric, "Bishop and Pawn: New Documents for the Chapel of the Cardinal of Portugal at S. Miniato al Monte, Florence," in *Cultural Links between Portugal and Italy in the Renaissance,* ed. K. J. P. Lowe, 183–203 (Oxford: Oxford University Press, 2000).

Avery, Charles, *Florentine Renaissance Sculpture* (London: Murray, 1970).

———, *Giambologna: The Complete Sculpture* (Oxford: Phaidon, 1987).

———, "Giambologna's *Horse and Rider,*" *SMI Review* 17 (1993), 19–27.

———, *Donatello: An Introduction* (New York: Icon Editions, 1994).

———, *Studies in Italian Sculpture* (London: Pindar, 2001).

———, Andrew Butterfield, and Ulrich Middeldorf, *Early Renaissance Reliefs,* exh. cat., Salander-O'Reilly Galleries, New York (2001).
Balchin, Paul N., *Urban Development in Renaissance Italy* (Chichester: John Wiley, 2008).
Baldassarri, Stefano Ugo, and Arielle Saiber, *Images of Quattrocento Florence: Selected Writings in Literature, History, and Art* (New Haven: Yale University Press, 2000).
Baldini, Umberto, *Giorgio Vasari, pittore* (Florence: Il Fiorino, 1994).
——— and Ornella Casazza, *La Cappella Brancacci* (Milan: Electa, 1990).
——— and P. A. Vigato, *The Frescoes of Casa Vasari in Florence: An Interdisciplinary Approach to Understanding, Conserving, Exploiting and Promoting* (Florence: Polistampa, 2006).
Bambach, Carmen C., *Drawing and Painting in the Italian Renaissance Workshop: Theory and Practice, 1300–1600* (New York: Cambridge University Press, 1999).
———, *Leonardo da Vinci: Master Draftsman,* exh. cat., Metropolitan Museum of Art, New York (New Haven: Yale University Press, 2003).
Barasch, Moshe, and Lucy Freeman Sandler, eds., *Art the Ape of Nature: Studies in Honor of H. W. Janson* (New York: Abrams, 1981).
Barkan, Leonard, *Unearthing the Past: Archaeology and Aesthetics in the Making of Renaissance Culture* (New Haven: Yale University Press, 1999).
Barker, Emma, Nick Webb, and Kim Woods, eds., *The Changing Status of the Artist* (New Haven: Yale University Press, 1999).
Barocchi, Paola, ed., *Trattati d'arte del Cinquecento fra manerismo e controriforma,* 3 vols. (Bari: Laterza, 1960–62).
———, ed., *Scritti d'arte del Cinquecento,* 3 vols. (Milan: Ricciardi, 1971–77).
———, ed., *Palazzo Vecchio: Committenza e collezionismo mediceo,* exh. cat., Palazzo Vecchio, Florence (Milan: Electa, 1980).
———, ed., *Il giardino di San Marco: Maestri e compagni del giovane Michelangelo,* exh. cat., Casa Buonarroti, Florence (Florence: Silvana, 1992).
——— and Giovanna Gaeta Bertelà, *Collezionismo mediceo e storia artistica,* 2 vols. (Florence: Studio per edizione scelte, 2002).
Barolsky, Paul, *Michelangelo's Nose: A Myth and Its Maker* (University Park: Pennsylvania State University Press, 1990).
———, *Why Mona Lisa Smiles and Other Tales by Vasari* (University Park: Pennsylvania State University Press, 1991).
———, *Giotto's Father and the Family of Vasari's Lives* (University Park: Pennsylvania State University Press, 1992).
———, *The Faun in the Garden: Michelangelo and the Poetic Origins of Italian Renaissance Art* (University Park: Pennsylvania State University Press, 1994).
———, "Botticelli's *Primavera* and the Poetic Imagination of Italian Renaissance Art," *Arion* 8 (2000), 5–35.
Barriault, Anne B., *Spalliera Paintings of Renaissance Tuscany: Fables of Poets for Patrician Homes* (University Park: Pennsylvania State University Press, 1994).
Barzman, Karen-edis, *The Florentine Academy and the Early Modern State: The Discipline of Disegno* (Cambridge: Cambridge University Press, 2000).
Baskins, Cristelle L., *Cassone Painting, Humanism, and Gender in Early Modern Italy* (Cambridge: Cambridge University Press, 1998).
——— et al., *The Triumph of Marriage: Painted Cassoni of the Renaissance,* exh. cat., Isabella Stewart Gardner Museum, Boston (Pittsburgh: Gutenberg Periscope, 2008).
Baxandall, Michael, *Giotto and the Orators: Humanist Observers of Painting in Italy and the Discovery of Pictorial Composition, 1350–1450* (Oxford: Clarendon Press, 1971).
———, *Painting and Experience in Fifteenth-Century Italy* (Oxford: Clarendon Press, 1972).
———, *Patterns of Intention: On the Historical Explanation of Pictures* (New Haven: Yale University Press, 1985).
———, *Words for Pictures: Seven Papers on Renaissance Art and Criticism* (New Haven: Yale University Press, 2003).
Bayer, Andrea, ed., *Art and Love in Renaissance Italy,* exh. cat., Metropolitan Museum of Art, New York (New Haven: Yale University Press, 2008).
Belluzzi, Amedeo, ed., *Palazzi fiorentini del Rinascimento, Atti della giornata di studi, Firenze, Archivio di Stato, 16 dicembre 2005* (Florence: Polistampa, 2008).
Benedictis, Cristina De, ed., *Altari e committenza: Episodi a Firenze nell'età della controriforma* (Florence: Pontecorboli, 1996).
Bent, George R., *Monastic Art in Lorenzo Monaco's Florence: Painting and Patronage in Santa Maria degli Angeli, 1300–1415* (Lewiston, NY: Edwin Mellen Press, 2006).
Berdini, Paolo, "Women under the Gaze," *Art History* 21 (1998), 565–90.
Berger, Harry, Jr., *Fictions of the Pose: Rembrandt against the Italian Renaissance* (Stanford: Stanford University Press, 2002).
Bergstein, Mary, *The Sculpture of Nanni di Banco* (Princeton: Princeton University Press, 2000).
Bertelli, Sergio, Nicolai Rubinstein, and Craig Hugh Smyth, eds., *Florence and Venice: Comparisons and Relations,* Acts of Two Conferences at Villa I Tatti, 1976–77, 2 vols. (Florence: Nuova Italia, 1980).
Berti, Luciano, *Il principe dello studiolo: Francesco I dei Medici e la fine del rinascimento fiorentino* (Florence: Edam, 1967; repr. Pistoia: Machietto & Musolino, 2002).
——— and Umberto Baldini, *Filippino Lippi* (Florence: Il Fiorino, 1991).
Beyer, Andreas, and Bruce Boucher, eds., *Piero de' Medici il Gottoso (1416–1464): Kunst im Dienste der Mediceer* (Berlin: Akademie Verlag, 1993).
Blœdé, James, *Paolo Uccello et la représentation du mouvement: Regards sur la Bataille de San Romano* (Paris: École nationale supérieure des beaux-arts, 1996).

Blunt, Anthony, *Artistic Theory in Italy, 1450–1600* (Oxford: Oxford University Press, 1962).
Boase, T. S. R., *Giorgio Vasari: The Man and the Book* (Princeton: Princeton University Press, 1979).
Bober, Phyllis Pray, *Drawings after the Antique by Amico Aspertini: Sketchbooks in the British Museum* (London: Warburg Institute, 1957).
——— and Ruth O. Rubinstein, *Renaissance Artists and Antique Sculpture: A Handbook of Sources* (New York: Oxford University Press, 1986; rev. ed., Turnhout: Harvey Miller, 2009).
Boccaccio, Giovanni, *Famous Women,* trans. Virginia Brown (Cambridge, MA: Harvard University Press, 2003).
Bolzoni, Lina, *The Gallery of Memory: Literary and Iconographic Models in the Age of the Printing Press* (Toronto: University of Toronto Press, 2001).
Bonsanti, Giorgio, ed., *Palazzo Strozzi: Cinque secoli di arte e cultura* (Florence: Nardini, 2005).
Borghini, Raffaelo, *Il Riposo* [Florence, 1584], ed. M. Rosci (Milan, 1968).
Bormand, Marc, Beatrice Paolozzi Strozzi, and Nicholas Penny, *Desiderio da Settignano: Sculptor of Renaissance Florence,* exh. cat., National Gallery of Art, Washington (Milan-Paris: 5 Continents, Musée du Louvre Editions, 2007).
Borsi, Franco, and Stefano Borsi, *Paolo Uccello,* trans. Elfreda Powell (New York: Abrams, 1994).
Borsi, Stefano, *Giuliano da Sangallo: I disegni di architettura e dell'antico* (Rome: Officina, 1985).
Borsook, Eve, *The Mural Painters of Tuscany: From Cimabue to Andrea del Sarto,* rev. ed. (Oxford: Clarendon Press, 1980).
——— and Johannes Offerhaus, *Francesco Sassetti and Ghirlandaio at Santa Trinita, Florence: History and Legend in a Renaissance Chapel* (Doornspijk: Davaco, 1981).
——— and Fiorella Superbi Gioffredi, eds., *Italian Altarpieces, 1250–1500: Function and Design* (Oxford: Clarendon Press, 1994).
Bradshaw, Marilyn, *Italian Renaissance Art: A Source Book* (Upper Saddle River, NJ: Pearson Prentice Hall, 2009).
Brandt, Kathleen Weil-Garris, Cristina Acidini Luchinat, James David Draper, and Nicolas Penny, eds., *Giovinezza di Michelangelo,* exh. cat., Casa Buonarroti, Florence (Milan: Skira, 1999).
Branko, Mitrovic, *Serene Greed of the Eye: Leon Battista Alberti and the Philosophical Foundations of Renaissance Architectural Theory* (Munich: Deutscher Kunstverlag, 2005).
Brann, Noel L., *The Debate over the Origins of Genius during the Italian Renaissance: The Theories of Supernatural Frenzy and Natural Melancholy in Accord and in Conflict on the Threshold of the Scientific Revolution* (Leiden: Brill, 2002).
Brock, Maurice, *Bronzino,* trans. David Pool Radzinowicz and Christine Schultz-Touge (Paris: Flammarion, 2002).
Brothers, Cammy, *Michelangelo, Drawing, and the Invention of Architecture* (New Haven: Yale University Press, 2008).
Broude, Norma, and Mary D. Garrard, eds., *Feminism and Art History: Questioning the Litany* (New York: Harper & Row, 1982).
———, eds., *The Expanding Discourse: Feminism and Art History* (New York: HarperCollins, 1992).
Brown, Alison M., "The Humanist Portrait of Cosimo de' Medici Pater Patriae," *Journal of the Warburg and Courtauld Institutes* 24 (1961), 186–94.
———, ed., *Language and Images of Renaissance Italy* (Oxford: Clarendon Press, 1995).
Brown, David Alan, *Leonardo da Vinci: Origins of a Genius* (New Haven: Yale University Press, 1998).
———, *Virtue and Beauty: Leonardo's Ginevra de' Benci and Renaissance Portraits of Women,* exh. cat., National Gallery of Art, Washington (Princeton: Princeton University Press, 2001).
Brown, Judith C., and Robert C. Davis, eds., *Gender and Society in Renaissance Italy* (New York: Addison-Wesley, 1998).
Brucker, Gene A., *Renaissance Florence* (Berkeley: University of California Press, 1983).
———, *Florence: The Golden Age, 1138–1737* (Berkeley: University of California Press, 1998).
Bruschi, Arnaldo, *Storia dell'architettura italiana: Il primo Cinquecento* (Milan: Electa, 1999).
———, *Filippo Brunelleschi* (Milan: Electa, 2006).
Bule, Steven, Alan Phipps Darr, and Fiorella Superbi Gioffredi, eds., *Verrocchio and Late Quattrocento Italian Sculpture* (Florence: Le Lettere, 1992).
Bull, Malcolm, *The Mirror of the Gods: How the Renaissance Artists Rediscovered the Pagan Gods* (New York: Oxford University Press, 2005).
Burckhardt, Jacob, *The Civilization of the Renaissance in Italy,* trans. S. G. Middlemore (New York: Phaidon, 1955).
Burioni, Matteo, *Die Renaissance der Architekten: Profession und Souveränität des Baukünstlers in Giorgio Vasari Viten* (Berlin: Mann, 2007).
Burke, Peter, *The Italian Renaissance: Culture and Society in Italy,* rev. ed. (Princeton: Princeton University Press, 1986).
Burns, Howard, "San Lorenzo in Florence before the Building of the New Sacristy: An Early Plan," *Mitteilungen des Kunsthistorichen Institutes in Florenz* 23 (1979), 145–59.
Burroughs, Charles, *The Italian Renaissance Palace Façade: Structures of Authority, Surfaces of Sense* (Cambridge: Cambridge University Press, 2002).
Bush, Virginia, *The Colossal Sculpture of the Cinquecento, from Michelangelo to Giovanni Bologna* (New York: Garland, 1976).
———, "Bandinelli's *Hercules and Cacus* and Florentine Tradition," in *Studies in Italian Art History and Architecture, 15th through 18th Centuries,* ed. Henry A. Millon, 163–206. Memoirs of the American Academy in Rome 35 (Cambridge, MA: MIT Press, 1979).
Butterfield, Andrew, "Verrocchio's *Christ and St. Thomas:* Chronology, Iconography and Political Context," *Burlington Magazine* 134 (1992), 225–33.

———, "Documents for the Pulpits of San Lorenzo," *Mitteilungen des Kunsthistorischen Institutes in Florenz* 38 (1994), 147–53.
———, *The Sculptures of Andrea del Verrocchio* (New Haven: Yale University Press, 1997).
——— and Caroline Elam with a contribution from Victor Coonin, "Desiderio da Settignano's Tabernacle of the Sacrament," *Mitteilungen des Kunsthistorischen Institutes in Florenz* 43 (1999), 333–57.
Cadogan, Jean K., *Domenico Ghirlandaio: Artist and Artisan* (New Haven: Yale University Press, 2000).
Caglioti, Francesco, "Donatello, I Medici e Gentile de' Becchi: Un po' d'ordine intorno all 'Giuditta' (e al 'David') di Via Larga: I, II, III," *Prospettiva* nos. 75/76 (July–Oct. 1994), 14–49; 78 (Apr. 1995), 22–55; 80 (Oct. 1995), 15–58.
———, *Donatello e i Medici: Storia del David e della Giuditta* (Florence: Olschki, 2000).
———, "Nouveautés sur la *Bataille de San Romano* de Paolo Uccello," *Revue du Louvre* 4 (2001), 37–54.
Calabi, Donatella, ed., *Il mercante patrizio: Palazzi e botteghe nell"Europa del Rinascimento* (Milan: Mondadori, 2008).
Callmann, Ellen, *Apollonio di Giovanni* (Oxford: Clarendon Press, 1974).
———, "The Growing Threat to Marital Bliss as Seen in Fifteenth-Century Florentine Paintings," *Studies in Iconography* 5 (1979), 73–92.
Calvi, Giulia, and Riccardo Spinelli, eds., *Le donne Medici nel sistema europeo delle corti XVI–XVIII secolo,* Atti del convegno internazionale, Firenze–San Domenico di Fiesole, 6–8 ottobre 2005 (Florence: Polistampa, 2008).
Calzona, Arturo, Joseph Connors, et al., eds., *Leon Battista Alberti: Architetture e committenti. Atti dei Convegni internazionali del Comitato Nazionale VI Centenario della nascita de Leon Battista Alberti (Firenze, Rimini, Mantova, 12–16 ottobre 2004),* 2 vols. (Florence: Olschki, 2009).
Camerota, Filippo, ed., *Nel segno di Masaccio: L'invenzione della prospettiva* (Florence: Giunti, 2001).
——— and Mara Miniati, eds., *I Medici e le scienze: Stumenti e macchine nelle collezioni granducali,* exh. cat., Museo degli Argenti, Florence (Florence: Giunti, 2008).
Campbell, Caroline, *Love and Marriage in Renaissance Florence: The Courtauld Wedding Chests* (London: Courtauld Gallery in association with Paul Holberton, 2009).
Campbell, Gordon, ed., *The Oxford Dictionary of the Renaissance* (Oxford: Oxford University Press, 2003).
Campbell, Lorne, *Renaissance Portraits: European Portrait Painting in the Fourteenth, Fifteenth, and Sixteenth Centuries* (New Haven: Yale University Press, 1990).
——— et al., *Renaissance Faces: Van Eyck to Titian,* exh. cat., National Gallery, London (New Haven: Yale University Press, 2008).
Campbell, Stephen J., and Stephen J. Milner, eds., *Artistic Exchange and Cultural Translation in the Italian Renaissance City* (Cambridge, Cambridge University Press, 2004).
Campbell, Thomas, *Tapestry in the Renaissance: Art and Magnificence,* exh. cat. (New York: Metropolitan Museum of Art, 2002).
Caneva, Caterina, ed., *Il Corridoio vasariano agli Uffizi* (Milan: Silvana, 2008).
Capecchi, Gabriella, Amelio Fara, Detlef Heikamp, and Vincenzo Saladino, eds., *Palazzo Pitti: La reggia revelata,* exh. cat., Palazzo Pitti, Florence (Florence: Giunti, 2003).
Caplow, Harriet McNeal, *Michelozzo,* 2 vols. (New York: Garland, 1977).
Capretti, Elena, and Serena Padovani, eds., *Domenico Puligo, 1492–1527: Un protagonista dimenticato della pittura fiorentina* (Livorno: Sillabe, 2002).
Cardini, Roberto, and Mariangela Regoliosi, eds., *Alberti e la cultura del Quattrocento,* 2 vols., Atti del Convegno internazionale svoltosi a Firenze tra il 16 e il 18 dicembre 2004 (Florence: Polistampa, 2008).
———, *Leon Battista Alberti umanista e scrittore: Filologia, esegesi, tradizione,* 2 vols. (Florence: Polistampa, 2008).
Carl, Doris, *Benedetto da Maiano: A Florentine Sculptor at the Threshold of the High Renaissance,* 2 vols. (Turnhout, Belgium: Brepols, 2006).
Carli, Cecilia de, *I Deschi da Parto e la pittura del primo rinascimento toscano* (Turin: Allemandi, 1997).
Carlino, Andrea, *Books of the Body: Anatomical Ritual and Renaissance Learning,* trans. John Tedeschi and Anne C. Tedeschi (Chicago: University of Chicago Press, 1999).
Carpeggiani, Paolo, and Anna Maria Lorenzoni, *Carteggio di Luca Fancelli con Ludovico, Federico e Francesco Gonzago, marchesi di Mantova* (Mantua: Arcari, 1998).
Carroll, Eugene A., *Rosso Fiorentino: Drawings, Prints and Decorative Arts,* exh. cat. (Washington, DC: National Gallery of Art, 1987).
Caruso, Carlo, and Andrew Laird, eds., *Italy and the Classical Tradition* (London: Duckworth, 2008).
Cassigoli, Iacopo, *Pontormo: Percezione e rappresentatione del corpo nella pittura e negli scritti* (Florence: Pagnini, 2007).
Cast, David, *The Delight of Art: Giorgio Vasari and the Traditions of Humanist Discourse* (University Park: Pennsylvania State University Press, 2009).
Cecchi, Alessandro, *Botticelli* (Milan: Motta, 2005).
Cellini, Benvenuto, *Autobiography,* trans. George Bull, rev. ed. (Harmondsworth: Penguin, 1998).
———, *The Treatises of Benvenuto Cellini on Goldsmithing and Sculpture,* trans. C. R. Ashbee (London: Arnold, 1888: repr. New York: Dover, 1967).
Cennino, Cennini, *The Craftsman's Handbook: Il libro dell' arte,* trans. David V. Thompson (New York: Dover, 1989).
Chambers, David S., *Patrons and Artists in the Italian Renaissance* (Columbia: University of South Carolina Press, 1971).
——— and François Quiviger, eds., *Italian Academies of the Sixteenth Century* (London: Warburg Institute, 1995).
Chapman, Hugo, Tom Henry, Carol Plazzotta, et al., *Raphael: From Urbino to Rome,* exh. cat. (London: National Gallery, 2004).

Chastel, André, *Art et humanisme à Florence au temps de Laurent le Magnifique: Études sur la Renaissance et l'humanisme platonicien,* 2nd ed. (Paris: Presses Universitaires de France, 1961).
Cheney, Liana de Girolami, *Neoplatonism and the Arts* (Lewiston, NY: Mellen Press, 2002).
———, *The Homes of Giorgio Vasari* (New York: Peter Lang, 2006).
———, *Giorgio Vasari's Teachers: Sacred and Profane Art* (New York: Peter Lang, 2007).
Cherubini, Giovanni, and Giovanni Fanelli, eds., *Il Palazzo Medici Riccardi di Firenze* (Florence: Giunti, 1990).
Ciappelli, Giovanni, and Patricia Lee Rubin, eds., *Art, Memory, and Family in Renaissance Florence* (Cambridge: Cambridge University Press, 2000).
Ciatti, Marco, Cecilia Frosini, Antonio Natali, and Patrizia Riitano, eds., *Raffaello, la rivelazione del colore: Il restauro della Madonna del Cardellino della Galleria degli Uffizi* (Florence: Edifir, 2008).
Clark, Kenneth, *Leonardo da Vinci: An Account of His Development as an Artist* (Cambridge, 1939; rev. ed., with Martin Kemp, New York: Viking Penguin, 1988).
Clarke, Georgia, *Roman House—Renaissance Palaces: Inventing Antiquity in Fifteenth-Century Italy* (Cambridge: Cambridge University Press, 2003).
Clausse, Gustave, *Les San Gallo: Architectes, peintres, sculpteurs, medailleurs, XVeme et XVIeme siècles,* 3 vols. (Paris: E. Leroux, 1900–1902).
Clearfield, Janis, "The Tomb of Cosimo de' Medici in San Lorenzo," *Rutgers Art Review* 2 (1981), 13–30.
Climent-Delteil, Pascale, *Il Rosso Fiorentino, pittore della Maniera* (Montpellier: Presses universitaires de la Méditerranné, 2007).
Cochrane, Eric, *Florence in the Forgotten Centuries, 1527–1800: A History of Florence and the Florentines in the Age of the Grand Dukes* (Chicago: University of Chicago Press, 1973).
Cohen, Simona, *Animals as Disguised Symbols in Renaissance Art* (Leiden: Brill, 2008).
Cole, Bruce, *Masaccio and the Art of the Early Renaissance* (Bloomington: Indiana University Press, 1980).
———, *The Renaissance Artist at Work: From Pisano to Titian* (New York: Harper & Row, 1983).
———, *Italian Art, 1250–1550: The Relation of Renaissance Art to Life and Society* (New York: Harper & Row, 1987).
———, ed., *Sixteenth-Century Italian Art* (Oxford: Blackwell, 2006).
Cole, Michael, "The *Figura Sforzata:* Modeling, Power and the Mannerist Body," *Art History* 24 (2001), 520–51.
———, *Cellini and the Principles of Sculpture* (Cambridge: Cambridge University Press, 2002).
——— and Mary Pardo, eds., *Inventions of the Studio: Renaissance to Romanticism* (Chapel Hill: University of North Carolina Press, 2005).
Collobi, Licia Ragghianti, *Il Libro de' disegni del Vasari,* 2 vols. (Florence: Vallecchi, 1974).
Comanducci, Rita Maria, "L'altare nostro de la Trinità: Masaccio's Trinity and the Berti Family," *Burlington Magazine* 145 (2003), 14–21.
Condivi, Ascanio, *The Life of Michelangelo,* trans. Alice Sedgwick Wohl, ed. Hellmut Wohl (University Park: Pennsylvania State University Press, 1999).
Conforti, Claudia, *Giorgio Vasari architetto* (Milan: Electa, 1993).
——— and Richard J. Tuttle, eds., *Storia dell'architettura italiana: Il secondo Cinquecento* (Milan: Electa, 2001).
——— and Andrew Hopkins, eds., *Architettura e tecnonlogia: Acque, tecniche e cantieri nell'architettura rinascimentale e barocca* (Rome: Nuova Argos, 2002).
Connell, William J., and Giles Constable, *Sacrilege and Redemption in Renaissance Florence: The Case of Antonio Rinaldeschi* (Toronto: Centre for Reformation and Renaissance Studies, 2005).
Conticelli, Valentina, *"Guardaroba di Cose Rare et Preziose." Lo studiolo di Francesco I de' Medici: Arte, storia e significati* (Lugano: Agorà, 2007).
Convegni internazionale del comitato nazionale VI centenario della nasciata di Leon Battista Alberti, *La vita e il mondo di Leon Battista Alberti: Atti dei convegni internazionale del comitato nazionale VI centenario della nasciata di Leon Battista Alberti, Genova, 19–21 febbraio 2004,* 2 vols. (Florence: Olschki, 2008).
Corti, Gino, and Piero Morselli, *La Chiesa di S. Maria delle Carceri in Parto* (Florence: EDAM, 1982).
Costamagna, Philippe, *Pontormo* (Milan: Electa, 1994).
Covi, Dario A., *Andrea del Verrocchio: Life and Work* (Florence: Olschi, 2005).
Cox-Rearick, Janet, *The Drawings of Pontormo,* 2 vols, rev. ed. (New York: Hacker Art Books, 1981).
———, *Dynasty and Destiny in Medici Art: Pontormo, Leo X, and the Two Cosimos* (Princeton: Princeton University Press, 1984).
———, *Bronzino's Chapel for Eleonora di Toledo in the Palazzo Vecchio* (Berkeley: University of California Press, 1993).
Cozzi, Mauro, *Antonio da Sangallo il Vecchio e l'architettura del Cinquecento in Valdichiana* (Genoa: Sagep, 1992).
Cranston, Jodi, *The Poetics of Portraiture in the Italian Renaissance* (New York: Cambridge University Press, 2000).
Cropper, Elisabeth, "On Beautiful Women, Parmigianino, *Petrarchismo,* and the Vernacular Style," *Art Bulletin* 58 (1976), 374–94.
———, *Pontormo: Portrait of a Halberdier* (Los Angeles: J. Paul Getty Museum, 1997).
Cross, F. L., and E. A. Livingstone, *The Oxford Dictionary of the Christian Church,* 2nd ed. (Oxford: Oxford University Press, 1978).
Crum, Roger J., "'Cosmos, the World of Cosimo': The Iconography of the Uffizi Facade," *Art Bulletin* 71 (1989), 237–53.
———, "Donatello's *Ascension of St. John the Evangelist* and the Old Sacristy as Sepulchre," *Artibus et historiae* 32 (1995), 141–61.

——— and D. G. Wilkins, "In Defence of Florentine Republicanism: Saint Anne and Florentine Art 1343–1575," in Kathleen Ashley and Pamela Sheingorn, eds., *Interpreting Cultural Symbols: Saint Anne in Late Medieval Society* (Athens: University of Georgia Press, 1990).

——— and John T. Paoletti, eds., *Renaissance Florence: A Social History* (Cambridge: Cambridge University Press, 2006).

Currie, Stuart, and Peta Motture, eds., *The Sculpted Object, 1400–1700* (Aldershot: Scolar Press, 1997).

———, ed., *Drawing, 1400–1600: Invention and Innovation* (Brookfield, VT: Ashgate, 1998).

Danti, Cristina, ed., *La Trinità di Masaccio: Il restauro dell'anno Duemila* (Florence: Edifir, 2002).

Debby, Nirit Ben-Aryeh, *The Renaissance Pulpit: Art and Preaching in Tuscany, 1400–1550* (Turnhout: Brepols, 2007).

Dempsey, Charles, *The Portrayal of Love: Botticelli's Primavera and Florentine Humanist Culture at the Time of Lorenzo the Magnificent* (Princeton: Princeton University Press, 1992).

Denley, Peter, and Caroline Elam, eds., *Florence and Italy: Renaissance Studies in Honour of Nicolai Rubinstein,* Westfield Publications in Medieval Studies 2 (London: Westfield College, 1988).

Depth of Field: The Place of Relief in the Time of Donatello, exh. cat., Henry Moore Institute, Leeds (London: Victoria and Albert Museum, 2004).

Didi-Huberman, Georges, *Fra Angelico: Dissemblance and Figuration,* trans. Jane Marie Todd (Chicago: University of Chicago Press, 1995).

Digiesi, Cristina, Roberto Lunardi, and Giuseppe Raspini, *La bottega di Giuliano e Benedetto da Maiano nel Rinascimento fiorentino,* exh. cat. (Florence: Octavo, 1994).

Dizionario biografico degli Italiani, ed. Alberto M. Chisalberti (Rome: Istituto della Enciclopedia italiana, 1960–).

Dolcini, Lorettta, *Verrocchio's Christ and St. Thomas: A Masterpiece of Sculpture from Renaissance Florence,* exh. cat., Palazzo Vecchio, Florence, and the Metropolitan Museum of Art, New York (New York: Abrams, 1992).

Draper, James David, *Bertoldo di Giovanni, Sculptor of the Medici Household: Critical Reappraisal and Catalogue Raisonné* (Columbia: University of Missouri Press, 1992).

Dressen, Angelo, *Pavimenti decorate del Quattrocento in Italia* (Venice: Marsilio, 2008).

Dumont, Catherine, *Francesco Salviati au Palais Sacchetti de Rome et la décoration murale italienne (1520–1560)* (Geneva: Institut Suisse de Rome, 1973).

Dussler, Luitpold, *Raphael: A Critical Catalogue of His Pictures, Wall-Paintings and Tapestries,* trans. Sebastian Cruft (London: Phaidon, 1971).

Eckstein, Nicholas A., ed., *The Brancacci Chapel: Form, Function and Setting,* Acts of an International Conference, Florence, Villa I Tatti, June 6, 2003 (Florence: Olschki, 2007).

Edgerton, Samuel Y., Jr., *The Renaissance Rediscovery of Linear Perspective* (New York: Harper & Row, 1976).

———, *Pictures and Punishment: Art and Criminal Prosecution during the Florentine Renaissance* (Ithaca: Cornell University Press, 1985).

———, *The Mirror, the Window, and the Telescope: How Renaissance Linear Perspective Changed Our Vision of the Universe* (Ithaca: Cornell University Press, 2009).

Einem, Herbert von, *Michelangelo* (London: Methuen, 1973).

Eisenberg, Marvin, *Lorenzo Monaco* (Princeton: Princeton University Press, 1989).

Eisenbichler, Konrad, ed., *The Cultural Politics of Duke Cosimo I de' Medici* (Aldershot: Ashgate, 2001).

———, ed., *The Cultural World of Eleonora di Toledo, Duchess of Florence and Spain* (Aldershot: Ashgate, 2004).

Elam, Caroline, "Lorenzo de' Medici and the Urban Development of Renaissance Florence," *Art History* 1 (1978), 43–66.

———, "The Site and Early Building History of Michelangelo's New Sacristy," *Mitteilungen des Kunsthistorichen Institutes in Florenz* 23 (1979), 155–86.

———, "Lorenzo de' Medici's Sculpture Garden," *Mitteilungen des Kunsthistorichen Institutes in Florenz* 36 (1992), 41–84.

Emison, Patricia A., *Creating the "Divine" Artist: From Dante to Michelangelo* (Leiden: Brill, 2004).

Ettlinger, Leopold D., "Hercules Florentinus," *Mitteilungen des Kunsthistorichen Institutes in Florenz* 16 (1972), 119–42.

———, *Antonio and Piero Pollaiuolo* (London: Phaidon, 1978).

———, "The Liturgical Function of Michelangelo's Medici Chapel," *Mitteilungen des Kunsthistorichen Institutes in Florenz* 22 (1978), 287–304.

Fabbri, Patrizia, *Palaces of Florence* (Venice: Arsenale, 2000).

Falomir, Miguel, ed., *The Renaissance Portrait: From Pisanello to Rubens,* exh. cat., Museo Nacional del Prado, Madrid, and National Gallery, London (Madrid: El Viso, 2008).

Fanelli, Giovanni, *Firenze: Architettura e città,* 2 vols. (Florence: Vallechi, 1973).

———, *Firenze: La città nella storia d'Italia* (Bari: Laterza, 1980).

——— and Michele Fanelli, *Brunelleschi's Cupola: Past and Present of an Architectural Masterpiece* (Florence: Mandragora, 2004).

Fantoni, Marcello, Louisa C. Matthew, and Sara F. Matthews-Grieco, eds., *The Art Market in Italy, 15th–17th Centuries / Il mercato dell'arte in Italia secc. XV–XVII* (Modena: Panini, 2003).

Fara, Amelio, *Bernardo Buontalenti e Firenze: Architettura e disegno dal 1576 al 1607,* exh. cat., Gabinetto disegni e stampe degli Uffizi, Florence (Florence: Olschki, 1998).

Farago, Claire J., *Leonardo da Vinci's Paragone: A Critical Interpretation with a New Edition of the Text in the Codex Urbinas* (Leiden: Brill, 1992).

———, ed., *Reframing the Renaissance: Visual Culture in Europe and Latin America, 1450–1650* (New Haven: Yale University Press, 1995).
———, ed., *Biography and Early Art Criticism of Leonardo da Vinci* (New York, Garland, 1999).
———, ed., *Leonardo's Projects, c. 1500–1519* (New York, Garland, 1999).
———, ed., *Leonardo's Science and Technology: Essential Readings for the Non-Scientist* (New York, Garland, 1999).
———, ed., *Leonardo's Writings and Theory of Art* (New York, Garland, 1999).
———, ed., *An Overview of Leonardo's Career and Projects until c. 1500* (New York, Garland, 1999).
———, ed., *Leonardo da Vinci and the Ethics of Style* (Manchester: Manchester University Press, 2008).
———, ed., *Re-reading Leonardo: The Treatise on Painting across Europe, 1550–1900* (Aldershot: Ashgate, 2009).
Ferguson, Margaret W., Maureen Quilligan, and Nancy Vickers, eds., *Rewriting the Renaissance: The Discourses of Sexual Difference in Early Modern Europe* (Chicago: Chicago University Press, 1986).
Fidanza, Giovan Battista, *Vincenzo Danti, 1530–1576* (Florence: Olschki, 1996).
Filardi, Domenico, *Orto de' Pitti: The Architects, Gardeners and Botanical Design of the Boboli Gardens* (Florence: Centro Di, 2007).
Findlen, Paula, *Possessing Nature: Museums, Collecting, and Scientific Culture in Early Modern Italy* (Berkeley: University of California Press, 1994).
Fischer, Chris, *Fra Bartolommeo: Master Draughtsman of the High Renaissance,* exh. cat., Museum Boymans-van Beumingen, Rotterdam (Seattle: University of Washington Press, 1990).
Fleming, John, Hugh Honour, and Nikolaus Pevsner, *Dictionary of Architecture* (Harmondsworth: Penguin, 1976).
Forster, Kurt W., "Metaphors of Rule: Political Ideology and History in the Portraits of Cosimo I de' Medici," *Mitteilungen des Kunsthistorishen Institutes in Florenz* 15 (1971), 65–104.
Foster, Philip, *A Study of Lorenzo de' Medici's Villa at Poggio a Caiano* (New York: Garland, 1978).
France, Robert G. La, *Bachiacca: Artist of the Medici Court* (Florence: Olschki, 2008).
Francini, Carlo, and Francesco Vossilla, *Baccio Bandinelli's "Hercules and Cacus"* (Florence: Alinea, 1999).
Frangenberg, Thomas, ed., *Poetry on Art: Renaissance to Romanticism* (Donington: Shaun Tyas, 2003).
——— and Robert Williams, eds., *The Beholder: The Experience of Art in Early Modern Europe* (Aldershot: Ashgate, 2006).
Franklin, David, *Rosso in Italy: The Italian Career of Rosso Fiorentino* (New Haven: Yale University Press, 1994).
———, *Painting in Renaissance Florence, 1500–1550* (New Haven: Yale University Press, 2001).
Fredianelli, Antonio, *I palazzo storici di Firenze: Dalla austere dimore dei banchieri e dei mercanti agli splendori degli edifici rinascimentali, dai "capricci" del Barocco all'eclettismo dell'Ottocento e oltre* (Rome: Newton Compton, 2007).
Freedberg, Sydney J., *Painting of the High Renaissance in Rome and Florence,* 2 vols. (Cambridge, MA: Harvard University Press, 1961).
———, *Andrea del Sarto* (Cambridge, MA: Harvard University Press, 1963).
———, *Painting in Italy, 1500–1600* (Harmondsworth: Penguin, 1971, rev. ed. 1975).
Freedman, Luba, *The Revival of the Olympian Gods in Renaissance Art* (Cambridge: Cambridge University Press, 2003).
Frommel, Christoph Liutpold, and Nicolas Adams, eds., *The Architectural Drawings of Antonio da Sangallo the Younger and His Circle,* vol. 1: *Fortifications, Machines and Festival Architecture;* vol. 2: *Churches,Villas, the Pantheon, Tombs, and Ancient Inscriptions* (New York: Architectural History Foundation; Cambridge, MA: MIT Press, 1994–2000).
Frommel, Sabine, *Sebastiano Serlio Architect,* trans. Peter Spring (Milan: Electa; London: Phaidon, 2003).
Gabrielli, Edith, *Cosimo Rosselli: Catalogo ragionato* (Turin: Allemandi, 2007).
Gallucci, Margaret A., *Benvenuto Cellini: Sexuality, Masculinity, and Artistic Identity in Renaissance Italy* (New York: Palgrave Macmillan, 2003).
——— and Paolo L. Rossi, eds., *Benvenuto Cellini: Sculptor, Goldsmith, Writer* (Cambridge: Cambridge University Press, 2004).
Garfagnini, Giancarlo, ed., *Firenze e la Toscana dei Medici dell'Europa del '500, Convegno internazionale di studio tenutosi a Firenze dal 9 al 14 giugno 1980 nell' ambito della XVI Esposizione europea di Arte, scienza e cultura,* 3 vols. (Florence: Olschki, 1983).
———, ed., *Giorgio Vasari: Tra decorazione ambientale e storiografia artistica,* Convegno di studi, Arezzo, 8–10 ottobre 1981 (Florence: Olschki, 1985).
Garibaldi, Vittoria, *Perugino* (Milan: Silvana, 2005).
Gebhardt, Volker, "Some Problems in the Reconstruction of Uccello's Rout of San Romano," *Burlington Magazine* 133 (1991), 179–88.
Gentili, Augusto, Philippe Morel, and Claudia Cieri Via, eds., *Il ritratto e la memoria* (Florence: Bulzoni, 1994).
Gentilini, Giancarlo, *I Della Robbia: La scultura invetriata nel Rinascimento,* 2 vols. (Florence: Cantini, 1992).
Geronimus, Dennis, *Piero di Cosimo: Visions Beautiful and Strange* (New Haven: Yale University Press, 2006).
Ghiberti, Lorenzo, *I Commentarii,* ed. Lorenzo Bartoli (Florence: Giunti 1998).
Giambologna tra Firenze e l'Europa: Atti del Convegno Internazionale, Firenze, Istituto Universitario Olandese di Storia dell'Arte (Florence: Centro Di, 2000).
Giampaolo, Mario Di, and Elisabetta Saccomani, eds., *Scritti di storia dell'arte in onore di Sylvie Béguin* (Naples: Paparo, 2001).
Giannetto, Raffaella Fabiani, *Medici Gardens: From Making

to Design (Philadelphia: University of Pennsylvania Press, 2008).
Giannotti, Alessandra, *Il teatro di natura: Niccolo Tribolo e le origini di un genere. La scultura di animali nella Firenze del Cinquecento* (Florence: Olschki, 2007).
Giavarina, A. Ghisetti, *Aristotile da Sangallo: Architettura, scenografia e pittura tra Roma e Firenze nella prima metà del Cinquecento* (Rome, 1990).
Gilbert, Creighton E., "When Did a Man in the Renaissance Grow Old?" *Studies in the Renaissance* 14 (1967), 7–32.
———, *Italian Art, 1400–1500: Sources and Documents in the History of Art* (Englewood Cliffs, NJ: Prentice-Hall, 1980).
———, ed. and trans., *Complete Poems and Selected Letters of Michelangelo* (Princeton: Princeton University Press, 1980).
Gill, Anton, *Il Gigante: Michelangelo, Florence, and the David, 1492–1504* (New York; St. Martin's Press, 2003).
Giovannoni, Gustavo, *Antonio da Sangallo il Giovane,* 2 vols. (Rome: Centro studi di storia dell'architettura e della Facoltà di architettura dell'Università di Roma, 1959).
Goffen, Rona, *Renaissance Rivals: Michelangelo, Leonardo, Raphael, Titian* (New Haven: Yale University Press, 2002).
———, ed., *Masaccio's Trinity* (Cambridge: Cambridge University Press, 1998).
Goguel, Catherine Monbeig, ed., *Francesco Salviati (1510–1563) o la bella maniera,* exh. cat., Villa Medici, Rome, and Musée du Louvre, Paris, 1998 (Milan: Electa, 1998).
Goldthwaite, Richard A., "The Building of the Strozzi Palace: The Construction Industry in Renaissance Florence," *Studies in Medieval and Renaissance History* 10 (1973), 99–194.
———, *The Building of Renaissance Florence* (Baltimore: Johns Hopkins University Press, 1980).
———, *Wealth and the Demand for Art in Italy* (Baltimore: Johns Hopkins University Press, 1993).
———, *Banks, Palaces and Entrepreneurs in Renaissance Florence* (Brookfield, VT: Variorum, 1995).
———, *The Economy of Renaissance Florence* (Baltimore: Johns Hopkins University Press, 2009).
Gombrich, Ernst H., "Botticelli's Mythologies: A Study in the Neoplatonic Symbolism of His Circle," *Journal of the Warburg and Courtauld Institutes* 8 (1945), 7–60.
———, *Norm and Form: Studies in the Art of the Renaissance* (London: Phaidon, 1971).
———, *The Heritage of Apelles: Studies in the Art of the Renaissance* (Ithaca: Cornell University Press, 1976).
———, *Symbolic Images: Studies in the Art of the Renaissance* (Oxford: Phaidon, 1978).
———, *New Light on Old Masters* (Chicago: University of Chicago Press, 1986).
———, *The Uses of Images: Studies in the Social Function of Art and Visual Communication* (London: Phaidon, 2000).
Gomez, Margarita Fernandez, *Codex Escurialensis 28-II-12: Libro de dibujos o antiquedades,* 2 vols. (Madrid: Patrimonio Nacional, 2000).
Goy, Richard, *Florence: The City and Its Architecture* (London: Phaidon, 2002).
Grafton, Anthony, *Leon Battista Alberti: Master Builder of the Italian Renaissance* (New York: Hill & Wang, 2000).
Grazia, Margreta de, Maureen Quilligan, and Peter Stallybrass, eds., *Subject and Object in Renaissance Culture* (Cambridge: Cambridge University Press, 1996).
Grendler, Paul, *Schooling in Renaissance Italy: Literacy and Learning, 1300–1600* (Baltimore: Johns Hopkins University Press, 1989).
Greve, David, *Status und Statue: Studien zu Leben und Werke des Florentiners Bildhauers Baccio Bandinelli* (Berlin: Frank & Timme, 2008).
Griffiths, Gordon, "The Political Significance of Uccello's *Battle of San Romano,*" *Journal of the Warburg and Courtauld Institutes* 41 (1978), 313–16.
Guillaume, Jean, ed., *Les traités d'architecture de la Renaissance: Actes du colloque tenu à Tours du 1er au 11 juillet 1981* (Paris: Picard, 1988).
———, ed., *L'Invention de la Renaissance: La reception des formes "à l'antique" au debut de la Renaissance,* Actes du colloque tenu à Tours du 1er au 4 juin 1994 (Paris: Picard, 2003).
Gurrieri, Francesco, Patrizia Fabbri, and Stefano Giraldi, *Palaces of Florence* (New York: Rizzoli, 1996).
Haines, Margaret, *The Sacrestia delle Messe of the Florentine Cathedral* (Florence: Cassa di Risparmio di Firenze, 1983).
———, ed., *Santa Maria del Fiore: The Cathedral and Its Sculpture,* Acts of the International Symposium for the VII Centenary of the Cathedral of Florence, Florence, Villa I Tatti, 5–6 June 1997 (Fiesole: Cadmo, 2001).
Hale, John R., *Florence and the Medici: The Pattern of Control* (London: Thames and Hudson, 1977).
Hall, James, *Dictionary of Subjects and Symbols in Art,* rev. ed. (New York: Harper & Row, 1979).
———, *Michelangelo and the Reinvention of the Human Body* (New York: Farrar, Straus & Giroux, 2005).
Hall, Marcia B., "The *Tramezzo* in S. Croce, Florence, and Domenico Veneziano's Fresco," *Burlington Magazine* 112 (1970), 797–99.
———, "The Ponte in Sta. Maria Novella: The Problem of the Rood Screen in Italy," *Journal of the Warburg and Courtauld Institutes* 37 (1974), 157–73.
———, *Renovation and Counter-Reformation: Vasari and Duke Cosimo in S. Maria Novella and S. Croce, 1565–1577* (Oxford: Clarendon Press, 1979).
———, *Color and Meaning: Practice and Theory in Renaissance Painting* (New York: Cambridge University Press, 1992).
———, ed., *The Cambridge Companion to Raphael* (New York: Cambridge University Press, 2005).
Hart, Vaughan, and Peter Hicks, eds., *Paper Palaces: The Rise of the Renaissance Architectural Treatise* (New Haven: Yale University Press, 1998).
Hartt, Frederick, *The Drawings of Michelangelo* (London: Thames & Hudson, 1971).

———, Gino Corti, and Clarence Kennedy, *The Chapel of the Cardinal of Portugal, 1434–1459, at San Miniato in Florence* (Philadelphia: University of Pennsylvania Press, 1964).

——— and David G. Wilkins, *History of Italian Renaissance Art: Painting, Sculpture, Architecture* (New York: Abrams, 2003).

Haskell, Francis, and Nicholas Penny, *Taste and the Antique: The Lure of Classical Sculpture, 1500–1900* (New Haven: Yale University Press, 1981).

Hatfield, Rab, "The Compagnia de' Magi," *Journal of the Warburg and Courtauld Institutes* 33 (1970), 107–61.

———, *Botticelli's Uffizi Adoration: A Study in Pictorial Content* (Princeton: Princeton University Press, 1976).

———, *The Wealth of Michelangelo* (Rome: Grafica Editrice Romana, 2002).

———, *Finding Leonardo: The Case for Recovering the Battle of Anghiari* (Florence: The Florentine Press, 2008).

———, ed., *Sandro Botticelli and Herbert Horne: New Research* (Florence: Syracuse University in Florence, 2009).

Hegarty, Melinda, "Laurentian Patronage in the Palazzo Vecchio: The Frescoes of the Sala dei Gigli," *Art Bulletin* 78 (1996), 264–85.

Hegener, Nicole, *Divi Iacobi Eqves: Selbstdarstellung im Werk des Florentiner Bildhauers Baccio Bandinelli* (Munich-Berlin: Deutscher Kunstverlag, 2008).

Heikamp, Detlef, "Baccio Bandinelli nel Duomo di Firenze," *Paragone* 15, no. 169 (1964), 32–42.

———, "Ammannati's Fountain for the *Sala Grande* of the Palazzo Vecchio in Florence," *Fons sapientiae: Renaissance Garden Fountains,* ed. Elizabeth B. MacDougall, 117–73. Dumbarton Oaks Colloquium on the History of Landscape Architecture, 1977 (Washington, DC: Dumbarton Oaks, Trustees for Harvard University, 1980).

Henderson, John, *The Renaissance Hospital: Healing the Body and Healing the Soul* (New Haven: Yale University Press, 2006).

Hersey, George, *Pythagorean Palaces: Magic and Architecture in the Italian Renaissance* (Ithaca: Cornell University Press, 1976).

Heydenreich, Ludwig H., and Wolfgang Lotz, *Architecture in Italy, 1400 to 1600,* trans. Mary Hottinger (Harmondsworth: Penguin, 1974).

Hibbard, Howard, *Michelangelo* (New York: Harper & Row, 1974).

Hochmann, Michel, Julian Kliemann, Jérémie Koering, and Philippe Morel, eds., *Programme et invention dans l'art de la Renaissance* (Paris: Somogy, Academie de France à Rome, 2008).

Hollingsworth, Mary, *Patronage in Renaissance Italy from 1400 to the Early Sixteenth Century* (Baltimore: Johns Hopkins University Press, 1994).

———, *Patronage in Sixteenth-Century Italy* (London: John Murray, 1996).

Holmes, Megan, *Fra Filippo Lippi: The Carmelite Painter* (New Haven: Yale University Press, 1999).

Hood, William, *Fra Angelico at San Marco* (New Haven: Yale University Press, 1993).

Hornik, Heidi J., *Michele Tosini and the Ghirlandaio Workshop in Cinquecento Florence* (Eastbourne: Sussex Academic Press, 2008).

Horster, Marita, *Andrea del Castagno* (Ithaca: Cornell University Press, 1980).

Hudson, Hugh, *Paolo Uccello: Artist of the Florentine Renaissance Republic* (Saarbrücken: Müller, 2008).

Hughes, Diane Owen, "Representing the Family: Portraits and Purposes in Early Modern Italy," *Journal of Interdisciplinary History* 17 (1986), 7–38.

Hughes, Graham, *Renaissance Cassoni, Masterpieces of Early Italian Art: Painted Marriage Chests, 1400–1550* (London: Art Books International, 1997).

Humfrey, Peter, and Martin Kemp, eds., *The Altarpiece in the Renaissance* (New York: Cambridge University Press, 1991).

Hunt, Alan, *Governance of the Consuming Passions: A History of Sumptuary Law* (New York: St. Martin's Press, 1996).

Hyman, Isabelle, *Fifteenth-Century Florentine Studies: The Palazzo Medici and a Ledger for the Church of San Lorenzo* (Ann Arbor: UMI, 1977).

Jacks, Philip, ed., *Vasari's Florence: Artists and Literati at the Medicean Court* (Cambridge: Cambridge University Press, 1998).

Jacobs, Fredrika H., *Defining the Renaissance Virtuosa: Women Artists and the Language of Art History and Criticism* (Cambridge: Cambridge University Press, 1997).

———, *The Living Image in Renaissance Art* (Cambridge: Cambridge University Press, 2005).

Janson, H. W., *The Sculpture of Donatello* (Princeton: Princeton University Press, 1963; repr. 1979).

Jarzombek, Mark, *On Leon Baptista Alberti: His Literary and Aesthetic Theories* (Cambridge, MA: MIT Press, 1989).

Jenkins, A. D. Fraser, "Cosimo de' Medici's Patronage of Architecture and the Theory of Magnificence," *Journal of the Warburg and Courtauld Institutes* 33 (1970), 162–70.

Joannides, Paul, *The Drawings of Raphael with a Complete Catalogue* (Berkeley: University of California Press, 1983).

———, *Masaccio and Masolino: A Complete Catalogue* (London: Phaidon, 1993).

———, *The Drawings of Michelangelo and His Followers in the Ashmolean Museum* (Cambridge: Cambridge University Press, 2006).

Johannsen, Birgitte B., and Marianne Marcussen, "A Critical Survey of the Theoretical and Practical Origins of Renaissance Linear Perspective," *Acta ad archaeologiam et atrium historiam pertinentia,* ser. 8, 1 (1981), 191–227.

Johnson, Geraldine A, and Sara F. Matthews-Grieco, eds., *Picturing Women in Renaissance and Baroque Italy* (Cambridge: Cambridge University Press, 1997).

Jones, Lars R., and Louisa C. Matthew, eds., *Coming About . . . : A Festschrift for John Shearman* (Cambridge, MA: Harvard University Art Museums, 2002).

Jones, Roger, and Nicholas Penny, *Raphael* (New Haven: Yale University Press, 1983).
Jungmann, J. A., *The Mass of the Roman Rite: Its Origins and Development,* 2 vols., trans. Francis A. Brunner (New York: Benziger, 1951–52).
Kanerva, Lisa, *Defining the Architect in Fifteenth-Century Italy: Exemplary Architects in L. B. Alberti's* De re aedificatoria (Helsinki: Suomalainen Tiedeakatemia, 1998).
———, *Between Science and Drawings: Renaissance Architects on Vitruvius's Educational Ideas* (Helsinki: Finnish Academy of Science and Letters, 2006).
Katz, Dana E., *The Jew in the Art of the Italian Renaissance* (Philadelphia: University of Pennsylvania Press, 2008).
Kemp, Martin, *Leonardo da Vinci: The Marvellous Works of Nature and Man* (London: Dent, 1981; rev. ed., 1988).
———, *The Science of Art: Optical Themes in Western Art from Brunelleschi to Seurat* (New Haven: Yale University Press, 1992).
——— and M. Walker, eds., *Leonardo on Painting: An Anthology of Writings by Leonardo da Vinci with a Selection of Documents Relating to His Career as an Artist* (New Haven: Yale University Press, 1989).
Kempers, Bram, *Painting, Power and Patronage: The Rise of the Professional Artist in the Italian Renaissance* (London: Penguin, 1992).
Kennedy, Ruth Wedgwood, *Alesso Baldovinetti: A Critical and Historical Study* (New Haven: Yale University Press, 1938).
Kent, Dale, *Cosimo de' Medici and the Florentine Renaissance: The Patron's Oeuvre* (New Haven: Yale University Press, 2000).
Kent, Francis William, "'Più superba di quella de Lorenzo': Courtly and Family Interest in the Building of Filippo Strozzi's Palace," *Renaissance Quarterly* 30 (1977), 311–23.
———, "Palaces, Politics and Society in Fifteenth-Century Florence," *I Tatti Studies* 2 (1987), 41–70.
———, *Lorenzo de' Medici and the Art of Magnificence* (Baltimore: Johns Hopkins University Press, 2004).
———, Alessandro Perosa, Brenda Preyer, et al., *Giovanni Rucellai ed il suo Zibaldone,* vol. 2: *A Florentine Patrician and His Palace* (London: Warburg Institute, 1981).
———, Patricia Simons, and J. C. Eade, eds., *Patronage, Art and Society in Renaissance Italy* (Oxford: Clarendon Press, 1987).
Kiene, Michael, *Bartolomeo Ammannati* (Milan: Electa, 1995).
King, Catherine E., *Representing Renaissance Art, c. 1500–c. 1600* (Manchester: Manchester University Press, 2007).
King, Margaret L., *Women of the Renaissance* (Chicago: University of Chicago Press, 1991).
Klapisch-Zuber, Christiane, *Women, Family, and Ritual in Renaissance Italy,* trans. Lydia Cochrane (Chicago: University of Chicago Press, 1985).
Klein, Robert, and Henri Zerner, *Italian Art, 1500–1600: Sources and Documents in the History of Art* (Englewood Cliffs, NJ: Prentice Hall, 1966).
Kliemann, Julian, *Gesta dipinte: La grande decorazione nelle dimore italiane dal Quattrocento al Seicento* (Milan: Silvana, 1993).
——— and Michael Rohlmann, *Italian Frescoes: High Renaissance and Mannerism, 1510–1600* (New York: Abbeville Press, 2004).
Koch, Linda A., "The Early Christian Revival at S. Miniato al Monte: The Cardinal of Portugal Chapel," *Art Bulletin* 78 (1996), 527–55.
Kohl, Jeanette, and Rebecca Miller, eds., *Kopf Bild: Die Büste in Mittelalter und Früher Neuzeit* (Munich-Berlin: Deutscher Kunstverlag, 2007).
Kostof, Spiro, ed., *The Architect: Chapters in the History of the Profession* (Oxford: Oxford Universtiy Press, 1977).
Krautheimer, Richard, and Trude Krautheimer-Hess, *Lorenzo Ghiberti* (Princeton: Princeton University Press, 1956; rev. ed. 1982).
Kraye, Jill, ed., *The Cambridge Companion to Renaissance Humanism* (New York: Cambridge University Press, 1996).
Kris, Ernst, and Otto Kurz, *Legend, Myth, and Magic in the Image of the Artist,* trans. Alastair Laing and Lottie M. Newman (New Haven: Yale University Press, 1979).
Kuhn, Jehane R., "Measured Appearances: Documentation and Design in Early Perspective Drawing," *Journal of the Warburg and Courtauld Institutes* 53 (1990), 114–32.
Kusch-Arnhold, Britta, *Pierino da Vinci* (Münster: Rhema, 2008).
Ladis, Andrew, *Victims and Villains in Vasari's Lives* (Chapel Hill: University of North Carolina Press, 2008).
———, Carolyn Wood, and William U. Eiland, eds., *Craft of Art: Originality and Industry in the Italian Renaissance and Baroque Workshop* (Athens: University of Georgia Press, 1995).
Lahanier, Christian, ed., *La Joconde: Essai scientifique* (Paris: Codex Images International, 2007).
Land, Norman E., *The Viewer as Poet: The Renaissance Response to Art* (University Park: Pennsylvania State University Press, 1994).
Landau, David, and Peter Parshall, *The Renaissance Print, 1470–1550* (New Haven: Yale University Press, 1994).
Landini, Roberta Orsi, *Moda a Firenze, 1540–1580: Lo stile di Eleonora di Toledo e la sua influenza* (Florence: Pagliai Polistampa, 2005).
Landucci, Luca, *A Florentine Diary from 1450 to 1516* (New York: Arno Press, 1969).
Langdon, Gabrielle, *Medici Women: Portraits of Power, Love, and Betrayal from the Court of Duke Cosimo I* (Toronto: University of Toronto Press, 2006).
Langedijk, Karla, "Baccio Bandinelli's *Orpheus*: A Political Message," *Mitteilungen des Kunsthistorischen Institutes in Florenz* 20 (1976), 33–52.
———, *The Portraits of the Medici: Fifteenth to Eighteenth Centuries,* 3 vols. (Florence: Studio per Edizioni Scelte, 1981–87).
Lavin, Irving, "On the Sources and Meaning of the Renaissance Portrait Bust," *Art Quarterly* 33 (1970), 207–26.

———, "The Sculptor's Last Will and Testament," *Allen Memorial Art Museum Bulletin* 35 (1977–78), 4–16.
———, *Past and Present: Essays on Historicism in Art from Donatello to Picasso* (Berkeley: University of California Press, 1993).
———, *Santa Maria del Fiore: Il Duomo di Firenze e la Vergine incinta,* trans. Silvia Panichi (Rome: Donzelli, 1999).
———, ed., *World Art: Themes of Unity in Diversity* (University Park: Pennsylvania State University Press, 1989).
Lavin, Marilyn Aronberg, *The Place of Narrative: Mural Decoration in Italian Churches, 431–1600* (Chicago: University of Chicago Press, 1990).
Lee, Rensselaer W., *Ut pictura poesis: The Humanist Theory of Painting* (New York: Norton, 1967).
Levy, Allison M., *Re-membering Masculinity in Early Modern Florence: Widowed Bodies, Mourning and Portraiture* (Aldershot: Ashgate, 2006).
Liebenwein, Wolfgang, *Studiolo: Storia e tipologia di uno spazio culturale,* trans. Alessandro Califano, ed. Claudia Cieri Via (Modena: Panini, 1988).
Lightbown, Ronald, *Sandro Botticelli,* 2 vols. (Berkeley: University of California Press, 1978).
———, *Donatello and Michelozzo: An Artistic Partnership and Its Patrons in the Early Renaissance* (London: Miller, 1980).
Lillie, Amanda, *Florentine Villas in the Fifteenth Century: An Architectural and Social History* (New York: Cambridge University Press, 2000).
Lindley, Phillip, and Thomas Frangenberg, *Secular Sculpture, 1300–1550* (Stamford, CT: Tyas, 2000).
Lindow, James R., *The Renaissance Palace in Florence: Magnificence and Splendor in Fifteenth-Century Italy* (Aldershot: Ashgate, 2007).
Looper, Matthew G., "Political Messages in the Medici Palace Garden," *Journal of Garden History* 12 (1992), 255–68.
Lotz, Wolfgang, *Studies in Italian Renaissance Architecture* (Cambridge, MA: MIT Press, 1981).
Luchinat, Christina Acidini, *Michelangelo pittore* (Milan: Motta, 2007).
——— et al., *Magnificenza alla corte dei Medici: Arte a Firenze alla fine del Cinquecento,* exh. cat., Palazzo Pitti, Museo degli Argenti, Florence (Milan: Electa, 1997).
——— et al., *The Medici, Michelangelo, and the Art of Late Renaissance Florence,* exh. cat., Art Institute of Chicago (New Haven: Yale University Press, 2002).
———, ed. *Benozzi Gozzoli: La Cappella dei Magi* (Milan: Electa, 1993).
———, ed., *Renaissance Florence: The Age of Lorenzo de'Medici,* exh. cat., Accademia Italiana, London (Florence: Charta, 1993).
———, ed., *Giardini Medicei: Giardini di palazzo e di villa nella Firenze del Quattrocento* (Milan: Motta, 1996).
——— and Rosanna Caterina Proto Pisani, eds. *La tradizione fiorentina dei Cenacoli* (Florence: Cassa di Risparmio di Firenze, 1997).
Lytle, Guy Fitch, and Stephen Orgel, eds., *Patronage in the Renaissance* (Princeton: Princeton University Press, 1981).
Mallett, Michael, and Nicholas Mann, eds., *Lorenzo the Magnificent: Culture and Politics* (London: Warburg Institute, 1996).
Manetti, Antonio di Tuccio, *The Life of Filippo Brunelleschi,* ed. Howard Saalman, trans. Catherine Enggass (University Park: University of Pennsylvania Press, 1970).
Maniura, Robert, Gabriele Neher, and Rupert Shepherd, eds., *Italian Art of the Fifteenth Century* (Malden: Blackwell, 2008).
Mann, Nicholas, and Luke Syson, eds., *The Image of the Individual: Portraits in the Renaissance* (London: British Museum Press, 1998).
Marani, Pietro, Francoise Viatte, and Varena Forcione, *L'opera grafica e la fortuna critica di Leonardo da Vinci,* Atti del Convegno internazionale, Parigi, Musée du Louvre, 16–17 maggio 2003 (Florence: Giunti, 2006).
Marchand, Eckart, and Alison Wright, *With and without the Medici: Studies in Tuscan Art and Patronage, 1434–1530* (Aldershot: Ashgate, 1998).
Marino, Eugenio, *La Trinità di Masaccio: Saggio storico ed interpretative degli schemi stilistici, iconografici ed iconoteologici* (Florence: Nerbini, 2008).
Massey, Lyle, *The Treatise on Perspective: Published and Unpublished,* Studies in the History of Art 59 (Washington, DC: National Gallery of Art, Center for Advanced Study in the Visual Arts, 2003).
McGee, Timothy J., *The Ceremonial Musicians of Late Medieval Florence* (Bloomington: Indiana University Press, 2009).
McHam, Sarah Blake, "Donatello's Bronze *David* and *Judith* as Metaphors of Medici Rule in Florence," *Art Bulletin* 83 (2001), 32–47.
———, ed., *Looking at Italian Renaissance Sculpture* (New York: Cambridge University Press, 1998).
Medici, Lorenzo de', *Lorenzo de' Medici: Selected Poems and Prose,* eds. and trans. Jon Thieme et al. (University Park: Pennsylvania State University Press, 1991).
Medri, Litta Maria, *Il Mito di Lorenzo il Magnifico nelle decorazioni della villa di Poggio a Caiano* (Florence: Medicea, 1992).
———, ed., *Il giardino di Boboli* (Milan: Silvana, 2003).
Meijer, Bert W., ed., *Firenze e gli antichi Paesi Bassi, 1430–1530. Dialoghi tra artisti: Da Jan van Eyck a Ghirlandaio, da Memling a Raffaello,* exh. cat., Palazzo Pitti, Florence (Livorno: Sillabe, 2008).
Meller, Peter, "Physiognomical Theory in Renaissance Heroic Portraits," *Renaissance and Mannerism: Studies in Western Art,* Acts of the Twentieth International Congress of the History of Art, vol. 2, 53–69 (Princeton: Princeton University Press, 1963).
Meltzoff, Stanley, *Botticelli, Signorelli and Savonarola: Theologia Poetica and Painting from Boccaccio to Poliziano* (Florence: Olschki, 1987).
Mendelsohn, Leatrice, *Paragone: Benedetto Varchi's Due*

Lezzioni and Cinquecento Art Theory (Ann Arbor: UMI Research Press, 1982).
Meyer zur Capellen, Jürg, *Raphael: The Paintings,* vol. 1, *The Beginning in Umbria and Florence, ca. 1500–1508,* trans. Stefan B. Polter (Würzburg: Arcos, 2001).
Millon, Henry A., and Craig Hugh Smyth, *Michelangelo Architect: The Façade of S. Lorenzo and the Cupola of St. Peter's,* exh. cat., National Gallery of Art, Washington, DC (Milan: Olivetti, 1988).
——— and Linda Nochlin, eds., *Art and Architecture in the Service of Politics* (Cambridge, MA: MIT Press, 1978).
——— and Vittorio Magnago Lampugnani, eds., *Renaissance from Brunelleschi to Michelangelo: The Representation of Architecture,* exh. cat., Palazzo Grassi, Venice (London: Thames & Hudson, 1994).
Minor, Andrew C., and Bonner Mitchell, *A Renaissance Entertainment: Festivities for the Marriage of Cosimo I, Duke of Florence, in 1539* (Columbia: University of Missouri Press, 1968).
Mitrovic, Branko, *Serene Greed of the Eye: Leon Battista Alberti and the Philosophical Foundations of Renaissance Architectural Theory* (Munich: Deutscher Kunstverlag, 2005).
Moffitt, John F., *Painterly Perspective and Piety: Religious Uses of the Vanishing Point from the 15th to the 18th Century* (Jefferson, NC: McFarland, 2008).
Molho, Anthony, "The Brancacci Chapel: Studies in Its Iconography and History," *Journal of the Warburg and Courtauld Institutes* 40 (1977), 50–98.
Monfasani, John, and Ronald G. Musto, eds., *Renaissance Society and Culture: Essays in Honor of Eugene F. Rice, Jr.* (New York: Ithaca Press, 1991).
Morel, Philippe, *Les grotesques: Les figures de l'imaginaire dans la peinture italienne de la fin de la Renaissance* (Paris: Flammarion, 1997).
Morolli, Gabriele, *Leon Battista Alberti, Florence and Tuscany: Itineraries through Architecture and Ideas* (Florence: Maschietto, 2006).
———, *Michelangelo e la facciata di San Lorenzo: Dai progetti alla realtà virtuale, le colonne ritrovate* (Florence: Maschietto, 2007).
———, ed., *Michelozzo: Scultore e architetto (1396–1472): Atti del Convegno Internazionale Michelozzo. Scultore e Architetto nel suo tempo (1396–1472)* (Florence: Centro Di, 1996).
———, Cristina Acidini Luchinat, and Luciano Marchetti, eds., *L'Architettura di Lorenzo il Magnifico,* exh. cat., Spedale degli Innocenti, Florence (Milan: Silvana, 1992).
——— and P. Ruschi, eds., *San Lorenzo, 393–1993, l'architettura: Le vicende dalla fabbrica* (Florence: Alinea, 1993).
Morrogh, Andrew, Fiorella Superbi Gioffredi, Piero Morsella, and Eve Borsook, eds., *Renaissance Studies in Honor of Craig Hugh Smyth,* 2 vols. (Florence: Giunti, 1985).
Mortari, Luisa, *Francesco Salviati* (Rome: De Luca, 1992).
Motture, Peta, ed., *Large Bronzes in the Renaissance,* Studies in the History of Art 64 (Washington, DC: National Gallery of Art, Center for Advanced Study in the Visual Arts, 2003).
Mozzati, Tommaso, *Giovanfrancesco Rustici: Le Compagnie del Paiuolo e della Cazzuola. Arte, letterature, festa nell'età della maniera* (Florence: Olschki, 2008).
Muccini, Ugo, *The Salone del Cinquecento of Palazzo Vecchio* (Florence: Le Lettere, 1990).
———, *The Apartment of the Priori in Palazzo Vecchio* (Florence: Le Lettere, 1992).
——— and Alessandro Cecchi, *The Apartment of Cosimo in Palazzo Vecchio* (Florence: Le Lettere, 1991).
Murray, Alexander, *Doubting Thomas in Medieval Exegesis and Art* (Rome: Unione internazionale degli istituti di archeologia, storia e storia dell'arte in Roma, 2006).
Musacchio, Jacqueline Marie, *The Art and Ritual of Childbirth in Renaissance Italy* (New Haven: Yale University Press, 1999).
———, *Art, Marriage, and Family in the Florentine Renaissance Palace* (New Haven: Yale University Press, 2008).
Nagel, Alexander, *Michelangelo and the Reform of Art* (New York: Cambridge University Press, 2000).
Natali, Antonio, *Andrea del Sarto: Maestro della "maniera moderna"* (Milan: Leonardo arte, 1998).
———, *Lo squardo degli angeli: Verrocchio, Leonardo e il "Battesimo di Cristo"* (Milan: Silvana, 1998).
———, *Annunciazione di Leonardo: La Montagna sul mare* (Milan: Silvana, 2000).
———, *Rosso Fiorentino: Leggiadra maniera e terribilità di cose stravaganti* (Milan: Silvana, 2006).
———, ed., *L'onestà dell'invenzione: Pittura della riforma cattolica agli Uffizi* (Milan: Silvana, 1999).
Neher, Gabriele, and Rupert Shepherd, eds., *Revaluing Renaissance Art* (Brookfield, VT: Ashgate, 2000).
Nelson, Jonathan K., "The High Altarpiece of SS. Annunziata in Florence: History, Form and Function," *Burlington Magazine* 139 (1997), 84–91.
———, *Leonardo e la reinvenzione della figura femminile: Leda, Lisa e Maria,* Lettura Vinciana 46 (Città di Vinci: Giunti, 2006).
———, ed., *Plautilla Nelli, 1523–1588: The Prioress Painter of Renaissance Florence,* The Villa Rossa Series 4 (Florence: Syracuse University in Florence, 2008).
——— and Patrizia Zambrano, *Filippino Lippi* (Milan: Electa, 2003).
——— and Richard J. Zeckhauser, eds., *The Patron's Payoff: Conspicuous Commissions in Italian Renaissance Art* (Princeton: Princeton University Press, 2008).
Nova, Alessandro, and Anna Schreurs, eds., *Benvenuto Cellini: Kunst und Kunsttheorie im 16. Jahrhundert* (Cologne: Böhlau Verlag, 2003).
Nuttall, Paula, *From Flanders to Florence: The Impact of Netherlandish Painting, 1400–1500* (New Haven: Yale University Press, 2004).
Oberhuber, Konrad, *Raphael: The Paintings* (Munich: Prestel, 1999).

Ohlig, Stefanie Felicitas, *Florentiner Refektorien: Form, Funktion und die Programme ihrer Fresken* (Egelsbach: Hänsel-Hohenhausen, 2000).
Olsen, Christina, "Gross Expenditure: Botticelli's *Nastagio degli Onesti* Panels," *Art History* 15 (1992), 146–70.
Olson, Roberta J. M., *The Florentine Tondo* (Oxford: Oxford University Press, 2000).
O'Malley, Michelle, *The Business of Art: Contracts and the Commissioning Process in Renaissance Italy* (New Haven: Yale University Press, 2005).
Onians, John, "Alberti and Filarete: A Study in Their Sources," *Journal of the Warburg and Courtauld Institutes* 34 (1971), 96–114.
———, *Bearers of Meaning: The Classical Orders in Antiquity, the Middle Ages and the Renaissance* (Princeton: Princeton University Press, 1988).
———, ed., *Sight and Insight: Essays on Art and Culture in Honour of E. H. Gombrich at 85* (London: Phaidon, 1994).
Paatz, Walter, and Elizabeth Paatz, *Die Kirchen von Florenz,* 6 vols. (Frankfurt am Main: Klostermann, 1940–54).
Padovani, Serena, ed., *Età di Savonarola: Fra Bartolomeo e la Scuola di San Marco,* exh. cat., Palazzo Pitti and Museo di S. Marco, Florence (Florence: Marsilio, 1996).
——— and Bert W. Meijer, *Firenze e gli antichi Paesi Bassi, 1430–1530, tra Jan van Eyck e Raffaello* (Livorno: Sillabe, 2008).
Panizza, Letizia, ed., *Women in the Italian Renaissance Culture and Society* (Oxford: European Humanities Research Centre, 2000).
Panofsky, Erwin, *Tomb Sculpture: Four Lectures on Its Changing Aspects from Ancient Egypt to Bernini* (New York: Abrams, 1964).
———, *Idea: A Concept in Art Theory,* trans. Joseph J. S. Peake (Columbia: University of South Carolina Press, 1968).
———, *Renaissance and Renascences in Western Art* (New York: Harper & Row, 1972).
———, *Studies in Iconology: Humanistic Themes in the Art of the Renaissance* (New York: Harper & Row, 1972).
———, *Meaning in the Visual Arts* (Chicago: University of Chicago Press, 1982).
———, *Perspective as Symbolic Form,* trans. Christopher Wood (New York: Zone Books, 1991).
Paoletti, John T., "Donatello's Bronze Doors for the Old Sacristy of San Lorenzo," *Artibus et historiae* 21 (1990), 39–69.
Paolucci, Antonio, et al., *The Statues of the Loggia della Signoria in Florence: Masterpieces Restored* (Florence: Giunti, 2002).
Parker, Deborah, *Bronzino: Renaissance Painter as Poet* (New York: Cambridge University Press, 2000).
Partridge, Loren, "Art," in *A Companion to the Worlds of the Renaissance,* ed. Guido Ruggiero, 349–65. (Oxford: Blackwell, 2002).
Pecchioli, Eleonora, *The Painted Facades of Florence: From the Fifteenth to the Twentieth Century* (Florence: Centro Di, 2005).
Pedretti, Carlo, *Leonardo da Vinci: The Battle of Anghiari and the Fanciful Weapons* (Florence: Giunti, 2000).
——— and Margherita Melani, *Leonardo: The European Genius, Paintings and Drawings* (Foligno: Cartei & Bianchi, 2007).
Peterson, David S., and Daniel E. Bornstein, eds., *Florence and Beyond: Culture, Society and Politics in Renaissance Italy: Essays in Honour of John M. Najemy* (Toronto: Centre for Reformation and Renaissance Studies, 2008).
Pevsner, Niklaus, *Academies of Art: Past and Present* (New York: Macmillan, 1940).
Pieri, Elisabetta, and Luigi Zangheri, eds., *Niccolò detto il Tribolo tra arte, architettura e paessagio,* Atti del Convegno di Studi per il Centenario della Nasciata, Poggio a Caiano, 10–11 novembre 2000 (Signa: Nova, 2001).
Pilliod, Elizabeth, *Pontormo, Bronzino, and Allori: A Genealogy of Florentine Art* (New Haven: Yale University Press, 2001).
Pinelli, Antonio, *La bellezza impura: Arte e politica nell'Italia del Rinascimento* (Rome: Laterza, 2004).
Plakolm-Forsthuber, Sabine, *Florentiner Frauenklöster: Von der Renaissance bis zur Gegenreformation* (Petersberg: Imhof, 2008).
Poeschke, Joachim, *Michelangelo and His World: Sculpture of the Italian Renaissance,* trans. Russell Stockman (New York: Abrams, 1992).
———, *Donatello and His World: Italian Renaissance Sculpture,* trans. Russell Stockman (New York: Abrams, 1993).
——— and Candida Syndikus, eds., *Leon Battista Alberti: Humanist—Architeckt—Kunsttheoretiker* (Münster: Rhema, 2007).
Poletti, Federico, *Antonio e Piero Pollaiuolo* (Florence: Silvana, 2001).
Poliziano, Angelo, *The Stanze of Angelo Poliziano,* trans. David Quint (University Park: Pennsylvania State University Press, 1993).
Pope-Hennessy, John, *The Portrait in the Renaissance,* Bollingen Series 35, A. W. Mellon Lectures in the Fine Arts 12 (New York: Pantheon, 1966).
———, *Essays on Italian Sculpture* (London: Phaidon, 1968).
———, *Italian Renaissance Sculpture* (London: Phaidon, 1970; repr. New York: Vintage, 1985).
———, *Italian High Renaissance and Baroque Sculpture* (London: Phaidon, 1970: repr. New York: Vintage; 1985).
———, *Luca della Robbia* (Ithaca: Cornell University Press, 1980).
———, *The Study and Criticism of Italian Sculpture* (New York: Metropolitan Museum of Art, 1980).
———, *Cellini* (New York: Abbeville Press, 1985).
———, *Donatello: Sculptor* (New York: Abbeville Press, 1993).
——— and Keith Christiansen, "Secular Painting in 15th-Century Tuscany: Birth Trays, Cassone Panels, and Portraits," *Bulletin of the Metropolitan Museum of Art* 38 (1980), 4–64.

——— and Ronald Lightbown, *Catalogue of Italian Sculpture in the Victoria and Albert Museum,* 2 vols. (London: Her Majesty's Stationery Office, 1964).
Popham, A. E., *The Drawings of Leonardo da Vinci* (New York: Reynal & Hitchcock, 1945).
Prager, Frank D., and Gustina Scaglia, *Brunelleschi: Studies of his Technology and Inventions* (Cambridge, MA: MIT Press, 1970).
Preyer, Brenda, "Planning for Visitors at Florentine Palaces," *Renaissance Studies* 12 (1998), 357–74.
Radke, Gary M., *The Gates of Paradise: Lorenzo Ghiberti's Renaissance Masterpiece,* exh. cat., High Museum of Art, Atlanta (New Haven: Yale University Press in asssociation with the Opera di S. Maria del Fiore, Florence, 2007).
——— et al., *Verrocchio's David Restored: A Renaissance Bronze from the National Museum of the Bargello, Florence,* exh. cat., High Museum of Art, Atlanta (Prato: Giunti, 2003).
——— et al., *Leonardo da Vinci and the Art of Sculpture,* exh. cat. High Museum of Art, Atlanta (New Haven: Yale University Press, 2009).
Ragionieri, Pina, *Michelangelo: The Man and the Myth* (Philadelphia: University of Pennsylvania Press, 2008).
Ramsden, E. H., ed., *The Letters of Michelangelo,* 2 vols. (London: Owen, 1963).
Randolph, Adrian W. B., "Performing the Bridal Body in Fifteenth-Century Florence," *Art History* 21 (1998), 182–200.
———, *Engaging Symbols: Gender, Politics, and Public Art in Fifteenth-Century Florence* (New Haven: Yale University Press, 2002).
———, "Gendering the Period Eye: *Deschi da Parto* and Renaissance Viusal Culture," *Art History* 27 (2004), 538–62.
Réau, Louis, *Iconographie de l'art chrétien,* 3 vols. in 6 (Paris: Presses Universitaires de France, 1955–59).
Rebecchini, Guido, *Le ville dei Medici da Firenze a Roma* (Rome: Istituto Poligrafico e Zecca dello Stato, 2008).
Reiss, Sheryl E., and David G. Wilkins, eds., *Beyond Isabella: Secular Women Patrons of Art in Renaissance Italy* (Kirksville, MO: Truman State University Press, 2001).
Rice, Eugene F., Jr., "St. Jerome's *Vision of the Trinity:* An Iconographical Note," *Burlington Magazine* 125 (1983), 151–55.
———, *Saint Jerome in the Renaissance* (Baltimore: John Hopkins University Press, 1985).
Richelson, Paul William, *Studies in the Personal Imagery of Cosimo I de' Medici, Duke of Florence* (New York: Garland, 1978).
Richter, Jean Paul, with commentary by Carlo Pedretti, *The Literary Works of Leonardo da Vinci,* 2 vols. (Berkeley: University of California Press, 1977).
Rizzo, Anna Padoa, *Benozzo Gozzoli: Un pittore insigne, "pratico di grandissima invenzione"* (Milan: Silvana, 2004).
Robertis, Teresa De, Giuliano Tanturli, and Stefano Zamponi, eds., *Coluccio Salutati e l'invenzione dell'umanesimo,* exh. cat., Biblioteca medicea Laurenziana (Florence: Mandragora, 2008).
Roccasecca, Pietro, *Paolo Uccello: Le Battaglie* (Milan: Electa, 1997).
Rocke, Michael J., *Forbidden Friendships: Homosexuality in Renaissance Florence* (New York: Oxford University Press, 1996).
Roettgen, Steffi, *Italian Frescoes: The Early Renaissance, 1400–1470,* trans. Russell Stockman (New York: Abbeville Press, 1996).
———, *Italian Frescoes: The Flowering of the Renaissance 1470–1510,* trans. Russell Stockman (New York: Abbeville Press, 1997).
Rogers, Mary, ed., *Fashioning Identities in Renaissance Art* (Aldershot: Ashgate, 2000).
Rosenauer, Autur, *Donatello* (Milan: Electa, 1993).
Rosenfeld, Myra N., ed., *Sebastiano Serlio on Domestic Architecture* (New York: Architectural History Foundation, 1978).
Rosenthal, Earl, "A Renaissance 'Copy' of the Holy Sepulcher," *Journal of the Society of Architectural Historians* 17 (1958), 2–11.
Rowe, Colin, and Leon Satkowski, *Italian Architecture of the Sixteenth Century* (New York: Princeton Architectural Press, 2002).
Roy, Ashok, and Marika Spring, eds., *Raphael's Painting Technique: Working Practices before Rome / La tecnica pittorica di Raffaello* (Florence: Nardini, 2007).
Rubin, Patricia Lee, *Giorgio Vasari: Art and History* (New Haven: Yale University Press, 1995).
———, *Images and Identity in Fifteenth-Century Florence* (New Haven: Yale University Press, 2007).
Rubinstein, Nicolai, *The Palazzo Vecchio, 1298–1532: Government, Architecture and Imagery in the Civic Palace of the Florentine Republic* (New York: Oxford University Press, 1995).
Ruda, Jeffery, *Fra Filippo Lippi: Life & Work with a Complete Catalogue* (London: Phaidon, 1993).
Ruschi, Pietro, ed., *Michelangelo architetto a San Lorenzo: Quattro problemi aperti,* exh. cat., Casa Buonarroti, Florence (Florence: Mandragora, 2007).
Ruvoldt, Maria, *The Italian Renaissance Imagery of Inspiration: Metaphors of Sex, Sleep, and Dreams* (Cambridge: Cambridge University Press, 2004).
Saalman, Howard, *Filippo Brunelleschi: The Cupola of Santa Maria del Fiore* (London: Zwemmer, 1980).
———, *Filippo Brunelleschi: The Buildings* (University Park: Pennsylvania State University Press, 1993).
Sale, J. Russell, *Filippino Lippi's Strozzi Chapel in Santa Maria Novella* (New York: Garland, 1979).
Sandström, Sven, *Levels of Unreality: Studies in Structure and Construction in Italian Mural Painting during the Renaissance* (Uppsala: Almquist and Wiksell, 1963).
Saslow, James M., *Ganymede in the Renaissance: Homosexuality in Art and Society* (New Haven: Yale University Press, 1986).

———, *The Medici Wedding of 1589: Florentine Festival as Theatrum Mundi* (New Haven: Yale University Press: 1996).
———, trans., *The Poetry of Michelangelo: An Annotated Translation* (New Haven: Yale University Press, 1991).
Satkowski, Leon, "The Palazzo Pitti: Planning and Use in the Grand-Ducal Era," *Journal of the Society of Architectural Historians* 42 (1983), 336–49.
———, *Giorgio Vasari: Architect and Courtier* (Princeton: Princeton University Press, 1993).
Satzinger, Georg, *Antonio da Sangallo der Ältere und die Madonna di San Biagio bei Montepulciano* (Tübingen: Wasmuth, 1991).
Scaillieriz, Cecile, *Leonard de Vinci: La Joconde,* exh. cat., Musée du Louvre, Paris (Paris: Musée du Louvre, 2003).
Schedler, Uta, *Filippo Brunelleschi: Synthese von Antike und Mittelalter in der Renaissance* (Petersberg: Imhof, 2004).
Schiapparelli, Attilio, *La casa fiorentina e i suoi arredi nei secoli XIV e XV* (Florence, 1908; repr. with tables, ed. Mina Gregori, Maria Sframeli and Laura Pagnotta, Florence: Le Lettere, 1983).
Schiller, Gertrud, *Iconography of Christian Art,* 2 vols., trans. Janet Seligman (Greenwich, CT: New York Graphic Society, 1972).
Schlosser, Julius von, *La letteratura artistica: Manuale dei fonti della storia dell'arte moderna,* trans. Filippo Rossi (Florence: Nuova Italia, 1964; repr. 1977).
Schmitt, Charles B., and Quentin Skinner, *The Cambridge History of Renaissance Philosophy* (Cambridge: Cambridge University Press, 1988).
Schubring, Paul, *Cassoni: Truhen and Truhenbilder der italienischen Frührenaissance* (Leipzig: Hiersemann, 1915, supp. 1923).
Schulz, Anne Markham, *The Sculpture of Bernardo Rossellino and His Workshop* (Princeton: Princeton University Press, 1977).
Schultz, Bernard, *Art and Anatomy in Renaissance Italy* (Ann Arbor: UMI Research Press, 1985).
Schuyler, Jane, *Florentine Busts: Sculpted Portraiture in the Fifteenth Century* (New York: Garland, 1976).
Sciolla, Gianni Carlo, *La scultura di Mino da Fiesole* (Turin: Giappichelli, 1970).
Sellink, M., and S. Janssens, *Stradanus (1523–1605), Court Artist of the Medici* (Turnhout: Brepols, 2008).
Senechal, Philippe, *Giovan Francesco Rustici, 1475–1554: Un sculpteur de la Renaissance entre Florence et Paris* (Paris: Arthena, 2008).
Settis, Salvatore, ed., *Memoria dell'antico nell'arte italiana,* 3 vols., Biblioteca di storia dell'arte (Turin: Einaudi, 1984–86).
Seymour, Charles, Jr., *Sculpture in Italy, 1400–1500* (Harmondsworth: Penguin, 1966).
———, *Michelangelo's David: A Search for Identity* (Pittsburgh: University of Pittsburgh Press, 1967).
Seznec, Jean, *The Survival of the Pagan Gods: The Mythological Tradition and Its Place in Renaissance Humanism and Art,* trans. Barbara F. Sessions (Princeton: Princeton University Press, 1972).
Sheard, Wendy Steadman, and John Paoletti, eds., *Collaboration in Italian Renaissance Art* (New Haven: Yale University Press, 1978).
Shearman, John, "Leonardo's Colour and Chiaroscuro," *Zeitschrift für Kunstgeschichte* 25 (1962), 13–47.
———, *Andrea del Sarto,* 2 vols. (Oxford: Oxford University Press, 1965).
———, *Mannerism* (Harmondsworth: Penguin, 1967).
———, *Pontormo's Altarpiece in S. Felicità* (Newcastle upon Tyne: University of Newcastle upon Tyne, 1971).
———, *"Only Connect . . .": Art and the Spectator in the Italian Renaissance,* A. W. Mellon Lectures in the Fine Arts, 1988, National Gallery Art, Washington, DC (Princeton: Princeton University Press, 1992).
———, *Raphael in Early Modern Sources (1483–1602),* 2 vols., ed. Julian Kliemann (New Haven: Yale University Press, 2003).
——— and Marcia B. Hall, eds., *Science in the Service of Art History: The Princeton Raphael Symposium* (Princeton: Princeton University Press, 1990).
Sheingorn, Pamela, and Kathleen Ashley, eds., *Interpreting Cultural Symbols: St. Anne in Late Medieval Society* (Athens: University of Georgia Press, 1990).
Shenfield, Larry, *How Much of the Florence Baptistery Is a Surviving Roman Building?: A Reevaluation of the Archaeological, Architectural and Artistic Evidence* (Oxford: British Archaeological Reports, 2008).
Sica, Graz Gobbi, *The Florentine Villa,* Architecture History Society: The Classical Tradition in Architecture (London: Routledge, 2007).
Smith, Christine, *Architecture in the Culture of Early Humanism: Ethics, Aesthetics and Eloquence, 1400–1470* (New York: Oxford University Press, 1992).
——— and Joseph F. O'Connor, *Building the Kingdom: Giannozzo Manetti on the Material and Spiritual Edifice,* Arizona Studies in the Middle Ages and the Renaissance 20; Medieval and Renaissance Texts and Studies 317 (Tempe: Arizona Center for Medieval and Renaissance Studies, 2006).
Smith, Webster, "On the Original Location of the *Primavera,*" *Art Bulletin* 57 (1975), 31–40.
Smyth, Craig Hugh, *Mannerism and Maniera* (Locust Valley, NY: Augustin, 1963).
———, *Bronzino as Draughtsman: An Introduction with Notes on His Portraiture and Tapestries* (Locust Valley, NY: Augustin, 1971).
Sohm, Philip, *Style in the Art Theory of Early Modern Italy* (Cambridge: Cambridge University Press, 2001).
———, *The Artist Grows Old: The Aging of Art and Artists in Italy, 1500–1800* (New Haven: Yale University Press, 2007).
Solum, Stefanie, "Attributing Influence: The Problem of Female Patronage in Fifteenth-Century Florence," *Art Bulletin* 90 (2008), 76–100.
Spagnesi, Gianfranco, ed., *Antonio da Sangallo il Giovane: La vita e l'opera* (Rome: Centro di studi per la storia dell'architettura, 1986).

Spallanzani, Marco, *Oriental Rugs in Renaissance Florence* (Florence: SPES, 2007).
Spencer, John, *Andrea del Castagno and His Patrons* (Durham, NC: Duke University Press, 1991).
Spike, John T., *Masaccio* (New York: Abbeville Press, 1995).
———, *Fra Angelico* (New York: Abbeville Press, 1996).
Spini, Giorgio, "Politicità di Michelangelo," *Rivista storica italiana* 76 (1964), 557–600.
———, ed., *Architettura e politica da Cosimo I a Ferdinando I* (Florence: Olschki, 1976).
Starn, Randolph, and Loren Partridge, "Representing War in the Renaissance: The Shield of Paolo Uccello," *Representations* 5 (1984), 32–65.
———, *Arts of Power: Three Halls of State in Italy, 1300–1600* (Berkeley: University of California Press, 1992).
Stefaniak, Regina, *Mysterium Magnum: Michelangelo's Tondo Doni* (Leiden: Brill, 2008).
Stegmann, Carl von, and Heinrich von Geymüller, *Die Architektur der Renaissance in Toscana,* 11 vols. (Munich: Bruckmann, 1885–1908).
Steinberg, Leo, "Michelangelo's Florentine Pietà: The Missing Leg," *Art Bulletin* 50 (1968), 343–59.
———, "The Metaphors of Love and Birth in Michelangelo's Pietàs," in *Studies in Erotic Art,* ed. Theodore Bowie and Cornelia Christenson, 231–85 (New York: Basic Books, 1970).
———, "Pontormo's Capponi Chapel," *Art Bulletin* 56 (1974), 385–99.
———, *The Sexuality of Christ in Renaissance Art and in Modern Oblivion,* 2nd ed. (Chicago: Chicago University Press, 1996).
Steinberg, Ronald, *Fra Girolamo Savonarola: Florentine Art and Renaissance Historiography* (Athens: Ohio University Press, 1977).
Stimato, Gerarda, *Autoritratti letterari nella Firenze di Cosimo I: Bandinelli, Vasari, Cellini e Pontormo* (Bologna: Bononia University Press, 2008).
Strehlke, Carl Brandon, et al., *Pontomo, Bronzino, and the Medici: The Transformation of the Renaissance Portrait in Florence,* exh. cat., Philadelphia Museum of Art (University Park: Pennsylvania State University Press, 2004).
Strocchia, Sharon T., *Death and Ritual in Renaissance Florence* (Baltimore: Johns Hopkins University Press, 1992).
Strozzi, Beatrice Paolozzi, *Donatello: Il David restaurato,* exh. cat., Museo nazionale del Bargello, Florence (Florence: Giunti, 2008).
Summers, David, "*Maniera* and Movement: The *Figura Serpentinata,*" *Art Quarterly* 35 (1972), 264–301.
———, "Contrapposto: Style and Meaning in Renaissance Art," *Art Bulletin* 59 (1977), 336–61.
———, *The Sculpture of Vincenzio Danti: A Study in the Influence of Michelangelo and the Ideals of the Maniera* (New York: Garland, 1979).
———, *Michelangelo and the Language of Art* (Princeton: Princeton University Press, 1981).
———, *The Judgment of Sense: Renaissance Naturalism and the Rise of Aesthetics* (Cambridge: Cambridge University Press, 1987).
———, *Vision, Reflection, and Desire in Western Painting* (Chapel Hill: University of North Carolina Press, 2007).
Summerson, John, *The Classical Language of Architecture* (London: BBC, 1963; reprinted many times by Cambridge, MA: MIT Press).
Syson, Luke, and Dora Thornton, *Objects of Virtue: Art in Renaissance Italy* (London: British Museum Press, 2001).
Tafuri, Manfredo, *L'architettura dell'umanesimo* (Bari: Laterza, 1969).
———, *Ricerca del Rinascimento: I principi, città, architetti* (Turin: Einaudi, 1992).
Talvacchia, Bette, *Taking Positions: On the Erotic in Renaissance Culture* (Princeton: Princeton University Press, 1999).
Tavernor, Robert, *On Alberti and the Art of Building* (New Haven: Yale University Press, 1998).
Tempesti, Anna Forlani, and Elena Capretti, *Piero di Cosimo: Catalogo completo* (Florence: Otavo, 1996).
Tervarent, Guy de, *Attributs et symbols dans l'art profane, 1450–1600: Dictionnaire d'un language perdu* (Geneva: Droz, 1958).
Tetel, Marcel, Ronald G. Witt, and Rona Goffen, eds., *Life and Death in Fifteenth-Century Florence* (Durham, NC: Duke University Press, 1989).
Thiem, Gunther, and Christel Thiem, *Toskanische Fassaden-Dekoration in Sgraffito und Fresco: 14 bis 17. Jahrhundert* (Munich: Bruckmann, 1964).
Thomas, Anabel, *The Painter's Practice in Renaissance Tuscany* (New York: Cambridge University Press, 1995).
Thomson, David, *Renaissance Architecture: Critics, Patrons, Luxury* (Manchester: Manchester University Press, 1993).
Thornton, Dora, *The Scholar in His Study: Ownership and Experience in Renaissance Italy* (New Haven: Yale University Press, 1997).
——— and Timothy Wilson, *Italian Renaissance Ceramics: A Catalogue of the British Museum Collection,* 2 vols. (London: British Museum Press, 2009).
Thornton, Peter, *The Italian Renaissance Interior, 1400–1600* (New York: Abrams, 1991).
———, *Form and Decoration: Innovation in the Decorative Arts, 1470–1870* (London: Weidenfeld & Nicolson, 1998).
Thunø, Erik, and Gerhard Wolf, eds., *The Miraculous Image in the Late Middle Ages and Renaissance,* Papers from a Conference held at the Accademia di Danimarca in Collaboration with the Bibliotheca Hertziana (Rome: "L'Erma" di Bretschneider, 2004).
Tofani, Annamaria Petrioli, *Andrea del Sarto: Disegni* (Florence: Nuova Italia, 1985).
———, *Il disegno fiorentino del tempo di Lorenzo il Magnifico,* exh. cat., Gabinetto disegni e stampe degli Uffizi, Florence (Milan: Silvana, 1992).
———, *Michelangelo, Vasari, and Their Contemporaries: Drawings from the Uffizi* (New York: Pierpont Morgan Library, 2008).

Tolnay, Charles de, *Michelangelo,* 5 vols. (Princeton: Princeton University Press, 1943–60).
———, *Corpus dei disegni di Michelangelo,* 4 vols. (Novara, 1975–80).
Tomas, Natalie R., *The Medici Women: Gender and Power in Renaissance Florence* (Burlington, VT: Ashgate, 2003).
Tönnesmann, Andreas, *Der Palazzo Gondi in Florenz* (Worms: Wernersche Verlagsgesellschaft, 1983).
Toscani, Bernard, ed., *Lorenzo de' Medici: New Perspectives,* Proceedings of the International Conference Held at Brooklyn College and the Graduate Center of the City University of New York, April 30–May 2, 1992 (New York: Lang, 1993).
Trachtenberg, Marvin, *The Campanile of Florence Cathedral: Giotto's Tower* (New York: New York University Press, 1971).
———, *Dominion of the Eye: Urbanism, Art and Power in Early Modern Florence* (Cambridge: Cambridge University Press, 1997).
———, "Michelozzo and the Pazzi Chapel, Santa Croce, Florence," *Casabella* 61 (1997), 56–75.
———, *Brunelleschi, Michelozzo, and the Problem of the Pazzi Chapel* (New Haven: Yale University Press, 2008).
Trexler, Richard C., *Public Life in Renaissance Florence* (New York: Academic Press, 1980).
———, *Journey of the Magi: Meanings in History of a Christian Story* (Princeton: Princeton University Press, 1997).
——— and Mary E. Lewis, "Two Captains and Three Kings: New Light on the Medici Chapel," *Studies in Medieval and Renaissance History,* n.s. 4 (1981), 91–177.
Trinkaus, Charles, *In Our Image and Likeness: Humanity and Divinity in Italian Humanist Thought* (Chicago: University of Chicago Press, 1970).
Turco, Niccolò Rosselli del, and Federica Salvi, eds., *Bartolomeo Ammannati: Scultore e architetto (1511–1592)* (Florence: Alinea, 1995).
Turner, A. Richard, *The Vision of Landscape in Renaissance Italy,* rev. ed. (Princeton: Princeton University Press, 1974).
———, *Renaissance Florence: The Invention of a New Art* (New York: Abrams, 1997).
Turner, James G., ed., *Sexuality and Gender in Early Modern Europe: Institutions, Texts, Images* (New York: Cambridge University Press, 1993).
Turner, Jane, ed., *Encyclopedia of Italian Renaissance and Mannerist Art,* 2 vols. (London: Macmillan, 2000).
Tuyll van Serooskerken, Carel van, *Baccio Bandinelli,* exh. cat., Cabinet des Dessins, Musée du Louvre, Paris (Milan: 5 Continents, 2008).
Unger, Miles J., *Magnifico: The Brilliant Life and Violent Times of Lorenzo de' Medici* (New York: Simon and Schuster, 2008).
Valtieri, Simonetta, ed., *Il palazzo del principe, il palazzo del cardinale, il palazzo del mercante nel rinascimento* (Rome: Gangemi, 1988).
Vasari, Giorgio, *Lives of the Painters, Sculptors and Architects,* 2 vols., trans. Gaston du C. de Vere, (New York: Knopf, 1996; repr. of 1912 ed.).
———, *Vasari on Technique,* trans. Louisa S. Maclehose, ed. G. Baldwin Brown (New York: Dover, 1960).
Vatovec, Corinna Vasić, *Luca Fancelli architetto: Espistolario gonzaghesco* (Florence: Uniedit, 1979).
Veen, Henk Th. van, *Cosimo I de' Medici and His Self-Representation in Florentine Art and Culture* (Cambridge: Cambridge University Press, 2006).
Veit, Probst, *Zur Enstehungsgeschichte der Mona Lisa: Leonardo da Vinci trifft Niccol Machiavelli und Agostino Vespucci* (Ubstadt-Weiher: Verlag Regionalkultur, 2008).
Ventrone, Paola, ed., *Le temps revient. Il tempo si rinnova. Feste e spettacoli nella Firenze di Lorenzo il Magnifico,* exh. cat. (Florence: Palazzo Medici-Riccardi, 1992).
Verdon, Timothy, "Donatello and the Theater: Stage Space and Projected Space in the San Lorenzo Pulpits," *Artibus et historiae* 14 (1986), 29–55.
——— and John Henderson, eds., *Christianity and the Renaissance: Images and Religious Imagination in the Quattrocento* (Syracuse: Syracuse University Press, 1990).
——— et al., *Sotto il cielo della cupola: Il coro di Santa Maria del Fiore dal Renascimento al 2000* (Milan: Electa, 1997).
———, Alessandro Coppellotti, and Patrizia Fabbri, *Churches of Florence* (Venice: Arsenale, 2000).
——— and Annalisa Innocenti, eds., *Atti del VII Centenario del Duomo di Firenze,* 3 vols. in 5 (Florence: Edifir, 2001).
———, ed., *Le chiese e la città* (Florence: Centro Di, 2002).
——— and Severino Dianich, eds., *La Trinità di Masaccio: Arte e teologia* (Bologna: Dehoniane, 2004).
———, ed., *Alla riscoperta delle chiese di Firenze,* 4: *Santissima Annunziata* (Florence: Centro Di, 2005).
———, ed., *Alla riscoperta delle chiese di Firenze,* 5: *San Lorenzo* (Florence: Centro Di, 2007).
Vespasiano da Bisticci, *Renaissance Princes, Popes and Prelates: The Vespasiano Memoirs, Lives of Illustrious Men of the 15th Century,* trans. William George and Emily Waters (New York: Harper & Row, 1963).
Vitruvius, *Ten Books on Architecture,* trans. Ingrid D. Rowland with commentary by Thomas Noble Howe (New York: Cambridge University Press, 1999).
Voragine, Jacobus de, *The Golden Legend,* trans. William Granger Ryan, 2 vols. (Princeton: Princeton University Press, 1993).
Vossilla, Francesco, "L'Altar Maggiore di Santa Maria del Fiore di Baccio Bandinelli," in *Architettura di altari e spazio ecclesiale: Episodi a Firenze, Prato e Ferrara nell'età della Controriforma,* ed. Carlo Cresti (Florence: Pontecorboli, 1995), 37–79.
———, "Baccio Bandinelli e Benvenuto Cellini tra il 1540 e il 1560: Disputa su Firenze e su Roma," *Mitteilungen des Kunsthistorischen Institutes in Florenz* 41 (1997), 254–313.
Wackernagel, Martin, *The World of the Florentine Renaissance Artists: Projects and Patrons, Workshop and Art Market,* trans. Alison Luchs (Princeton: Princeton University Press, 1981).
Waldman, Louis A., ed., *Baccio Bandinelli and Art at the Medici Court: A Corpus of Early Modern Sources,*

Memoirs of the American Philosophical Society 251 (Philadelphia: American Philosophical Society, 2004).
Wallace, William E., *Michelangelo at San Lorenzo: The Genius as Entrepreneur* (Cambridge: Cambridge University Press, 1994).
———, *Michelangelo: The Complete Sculpture, Painting, Architecture* (New York: Hugh Lauter Levin Associates, 1998).
———, *Michelangelo: The Artist, the Man and His Times* (Cambridge: Cambridge University Press, 2009).
———, ed., *Michelangelo: Selected Scholarship in English,* 5 vols. (New York: Garland, 1995).
Warnke, Martin, *The Court Artist: On the Ancestry of the Modern Artist,* trans. David McLintock (Cambridge: Cambridge University Press, 1993).
Watkins, R. N., "L. B. Alberti's Emblem, the Winged Eye, and His Name Leo," *Mitteilungen des Kunsthistorishen Instituts in Florenz* 9 (1960), 256–58.
Watson, Paul F., *The Garden of Love in Tuscan Art of the Early Renaissance* (Philadelphia: Art Alliance Press and Associated University Presses, 1979).
Waźbiński, Zygmunt, *L'Accademia medicea del disegno a Firenze nel Cinquecento: Idea e istituzione,* 2 vols. (Florence: Olschki, 1987).
Weil-Garris, Kathleen, "On Pedestals: Michelangelo's *David,* Bandinelli's *Hercules and Cacus,* and the Sculpture of the Piazza della Signoria," *Römisches Jahrbuch für Kunstgeschichte* 20 (1983), 377–415.
Weinberger, Martin, *Michelangelo the Sculptor,* 2 vols. (New York: Columbia University Press, 1967).
Weinstein, Donald, *Savonarola and Florence: Prophecy and Patriotism in the Renaissance* (Princeton: Princeton University Press, 1970).
Weiss, Roberto, *The Renaissance Discovery of Classical Italy* (Oxford: Blackwell, 1969).
Welch, Evelyn, *Shopping in the Renaissance: Consumer Cultures in Italy, 1400–1600* (New Haven: Yale University Press, 2005).
White, John, *The Birth and Rebirth of Pictorial Space* (London: Faber & Faber, 1957; rev. ed. Cambridge, 1987).
Wilde, Johannes, "The Hall of the Great Council in Florence," *Journal of the Warburg and Courtauld Institutes* 7 (1944), 65–81.
Wiles, B. Harris, *The Fountains of Florentine Sculptors and Their Followers from Donatello to Bernini* (Cambridge: Cambridge University Press, 1933).
Wilinski, Stanislaw, "La Serliana," *Bolletino del Centro Internazionale di Studi di Archittetura Andrea Palladio* 11 (1969), 399–429.
Williams, Robert, *Art, Theory, and Culture in Sixteenth-Century Italy: From Techne to Metatechne* (Cambridge: Cambridge University Press, 1997).
Wilson, Carolyn C., *St. Joseph in Italian Renaissance Society and Art: New Directions and Interpretations* (Philadelphia: Saint Joseph's University Press, 2001).
Wind, Edgar, *Pagan Mysteries in the Renaissance: An Exploration of Philosophical and Mystical Sources of Iconography in Renaissance Art* (New York: Norton, 1958).
Windt, Franziska, *Andrea del Verrocchio und Leonardo da Vinci: Zusammenarbeit in Skulptur und Malerei* (Münster: Rhema, 2003).
Wisch, Barbara, and Diane Cole Ahl, eds., *Confraternities and the Visual Arts in Renaissance Italy: Ritual, Spectacle, Image* (New York: Cambridge University Press, 2000).
Witthoff, Brucia, "Marriage Rituals and Marriage Chests in Quattrocento Florence," *Artibus et historiae* 5 (1982), 43–59.
Wittkower, Rudolph, "Michelangelo's Biblioteca Laurenziana," *Art Bulletin* 16 (1934), 123–218.
——— and Margot Wittkower, *Born under Saturn: The Character and Conduct of Artists. A Documented Study from Antiquity to the French Revolution* (New York, 1963).
——— and Margot Wittkower, trans., *The Divine Michelangelo: The Florentine Academy's Homage on His Death in 1564* (London: Phaidon, 1965).
———, *Architectural Principles in the Age of Humanism* (New York: Norton, 1971).
Wohl, Helmut, *The Paintings of Domenico Veneziano, ca. 1410–1461: A Study in Florentine Art of the Early Renaissance* (New York: New York University Press, 1980).
———, *The Aesthetics of Italian Renaissance Art: A Reconsideration of Style* (Cambridge: Cambridge University Press, 1999).
Woodall, Joanna, ed., *Portraiture: Facing the Subject* (Manchester: Manchester University Press, 1997).
Woods-Marsden, Joanna, *Renaissance Self-Portraiture: The Visual Construction of Identity and the Social Status of the Artist* (New Haven: Yale University Press, 1998).
Wright, Alison, *The Pollaiuolo Brothers: The Arts of Florence and Rome* (New Haven: Yale University Press, 2004).
Zervas, Diane Finiello, *The Parte Guelfa: Brunelleschi and Donatello* (Locust Valley, NY: Augustin, 1988).
——— and Paola, Grifoni, *Orsanmichele a Firenze,* 2 vols. (Modena: Panini, 1996).
Zirpolo, Lilian H., *Historical Dictionary of Renaissance Art* (Lanham, MD: Scarecrow Press, 2008).
Zöllner, Frank, *Leonardo da Vinci, 1452–1519: The Complete Paintings and Drawings* (Cologne: Taschen, 2003).
———, "The 'Motions of the Mind' in Renaissance Portraits: The Spiritual Dimension of Portraiture," *Zeitschrift für Kunstgeschichte* 68 (2005), 23–40.
———, Christof Thoenes, and Thomas Pöpper, *Michelangelo, 1475–1564: Complete Works* (Cologne: Taschen, 2007).
Zorzi, Renzo, *Le Metamorfosi del ritratto* (Olschki, 2002).
Zuccari, Alessandro, Giovanni Morello, and Gerardo de Simone, eds., *Beato Angelico: L'alba del Rinascimento* (Milan: Skira, 2009).

ILLUSTRATIONS AND PICTURE CREDITS

N.B.: Picture credits in brackets. Insert (enlarged fig. 12) follows p. 148.

INDEX

N.B.: An asterisk before a name indicates the artist is included in the Artists' Biographies. Saints are listed under "Saint" (abbreviated "St.").

TEXT 9.75/12 Garamond
DISPLAY Garamond and Requiem

SPONSORING EDITOR Stephanie Fay
ASSISTANT EDITOR Eric Schmidt
PROJECT EDITOR Sue Heinemann
EDITORIAL ASSISTANTS Erica Lee Lynn Meinhardt
COPYEDITOR Charles Dibble

DESIGNER Claudia Smelser
PRODUCTION COORDINATOR Pam Augspurger
COMPOSITOR Integrated Composition Systems
PRINTER AND BINDER Friesens